The Social Contract
in the Ruins

The Social Contract in the Ruins

Natural Law and Government by Consent

Paul R. DeHart

UNIVERSITY OF MISSOURI PRESS
COLUMBIA

Copyright © 2024 by
The Curators of the University of Missouri
University of Missouri Press, Columbia, Missouri 65211
Printed and bound in the United States of America
All rights reserved. First printing, 2024.

Library of Congress Cataloging-in-Publication Data

Names: DeHart, Paul R., 1975- author.
Title: The social contract in the ruins : natural law and government by
    consent / by Paul R. DeHart.
Description: Columbia, Missouri : University of Missouri Press, [2024] |
    Includes bibliographical references and index.
Identifiers: LCCN 2023050102 (print) | LCCN 2023050103 (ebook) | ISBN
    9780826223050 (hardcover) | ISBN 9780826275004 (ebook)
Subjects: LCSH: Social contract--Philosophy. | Natural law. | Political
    science--Philosophy. | BISAC: POLITICAL SCIENCE / Political Ideologies /
    Conservatism & Liberalism | PHILOSOPHY / Political
Classification: LCC JC336 .D387 2024 (print) | LCC JC336 (ebook) | DDC
    320.1/1--dc23/eng/20240214
LC record available at https://lccn.loc.gov/2023050102
LC ebook record available at https://lccn.loc.gov/2023050103

♾™ This paper meets the requirements of the
American National Standard for Permanence of Paper
for Printed Library Materials, Z39.48, 1984.

Cover art by Wilhelmina Joy DeHart

Typefaces: Iowan Old Style and Adobe Caslon Pro

To Hadley Arkes, J. Budziszewski, Ronald J. Oakerson, and Nicholas Wolterstorff,

pillars of scholarship, who are ἀληθῶς φιλόσοφοι,

in unwavering admiration and deep gratitude for the example each has set,

eternal monuments for those who would follow in their stead.

To my wife, Robyn,

because I'm utterly inept without my person.

To my daughters, Wilhelmina Joy and Abigail Zoe,

that you may discover the sheer Goodness and unfailing Love

at the foundation of all things.

"As for those, then, who look at many beautiful things but do not see the beautiful itself, and are incapable of following another who would lead them to it; or many just things but not the just itself, and similarly with all the rest—these people, we will say, have beliefs about all these things, but have no knowledge of what their beliefs are about."

—Plato, *Republic*

Contents

Part III: Covenantal Realism: The Essential Dependence of Covenant and Consent on Classical Natural Law

Acknowledgments

ABOUT TWO DECADES AGO I read a paper by Nick Wolterstorff and a reply by J. Budziszewski that launched me on this project. A few years later, in 2007, I delivered a paper entitled "Covenantal Realism: Reclaiming the Possibility of Realist Social Contract Theory from the Ruins of Conventionalist and Voluntaristic Contractarianism" at the Midwest Political Science Association, and the current project officially embarked. When I first set sail, my focus was initially on the question of consent and its relation to political authority and obligation—which, of course, remains at the center of this project. But (as the title of the very first installment of the first part of the argument suggests) my vision for the project quickly expanded. When it comes to the coherence of government by consent, the crux of the matter is whether one *begins* with covenant and proceeds from there (in both ethics and politics) or, instead, with Goodness as the ultimate ontological ground. For a long time, I called this project *Covenantal Realism* because beginning with covenant—with will, artifice, construction—and making all else (including the good and the right) depend on it is self-referentially incoherent. Any coherent account of covenant and also of government by consent requires starting with an uncreated, unmade Goodness at the deepest foundation of things. Put another way, any intelligible account of covenant and of government by consent depends on moral and metaphysical realism for its coherence. There is no more comprehensive or thoroughgoing theorist of covenant than Thomas Hobbes, who says ethics and politics—just and unjust—are entirely the products of principles that we make. He also claims that the basis of divine sovereignty over us (exercised in commanding the laws of nature) derives entirely from

God's irresistible power and omnipotence. However one fits these two pieces of his thought together, in both claims Hobbes makes artifice and will prior to goodness and right. He denies any good or right founded in the nature of things.

So in this work, I argue that any approach to ethics and politics that begins with will and artifice, with construction, rather than with an uncreated goodness is self-referentially incoherent. We find this self-referential incoherence in the work of ancient Greek Sophists like Protagoras, Antiphon, Callicles, and Thrasymachus, medieval nominalists like William of Ockham, modern theorists like Thomas Hobbes and David Hume, and contemporary moral and political philosophers like J. L. Mackie, David Gauthier, and John Rawls. It obtains in conventionalist accounts of justice, purely constructivist accounts of morality (normative constructivism, morals by agreement), normative positivism, and metaethical voluntarist accounts of natural law. This self-referential incoherence obtains whether the good and right are said to be made by human beings—and whether by each of us, by all of us together, or by a sovereign power over us—or by omnipotent, divine will. The only way out of the incoherence is to give up the proposition that goodness is created or made.

A good many scholars associate government by consent or the necessity of consent for political authority and obligations with the priority of will and artifice to goodness and nature. If they're right, my argument entails the incoherence of government by consent (or political contractarianism). Yet the necessity of consent for political authority and obligation arguably follows from the natural equality of human beings. If so, the possibility of rightful political authority and genuine obligations to obey rightful authority depends on consent. Put another way, given human equality, the possibility of legitimate political authority (and also of political obligations) depends on government by consent—in which case the principle of consent must be salvaged from the ruins of the will and artifice tradition in ethical and political thought. Rescuing the principle of consent, in turn, requires grounding it on moral and metaphysical realism—requires starting with goodness rather than raw will.

A number of people read parts of this manuscript and provided insightful comments along the way. When I presented the very first part of this project at the Midwest Political Science Association meeting in 2007, a comment made by the discussant, Steven DeLue of Miami University of Ohio, led not only to revisions of what is now chapter 1 but also to the writing of chapters 2 and 3. Carson Holloway provided feedback, insight, and encouragement for the article version of chapter 1. Micah Watson read and provided helpful commentary on earlier versions of chapters 2 and 6. Justin Dyer read and discussed with me earlier versions of the arguments in multiple chapters, and in particular chapters 6 and 7. Chris Esh, Mark Hall, Michael Pakaluk, and David Williams all read parts of the current manuscript and provided insightful comments. Nick Wolterstorff and J. Budziszewski read the whole thing and provided sage counsel. Nick and J. have invested considerable time in reading and commenting on many things that I've written over the years; I've benefited immensely from their wisdom and generosity. I am profoundly grateful for all the ways in which these individuals have made this project better.

I started thinking about social contract theory, government by consent, and Thomas Hobbes (in particular, *Leviathan*) under the tutelage of Ron Oakerson at Houghton College (now Houghton University) in 1994 and 1995. Oakerson began his Introduction to Politics class with Stephen Nathanson's *Should We Consent to Be Governed?* I've been wrestling with social contract theory and the difficulties surrounding consent-based justifications of political authority ever since. Likewise, somewhere in the 1996–97 academic year, at a time when I was grappling with the voluntarism of Martin Luther's *Bondage of the Will*, Carlton Fisher gave me a copy of his essay "Because God Says So." Fisher's argument persuaded me that voluntarism and affirmation of divine goodness are utterly irreconcilable. That realization ultimately launched me on the quest for the argument that voluntarism fails on its own terms. The framing of that argument, along with, government by consent and the normative foundations of American constitutionalism, has been at the center of my scholarly career. Since 1994 I have been discussing covenant, political theory, political history, the American founding, theology, and everything else under the sun—and several of the matters addressed in this book—with my good friend Chris Esh. Over the last fifteen years I have likewise benefited from numerous conversations that pertained directly or indirectly (and, of course, sometimes not at all) to the present work with Frank Beckwith, Josh Bowman, Steven Brust, Lee Cheek, Justin Dyer, Jeff Fish, Darren Guerra, Gunnar Gundersen, Mark Hall, Rudy Hernandez, Robert Miller, Michael Pakaluk, James Patterson, Jeff Peterson, Will Ruger, Kevin Stuart, Tom Varacalli, Micah Watson, David Williams, Matthew Wright, and friends and colleagues at Texas State University in San Marcos including Bob Fischer, Ken Grasso, Ashleen Menchaca-Bagnulo and Vince Bagnulo, Pat Shields, and Ken Ward. For several years students at Texas State in Senior Seminar and in a graduate course entitled Social Contract Theory have allowed me to lay out the arguments of the social contract theorists and their critics, contemporaneous and today. They have raised interesting questions for both social contract theorists and their critics. Students in Ancient Political Theory, Modern Political Theory, Contemporary Political Theory, and directed studies during my brief time at Lee University in Tennessee likewise asked insightful questions about many of the theorists I engage in this text. This book is far better for my having taught them.

Along the way, I received helpful feedback and tremendous encouragement on the Locke material from the late Brian Tierney. I benefited from a number of exchanges with Frank Oakley, who in 2008 sent me a signed copy of his important book *Omnipotence, Covenant, & Order*, a work that continues to shape my thinking. Very early in this project I applied for a Summer Stipend from the National Endowment for the Humanities. At that point and at others along the way Hadley Arkes provided valuable input and encouragement. Hadley (like James Wilson) has long affirmed both (morally and metaphysically realist) natural law and government by consent, on account of human equality. That contention has long influenced my own thinking. And for the last decade Hadley, Garrett Snedeker and the James Wilson Institute have provided the sort of intellectual engagement, fellowship, and friendship that fills the well on which projects like this draw. Bill McClay has been a tremendous supporter of my work and of this project since its inception. Though we use different tools, I think of my work like he once described his own: as intellectual archeology (archeology in the proper sense of the word).

Paul Kerry invited me to give a talk at Oxford on my work on the Constitution's moral design, which allowed me to update my argument on that matter in light of theoretical developments central to this project.

My wife, Robyn, has been with me at every step of this project, especially those twists and turns where I despaired of ever bringing this project to completion. I'm certain I could not have done so without her unfailing encouragement and support (I say this, of course, in the hope that she will continue to feed me even though this project is done, especially given my general ineptitude in the culinary arts . . .). My parents have supported my decision to take up the vocation of political philosophy from the very start, in 1994. My daughters provide a constant reminder of that bit of wisdom from C. S. Lewis: politics and political order exist for the sake of ordinary goods, like art showings, choral concerts, and theater performances of which one's children are a part. The front cover of this volume is from one of my eldest daughter's color studies, in which she mixed the colors herself as part of thinking about a painting of the Parthenon on a larger canvas. The color study reminds me that even the ruins of something beautiful can transport us to Beauty itself. Indeed, I hope the major premise of this volume—that our ability to distinguish some instances of will, agreement, convention, interest, desire, or preference from others depends on a real, uncreated good that transcends these—might provide readers with a path to the Good itself, much as passages in Lewis and Plato (though I would never put my work on a level with theirs) have done for me.

Finally, I received a Summer Stipend from the National Endowment for the Humanities in the summer of 2008 that supported research for the very first part of this. I owe the NEH a debt of thanks. While the vast majority of the material in this volume was written specifically for and is entirely original to this volume (all of chapters 2, 4, 8, and 9, and almost all of chapters 3 and 7), some chapters contain substantially revised passages from previously published work or draw on portions of it. About half of chapter 1 appeared in "Covenantal Realism: The Self-Referential Incoherency of Conventional Social Contract Theory and the Necessity of Consent" in *Perspectives on*

Political Science 41, no. 3 (July 2012): 165–77, https://www.tandfon line.com/journals/vpps20. The material from "Covenantal Realism" used here is used by permission from Taylor & Francis.

A few paragraphs of chapter 3 dealing with Rawlsian political liberalism draw on material published in "Political Philosophy after the Collapse of Classical, Epistemic Foundationalism" in *Reason, Revelation, and the Civic Order: Political Philosophy and the Claims of Faith*, edited by Paul R. DeHart and Carson Holloway (Dekalb: Northern Illinois University Press, 2014), 33–63. Copyright (c) 2014 by Northern Illinois University Press. Used by permission of the publisher.

An earlier version of chapter 5 appeared as "Fractured Foundations: The Contradiction between Locke's Ontology and His Moral Philosophy" in *Locke Studies* 12 (2012): 111–48. Material from the article is used here with permission from *Locke Studies*. Some paragraphs of chapter 6 draw from material previously published in "Reason and Will in Natural Law" in *Natural Law and Evangelical Political Thought*, edited by Jesse Covington, Bryan McGraw, and Micah Watson (Lanham, MD: Lexington Books, 2013), 125–52. That material is used here by permission of Rowman and Littlefield, all rights reserved.

A few paragraphs in chapter 6 are drawn from "Nature's Lawgiver: On Natural Law as *Law*," *The Catholic Social Science Review* 22 (2017): 53–71. While all of chapter 7 was originally written for this volume, revised versions of a few paragraphs were drawn upon and published in "Whose Social Contract?: Hobbes versus Hooker and the Realist Contract Tradition," *The Catholic Social Science Review* 26 (2021): 3–21. These two pieces are used by permission of the Society of Catholic Social Scientists.

While all previously published material has undergone substantial revision for this project, I am grateful to these journals and presses for allowing me to use paragraphs and arguments that in places will be quite similar to material they published first.

Last but certainly not least, I would be remiss if I failed to express the depth of my gratitude to editor in chief Andrew Davidson, as well as to Drew Griffith and everyone else I worked with at the University of Missouri Press. I am ever grateful and in their debt.

The Social Contract
in the Ruins

INTRODUCTION

Natural Law, Modernity, and Government by Consent:
Where the Conflict Really Lies

MOST SCHOLARS WHO WRITE ON social contract theory and classical natural law today (and for the better part of the last century) perceive an irreconcilable tension between them.[1] Against the regnant view, I maintain that they are not only logically and metaphysically compatible but also that political contractarianism and the principle of consent necessarily and essentially depend upon classical natural law for their very intelligibility.

According to the American Declaration of Independence, governments derive "their just powers from the consent of the governed."[2] This statement and affirmations like it in various state declarations of rights, reports issued by committees of correspondence, and pamphlets that gained wide circulation from the 1760s through the 1780s embody the theoretical commitment of Revolutionary-era Americans to social contract theory and to the principle of consent as the proper account of political authority and obligation and their ground.[3] Social contract theorists of the preceding century rejected previous grounds of political authority and obligation such as the divine ordination of rulers, natural subordination, and the right of the wise and good to exercise political rule.[4] In place of these, early modern social contract theorists emphasized the necessity of consent for political authority and obligations. They inferred the necessity of consent from the natural equality of individuals (though they quite disagreed as to that in which this equality consists).[5] According to their argument, broadly framed, precisely because human beings are naturally equal (when it comes to ruling and being ruled), relations of political authority and obligation are not given by nature. Rather, human beings must construct them. Consequently, such relations are

artificial (constructed or made) rather than given by nature. If human
equality entails the necessity of consent for political authority and
obligation, the principle of consent must be coherent and must rest
upon a coherent foundation.

Early modern social contract theory—especially in the paradigmatic instances of Thomas Hobbes and John Locke—has often been
linked to the modern turn in metaphysics, physics, ethics, and philosophical anthropology. A number of theorists connect social contract
theory and the insistence on consent as a necessary condition of political authority and obligation to metaphysical nominalism, mechanistic philosophy, metaethical voluntarism, and radical individualism.[6]
Social contract theory and government by consent have often been
considered the political-theoretic concomitant of the modern rejection of classical metaphysics, ethics, and philosophical anthropology.[7]
The relation of classical philosophy—its account of fundamental reality (including universals and formal and final causality), ethics (the
objectivity of goodness and justice and their connection to human
nature), and its view of the human person (as social and political by
nature)—to the social contract theory of the early moderns has been
viewed as one of deep conflict and even contradiction rather than as
one of compatibility or essential connection.

Now as some scholars see it, social contract theory lies downstream
from the federal, or covenantal, theology of the Reformation era,
which in turn has roots in Hebrew scripture and theology.[8] Moreover,
some important scholars of covenant hold that covenant includes
its own conception of natural law. Some even claim that covenant
is not necessarily wed to nominalist metaphysics and may in some
sense be compatible with moral realism. But these scholars also hold
that covenantal theory rejects *classical* natural law or natural right—
whether Aristotelian, Stoic, or Scholastic (especially Thomistic).[9]
Early modern proponents of the covenant idea, the argument goes,
reconfigured natural law to fit with the primacy of covenant and divine will to nature and reason. Thus, even those scholars who speak
of the compatibility of covenant and natural law emphatically reject
classical or traditional natural law as the proper moral ontology for
covenant (in theology or political theory).[10] Classical natural law and
covenant remain completely at odds.

In this book, I argue that the received wisdom is wrong. The relation between the principle of consent (the necessity of the consent of the governed for legitimate government) and classical natural law is one of concord rather than conflict. I will argue that the principle of consent, and so covenantal models of political organization, are compatible with the claims that human persons are by nature political and that political association exists by nature. More strongly, I will argue that any intelligible account of covenant and of the claim that consent forms a necessary condition for political authority and obligation depends necessarily on the sort of morally and metaphysically realist account of natural law that one finds in, say, Thomas Aquinas. Correlatively, the real conflict and, indeed, contradiction, lies between any intelligible social contract or consent theory and modernist metaphysics (nominalism and conceptualism) and ethics (voluntarism or normative constructivism).[11]

Two main concerns motivate the argument advanced in these pages. First, where early modern contractarians insisted that human equality entails the necessity of consent for political authority and obligation, prominent political and legal theorists of the last half century (e.g., A. John Simmons, Leslie Green) have argued that contractarianism or consent theory is unworkable.[12] But, as Simmons argues, if consent is necessary *and* consent theory incoherent or impracticable, philosophical anarchism (the rejection of political authority and obligations) seems necessarily to follow.[13] The necessity of consent and the problems attendant to consent theory seem to entail that political authority and obligations cannot (at least for the most part) be justified.

Second, theorists such as Wilson Carey McWilliams and Patrick Deneen claim that social contract theory gives expression to moral skepticism, normative constructivism, and a subjectivist view of the good.[14] The American order, they maintain, was therefore conceived in moral subjectivism and predicated upon the rejection of classical natural law.[15] I will argue that every attempt to make or construct morality, to predicate it on will—as in ancient or modern conventionalism concerning justice, normative constructivism, normative positivism, voluntarist accounts of obligation (theistic or secular)—and every account of morality that does not include an objective, uncreated

good at its foundation ultimately collapses into self-referential incoherence. Morality cannot be constructed or otherwise derived from
nonmoral building blocks. But if social contract theory instantiates or
is predicated on normative constructivism, metaethical voluntarism,
or subjectivism concerning the good, *and* if the constitutional order
established by the American founders and framers is predicated on
social contract theory, then that political order is incoherent as well.

Both criticisms entail a conceptual crisis when it comes to the
justification of political authority and obligation. This book responds
to that crisis by grounding political authority and obligation and
contractarian or consent-based justifications of these on moral and
metaphysical realism. Such grounding retrieves an understanding
of consent and political foundations older than Hobbes and Locke,
an understanding present in the work of Richard Hooker, Francisco
Suárez, and Johannes Althusius, among others. To that retrieval, I
add an analytic defense of the necessity of moral and metaphysical
realism for any coherent *political* contractarianism or justification of
political authority and obligation by means of consent.

In the pages that follow I argue that *conventional* social contract
theory and any sort of pure contractualism fails on its own terms, and
that early modern political thought (e.g., that of Hobbes or, when it
comes to metaphysics, Locke) and contemporary moral contractarianism (e.g., that of David Gauthier and John Rawls) lack the metaphysical resources to eliminate the incoherence—especially when it
comes to moral and political obligation. I also aim to show not only
the compatibility of the claim that consent is necessary for political
authority and obligation with classical natural law (and moral and
metaphysical realism) but also the essential dependence of the former
on the latter.

According to Michael Oakeshott, "three great traditions of thought"
have "impressed upon the intellectual history of Europe." Two trace
their roots to classical antiquity. The "master-conceptions" of the first
tradition are "Reason and Nature." Oakeshott places Plato's *Republic*
at the head of this tradition. In contrast, "The master-conceptions of
the second [tradition] are Will and Artifice," and Hobbes's "*Leviathan*
is [its] head and crown."[16] In the first tradition, justice (or right) and
goodness are given by nature and prior to and normative for will

and construction. If human beings make covenants or agreements, these must accord with a real goodness and an objective right in order to bind. Divine will itself exemplifies, is an expression of, divine Goodness. On the second tradition, will, construction, and covenant precede and even make goodness and right. Will, construction, covenant determine what counts as just or unjust, what counts as evil or good. According to Hobbes in *De Homine*, politics and ethics—"the sciences of *just* and *unjust*"—"can be demonstrated *a priori*; because we ourselves make the principles," by which he means, we make "the causes of justice (namely laws and covenants). . . . For before covenants and laws were drawn up, neither justice nor injustice, neither public good nor public evil, was natural among men any more than it was among beasts."[17] To be sure, Hobbes also claims that the laws of nature are the commands of God and therefore laws properly speaking. But God's "right to rule" or "the right of God's sovereignty" over us "derives," as Hobbes puts it, from His "omnipotence" or "irresistible power"—that is, solely from His omnipotent and irresistible will.[18] In this book, I demonstrate the fundamental incoherence of the tradition that places artifice and will—human or divine—at the foundation not only of political authority and obligation but also of morality, goodness, and right. The very possibility of covenant and construction when it comes to political order, morality, or, for that matter, theology, depends for its coherence on an uncreated, unmade goodness at the foundation of things. When it comes to morality, moral norms, obligation, rightness—it's that or nothing.

PART I

THE SOCIAL CONTRACT IN THE RUINS?

CHAPTER I

The Self-Referential Incoherence of *Conventional* Social Contract Theory

Introduction

In this chapter I contend that *conventional* social contract theory—a variant of social contract theory that makes *agreement* and therefore will the *ultimate* ground of political authority and obligation—is self-referentially incoherent, that it presupposes its own denial. Since the mid-seventeenth century, social contract theory has been the prevailing justification of political authority in the West.[1] Social contract theory pervaded the political thought of the American founding.[2] In a letter to Nicholas Trist dated February 15, 1830, James Madison captured the Revolutionary vision: "The idea of a compact among those who are parties to a Govt. is a fundamental principle of free Govts." He continued, "The original compact is the one implied or presumed, but nowhere reduced to writing, by which a people agree to form one Society. The next is a compact, here for the first time reduced to writing, by which the people in their Social State agree to a Govt. over them. These two compacts may be considered as blended in the Constitution of the U.S., which recognizes a Union or Society of States, and makes it the basis of the Govt. formed by the parties to it."[3] Five decades earlier, the Second Continental Congress had asserted in the Declaration of Independence that governments derive their just powers from the consent of the governed—that is, government derives its rightful authority from the consent of those it governs.[4] Madison in his letter to Trist and the Second Continental Congress in the Declaration of Independence clearly took authority to govern to depend in some way upon the consent of the governed. But what is the nature of the connection between political authority and consent? Is consent simply necessary for political authority (and correlatively, for the obligations of citizens to obey)? Or is it both necessary and sufficient for the authority to govern? According to a position I will call *conventional social contract theory* (or *conventional contractarianism*), popular consent is both necessary and sufficient for the authority of the state: The state has authority or legitimacy *if and only if* the people have consented to it. Authority to govern requires consent, but it doesn't require anything else. Consent is all you need (apologies to the Beatles).

Why should we think consent is necessary? According to a wide array of theorists in early modernity—including Richard Hooker, Robert Bellarmine, Francisco Suárez, Algernon Sidney, John Locke, and the American founders—consent is necessary just because human beings are equal by nature.[5] The necessity of consent for political authority derives from the natural equality of human beings.[6] Human beings are naturally equal in the sense that none are naturally superior to others and none naturally inferior *with respect to fitness to rule*. Thus, human beings can exercise political authority over their natural equals *only if* those over whom they exercise authority have given their consent. To formalize this relation: If human beings are naturally equal *and* if some human beings exercise rightful authority over others, then those others must have consented to it. Given this conditional and the laws of inference (modus tollens and DeMorgan's rule), rejecting the necessity of consent for political authority (and, correlatively, for the obligations of individuals to obey) necessarily entails either rejecting political authority or rejecting human equality.[7]

Why, as some contractarians seem clearly to do, go beyond the claim that consent is *necessary* for political authority to the further claim of conventional contractarianism that consent is also *sufficient* for it?[8] According to proponents of conventional social contract theory, no other ground of political authority is available to us. Many political and legal theorists and social scientists today take for granted that natural law or a real and substantive common good transcendent of and normative for human willing and human behavior do not exist or, if they do exist, that they are irrelevant to the authority of the state.[9] According to one line of argument (call it the Hobbesian Story), good and evil are names that express desires and aversion, tastes, preferences, or emotions, which vary not only across time and place but also across individuals within a society and within particular individuals over time. Clashes produced by divergent and incompatible views concerning good and evil cannot be resolved by appealing to one particular view of what counts as good (or evil). Consequently, those who disagree about good and evil and who wish to avoid a violent resolution to their conflict must establish and agree to abide by the decision(s) of a common judge whose public judgment concerning good and evil (what should or should not be done) replaces—or, more aptly, trumps—the private (i.e., particular) views of individuals or groups.

According to another—similar but also distinct—line of argument (call it the Rawlsian Story), modern constitutional democracies are characterized by an ineliminable pluralism of incommensurable views of the good affirmed by various individuals and groups within the society. The only basis for shared principles to govern such a society is agreement (or consent), where the agreement—and the principles agreed to—make no assumption about whether any particular view affirmed by individuals or groups within the society is true or false (and without assuming that the principles agreed to are true or good). That is, the basis of political order must be an agreement that refrains from presupposing that either moral realism or expressivism (or emotivism or noncognitivism) is true or false (and so also for metaphysical realism or metaphysical nominalism or Protagorean antirealism, and for any epistemic position).

On both stories—whether the one that rejects a realist account of the good as an objective reality, transcendent of and normative for human willing, in favor of an account of good and evil, right and wrong, as creations or expressions of human will, tastes, or emotions, *or* the one that seeks basic principles of political order that presume neither the truth nor falsity of any particular view of the good, or of the nature of reality or knowledge more broadly—consent is not based on prior moral principles or a logically antecedent view of the good. Social contract theory, so understood, provides a way to derive political obligation absent the existence of any prior moral obligation or in light of an ineliminable pluralism of incommensurable and conflicting comprehensive views, none of which command broad assent.

Consequently, on this view political obligation is said to derive from human consent *rather than* from an antecedent moral obligation.

Now, the consent operative in social contract theory is of various kinds. According to the various conceptions of the social contract, consent might be actual or hypothetical. And actual consent might be tacit or express. In the latter half of the twentieth century every variant of social contract theory came under withering assault. Since these attacks were leveled by analytic philosophers and analytic legal theorists, they went largely unnoticed, or at least were not substantially engaged, by many historians of thought, political theorists, and social scientists. Nevertheless, these attacks—brought to a culmination in the works of A. John Simmons, Leslie Green, Jean Hampton, and Nicholas Wolterstorff—were devastating for social contract theory and consent theory, at least insofar as we inherit these from modernity. In this chapter, I want to suggest that social contract theory, on the standard accounts, is in even worse shape than many have realized. I contend that conventional social contract theory incorporates a logical incoherency into its very foundation.[10] Conventional social contract theory is self-referentially incoherent. It fails on its own terms.[11]

But if the Bastille that was conventional social contract theory has been successfully stormed, then we face a crisis concerning how to justify the authority of the state. As many late modern people (especially in the West) see it, the great social contract theorists of early and mid-modernity demolished other putative bases of political authority such as natural hierarchy or the divine delegation of regal authority to particular individuals.[12] If social contract theory and the principle of consent also fail, on what basis can the authority of government be justified? What justifies the obligation of citizens to obey (even just) laws enacted by the state? Moreover, recall that the necessity of consent follows from human equality. Insofar as this connection between consent and political authority holds and insofar as human beings really are naturally equal, it seems to follow that political authority really does require consent and cannot be justified without it.[13] But in that case, the fall of conventional social contract theory seems to put the very consent required for political authority and obligation out of reach. Philosophical anarchism—understood as the denial of political authority and the obligation of citizens to obey—seems clearly to follow.[14] If we are to justify political authority—given human equality—we must have consent. If we must have consent, then we will have to ground the principle on something other than the cracked foundation of conventional social contract theory. Though the prospects for such an undertaking initially appear quite bleak, there is hope yet. For the principle of consent predates the sort of *conventional* social contract theory that became its predominant justification.

Conventional Social Contract Theory in the Ruins
A BRIEF OVERVIEW OF THE RISE AND DEVELOPMENT
OF MODERN SOCIAL CONTRACT THEORY

Scholars have long debated the roots of social contract theory. While agreeing on the central importance of contractarian (or consent-based) justifications of political authority in the sixteenth, seventeenth, and eighteenth centuries, scholars—as Harro Höpfl and Martyn P. Thompson demonstrate—dispute whether contractarianism originated in ancient Greece, in the Latin Middle Ages (with William of Ockham and later conciliarists), with Protestant resistance theorists in France and Holland, with Catholic Counter-Reformation theorists, in some combination of all of these, or with Thomas Hobbes and distinctively modern political thought.[15] Still others trace the headwaters of social contract theory to the covenantal order of ancient Israel.[16] Without rejecting the importance of other sources (such as Counter-Reformation theorists), it seems undeniable that modern contractarianism—in particular, its insistence on the necessity of *individual* consent as not simply the occasion of but also the ground for the authorization of civil power—has deep roots in the covenantal theology of Reformed Protestantism.[17]

The idea of a covenantal foundation for political authority arguably begins with Heinrich Bullinger's reframing of Christian theology in terms of covenantal relations in *De testamento seu foedere Dei unico et aeterno*.[18] According to Charles S. McCoy and J. Wayne Baker, "Bullinger viewed the covenant as the divine framework for human life, both religious and civil, from the beginning of the world until the last judgment."[19] The Latin *foedus* corresponds to the Hebrew *berith*, which, says Bullinger, stipulates terms or "conditions." In the covenant binding together God and Abraham's descendants, the principal condition for Abraham and his descendants is "to walk uprightly before God."[20] What does it mean to walk before God *and* uprightly? Bullinger suggests that "the Decalogue . . . seems to be almost a paraphrase of the conditions of the covenant."[21] According to McCoy and Baker, Bullinger holds, "the moral law was a restatement of these conditions."[22] And Christ, ultimately, "renewed and confirmed" it and "left for us a living example which we might follow."[23] Some scholars, notably Heiko Oberman, endeavor to connect covenantal (or federal) theology to late medieval nominalism and the *via moderna*, which rejected the real existence of universal essences and subordinated good and evil to omnipotent will.[24] Bullinger, however, was educated and remained grounded in the *via antiqua*, at least insofar as he affirmed moral realism (i.e., insofar as he affirmed that a goodness not reducible to will—even omnipotent will—really exists) and the realist understanding of God's relation to morality.[25] Thus, he speaks of "the sheer goodness which is God's nature" and of "divine goodness" that created "all things for the benefit of human beings."[26] Alongside the divine perfections of unity and omnipotence, he notes that "the Hebrew word *Shaddai*" also "comprehends . . . all his moral excellence and goodness."[27] Further, from God's promises to Abraham, "we are able to gain a full understanding that this God is the highest good."[28] For Bullinger there is an objective, real, highest good—God Himself—whose prescriptions redound to human well-being. Goodness is the beginning and end (or telos) of the covenant.

The Reformation was an earthquake of great magnitude not only in theology but in ecclesiology as well. Not long after the advent of covenant as *the* central motif for understanding and interpreting Scripture, the covenant idea led to a revolution in the design of church government. Covenantal or federal theorists within Reformed Protestantism developed a congregational model of church formation and organization. In 1613 an English Separatist named Henry Jacob contended that a "visible Church of Christ under the Gospel" is "a Spiritual Body Politike" in which "the people" have "power of free consent in their ordinary government."[29] The "Platform of Church Discipline," adopted by a synod of churches that met in Cambridge, Massachusetts in 1649, provides a detailed account of the congregationalist model of church governance.[30] According to the "Platform," particular churches (or congregations) can only be distinguished from each other by their respective forms. And the form of a particular church (or congregation) is its "visible covenant." The authors of the "Platform" maintain that "voluntary agreement" or "consent" ("for all these are here taken for the same") provide the only way by which some members of a congregation can come to have authority ("church-power") over others. A congregation is formed or established when "there is real agreement and consent of a company of faithful persons to meet constantly together in one congregation, for the public worship of God, and their mutual edification."[31] On this model, then, congregations are created or *formed* by voluntary consent.

This model of church *formation* implies a model of church *government*.[32] The "Platform" informs its readers that a congregation exists as a church prior to the appointment of officers and remains a congregation or church even without them.[33] Thus, while supreme power ultimately belongs with Christ, in the local church, officials are subordinate to the congregation. The congregation controls membership— it possesses authority over admission to membership as well as to admonish, censure, or remove "an offending brother" from the church: "the whole church has the power to proceed to censure him, whether by admonition or excommunication . . . and upon his repentance to restore him again unto his former communion." The congregation also appoints "their own officers, whether elders or deacons," and if an official "offend incorrigibly . . . as the church had the power to call him to office, so they have the power . . . to remove him from his office" and return him to the status of an ordinary congregant. In cases of "contumacy," after removal from office, "the church, that had power to receive him into their fellowship, hath also the same power to cast him out that they have concerning any other matter."[34]

According to Höpfl and Thompson, "separatist congregations" "interpreted their churches as free and voluntary associations founded on covenants. And, by a process that has yet to be fully explained, they appear, having compared their congregations to bodies politic, to have gone on to interpret bodies politic as if they were sectarian congregations."[35] Thus in 1616 Henry Jacob asked, "How is a Visible

Church constituted and gathered?" He answered: "By a free mutuall consent of Believers joyning and covenanting to live as members of a holy Society together in all religious and vertuous duties as Christ and his Apostles did institute and practise in the Gospell. *By such free mutuall consent also all perfect Corporations did first beginne.*"[36] Indeed, say Höpfl and Thompson, "The Covenant of the 'Pilgrim Fathers' of 1620 simply converted the church into a civil society: 'We . . . do, by these presents, solemnly and mutually in the presence of God and one another, covenant and combine ourselves together into a civil Body Politick, for our better Ordering and Preservation.' "[37] Henry Wolcott's notes of an election sermon delivered by Thomas Hooker, generally considered the founder of Connecticut, in 1638 recount Hooker arguing, "that the choice of public magistrates belongs unto the people by God's allowance" and "they who have the power to appoint officers and magistrates, it is in their power also to set the bounds and limitations of power and place unto which they call them." Why? Hooker says, "because the foundation of authority is laid, firstly, in the free consent of the people."[38] Because political authority is founded in free consent, the people who appoint may limit or set boundaries to the authority of those they choose to govern them.

In his *Politica methodice digesta*, first published in 1603 and culminating in the third edition of 1614, Johannes Althusius laid out the first systematic, thoroughly covenantal account of political order.[39] For Althusius, human relations are founded on covenants. According to Höpfl and Thompson:

> Althusius thus interpreted civil society as an association of lesser associations. The elementary association was the family, which was initiated by a *pactum* and involved a *mutua obligatio* [mutual obligation]. After family came private associations (*collegia, societas*, and the like), all joined together by *pacta* and laws. The association of private associations was a city; an association of cities was a province; and an association of provinces, cities, and estates was the "the universal public association." Sovereignty in the public association was not vested . . . in some absolute monarch but in the public association—that is, in the people or their

representatives. Indeed, for Althusius the sovereignty was not absolute at all, since it was limited by natural and divine law.[40]

Althusius's covenantal account of political order includes the proposition that government is legitimate *only if* it is erected on the basis of covenant (or consent).[41] By way of illustration, consider the following passage: "Politics is the art of associating (*consociandi*) men for the purpose of establishing, cultivating, and conserving social life among them. Whence it is called 'symbiotics.' The subject matter of politics is therefore association (*consociato*), in which the symbiotes pledge themselves each to the other, by explicit or tacit agreement, to mutual communication of whatever is useful and necessary for the harmonious exercise of social life."[42]

A few pages later Althusius writes, "We further conclude that the efficient cause of political association is consent and agreement among the communicating citizens."[43] According to this passage, consent constitutes the efficient cause of political association qua political association or just as such. It follows from this proposition that consent constitutes a necessary condition for all political associations among human beings.[44] Moreover, Althusius weds the covenantal foundation of all political authority to a substantially classical understanding of natural law. His affirmation of a rather traditional moral realism is apparent in his denial of absolute power: "Absolute power is wicked and prohibited. For we cannot do what can only be done injuriously. Thus even almighty God is said to be unable to do what is evil and contrary to his nature.' "[45]

According to Daniel Judah Elazar, the covenant idea, which "received its first full exposition" in the 1603 edition of Althusius's *Politica methodice digesta*, "subsequently . . . appeared in various secular forms, mainly as the idea of the social contract or compact" in the work of Thomas Hobbes, James Harrington, and John Locke in England and Benedict Spinoza, Hugo Grotius, Samuel von Pufendorf, Baron de Montesquieu, and Jean-Jacques Rousseau on the Continent.[46] A. John Simmons contends that Althusius, Grotius, and John Milton "were authors of the first important consent theories, on the foundation of which the classic works of Hobbes, Locke, and Rousseau were constructed."[47] Moreover, Hobbes's *Leviathan* (1651), Locke's

Two Treatises of Government (1689), and Rousseau's *Du contrat social* (1762) arguably demolished alternative grounds for political authority such as Aristotle's putative natural subordinationism (though natural subordination is only one element of Aristotle's theory of authority) and the sort of divine right theory promulgated in Robert Filmer's *Patriarcha* (1680).[48]

But just here a word of caution is in order. Whereas Otto von Gierke contends that Althusius first crossed the Rubicon to social contract theory—Althusius, he says, "was the first to construct in a logical way a scientific system of general politics on the assumption of definite original contracts"[49]—Höpfl and Thompson maintain that "Althusian theory was a historical anticlimax; it appeared only to be ignored."[50] I think the claims of Gierke and of Höpfl and Thompson too strong on this count. I would adapt Brian Tierney's insight concerning the relation of Althusius to American federalism. On that subject, he writes, "Americans had to reinvent federalism for themselves, guided by their own special needs and experiences; but they were working within the same tradition of thought as Althusius."[51] So also Althusius and the congregationalists and, downstream from them, John Locke (whose parents, after all, seem to have held Puritan views and whose father fought on the side of Parliament in the war between Parliament and the Crown).[52] My point is simply that Althusius shows what covenantal theology looks like when applied to the foundations of political order.

The contention of Höpfl and Thompson and of Oakley, that the principal development in terms of influence occurred not with Althusius but with the advent of congregationalism as a model of church government that was almost immediately applied to political order in British North America, strikes me as compelling. But here again caution is in order. Some scholars have too quickly dismissed the influence of the judicious Hooker on social contract theory by treating him either as a theorist of corporate *rather than* individual consent or as a consent *rather than* a covenant theorist.[53] Yet, as I show later, Hooker not only insists on the necessity of individual consent for the original establishment of political authority but also infers its necessity from the equality of human beings. Moreover, the state of nature factors into the political thought of the later Thomists

of the latter sixteenth and early seventeenth centuries and especially
of those associated with the Salamancan school in Spain. According
to Quentin Skinner, these "later Jesuit writers . . . lay the foundation
for the so-called 'social contract' theories of the seventeenth century."[54] They did so by positing a state of nature populated by naturally
free individuals who were "subject to no one" (as Suárez puts it),[55] a
miserable state of affairs in which men and women lack those things
requisite for human preservation and in which human selfishness
precludes preserving peace among them,[56] and by invoking the
"concept of consent . . . to explain how it is possible for a free individual to become the subject of a legitimate commonwealth."[57] Thus,
"the counter-reformation theorists not only arrived at a number of
radically populist conclusions, but also served as the main channel
through which the contractarian approach to the discussion of political obligation came to exercise its decisive influence in the course
of the following century."[58] Filmer's express criticism of Bellarmine
and Suárez in *Patriarcha* and Locke's close reading of Filmer's text,
Sidney's express invocation of them in his *Discourses*, and Althusius's
invocation of Fernando Vázquez (and of Vázquez's treatment of
Bartolus) in *Politica* all provide substantial evidence that theorists
of covenant and social contract knew the works of these writers and
were influenced by them.[59]

The destruction of natural subordination and the divine right of
kings paved the way for the ascendancy of social contract justifications
of the authority of the state and of the obligations of citizens to obey.
But it was not merely social contract theory that became ascendant.
Nor was it Althusius's metaphysically and morally realist and natural
law covenantal model that emerged as the dominant modern way
of justifying the state's authority. Rather, Hobbesian and Lockean
theories, theories wedded to nominalist metaphysics (in both Hobbes
and Locke) and voluntaristic metaethics[60] (certainly in Hobbes and
some say Locke, though here the matter is vexed), became the dominant justification of state authority.[61] The voluntaristic ethical theory
of Hobbes (and perhaps Locke), at least on its face, was a kind of
divine-command theory of natural law in which things are right or
good because God wills them to be so. For Hobbes, in particular, it
is God's irresistible and absolute power that makes his commands

binding on his creatures.[62] In its secularized form, social contract theory retained its nominalist and voluntarist underpinnings, while shedding the will of God as the source of moral and political obligation. Human will and convention replaced divine will.[63] A secularized Hobbesian contractarianism came to be the dominant justification of the authority of the state among contemporary scholars. Indeed, one encounters (not only in scholarly work but also in introductory political science texts, conference panel presentations, the comments of panel discussants, and so forth) social contract justifications of the state predicated on the fall of religious and natural law justifications of the political authority.

What I have denominated *conventional social contract theory* is essentially Hobbesian in nature. As a result, the foregoing discussion allows us to define conventional contractarianism in broad outline. Conventional social contract theory is committed to a conventionalist understanding (or a voluntarist ontology) of obligation.[64] Moral and political obligations derive solely from some act or exercise of will. In conventionalism's religious form, God's omnipotent will ultimately underwrites all moral and political obligation. On this view, God's omnipotent power alone is sufficient to obligate or bind individuals to observe the terms of the contract, whether hypothetical or actual. In its secularized form, human agreement (i.e., human willing) alone makes the social contract binding.[65]

THE CONTEMPORARY PHILOSOPHICAL CRITIQUE
OF SOCIAL CONTRACT THEORY

Social contract theory reigned as the prevailing justification of the modern state into the twentieth century. But the hypothetical social contract of Thomas Hobbes (and, for that matter, Immanuel Kant) and the actual social contract of John Locke (and, for that matter, Jean-Jacques Rousseau) began to draw fire from political and legal theorists. David Gauthier's early work, in particular *The Logic of Leviathan* and "The Social Contract as Ideology," attacked the practical viability of the hypothetical Hobbesian contract by arguing that Hobbesian moral theory is subverted by Hobbesian psychology.[66] To be sure, Gauthier subsequently defended Hobbesian moral theory, calling Hobbes the "greatest of English moral philosophers."[67] And in

Morals by Agreement he defends a contractarian account of right and wrong.[68] But I find his earlier argument—that the ideology of social contract (or, at least, the Hobbesian ideology of social contract) fails to provide sufficient justification for the authority of the state, at least from the standpoint of the citizen—instructive.[69]

Gauthier's argument in "The Social Contract as Ideology" goes something like this: The contract of Hobbes's *Leviathan* is hypothetical rather than real. His argument is designed to highlight the fact that human beings are utility maximizers, that they are not naturally sociable but rather (given a world in which human desire for more outstrips the number of goods in the world) naturally opposed, and that all relationships (including political ones) must therefore be a matter of a contract between nonsociable, utility-maximizing human beings.[70] Given human nature, such relationships must therefore be in the self-interest of those who contract together. But, as Gauthier notes, true utility maximizers will defect from contractual agreements any time that (1) they can get away with it, and (2) it is in their self-interest to do so. To this he adds the premise that there will be many opportunities to get away with defecting on a "contract" to obey the commands of the sovereign (i.e., to get away with disobeying the edicts of the state). He also notes that the state lacks the resources to compel people to obey its edicts much of the time.[71] States have therefore relied on motives like love and patriotism (both of which Gauthier says are myths to the contractarian) rather than the threat of punishment to get most people to obey most of the time. In view of the foregoing, Gauthier concludes that the more people are aware of their utility maximizing, antisocial nature and the more they act consistent with that nature, the less compelling social contract ideology becomes as a reason for individuals to obey the commands of the state. The ideology of social contract and the psychology presupposed by that very ideology are at cross-purposes such that the latter defeats the former. In later work (especially *Morals by Agreement*) Gauthier proposes a way out of this dilemma: individuals (altogether hypothetical) who see that utility maximization produces a state of nature dominated by conflict would choose to *adopt* constrained rationality rather than straightforward maximization. He considers this agreement to adopt principles constraining utility maximization a moral point of view. Put briefly, to solve the problems of *political* contractarianism identified in his earlier work, he adopts a *moral* contractarian (or moral conventionalist) position in his later work. I believe intractable difficulties accompany the moral contractarianism (or moral conventionalism) advanced by the later Gauthier. But I take that up in chapter 3.

In *Hobbes and the Social Contract* and *Political Philosophy*, Jean Hampton attacks both the theoretical coherence and the practical viability of the Hobbesian hypothetical contract.[72] Hampton's argument has two stages. First, while the Hobbesian contract seems to be an alienation theory of contract, it is in reality an agency theory of contract pretending to be an alienation theory (i.e., to make key Hobbesian premises work, logical consistency demands, as John Bramhall saw, that Hobbes adopt—though he wants to reject—the agency theory).[73] Second, agency contract theory (like the explicit agency contract between society and the government created by society in Locke's Second Treatise) can't be made to work. Let's elaborate each stage of her argument.

Concerning the first stage of Hampton's argument, we need only remind ourselves that Hobbes maintained the following: First, individuals, according to Hobbes, principally seek their own preservation.[74] Second, the reason for seeking peace with others by means of establishing a sovereign power is for the sake of self-preservation.[75] Third, the establishment of sovereign power requires individuals to alienate their right to all things (i.e., the right of nature) by surrendering it to a sovereign power via covenant or agreement.[76] Fourth, the sovereign power is created by the covenant, is not party to the covenant and so not bound by it, and thus nothing the sovereign does violates the covenant. Correlatively, no action of the sovereign forfeits power by means of violating a covenant between the sovereign and the people; no such covenant exists.[77] The covenant is only between those who become subjects—they covenant to obey the sovereign power they will establish and by this covenant authorize. Fifth, according to what Hampton calls Hobbes's "regress argument," the psychology of Hobbesian individuals entails that conflicts among them cannot be resolved without an arbiter or judge.[78] But the notion of a judge possessed of power to determine the terms by which conflicts are resolved, requires *final* judgment. A final judge cannot be limited by some yet greater power and, consequently, is absolute. To put all this another way, the only power capable of rescuing Hobbesian individuals from the state of nature is an absolute sovereign to which Hobbesian individuals give up or *alienate* their right to all things (a right entailed by the fact that in the state of nature nothing is just or unjust—neither right nor wrong have any place in that state of affairs; and given the absence of justice, no one has property in or exclusive title to anything).

But, sixth, precisely because Hobbesian individuals aim principally at the conservation of their own lives, subjects possess the liberty (or right) to resist those commands of the sovereign that threaten their preservation, and "The obligation of subjects to sovereign, is understood to last as long, and no longer than the power lasteth, by which he is able to protect them. . . . The end of obedience is protection."[79] Hobbes's concession on this point undoes his alienation argument. As Hampton observes, "If the people are always going to be concerned to preserve themselves and if the sovereign begins to rule such that their self-preservation is threatened, then their interests are such that they will do what they can to evade his commands, lest their lives be put at risk. Note that *the subjects* decide whether or not the ruler's commands are life-threatening; since it is *their* lives that are at stake, they are the ones who will (and must) make the determination about whether or not they are at risk."[80] To be sure, "If only one person concluded that a sovereign's rule is inconsistent with her self-preservation and thus refused to obey one or more of the sovereign's commands, the sovereign's power and authority would not be threatened." Nevertheless,

> if many or most people make that determination and decide not to obey him, then the sovereign is in trouble. For such a massive refusal to follow his commands would effectively amount to rebellion. Not only would he lose all or most of the support of those parts of the society that enforce his commands (e.g., the police, the court system, the army), but he would also lose the compliance of the population on which any regime relies to function efficiently and cooperatively. Moreover, if all or most of

the people decide to start obeying someone else, the sovereign would be effectively deposed, and this new individual would be invested with power and authority.[81]

"In the end," Hampton concludes, "it is Hobbes's effectively granting that the people will (and ought to) judge the ruler's performance that is the ruin of his attempt to mount a viable alienation argument."[82] After all, "if each subject judges when he is entitled to disobey the sovereign's commands and when he is not, then to all intents and purposes the sovereign reign depends upon the judgment of the subjects that his commands are worth obeying, in which case he rules at their pleasure."[83] And, consequently, Hobbesian social contract theory turns out to be an agency theory masquerading as an alienation theory of sovereign power.[84]

On agency social contract theory, the so-called rulers of the people are actually their agents, their delegates, or, as Hampton suggests, their "employees" who "remain under [the people's] control."[85] But agency social contract theory, such as we find in Locke, presents problems of its own. As Hampton argues,

> If there is such an agency relationship between ruler and people, how does it make sense to consider the people "ruled"? And if the people who are being "ruled" are themselves in charge of their rulers, how can their political society last? If babysitters are hired to supervise a bunch of unruly children and in reality the babysitters turn out to *be* the unruly children, the supervision is useless. And similarly, if the reason for creating a political institution is that people cannot govern themselves satisfactorily and the political regime that is created is one in which the people rule, the exercise appears useless.[86]

According to Hampton, the problem is only worse if the agency relationship is between individuals and the political society, "because then it would seem that the political society cannot hope to keep its noncompliant members in line if they insist that both the government and the majority of the society who support it are failing to secure effectively the preservation of person and property." Hampton returns us to the seventeenth-century political conservative criticism of agency social contract theory: "How, they ask, can we conceive of the state as one in which people have ultimate control over their rulers when the reason this argument gives for creating and maintaining the state is that the people need controlled?"[87] Having made this argument, Hampton nevertheless maintains that consent is essential to legitimate authority. But the damage to standard forms of social contract theory seems already done.[88]

Some critics of social contract theory consider Leslie Green's famous work *The Authority of the State* to deliver the fatal blow.[89] In what follows, I borrow from Nicholas Wolterstorff's treatment of Green's argument. Green considers *conventionalism* (which he defines differently than I do for the purposes of this volume), *contractarianism*, and *consent theory*.[90] According to Wolterstoff, summarizing Green, conventionalist and contractarian theories both seek "to ground the political authority of the state in some common good served by compliance with the directives it issues." Conventionalist accounts of political authority, on Green's definition of conventionalism, "focus on the need for conventions to which all conform." Conventionalists claim that "the political authority of the state supervenes on its securing and establishing the common good of coordination," which is requisite for securing some public good (for instance, defense of the community). "Contractualist accounts" of political authority "focus on the importance of coercion for insuring the performance of mutually beneficial actions when adequate internal motivation is lacking in some people." Contractualists proceed to "argue that the political authority of the state supervenes on the good that ensues from its exercise of coercion."[91] Put another way, contractualism, for Green, underscores the necessity of using coercion to ensure that mutually beneficial actions are performed when some individuals (or a group of individuals) in a given society that stand to benefit from such an action also have an incentive not to cooperate. The authority of the state is justified by the necessity of state authority for establishing a social order in which individuals cooperate to perform mutually beneficial acts.

There is a significant problem with the foregoing justification of state authority. Government (or the state) can secure the requisite cooperation and the goods produced by such cooperative action by issuing directives (including sanction or the threat of sanction for noncompliance) *whether or not* it possesses—and whether or not anyone *believes* it possesses—authority to issue these directives. The state possessing authority to issue directives, beliefs about government's or the state's authority to issue directives, the agreement of the subjects or citizens of a state to treat the state as possessing authority to issue directives—all these are unnecessary for the state to ensure the requisite cooperation. As Wolterstorff frames Green's argument in an earlier essay:

> The social good will be achieved if the members of the group act in conformity to the directives for whatever reason—out of prudence (rational self-interest), for example, or because they regard it as a morally good thing to act thus. The point seems to me decisive. The social good in question can be achieved without the institution that issues directives having, or being seen as having, genuine authority—that is, without its being able to generate, or being seen as able to generate, obligations to obedience in the group. The rabbit of authority cannot be pulled from this hat.[92]

In a later essay, Wolterstorff writes: "From the fact that the social good [or mutual benefit] in question is secured by the state issuing directives and the recipients complying, it does not follow that those directives generate in the recipients an obligation to comply. All that follows is that it is instrumentally good that they comply."[93] We might put Wolterstorff's later point this way: conventionalism and contractualism (as Green defines these terms) both describe causal connections; cooperation is (causally) necessary to obtain public or common goods (collective goods, in the parlance of contemporary economic theory); cooperation requires coordination given the multiplicity of ways any good or mutually beneficial action might be pursued; coordination requires an agent—or agency—that can issue directives and secure the compliance of members of the community with those directives; getting members of the community to comply with directives requires coercion or the power to coerce—the power to impose sanctions on individuals who refuse to comply with the agency's directives. But the governing agency of a community can obtain compliance with its directives, thereby securing the requisite cooperation, by coercion—threatening and imposing sanction for noncompliance—without actually possessing authority and without anyone believing that it does. Green concludes, "Neither the power of government to create conventions serving the common good, nor its capacity to solve certain problems of collective action warrants citizens taking its directives as binding. These are, indeed, among the important functions of government and they do contribute to its value. But they do not justify its authority."[94]

Having rejected conventionalism and contractarianism, Green embraces consent as sufficient to ground the authority of the state. But Green rejects both hypothetical and tacit consent—and for good reason. As David Lay Williams argues, if a social contract binds me, then the contract must be real rather than hypothetical.[95] For hypothetical contracts cannot answer the question "Why should I obey?" in a convincing way. Real and express contracts have an easy answer to the question: "I should obey because I pledged to do so." Building on Williams's point, I would add that hypothetical agreements fail *actually* to bind me here and now to some command of government because they lack binding power or normative force (*potestas*). They lack normative force just because there is no obligation or moral norm that I ought to keep agreements I would have but did not actually make and, therefore, no obligation to obey a sovereign or government that I *would have* agreed to obey, even though I actually did no such thing. Moreover, even if such a norm exists, it is entirely implausible that the norm is grounded in convention—that is, in will alone. If, however, there is a real *moral* obligation to keep my word *and* if, in an express agreement, I give my word to obey the commands of the sovereign or at least the sovereign's just commands, then I am really bound to do so.[96]

Tacit consent fares little better than the hypothetical variety. As Stephen Nathanson has pointed out, tacit consent is notoriously ambiguous, too ambiguous for contracting parties to understand what they have putatively pledged themselves to do.[97] Moreover, as Simmons argues, the only signs of tacit consent (residence or enjoying benefits like protection or use of inns and roads) seem to entail that all states are legitimate or, at least, possess the consent of those they rule.[98] Put another way, tacit consent seems incapable of distinguishing regimes that possess the consent of the governed from those that do not. Moreover, as Simmons suggests, all the proposed signs of tacit consent to authorize political authority or to take on political obligations seem clearly to eliminate voluntary choice—in which case we might wonder whether we're still talking about consent at all.

In light of the foregoing considerations, Green seems entirely right to conclude that consent theory or government by consent requires *express* consent—where express consent constitutes an explicit promise to obey the decrees of the government. But Green also acknowledges that few, if any, governments are founded on express consent. Even regimes that incorporate the principle of consent receive the express consent only of a very few members of the society over which they purportedly govern. But in this case, the putative government of a society exercises authority only over a few members of the society— only over those few who *expressly consented* to its authority by promising to obey.[99] As Wolterstorff concludes, "On this view, the authority of the state has become—so it seems to me—an altogether quirky pointless thing. . . . If almost everybody around me is conforming to the valid directives of the state out of rational self-interest or because it's a morally good thing to do, why would I take that additional step of *promising* to obey those directives?"[100] The authority of the state together with its authorization by consent, on this view, has become entirely superfluous.[101]

I find the arguments above compelling. Individually they are damaging. Together they provide powerful grounds for embracing the conclusion to which they point—to wit, the rejection of social contract theory. Yet one cannot help but notice two things: (1) the frequency with which social contract theory's great critics, having leveled such damaging attacks upon the fortress, still seek refuge in the principle of consent; and (2) many (if not all) of their most impressive arguments turn upon the impracticability of obtaining meaningful consent. In either instance, there seems to be an operative assumption that consent might be considered requisite for political authority if only meaningful consent can be obtained. Put another way, many philosophical objections to conventional social contract theory are *de facto* rather than *de jure* (albeit not Hampton's). I find the de facto arguments powerful. But I am persuaded that conventional social contract theory is problematic for more than merely pragmatic reasons. I am persuaded that conventional social contract theory fails on its own terms. It is to that argument that I now turn.

THE SELF-REFERENTIAL INCOHERENCE OF
CONVENTIONAL SOCIAL CONTRACT THEORY

Above I noted that social contract theory, as we have received it, is wedded to nominalist metaphysics and to a voluntarist ontology of obligation (i.e., to a voluntarist metaethic). In its secularized form, this involves a denial of any standard or measure of human acts independent of *human* will and normative for human willing. Consequently, ethics and moral obligation are nothing other than human conventions. Justice, for instance, is taken to result from human agreement, an agreement upon the rules by which we will live together. There are various mechanisms for producing this agreement. For instance, there is John Rawls's veil of ignorance or Jürgen Habermas's or James Fishkin's dialogue of justice.[102] All of these theories posit that the proper standards for human behavior are creations of human will, a will exercised either hypothetically or actually. So they posit; so they fall. For, logically speaking, it is impossible to distinguish intelligibly among exercises of will on the basis of will alone. With respect to acts (or exercises) of will just as such, we have nothing but this exercise of will and that one. Consequently, in order to judge that some exercises of will bind us where others do not, there must be a source of obligation independent of will. This conclusion is the ruin of conventional social contract theory, for, to underscore the point, conventional theories of social contract make the good and the just dependent on human will alone.[103]

To make the preceding point more precise, consider possible exercises of will. Some are those of an individual—to purchase a soda or savor a glass of Chianti; to watch the Cleveland Guardians play baseball; to contemplate the argument of Plato's *Republic*; to immerse oneself in the world of C. S. Lewis's *Till We Have Faces*; to engage in a dual with one's archnemesis; to perform "Amor ti vieta" from *Fedora* before a panel of judges for a vocal jury; to admire the ancient

Assyrian colossal winged bulls at the British Museum; to prepare filet mignon with a red wine, shallot reduction; to go rock climbing and rappelling at Rattlesnake Point in Canada; to provide food for the hungry; to give money to a mendicant who tells one of their dire need; to lay down one's life to save a friend. Others are those of a group (i.e., a corporate entity or a community)—to build and maintain a road; to raise taxes for the school district in order to fund construction of a new school building; to designate a parcel of land for a park; to defend the village or city or nation from invaders; to erect a protective wall around the polis or, in polities of a grander scale, to make other provisions for national defense; to provide a measure of relief for members of the community in serious need. Of those that are made by a group, some reflect the unanimous consent of the community, others only the consent of the majority, still others the will of some minority with sufficient power to compel the rest (for instance, the cloture rule of the US Senate allows a minority with at least forty-one votes to exact concessions from a majority to allow passage of a bill). Moreover, some exercises of the will involve *voluntary* consent—to buy a soda or to build a road—and other exercises of will are *coerced*—to hand over one's wallet to the attacker or to walk the plank when ordered to do so at sword's point.

  Abstractly, we might posit a set of every conceivable exercise of will that looks something like this: $(W_1, W_2, W_3, W_4, W_5, \ldots W_n)$. *In terms of will alone* it makes no sense—it is utter nonsense—to suggest that any particular exercise of will is binding or obligatory. It makes no sense to say that W_4 should be favored over or considered normative for W_1, W_2, W_3, and W_5 such that all subsequent exercises of will (or even just some) must now conform to it (i.e., that they must be consistent with it or not contradictory to it). To do so would be to posit a new exercise of will—call it W_6—that designates W_4 as normative for the rest. But W_6 is also an exercise of will. In fact, W_6 is a member of our set. As such, the selection of W_4 by W_6 cannot establish W_4 as binding, for W_6 itself lacks normative force, it being nothing other than an exercise of mere will. And it cannot pass on to some exercise of will what it does not have to give. To suggest that some exercise of will or other binds me (perhaps the exercise of majority will or an exercise of will in accordance with voluntary consent) whereas others do not (for instance, a will constrained by violent coercion or the will of an oligarchic and oppressive minority) is to introduce into the consideration of will a property that is not itself reducible to mere will or made by will. To reiterate my point from the previous paragraph, we cannot, in a rationally coherent way, discriminate among exercises of will on the basis of will alone.[104] If W_4 is to be able to serve as a rule and measure for other acts of will, it must be set apart by something outside the set—it must conform to some standard that transcends the set. More generally, any distinction among exercises of will must be made on the basis of some standard external to—that transcends—the set.

The principle that we cannot distinguish among exercises of will on the basis of will alone is an instance of a more general principle that applies to other domains of thought, such as mathematics. Consider mathematical sets—the set of all even, positive integers beginning with two and running to infinity or the set of all prime numbers beginning with two and also running to infinity. We cannot intelligibly distinguish 2 from 4 on the basis of the evenness of 2—for 4 is also even (equally so). Nor can we distinguish 31 from 7 and 13 on the basis of the primeness of 31, for 7 and 13 are just as prime. It is a general principle of sets—and not only of mathematical sets— that one cannot intelligibly distinguish among the members of the set on the basis of predication of the property or properties that define it. Put another way, one cannot distinguish one thing from another, whether it be a number or anything else, on the basis of a property they both or all share (insofar as they share it; insofar as the property is predicated of both).[105] And this general principle of sets necessarily entails the principle I've been articulating—that one cannot distinguish among exercises of will on the basis of will alone.

The implication of the foregoing is that *human* will cannot be the source of political, legal, or moral obligation precisely because will, all by itself, cannot be the source of obligation at all.[106] Consequently, to posit that some exercise of will, x, is binding vis-à-vis all (or any) other exercises of will, y, we need a standard or property of obligation, o, external to (or transcendent of) exercises of will and normative for them. Moreover, we cannot intelligibly appeal to the distinction between higher and lower order preferences to salvage the project of grounding obligation in human will. For that very distinction pre-supposes a standard external to human preferences by which some preferences can be deemed of a higher order while others are not.[107] As with the argument concerning acts of will, some preferences cannot coherently be deemed higher than other preferences on the basis of preference alone. To hold that some could be higher on the basis of preference alone would be equivalent to saying that some prime numbers could be distinguished from others on the baseness of primeness alone, would be to distinguish some member(s) of the set based on the predication of the property by which the set is defined, which is nonsense. Consequently, if some preferences are of a higher order than others, it must be on the basis of a property, of a rule and measure transcendent of preference alone. Ultimately, the attempt to derive obligation from mere will is self-referentially incoherent. It must therefore be rejected.

Locke understood perfectly well the point in view. For he strongly rejected the notion that good (and consequently moral good or right) can be produced by human agreement: "Nor, further, can those very men who agree among themselves know that something is good because they agree it is, but [rather], they agree because they know from natural principles that something is good. And [this] knowl-edge precedes agreement, for otherwise the same thing would be both cause and effect at the same time, and the consent of all [i.e., an effect] would result in the consent of all [i.e., a cause] which is plainly absurd."[108] Moreover, Locke clearly perceived the implication of this argument. For human laws to be binding (i.e., for them to have normative force), they must receive their binding power from a source of obligation external to human will, a source he refers to as the law of nature, the *lex naturale*. The law of nature, he argued, constitutes a *necessary* (though not sufficient) condition for human law that is *obligatory* in any meaningful sense:

> If the law of nature is not binding on men, neither can any hu-man positive law bind them, since the laws of the civil magistrate derive all their force from the binding power of this law. . . . if you would abolish the law of nature, you overturn at one blow all government among men, [all] authority, rank, and society. Nor

must we obey a king out of fear, because he is more powerful and can compel us. For this would be to establish the power of tyrants, thieves, and pirates; but [we must] out of conscience, because he obtains his rule over us by right, that is, at the command of the law of nature. . . . Thus, the obligation of civil law depends on the law of nature.[109]

Put another way, moral obligation is antecedent to political or legal obligation in the sense that moral obligation is logically prior legal obligation. Moral obligation (or natural law) forms a necessary, though not sufficient, condition of legal obligation: If some person, p, is legally bound to observe some law, l, then p is also morally bound to observe l.[110] Moral and legal obligation are not coextensive. We can have moral obligations that are not also legal obligations. But we cannot have a legal obligation unless that obligation is, in some way, underwritten by an antecedent moral obligation.[111]

Elsewhere I make this point elsewhere in different language:

All constitutions and written laws are human creations. Either it is possible for human beings to frame these laws inappropriately or not. If not, then the law itself is devoid of obligation. For if there no such thing as a good or bad law because there is no such thing as good or bad, then there is no such thing as good or bad behavior with respect to the law. One could not do wrong in failing to follow the law, and therefore one could not be said to behave inappropriately towards others in failing to adhere to a law or constitution. That is, one could not be said to behave unjustly, either towards a ruler or one's fellow citizens or anyone at all. In short, if there is no standard outside of the law telling us that we must obey good laws and render people their due, then it makes little sense to say that we are obligated to render people their due according to some law. For whatever that law is, it has no claim on our obedience. In such a situation law lacks any normative force (*potestas*).[112]

Whether one speaks of constitutions and written laws or of social contracts, the argument works just the same. For there to be good or bad behavior under the terms of the social contract, we must first be bound to observe the terms of the social contract. But we cannot, without reasoning in a circle, maintain that the social contract is the source of our obligation to observe the social contract. Such an idea is, as Locke saw, sheer nonsense.

Perhaps Hobbes also apprehended the point I have in view. His third law of nature dictates that human beings keep their covenants. Moreover, he implies that this law of nature obtains in the state of nature: "Covenants entered into by fear, in the condition of mere nature, are obligatory."[113] Despite what Hobbes contends in other passages—that no action in the state of nature is just or unjust, right or wrong—here and elsewhere he affirms that a moral obligation to keep covenants obtains even in the state of nature and even if the psychological motive inducing one of the parties to enter the covenant is fear for their very life. Moreover, it's not hard to see why Hobbes makes this point. If the law of nature prescribing that all men keep their covenants made does not obtain in the state of nature (i.e., if moral obligation does not precede human agreement—which is what the covenant that creates a political society is), then there is no hope for creating a covenant in the state of nature (which follows from my argument above). But Hobbes's theory collapses into incoherence if binding covenants cannot be made in the state of nature. For, as A. P. Martinich observes, unless binding covenants can be made in the state of nature, there is no possibility of grounding political authority by covenant or consent:

> There is even a sharper way of putting the problem of interpreting Hobbes to mean that it is impossible for people to make covenants in the state of nature. If he is interpreted in this way, then his account of the origin of government is hopelessly incoherent. According to Hobbes, the origin of civil government requires a covenant. If every covenant requires a coercive power, and if there is no coercive power in the state of nature, then no covenant can be made in the state of nature. In particular, no covenant creating a government could be made in the state of nature. The upshot of this argument is that if Hobbes's philosophy is to have any chance for success, he must allow that some covenants can be made in the state of nature.[114]

In sum, if covenants cannot be made in the state of nature, then there is no way for people to exit it.[115] The very concept of a covenant between parties presupposes an obligation of the parties to observe the terms of the covenant. As Hobbes seems to understand, if such an obligation is lacking, then, in fact, no covenant has been made. Therefore, antecedent to the making of any covenant (or agreement) there must first exist an obligation that covenants, once made, are to be kept. That obligation to keep our agreements, however, cannot come from an agreement—cannot, that is, so long as we want to avoid reasoning in a circle.

Prima facially, Hobbes and Locke appear to provide conventional contractarianism a way out of a vicious circle and out of self-referential incoherence when they posit a law of nature normative for human willing. We cannot distinguish among exercises of human will on the basis of *human* will, but we can distinguish some exercises of human will from others based on whether or not human will (or behavior) conforms to *God's* will. God's will can serve as rule and measure for human acts. Moreover, Hobbes and Locke maintain that humans have access to knowledge of God's will for human behavior through the law of nature, a standard operating through human reason (though the reason in question may be purely instrumental in the case of Hobbes). Those who subscribe to a secularist interpretation of Hobbes (either because they think him insincere in his religious pronouncements or because they think the character of his political theory secular, whatever his personal beliefs may have been) will not be happy with such a resolution, to be sure. But some measure for human acts independent of human will is necessary if social contract theory is to escape a vicious circle.

But just here a significant problem emerges with what seems to be the Hobbesian way out of this dilemma. Suppose we ask Hobbes just why we should obey God. Hobbes's answer is that God has a right to rule us as a result of his irresistible power: "In the *Natural Kingdom* God's right to Reign and to punish those who break his laws is from *irresistible power* alone."[116] Were we to ask Locke the same question, there are passages within the Lockean corpus in which he seems to concur. For instance, Locke says, "The foundation of obligation [in both the natural law and divine positive law] is the same, that is, the will of the supreme divine power [*numen*]."[117] To be sure, certain passages within the Lockean corpus indicate a more complex moral theory—passages suggesting that the relevant thing about God's will is that it is God's and the relevant thing about God is that He is good and wise.[118] For the sake of argument, however, let us take this passage as indicative of the Lockean position. If we do that, social contract theory cannot escape falling into self-referential incoherence.

Recall that we cannot intelligibly distinguish among exercises of will on the basis of will alone. By implication, obligation (moral or political) cannot be created solely by the sheer *will* of God, qua will. Will (sheer will; will just as such) provides no basis for distinguishing among exercises of will and consequently cannot distinguish among any of the following: an omnipotent will, an incontinent will, God's will, the devil's will, a good will, an evil will, human will, the unanimous will of society, the majority will of a society, the will of some minority within the society, the will of each individual within the society, the strongest will, the weakest will, and every will between strongest and weakest. The very act of distinguishing among exercises of will presupposes a standard external to will—some ground or property that transcends the set of exercises of will. Suppose, for a moment, that we know that some instance of will within this set is binding upon us. Consideration of will alone cannot tell us which one is, precisely because obligation and will are distinct properties. Suppose someone tells us the strongest will is binding (perhaps because the strongest will is omnipotent). And suppose, additionally, that we ask her why this is so. So far as I can tell, her reason must be because the will is the *strongest* will, not because it's the strongest *will*. In which case strength rather than will is taken to be the source of obligation. Strength, however, is not a moral property and so, qua strength, cannot impose any obligation upon us.[119] As Hadley Arkes puts it, moral propositions "cannot be drawn from distinctly nonmoral attributes as brute physical strength."[120] Now, suppose someone maintains that *God's* will is obligatory—a proposition to which some highly regarded philosophers, such as Leibniz and Robert Merrihew Adams, have subscribed.[121] What matters in this proposition is not sheer will or even strength (in this case omnipotence) of will, but, rather, that the will is God's. It is the fact that *God* has willed that makes His commands binding, not the fact that God has *willed*.[122]

Indeed, it is the fact that a *good* God—more aptly, a God that is Goodness—has commanded that makes His commands obligatory. The point, again, is that will alone cannot ground obligation. The implication is that political authority cannot derive from mere will precisely for the reason that obligation cannot be based on will alone. The inability of will alone to ground obligation per se and to ground moral obligation in particular also entails that voluntarist ontologies of moral obligation are in fact false. But, more importantly for our considerations, because the giving of consent is nothing other than an exercise of will, it follows that consent alone (even unanimous consent) is incapable of grounding obligation, whether moral or political. Consent cannot, therefore, provide a *sufficient* condition for political authority. By implication, it would be wrong to claim that consent can form both a necessary and sufficient condition for political authority. Consent alone will not do.

So the problem is this:

(1) It is logically impossible to distinguish among exercises of will on the basis of sheer will.

(2) Because it is logically impossible to distinguish among exercises of will on the basis of will alone, any distinction among exercises of will presupposes a standard external to and transcendent of mere will (a standard also normative for will)—put another way, to distinguish among exercises of will in the set comprised of all exercises of will, we require a criterion (a rule and measure; a norm) or property external to the set.

(3) Conventional social contract theory posits no other basis for obligation (moral, legal, or political) than will by virtue of its subscription to conventionalism.[123]

(4) A conventionally grounded social contract theory attempts to distinguish some exercises of will on the basis of mere will *because* the social contract makes a particular exercise of the society's will binding upon subsequent exercises of a society's will and on the wills of its members.

(5) By implication of (1), (2), and (4), a conventional social contract presupposes a standard transcendent of and normative for acts of will.

(6) Premise (5) entails the denial of conventionalism.

(7) Conventional social contract theory therefore presupposes its own denial.

(8) Conventional social contract theory is therefore self-referentially incoherent.

THE DILEMMA POSED BY THE FALL OF
CONVENTIONAL SOCIAL CONTRACT THEORY

The incoherence of conventional social contract theory presents us with a real crisis. The reason for the crisis is twofold. First, human equality, as Locke saw, seems to imply that consent is a necessary condition for the legitimate exercise of political authority. As Arkes characterizes Locke's reasoning, "No man can be, by nature, the ruler of other men in the same way that God is by nature the ruler of men, and men are by nature the rulers of dogs, horses and monkeys. Therefore, if a situation has come about in which some men have been placed in the position of exercising power over others, that situation could not have arisen from *nature*. It had to arise from convention or agreement; it had to arise, one might say, from *consent*."[124] The *necessity* of consent follows from human equality. If that inference is correct, then, given modus tollens, denying that consent is necessary to ground political authority, entails denying human equality.[125] As I see it, the arguments for human equality are sound.[126] Consequently, we seem bound to hold that consent is a necessary condition for political authority and obligation while simultaneously recognizing that social contract theory, in its conventional form, is logically incoherent. At first glance it seems impossible to hold to the principle of consent and that we are bound to hold to it.

Nor is the necessity of human consent for political authority obviated by reframing political authority as a delegation from God. As J. Budziszewski observes, "Had God transmitted authority *directly* to government, then short of revelation in words, He could have made this clear only by making the created nature of the rulers distinct in kind from the created nature of the subjects. Plainly He has not done this, and Locke's theory is a plausible alternative: Authority is transmitted directly from God to individuals, and directly from individuals to the state—which is the same as to say that it is transmitted *indirectly* from God to the state."[127]

The consequence of Budziszewski's point is that consent remains a necessary condition of the authority of some over others, given that God has not clearly marked out specific persons as having specially delegated power. Second, the early and mid-modern political theorists seem to have left us with no other justification of political authority. That is, the fall of social contract theory may seem to entail the end of political authority altogether. To be sure, "governments" and "states" will remain, and they will try (probably successfully) to compel us in a great many of our actions. But they will lack authority—if, that is, modern political thought left us only with consent for a basis of authority, a basis that has now fallen.

CAN THE PRINCIPLE OF CONSENT SURVIVE THE
FALL OF THE SOCIAL CONTRACT?

But is social contract theory damaged beyond repair? Is government by consent irretrievably lost? At this point I would like to argue that the principle of consent is not necessarily lost and that it may be possible to rebuild a different sort of social contract theory from amid the ruins. The problem with conventional social contract theory, as it turns out, is quite clear. It is conventional social contract theory's *conventionalism* that renders it incoherent. Obligation cannot be generated from conventions or constructed from will alone. Authority cannot be justified by sheer power shorn of any normative property.

I suggest that we begin the work of reconstructing social contract theory, first, by rejecting conventionalism and, second, by embracing moral and metaphysical realism. One might perhaps wonder how I've arrived at the second part of the conjunct. The argument, adumbrated here and elaborated later in this volume, runs as follows: The only possible account of obligation consonant with metaphysical nominalism (the position that only particular or individual things have real existence and that universals are only general *names* that stand for a group of particulars and creatures or inventions of the understanding made by us) is a conventionalist or voluntaristic account.[128] Consequently, nominalism together with obligation entails conventionalism (or voluntarism) such that if nominalism constitutes the correct ontology, and if anyone is ever possibly under any obligation to do anything, then conventionalism (or voluntarism) must also be true. But given that the foregoing argument for the self-referential incoherence of conventional social contract theory entails the self-referential incoherence not only of conventionalism (broadly construed) but also of metaethical voluntarism, it follows that conventionalism/voluntarism and obligation are mutually exclusive.[129] If there is any such thing as obligation (indeed, if there is any such thing as the possibility—even just the conceptual possibility—of anyone, anywhere, ever being under any obligation), then we must deny conventionalism. Given modus tollens, if we posit the existence or possibility of some obligation obtaining for some person, then we must reject nominalism as well. But I submit that either nominalism is true or realism is.[130] If I am right, then, by application of the disjunctive syllogism, a rejection of nominalism requires embracing realism.[131] That is, affirming obligation, of any sort and for anyone, entails affirming moral, and so also ontological, realism.[132]

I have proposed the rejection of nominalism, along with its close allies, voluntarism and conventionalism. These isms are so widely accepted in political theory, and in social science more generally, that the proposal may seem shocking. Allow me to suggest, in conclusion, that it is not so shocking as one may think. First, within political theory, and in social science more generally, the nominalist turn consisted in a *historical* turn away from realism rather than in a *logical* repudiation of the realist position or a philosophical defense of the nominalist one. It is frequently supposed that early moderns such as Hobbes and Locke provided arguments against realism or on behalf of nominalism. In fact, they did little more than *assert* the denial of real universals.[133] What is perhaps most noteworthy about these passages (discussed in chapters 4 and 5) is the distinct lack of *argumentation* for nominalism within them. Instead of arguments, Hobbes and Locke simply stipulate that only particulars exist and that universal essences lack real existence. And there is no reason on the basis of assertion or stipulation for those not already convinced of nominalism to accept it. And so there is no reason for those who are not already nominalists to reject realism on account of nominalism.[134]

Second, we live after the fall of logical and scientific positivism and after the substantive turn in analytic philosophy.[135] Thus, though oft neglected in political theory, there are, in fact, a number of serious contemporary philosophers who reject nominalism, conventionalism, normative positivism, and voluntarism on account of the philosophical difficulties with such metaphysical and normative positions and who have constructed compelling arguments for metaphysical and moral realism.[136] Even at the height of the modern period, the penetrating intellect of Leibniz (*pace* Voltaire's naive caricature) rejected not only the metaethical voluntarism of Thomas Hobbes and Samuel von Pufendorf but also the metaphysical nominalism of Hobbes and Locke.[137] Nor was Leibniz alone, during the Enlightenment, in his resistance to Hobbesian moral theory with its nominalistic foundation.[138] I suggest, in light of the argument advanced herein, that we set aside the anti moral realist prejudice of the moment and begin the hard work of thinking about political authority from the ground up—placing moral realism back on the table as the starting point for such an endeavor.[139]

CHAPTER 2

Unconventional Justice:
The Incoherence of Conventionalist Accounts of
Justice in Antiquity and Modernity

Introduction

IN CHAPTER 1, I ARGUED that conventional social contract theory—a theory that takes our political obligations to be created wholly by human agreement or consent and therefore wholly by human will— is self-referentially incoherent. Any act of will and, by implication, any agreement or consent capable of underwriting genuine political authority or the obligation of citizens to obey requires a logically prior moral obligation. One prominent account of morality takes moral principles to be the products of agreement, to be conventional. In the "Two Faces of Contractarian Thought," Jean Hampton distinguishes between those who use the idea of a social contract to argue for the legitimacy of the state, on the one hand, and those who use contractarian arguments "to identify the best available conception of justice," on the other.[1] The first group (Hobbes, Locke, Rousseau, and Robert Nozick) she refers to as "state contractarians" (I'll call them *political contractarians*). The second group (Kant, Rawls, Gauthier) she calls "moral contractarians." If the intelligibility of political contractarianism requires an antecedent moral grounding to avoid collapse into self-referential incoherence, we might ask whether moral contractarianism can provide this ground. Over the course of chapters 2 and 3, I will argue that it cannot. For moral contractarianism, like conventional political contractarianism, is self-referentially incoherent.

To paint with broad strokes, over the history of Western thought two camps have contended with each other about the nature of justice. One camp includes those who reduce justice, whether defined as rendering to each their due or as the proper order of things, to convention (whether *convention* refers to the customs of each community, or to the laws the strong lay on those they govern, or to the shackles the weak lay about the strong). For this group (call them *conventionalists*) just and unjust, right and wrong, are human creations, communal conventions perhaps, or the decrees of those who possess the power to rule over others. The other camp (call them *moral realists*) includes those who maintain that some acts are intrinsically (or simply and absolutely) right, and other acts intrinsically wrong. Moral realists affirm the objectivity of moral value or, more aptly, the objective reality of goodness and justice. On this view, then, some acts are really just and others really unjust, whatever we may think and whatever our community may say. Ancient conventionalists include Greek Sophists such as Protagoras, Antiphon, Thrasymachus, and Callicles.[2] Proponents of conventionalism in the modern period include Thomas Hobbes and David Hume.[3] Contemporary conventionalists preeminently include David Gauthier and John Rawls (at least in work after *A Theory or Justice*) as well as J. L. Mackie and Hans Kelsen.[4] Moral realists include Plato, Aristotle, Cicero, Augustine, and Aquinas (who holds that to say justice depends simply on the will is blasphemous)[5] in antiquity and the Middle Ages, Ralph Cudworth and the Cambridge Platonists and Leibniz in the modern period, and Nicholas Wolterstorff, Robert Merrihew Adams, John Rist, and T. K. Seung today.[6] Ronald Dworkin belongs in this second camp insofar as he affirms the objectivity of moral value generally and of justice in particular.[7] At the same time, he rejects the term *realism* and quite emphatically contends that the objectivity of moral value does not presuppose *metaphysical* realism.

Over the course of the next two chapters, I will argue that conventionalists and moral contractarians fail to provide any coherent view of justice. Their accounts of justice either endeavor to establish moral norms binding on individuals on the basis of will alone, in which case the position is self-referentially incoherent, *or*, in the case of contemporary moral contractarianism, presuppose normative constraints on any agreement as to principles of justice for a community where those constraints are prior to the choice of principles and normative for it, in which case the position is not really a contractarian account of morality at all. Consequently, a coherent account of justice requires the objective reality of justice, of right and wrong. Conventionalist, constructivist, and antirealist accounts of justice fail as accounts of justice per se, and therefore fail both as possible grounds of political authority and obligations generally and as a possible ground of political contractarianism in particular.

Conventionalism in Ancient Thought[8]
AN OVERVIEW OF CONVENTIONALIST ACCOUNTS
OF JUSTICE IN ANCIENT GREEK THOUGHT

At the headwaters of the conventionalist view of justice in antiquity stands Protagoras. Protagoras traveled from his native Thrace to Athens in the mid-fourth century B.C., where Pericles apparently commissioned him to draft a constitution for the colony of Thurii, in 431. He was visiting Athens again when the Peloponnesian War commenced, and finally in 430, when Athens was being ravaged by the plague.[9] According to Diogenes Laërtius, controversy over Protagoras's book on the gods got him indicted for blasphemy, necessitating his flight from Athens before the trial could take place. The controversy notwithstanding, Protagoras's influence was substantial. He remains most famous for his contention, recounted in the Platonic dialogue named for him, that "a human being is the measure of all things—of things that are, that they are, and of things that are not, that they are not."[10] There has long been some debate as to how to understand this statement. Some take Protagoras to mean that reality is a function of *individual* perception. Others, writes Frederick Copleston, contend that "by 'man' Protagoras does not mean the individual man, but man in the specific sense." In that case, "the meaning of [Protagoras's] dictum would not be that 'what appears to you to be true is true for you, and what appears to me to be true is true for me,' but rather that the community or group or the whole human species is the criterion of truth" or reality.[11] On either interpretation, however, Protagoras clearly seems to make a claim about reality as such. He seems to say that reality is a function of human perception or construction.[12] By implication, on either interpretation he appears to deny that there is an objective reality, external to human perception, and that human beings might rightly or wrongly perceive. Thus Protagoras's famous *homo mensura* seems to connote a kind of *metaphysical* conventionalism or antirealism, according to which reality is relative to human perception, whether that of the individual or the community.

The interpretative debate notwithstanding, Protagoras's antirealism seems to be individualist.[13] That is, he seems to hold that reality is a function of each individual's perception rather than of collective perception. In one fragment he writes, "I do say that the truth is as I've written: each of us is the measure of the things which are and the things which are not. Nevertheless, there's an immense difference between one man and the other in just this respect: the things which are and appear to one man are different from those which are and appear to another." Now this view of reality, as Protagoras sees it, has some clear implications for morality—especially when it comes to wisdom and justice. He describes a wise person as one "who can effect a change in one of us, to whom bad things appear and are, and make good things both appear and be for him." As to justice, "If any sort of thing seems just and admirable to any state, then it actually is just and admirable for it, as long as that state accepts it." Consequently (as he sees it), the work of the wise man is to make "the beneficial things be and seem just and admirable to them, instead of any harmful things which used to be so for them."[14] What Protagoras means by "better" and "harmful" is mysterious save that he rejects any identification of "better" with "truer." Here we have an identification of justice with what a given polis views as just.

In keeping with Protagorean conventionalism, the Sophist Antiphon held that "justice is a matter of not transgressing what the *nomoi* [laws] prescribe in whatever city you are a citizen of." From this he deduced an interest-maximizing strategy: "A person would make the most advantage of justice for himself if he treated the *nomoi* as important in the presence of witnesses, and treated the decrees of *physis* [nature] as important when alone and with no witnesses present. For the decrees of *nomoi* are extra additions, those of *physis* necessary; those of *nomoi* are the products of agreement, not of natural growth, whereas those of *physis* are the products of natural growth, not agreement."[15] Laws and justice result from agreement and are not natural (perhaps they are even agreements contrary to nature such that keeping them is sometimes contrary to nature). Following such laws or justice may be contrary to our self-interest. Consequently, persons moved by self-interest should refrain from following the laws (or the requirements of justice) whenever (1) they can get away with it and (2) it is in their interest so to do.

But if laws (*nomoi*) and justice are the products of agreement, as Antiphon contends, how is it that these might fail to promote the interest of those the laws and justice purport to govern? One answer given by some ancient Greeks is that justice denominates obedience to laws laid down by the strong, by those in power, in order to benefit themselves at the expense of those they rule. Without framing justice in precisely these terms, the Athenians depicted in the Melian Dialogue of Thucydides's *Peloponnesian War* take significant strides in this direction. Presented with the Athenian offer of a choice between total subjugation to Athens or complete destruction, the representatives of Melos protest that the Athenians's demand is unjust. As the Athenians see it, however, the Melians misunderstand the nature of justice. Justice, they say, does not govern the relation between the strong and the weak: "decisions about justice are made in human discussions only when both sides are under equal compulsion; but when one side is stronger, it gets as much as it can, and the weak must accept that."[16] The representatives of Melos contend that Athens is putting her "interest in the place of justice."[17] Indeed, the Melians appeal to a common standard of justice—one that is normative for Athenians and Melians and that is in the ultimate interest of all to follow. The Athenians reply that it is in their interest to exercise power or dominance over the inhabitants of Melos. Moreover, "Nature always compels gods (we believe) and men (we are certain) to rule over anyone they can control. We did not make this custom [nomos], and we were not the first to follow it; but we will take it as we found it and leave it to posterity forever, because we know that you [Melians] would do the same if you had our power, and so would anyone else."[18] In other words, the so-called law of nature underwrites the pursuit of interest or advantage. And, at the end of the day, that means that the strong dominate the weak by right—which is to say, in accordance with, or at least not contrary to, justice.

While Thucydides's Athenians claim that justice only applies to equals and not to relations between the strong and weak, in Plato's *Republic* Thrasymachus defines justice as nothing but the interest of the stronger party.[19] This account of justice requires filling in. According to Thrasymachus, in each city the stronger element rules—in some the one strongest, in others the wealthy few, in others the demos:

> And each type of rule makes laws that are advantageous for itself: democracy makes democratic ones, tyranny tyrannical ones, and so on with the others. And so by legislating, each declares that what is just for its subjects is what is advantageous for itself—the ruler [or rulers]—and it punishes anyone who deviates from this as lawless and unjust. That, Socrates, is what I say justice is, the same in all cities [*poleis*]: what is advantageous for the established rule. Since the established rule is surely stronger, anyone who does the rational calculation correctly will conclude that the just is the same everywhere—what is advantageous for the stronger.[20]

In Plato's *Laws*, the Athenian Stranger addresses the same position in an exchange with Cleinias:

> You realize that some people maintain that there are as many different kinds of laws as there are political systems? . . . Don't think the question at issue is a triviality: it's supremely important, because in effect we've got back to arguing about the criteria of justice and injustice. These people take the line that legislation should be directed not to waging war or attaining complete virtue, but to safeguarding the interests of the established political system, whatever that is, so that it is never overthrown and remains permanently in force. They say that the definition justice that measures up to the facts is best formulated like this. . . . It runs: "Whatever serves the interest of the stronger." . . . The point is this: according to them, the element in control at any given moment lays down the law of the land. . . . "So do you imagine," they say, "that when a democracy has won its way to power, or some other constitution has been established (such as dictatorship), it will ever pass any laws, unless under pressure, except those designed to further its own interest and ensure that it remains permanently in power? That'll be its main preoccupation, won't it?" . . . So the author of these rules will call

them "just" and claim that anyone who breaks them is acting "unjustly," and punish him. . . . So this is why such rules will always add up to "justice."[21]

The Athenian Stranger says that the account of justice elaborated above has to do with one of those "claims to authority" concerning "who should rule whom." These putative titles to authority include claims that "parents should rule children, the elder the younger, and the noble those of low birth; and there was a large number of other titles to authority, if you remember, some of which conflicted with others." The account of justice in the passage above turns out to be a claim of this sort. It's the claim that the strong should rule and the weak obey: "The claim we're talking about now was certainly one of these: we said, I think, that Pindar turned it into a law of nature— which meant that he 'justified the use of force extreme,' to quote his actual words."[22]

Over and against Thucydides's Athenians, Thrasymachus, and the Theban poet Pindar, Plato's Athenian Stranger rejects the notion that strength (or power) confers any title or claim to authority. Putative laws that are really nothing more than the "commands" of the stronger party are not really laws at all:

When offices are filled competitively, the winners take over the affairs of the state so completely that they totally deny the losers and the losers' descendants any share of power. Each side passes its time in a narrow scrutiny of the other, apprehensive lest someone with memories of past injustices should gain some office and lead a revolution. Of course, our position is that this kind of arrangement is very far from being a genuine political system; we maintain that laws which are not established for the good of the whole state [polis] are bogus laws, and when they favour particular sections of the community their authors are not citizens but party-men; and people who say those laws have a claim to be obeyed are wasting their breath.[23]

The Athenian Stranger's argument relies on the notion that force or strength or will (just as such) lacks normative force. Put another way, given the distinction between *potentia* (the capacity to do something) and *potestas* (normative power or right or authority), force or strength or will (just as such) are instances of *potentia*, of the capacity to do something. They are not, on account of being instances of force or strength or will (that is, on account of being instances of *potentia*), instances of *potestas*. Thus, from differences in strength or power, nothing of normative consequence follows. The analysis of justice proffered by Thrasymachus at best gives us a purely descriptive or causal account (about how laws and the word justice function in different societies) that has no implication about what ought to be the case. If it did, there would be no distinction between what ought to happen and what does—there would be here a distinction without difference, rendering normative language altogether superfluous.

In contrast to Thrasymachus, the Callicles of Plato's *Gorgias* views conventional justice as an imposition of the weak upon the strong:

> I think, those who set down the laws are the weak human beings and the many. It is therefore in reference to themselves and their own advantage that they set down the laws and praise their praises and blame their blames: frightening away the more forceful human beings and those with power to have more, so that they won't have more than themselves, they say that taking more is shameful and unjust, and that doing injustice is this—seeking to have more than the others. For they are quite contented, I think, if they themselves have an equal share, since they are lowlier.

He concludes that "it's on account of these things that this, seeking to have more than the many, is said to be unjust and shameful, and they call it doing injustice." Callicles contrasts this *conventional justice*, by which the weak shackle the strong, with *natural justice*, which, as he defines it, echoes the rule of nature that Thucydides's Athenians claim to have discovered (but not to have invented):

> But nature herself, I think, reveals that this very thing is just, for the better to have more than the worse and the more powerful than the less powerful. And it is clear in many places that

these things are so: both among the other animals and in whole cities and races of human beings, the just has been decided thus, for the stronger to rule and the weaker to have more. Indeed, making use of what kind of justice did Xerxes lead his army against Greece or his father against the Scythians? . . . Indeed I think these men do these things according to the nature of the just, and yes, by Zeus, according to the law of nature—though perhaps not according to this one that we set down. By molding the best and most forceful of us, catching them young like lions, subduing them by charms and bewitching them, we reduce them to slavery, saying that one must have an equal share and that this is the noble and the just. But, I think, if a man having a sufficient nature comes into being, he shakes off and breaks through all these things and gets away, trampling underfoot our writings, spells, charms, and the laws that are all against nature, and the slave rises up to be revealed as our master; and there the justice of nature shines forth.[24]

Thus Callicles presents us with a distinction between conventional and natural justice and argues that conventional justice and natural justice are opposed. Conventional justice is the means by which the weak shackle the strong; natural justice approves the strong dominating the weak. This opposition notwithstanding, there are two profound similarities between these kinds of justice. First, conventional and natural justice, on Callicles's account, are both impositions by one group upon another—by the weak shackling the strong or the strong imposing their order upon the weak. In both cases, the ontological ground of justice is nothing other than an assertion of sheer will. Second, for both sorts of justice, the rules called just or right constitute the means by which each group, the many weak or few strong, seeks its own gain at the expense of the other. Thus, the weak shackle the strong with traditional morality for the sake of their own advantage. Likewise, natural justice advances the advantage of the strong against the weak because it putatively justifies the powerful having more and better than the weak.

Finally, for our brief overview of the Sophist's conventionalist accounts of justice, consider Glaucon's account of the origin and nature of justice in book 2 of *The Republic*. Glaucon poses three challenges to Socrates's claim that justice is both good for its own sake and beneficial to the just soul: the origin of justice in an agreement, the ring of Gyges of Lydia's ancestor, and the two lives (of the consummately unjust and consummately just persons). For our purposes we need only consider the first:

> People say. . . that to do injustice is naturally good and to suffer injustice bad. But the badness of suffering it far exceeds the goodness of doing it. Hence, those who have done and suffered injustice and who have tasted both—the ones who lack the power to do it and avoid suffering it—decide that it is profitable to come to an agreement with each other neither to do injustice nor to suffer it. As a result, they begin to make laws and covenants; and what the law commands, they call lawful and just. That, they say, is the origin and very being of justice. It is in between the best and the worst. The best is to do injustice without paying the penalty; the worst is to suffer it without being able to take revenge. Justice is in the middle between these two extremes. People love it, not because it is a good thing, but because they are too weak to do injustice with impunity. Someone who has the power to do it, however—someone who is truly a man—would not make an agreement with anyone, neither to do injustice nor to suffer it. For him, that would be insanity.[25]

As it stands, some vicious circularity stalks Glaucon's argument (how can justice be the product of an agreement *for the sake of preventing* injustice?). We might try to eliminate it along the following lines. To be able to harm (or hurt) others with impunity is good (or advantageous). To suffer harm (or hurt) from others—for others to be able to harm (or hurt) one with impunity—is bad. The badness of being harmed by others with impunity exceeds the good of being able to harm (or hurt) others with impunity. Thus, those who have harmed others (for their own gain) and suffered harm at the hands of others conclude that it is beneficial to enter an agreement or covenant with others in which they all agree to refrain from harming (or hurting) each other. Thus, they "make laws and covenants" and call "what the law commands" "lawful and just." The agreement or covenant is the origin of justice (and so of injustice). The content or requirements of justice are the terms stipulated in the agreement or the laws laid down pursuant to it. On this account, when everyone pursues their own gain without restraint, each person is vulnerable to being trampled by others who are likewise unrestrained. Thus, weak or vulnerable individuals seek to constrain others by agreeing to be constrained.[26]

THE FAILURE OF CONVENTIONALIST ACCOUNTS
OF JUSTICE IN ANTIQUITY

How might we reply to conventionalist accounts of justice offered in antiquity? Let's begin with Protagorean conventionalism. Recall that Protagoras weds conventionalism concerning justice to metaphysical antirealism.[27] According to Protagoras's antirealist metaphysics, all reality (what is and what is not) is a function of human perception (whether of each individual or of a community of individuals). Consequently, justice is just a matter of human perception. Thus, conventionalism concerning justice is an entailment (or simply part) of metaphysical antirealism (or creative antirealism or perspectivism).[28] But Protagoras's antirealism either presupposes or entails its own denial and is therefore self-refuting.[29]

According to Protagoras, human perception determines what is and what is not. But is this a statement about reality just as such? That is, does Protagoras mean to claim that man is the measure *whether or not* we perceive him to be so? Only two answers are possible. If Protagoras says yes, then reality (what is and what is not) is not entirely a function of human perception or construction. That is, if it is true, *independent of perception*, that all reality depends on perception, then, necessarily, it is *not* true that all reality depends on perception—for something that *is* the case (namely, that all reality depends on human perception) is so independent of human perception. In that case, in order to be a Protagorean antirealist (or perspectivist), one must reject Protagorean antirealism (or perspectivism), making the position self-referentially incoherent.[30]

In light of this difficulty, suppose Protagoras answered the question negatively. In that case, the claim that reality is a function of human perception would just be one perception among others. Now, some of us (e.g., Plato, Aristotle, Aquinas, Locke) clearly perceive the Protagorean account of reality—that reality depends on human perception—to be false.[31] Such objectors to Protagorean antirealism (or perspectivism) hold that some things really are or really are not the case independent of human perception. It follows that if all reality is a function of human perception, including the claim that all reality is a function of human perception, then it is equally true that reality both is and is not a function of human perception. That is, given that I (and others) perceive that there is some reality independent of human perception *and* that the Protagorean does not (but perceives what is and what is not is entirely a function of human perception), the Protagorean must both affirm and reject the proposition that all reality depends on human perception. That proposition quite obviously violates the law of noncontradiction. Moreover, given rules of logical inference (commutativity and simplification), the proposition that all reality both is and is not a function of human perception necessarily entails that not all reality depends upon human perception.[32] Thus, Protagorean antirealism entails its own denial. Either answer the Protagorean gives to the question about whether human perception determines reality is or is not itself simply a matter of perception collapses into incoherence.

The only way out for someone committed to a conventionalist account of justice is to reject antirealism (and perspectivism) about reality as such. Proponents of a conventionalist account of justice must affirm some objective reality, external to the human mind, for their account to have a shot at coherence—though I maintain that no coherent conventionalist account exists. Put another way, rejection of the claim that reality is a function of human perception comprises a necessary (though *not* a sufficient) condition of conventionalism concerning justice. And the accounts of justice advanced by Thucydides's Athenians, Thrasymachus, Pindar, Callicles, and Glaucon are all potentially compatible with affirming the existence of an external world, other minds, and the objective reality of descriptive claims (e.g., that the strong dominate the weak or that the weak shackle the strong). On their views, there are or may be realities external to the human mind and independent of human perception. They deny that justice is one of those realities. That is, on their different views, there is no external or perception-independent reality that corresponds to justice. Rather, justice is constructed by human beings. Can such views be refuted?

In *De legibus*, Marcus Tullius Cicero affirms the universality, objective reality, and intrinsic goodness of justice and rejects the conventionalist account of it:

> Most foolish of all is the belief that everything decreed by the institutions or laws of a particular country is just. What if the laws are the laws of tyrants? If the notorious Thirty had wished to impose their laws on Athens, even if the entire population of Athens welcomed the tyrants' laws, should those laws on that account be considered just? No more . . . should that law be considered just which our interrex passed, allowing the Dictator to execute with impunity any citizen he wished, even without trial. There is one, single, justice. It binds together human society and has been established by one, single, law. That law is right reason in commanding and forbidding. A man who does not acknowledge this law is unjust, whether it has been written down anywhere or not. If justice is a matter of obeying the written laws and customs of particular communities, and if, as our opponents allege, everything is to be measured by self-interest, then a person will ignore and break the laws when he can, if he thinks it will to be to his own advantage. That is why justice is completely nonexistent if it is not derived from nature, and if that kind of justice which is established to serve self-interest is wrecked by that same self- interest. And that is why every virtue is abolished if nature is not going to support justice.[33]

Furthermore:

> What room will there be for liberality, patriotism, and devotion; or for the wish to serve others or to show gratitude? These virtues are rooted in the fact that we are inclined by nature to have a regard for others; and that is the basis of justice. Moreover, not just our services to other men, but also ceremonies and rituals in honour of the gods will be abolished—practices which, in

my view, should be retained, not out of fear, but in consequence of the association between man and God. If on the other hand laws were validated by the orders of peoples, the enactments of politicians, and the verdicts of judges, then it would be just to rob, just to commit adultery, just to introduce forged wills, provided those things were approved by the votes or decrees of the populace.[34]

Now, the conventionalist's position is that "justice" does not refer to any reality independent of human perception or construction. And Cicero's argument here might be taken to mean that founding justice only on self-interest negates its objectivity. Suppose justice is only a convention founded on the interests of individuals. Interests vary from person to person. Consequently, if justice is founded on interest, then right and wrong vary from one person to another. Nothing is always right—nothing simply or intrinsically right or wrong. Doubtless Cicero means to include that claim. But I think he may mean to say something stronger too. I think he may mean that the implication of the conventionalist account of justice is that there is no such thing as justice at all—that is, on conventionalism there's *nothing* to which the word *justice* refers; it's an empty signifier.[35]

What might Cicero's stronger albeit implicit argument be? Well, consider why justice is invented according to Thrasymachus or Callicles. The reason for justice, on their accounts, is to advance the interest of those who impose rules of action upon others (the interest of the stronger or the weaker party, as the case may be). Now, if justice is nothing but the interest of the stronger party imposed on those they rule, then it might well be in your interest, ceteris paribus, to follow its dictates whenever you might suffer punishment for acting unjustly. However, there may be many times when (1) you can get away with acting contrary to justice or the law, and (2) you consider it in your interest to do so.[36] In those cases, the Sophist Antiphon counseled following your own advantage rather than the dictates of justice. Yet every time someone acts in this way, justice (as conceived and imposed by those who rule) fails to serve the advantage of the ruling class. Those who rule others invented or constructed justice for their own gain. But, in fact, the rules of justice don't always advance the interest of those who rule. They do so only to the extent that those in power correctly ascertain and lay down rules that, when followed, really do redound to their gain *and* only to the extent those rules are reliably obeyed.[37]

Assume *arguendo* that those in power get the rules right so far as their own advantage is concerned. The conventional view must still take into account that the so-called rules of justice will or at least might frequently be ignored. But these rules, insofar as they are purely conventional—insofar as they are *conventions*—and founded upon interest, are not rules of action, if they are not followed. The moral realist can posit moral rules for action that really exist whether or not they are followed—that hold whatever anyone in fact does. The conventionalist cannot.[38] For if the rules of justice are not followed, then they do not advance the interest of those who rule. In which case, they do not *refer* to generalizations of actual human behavior or to the actual advantage of the strong (especially if the dictates of the strong may or may not redound to their advantage). If putative rules of justice do not refer to generalizations of actual behavior, then they do not refer to actual *conventions*. And if the only rules of action are conventions, then they don't refer to any *rules* at all.

To what solution can our rulers recur in the absence of anything intelligible as rules of action? Well, they could try to compel action that is to their advantage in each and every instance. But at that point, rules of justice have become entirely superfluous.[39] At that point, it is compulsion and not rules about right action or following the law that serves the interest of the ruling party. The raison d'être for rules of justice—as a device to promote the advantage of our rulers—is to avoid the cost of constant enforcement. But justice founded on self-interest alone seems to presuppose the sort of behavioral patterns that require constant enforcement. Thus, justice founded on interest alone turns out to be an empty concept.

In sum, if justice is a matter of interest, then one will follow its requirements whenever it is in one's interest to do so and one will act contrary to justice whenever one thinks that's in one's interest and one can get away with it. Justice can only work to advance mutual advantage or the advantage of the regnant class or group to the extent that they (or all of us) can expect it to be followed. But if humas are driven only by self-interest, then we must expect individuals to act contrary to justice whenever they perceive that it's in their interest to do so—in which case the rules of justice are not a reliable guide to action. The only solution for the regnant class (whether the strong, the weak, or all of us trying to constrain each other) is to rely on total enforcement of their will in every instance. But in that case, *rules* of justice never actually come into play.

Hobbes's response to the Foole in chapter 15 of *Leviathan* can be understood as a reply to Cicero's contention that founding justice on interest actually eviscerates it. Gauthier reads Hobbes that way. Given the deficiencies of Hobbes's reply (to his own imagined objection), Gauthier seeks to improve it. I contend that Hobbes and Gauthier both fail.

Moral Conventionalism in Modernity
THE CONVENTIONALIST STRAIN IN THOMAS HOBBES'S MORAL PHILOSOPHY

Though not a "commonplace," David Gauthier maintains it is nevertheless "true" that Thomas Hobbes "is the greatest of English moral philosophers." Just what accounts for Hobbes's greatness as a moral (and not only as a political) theorist? According to Gauthier, "The problematic of modern moral theory is set by three dogmas which philosophy receives from economics. The first is that value is utility—a measure of subjective, individual preference. The second is that rationality is maximization: the rational individual 'will maximize the extent to which his objective is achieved.' The third is that interests are non-tuistic: interacting persons do not take 'an interest in one another's interests.'"[40] Gauthier claims that "modern moral theory determines the possibility of morality in relation to these dogmas" and that "the majority of moral theorists have, of course, sought to establish the possibility of morality by rejecting one or more account of the economists' presuppositions. They have offered alternative accounts of value, or reason, or interest." And yet "the bolder course" is to embrace all three dogmas. And "this is what Hobbes does, establishing a place for morality as a conventional constraint on our natural behavior. The *tour de force* in his theory is the reconciliation of maximizing rationality with constraining morality." Hobbes's "true moral theory is a dual conventionalism, in which a conventional reason, superseding natural reason, justifies a conventional morality, constraining natural behavior. And this dual conventionalism is Hobbes's enduring contribution to moral theory."[41] While I don't think that conventionalism or moral contractarianism is the only strain in Hobbes's political and ethical thought, I nevertheless think that it's a real and important strain of his thought. In what follows, I maintain that this moral contractarian strain fails to provide a coherent account of justice.[42]

As part of his case for Hobbes's moral contractarianism, Gauthier adduces as evidence Hobbes's subjectivism concerning good and evil and his instrumentalist account of reason. I'll begin by discussing some passages that I think make the case for Hobbesian conventionalism (or moral contractarianism) even more strongly than the ones on which Gauthier focuses. According to Hobbes in *De Homine*,

> The common name for all things that are desired, insofar as they are desired, is *good*; and for all things we shun, *evil*. . . . But, since different men desire and shun different things, there must needs be many things that are *good* to some and *evil* to others; so that which is *good* to us is *evil* to our enemies. There can be a common good, and it can rightly be said of something that *it is commonly a good*, that is, useful to many, or good for the state. At times one can also talk of a good for everyone, like health: but this way of speaking is relative; therefore one cannot speak of something as being *simply* good; since whatever is good is good for someone or other. . . . Therefore good is said to be relative to person, place, and time. What pleaseth one man now, will displease another later; and the same holds for everyone else.[43]

If "good is . . . relative to person, place, and time," it would seem that common principles of justice likewise are not given by nature and can only be established by convention. And Hobbes holds precisely this. Thus, a few chapters later he writes, "Since . . . good and evil are not the same to all, it happens that the same manners are praised by some and condemned by others, that is, are called good by some, evil by others, virtues by some, vices by others. So, just as the proverb hath it, 'So many men, so many opinions,' one can also say, 'Many men, many different rules for vice and virtue."[44] Now, those "who consider men by themselves and as though they existed outside of civil society, can have no moral science because they lack any certain standard against which virtue and vice can be judged and defined."[45] Indeed, "a common standard for virtues and vices" *only* appears "in civil life." And "this standard cannot . . . be other than the law of each and every state." Moreover, there is no "impediment to such a thesis in the fact that laws are innumerable and that once there were states with different laws. For whatsoever the laws are, not to violate them is always and everywhere held to be a virtue in citizens, and to neglect them a vice. *Although it is true that certain actions may be just in one state, and unjust in another, nevertheless, justice (that is, not to violate the laws) is and shall be everywhere the same.*"[46] The degree to which this passage echoes Thrasymachus's conventionalism in book 2 of Plato's *Republic* is striking.

In his earlier work *De Cive*, Hobbes argued that although "theft, murder, adultery, and all injuries are forbid by the law of nature," what counts as theft, murder, adultery, and injury "is not to be determined by natural, but by the civil law." Not every taking of another's possessions counts as theft, not every killing of another person counts as murder, not every intimate encounter with another woman counts as adultery—"but only that which the civil law prohibits." Consequently, writes Hobbes, the city of Sparta legislated that young men (in training) who could take "certain goods from others," without getting caught, should not be punished—"for it was nothing else but to make a law, that what was so acquired should be their own and not another's." Likewise, "that copulation which in one city is matrimony, in another will be judged adultery."[47]

Hobbes's invocation of Lacedaemon is apropos. With respect to adultery, writes Carl Richard, "A Spartan husband would not think of denying his wife to another male, nor would the wife consider refusing such a request, if the suitor were an honorable man. The point was to produce more children, but without the passionate feuds that resulted from surreptitious sex. By institutionalizing adultery, the Spartans hoped to rob it of its power to destabilize society."[48] On Hobbes's argument, such spousal sharing in Sparta could not be *adultery* because Spartan law permitted it. The same action, however, was certainly adultery in seventeenth-century England because (and only because) the laws there forbid it. With respect to killing, Richard writes, "When a Spartan child was born, the ephors inspected him for signs of illness. If the child was weak or deformed in any way, he was hurled from the top of Mount Taygetus [in] a crude form of genetic engineering." During the year of concealment (*krypteia*), from twenty to twenty-one, Spartan males, who at night left hiding to procure food, were permitted (indeed, expected) "to kill any helots who were out after curfew."[49] On Hobbes's argument, these killings in Sparta were not murder because they were permitted and (in the case of the *ephori* killing "weak and deformed" infants, at least) even required. But the laws of England in Hobbes's day prohibited infanticide, *thereby making it murder.* If the foregoing passages in Hobbes don't count as a conventionalist account of justice (or as moral contractarianism), it's hard to know what does.

Chapter 13 of *Leviathan* has also been considered evidence of Hobbes's moral conventionalism:

> To this war of every man against every man, this also is consequent: that nothing can be unjust. The notions of right and wrong, justice and injustice, have there no place. Where there is no common power, there is no law; where no law, no injustice. Force and fraud are the two cardinal virtues. Justice and injustice are none of the faculties neither of the body, nor mind. If they were, they might be in a man that were alone in the world, as well as his senses and passions. They are qualities that relate to men in society, not in solitude. It is consequent also to the same condition that there be no propriety, no dominion, no *mine* and *thine* distinct, but only that to be every man's that he can get, and for so long as he can keep it.[50]

To the foregoing we must add Hobbes's claim in chapter 14 that individuals in the state of nature/war possess the morally unregulated right of nature—the right to everything and to do anything, even make use of another's body, in order to survive (or, as he also sometimes defines it, the right to everything).[51] In the next century, Alexander Hamilton took Hobbes's correlative contentions that

justice has no place in the state of nature/war and that justice and injustice are properties that relate to men in society, and so not to men
as men, to express moral conventionalism. In his riposte to Samuel
Seabury, Hamilton writes, "Mr. Hobbs" held that "man in a state
of nature . . . was, then, perfectly free from all restraint of *law* and
government. Moral obligation, according to him, is derived from the
introduction of civil society; and there is no virtue, but what is purely
artificial, the mere contrivance of politicians, for the maintenance of
social intercourse."[52]

Finally, consider Hobbes's discussion of the third law of nature,
"*that men perform their covenants made*, without which covenants are in
vain, and but empty words, and the right of all men to all things [i.e.,
the right of nature] remaining, we are still in the condition of war."[53]
Moreover, this law of nature constitutes "the fountain and original of
JUSTICE. For where no covenant hath preceded, there hath no right
been transferred, and every man has a right to everything; and consequently, no action can be unjust. But when a covenant is made, then
to break it is *unjust*; and the definition of INJUSTICE is no other
than *the not performance of covenant*. And whatsoever is not unjust is
just."[54] So we might say that the third law of nature contains the definition of justice—namely, the performance of one's covenants. And
Hobbesian covenants are artifacts designed to save us from nature.

Whether or not a covenant is or can be made, however, depends
upon the circumstances. "Covenants of mutual trust," he says, "are invalid" whenever either party has "a fear" the other won't perform their
part of the agreement. Thus, even though the origin of justice is "the
making of covenants," "yet injustice actually there can be none till the
cause of such fear be taken away, which while men are in the natural
condition of war, cannot be done." Consequently, "before the names
of just and unjust can have place, there must be some coercive power
to compel men equally to the performance of their covenants, by the
terror of some punishment greater than the benefit they expect by the
breach of their covenant, and to make good that propriety which by
mutual contract men acquire, in recompense of the universal right
they abandon; and such power there is none before the erection of a
commonwealth."[55] Not only the meaning of *just* and *unjust* generally
but also their specific content (the specific actions denominated just

and unjust) depend so much on covenant, or agreement, that these words have no meaning unless some coercive power exists to punish injustice—precisely because, as Hobbes later says, "covenants without the sword are but words."[56]

Hobbes doesn't think his definition of justice excludes that of Aristotle and the Scholastics. Rather, he thinks their account of justice must be subsumed under his in order for their account to be intelligible:

> And this is to be gathered out of the ordinary definition of justice in the Schools; for they say that *justice is the constant will of giving to every man his own.* And therefore where there is no *own*, that is, no propriety, there is no injustice; and where there is no coercive power erected, that is, where there is no commonwealth, there is no propriety, all men having right to all things; therefore where there is no commonwealth, there nothing is unjust. So that the nature of justice consisteth in the keeping of valid covenants; but the validity of covenants begins not but with the constitution of a civil power sufficient to compel men to keep them; *and then it is also that propriety begins.*[57]

That is, covenants are valid *only if* a civil power capable of compelling their observance has been constituted—and only then does propriety begin. In chapter 15, Hobbes seems clearly to claim that what individuals are *due*—what is owed them (in terms of goods or treatment from others)—depends on, is *determined* by, covenant and therefore agreement. Agreement backed up by threat of sanction for failure to perform one's end of the bargain, to be sure. But agreement nevertheless. And prior to covenant, everyone has a right to everything and no action whatsoever is unjust.[58] Moreover, as we saw with *De Cive*, Hobbes clearly apprehends the upshot of predicating justice on covenant or agreement for law, where no prior natural justice constrains the terms of agreement. In *Leviathan* he writes, "No law can be unjust. The law is made by the sovereign power, and all that is done by such law is warranted and owned by every one of the people; and that which every man will have so, no man can say is unjust. It is in the laws of a commonwealth as in the laws of gaming: whatsoever the gamesters all agree on is injustice to none of them."[59] When "no action can be unjust" prior to covenant and when covenant creates sovereign power, it follows that "no law can be unjust" after the establishment of sovereign power.

In sum, justice consists in keeping one's covenants. And a necessary condition of valid covenants is the establishment of a civil power "sufficient to compel men to keep them." But this would seem to leave open the possibility that interest and justice conflict *or* to reduce justice to self-interest, thereby implying, as Cicero maintained, that justice does not really exist. As Hobbes sees it, however, there is such a thing as justice (the keeping of covenants), and justice and interest never conflict. He seeks to demonstrate this in his reply to the Foole.

According to Hobbes, "The Foole hath said in his heart: 'there is no such thing as justice'; and sometimes also with his tongue, seriously alleging that: 'every man's conversation and contentment being committed to his own care, there could be no reason why every man might not do what he thought conduced thereunto, and therefore also to make or not make, keep or not keep, covenants was not against reason, when it conduced to one's benefit.'" The Foole "does not therein deny that there [are] covenants, [or] that they are sometimes broken, sometimes kept, [or] that such breach of them may be called injustice, and the observance of them justice." Rather, "he questioneth whether injustice . . . may not sometimes stand with that reason which dictateth to every man his own good," especially "when it conduceth to such a benefit as shall put a man in a condition to neglect, not only the dispraise and revilings, but also the power of other men."[60]

But, says Hobbes, "This specious reasoning is nevertheless false":

> For the question is not of promises where there is no security of performance on either side (as when there is no civil power erected over the parties promising), for such promises are no covenants, but either where one of the parties has already performed, or where there is a power to make him perform, there is the question whether it be against reason, that is, against the benefit of the other to perform or not. And I say it is not against reason. For . . . in a condition of war wherein every man to every man (for want of a common power to keep them all in awe) is an

enemy, there is no man [who] can hope by his own strength or wit to defend himself from destruction without the help of confederates ... and therefore, he which declares he thinks it reason to deceive those that help him can in reason expect no other means of safety than what can be had from his own single power. He therefore that breaketh his covenant, and consequently declareth that he thinks he may with reason do so, cannot be received into any society that unite themselves for peace and defence but by the error of them that receive him; nor when he is received, be retained in it without seeing the danger of their error; which errors a man cannot reasonably reckon upon as the means for his security; and therefore, if he be left or cast out of society, he perisheth; and if he live in society, it is by the errors of other men, which he could not foresee nor reckon upon; and consequently [he has acted] against reason of his preservation, and so as all men that contribute not to his destruction forbear him only out of ignorance of what is good for themselves.[61]

So as Hobbes sees it, the Foole fails to calculate interest correctly. Someone who behaves as the Foole recommends either makes it impossible for others to covenant and enter into society with him or relies entirely on others covenanting with him because they misjudge their own interest. And he thinks it unreasonable for anyone to count on the miscalculation of others as a basis for their own preservation.

Few, however, have found Hobbes reply to the Foole convincing. Gauthier contends that "The Foole's reasoning contains an argument seemingly fatal to moral conventionalism":

If morality is to be a rational and conventional constraint on natural behavior, then it must be rationally stable, and this requires that each [person] have reason to follow [morality] provided others do. Since reason enjoins the maximization of advantage, morality is rationally stable only if it is most advantageous for each to follow it provided others do. But if this holds, then in what sense is morality a *constraint*? If each person's good is best furthered by some course of action, then each [person], rationally exercising his or her unlimited right of nature, will follow that course of action. No laying down of right is needed. The role of so-called "moral" conventions can then be not to constrain our behavior, but rather to enable us to coordinate that behavior to maximal advantage, effecting, like the perfectly competitive market, the harmony of non-tuisms. The conception of morality as a rational and conventional *constraint* has no place. On the other hand, if each does worse, in terms of advantage, to follow morality provided others do, then, although morality constitutes a constraint on our natural behavior, the constraint is irrational. And so again, the conception of morality as a *rational* and conventional constraint has no place.[62]

Yet Gauthier believes Hobbes has a viable reply to the Foole contained within his account of "right reason." The Hobbesian position includes not only moral conventionalism but *rational* conventionalism as well. Here Gauthier cites Hobbes's treatment of right reason in chapter 5 of *Leviathan*. In the relevant passage, Hobbes rejects the existence or reality of a right reason established by nature capable of resolving disputes. Consequently, the resolution of conflicts requires establishing the reason of a judge or arbitrator as right (i.e., decisive) reason: "no mans Reason, nor the Reason of any one number of men, makes the certaintie; no more than account is there well cast up, because a great many men have unanimously approved it. And therefore, as when there is a controversy in an account, the parties must by their own accord, set up for right Reason, the Reason of some Arbitrator, or Judge, to whose sentence they will both stand, or their controversie must either come to blowes, or be undecided, for want of a right Reason constituted Nature; so is it also in all debates of what kind soever."[63] Gauthier (convincingly) takes Hobbes to mean we must set aside individual reason in favor of a "conventional standard of right reason."[64]

The Foole's objection to Hobbes's conventional justice—that all men keep their covenants made—derives from an appeal to natural reason, the sort of reasoning appropriate to the state of nature. But in order to seek peace with others and to establish civil society, we must replace "natural reason" with conventional right reason: "The Foole appeals to that reason which dictates to every man his own good—to natural reason, so that he may show injustice to be rational. But injustice is a violation of the covenant, and, in covenanting, in laying down one's right, one has renounced natural reason as the court of appeal, in favor of a reason that dictates to every man what all *agree* is good."[65] Put another way, we are to "[base] reason on peace, rather than on individual preservation" insofar as others do. This is compatible with maximizing rationality precisely because one's own interests or goals can only adequately be pursued (or maximized) by bracketing natural rationality for reason based on peace. If everyone maximizes their own interest in an unconstrained way, this creates a state of affairs contrary to the interest of each—in which each individual is not only deeply hampered in the pursuit of his own interests but also subject to being trampled by others in the unconstrained pursuit of theirs. Perhaps counterintuitively, only the constrained pursuit of interest (i.e., only a pursuit constrained by impartial rules of right) is compatible with one's greatest advantage. And Hobbes's Foole fails to see this.

Has Gauthier improved on Hobbes's reply to the Foole? One might argue that he's more or less restated it in somewhat different phraseology. But even if Gauthier has improved upon Hobbes's reply to the Foole (by drawing upon another line of thought within the Hobbesian corpus), this reconstructed Hobbes (call him Gauthier's Hobbes) is not without problem. Gauthier suggests that Hobbes's best reply to the Foole consists in distinguishing between interest maximization as construed by natural reason, on the one hand, and interest maximization as based on peace, on the other—that is, in distinguishing between unconstrained and constrained rational maximization. Yet it is quite impossible to distinguish between different kinds of self-interest on the basis of self-interest alone.

In chapter 1, I argued that it's impossible to distinguish among instances or exercises of will on the basis of will alone, for the same reason that one cannot distinguish some prime numbers from others on the basis of primeness. One cannot intelligibly distinguish among the members of the set on the basis of the predication of the property or properties by which the set is defined. This principle also applies to interest and self-interest. We can conceive of a set of all our interests: $(I_1, I_2, I_3, I_4, I_5 \ldots I_n)$. It is impossible to distinguish I_3 from I_5 on the basis of interest alone, for both are equally a matter of interest. More generally, no member of the set of interests (or from the set of one's own interests) can intelligibly be distinguished from any other member of the set on the basis of interest alone. It follows that the constrained maximization of one's interest cannot intelligibly be distinguished from the unconstrained maximization of it based only on interest. And Gauthier's reconstructed Hobbes falls into this very incoherence.

In chapter 1 we also saw that some instances of will can only be *normative* for others, on the basis of some property distinct from sheer will and normative for exercises of it. The same goes for self-interest. If some instances of self-interest (say constrained self-interest or rational self-interest as based on peace) are taken as normative for others (say self-interest as interpreted by natural reason), then this distinction can only be made on the basis of some property distinct from self-interest. But if justice is grounded in self-interest and if the interest in question is constrained rather than unconstrained self-interest, then (given the foregoing) justice cannot be based on self-interest alone. If justice were based on nothing but interest, it would have to be completely indifferent to different kinds of self-interest and therefore indifferent with respect to constrained or unconstrained self-interest.[66]

Can Gauthier's Hobbes avoid falling into self-referential incoherence? Gauthier would doubtless reply by pointing us to the concept of *maximization*. No one can maximize their self-interest in a situation in which everyone pursues their own interest in an unconstrained way. Such a state of affairs is a state of nature, which, according to Hobbes, *is* in essence a state war, a condition that puts in jeopardy the attainment of any object of desire. We can maximize the pursuit of self-interest *only if* we pursue our interests in a constrained manner and *only insofar* as others do the same. The idea is that interest maximization is sufficient for a coherent distinction between the constrained and unconstrained pursuit of interest and to ground the preference for the former over the latter.

Nevertheless, such a reply ultimately fails. First, interest maximization (or rational maximization) is an equivocal idea. One can, for instance, maximize one's interests now or over the long term. Presumably Gauthier's constrained pursuit seeks the maximization of long-term interest (or of interest over the long term) rather than immediate interest. But there is no basis in self-interest alone to prefer the maximization of long-term over immediate interest. Any decision to maximize one's interest over the course of $T_1, T_2, T_3 \ldots T_n$ rather than just at T_1 or rather than just over the course of T_1 and T_2 is a decision that cannot be based on interest maximization alone. Moreover, given the distinction between interests as perceived by natural reason and interest as perceived by conventional reason (i.e., reason based on peace), we should immediately note that it's possible to maximize in accordance with either of these or in accordance with some conjunction in which one goes back and forth (let's call this the Antiphonic Position). But interest maximization all by itself cannot tell you which sort of maximization to pursue. Maybe you just want to maximize some interest according to natural reason, in a morally unconstrained way, *even if* the end result is that you are unable to maximize interest over the long term with any success. Maybe you're willing to hazard the state of war. Maybe you believe you can successfully free ride on others, maximizing according to conventional rather than natural reason. Hobbes says you shouldn't expect to succeed in this. But maybe your assessment is correct. At any rate, Hobbes's (and Gauthier's) advice turns on a distinction between perceived interests and true interests. And one cannot distinguish between these on the basis of interest alone either.

But the conventionalist may have an even worse problem. Earlier I noted that self-interest all by itself, self-interest qua self-interest, is devoid of normative content. Gauthier (in his treatment of Hobbes and in his own work) seems to want self-interest (or the three dogmas he outlined above) to be generative of justice. But when Hobbes speaks of self-interest and when he replies to the Foole, he seems to speak of *motives* for keeping covenants or observing justice, in the context of civil society, rather than of the ground or generation of justice. That is, when it comes to the conventionalist view of justice, we should speak of *motivational* principles on the one hand—motives that impel us to follow the principles chosen—and *generative* principles on the other—the ground from which the principles of justice are generated. But how can self-interest generate justice or right and wrong? Even if Hobbes's argument gets the reasons for doing what justice requires—keeping one's covenants—entirely right, the reasons for following justice cannot, on the Hobbesian or on any convention-alist view, be identical with justice or the grounds from which it is constructed. Not without viciously begging the question.

Indeed, I suspect that Hobbes and Gauthier have a different ontological ground in mind. Self-interest rightly understood may motivate us to be just or even motivate us to construct principles of justice. Self-interest rightly understood may deliver to us the content of justice. But self-interest rightly understood is not the real ground of justice for Gauthier or Hobbes. Self-interest rightly understood (i.e., constrained self-interest) motivates us to choose in a certain way or to agree to constrain our self-interest. Self-interest is a motive that impels or directs our will—to enter into an agreement (whether actual or, as Gauthier maintains, entirely hypothetical). But the *ontological ground* of justice is agreement or willing. In *De Homine* Hobbes says a priori demonstration is possible "only of those things whose gen-eration depends on the will of men."[67] He adds, "politics and ethics (that is, the sciences of *just* and *unjust*, of *equity* and *inequity*) can be demonstrated because we ourselves make the principles—that is, the causes of justice (namely laws and covenants)—whereby it is known what *justice* and *equity*, and their opposites *injustice* and *inequity*, are."[68] Now, if conventionalists make will or agreement the ontolog-ical ground of justice, then the conventionalist account of justice is a species of metaethical voluntarism—a species of voluntarism in which will motivated by conventional reason or reason based on peace is set up as normative for will guided by natural reason. This is done on the basis of nothing but agreement—which is to say, on the basis of nothing but will. And is therefore self-referentially incoherent.

A generation after Hobbes, Samuel Clarke sought to demonstrate the self-refuting nature of Hobbes's account of justice. Clarke took Hobbes to be a conventionalist (or a moral contractarianism) who did not—because logically he could not—consistently adhere to the position.[69] Clarke's objection to Hobbes's moral conventionalism (at least as he understood Hobbes) is most clearly explicated by Terence Cuneo: "Clarke's point is that if agents in the state of nature are to make a compact with one another—if they are genuinely to *prom-ise* certain things to one another—moral obligations must already exist. . . . Clarke adverts to the obligation that promises be faithfully performed. An obligation of this sort, Clarke intimates, is not generated by promising but is a condition of performing a promise in the first place. Accordingly, Clarke maintains, Hobbes' contractualism does not explain the emergence of moral norms. Rather, it presupposes their existence." We might put the point this way: agreements cannot coherently generate the obligation to keep our agreements; rather, the obligation to keep our agreements supplies a necessary condition of there being binding agreements at all. Or, as Cuneo puts it, the obligation to keep my promises "is not generated by my promising anything. Rather, it is a normative condition thereof."[70]

CONVENTIONAL JUSTICE WITHOUT MAXIMIZATION OR THE STATE OF NATURE: THE CASE OF DAVID HUME

Hume avoids basing morality *entirely* on self-interest, and therefore might seem to avoid the foregoing critique of Hobbes's position (and especially of Gauthier's Hobbes). His account of justice as conventional does not require the dubious claim that we are rational maximizers (or, if we are, that an account of justice ought to be built on this assumption). Rather, he seeks to show that justice is conventional by showing that nothing is intrinsically right or wrong. And he seeks to demonstrate this by showing that justice is contingent or conditional—it applies only to certain circumstances. Human beings, as he sees it, construct or invent justice solely because of its utility. And its utility applies only to particular circumstances; which is to say, justice doesn't govern human life in all *conceivable* circumstances.

So what are the circumstances to which justice applies? Those circumstances have to do, in part, with human nature. We are, on the one hand, selfish—desirous of our own good or preservation. On the other hand, we are also moved by benevolence or generosity. But our generosity is limited. We are not generous to the point of sacrificing our own interests. Finally, we inhabit a world in which the goods of the world are scarce vis-à-vis our wants (or needs). These three claims constitute what might be called the circumstances of justice. Thus, Hume: "Here then is a proposition, which, I think may be regarded as certain, *that 'tis only from the selfishness and confin'd generosity of men, along with the scanty provision nature has made for his wants, that justice derives its origin.*"[71] On the Humean view, if any of these three claims does not hold, justice is unnecessary or useless.

Hume situates the social state, for which justice is invented, between the *poetical golden age* and the *philosophical state of nature.* The poetical golden age, is a state of abundance and goodwill. Benevolence is unlimited. Consequently, rules of right and wrong in the governance of human relations are unnecessary. Such rules are needed only when there is competition and conflict among individuals. But in the poetical golden age, the goods of the world are plentiful. So there would be no competition or conflict over them in that state of affairs. There would be no need for property, and so no need for rules concerning the regulation of property. The bounty of the world eliminates competition, and seems to do so even if individuals are self-interested rather than benevolent. Of course, if people were benevolent to the point of being self-abdicating, even scarcity of goods would not produce the sort of conflict that necessitates rules of right and wrong. Thus, Hume suggests that such rules are only needed and therefore only exist when there is competition or conflict—in a state of affairs that is populated by individuals whose benevolence is limited by self-interest and that is characterized by the scarcity of goods.

As for the philosophical state of nature, "a state of mutual war and violence" and in which "there is no mutual trust" (as he puts it in his later *Enquiries*), Hume follows Hobbes in claiming that rules of justice would not exist in that state of affairs. But he doubts such a state ever existed. Human beings as we have them are, and perhaps have always been, born into society (at least the society of families). Nevertheless, if such a state ever existed, justice would have no place in it.

Consequently, justice only has a place, and so only exists, in civil society, a state of affairs in which persons are motivated by both self-interest and a limited benevolence *and* in which goods are scarce relative to human wants and needs. "Thus," writes Hume, "the rules of equity or justice depend entirely on the particular state and condition in which men are placed, and owe their origin and existence to that utility, which results to the public from their strict and regular observance. Reverse, in any considerable circumstance, the condition of men. Produce extreme abundance or extreme necessity. Implant in the human breast perfect moderation and humanity, or perfect rapaciousness and malice. By rendering justice totally *useless*, you thereby totally destroy its essence, and suspend its obligation upon mankind."[72] Justice only exists where it has a point. And it only has a point in civil society—*not* in the golden age of the poets or the state of nature painted by Hobbes.

Hume takes the foregoing to mean that justice is *conditional*. It does not apply to or obtain in every state of affairs. The rules of justice do not apply always and to everyone, everywhere. In the language of contemporary analytic philosophy, rules of justice do not obtain in every (logically or metaphysically) possible world. Hume takes the conditionality of justice to imply that justice is artificial or conventional *rather than* natural, constructed by human beings to address the necessities of certain circumstances. More precisely, he infers that justice is artificial or conventional from the proposition that nothing is inherently right or wrong; he infers that nothing is inherently or intrinsically right or wrong from the claim that justice only has a point, is only useful, under certain conditions.

Hume's argument is a bridge too far. Even if justice is conditional—only applicable to a certain set of circumstances or under certain conditions (say, of men in society)—it does not follow that justice is artificial. Even if justice is only advantageous in civil society, and not in the poetical golden age or in the philosophical state of nature, it does not follow that justice is constructed rather than given in the nature of things. It might be that justice is both conditional and objective.[73] For instance, one can conceive of duties or obligations applicable to persons who are married but not to individuals who are not, or to parents but not to others. Such obligations are conditional. They do not apply to all people at all times and places. They apply to people in the condition of marriage or parenthood. But it does not follow that these obligations (of spouses to each other or of parents to children) are not objective, that they are not right in and of themselves, that they are simply constructed or artificial. As it happens, I think justice (or right and wrong in the treatment of others) includes both general duties owed to everyone and special duties owed only to some (i.e., that attach to specific relations in which one stands to certain persons but not to others), *and* that justice is not conventional (or is not purely conventional) in either case. But even if justice only fit the category of special duties or obligations, it would *not*, on account of that, be artificial rather than natural, objective, or real. Minimally, Hume's argument is a non sequitur.

But Hume's conventionalism faces a far greater problem. For, as with Hobbes, Hume's conventional justice is an artifact, a creation of sheer will. The will in question may be the tacit will of the community expressed in customs. Or it may be expressed in agreement. But given that Humean justice is conventional rather than natural, its normative force rests on will alone. To be sure, Hume says justice derives its merit and moral obligation from its utility or usefulness alone. But he also says that "justice takes its rise from human conventions" (here he includes promises and rules governing property).[74] Consider that usefulness (or utility) and moral obligation are analytically distinct. It's one thing for x to be useful and another for x to be morally obligatory, perhaps on account of its being useful. The "morally obligatory" part is not analytically packed into the "useful" part. That means something must be added to "useful" or "utility" to get "morally obligatory" and so to get justice. Since for Hume justice is "not natural," conformity to nature or intrinsic rightness cannot be what is added. As Hume sees it, the community, through its conventions, has made useful actions (or some subset thereof) morally obligatory. That is, the ground of the moral obligatoriness of that which is useful to humans in society is the will of the community as expressed in its conventions. Thus, even though Hume has abandoned the problematic Hobbesian (and Sophist) project of wedding justice to self-interest, he has nevertheless kept company with Hobbes in making *will* the ground of obligation or rightness (or of normativity). The will in question is communal or corporate and expressed in agreement and conventions—but it is will nevertheless that serves to ground what is right. So Hume's moral contractarianism, too, is a species of metaethical voluntarism, in which will is treated either as sufficient or as necessary and sufficient for moral obligation. As such, the position is self-referentially incoherent. But if conventional accounts of justice are self-referentially incoherent, then it follows that only *unconventional* (to wit, realist) accounts are possibly intelligible.

Conclusion

Conventionalisms ancient and modern fail to provide coherent accounts of justice or of moral norms more generally. The antirealist conventionalism of Protagoras, the reduction of justice to self-interest in Thrasymachus and Hobbes, the ultimate grounding of justice in utility and agreement in Hobbes and Hume, with no further foundation and that consequently ultimately rest justice, and morality more generally, entirely on human will, all turn out to be incoherent, either self-contradictory, as in the case of Protagoras, or self-referentially incoherent, as in the case of Hobbes and Hume. In the next chapter we consider whether moral contractarianism in the twentieth century saved the position from logical collapse. I maintain it did not.

CHAPTER 3

Moral Constructivism in the Dock:
Moral Contractarianism's Normative Failure

We cannot defend a theory of justice without also defending,
as part of the same enterprise, a theory of moral objectivity.

—Ronald Dworkin, *Justice for Hedgehogs*

IN WHAT FOLLOWS, I WILL argue that the moral contractarian theories
of Gauthier (in *Morals by Agreement* and "Why Contractarianism?")
and Rawls (in *A Theory of Justice*, the Dewey Lectures, published as
"Kantian Constructivism in Moral Theory," and *Political Liberalism*)
fare no better than conventionalist accounts of justice in modernity
or antiquity. According to Gauthier, morality is made by rational
agreements, where rational agreements can be made only by individuals capable of entering and participating in mutually beneficial
relations. With Annette Baier, I hold that Gauthier affirms a severely
minimalist morality that excludes whole classes of human beings
from the domain of moral obligations and of morality more generally.
He expressly excludes the unborn and those who are congenitally
handicapped or defective from the class of those to whom we have
moral obligations. But his account seems clearly to entail exclusion
of newborns, toddlers, young children for some years beyond tod-
dlerhood, and perhaps those elderly in serious decline (mentally,
physically, or both) as well. Moreover, his position must be not only
that we have no obligations to help such individuals but also that we
have no moral obligations to them at all—and therefore no obligation to refrain from harming them, including harming them just for
fun. I contend that this abhorrent implication of Gauthier's theory
provides a reductio ad absurdum refutation of it. But Gauthier holds

that if reason conflicts with our fundamental intuitions concerning right and wrong in the treatment of others, then so much the worse for our intuitions. Though I quite disagree with Gauthier here (and hold that our intuitions may provide better guidance concerning right and wrong than rational maximization, constrained or not), I turn to whether Gauthier's moral contractarianism fails on its own terms. Gauthier seeks to build morality—as a rational constraint on the pursuit of interest—from *nonmoral* building blocks. Insofar as the ultimate foundation of morality is agreement, where the agreement constitutes a nonmoral foundation, and agreement is an exercise of human will, then Gauthier grounds morality in nothing other than human will. This grounding renders his position self-referentially incoherent. Moreover, the incoherence of Gauthier's will-based attempt to create morality entails that he in fact smuggles moral building blocks into the foundation of his theory—while denying that he does.

With respect to Rawls, I argue that his account of the original position in *A Theory of Justice* begs the question. I follow T. K. Seung's contention that Rawls extracts his fair principles of justice from the original position because he has constructed that position (and the veil of ignorance) by means of (what he considers to be) fair principles of justice. In Rawls's construction of the original position, principles about the right treatment of others—especially concerning fairness and impartiality—determine what knowledge is withheld from hypothetical individuals behind the veil of ignorance. Additionally, I note that the coherence of reflective equilibrium, in which our description of the original position and our considered convictions are revised in light of each other, necessarily depends upon a standard of what is good or right that transcends both the original position and our considered convictions, and which either might, in any given instance, better instantiate, or to which either might better conform. Without such a standard, revising our description of the original position in light of our considered convictions or revising our considered convictions in light of our description of the original position would be entirely ungrounded, would be rationally arbitrary, and therefore unintelligible. Finally, with respect to *A Theory of Justice*, Rawls claims to derive the original position from norms and ideas that are widely shared *assumptions*, embedded deeply in our culture. According to Seung, these deeply embedded norms, though conventions, either instantiate transcendent norms of justice or are purely positive and merely conventional. I contend that if the ideas on which Rawls relies instantiate transcendent norms, then his theory is not fundamentally constructivist (even if it has a constructivist *element*, as Seung says we find in Plato and Aquinas).[1] But if the norms are purely positive and thoroughly conventional (i.e., these ideas do not instantiate transcendent norms), then the theory is voluntarist and self-referentially incoherent. In "Kantian Constructivism," "Justice as Fairness: Political not Metaphysical," and *Political Liberalism*, the rejection of metaphysical foundations renders agreement—an instance of human will (and *sheer* will at that)—the ultimate foundation or final ground of the public conception of justice for modern constitutional democracies characterized by an ineliminable pluralism of incommensurable and conflicting metaphysical views and conceptions of the good. And this makes the political liberalism of the later Rawls unequivocally (metaethically) voluntarist and therefore self-referentially incoherent.

In view of the foregoing, *moral* contractarianism fails to provide a coherent foundation for *political* contractarianism and government by consent. Rather than being essentially connected, political and moral contractarianism are necessarily opposed. Any coherent account of justice—of right and wrong—and of moral norms more generally requires rejecting moral contractarianism and normative constructivism (at least all the way down). We cannot build principles of justice from nonmoral building blocks or derive them from purely conventional ideas or norms. Ronald Dworkin, for his part, realizes that a coherent account of justice requires affirming morality all the way down—that the foundation of justice or moral norms must itself be moral. And he affirms the objectivity of moral value and of justice. At the same time, he rejects the term *realism* and quite emphatically contends that the objectivity of moral value does not presuppose *metaphysical* realism. I argue that Dworkin gets this wrong. The objectivity of moral value entails (or instantiates) moral realism. Moreover, both the objectivity of value and moral realism necessarily presuppose metaphysical realism. Thus, any intelligible account of justice presupposes metaphysical realism. Consequently, given modus tollens, to reject metaphysical realism entails giving up the objectivity or reality of justice and moral value altogether.

For the past half century or so, a number of scholars working in the areas of moral and political philosophy and legal theory have found themselves drawn to moral contractarianism. The reason for that allure, I suspect, is moral contractarianism's rejection of the metaphysics upon which classical natural law depends. For Gauthier, moral contractarianism rejects the existence of an intrinsic good or evil, embraces subjectivism concerning these, affirms an instrumentalist and maximizing account of rationality, and, concomitantly, rejects a teleological world—a cosmos constituted by things with final causes (i.e., of substances with final ends or *teloi*). For Rawls (at least in the essays after *A Theory of Justice* and in *Political Liberalism*), moral contractarianism (which he calls Kantian constructivism) neither affirms nor rejects classical ethical theory or metaphysics. Rather, it completely avoids making any truth claims about such things. So I suspect the contemporary attraction to moral contractarianism has much to do with the modernist metaphysics of Gauthier or the Rawlsian methodical avoidance of controversial metaphysical claims.

Ex Nihilo Nihil: The Case against Gauthier's Moral Contract
DAVID GAUTHIER RECONSIDERED

After John Rawls, David Gauthier is perhaps the most important moral contractarian of the last half century. In an essay entitled "Why Contractarianism?" Gauthier contends, "Contractarianism offers the only plausible resolution" to the "foundational crisis" morality presently faces. What is this crisis? "Moral language" seems only to fit "a world view that we have abandoned—a view of the world as purposively ordered" and that affirms "objective values."[2] Gauthier concurs in rejecting both a "purposively ordered" cosmos and the objectivity of values. He also rejects emotivist or expressivist accounts of morality, since these lack any *prescriptive* force. We need not, he thinks, draw the Nietzschean conclusion that morality will ultimately perish. Rather, moral contractarianism provides an "alternative mode" of "moral justification."[3]

In *Morals by Agreement* Gauthier argues, "Morality . . . can be generated as a rational constraint from the non-moral premises of

rational choice."[4] This statement incorporates several points fundamental to Gauthier's argument. First, Gauthier's theory assumes the
"maximizing conception of rationality"[5]—that is, human beings as
we have them are rational maximizers.[6] The "person is conceived as
an independent centre of activity, endeavoring to direct his capacities
and resources to the fulfilment of his interests."[7] Second, morality
consists in impartial rational *constraints* on the pursuit of interest.[8]
Duty cannot be reduced to interest or advantage alone: "Were duty
no more than interest, morals would be superfluous. Why appeal to
right or wrong, to good or evil, to obligation or duty, if instead we
may appeal to desire or aversion, to benefit or cost, to interest or to
advantage? An appeal to morals takes its point from the failure of
these latter considerations as sufficient guides to what we ought to
do."[9]

Third, these moral constraints do not reflect or derive from any
sort of objective value or any real good: "Value . . . we take to be a
measure of individual preference—subjective because it is a measure
of preference and relative because it is a measure of individual preference. What is good is good ultimately because it is preferred, and it
is good from the standpoint of those and only those who prefer it."[10]
Fourth, moral constraints are the product of a rational, *hypothetical*
agreement, not an actual one. Gauthier connects the third and fourth
propositions multiple times in *Morals by Agreement*. For instance, in
chapter 1, he writes, "Moral principles are introduced as the objects
of fully voluntary *ex ante* agreement among rational persons. Such
agreement is hypothetical, in supposing a pre-moral context for the
adoption of moral rules and practices."[11] In chapter 9 he writes, "If
morality is a matter of agreement, then prior to agreement nothing is
either just or unjust." On the account of justice that Glaucon poses as
a challenge to Socrates, says Gauthier, "natural man is pre-social and
pre-moral."[12] Thus, on moral contractarianism, morality is generated
"as a rational constraint on choice and action, from a non-moral, or
morally neutral, base."[13] But this requires justifying moral constraints
on the pursuit of interests or desires to persons who are preference
maximizers—*and doing so on nonmoral grounds*. What could possibly motivate such individuals to enter such an agreement or, given
the hypothetical nature of the agreement, to recognize its binding

nature? This brings us to the fifth element of Gauthier's theory: recognition of the mutual advantage to be found in *constrained* rather than *straightforward* maximization (i.e., recognition of the benefits of cooperation). Why constrained maximization? Because it often happens that when each person acts to maximize his own gain, the result is a state of affairs that disadvantages everyone. Consequently (or correlatively, as Gauthier sees it), everyone gains if each person is constrained in the quest to satisfy his own preferences. Rational, preference-maximizing individuals would therefore accept constraints on their behavior.[14] At the same time, preference-maximizing humans (Gauthier also uses the phrase "economic man") would only enter mutually advantageous agreements—that is, they would only enter agreements with those whose compliance with the agreement provides some benefit to them.[15] Thus, morals (or justice) by agreement extends only to those with whom we can enter mutually beneficial arrangements. This leads to the problem of the potentially very minimal morality that morals by agreement can supply. But let's postpone that for now.

Sixth, when it comes to the sorts of agreements that preference-maximizing individuals can rationally enter, Gauthier maintains that rational maximizers seek a bargain in which "the greatest concession" each person makes, "measured as a proportion of the conceder's stake," is "as small as possible." He calls this the "minimax relative concession." The corollary is that rational maximizers will only enter agreements where "the least relative benefit" is "as great as possible," which he calls the "maximin relative benefit."[16] Seventh, he stipulates a proviso that serves as "a condition" that each individual must accept for any agreement "to be possible."[17] The proviso "prohibits bettering one's position through interaction worsening the position of another" and functions as a constraint on "the initial bargaining position."[18] According to Gauthier's proviso, "No person should be worse off in the initial bargaining position than she would be a non-social context of no interaction."[19]

The eighth element of Gauthier's moral contractarianism concerns the vantage from which a binding agreement can be reached for impartial, rational constraints on the actions of preference-maximizing individuals. In *Morals by Agreement* (see chapter 8) he calls this vantage the Archimedean point. The Archimedean point provides a point "from which an individual can move to the moral world." But "to confer this moral power, the Archimedean point must be one of assured impartiality."[20] That particular language vanishes from the later essay, "Why Contractarianism?" (which presents the core argument in a more direct and clearer light). But therein he seeks to show how rational maximizers move from the given norms of their society to agreement on norms and finally to hypothetical agreement in this putatively impartial position. Gauthier begins with the *given moral practices* of a community. These moral practices constrain the behavior of individuals. And preference-maximizing persons recognize the necessity of constraints. But insofar as individuals are reflective "rational maximizers," "they will recognize that the set of actual [i.e., given] moral practices is not the only possible set of constraining practices that would yield mutually advantageous, optimal outcomes." That is, "they will recognize the possibility of alternative moral orders."[21] And rational maximizers, still recognizing the necessity of constrained preference maximization, will ask whether or not a different set of moral constraints might serve them better (i.e., might provide greater utility). Consequently, "the existing moral order must be assessed . . . against . . . alternative compliance."[22] Thus we move from the given moral order to what rational maximizers could agree to, given other possible sets of moral constraints: "although in the real world, we begin with an existing set of moral practices as constraints on our maximizing behavior, yet we are led by reflection to the idea of an amended set that would obtain the agreement of everyone." Moreover, "this amended set has, and will be recognized to have, a stability lacking in existing a morality"—presumably because individuals see this amended set of moral constraints as better redounding to their ultimate advantage.[23]

But an actual agreement among rational maximizers remains problematic. For "what a rational person would agree to in existing circumstances depends in large part on her negotiating position vis-à-vis her fellows. Her negotiating position is significantly affected by the existing social institutions, and so by the currently accepted moral practices embodied in those institutions."[24] The agreement of individuals in a community to amend their current moral practices or current set of moral constraints in order to adopt an altered set that better serves their advantage is "influenced" by the very practices they amend—a fact that calls into question the set of practices to which they would agree. Thus, "although rational agreement is in itself a source of stability, yet this stability is undermined by the arbitrariness of the circumstances in which it takes place." The only way to avoid this arbitrariness is for "rational persons" to "revert from actual to hypothetical agreement." Now, "the content of a hypothetical agreement is determined by an appeal to the equal rationality of persons." Consequently, "Rational persons will voluntarily accept an agreement only insofar as they perceive it to be equally advantageous to each." Any preference-maximizing person would of course readily "accept an agreement more advantageous to herself than to her fellows." But no such person "will accept an agreement perceived to be less advantageous." Insofar as each person recognizes others as rational maximizers, each realizes "the futility of holding out for more," and consequently rational agents "minimize their bargaining costs by coordinating at the point of equal advantage." In sum, "to neutralize this arbitrary element" in the given social practices of a society or its institutions or in an actual agreement reached by rational maximizers that is nevertheless influenced by the society's initially given practices and institutions, "moral practices to be fully acceptable must be conceived as constituting a possible outcome of a hypothetical agreement under circumstances that are unaffected by social institutions that themselves lack full acceptability."[25]

In *Morals by Agreement*, Gauthier holds that "as the heir of the Homeric *agathos*, economic man sees the moral and political orders as conventional constraints, curbing the natural expression of his desires." Thus, "The rational defense of these [moral] constraints reveals them to be necessary evils." To be sure, *homo economicus* "is properly a theoretical entity, entering into our best theories for conceptualizing and explaining human interaction." Nevertheless, "economic man has entered into the ground of our self-consciousness." Indeed, "Economic man is a caricature, or distortion, who has come more and more to shape our reality." Yet "moral constraints can have no hold on those who see in them only instruments of domination."[26] Thus, "it may be that the very characteristics of human nature that enter into the grounding of these constraints, serve also to undermine the conditions under which compliance with them would be rational. It may seem that we need moral constraints because of asociality and non-tuism, but that, being asocial and non-tuistic, we act to bring about circumstances in which the alleged impartiality of these constraints is an imposture. And if the imposture is recognized, the constraints cease to be effective."[27] Gauthier contends, "Morals by agreement would afford economic man a beneficial constraint, if only he could be constrained." But to the extent that "economic man is part of our way of understanding ourselves, part of our idea of what it is to be human, and in so far as this idea persists even in the face of conscious disavowal, then the rational bonds of morals by agreement may be too weak to hold us. We need exorcism in addition to argument."[28] Gauthier's point here echoes the argument from "The Social Contract as Ideology," which he references.[29]

I might have put the point somewhat differently—or at least added to the foregoing: actual preference-maximizing individuals lack any reason to abide constraints affirmed in a hypothetical agreement rather than to adopt Antiphon's position, ignoring moral constraints whenever it both serves their (perceived) interest and they can get away with it. Hobbes's reply to the Foole seems to rest on denying the possibility of getting away with it. But why think that? Consider Glaucon's consummately unjust individual who always succeeds in getting away with it—who always succeeds in procuring his own advantage by acting unjustly while also securing a reputation for justice.[30] Maybe many individuals are capable of disregarding moral constraints when it benefits them and also without being detected in their noncompliance with moral constraints.

Gauthier certainly recognizes this problem. And this brings us to the ninth element of Gauthier's theory: conversion. Preference-maximizing human beings must become *liberal individuals*, individuals who no longer view morality as "a necessary evil" or "an instrument of domination."[31] Since Gauthier thinks that actual human beings are only partially *homo economicus*, there is something in us that allows for the "exorcism" or conversion of human beings so that we become capable of morality. In "Why Contractarianism?" he concludes, "morality requires that a person have the capacity to commit himself" and that "In developing '*the right to make promises*,' we human beings have found a contractarian bulwark against the perishing of morality."[32] Thus, Gauthier concludes that human beings developed (or invented) the capacity to make promises and so doing created the foundation for morality: promising and agreement.

THE CASE AGAINST GAUTHIER: MORALITY CANNOT BE CREATED FROM NONMORAL BUILDING BLOCKS

Several criticisms can be advanced against Gauthier's moral contractarianism. I will focus on three. First, Gauthier clearly rests his moral contractarianism on metaphysical premises—rejection of a purposively ordered universe, affirmation of the subjectivity and relativity of good and evil (and of value more generally), and reason conceived as preference maximizing and in entirely instrumental terms—that he alleges *we* affirm. But, in fact, Gauthier's contention is dubious. The propositions he says *we* affirm or reject do not clearly command universal or even widespread assent or condemnation, as the case may be. Second, moral contractarianism radically constricts justice and moral obligation, leaving us with an exceedingly minimal morality that excludes whole classes of human beings from the realm of moral obligation or even from normative relations at all. Third, moral contractarianism fails to escape the criticisms already advanced of ancient and modern moral conventionalism—namely, the impossibility of grounding right or obligation upon will alone. Fourth, given the impossibility of grounding moral obligation in acts of will alone, it is logically impossible to construct normative or moral requirements from nonmoral building blocks. Fifth, given the impossibility of constructing normative or moral requirements from nonmoral building blocks, Gauthier in fact smuggles normative building blocks in while calling them nonmoral.

Let's take the foregoing criticisms in order. Gauthier's moral contractarianism presumes the subjectivity and relativity of good and evil and, concomitantly (and perhaps correlatively), the rejection of a purposively ordered universe. By this he means, I think, to reject final causality (or classical teleology)—especially as one finds that teleology in Aristotle or Aquinas.[33] That is, he means, I think, to reject claims that the world is constituted by things that have inbuilt purposes ordered to the attainment of some aim, goal, or end (telos) where the attainment of the intrinsic end of a thing constitutes its highest or greatest good (e.g., an acorn growing into an oak or the heart pumping to circulate blood through the body or a rational creature seeking to understand the proof for the Pythagorean theorem). Gauthier predicates moral contractarianism on the rejection of a purposively ordered world and a rejection of the objectivity of moral value because, he says, *we* reject or can no longer accept such an understanding of the world.[34] Gauthier also contends that we must conceive of reason or rationality entirely in instrumental terms: "We order our preferences, in relation to decision and action so that we may choose in a way that maximizes our expectation of preference fulfillment. And in so doing, we show ourselves to be rational agents, engaged in deliberation and deliberative justification. There is simply nothing else for reason to be."[35] Let's call the foregoing *Gauthier's metaphysics*—the metaphysical basis of his moral contractarianism. Doubtless his metaphysics includes more (perhaps materialism or the rejection of classical theism).[36] But it certainly includes the foregoing, and the foregoing propositions are certainly metaphysical.

At the same time, Gauthier insists that moral requirements must be understood as *constraints* on preference maximization or the pursuit of self-interest and the satisfaction of desire precisely because "morality, as we, heirs to the Christian and Kantian traditions, conceive it, constrains the pursuits to which even our reflective desires would lead us."[37] Now *if* we today in fact reject final causality (as understood in classical ancient or medieval thought), why retain the Christian or Kantian notion of morality as a *constraint* on preference maximization, on seeking to satisfy as many of our desires as possible, on the pursuit of self-interest however each of us conceives it? Why not abandon thinking of morality in terms of constraints altogether? Why not hold instead that constraints on the satisfaction of preferences—satisfying as many of them as possible—are neither obligatory nor properly normative at all? To be sure, one might hold that all such constraints are merely prudential *and* that prudent individuals realize that the Antiphonic position is impossible for humans as we have them. That is, prudent individuals might realize that no one is in fact or should take himself to be Glaucon's consummately unjust man, someone who can always get away with injustice with impunity while maintaining a reputation for justice; rather, everyone always risks the possibility of getting caught and losing out on the benefits of cooperating with others in the future. Perhaps morality is superfluous (as Gauthier suggests) if not conceived as constraints on the pursuit of our interests.[38] But in that case, why not simply conclude that it is in fact superfluous—that all judgments about what to do in fact lack normativity? In sum, why think the idea of moral constraints survives the collapse of a purposively ordered universe or the loss of final causes? Insofar as Gauthier's argument turns on what *we* affirm or reject, he must hold that *we* overwhelmingly *reject* a purposively ordered universe and *affirm* that morality consists in constraints on pursuit of self-interest or the maximal satisfaction of our preferences. Whether or not such a *we* exists is an empirical question for which any evidence seems to be lacking—a problem Gauthier elides by simply stipulating this *we*.

We are compelled to ask Gauthier, who is this *we* that rejects the objectivity or reality of moral values? Who is this *we* that rejects the notion that some acts are simply and intrinsically good and others simply and intrinsically evil or bad, for instance—or the notion that the world is constituted by things with inbuilt purposes the realization of which is their aim or end and good? Who is this *we* for whom rationality can only be calculation about the best way to satisfy our preferences or desires and who reject alternative conceptions of reason? Do not a good many people still affirm a purposively ordered universe and the objective reality of moral values? Do not many people reject the notion that reason is purely instrumental? Perhaps Gauthier means to confine this *we* to educated people. But many educated people seem to reject what Gauthier affirms and to affirm what he rejects. And surely Gauthier knows this too. Does his *we* refer only to contemporary academics? But even then, there are gifted scholars who affirm a purposively ordered universe: physicists such as Stephen Barr, John Polkinghorne, John Barrow, and Paul Davies;[39] philosophers like Étienne Gilson, Frederick Copleston, Peter van Inwagen, Thomas Nagel, Anthony Flew, Robert Koons, and Edward Feser;[40] sociologists like Christian Smith, to name just a few.[41] As well (and with some overlap with the group just listed), many scholars reject subjectivity and relativism concerning good and evil and affirm instead the objective reality of good and evil and moral values more generally: philosophers such as Robert Merrihew Adams, Charles Taylor, Alasdair MacIntyre, John Rist, Terence Cuneo, John Finnis, Elizabeth Anscombe, and Eleonore Stump;[42] literary scholars like C. S. Lewis;[43] political theorists such as Hadley Arkes, J. Budziszewski, and Carson Holloway;[44] sociologists like Christian Smith.[45] Finally, there are scholars (and some rather luminary epistemologists) who reject construing reason in wholly instrumentalist terms: political philosophers like Jean Hampton, Robert George, and T. K. Seung;[46] and analytic epistemologists such as Alvin Plantinga, Nicholas Wolterstorff, and Terence Cuneo.[47] My point is not that most scholars disagree with Gauthier. Some do and some don't. Consequently, his *we* is now restricted to a subset of scholars and a subset of educated people more generally. We can say at least this: many individuals today reject his rejection of a purposively ordered universe and reject his affirmation of the subjectivity and relativity of good and evil and his reduction of reason or rationality to preference maximization.

Gauthier might reply that most scholars or most educated people are with him, after all. But even if he's right, what follows? The counting game is entirely beside the point. What counts is the truth of the matter. And on this score Alasdair MacIntyre argues in *After Virtue* that moral obligation in particular and right or normativity more generally absolutely require teleology (i.e., final causes), the prescription of divine law, or both to be intelligible at all.[48] I think MacIntyre is right about this. And the next three chapters aim to support this conclusion, albeit from a different angle of argument. In particular, if we give up final causes and the objective reality of moral values, then, I maintain, we are left with only the possibility of hypothetical imperatives at best (though on the subjectivity and relativity of good and evil, it is exceedingly difficult to see how we're left with even that). But, as Hampton argues and as I will also argue in the next chapter, hypothetical imperatives fail to ground normativity.[49] Here I'll only note that the alleged fact that *we* today—or, more aptly, *some* today—can no longer take seriously a purposively ordered universe or the objective reality of moral values is neither here nor there. Either the universe is purposely ordered, or it isn't. Whether *we*—or only some of us—can think of it in these terms has nothing to do with the ontological requirements of good and evil, right and wrong.

Let's turn to the objection that moral contractarianism problematically constricts morality. Gauthier himself notes Locke's critique of the Hobbesian account of morality. According to Locke, "an Hobbist . . . *will not easily admit a great many plain duties of morality.*"[50] In apparent corroboration of Locke's contention, Gauthier holds that moral requirements established by agreement apply only to mutually beneficial relations. And "only beings whose physical and mental capacities are either roughly equal or mutually complementary can expect to find cooperation beneficial to all."[51] Consequently, on Gauthier's view, "Animals, the unborn, the congenitally handicapped and defective, fall beyond the pale of a morality tied to mutuality. . . . The disposition to comply with moral constraints . . . may be rationally defended only within the scope of expected benefit."[52] Now, Gauthier's theory includes a proviso that prohibits any person from improving their position through interactions that leave others worse off—or from entering agreements or making bargains that benefit oneself at the expense of others. Annette Baier interprets Gauthier's proviso to prohibit each person from bettering his position through interactions that would leave another worse off *relative to what that person's position would have been in one's absence.*[53] Put another way, as Baier understands Gauthier, the proviso constraining the agreements that Gauthier's individuals can enter says, "Don't push a fellow further down than he'd sink anyway, in your absence."[54] Baier contends that this results in an exceedingly minimal morality. Here she notes Locke's discussion, in his First Treatise, of Garcilaso de la Vega's account of cannibalism in his *History of the Incas of Peru.*[55] In that work, Garcilaso claimed the Inca "made their Captives their mistresses and choicely nourished their Children they had by them, till about thirteen years old they Butcher'd and Eat them; and they served the Mothers after the same fashion when they grew past child bearing and ceas'd to bring them any more Roasters."[56] After quoting this passage, Baier notes, "As far as I grasp Gauthier's version of a rational morality, such a practice would not have to be condemned either by [Gauthier's] proviso or by the morality that grows from it."[57]

Gauthier contends that "Baier misstates the proviso. It does not say 'don't push a fellow further down than he'd sink anyway, in your absence,' but rather, 'don't push, etc. *except* to avoid being pushed further down than you'd sink in his absence.' Don't *better* yourself by your fellow's presence, by *worsening* him by your own presence." On the one hand, "This rules out eating other people's children (unless they are better off eaten, which seems unlikely)." On the other hand, this does *not* rule out "eating one's own (unless their lives are thereby made not worth living, which of course is not altogether improbable)." Gauthier says his proviso also "rules out using women as breeders, since," in Baier's example (taken from Locke's quotation of Garcilaso), "this betters the situation of the cannibals by worsening that of the women." Gauthier concludes, "Even if the proviso permits eating the children"—presumably where they are one's own rather than someone else's—"it does not permit breeding with the mother"—"unless, of course, she too were to be a happy party to the future feast, eager to enjoy the fruit of her womb."[58] So far as I can tell, Gauthier's objection to Baier's interpretation is that women have been taken captive and compelled to breed and raise children for the purpose of eating them. That is, the women have been coerced, or the children of others have been taken (or both). The execution of children in order to eat them, however, is not, on his account, morally untenable per se.

Setting aside perhaps fanciful claims about cannibalism, Baier might have mentioned the practice of child sacrifice—something carried out by the Inca but also arguably widespread in the ancient Near East and a practice the ancient Romans claimed was extensive in Carthage.[59] We might also consider the practice of exposing infants, something pervasive in ancient Sparta and common in ancient Rome, and the sale of children.[60] Since the unborn (and apparently the congenitally handicapped) cannot benefit mature, fully functioning human beings *and* since on account of that the latter have no moral obligations to the former, then we might ask on what ground anyone has moral obligations to newborns or, for that matter, toddlers. John Locke in fact maintained that human parents have a moral obligation, imposed by the law of nature, to take care of their dependent children. And he maintained that we have a moral obligation to refrain from murdering any human being—which rules out infanticide and exposure (*expositio*). In the First Treatise of Government, Locke excoriates those who argue for the absolute power of parents over children and who invoke as evidence for this absolute power the practice in various societies of parents "*exposing or selling* their Children." Locke describes this practice as the "most unnatural Murder" of which humans are capable: "The Dens of Lions and Nurseries of Wolves know no such Cruelty as this. . . . And is it the Priviledge of Man alone to act more contrary to Nature than the Wild and most Untamed part of Creation?"[61] Locke finds these practices of exposing and selling children *especially* contrary to the moral law. But Locke, though a *political* contractarian, is not, as Gauthier notes, a *moral* contractarian.[62]

What Locke denounces as the "most unnatural murder," the moral contractarian Hobbes considers consonant with right of nature—that is, the exposure of infants would not be wrong or unjust in the state of nature.[63] Thus, in *Leviathan*, he argues that "in the condition of mere nature," so long as there is no contract between the mother and father concerning a dependent child such as a newborn, then the child is under the mother's absolute control: "In the condition of mere nature . . . the right of dominion over the child dependeth on her will, and is consequently hers." And since "the infant is first in the power of the mother, so as she may either nourish or expose it, if she nourish it, it oweth its life to the mother, and is therefore obliged to obey her rather than any other, and by consequence the dominion over it is hers. But if she expose it, and another find and nourish it, the dominion is in him that nourisheth it."[64] There is, on the Hobbesian view, no obligation given by nature of parents to dependent children. Implicit in Hobbes's position, so strongly rejected by Locke, is the idea that the benefit between mother and the infant runs only one way. Newborns cannot enter into mutually beneficial agreements with their parents or anyone else. And so, on Gauthier's argument, there seems just as much reason to deny the obligations of parents or anyone else to newborns (or toddlers) as there is to the unborn. Consequently, Gauthier's argument entails that parents that kill their own newborns (infanticide) or who expose them (in which case they die or are taken into the care of others) or sell them to others (to do with them as they please) do not thereby wrong their children or do them any injustice. For, again, in terms of mutual benefit, there is no substantial or significant difference between a newborn and an unborn child.

Nor is there much difference between a toddler and a newborn. So it seems on Gauthier's view that parents have no moral obligations to toddlers either. To this group, Gauthier adds (as we've seen) "the congenitally handicapped and the defective." We cannot enter mutually beneficial agreements with them and, consequently, do not have moral obligations to them. Two criticisms immediately emerge. Suppose arguendo that Gauthier is right that we can only have moral obligations toward those with whom we can enter mutually beneficial agreements. And suppose there are some human beings with whom we cannot enter such relations. Nevertheless, is it not the case that for the most part other humans benefit us more or less? That is, by and large, doesn't the ability to benefit come in degrees? In that case, wouldn't Gauthier's position entail that moral obligations are stronger or weaker, depending on whether or not people can (or have) benefited us and we them? And if the capacity of individuals to benefit others comes in degrees (perhaps of maturation), Annette Baier's query has teeth, Gauthier's dismissal of it notwithstanding: "We are told that unborn children 'fall beyond the pale of morality tied to mutuality,' and the proviso, as much as the bargain, is tied to mutuality. Just when do children acquire any rights, by Gauthier's account? Only when they are large enough to pose a threat of predation unless they are granted some rights?"[65] Moreover, it would seem that our obligations to others must diminish the less they are capable of benefiting us—and so also for them in relation to us.

Thus, Gauthier expressly excludes the unborn and the congenitally handicapped and defective from the class of those to whom other human beings have obligations. And on his premises this group must be expanded to include newborns, infants, and toddlers (and maybe young children older than toddlers). Here it might be tempting to think that his position entails only that we have no obligation to help such individuals. But Gauthier's position is that we have *no* obligations to them at all. It follows that we owe them *nothing*. We have no duties or obligations to them; they have no claim-rights in relation to the rest of us. But in that case, we have no moral obligation to refrain from harming such individuals. On Gauthier's view, it seems there is no obligation not to torture infants, toddlers, or "the congenitally handicapped and defective." And in that case, there would be no obligation to refrain from torturing such humans just for fun.

Suppose, following Locke, we reply to Gauthier that this implication of his theory violates the plain requirements of morality, or suppose we say that these implications offend deeply held moral convictions or intuitions, that the implications of his theory are abhorrent, and that his theory is therefore reductio ad absurdum false. Gauthier would insist that moral constraints on our behavior are *only* justified as agreements (or the product of a hypothetical agreement) made by those capable of entering mutually beneficial relations and therefore only obtain among such persons. Consequently, he seems to suggest that we should give up or substantially revise our deeply held moral convictions or intuitions in light of the demands of a morality justified by the theory of rational choice: "We shall find no simple fit, or lack of fit, between our theory and the supposedly 'plain duties' of conventional morality. . . . If the reader is tempted to object to some part of this view, on the ground that his moral intuitions are violated, then he should ask what weight such an objection can have, if morality is to fit within the domain of rational choice."[66]

So far as I can tell, those who follow Gauthier's morals by agreement must sacrifice their most fundamental moral convictions and intuitions to the requirements of his rational choice account of moral foundations *rather than* reject his theory in favor of their deepest and most fundamental moral convictions. But why think that? Faced with a choice between the two, why not reject his rational choice account of morality instead? Note well: such a decision cannot be made intelligibly on the basis of his theory or his elaboration of its moral requirements. Note also that Gauthier's entire project turns on rejection of a purposively ordered universe and the objective reality of good and evil and, correlatively, on affirmation of a purely instrumentalist account of rationality. If Gauthier's theory entails abandoning fundamental moral convictions, we might say so much the worse for Gauthier's theory—and also for the metaphysical basis on which he grounds it. If rejecting moral and metaphysical realism entails—*at most*—a morality that allows parents to kill, expose, or sell their infants or toddlers, or to torture them for fun, or to treat others (the congenitally handicapped or defective) this way, then that gives us good reason to affirm what Gauthier rejects and to reject what he affirms.[67]

Do we have reason to reject Gauthier's moral conventionalism in addition to its abhorrent implications? I think we do. In chapter 1, I argued that *political* obligation cannot be established by convention or agreement alone, while also suggesting that the argument has broader implications. That argument entails, necessarily, that *moral* obligation cannot be created by agreement alone. Recall Locke's argument: "Nor . . . can those very men [who] agree among themselves know something is good *because they agree it is*, but [rather], they agree because they know from natural principles that something is good. And [this] knowledge precedes the agreement, *for otherwise the same thing would be both cause and effect at the same time*, and the consent of all [i.e., an effect] would result in the consent of all [i.e., a cause] which is plainly absurd."[68] Locke's argument shows that moral contractarianism viciously begs the question.

Moreover, in order for any of our agreements (whether hypothetical or actual) to bind us, there must be an antecedent obligation to keep our agreements. If we have no prior obligation to keep our agreements, then no agreement we (hypothetically or actually) enter binds us. Now either the obligation to keep our agreements is created by agreement or not. If not, then we have taken leave of moral contractarianism. If so, we must again ask whether the obligation to keep our agreements is created by agreement or not. Either we go to infinity asking this question in each instance of an agreement (to keep our agreement)—in which case moral obligation is never grounded, never justified—*or* we reach a terminus at which point the obligation to keep our agreements is not itself founded on agreement—in which case all moral obligations founded on agreement rest on an obligation itself not founded on agreement. And in that case morals by agreement is self-refuting. I don't see how Gauthier can escape the horns of this dilemma, and his theory is impaled by either horn.

Nor can moral contractarianism escape the self-referential incoherence argument of the first chapter—and this demonstrates, ultimately, the impossibility of generating morality (or oughtness or normativity more generally) from nonmoral premises or foundations. The alternatives are embracing moral premises all the way down or giving up morality and the project of moral justification altogether. Central to the argument is the fact that agreement is an instance of human will—collective or corporate rather than individual will, but *will* nevertheless. Given the subjectivity and relativity of good and evil (according to Hobbes and Gauthier) and the rejection of a purposively ordered cosmos, human agreement cannot be considered binding because it is good or an ultimate (or real) aim or end (telos) of human willing. There is nothing other than the agreement—the act of will in agreeing—itself. But then recall that it's impossible to distinguish among instances of will on the basis of will alone. Some exercise of will cannot intelligibly be considered normative for other exercises of will on the basis of will alone. Consequently, agreement, as an instance of will, cannot be considered normative or obligatory for other instances of willing—the will of the group cannot be considered normative or obligatory for the willing of individuals (or groups)—on the basis of will alone. If agreement or the will of the group binds individuals (or groups) or in some other way provides a rule and measure for individual behavior, it must be on the basis of some property or reality of goodness or justice or right that transcends human will, that transcends the set.

Moreover, Gauthier doesn't intend morals by agreement to make all agreements binding but only some. With respect to moral foundations, he ultimately has in view hypothetical rather than actual agreements. And this hypothetical agreement is not universal but only includes those individuals capable of mutually beneficial relations. So he takes some agreements to be normative and others not to be. As with will or interest, we can conceive a set of all agreements (hypothetical, actual, tacit, express, etc.). We can represent the set abstractly: $(A_1, A_2, A_3, A_4, A_5 \ldots A_n)$. And we cannot intelligibly distinguish any member of the set as normative for the rest on the basis of the property the predication of which defines the set—namely, agreement. Thus, we cannot take A_3 to be normative for A_1, A_2, A_4 and the rest on the basis of agreement. Necessarily, then, we cannot coherently distinguish some agreements from others on the basis of agreement alone. If some agreements bind and others do not, then it must be on the basis of some moral property or reality—some rule and measure, some good, some standard of right—that itself is not an agreement. Thus, morals by agreement in fact presupposes moral properties (more aptly, moral realities) not reducible to agreement or will.

The upshot is that the endeavor to create morals by agreement is self-referentially incoherent. Any intelligible account of norms or obligations founded on agreement presupposes moral properties or realities that are *not*. It follows that moral obligation (or moral ought or normativity more generally) cannot be built from nonmoral building blocks. Again, the alternative is between a nonconventional, real ground of morality or no morality at all. Moral contractarianism provides no plausible middle ground.[69]

Rawlsian Moral Construction in the Dock

John Rawls offers two accounts of moral contractarianism. In both, his theory is aptly described as Kantian and, indeed, as Kantian constructivism. But the account proffered in *A Theory of Justice* can be interpreted as advancing not only Kantian conventionalism but also Kantian transcendentalism.[70] In essays subsequent to *A Theory of Justice* and in *Political Liberalism* he offers a political theory that explicitly disavows metaphysical foundations of any kind. Thus, his Kantian constructivism ultimately resolves into a thoroughgoing, deep conventionalism.[71] Below I discuss the moral contractarianism of *A Theory of Justice* with an eye to treating the deep conventionalism of *Political Liberalism* and the essays written prior to it and incorporated within its pages.

Gauthier, as we saw, predicated moral contractarianism on a particular metaphysics—on a comprehensive view that included the rejection of a purposively ordered universe, affirmation of the subjectivity and relativity of moral value and, correlatively, the rejection of any objective or real good, and affirmation of reason or rationality purely instrumental and preference-maximizing. These are not the whole of Gauthier's view. But they represent a particular metaphysical view. Indeed, we might consider these part and parcel of a view called metaphysical naturalism (whereas Protagoras and his later heirs espoused a view that's been called creative antirealism and Aquinas affirmed classical theism). The moral contractarianism of the later Rawls, by way of contrast, refuses to affirm or reject any particular metaphysical or moral view. No particular account of the nature or reality of the good or of reality itself is presupposed by his political conception of justice. And yet this leaves the political justice of the later Rawls as dependent on sheer will as Gauthier's morals by agreement, and therefore subject to the same fate.

MORAL CONSTRUCTION, THE ORIGINAL POSITION, AND REFLECTIVE EQUILIBRIUM IN *A Theory of Justice*

In *A Theory of Justice*, Rawls sought to provide a means of discerning principles of justice that could provide a basis for assessing the degree to which any given social and political order is in fact just. The mechanism on which he landed was the original position, the central feature of which is the veil of ignorance. According to Rawls, principles of justice binding on us are those to which (hypothetical) individuals behind a veil of ignorance would agree. Rawls deprives these individuals (which he calls "moral personalities") of any particular knowledge about themselves: "No one knows his place in society, his class position or social status; nor does he know his fortune in the distribution of natural assets and abilities, his intelligence, and the like. Nor . . . does anyone know his conception of the good, the particulars of his rational plan of life, or even the special features of his psychology such as his aversion to risk or liability to optimism or pessimism." Further "the parties [in the original position] do not know the particular circumstances of their own society. . . . They do not know its economic or political situation, or the level of civilization it has been able to achieve." Nor do they know "to which generation they belong." In short, Rawls seeks to strip parties in the original position of all those "contingencies that set [humans] in opposition" to each other.[72] He aims to create a situation in which any individual behind the veil of ignorance might turn out to be anyone at all in a society, just because they are stripped of everything contingent about themselves. For in that case they must choose principles for that society that are in the interest of everyone in that society.

Rawls does not think that any actual individuals can get behind the veil of ignorance. Rather, he holds that the choices of these *moral personalities* would be normative or authoritative for us, and he seeks to show what they would choose. Since these hypothetical individuals don't know who they might turn out to be—and since they are to reason not only with their own interest in view but also that of their progeny (actual, future, or merely possible)—Rawls says they must adopt a rational principle for deciding under conditions of radical uncertainty. He calls what he considers the appropriate decision rule the maximin principle: one should choose principles of justice that maximize one's minimum prospects in society.[73] That is, make your worst-case scenario as good as possible *given that you might turn out to be anyone in society.* This principle for reasoning in the original position entails his two principles of justice, the second of which runs as follows: "Social and economic inequalities are to be arranged so that they are both (a) reasonably expected to be to everyone's advantage, and (b) attached to positions and offices open to all."[74] The upshot of this principle is this: inequalities in wealth, status, authority (or anything else) are justifiable only if those inequalities benefit everyone, especially the least advantaged (the least well off) in society. This principle rejects utilitarianism, which is its point (we might say its telos). According to Rawls, "it is not just that some should have less in order that others may prosper"; though "there is no injustice in the greater benefits earned by a few provided that the situation of persons not so fortunate is thereby improved."[75] A few pages later he contends, "Utilitarianism does not take seriously the distinction between persons." Instead, it "conflat[es] all persons into one through," failing to perceive "separate individuals" to which "rights and duties are assigned."[76] We might say Rawls holds that Utilitarianism treats some individuals *unfairly.* Its "maximalist" principle of the greatest good (or happiness) for the greatest number entails using or sacrificing some persons for the advantage of others, which is morally unacceptable. At the commencement of *A Theory of Justice,* he states, "Each person possesses an inviolability founded on justice that even the welfare of society as a whole cannot override."[77]

In sum, the principles of justice chosen in—and necessarily entailed by—the original position entail that any inequality can be justified *only if* the inequality is to the advantage of everyone (and, in particular, the least advantaged) and, consequently, that Utilitarianism must be rejected. Rawls's original position justifies his principles of justice, which in turn grounds his rejection of utilitarianism.[78] Assume arguendo (and not implausibly) that the derivation of Rawls's principles of justice validly follows from the original position. The soundness of his argument—and the normativity of his principles—depends on whether or not the original position itself can be justified. After all, the original position is neither epistemically nor ontologically basic; on Rawls's own terms, it is not *per se nota*.[79] So what is its justification?

Rawls claims that "the original position is the appropriate initial status quo which insures that the fundamental agreements reached in it are fair."[80] He assumes "that there is a *broad measure of agreement* that principles of justice should be chosen under certain conditions. *To justify a particular description of the initial situation one shows that it incorporates these commonly shared presumptions.* One argues from widely accepted but weak premises to more specific conclusions."[81] For instance,

> it seems reasonable and *generally acceptable* that no one should be advantaged or disadvantaged by natural fortune or social circumstances of one's case. We should insure further that particular inclinations and aspirations, and persons' conceptions of their good do not affect the principles adopted. The aim is to rule out those principles that it would be rational to propose for acceptance, however little their chance of success, only if one knew certain things that are irrelevant from the standpoint of justice. For example, if a man knew that he was wealthy, he might find it rational to advance the principle that various taxes for welfare measures be counted unjust; if he knew that he was poor, he would most likely propose the contrary principle. To represent the desired restrictions one imagines a situation in which everyone is deprived of this sort of information. *One excludes the knowledge of those contingencies which sets men at odds and allows them to be guided by their prejudices.* In this manner the veil of ignorance is arrived at in a natural way.[82]

We might consider the foregoing Rawls's *conventional* justification of the original position. What justifies reasoning in this way is that it derives from widely shared assumptions, about what fairness in the treatment of each other requires, that are deeply embedded in *our* way of thinking—which is to say, embedded deeply in our culture. Thus, when Rawls considers the question of why we should be interested in a hypothetical agreement in the original position—an agreement no one actually enters—"the answer," he says, "is that the conditions embodied in the description of the original position are ones *that we do in fact accept*. Or if we do not, then perhaps we can be persuaded to by philosophical reflection."[83] I find the soundness of this claim dubious. But this is not the only part of Rawls's justification.

Rawls says, "another side to justifying a particular description of the original position" involves seeing "if the principles which would be chosen match our considered convictions of justice or extend them in an acceptable way." That is, "We can note whether applying these principles would lead us to make the same judgments about the basic structure of society which we now make intuitively and in which we have the greatest confidence; or whether, in cases where our present judgments are in doubt and given with hesitation, these principles offer a resolution which we can affirm on reflection."[84] Rawls calls our most fundamental or deeply held moral convictions "provisional fixed points which we presume any conception of justice must fit."[85] He adds that in our search for the "most favored description" or the initial status quo, "we work from both ends":

> We begin by describing [the original position] so that it represents generally shared and preferably weak conditions. We then see if these conditions are strong enough to yield a significant set of principles. If not, we look for further premises equally reasonable. But if so, and these principles match our considered convictions of justice, then so far well and good. But presumably there will be discrepancies. In this case we have a choice. We can either modify the account of the initial situation or we can revise our existing judgments, for even the judgments we take provisionally as fixed points are liable to revision. By going back and forth, sometimes altering the conditions of the contractual circumstances, at other times withdrawing our judgments and conforming them to principle, I assume that eventually we shall

find a description of the initial situation that both expresses reasonable conditions and yields principles which match our considered judgments duly pruned and adjusted. This state of affairs I refer to as reflective equilibrium. It is an equilibrium because at last our principles and judgments coincide; and it is reflective since we know to what principles our judgments conform and the premises of their derivation.[86]

Thus, in addition to the conventional justification or description of the original position, there is also a justification that derives from our deepest moral convictions or most fundamental intuitions (call it the *considered convictions justification*). And the best—"most *favored*"— description of the original position derives from a reflective interaction between the initial description of the original position and those principles of justice deduced from it, on the one hand, and our "considered convictions," on the other.

Several difficulties with Rawls's depiction of the original position and its justification immediately emerge. First, what is the ontological status of our most fundamental and deeply held or of our most reflectively considered moral convictions? Are they genuine insights into moral reality? Do we really intuit something in them? Or are they merely *our* convictions and intuitions, moral beliefs we happen to espouse and nothing else? Put another way, do we apprehend in our considered convictions a moral law or transcendent principles of right? Or, to the contrary, do they just reflect how we (individually or in our culture as a whole) happen to think about right and wrong? The intelligibility of Rawls's project depends on how he answers these questions. But let's bracket that query for the moment.

Second, suppose that we have a description of the original position together with principles of justice deduced from it, on the one hand, and our considered moral convictions on the other. *And* suppose there is a lack of fit between them.[87] On what basis can we revise one or the other so that they better cohere? We might simply choose to favor one over the other. In that case, the decision is made on the basis of ungrounded and arbitrary will. Perhaps our will is determined by a preference for one over the other. But if we decide merely on the basis of satisfying the preference, with no consideration of whether the preference is *good* or whether we *should* satisfy it, then our decision is made on the basis of arbitrary preference rather than on the basis of reason or reflection. If we decide to revise one (maybe our description of the original position) in light of the other (perhaps our considered convictions) on the basis of reflection rather than on the basis of arbitrary preference or *sheer* will, then there must be a basis for this decision—some standard of right that our description of the original position and the principles we derive from it *or* our considered convictions might better approximate (or that one might approximate worse than the other). With such a standard we can say that in some instances our description of the original position should be revised to fit better with our considered convictions, because in those instances our considered convictions better approximate a real standard of what is right and good than does our present description of the original position (and the principles derived from it), but in other cases that our description of the original position should not be revised to better fit our considered convictions, because in those cases our convictions do not better approximate that standard of right. Without such a standard, however, no basis for any such judgment exists. Likewise, with such a standard we can revise our considered convictions to better fit our description of the original position and the principles derived from it, because our description of the original position and the principles deduced from it better approximate the right or good than do our considered convictions, and in other cases choose not to revise our considered conviction in this way, because our description of the original position and its concomitant principles does not better approximate that standard. Again, absent a standard that transcends both and that each might better approximate, we lack a nonarbitrary basis for any such judgment. Thus, to go back and forth and to choose to revise one in light of the other, as putatively occurs in Rawlsian reflective equilibrium, we need an objective moral reality to which either might conform in order to make the back-and-forth nonarbitrary and rationally intelligible.

Suppose that the Spartans have considered convictions that require them to submit infants to the *ephori* for inspection and to hurl to their death, from Mount Taygetus, any infants in whom they detect any sign of illness, physical deformity, or substantial weakness. Suppose also (though improbable) that these same Spartans decide to evaluate the justice of their regime and its way of life and somehow land upon a description of an original position from which they derive principles of justice. Now suppose the principles they derive from this original position rule out, as unjust, their eugenicist infanticide. In this case there is a lack of fit between their considered convictions, on the one hand, and their description of the original position and the principles they derive from it, on the other. Now suppose these Spartans aim at the coherence of all their principles. Which should be revised to better fit with the other—their long and deeply held considered convictions or their account of the original position and its concomitant principles of right? How can they choose one over the other? If there is to be some basis other than what they've always done and their native hostility to change, on the one hand, or a sheer preference for their new moral reasoning device because (against all odds) they find they really enjoy thinking in this way, on the other, then there must be some reality about justice and its requirements that their practice of infanticide either violates or approximates. Suppose, for instance, that their practice violates the requirement of justice, that their considered convictions are therefore contrary to justice on this count, *and* that their account of the original position and the principles derived from it provides genuine insight into what justice here requires. Then the revision of their considered convictions to better fit the principles derived from this description of the original position has a rational basis and is nonarbitrary. Absent such a standard transcendent of both, then the decision to revise either to better fit with the other has no basis at all—it rests on nothing but sheer will or arbitrary, nonreflective preference.

Suppose, on the other hand, that we have a description of the original position more like Gauthier's Archimedean point, where the resulting principles of justice apply only to those capable of mutually beneficial relations—and that therefore, from that vantage, the Spartan practice of infanticide and the Roman practices of exposing and even selling young children are not wrong. Suppose also that we have considered convictions according to which these practices are deeply unjust. We find them morally abhorrent. Should we in this case bring our considered convictions in line with such a description of the original position and the moral principles derived from it? Or should we instead seek to revise our description of the original position so that it produces an outcome more in keeping with our considered convictions? If we decide to bring the original position and the principles derived from it in line with our considered convictions because those convictions better reflect a real moral standard according to which such practices are really wrong, then our decision has a basis. But if no such standard exists, then there is no rational or nonarbitrary basis for revising either.

Third, Rawls holds that the original position is justified because it is a *fair position*—one in which individuals are not influenced by partial or biased or otherwise unfair considerations in their selection of principles of justice.[88] And the principles deduced from the original position are themselves *fair principles*. Rawls's position is predicated on the *unfairness*—which is to say, the moral wrongness—of affirming principles of justice that could not be derived from a fair position. And a fair position seems to be one that renders each individual *due* consideration. In other words, Rawls derives (what he considers) fair principles of justice from an original position constructed by (what he considers) fair principles of justice. According to T. K. Seung, "The original position cannot be set up without presupposing the notion of fairness. To put it another way, the original position is based on the notion of fairness, or rather the original position is a fair position. Rawls' principles of justice are the principles of fairness. In short, his principles of fairness are derived from the notion of fairness. Therefore, their derivation is circular."[89] As Seung concluded in a talk a number of years ago, Rawls pulls the rabbit of his two principles of justice out of the hat of the original position because, as with all good magicians, the rabbit was stuffed into the hat right from the start.

The greatest difficulty with Rawls's position, I maintain, is the first one mentioned above. Let's turn there. Rawls is certainly a constructivist concerning justice. His principles of justice for evaluating a given social order are derived from, and the product of, agreement. But does the original position itself derive only from ideas embedded deeply in our culture (impartiality or the conception of persons as free and equal, for instance) but that do not in any sense transcend our cultural affirmation of them (i.e., that are purely conventional)?

Or, even if such principles are embedded deeply in our culture, do they also instantiate transcendent principles of right and good? The coherence of Rawls project in *A Theory of Justice* depends on which is the case.

According to Seung, if Rawls abandons transcendent norms or ideals, then the Kantian principles he affirms are purely positive. In that case, the back-and-forth of his reflective equilibrium aims only "to secure the coherence of all positive norms," which all "come from the same source, namely, our culture." If all our norms come from our culture, then in reflective equilibrium "some of our cultural ideals will be used to constitute the original position and others will be used for testing the principles derived from the original position." And "Because the original position is constituted by our cultural ideals, it cannot be independent of our considered judgments that belong to the same cultural ideals."[90] Without this independence, "Rawls has to resort to a positivistic justification of the original position." Thus, "In describing the conditions for the original position, Rawls says they are appropriate because they are widely accepted or commonly shared presumptions (*TJ* 18, 21, 587). The widely accepted views or commonly shared presumptions are none other than those ideas or institutions embedded in our culture." Yet "if the theory of the original position stands on Kantian conventionalism, it can be given no other justification than an empirical one. Positivism knows no other justification, and conventionalism is a form of positivism." So understood, "Rawls's program is basically Hobbesian rather than Kantian. The Kantian project begins with ideals; the Hobbesian approach begins with agreements." Moreover, "When Rawls says that the conception of moral persons as being free and equal is the Archimedean point, he appears to begin with an ideal. But when he says that he begins with the ideal because it is well accepted in our culture, he is shifting his point of departure from ideals to acceptance and agreement, from the Kantian to the Hobbesian basis."[91] Insofar as Rawls's project is Hobbesian and ultimately grounded in agreement, it is nothing more than the "systematization of our initial intuitions" in order to achieve coherence in the set of positive norms we affirm.[92] Now, if Rawls's theory is ultimately an instance of normative positivism—meaning that the only norms for any given community are those the community posits for itself—then his theory is an instance of metaethical voluntarism, according to which will alone grounds right, oughtness, or obligation. If so, Rawls's theory cannot escape self-referential incoherence. Either Rawls must embrace a real good and transcendent principles of right, or his theory collapses into incoherence.

Rawls insists that the principles of fairness he has in view are embedded in our political culture. Yet, according to Seung, "To say that that Kantian ideals are embedded in our political culture does not automatically deny their transcendence. To say that the idea of natural numbers is embedded in our culture does not automatically assert that this idea is no more than our provincial cultural product." Likewise, "Kantian ideas can have two modes of existence"; they can be both transcendent and "also immanent in our culture." And "in his two different accounts of Kantian ideals," as transcendent and as conventional, "Rawls is describing [Kantian ideals] in two modes of transcendence and immanence."[93] Seung calls this understanding of Rawls the "dual perspective thesis." Something much like this thesis is necessary (though I think not sufficient) to save Rawls's account of justice from the sort of logical failure to which Gauthier's theory falls prey.[94] Yet Rawls ultimately moves in the direction of a purely conventional account of political justice and, indeed, seeks a political philosophy detached completely from considerations of truth. And here we must ask why.

KANTIAN CONSTRUCTIVISM AND THE ATTEMPT TO CREATE
A POLITICAL PHILOSOPHY WITHOUT METAPHYSICS

Critical responses to *A Theory of Justice* revealed that what Rawls thought were widely shared, deeply embedded cultural assumptions are in fact quite controversial and not so widely shared as he thought. Rawls's individuals "think of themselves not as inevitably tied to the pursuit of the particular final ends they have at any given time, but rather as capable of revising and changing these ends on reasonable and rational grounds."[95] Scholars such as Alasdair MacIntyre, Charles Taylor, Michael Sandel, and John Rist (among others) have found this conception of the self quite implausible.[96] These scholars, and many others too, see Rawls's moral personalities as bereft, lacking any meaningful semblance to real human beings. Real humans, according to Sandel, inhabit a world thick with obligations, bound by moral principles that are antecedent to choice.[97] Rather than arguing against critics like MacIntyre, Taylor, and Sandel from the vantage of a Kantian idealism (or the dual perspective thesis), Rawls bracketed the dispute altogether. In *Political Liberalism* and the essays published between that work and *A Theory of Justice*, Rawls came to appreciate the pervasive and intractable pluralism, concerning incommensurable conceptions of the good and what he called comprehensive views, that characterizes modern constitutional democracies. The Kantian view he espoused in *A Theory of Justice* turned out to be just one view among many.[98]

According to philosopher (and former Rawls student) Michael Pakaluk, the major turn in Rawls's thought occurs in "Kantian Constructivism in Moral Theory."[99] Therein Rawls maintains that when we seek to justify a conception of justice,

> The search for reasonable grounds for reaching agreement rooted in our conception of ourselves and in our relation to society *replaces* the search for moral truth interpreted as fixed by a prior and independent order of objects and relations, whether natural or divine, an order apart and distinct from how we conceive of ourselves. The task is to articulate a public conception of justice that all can live with who regard their person and their relation to society in a certain way. . . . *What justifies a conception of justice is not its being true to an order antecedent to and given to us but its congruence with our deeper understanding of ourselves and our aspirations*, and our realization that, given our history and the traditions embedded in our public life, it is the most reasonable doctrine for us. . . . Kantian constructivism holds that moral objectivity is to be understood in terms of a suitably constructed social point of view that all can accept. *Apart from the procedure of constructing the principles of justice, there are no moral facts.* Whether certain facts are to be recognized as reasons of right and justice, or how much they are to count, can be ascertained only from within the constructive procedure.[100]

Later in these lectures he says, "The idea of approximating to moral truth has no place in a constructivist doctrine: the parties in the original position do not recognize any principles of justice as true or correct and so as antecedently given; their aim is simply to select the conception most rational for them, given their circumstances. This conception is not regarded as a workable approximation to the moral facts: there are no such moral facts to which the principles adopted could approximate."[101] Thus, "The parties in the original position do not agree on what the moral facts are, as if there already were such facts. It is not that, being situated impartially, they have a clear and undistorted view of a prior and independent moral order. Rather (for constructivism), *there is no such order*, and therefore no such facts apart from the procedure of construction as a whole; the facts are identified by the principles that result."[102] And in his conclusion to the lectures: "Thus, *the essential agreement in judgments of justice arises not from the recognition of a prior and independent moral order, but from everyone's affirmation of the same authoritative social perspective*."[103] I see no other way to read Rawls in these passages other than as saying that first principles of justice are agreed to, chosen, constructed in the original position *rather than* discerned (even though he also expressly denies that this choice of principles is radical, unconstrained, Nietzschean, or existentialist choice).[104]

This brings us to the matter of truth. Pakaluk claims (rightly, I believe) that Rawls has jettisoned the correspondence theory of truth. Indeed, Rawls says, "Given the various contrasts between Kantian constructivism and rational intuitionism, it seems better to say that in constructivism first principles are reasonable (or unreasonable) than that they are true (or false)—better still, that they are most reasonable for those who conceive of their persons as it is represented in the procedure of construction." Why *reasonable*? Perhaps because it coheres with the self-conception of such individuals. But also, reasonable insofar as "this Kantian doctrine as a whole, more fully than other views available to us, organize[s] our considered convictions." Rawls simultaneously holds that "particular judgments and secondary norms may be considered true when they follow from, or are sound applications of, reasonable first principles. These first principles may be said to be true in the sense that they would be agreed to if the parties in the original position were provided with all the relevant true general beliefs."[105] Here Rawls seems to beg the question and to yank the rug out from under the original position as one in which first principles are constructed or chosen rather than discerned.

Whatever we are to make of Rawls's position in the Dewey Lectures, by "Justice as Fairness: Political not Metaphysical," the method of political philosophy has become one of *avoidance* where questions of truth are concerned.[106] And this method of avoidance produces a moral contractarianism that differs, at least initially, from those forms of moral conventionalism on offer in antiquity, in modernity, or in the work of contemporary theorists like Gauthier. The moral contractarianism of all those theorists depended on metaphysical premises (such as the antirealism or perspectivism of Protagoras or the subjectivity and relativity of good and evil of Hobbes and Gauthier). In contrast, Rawls in his later work seeks to construct an account of justice free of any metaphysical foundations and neutral with respect to incommensurable and conflicting views of the good. Thus, the political conception of justice he advocates neither affirms nor denies either metaphysical realism or creative antirealism. It neither affirms nor denies the subjectivity and relativity of good and evil, on the one hand, or the existence of an objective and real good, on the other. From the standpoint of his later moral constructivism, the moral realist or the emotivist might be right (or wrong):

> Thus, the aim of justice as fairness as a political conception is practical and not metaphysical or epistemological. That is, *it presents itself not as a conception of justice that is true, but one that can serve as a basis of informed and willing political agreement between citizens viewed as free and equal persons.* . . . To secure this agreement we try, so far as we can, to avoid disputed philosophical, as well as disputed moral and religious, questions. We do this not because these questions are unimportant or regarded with indifference, but because we think them too important and recognize there is no way to resolve them politically. The only alternative to a principle of toleration is the autocratic use of state power. Thus, justice as fairness deliberately stays on the surface,

philosophically speaking. Given the profound differences in belief and conceptions of the good at least since the Reformation, we must recognize that, just as on questions of religious and moral doctrine, public agreement on the basic questions of philosophy cannot be obtained without the state's infringement of basic liberties. Philosophy as the search for truth about an independent metaphysical and moral order cannot, I believe, provide a workable and shared basis for a political conception of justice in a democratic society.[107]

Thus,

> in . . . "Kantian constructivism," we try to avoid the problem of truth and the controversy between realism and subjectivism about the status of moral and political values. This form of constructivism neither asserts nor denies these doctrines. Rather, it recasts ideas from the tradition of the social contract to achieve a practicable conception of objectivity and justification founded on public agreement in judgment on due reflection. The aim is free agreement, reconciliation through public reason. And similarly . . . a conception of the person in a political view, for example, the conception of citizens as free and equal persons, need not involve . . . questions of philosophical psychology or a metaphysical doctrine of the nature of the self. No political view that depends on these deep and unresolved matters can serve as a public conception of justice in a constitutional democratic state. . . . We must apply the principle of toleration to philosophy itself. The hope is that, by this method of avoidance . . . existing differences between contending political views can at least be moderated, even if not entirely removed, so that the social cooperation on the basis of mutual respect can be maintained.[108]

These statements from Rawls are astonishing. Justice as fairness, he says, avoids all questions of truth on matters of substance. Yet we might wonder whether Rawls has appreciated the degree to which he is presented with what William James called a *forced option*—a case where refusing to choose between two mutually exclusive alternatives is in fact to choose one of them.[109] A theory of justice that pretends to be neutral among conflicting and incommensurable views of the good *in effect* denies that anything is intrinsically or absolutely good (or evil), right (or wrong), binding for all people (whether individuals, groups, or polities), everywhere, always. That is, neutrality refuses to treat any moral norms as universal and absolute. So doing it sides with those who affirm the relativity of good and evil—Protagoras, Thrasymachus, Hobbes, John Stuart Mill, Gauthier, Mackie, A. J. Ayer, expressivists more generally. The impossibility of moral neutrality, however, is not the most devastating problem for Rawls's political liberalism.[110]

Why does Rawls seek a *political* rather than a metaphysical conception of justice? According to Rawls, "political liberalism supposes that there are many conflicting conceptions of the good, each compatible with the full rationality of human persons." Indeed, an ineliminable pluralism of incommensurable and conflicting conceptions of the good is the "normal result" of practical reason operating under "enduring free institutions." That is, pluralism of this sort is created by modern constitutional democracy. Consequently, "no comprehensive doctrine is appropriate as a political conception for a constitutional regime."[111] Rather, according to what Rawls calls the "liberal principle of legitimacy," "Our exercise of political power is fully proper only when it is exercised in accordance with a constitution the essentials of which all citizens as free and equal may reasonably be expected to endorse in light of the principles and ideals acceptable to their common human reason." And so, "only a political conception of justice that all citizens might be reasonably expected to endorse can serve as a basis of public reason and justification."[112] Put another way: some free and equal persons rightly (or legitimately) exercise power over other free and equal persons *only if* the exercise of that power can be justified in terms that could be viewed as reasonable by all members of the society.

Prima facially, an ineliminable pluralism of incommensurable and conflicting conceptions of the good (and of comprehensive views more broadly) would seem to eliminate the possibility of terms that all members of a society can view as reasonable. And that would seem to eliminate the possibility of a political conception of justice for modern, constitutional democracies—which, Rawls claims, as a result of their normal operation, produce these very conditions. How then are we to arrive at terms on which we all can live? One putative solution Rawls considers and rejects is the notion of a modus vivendi—Hobbesian terms of peace. We may define a modus vivendi as a purely pragmatic compromise between groups who view the world in fundamentally different ways and who affirm incommensurable conceptions of the good. These groups agree upon terms of peace by which all might live together, since their circumstances require them to live together and since no group, at present, is able to gain the upper hand. But these terms of peace are affirmed by each group only due to their weakness, only due to their inability to gain power over the others. Rawls contends this makes a mere modus vivendi unstable. For if some group gains the upper hand, the purely pragmatic justification for the compromise vanishes, in which case the terms of the compromise will no longer be affirmed or observed. Now, as Hampton contends, if modern constitutional democracies really are characterized by an *ineliminable* pluralism, then it seems no group can actually gain the upper hand.[113] But set that aside. The alleged instability of a mere modus vivendi leads Rawls to reject an agreement motivated by the self-interest of the parties to it as a basis of shared principles for living together.

Having rejected both the "dominant tradition" of political philosophy, according to which "institutions are justifiable to the extent that they effectively promote" the one "reasonable and rational" conception of the good,[114] on the one hand, *and* agreement motivated entirely by the self-interest of the parties to the agreement, on the other, where else can Rawls turn? Just here he introduces his idea of an overlapping consensus. In an overlapping consensus, each group in a liberal democracy subscribes (or might subscribe) to some principles or tenets concerning justice to which other groups in the society subscribe (or to which, on reflection, they might subscribe). Each group subscribes to the tenets or elements of the overlapping consensus for its own reasons—but also for reasons *essential* (and not accidental) to its own comprehensive doctrine, or at least derived from elements essential to its comprehensive doctrine. If the principles or ideas that constitute the overlapping consensus are only contingently related to each group in the society's comprehensive doctrine, then the overlapping consensus would be no more stable than a mere modus vivendi.[115]

Thus, from the vantage of each group, the overlapping consensus (and the conception of justice derived from it) is affirmed for reasons that are part of its own metaphysical view and its conception of the good. From the vantage of political philosophy and of the society as a whole, however, the overlapping consensus has no metaphysical presuppositions and no underlying conception of the good. Thus, while from the standpoint of each group there may be principles of the good and right prior to an agreement on the principles of justice by which our society should be governed, from the vantage of Rawlsian political liberalism just as such, there is no basis for principles of justice antecedent to agreement, prior to the choice of shared principles. And that makes political liberalism an instance of normative positivism and therefore of metaethical voluntarism.[116]

Consider again the liberal principle of legitimacy, which Rawls predicates on the ineliminable pluralism characteristic of modern constitutional democracies. Inferring this principle from ineliminable pluralism alone would be a glaring non sequitur. The principle of legitimacy must have some other foundation. And in fact, Rawls grounds this principle (and the correlative prescription that we make use of public reasons—or at least stand ready to offer public reasons—when discussing constitutional essentials or matters of basic justice) on the antecedent moral duties of civility and reciprocity.[117] His argument (to avoid being a non sequitur) must be something like this: given pluralism and because we ought to treat others with civility and respect, then laws (etc.) must be justified by reasons that can be understood and affirmed by all members of a society.

But the moral duties of reciprocity and civility are not affirmed by all comprehensive views or conceptions of the good. Some affirm these duties. Some don't. Moreover, the later Rawls of *Political Liberalism* cannot affirm that these are real duties or that we have an obligation to treat others with civility and to reciprocate because such behavior is good. When it comes to affirmation of duties to civility and reciprocity, one route is open to him. He must insist that civility and reciprocity are deep norms or conventions of *our* culture, shared by all groups or by all *reasonable* groups (whatever *reasonable* might mean given epistemic and metaphysical neutrality). On Kantian constructivism, political liberalism must refrain from holding that civility and reciprocity are real moral norms or objective duties (or, for that matter, that they are subjective convictions that each person or group affirms). The only thing that matters so far as political liberalism is concerned is that these norms are *ours*. But in that case, the ground of public reason and the liberal principle of legitimacy is nothing other than convention, agreement, will.

Let's now apply the argument of chapter 1 to Rawlsian political liberalism:

(1) Either (*a*) there are objective principles or norms of right and good prior to human choice and will and normative for these, *or* (*b*) all the norms of our society (or of any society) are purely positive (i.e., the only norms that exist are those that a given community posits for itself).

(2) It is logically impossible to distinguish among exercises of will on the basis of will alone.

(3) Consequently, it is impossible to distinguish normative or obligatory from non-normative or non-obligatory exercises of will on the basis of will alone.

(4) Consequently, any intelligible designation of some exercises of will as normative or obligatory for other exercises requires positing some standard external to or transcendent of mere will.

(5) The conventions of any given community (however intentional or reflective, on the one hand, or subconscious or latent on the other) can be construed as instances of communal will.

(6) It is therefore impossible to distinguish some instances of the community's will from others, such that a given instance of community will becomes normative for others, on the basis of community will alone.

(7) But if, per Rawls, the moral duties of civility and reciprocity are, at least for the purposes of political liberalism, nothing other than the deep conventions of the community, then these "moral duties" cannot obligate or otherwise be normative for other instances of willing. Put another way, if civility and reciprocity are merely conventions then they are in no sense normative. Thus we have:

(8) Given (2), (3), and (5), civility and reciprocity cannot coherently be normative for other exercises of human will on the basis of convention or will—for instance, by treating them as duties to which we must conform when publicly discussing constitutional essentials and matters of basic justice or as moral constraints upon a society's choice of its public conception of justice. Civility and reciprocity can only serve as norms for human behavior or agreements insofar as they are part of or derive from a standard external to (indeed, transcendent of) the community's will. For, as we've seen, any conventional account of justice or of moral duties more broadly is self-referentially incoherent. But Rawls ultimately seems to ground political liberalism in nothing else.

(9) Given (2), (3), and (5), and the argument of chapter 1 supporting (1) and (2), it follows, necessarily, that (1)(*b*) is self-referentially incoherent. But (1)(*b*) is correlative to the rejection of (1)(*a*), and (1)(*a*) correlative to the rejection of (1)(*b*). Put another way, (1)(*a*) and (1)(*b*) are mutually exclusive and exhaustive. Given the disjunctive syllogism, the incoherence (and therefore rejection) of (1)(*b*) entails the affirmation of (1)(*a*)—the necessity of transcendent norms of right or a transcendent good for any intelligible account of justice.[118]

Can We Have Moral Objectivity without Realism?: The Curious Case of Ronald Dworkin

The incoherence of moral contractarianism as a thoroughly conventionalist enterprise points to the necessity of moral norms that are not purely positive but that transcend the will, agreement, and conventions of any given society. The only way out of the problem of normative positivism or moral contractarianism is to affirm the existence of real or objective moral norms or values that obtain whether or not we affirm them. They don't depend on our perception. And they cannot be constructed from nonmoral building blocks or from a nonmoral foundation. Ronald Dworkin contends that there is no nonmoral foundation for moral norms, moral principles, and moral obligations. And he affirms that moral values are objective. There is an objective truth of the matter when it comes to the requirements of justice. For instance, it really would be wrong to torture a toddler just for fun (or at all). At the same time, he is deeply skeptical of moral realism. And he thinks the objectivity of values has no connection to or dependence on metaphysical realism. He wants objective morality without realism. I maintain that he is right to reject the possibility of any nonmoral foundation for moral values or moral truth. But he is wrong to think he can have the objectivity of moral value without metaphysical realism.

That Dworkin rejects moral contractarianism or a purely conventional account of justice (or normative positivism) is apparent from his critique of Michael Walzer's argument in *Spheres of Justice*.[119] According to Walzer,

> Justice is relative to social meanings. Indeed, the relativity of justice follows from the classic non-relative definition, giving each person his due. . . . We cannot say what is due to this person or that one until we know how these people relate to one another through things they make and distribute. There cannot be a just society until there is a society; and the adjective *just* doesn't determine, it only modifies, the substantive life of the societies it describes. There are an infinite number of possible lives, shaped by an infinite number of possible cultures, religions, political arrangements, geographical conditions, and so on. A given society is just if its substantive life is lived in a certain way—that is, in a way faithful to the shared understandings of its members.[120]

Thus, says Walzer, "in a society where social meanings are integrated and hierarchical, justice will come to the aid of inequality."[121] To be sure, he affirms that human beings are equals insofar as we are "culture-producing creatures" who "make and inhabit meaningful worlds." And, "since there is no way to rank and order these worlds with regard to their understanding of social goods, we do justice to actual men and women by respecting their particular creations." Thus, "justice is rooted in the distinct understandings of places, honors, jobs, things of all sorts, that constitute a shared way of life."[122]

According to Dworkin, Walzer's contention that justice depends on "the shared understandings" of the members of a society expresses his "deep relativism about justice. [Walzer] says, for example, that a caste system is just in a society whose traditions accept it, and that it would be unjust in such a society to distribute goods and other resources equally."[123] Dworkin rejects Walzer's relativism concerning right and wrong. He writes, "If justice is only a matter of following shared understandings, then how can the parties be debating about justice when there is no shared understanding? In that situation no solution can *possibly* be just, on Walzer's relativistic account, and politics can be only a selfish struggle. What can it mean even to say that people disagree about social meanings? The fact of disagreement shows that there is no shared social meaning to disagree about."[124] Moreover, "It is part of our common political life, if anything is, that justice is our critic not our mirror, that any decision about the distribution of any good—wealth, welfare, honors, education, recognition, office—may be reopened, no matter how firm the traditions that are then challenged, that we may always ask of some settled institutional scheme whether it is fair." Consequently, "Walzer's relativism is faithless to the single most important social practice we have: the practice of worrying about what justice really is."[125]

Having already laid out my own argument against conventional accounts of justice, I will not also lay out Dworkin's argument here. Rather, my argument to this point already shows the necessity of moral principles transcendent of human will and agreement *if we are to have moral norms and principles at all.* Here I simply want to treat Dworkin's claim that such principles or norms are not essentially bound up with metaphysics. He calls this thesis "the metaphysical independence of value." Consider the torturing of babies for fun. Dworkin says acts like this "are wrong in themselves, not just because people think them wrong. They would still be wrong even if, incredibly, no one thought so." So far so good. But Dworkin adds, "Most moral philosophers think . . . that the idea of what they call 'mind-independent' moral truth takes us outside morality into metaphysics"—a view he says posits "chimerical properties or entities 'in the world' that are half moral" and "half nonmoral."[126] He notes that while ordinary people sometimes use the language of moral facts (e.g., "It is a moral fact that torture is always wrong"), "trouble arrives . . . when philosophers make a meal of these innocent references" by taking them to refer to "moral particles or properties," which he pejoratively calls "morons."[127] Moral realists, he says, affirm the existence of these moral particles or properties and say that we interact with them (or can interact with them) in the formation of our moral beliefs. Antirealists deny that any such things exist or, if they do exist, that we can interact with them; they play no role in what moral values we affirm. Antirealists hold that "we make up values for ourselves." According to Dworkin, "Each of these different 'realist' and 'anti-realist' projects evaporates when we take the independence of value seriously."[128]

Dworkin contends, "The only intelligible case for the 'mind-independence' of some moral judgment is a moral argument showing that it would still be true even if no one thought it was."[129] That is, moral judgments can only be justified by *moral* reasons (Dworkin wrongly thinks realists deny this). Philosophers who deny the independence of moral values from metaphysics (e.g., realists and antirealists) distinguish substantive ethics and first-order moral questions (e.g., "Is torture always wrong?") from metaethics and second-order questions (e.g., "Which theory of morality—realism or antirealism—best lines up with the extant facts?"). Over and against realists and antirealists so understood, Dworkin contends that "there are no nonevaluative, second-order, metaethical truths about value," and therefore value judgments are not "true when they match special moral entities" or false "because there are no special entities for them to match." "The moral realm," he says, "is the realm of argument, not brute, raw fact."[130]

Dworkin's account of moral realism, so far as I can tell, describes no actual moral realist (at least not in the scholarly world). Indeed, it's very much as if he's converted moral realism into an instance of mechanistic philosophy.[131] And one wonders whether a particular conception of physics (quite modernist but also not obviously required by Newtonian physics and certainly not required by quantum mechanics) motivates his *metaphysical* independence thesis. The strangeness of Dworkin's account of moral realism notwithstanding, the objectivity of moral value necessarily takes us into the realm of ontology and metaphysics. For he posits the objectivity (or objective reality) of moral truth and, correlatively, rejects any claim that moral truths are merely constructions of human will, products of human agreement, or nothing other than the subjective perception of human minds (whether of individuals or a group or of everyone). But in that case Dworkin's position necessarily rejects Protagoras's antirealism about reality as a whole. Dworkin affirms mind-independent moral truths. Protagoras's (metaphysical) antirealism denies any such truths exist at all. That gives us this conditional: If Protagorean antirealism, then there are no mind-independent truths. Now, affirming mind-independent truths (moral or otherwise), as Dworkin does, necessarily entails rejecting the consequent of our conditional. Given modus tollens, denying the consequent (there are no mind-independent truths) entails denying the antecedent (Protagoras's metaphysical antirealism).[132] Thus, the mind-independence of moral values (or principles or truths) entails that they are *not* metaphysically independent. For the mind-independence of moral values necessarily rules out Protagorean antirealism, which is a metaphysical position.[133]

To put all this another way, one might argue that in the realm of metaphysics, realism (of any sort) and antirealism are mutually exclusive and exhaustive: either universal essences (or universal forms) really exist or they do not. If antirealism entails the rejection of universal essences and of all mind-independent truths (because antirealism makes all truth depend on our mental perceptions) *and* if Dworkin affirms mind-independent truths (which he repeatedly does), then he rejects antirealism. If we allow A to stand for antirealism and R to stand for realism *and* if A and R are mutually exclusive and exhaustive (just with respect to mind-independent truths), then we have this proposition: Either A or R. If A includes the claim that there are no mind-independent truths, then Dworkin denies A (for there are moral truths that are mind-independent, on his view). Given the disjunctive syllogism, that means affirming R (realism, insofar as realism is the affirmation of mind-independent truths or the affirmation of mind-independent truths is an instance of realism). But R is obviously a metaphysical view. Thus, Dworkin's claim about objective values rejects one metaphysics and implies (or presupposes) another.

Now, I would frame matters differently than Dworkin does. I would affirm something closer to moderate realism. But what the foregoing shows is that Dworkin's thesis concerning the independence of moral values and metaphysics fails on precisely the terms he laid out. To affirm a proposition about the nature of moral reality is to affirm something about the nature of reality. And moral realism—understood as the claim that moral judgments can really be true (or false)—entails metaphysical realism.

Conclusion

Chapters 2 and 3 together show that antirealist, conventionalist, and constructivist accounts of justice all fail. Insofar as they reject the objective reality of right and wrong, just and unjust, or seek to build or construct these from nonmoral and, indeed, nonnormative foundations, they collapse into logical incoherence. The contemporary moral contractarian accounts of Gauthier and Rawls fare no better than the conventionalist ones advanced by the Sophists in antiquity or by moderns like Hobbes and Hume. Consequently, human agreement—hypothetical or actual—cannot provide the moral foundation that political contractarianism requires for its intelligibility. Where most scholars seem to hold that political contractarianism and moral contractarianism are essentially connected—the former an expression or application of the latter—the arguments of chapters 1–3 together show that they are in fact logically opposed.

PART II

THE INESCAPABILITY OF THE GOOD:
ON THE NATURE OF MORAL OBLIGATION

CHAPTER 4

Thomas Hobbes and the
Failure of Modern Natural Law

Introduction

IN AN IMPORTANT ESSAY, DAVID Gauthier notes that Hobbes's work
(principally in the English and Latin editions of *Leviathan* and in his
replies to Bishop Bramhall), at least prima facially, gives rise to three
accounts of natural law.[1] The laws of nature might be construed as
dictates of natural reason or "theorems, tending to peace" (which is
to say, as counsels of prudence), as the commands of God (delivered
in the "word of God, that by right commandeth all things"), or as
"the commands of the commonwealth, and therefore also civil law,
for it is the sovereign power that obliges men to obey them." The task
Gauthier sets for himself is to ascertain the proper interpretation of
the laws of nature in Hobbes's most mature work. My task herein
is different. I want to suggest that Hobbesian natural law logically
fails on any plausible interpretation in which his natural law depends
on his metaphysics and his account of good and evil. Consequently,
Hobbes's account of the law of nature, on any plausible interpretation
given his philosophical commitments, cannot be used to ground any
intelligible theory of covenant or consent. Before proceeding, however, I should like to expand Gauthier's list.

As I see it, there are two initial possibilities. The laws of nature are
either laws in their own right, *or* they are not. If they are not, then
there are two possibilities: either the laws of nature are dictates of
reason or counsels of prudence and nothing more, *or* they may become laws proper. There are two accounts of how they may become
laws in the proper sense—the laws of nature become laws only when
they are commanded by the sovereign after the commonwealth has

been settled, *or* they become laws (that is, they become obligatory) only when they are assented to by individuals (such assent being given by laying down the right of nature). But until the laws of nature become laws (because either the sovereign commands or the subjects assent to them), they remain dictates or theorems of reason. If, on the other hand, the laws of nature are laws in the proper sense (that is, if they are laws in their own right), then they must be construed as commands (and who but God could be the relevant commander?). Even so, there are multiple ways the laws of nature might function. First, the laws of nature may obtain only in the civil state and so not in the state of nature, *or* they may obtain in both the civil state and the condition of mere nature. Second, the laws of nature may limit not only subjects but sovereigns as well, *or* they may underwrite absolute sovereign power and so not impose any meaningful limits on it.

We might represent these possible interpretations of Hobbesian natural law as follows:

1. The laws of nature, just as such, are not laws proper.

   a. *Interpretation I:* The laws of nature are dictates of reason (counsels of prudence or theorems concerning peace and preservation). As such, they are hypothetical imperatives. They direct individuals to take those steps necessary to preserve their lives and for seeking peace with others, given that individuals (at least insofar as they are rational) are motivated principally by self-preservation.

   b. *Interpretation II:* The laws of nature, qua laws of *nature*, are not real laws. But they can become laws proper *if and only if* they are commanded by a civil sovereign. Until such time as they are so commanded they remain rational theorems or counsels of prudence (that is, they remain hypothetical imperatives).

   c. *Interpretation III:* The laws of nature are not laws proper (they do not bind of their own accord). Rather, any person p comes under some obligation o if and only if p assents to o. The laws of nature become obligatory only when individuals assent to them. Obligation is analytically related to laying down one's right of nature.

2. The laws of nature are true laws—on account of being the commands of God.

    a. *Interpretation IV:* The laws of nature obtain only in civil society and not in the state of nature—they are conditionals but not hypothetical imperatives (they are, in a way, categorical imperatives).

    b. *Interpretation V:* The laws of nature are the commands of God, but instead of limiting the power of the sovereign vis-à-vis his (or, if an aristocratic or democratic council, then their) subjects, the laws of nature underwrite and establish absolute (or unlimited) sovereign power.

    c. *Interpretation VI:* The laws of nature apply in the state of nature and in the state of civil society, where they obligate subjects and sovereigns alike.

Are there any other interpretations of Hobbesian natural law that are significantly distinct from the ones just described? None of which I am aware.[2]

Hobbesian Metaphysics

The range of plausible interpretations of Hobbes on natural law is limited by certain tenets of Hobbesian philosophy. In particular, any viable interpretation of Hobbesian natural law must be compatible with his metaphysical nominalism and with his subjectivist and relativist account of good and evil.[3] As to his metaphysical nominalism, Hobbes says, "Of names, some are *proper,* and singular to one only thing, as *Peter, John, this man, this tree*; and some are *common* to many things, as *man, horse, tree,* every of which, though but one name, is nevertheless the name of divers particular things, in respect of all which together it is called an *universal,* there being nothing in the world universal but names; for the things named are every one of them individual and singular."[4] This is about as clear a statement of metaphysical nominalism as one could hope to find.[5] According to Hobbes, there are no real universal forms or essences; correlatively, only particulars exist. In what follows, this is what I mean by *metaphysical nominalism*, a position I take to originate with William of Ockham and certainly affirmed by late medieval Ockhamists or terminists (though nothing of substance in my argument in this chapter in fact turns on the correct interpretation of Ockham).[6]

Now, I hold that metaphysical nominalism precludes any account of moral obligation save a voluntaristic one.[7] Thus, if one is a nominalist and also affirms the existence of moral obligations (indeed, the existence of any obligations at all), then one must also be a metaethical voluntarist. A metaethical voluntarist is one who deems some act of will or other (God's or the sovereign's or the community's) necessary and sufficient for obligation (and for moral obligation in particular). Thus, on Suárez's interpretation (and I think Suárez has it right), Ockham held that divine will is both necessary and sufficient for moral obligation.[8] My position comes to this: the conjunction of nominalism and obligation entails metaethical voluntarism (or a voluntarist ontology of obligation).[9] Please note, I am not arguing that if one is a voluntarist, then one must also be a nominalist. Duns Scotus is frequently described as a metaphysical realist who was also an ethical voluntarist (or an ethical voluntarist about every proposition save one—namely, the love of God).[10] Perhaps this position is logically consistent. Perhaps not. For my purposes I need not enter that debate. I hold only that nominalism together with the affirmation of obligation entails voluntarism. As I argue in the next chapter, this is because will appears to be the only ground left for obligation once one rejects universals such as goodness or justice or once one denies that good is to be found in the nature of things.

Hobbes is also a subjectivist and relativist concerning the good, a position that seems inexorably to follow from his metaphysical nominalism.[11] Put another way, Hobbes's subjectivism and relativism concerning good and evil seems clearly to be an application of his metaphysical nominalism to ethics. Minimally, metaphysical nominalism precludes affirmation of the objective reality of goodness and so of acts that are intrinsically good or evil. In chapter 6 of *Leviathan*, he famously says,

> Whatsoever is the object of any man's appetite or desire that is it which he for his part calleth *good*; and the object of his hate

and aversion, *evil*; and of his contempt, *vile* and *inconsiderable*. For these words of good, evil, and contemptible are ever used with relation to the person that useth them, there being nothing simply and absolutely so, nor any common rule of good and evil to be taken from the nature of the objects themselves, but from the person of the man (where there is no commonwealth), or (in a commonwealth) from the person that representeth it, or from an arbitrator or judge whom men disagreeing shall by consent set up, and make his sentence the rule thereof.[12]

Hobbes here says nothing is simply or absolutely good. That is, nothing is good or evil in and of itself. Good and evil are not given in the nature of things. Rather, they consist entirely in *names* we give to certain relations—relations of desire and aversion insofar as we consider humans qua human. Thus, a few chapters later, Hobbes writes,

Good and *evil* are names that signify our appetites and aversions, which in different tempers, customs, and doctrines of men are different; and divers men differ not only in their judgment on the senses (of what is pleasant and unpleasant to the taste, smell, hearing, touch, and sight), but also of what is conformable or disagreeable to reason in the actions of common life. Nay, the same man in divers times differs from himself, and one time praiseth (that is, calleth good) what another time he dispraiseth (and calleth evil); from when arise disputes, controversies, and at last war.

Consequently, "so long as man is in the condition of mere nature (which is a condition of war) . . . private appetite is the measure of good and evil."[13] So Hobbes holds that good and evil vary not only across individuals but also within any given individual over the course of a life. There is but one good common to each individual: "All men agree on this, that peace is good."[14] But while the goodness of peace is universal, peace is good only insofar as it is an object of desire. And so this universally shared object of desire is nevertheless subjective.

Part and parcel of Hobbes's subjectivism concerning good and evil is his rejection of a greatest or highest good and final end that is desirable in and of itself: "The felicity of this life consisteth not in the repose of a mind satisfied. For there is no such *Finis ultimus* (utmost aim) nor *Summum Bonum* (greatest good) as is spoken of in the books of the old moral philosophers. Nor can a man any more live, whose desires are at an end, than he whose senses and imaginations are at a stand. Felicity is a continual progress of the desire from one object to another, the attaining of the former being still but a way to the latter."[15] That is to say, happiness does not consist in attaining an objectively desirable state of well-being—a state of affairs that is objectively good and desirable whether or not anyone actually desires it. Rather, happiness or well-being is found in the continual satisfaction of desire.[16] Quite clearly, then, this passage (taken in conjunction with those quoted above) rules out any account of Hobbesian natural law dependent upon a real or objective good found in the nature of things or desirable for its own sake and not for the sake of anything else.

Now, there are passages in Hobbes that seem to depend upon a real or objective good that is not merely the object of desire. For instance, Hobbes distinguishes that which is actually good from "*apparent* or *seeming good*" and that which is really evil for a person from "*apparent* or *seeming evil*."[17] Moreover, if good is just an object of appetite and peace (or preservation) is good, then the goodness of peace can consist only in the fact that it is desired. Hobbes is aware that not everyone desires it. To borrow a turn of phrase from Locke, some people quit or seek to quit their station willfully. Others, such as Achilles, court death on the field of battle for the sake of glory and fame. As Hobbes sees it, those who *fail* to seek their own preservation are irrational or unhealthy or mad.[18] In short, Hobbes seems to treat the end of preservation as regulative of human desire and not merely something at which desire is aimed. Be that as it may, Hobbes's rejection of any objectivist understanding of good (and evil) and his endorsement of the subjectivist understanding is apparent in the passages quoted above. Consequently, we can either find a way to construe those passages in which Hobbes appears to distinguish real from apparent good (and evil) in a subjectivist (or at least relativist) way, or we can conclude that Hobbes is deeply inconsistent. And, indeed, Hobbes may be deeply inconsistent (as Jean Hampton maintains). As I see it, Hobbes clearly intends to reject any objective or intrinsic or absolute good (and evil)—and this is so whether or not he is successful in achieving his goal. Thus, Hobbes cannot posit a good that ought to be desired whether or not anyone actually desires it. For Hobbes, something can be desirable only if (and only because) it is actually desired (the modal conflation involved in such a position notwithstanding). Consequently, any interpretation of Hobbes that affirms or implies moral or metaphysical realism must be rejected as implausible.

Part and parcel of Hobbes's rejection of a final end and greatest good in moral philosophy is his rejection of final causation more generally. In the part of *Elements of Philosophy* called *Concerning Body* (*De Corpore*), Hobbes says, "The writers of metaphysics reckon up two other causes besides the *efficient* and *material*, namely, the ESSENCE, which some call the *formal cause*, and the END, or *final cause*; both which are nevertheless efficient causes." Indeed, "A *final cause* has no place but in such things as have sense and will; and this also I shall prove hereafter to be an efficient cause."[19] As Frederick Copleston suggests, Hobbes reduces formal and final causes to efficient causes such that "to all intents and purposes we are left with efficient causality alone."[20] This passage indicates Hobbes's clear intention to reject final causes in any classical or Aristotelian sense—though whether he can consistently pull off that rejection is entirely another matter. But this rejection of final causes, in the classical sense, clearly coheres with and, I submit, grounds his rejection of a final end and greatest good in moral philosophy, on the one hand, and necessitates his instrumentalist account of reason, on the other.

Another boundary or framing consideration is Hobbes's account of the nature of rationality. Hobbes rejects the notion of noninstrumental (or substantive) reason, opting instead for an instrumentalist account. For Hobbes, reason does not perceive and is not motivated by the desirable itself or by that which is intrinsically reasonable. Rather, desire alone determines the objects (which are desirable only insofar as they are desired), and reason tells us how to attain the objects of desire. Thus, reason "is nothing but *reckoning* (that is, adding and subtracting) of the consequences of general names agreed upon for the *marking* and *signifying* our thoughts."[21] Early in *Leviathan*, Hobbes distinguishes between a "train of thought, or mental discourse" that is regulated and one that is not. The difference between them is that regulated mental discourse is "*regulated* by some desire, and design."[22] Reflecting on intellectual virtues (and vices), he writes, "The thoughts are to the desires as scouts and spies to range abroad and find the way to things desired."[23] We should recall here too Hobbes's contention that felicity, or happiness, is simply the satisfaction of one desire after another, where the satisfaction of any given desire is just a means to the satisfaction of a subsequent desire.[24] Additionally, Hobbes writes, "The *value* or WORTH of a man is, as of all other things, his price, that is to say, so much as he would be given for the use of his power; and therefore is not absolute, but a thing dependent on the need and judgment of another." Thus, "an able conductor of soldiers is of great price in time of war present or imminent; but in peace not so. A learned and uncorrupt judge is much worth in time of peace; but not so much in war. And as in other things, so in men, not the seller, but the buyer determines the price. For let a man (as most men do) rate themselves at the highest value they can; yet their true value is no more than it is esteemed by others."[25] As Hampton maintains, in this passage Hobbes says that human value is purely instrumental.[26] One's entire worth or value is only what others esteem it to be. Indeed, in this passage, he says the same goes for everything else. In *De Cive* he writes, "in the state of nature"—that is, by nature—"profit is the measure of right."[27] These passages clearly reflect an instrumentalist account of reason.

Some, notably Gert, have wondered how Hobbes can be construed as a proponent of instrumental rationality when he refers to those who desire (and so court) death as irrational or unhealthy or mad.[28] And this is indeed a thorny matter. Consonant with his claim that "reason is, and ought only to be the slave of the passions, and can never pretend to any other office than serve and obey them," Hume held, " 'Tis not contrary to reason to prefer the destruction of the whole world to the scratching of my finger. 'Tis not contrary to reason for me to chuse my total ruin, to prevent the least uneasiness of an *Indian* or person wholly unknown to me. 'Tis as little contrary to reason to prefer even my own acknowledg'd lesser good to my greater, and have a more ardent affection for the former than the latter."[29] These two statements together suggest this position: purely instrumental rationality entails the indifference of reason to the ends pursued. In that case, however, instrumental reason ought to be indifferent between pursuing peace and refusing to pursue it and indifferent between preferring the destruction of oneself to self-preservation. Hobbes holds that reason is not indifferent here. And it's exceptionally difficult to see how (on the purely instrumentalist view of reason) Hobbes is right and Hume is wrong. Nevertheless, we can clearly say at least this much. First, as the preceding paragraph demonstrates, Hobbes seems clearly to affirm the instrumentalist view of reason. Reason ascertains the means for attaining the objects of desire, the overriding desire being self-preservation. Second, the instrumental view of reason is consonant with (indeed, perhaps required by) his subjectivism concerning good and evil (which follows from his nominalism) in state of nature (and the relativity of good and evil to law in a commonwealth). Third, there is no ground in instrumental rationality for distinguishing among desires or the objects of desire; as to these, instrumental rationality, rightly understood, is indifferent. Hobbes himself holds that there is nothing simply or absolutely good, nothing intrinsically good—rather something is good just because it is desired.[30]

There is one last matter that deserves mention here. While there may be many places where certain persons now live in a relative state of nature (Hobbes says, "The savage people in many places of *America* . . . have no government at all, and live at this day in a brutish manner") and while the nations of the world exist in a state-of-nature relation to each other, the pure state of nature (the condition of mere nature) "never generally" obtained "over all the world."[31] Now Hobbes clearly intends his argument to be about the foundations of sovereign power per se and not only about how one might or must go about creating sovereign power in those places where the state of nature has actually obtained to some degree. This means that the state of nature is, for the purposes of his argument, a hypothetical state of affairs (we might say a possible world). I will return later to how and why this might matter for his argument.[32]

Interpretations of Hobbes's Account of Natural Law
INTERPRETATION I: THE LAWS OF NATURE
AS HYPOTHETICAL IMPERATIVES

With the foregoing tenets of Hobbesian philosophy in view, let's take the accounts of natural law enumerated above in order. While I will offer some evidence on behalf of each interpretation, my goal herein is less to defend any particular interpretation of Hobbesian natural law and more to argue that Hobbesian natural law is a resounding failure on any of them.

Howard Warrender famously maintained the following: "If the laws of nature in the State of Nature are not regarded as the commands of God, they may be taken to be merely rational principles of prudence. The atheist, presumably, would have some use for these maxims as they would be a guide to his preservation, but he could not consider them as laws, and, as we have seen, could not be obliged by them. There are some interpretations of Hobbes's doctrine which consist in identifying his whole theory or morals and politics virtually with this atheistical viewpoint." But "if it is denied that God plays an essential role in Hobbes's doctrine, the laws of nature in the State of Nature cannot be more than prudential maxims for those who desire their own preservation. Those commentators, therefore, who have seen the place of God in Hobbes's theory as the product of confusion or pretence on Hobbes's part, have taken this view."[33] Those who maintain that Hobbes's laws of nature are not *laws* in the proper sense rely on the following passages: "These dictates of reason men use to call by the name of laws, but improperly; for they are but conclusions or theorems concerning what conduceth to the conservation and defence of themselves, whereas law, properly, is the word of him that by right hath command over others."[34] Or, as Hobbes puts it in *De Cive*, "those which we call the laws of nature (since they are nothing else but certain conclusions, understood by reason, of things to be done and omitted), are not in propriety of speech laws, *as they proceed from nature*."[35] But as "delivered by God in holy Scripture," then they are laws in the proper sense.

Inspired by these lines, a number of scholars have treated Hobbes's laws of nature as an application of the instrumentalist account of rationality to the realm of politics and morals.[36] So understood, the laws of nature constitute hypothetical imperatives (rather than categorical imperatives or imperatives of right action binding on all persons and of their own accord). As Jean Hampton puts it, "Many philosophers and social scientists argue that the only acceptable theory of the nature of practical reason is what is called the 'instrumental' theory, which says, roughly, that reason's only practical role is working out and recommending action that best achieves the end of agent. Such theorists dismiss the idea that reason could ever play a noninstrumental role by dictating or determining ends themselves."[37] This view of reason and morality (and their relation) has had significant purchase with a number of prominent contemporary moral philosophers. Thus J. L. Mackie describes hypothetical imperatives this way: " 'If you want X, do Y' (or 'You ought to Y') will be a hypothetical imperative if it is based on the supposed fact that Y is, in the circumstances, the only (or the best) available means to X, that is, on a causal relation between Y and X. The reason for doing Y lies in its causal connection with the desired end, X; the oughtness is contingent upon the desire."[38] On this view, *oughtness* is contingent upon desire together with the necessity of using certain means (or refraining from certain kinds of actions) in order to obtain the object of desire. Such imperatives also appear to have a law-like causal structure that may seem analogous to the causal laws of the natural order (at least on a certain understanding of the cosmos). That's because hypothetical imperatives supply necessary and (at least ceteris paribus) sufficient conditions for attaining the desired object. Likewise, the physical laws of nature (at least on the common understanding of the models of Galileo and Newton and in contrast to the current model of bounded indeterminism so prevalent in modern physics) supply necessary and sufficient conditions for physical phenomena. Thus, when certain necessary and sufficient conditions are met, then rain falls upon storied Spanish plains. Hypothetical imperatives are such that (at least ceteris paribus) they must be followed for some desired object, *o*, to be obtained, and if they are followed, then *o* will in fact be obtained.

If the laws of nature are hypothetical imperatives, then they are the means (each) necessary and (together) sufficient for the attaining of some end.[39] Hobbes most commonly describes the end as peace. But peace among human persons is instrumental to self-preservation (or, perhaps more aptly, the avoidance of sudden and violent death). Construed as hypothetical imperatives, the laws of nature are necessary conditions for attaining peace and, through peace, preservation, given that preservation is what individuals desire most. Self-preservation and peace both require escaping (or avoiding) the state of nature, which is essentially a state of war—a state in which the survival of each individual is in jeopardy. Given that individuals most desire to survive and given that individuals cannot obtain that good in the state of nature, the laws of nature counsel individuals to seek to leave (or avoid) that state (to the extent that they can). The laws of nature constitute the necessary steps for achieving this goal. That is, the laws of nature specify the necessary conditions for exiting or avoiding the state of nature—by seeking peace with others, by laying down the right of nature, by transferring the right of nature to an absolute sovereign power, by keeping covenants (including the covenant to establish the sovereign), and so forth.

On this account the laws of nature do not govern the state of nature (Hobbes describes the condition of "mere nature" as morally ungoverned); but they are permanent and universal in that they tell each individual, "If you want to live, then you ought to leave the state of nature," and they specify the steps that must be taken in order to leave it or, more aptly, to forestall or avoid falling into it. If you want to live, then you ought to pursue peace with those that are willing to pursue it with you. If you want to pursue peace with others, then you must lay down the right of nature. If you want to lay down the right of nature, then you must do so by transferring it to a sovereign person(s). If you want to establish a sovereign power (especially as a final judge capable of resolving conflicts among individuals), then you must make the sovereign absolute (i.e., unlimited), et cetera. These laws are eternal and immutable in the sense that they always hold. They always counsel seeking peace with those who will seek peace with you. They always specify certain steps necessary for leaving or avoiding falling into the state of nature. Given the causal relation of the laws of nature to escaping or avoiding the state of nature, these hypothetical imperatives are not subjective. The good to which these laws are means is subjective. But the necessity (and at least ceteris paribus sufficiency) of these laws for the attainment of that good is not.

Now, there are passages in the Hobbesian corpus (and in *Leviathan* in particular) that are not easily harmonized with this account of the laws of nature. But let's set that to the side. Suppose this account of Hobbesian natural law is by and large correct. What then should we make of Hobbesian natural law? Following Hampton, I think the answer is clear. Either Hobbes seeks to use instrumental reason to account for or ground normative force (or oughtness), in which case instrumental reason imports metaphysical properties (like real universals) Hobbes wishes to deny (he calls such properties "nonsense" and "absurd"),[40] *or* instrumental reason yields a purely descriptive account of causal relations devoid of oughtness—devoid, indeed, of any prescriptive power at all—in which case we have a moral theory without prescription. But such a theory, arguably, "fails to be a moral theory at all."[41] Moreover, absent moral prescription and therefore obligation, the Hobbesian theory is unable to ground any of the rights attendant to sovereign power or the obligations of subjects to obey the sovereign or to keep their covenants. But in that case, civil society and sovereign power are without foundation—something Hobbes sought to provide.

Let's take these points in order. Recall that for Hobbes, good is subjective. Taking men insofar as they are men, as Hobbes puts it (that is, from the vantage of nature alone), for any person, p, and any object, o, if p desires o, then o is good for p, whatever o happens to be—for nothing is simply good or desirable as such.[42] On the instrumentalist account of rationality, hypothetical imperatives tell p how to attain o, whatever o happens to be. Hobbes also holds that self-preservation (and also peace) is a good (indeed, the most fundamental good) for every person. That should mean that each person desires his own self-preservation and, indeed, that each person desires his own self-preservation more than he desires anything else. But Hobbes was well aware that this claim is empirically false. Some individuals commit suicide. Others court death on the field of battle for the sake of attaining glory or fame. Hobbes refers to such persons as irrational, unhealthy, mad. But, as Hampton says, "to judge someone as sick or well, sane or mad, is to judge him using an ideal as one's yardstick. Hence, we cannot use these concepts to select which of our desires is value-defining without importing the normativity [the instrumentalist] had hoped the desires themselves would explain." Thus, "by calling a glory-prone person mad, Hobbes gives himself away as a man who cannot completely eschew Aristotelianism; by using this word he is illicitly relying on a norm to criticize this kind of human being, where this norm also justifies him in using only the desires of a person in a healthy and sane state to define value. But if a norm indirectly picks out what is supposed to be the 'non-normative' building blocks of Hobbes's normative theory, then his building blocks are normatively loaded from the start."[43]

Earlier I argued that it is impossible to distinguish among exercises of will on the basis of will alone because it is impossible intelligibly to distinguish among the members of any set on the basis of the property (or properties) by which the set is defined (or on the basis of the predication of that property). We can think of desires along the same lines. We can conceive of various desires, actual and potential, as comprising a set. As with prime numbers and exercises of will, it is impossible to distinguish among various desires on the basis of nothing but desire. From the standpoint of desires, all that matters is that p desires o. To distinguish some desires from others (on the basis of rationality or sanity or health) is to do so on the basis of some property other than desire. To make some desire (such as the desire to survive) normative for other desires (given the good of self-preservation, I ought not court glory on the field of battle, or I ought not quit my station willfully) is to introduce a rule and measure independent of desires and normative for them. But a rule and measure normative for desire cannot itself be subjective—cannot itself simply be a matter of desire. Such a standard tells us that there are goods (such as self-preservation or peace insofar as others will seek it with us) that we ought to desire, whether or not we do—goods desirable of their own accord. Hobbes denies that any such goods exist. Nothing is simply or absolutely good (or evil), he claims. Thus, Hobbes's account of instrumental rationality depends, for its intelligibility, on the very properties his subjectivism or relativism denies.

Could Hobbes amend his theory? Instead of treating self-preservation as normative—as something we ought to desire whether or not we do or as something only irrational or mad individuals do not desire—could Hobbes treat instrumental reason as indifferent to the good desired (even if the desired object is one's own destruction rather than one's preservation)? The moment Hobbes adopts the sort of indifference toward various goods that instrumental rationality requires (as Hume so clearly saw), his theory loses all prescriptive force (as Hampton maintains). Hypothetical imperatives tell one how to attain some good, whatever that good happens to be. If goods are morally indifferent, as the subjectivist must maintain, then hypothetical imperatives can do nothing more than *describe* causal relations between ends and means. If no goods are such that we ought to prefer them, then no means can be such that we ought to adopt them. In the case of self-preservation, instrumental rationality may tell me that if I want to survive, then I must do X, Y, and Z. But instrumental rationality cannot tell me that I ought (or am bound) to desire my own preservation (rather than, say, my destruction) and so cannot tell me that I ought to do X, Y, and Z. My point is this: hypothetical imperatives seem not to be imperatives at all. Indeed, the price of instrumental rationality seems clearly to be oughtness in general and obligation in particular. In which case Hampton is right—instrumental rationality yields a moral theory without prescription (of which instrumental rationality was intended to give a naturalistic account). But prescription is essential to morality. And so instrumental rationality yields a moral theory without morality.

What hypothetical imperatives are missing, then, is *prescription*. For hypothetical imperatives to be imperative, the good at which they aim must first be prescribed. In order for p to be bound to take certain (necessary) steps to attain some object o, p must first be bound to pursue o. But why should this matter? Can't Hobbes get by with a purely descriptive natural law? Does he really need oughtness or obligation or prescription? In particular, does he really need moral obligation and moral prescription? I think that he does. Why he does should become apparent in the next section.

INTERPRETATION II: SOVEREIGN COMMANDS

Interpretation II concedes that the laws of nature are, of themselves, not laws proper. Rather, they are hypothetical imperatives, and as hypothetical imperatives they lack the power to bind (or at least to obligate). On this view, the laws of nature become laws ("properly so-called") when they are commanded by the commonwealth, which is to say, by the sovereign power. Hobbes famously distinguishes counsel from command and treats law as a species of the latter rather than the former. As well, Hobbes says, "The law of nature and the civil law contain each other, and are of equal extent. For the laws of nature, which consist in equity, justice, gratitude, and other moral virtues on these depending, in the condition of mere nature . . . are not properly laws, but qualities that dispose men to peace and obedience. *When a commonwealth is once settled, then are they actually laws, and not before, as being then the commands of the commonwealth, and therefore also civil laws*; for it is the sovereign power that obliges men to obey them."[44] Later in the same chapter he says that "all laws, written and unwritten, have their authority from the force and will of the commonwealth, that is to say, from the will of the representative (which in a monarchy is the monarch, and in other commonwealths the sovereign assembly)."[45] These passages give rise to two main points. First, on this view, the laws of nature are not laws proper in the condition of mere nature. Consequently, they do not bind or obligate in that state of affairs. But the laws of nature do acquire binding force in the civil state, when they are commanded by the sovereign—"it is the sovereign power that obliges men to obey them." Second, Hobbes says the authority (the normative force or binding power) of "all laws"—*both written and unwritten*—derives from the "force and will of commonwealth" or, more aptly, of the sovereign. The force and will of the commonwealth or of the sovereign is the ground of the authority of the laws. In conjunction with the first quote, the second quote suggests that the authority of the laws includes (perhaps is preeminently manifest in) their power to oblige (or obligate). But in that case, the power of the laws (or the sovereign) to oblige is grounded in nothing other than the force and will of the sovereign. Sovereign will is taken to be both necessary and sufficient for the obligation of subjects to obey.

Suppose that Hobbes's position is that the laws of nature acquire the power to bind only when (if and only if) they are commanded by the civil sovereign. In that case, Hobbes has made the will of the sovereign normative (indeed, obligatory) for the will of subjects. But the binding power of the sovereign's will is found in nothing other than force and will. So, on this interpretation, Hobbes has made the will of the sovereign binding upon the will of subjects on the basis of nothing other than will. But, as we've already noted, this is to distinguish among exercises of will on the basis of nothing other than will, which cannot intelligibly be done. To make some exercises of will binding upon others on the basis of nothing but will is self-referentially incoherent. Consequently, any distinction among exercises of will must be made on the basis of something other than sheer will. If we distinguish between exercises of will that are obligatory and those that are not, between exercises of will that are authoritative or normative and those that are not, then we must do so on the basis of some rule and measure transcendent of human will and normative for it. That is, distinguishing some exercises of will from others implies a good that individuals ought to will (whether or not they do).

Now recall our earlier conditional: if both metaphysical nominalism and obligation, then metaethical voluntarism. Given this conditional and modus tollens, the incoherence of voluntarism entails rejecting nominalism or rejecting obligation and therefore that there is no account of obligation compatible with metaphysical nominalism—which is an essential part of the ontological ground of Hobbes's "moral science." One can be a nominalist and give up obligation. Or one can hold on to obligation and give up nominalism. Obligation as such, however, requires moral and metaphysical realism.[46] Consequently, if Hobbes wants the will of the sovereign to be obligatory, then the binding power of that will must be something other than just force and will. The will of the sovereign alone will not provide the sort of prescription that hypothetical imperatives so clearly lack.

I have a related but distinct point. There is some debate as to whether Hobbes is a positivist or, more aptly, a forerunner of the classical, legal positivism of Bentham and Austin.[47] And Hobbes clearly says some things that point in this direction (law is the command of the sovereign, the separation of law from goodness, resting the obligating power of law upon nothing other than the will and force of the sovereign). So perhaps Hobbes is a proto-positivist (though Mark C. Murphy and others claim he is a kind of natural law theorist).[48] But whether or not Hobbes is a proto-positivist, Interpretation II brings him into the positivist camp on the salient points. For on

Interpretation II there is no moral obligation antecedent to (or a necessary condition of) legal obligation. In prior work and earlier in this volume I have argued that moral obligation is a necessary condition of legal obligation.[49] I do not hold that moral obligation is sufficient or both necessary and sufficient for legal obligation. Thus, I do not hold that moral and legal obligation are coextensive. I hold only that moral obligation is a necessary (but *not* sufficient) condition of legal obligation. Moral obligation is the necessary ontological ground of there being legal obligation. This follows from the incoherence of legal positivism.[50] For absent an antecedent moral ground, legal norms can only instantiate or express a thoroughly voluntarist ontology of obligation—an ontology that, as we've seen, is self-referentially incoherent. We therefore have the following conditional: if legal obligation, then moral obligation.[51] That is, we can only have a legal obligation to perform some action if we have a prior moral obligation to fulfill our legal obligations. Otherwise, what we have are mere (legal) commands or injunctions. Now the problem with the protopositivist interpretation of Hobbes, which makes the binding power of all laws (including natural laws) depend upon the will of the civil sovereign, is that it entails that legal obligation is not dependent upon moral obligation. On this view, there is no moral obligation antecedent to legal obligation. But given the conditional above and given modus tollens, the upshot of rejecting moral obligation as necessary for legal obligation is the rejection of legal obligation itself—in this case, our obligation to obey the sovereign's commands.[52]

INTERPRETATION III: ASSENT AS THE GROUND OF OBLIGATION

The foregoing account of Hobbesian natural law (and of obligation in Hobbes) confronts some interpretative difficulties. Hobbes grounds the authority of the sovereign (and the power of the sovereign to oblige or obligate his subjects) in a covenant. The commonwealth and the sovereign representative are established by a covenant. Observance of this covenant and its terms must, for the Hobbesian argument to work, be obligatory. But the obligation to observe the covenant (or the covenantal authorization of sovereign power) cannot in turn derive from the command (or from the "force and will") of the sovereign or the commonwealth. So to posit would be to reason in a circle.

Any noncircular account of our obligation to observe the covenant that creates the commonwealth and establishes the sovereign power must rest on some ground other than the sovereign's will. And this means there must be a source of obligation independent of sovereign will and that grounds our obligation to obey the sovereign's commands. Based on passages in *Leviathan* and exchanges with Bishop Bramhall, Gauthier seeks to develop just such an interpretation.

Gauthier's account begins by noting "Hobbes's insistence that law is addressed 'to one formerly obliged to obey' the commander." He takes this to mean that "law is not the source of obligation. Rather, it makes prior obligation determinate."[53] But if law is not the source of our obligation to do what the law says or to obey the lawgiver, what is? Gauthier finds his answer in Hobbes's claim that "there [is] no obligation on any man which ariseth not from some act of his own; for all men equally are by nature free."[54] The terms of the Hobbesian covenant include authorization by the (soon-to-be) subjects of all the sovereign's actions. And Hobbes says, "the *obligation* and liberty of the subject *is to be derived . . . from those words*."[55] From the foregoing, Gauthier infers that "law is the command of some person whom one is formerly obliged to obey in virtue of some act of one's own—Hobbes speaks of 'the act of our *submission*.' " Gauthier concludes that for Hobbes, "*all* law depends on the assent of the subjects."[56] As Gauthier notes, in his reply to Bishop Bramhall in *Of Liberty and Necessity*, Hobbes explicitly includes the law of nature; in Part III of *Leviathan* he expressly includes the Decalogue.[57] On this view, then, obligation just as such depends upon the assent of the person who falls under it.

As I understand Gauthier, he seems to be saying that the assent of *p* to *o* is necessary and sufficient for *p* to fall under *o*. And how do individuals obligate themselves to obey the sovereign? According to Gauthier (citing *Leviathan* 14.7 in support), "Obligation enters with the renunciation or laying down of right. Given the right of nature [the right individuals possess in the state of nature to everything and to do anything] as a normative, moral primitive, then obligation is introduced by accepting a restriction on this right." Thus, "Hobbes . . . has no need to treat the law of nature as law, or as in itself binding or obliging, to explain how men come to be bound and obliged. Men oblige themselves by their own acts of laying down this right."[58]

We should note (as Gauthier does) that Hobbes explicitly rejects this account of obligation in *De Cive*. There he says, "It is manifest that the *divine laws* sprang not from the consent of men, nor yet the *laws of nature*. For if they had their original from the consent of men, they might also by the same consent be abrogated; but they are unchangeable."[59] But *Leviathan* and his reply to Bramhall in *Of Liberty and Necessity* reflects Hobbes's *mature* view of the matter. And his mature view is different from that expressed in *De Cive:* "Hobbes has since discovered how law may be unchangeable in its content, as expressing the will of God (in Scripture) or the conditions of preservation, yet owe its binding status to assent, whether by covenant of submission to the sovereign, or by natural reason determining the necessity of peace, and so the means, for self-preservation."[60]

On this view, the laws of nature become obligatory when we assent to them or when we, through a covenant, give our assent—thereby binding ourselves—to a sovereign power, which in turn commands obedience to the laws of nature. On this view, our assent (or consent)—an act of will—creates obligation. Any person p is obligated to do some act a if and only if p assents (or consents) to a. Or there is an analytic relation between assent and obligation. In particular, Gauthier seems to suggest an analytic connection between authorizing sovereign power and being obligated to do what the sovereign commands and (relatedly) between laying down the right of nature and being obligated to the person to whom that right is transferred.

This view is problematic for several reasons. First, grounding obligation (to the sovereign, to God, to the laws of nature) in the assent of individuals seems clearly to depend upon the soundness of self-imposed obligations. But Hobbes rejects the idea of self-imposed obligations as unsound. In *De Cive*, Hobbes argues "no one can . . . be obligated to oneself; for since *the obligated and the obligating party* would be the same, and the obligating party may release the obligated, obligation to oneself would be meaningless, because he can release himself at his own discretion, and anyone who can do this is in fact free."[61] Lest we think this passage reflects a position later rejected by a more mature Hobbes, in *Leviathan* he writes, "Nor is it possible for any person to be bound to himself, because he that can bind can release; and therefore, he that is bound to himself only is not bound."[62] So self-imposed obligation seems clearly to be one of those notions Hobbes considered nonsense. Yet to ground obligation in the assent of the person who is to fall under it is to make obligation self-imposed. Moreover, even if Hobbes had not endorsed the argument from *De Cive* in *Leviathan*, the argument in *De Cive* ought to be compelling for one with Hobbesian commitments (especially concerning the nature of sovereign power).

Second, there is a vicious circularity involved in the effort to ground obligation in assent. This view depends upon the very thing it seeks to explain. For us to incur obligations by assent (or consent), we must first be bound to honor our assent—bound to do those acts that we've assented to do and to refrain from doing those things we've assented not to do. If we've assented to *a* and are therefore obligated to *a*, it can only be because we have an antecedent moral obligation to do what we've assented to do. At the very least, there is a modal distinction between consenting or assenting to *a* and being obligated to *a*. It is one thing to undertake an obligation and another to be bound to perform those obligations I have voluntarily undertaken. So there must be at least one moral obligation antecedent to assent for our assent to have the power to bind. But then assent depends upon obligation—and, in particular, on moral obligation—rather than accounting for it.

Third, assent, taken by itself, is nothing but an exercise or instance of human will. To make assent the ground of obligation is, therefore, to make one act of will (assent) normative for others (I am obligated to conform my will to that initial assent) on the basis of will alone. Grounding obligation (and, in particular, moral obligation) in assent instantiates a voluntarist ontology of obligation and renders the position self-referentially incoherent.

INTERPRETATIONS I–III: THE LAWS OF NATURE
DO NOT OBTAIN IN THE STATE OF NATURE

Interpretations I–III all share something in common. They all hold that the laws of nature do not obtain as laws in the state of nature. There is no such thing as moral obligation in that state of affairs. And this seems to comport with Hobbes's account of the natural condition. Hobbes says that neither just nor unjust, neither right nor wrong, have any place therein.[63] On Interpretations I–III the laws of nature obtain only in the state of civil society—and then only when commanded by the sovereign or assented to by individuals in the act of laying down the right of nature in order to establish a commonwealth and sovereign power.

Interpretations I–III also reject the notion that the laws of nature bind us because they are the commands of God. In contrast, Interpretations IV–VI all hold that the laws of nature really are laws. They are really laws because they are divine commands.

INTERPRETATION IV: THE LAWS OF NATURE

OBTAIN ONLY IN THE CIVIL STATE

On Interpretation IV, Hobbes's laws of nature are laws in the proper sense because they are commanded by God. This interpretation also holds, however, that the laws of nature only apply in the civil state. That is, they do not apply in the state of nature. This interpretation endeavors to do justice to two claims Hobbes makes. The first is Hobbes's claim that norms of just and unjust, right and wrong, do not obtain in the condition of mere nature. The second is Hobbes's claim that the laws of nature are the commands of God.

Political theorist William E. Connolly construes Hobbes along the following lines. Hobbes holds that (1) the laws of nature really are laws "because they are commands of God relayed to humans through natural reason," (2) "the laws of nature are recognizable in the state of nature," and (3) the laws of nature are not "operative until there is a common power to fear and each can be assured that his own submission will not place him at a double disadvantage with others."[64] Connolly also says Hobbes holds that (4) "the sovereign, though created by an earthly pact, is accountable to God in the last instance." Thus, "while the monarch does not sin against his subjects in acting capriciously or ruthlessly, he sins against God if he breaks a law of nature."[65] On this view, the sovereign is accountable to (and indeed limited by) the laws of nature—as, of course, are subjects. So on this view, (a) the laws of nature do not obtain in the state of nature, (b) the laws of nature apply to both sovereign and subjects in the civil state, and (c) the laws of nature, in the civil state, remain laws in their own right—that is, whether or not they are commanded by the civil sovereign or assented to by subjects. For the obligatory power of the natural law is grounded in the command of God.

This interpretation has at least two virtues to commend it. First, it recognizes (at least implicitly) the insufficiency of human will (whether of the sovereign or of individuals by giving assent) to ground obligation or to give the laws of nature normative force. Second, it treats the laws of nature as conditionals without treating them as hypothetical imperatives. Or, perhaps more aptly, it treats the laws of nature as hypothetical imperatives (they are not prescribed for the state of nature but are prescribed, by God, for the civil state) without wedding such imperatives to a thoroughly instrumentalist account of rationality. In other words, this interpretation recognizes the apparent if-then structure of Hobbesian natural law but does so in a way that endeavors not to sacrifice prescription.

On this view, then, the laws of nature prescribe in the civil state but not in the state of nature. Is this view tenable? For reasons discussed by A. P. Martinich in *Two Gods of Leviathan*, I don't think that it is. First, Hobbes's third law of nature is "that men perform their covenants made."[66] But he also holds that "covenants entered into by fear, in the condition of mere nature, are obligatory."[67] Taken together, these entail that laws of nature obtain in the state of nature as laws—indeed, as laws that impose obligations. The Connolly interpretation of Hobbes cannot account for this fact. The best proponents of this interpretation can do is to hold that passages such as this are unnecessary to Hobbes's argument. Advocates of this interpretation (and of Interpretations I–III) must therefore downplay the significance of this passage from chapter 14 (para. 18) and emphasize Hobbes's claim, in chapter 13, that the state of nature is a state of war and that nothing is just or unjust, right or wrong, in the war of all against all. Would excising passages like this from Hobbes salvage this particular interpretation? It will not. If the laws of nature (and especially the third law of nature) do not apply in the state of nature, then covenants cannot be made in the state of nature. And, to be sure, in certain passages, Hobbes seems clearly to suggest precisely this.[68] But, as Martinich argues (in the passage referenced in chapter 1), if it is impossible for individuals to make covenants in the state of nature, "then his account of the origin of government is hopelessly incoherent." For Hobbes argues that "the origin of civil government requires a covenant." Now "if every covenant requires coercive power, and if there is no coercive power in the state of nature, then no covenant can be made in the state of nature." But in that case, "no covenant creating a government could be made in the state of nature." Consequently, "if Hobbes's philosophy is to have any chance for success, he must allow that some covenants can be made in the state of nature."[69] Put another way, the intelligibility of Hobbes's social contract theory requires positing that covenants can be made in the state of nature—otherwise individuals in the state of nature could never make a covenant by which the state of nature is left. But in that case, they could never enter the civil state or establish the sovereign power. In short, Hobbesian political theory depends upon the laws of nature obtaining in the state of nature.

There's another problem. According to Hobbes, the sovereign is not party to the social contract.[70] Often he speaks of subjects laying down the right of nature by transferring it to the sovereign—which then possesses it.[71] In one passage in *Leviathan* he suggests that the sovereign does not receive the right of nature (or the right to punish) on *transfer* from subjects but rather that the sovereign, since he is not party to the social contract, never laid it down (though the subjects did).[72] Either way, the sovereign retains the right of nature vis-à-vis his subjects. But Hobbes holds that persons (whether individuals or corporate) that hold the right of nature in relation to each other are in a state of nature (indeed, in a state of war) with respect to each other.[73] Consequently, if the laws of nature do not obtain in state-of-nature conditions or apply to those in a state-of-nature relation with respect to each other, then the laws of nature cannot obligate individuals in a commonwealth to obey the sovereign. The state of nature is, after all, a state of affairs. Thus, for instance, Hobbes says the nations of the world find themselves in such a state of affairs in relation to each other. And his argument entails that individuals in a commonwealth and their sovereign exist in such a relation with respect to each other. But then moral obligation has no place in their relation.

The defender of this interpretation of Hobbes has a reply here. Such a person might note that the state of nature, as Hobbes understands it, is not a historical state of affairs. The state of nature never generally obtained the world over. Hobbes seeks to account for sovereign power just as such—and not merely for societies that emerged from a state of nature. Now, if the state of nature is not actual or historic, then neither is the covenant by which the state of nature is left and that establishes the commonwealth and authorizes sovereign power. The authorization of the sovereign is a scientific proposition (meaning an a priori proposition) rather than an empirical phenomenon.[74] But if the state of nature and the covenant by which the commonwealth and the sovereign are made are not actual, then the laws of nature need not obtain in the state of nature to help individuals escape it.

I don't think this sort of reply will work. The laws of nature must obtain in the state of nature for the thought experiment to work. But let's set this hesitation aside and suppose, for the sake of argument, that such a reply can be made. Even so, if the state of nature is hypothetical and the covenant by which sovereign power is established is hypothetical as well, then the consent that authorizes sovereign power is hypothetical rather than actual. In that case, the transfer of the right of nature from individuals to the sovereign would be hypothetical rather than actual. The idea is that a rational person would choose to authorize an absolute sovereign rather than hazard the state of nature. But hypothetical consent, though rational, obligates no one. There is no moral norm that I should obey that power I would have consented to obey but in fact have not consented to obey.[75]

Construing the laws of nature as hypothetical imperatives or as laws proper only insofar as they were commanded by the civil sovereign or assented to by individuals fails to yield sound or coherent accounts of natural law and moral obligation (and, indeed, fails to ground legal obligation). Interpretation IV endeavors to remedy that failure by treating the laws of nature as the commands of God. But, in view of Hobbes's claims about the absence of just and unjust, right and wrong, in the condition of mere nature, Interpretation IV maintains that the laws of nature hold only in the civil state. The cost of this position, however, is the grounding of sovereign power. The implication of the preceding section is that, in order to ground the

Hobbesian sovereign, the laws of nature must obtain in the state of nature. Now suppose we hold (1) that the laws of nature really are laws because they are commanded by God and (2) that these laws obtain not only in the civil state but in the state of nature as well. We might be tempted to infer (3) that the laws of nature impose obligations upon individuals in the state of nature as well as upon sovereigns and subjects. And we might take this to mean that the law of nature imposes limits not only on subjects but on sovereigns as well. Such an inference would be hasty; (3) does not automatically follow from (1) and (2).

Suppose that the laws of nature really are laws and that their obligatory force derives not from some human will but rather from divine will. Even so, such laws may simply underwrite sovereign power and so may not impose limitations upon it. Thus, according to S. A. Lloyd, Hobbes's "Law of Nature directs us to submit to the rule of an unlimited sovereign power."[76] Arguing that there is no incompatibility between obedience to divine law and the civil sovereign, Hobbes writes, "All that is NECESSARY *to salvation* is contained in two virtues: *faith in Christ* and *obedience to the laws*."[77] Later in the same chapter he writes that "when the civil sovereign is an infidel, every one of his own subjects that resisteth him sinneth against the laws of God (for such are the laws of nature) and rejecteth the counsel of the apostles, that admonisheth all Christians to obey their princes."[78] As Jean Hampton puts it, "the bulk of [chapter 43] is taken up with showing that God's premier command (embodied in the second law of nature) is to obey unconditionally our earthly sovereign—no matter what the sovereign orders us to do."[79]

Several criticisms of this position can be made. First, if the laws of nature underwrite an unlimited power of the sovereign to command, then it seems the laws of nature underwrite an arrangement in which the will of the sovereign is necessary and sufficient for political and legal obligation. In that case, the critiques of positivism referenced earlier seem to apply. Now, there is some ambiguity as to whether the laws of nature here are entirely self-effacing (as Lloyd puts it) such that the will of the sovereign is not only necessary but also sufficient for obligation. Perhaps the will of the sovereign explains our legal and political (and moral) obligations *only if* we are antecedently bound to obey the sovereign. Yet there is no noncircular account of our obligation to obey the sovereign that originates with the sovereign's will. Consequently, we must have a ground for obligation to obey the sovereign that is independent of the sovereign's will. And perhaps the laws of nature as divine commands supply this ground. In that case, the laws of nature constitute a necessary condition of the binding power of the sovereign's will. And in that case, the will of the sovereign is *necessary* but *not sufficient* for legal or political (or moral) obligation—and that even if the ability of the sovereign to command is morally unrestricted. So the arguments against positivism may not be decisive against Interpretation V as an account of natural law.

Second, Hobbes holds several mutually inconsistent propositions. The laws of nature are deeply bound up with self-preservation. Martinich is surely right when he claims that self-preservation is not the first law of nature (the first law of nature is rather the first branch of the general rule of reason that Hobbes lays down in chapter 14). Even so, Hobbes says that "a law of nature (*lex naturalis*) is a precept or general rule, found out by reason, by which a man is forbidden to do that which is destructive of his life or taketh away the means of preserving the same, and to omit that by which he thinketh it may be best preserved."[80] The laws of nature are means to self-preservation (they are this by virtue of being means to peace; for peace is a means to self-preservation). Given that the state of nature is not conducive to self-preservation, the laws of nature command seeking peace with others insofar as they will seek peace with you. Seeking peace requires laying down the right of nature by transfer to a sovereign.[81] And, so says Hobbes, sovereign power just as such is absolute and unlimited.[82] Only an absolute and unlimited sovereign is sufficiently strong to stave off the state of nature by inspiring obedience through awe and fear. But just here a problem emerges. An absolute sovereign is installed for the sake of peace. And peace is pursued for the sake of self-preservation. Thus, the absolute power of the sovereign is for the sake of self-preservation.[83] But this ultimate purpose of sovereign power necessarily implies some limitations on its power to obligate. Hobbes famously holds that individuals are not obligated to obey the sovereign when the sovereign seeks to take the subject's life or endangers the life of the subject by ordering the subject to take the life of another.[84] And Hobbes holds that our obligation to obey the sovereign ceases when the sovereign is no longer able to protect us.[85] Given the ultimate (indeed, instrumental) purpose of sovereign power, these qualifications are necessary to his theory. But, as Hampton argues, these qualifications seriously undermine the absolute power of the sovereign.[86] For, as she asks, who judges whether or not the sovereign is able to preserve the life of the subject? The only intelligible answer is that the subjects themselves make this determination. But if enough subjects judge that the sovereign is unable to protect them, then the sovereign will in effect have been deposed. And a sovereign that can be deposed by his subjects is not absolute in relation to them. Such a sovereign is rather limited in his power by the judgment of his subjects. Indeed, if laws of nature are truly for the preservation of individuals, then they cannot underwrite an absolute sovereign. They can at best underwrite a limited sovereign power. But then this interpretation of the laws of nature as underwriting an absolute sovereign is incoherent. The only way to preserve this interpretation is to deny that the laws of nature are for the preservation of individuals.

Third, suppose the laws of nature do underwrite an absolute sovereign. We must ask about the source of our obligation to follow those laws. In order for the laws of nature to bind, they must rest on an ontologically sound foundation. My claim is that Hobbes's laws of nature do not. But let me postpone summarizing that argument for a moment.

INTERPRETATION VI: THE LAWS OF NATURE OBTAIN IN THE STATE OF NATURE AND THE CIVIL STATE, WHERE THEY OBLIGE SUBJECT AND SOVEREIGN ALIKE

The remaining interpretation of the laws of nature, one defended by Taylor and Warrender and, more recently, by Martinich, involves at least three claims. First, the laws of nature are laws in the proper sense because they are the commands of God. Second, the laws of nature obtain in the state of nature and in the civil state. Third, the laws of nature obligate sovereigns and subjects alike.[87]

What support is there for this interpretation? We've already seen Hobbes's insistence that covenants entered into by fear in the condition of mere nature are binding or obligatory. This entails that the third law of nature obtains in the state of nature as something rather stronger than a mere theorem or dictate of reason. Hobbes also holds that the third law follows from the first and second.[88] So if the third law of nature holds in the state of nature, the first and second do as well. Moreover, as noted above, the Hobbesian argument entails (and Hobbes expressly affirms) that the sovereign possesses the right of nature vis-à-vis subjects. And he holds that those who possess the right of nature in relation to each other exist in a state of nature/ war relation to each other. But then Hobbes's concession that the law of nature obligates sovereigns is telling. He says, "The office of the sovereign (be it a monarch or an assembly) consisteth in the end for which he was trusted with the sovereign power, namely, the procuration of *the safety of the people*, to which he is obliged by the law of nature, and to render him an account thereof to God, the author of that law, and to none but him."[89] Speaking of monarchs, he writes, "But if there be none that can give the sovereignty after the decease of him that was first elected, then has he power, nay he is obliged by the law of nature to provide, by establishing his successor, to keep those that had trusted him with the government from relapsing into the miserable condition of civil war."[90] In the first passage Hobbes argues that sovereigns in general are obligated by the law of nature to procure the safety of the people. In the second passage Hobbes argues that monarchs are bound by the law of nature to provide for the safety of their people by staving off civil war; the monarch is bound to stave off civil war by providing for his succession (save in the case of elective monarchy). Finally, though Hobbes holds that David did not wrong Uriah the Hittite when he had him killed (because no treatment of the subject by the sovereign can be an injustice to the subject), he nevertheless holds that David wronged God—"because *David* was *God's* subject, and prohibited all iniquity by the law of nature."[91]

So Hobbes holds that the sovereign—who exists in a state-of-nature relation and who possesses the right of nature vis-à-vis his subjects and other sovereigns—is bound by the law of nature. The law of nature thus obligates individuals (here sovereigns) in state-of-nature relations. Now, as I see it, the only intelligible account of moral obligation will hold that it binds all individuals, including sovereigns, and that moral obligation or moral law would bind in the state of nature, if ever such a state of affairs obtained. But this still leaves open the question of how Hobbes grounds moral obligation. Here the answer is clear—if the laws of nature are the commands of God, the reason they bind is because God is omnipotent and His will irresistible: "The right of nature whereby God reigneth over men, and punisheth those that break his laws, is to be derived, not from his creating them (as if he required obedience, as of gratitude for his benefits), but from his *irresistible power.*" And so, "To those . . . whose power is irresistible, the dominion of all men adhereth naturally by their excellence of power; and consequently it is from that power that the kingdom over men, and the right of afflicting men at his pleasure, belongeth naturally to God Almighty, not as Creator and gracious, but as omnipotent."[92] In his earlier work, *De Cive*, he says that God's "right of sovereignty" "derives" from His irresistible *power.* To wit, Hobbes predicates God's authority—indeed, His moral authority to command the laws of nature, thereby making them binding on us— on His sheer, omnipotent, irresistible will.[93]

For Hobbes, the ground of the obligation of the natural law is the irresistible power of God. Hobbes's metaethical position is therefore a species of metaethical voluntarism.[94] Metaethical voluntarism makes will (in this case, divine will) necessary and sufficient for moral obligation.[95] But, as we've seen, it is impossible to distinguish some exercise(s) of will from others on the basis of will alone. To hold that some exercise of will is normative for other exercises just is to do so on the basis of a property transcendent of will and normative for it. Consequently, Hobbes cannot coherently make irresistible will the ground of obligation. His attempt to make God's will or the will of the sovereign obligatory for our wills therefore entails a metaphysical ground of obligation that is not mere will, which makes his position self-defeating (as it happens, I think that prescriptive will is essential to obligation just as such but *not sufficient* for it).

There is one final criticism of Interpretation VI—one that brings us full circle. According to Warrender, "If the laws of nature are binding because they are commands of God *qua* irresistible power, the ground of obligation would appear to rest in the rewards and punishments that such a power may administer, rather than in the intrinsic character of the commands themselves. If, moreover, it is merely a contingent fact that God is the sole irresistible power, obligation will have more to do with the sanctions behind his commands than the consideration that these commands are his will. From this point of view, therefore, duties may be regarded as a special class of prudent actions." That is, "The laws of nature ought to be obeyed because they are the commands of God, but in turn, the commands of God ought to be obeyed because his rewards and punishments bring it about that obedience is in the highest interest of the individual."[96] To put all this another way, as Warrender notes, rather than assuming "that a duty to obey God's will is axiomatic," Hobbes seeks to justify it.[97] And the justification he provides is prudential. Thus, Hobbes frames our obligation to obey God as a hypothetical imperative. His account of our duty to obey God is an application of instrumental rationality to divine commands—Why do as God says? Because God is omnipotent and can inflict significant punishment if you don't. And, after all, you want to preserve yourself. But, as we noted in our discussion of Interpretation I, hypothetical imperatives fail to generate obligations. As Hampton suggests, hypothetical imperatives merely describe certain causal relations relative to the satisfaction of human desires. Such "imperatives" are not, in any meaningful sense, prescriptive. Consequently, such imperatives are not in any meaningful sense normative for human behavior. Instrumental rationality yields a "moral theory" without prescription or obligation. Now, on Warrender's accounting, Interpretation VI would seem to be formally identical to Interpretation I—in which case it fails as an account of natural law for just the same reasons.

Conclusion: The Failure of Hobbesian Natural Law

The upshot of the failure of these various interpretations of Hobbesian natural law is this: if Hobbes wants not only a viable theory of natural law but also a viable account of obligation, then he must import the sort of metaphysical properties his nominalism and subjectivism reject and that he considers nonsense or he must give up prescription and moral obligation altogether. That is, the failure of Hobbesian natural law (on any interpretation, given his metaphysics) drives home a dichotomy—we can either accept something very like the classical account of natural law and moral obligation (that is, we can accept moral and metaphysical realism) *or* we can reject the notion of obligation as incoherent. What we cannot do—and what Hobbes failed to do—is to find a third way.

Does consideration of plausible interpretations of Hobbesian natural law profit us in any other way? I think that it does. For I think Hobbes is clearly right to hold that moral obligation requires prescription and that prescription requires a prescriber.[98] Put another way, the moral law ontologically depends upon the lawgiver. Prescriptive will (exercised by one with the authority to prescribe), while not sufficient, is necessary for moral obligation. So I think that Hobbes is right (and H. L. A. Hart is wrong)—natural law requires a divine lawgiver.[99] But I also think that Hobbes is wrong—the binding power of the lawgiver's commands cannot reside in irresistible will alone.

Hobbes is wrong about something else. He holds that moral obligation depends upon knowing the source or ground of the obligation. To be bound by laws of nature as the commands of God, I must know not only what they are (the content of the laws of nature) but also that God commands them.[100] Hobbes here conflates epistemology and ontology. For it is sufficient for obligation that one knows the content of the laws of nature and that one is bound by them. One need not know *why* one is bound by them. And knowledge that the laws of nature are obligatory may be epistemically basic (even if the ground of the obligation to obey them is not). But that's another story—a story about how modern and even contemporary moral theory all too frequently fail to distinguish knowing that something is the case from knowing how or why it is.

CHAPTER 5

Fractured Foundations:
The Contradiction between Locke's Metaphysics
and Moral Ontology

Introduction

LOCKE'S THEORY OF CONSENT AND the constitutional design that flows
from it rest upon a logically and ontologically prior moral theory—
namely, his theory of natural law. But all theories of moral obligation,
including natural law theories, depend upon a prior theory of reality;
depend, that is, upon an ontology or theory of being. Just as political
philosophy depends on moral philosophy, so also moral philosophy
depends on metaphysics. And it is precisely this relation that poses
the fundamental problem for the viability of Lockean political philosophy. For while his metaphysics exhibit some degree of obscurity, in
certain passages of *An Essay Concerning Human Understanding*, Locke
seems clearly to affirm metaphysical nominalism.[1] And the only sort
of ontology of obligation or metaethics that coheres with metaphysical nominalism seems to be voluntarist. In the arguments of William
of Ockham and Thomas Hobbes, one finds metaphysical nominalism
and a voluntaristic account of obligation lying down together as lion
and lamb. Moreover, particular passages in the Lockean corpus have
led prominent historians of thought to claim that Locke affirms a
voluntarist ontology of moral obligation (i.e., a voluntarist metaethical position). Yet there are passages in the Lockean corpus in which
Locke outright rejects a voluntarist account of moral obligation and
embraces a realist one instead and other passages in which he does so
by clear and necessary implication—passages in which Locke maintains that divine justice and human moral obligation are grounded in
divine wisdom and goodness and not in divine will or power alone.
As a result, Locke's political theory rests upon a contradictory and
unintelligible moral and metaphysical foundation.[2] In what follows I

159

will lay out the metaphysical fissure in Locke's thought. The implication is this—either Lockean political and constitutional theory must be erected upon a better foundation, or it must be tossed. Given the incoherence of voluntarism, I suggest that realism is the only alternative to ground a coherent Lockean theory.

The Dependence of Locke's Political Philosophy on His Moral Philosophy

Following John Rawls, many today think that political philosophy should be done without metaphysics.[3] Doing political philosophy without metaphysics means doing political philosophy in a way that is neutral with respect to metaphysical commitments—and especially with respect to particular conceptions of the good and particular comprehensive doctrines of what reality is like. Comprehensive views about reality and the good, says Rawls, should be kept out of discussions of constitutional essentials and basic matters of justice.[4]

As we saw in chapter 3, the Rawlsian position is subject to deep and powerful criticisms. For instance, some (such as Rawls's protégé, the late Jean Hampton) argue that political philosophy ought not abandon metaphysics.[5] Borrowing the language of Williams James concerning forced options, I argued that it takes a certain metaphysics, a certain account of the nature of reality or comprehensive view, to maintain that metaphysics (or comprehensive views) should be debarred from the practice of political philosophy and from public discussion about what policies are just. If Hampton and I are right, then the Rawlsian position is self-referentially incoherent. Others (such as T. K. Seung) argue that the Rawlsian position is viciously circular.[6] I find the arguments of Hampton and Seung compelling. But self-referential incoherency and vicious circularity are not the only difficulties with the Rawlsian approach. Any theory concerning the grounds of rightful or legitimate authority must take into account the necessary conditions of that authority. To frame the matter in older terms, any theory of what law is and who can make it must give an account of the essential conditions of law. And there is good reason to believe that any viable conception of law and authority must stipulate as a necessary condition of human or positive law its groundedness in natural law. Or, as I put the matter earlier, any intelligible theory of legal obligation depends on an ontologically prior moral obligation as a necessary condition of political or legal obligation.[7] This point was also argued by John Locke.

Locke maintained that positive human enactments derive what normative force they have from the ontologically prior law of nature:

> If the law of nature is not binding on men, neither can any human positive law bind them, since the laws of the civil magistrate derive all their force from the binding power of this law. This is surely true so far as concerns the greatest part of mankind, to whom the certain knowledge of divine revelation has not penetrated. They have no other law but natural [law], which is divine, and binding by virtue of itself; consequently, if you would abolish the law of nature, you overturn at one blow all government among men, [all] authority, rank, and society. Nor must we obey a king out of fear, because he is more powerful and can compel us. For this would be to establish the power of tyrants, thieves, and pirates; but [we must] out of conscience, because he obtains his rule over us by right, that is, at the command of the law of nature, that we obey a king, princes, and a legislator, or whatever name you would give a superior. *Thus, the obligation of civil law depends upon the law of nature,* nor are we compelled so much to show obedience to a magistrate by virtue of his power as we are bound by the law [*jus*] of nature.[8]

In these lines, Locke echoes Augustine of Hippo and Cicero.[9] The broad contours of the argument are easy to follow: (1) The commands of a purported authority or superior—or speech in the injunctive mode by one who can force us to comply—are, by themselves, merely the exercises of physical capacity. To borrow a distinction from Latin terminology, they are instances of *potentia* and not *potestas*. (2) Superiority in terms of strength or the issuance of a command plus the ability to compel does not, by itself, contain any moral property. (3) Obligation is a moral property. Consequently, (4) if we are obligated to perform some action, the command requiring the action of us must be more than merely a command issued by someone stronger than us. (5) Speech in the injunctive mode directed to us by a putative but not actual superior can be distinguished from the binding command of a rightful superior *only if* the latter comports with or is ontologically grounded in the law of nature. Put more simply, the command of a "superior" party, absent natural law, is nothing other than a command (or speech in the injunctive mode), nothing other than an exercise of *potentia*. Absent natural law, such commands lack even the possibility of possessing *potestas* or of being exercises of rightful authority. But mere exercises of physical capacity have no moral property and hence cannot obligate. So, (6) absent natural law, it follows that civil or human law loses its power to bind. It becomes just one exercise of will among many. Without the natural law (or something much like it), the bottom falls out of the notion of obligation.

But doesn't Locke's theory of consent obviate the need for his political theory to rely upon a conception of natural law for its moral and metaphysical ground? It does not, and does not for reasons that Locke clearly saw when he composed his early lectures on natural law. Reflecting upon whether or not the law of nature can be grounded in self-interest and arguing that it cannot, Locke says this: "What reason [would there be] for keeping promises, what force for the preservation of society, what life and association among men, when all justice and equity is [only] what is useful?"[10] That is, if it is right for each person to do whatever she calculates as most beneficial to her, then the reason for keeping promises or working to preserve society has been removed. Absent the requirements of an objective natural law obligating us to keep our promises and to work to preserve humankind, Locke believes something like the tragedy of the commons will obtain.[11] In an earlier passage he writes, "Without the law of nature the other foundation of human society collapses as well—that is, the keeping of contracts and agreements, for there would be no reason to expect a man to abide by an agreement, because he made a promise, when a more advantageous arrangement offered itself elsewhere, unless the obligation to fulfill promises came from nature and not from the will of men."[12] To put all this another way, Locke sees the theory of consent as an application of the norm of promise keeping. And unless there is a prior precept of natural law such that we *ought* or are *obligated* to keep our promises, then the whole theory falls apart.

Now I think Locke's arguments on these matters—the ontological dependence of positive human law on natural law and the dependence of promise keeping and therefore of consent or compact accounts of sovereignty and of governmental legitimacy on natural law—both valid and sound. But all that matters for my purposes in this chapter is that Locke subscribes to these ideas. Here he advances them with what strike me as cogent arguments. And nowhere in the Lockean corpus does one find an express repudiation of either of these points or of the arguments proffered on their behalf.[13] For Locke, society, governmental authority, and the binding force of human enactments all depend upon natural law. But then it of course matters a great deal whether his theory of natural law is viable or whether it is fatally flawed. While I find the above arguments cogent, I think his theory of natural law suffers from self-contradiction.

Locke's Metaphysical Nominalism

Part of the argument I advance herein depends on the premise that Locke was a *metaphysical nominalist*. While many scholars affirm that Locke indeed was a metaphysical nominalist, it is a matter about which there is some dispute. According to Frederick Copleston, one of the twentieth century's foremost historians of philosophy, there are "several different strands or tendencies of thought" in what Locke "has to say about universal ideas." Indeed, "Sometimes he speaks in a nominalist fashion, but at other times he implies what the Scholastics call 'moderate realism'. And the result of all this is that under the *prima facie* simplicity of Locke's writing there is a certain amount of ambiguity and confusion." Moreover, "It is not that Locke was incapable of cleaning up these obscurities of thought: he himself has provided what is doubtless the true explanation, namely, that he was either too lazy or too busy to do so."[14] I think any careful reading of the *Essay* bears out Copleston's claim that the work embodies some ambiguity and confusion on this most pressing topic for an essay in epistemology.

Locke's ambiguity concerning the status of ideas notwithstanding, I concur entirely with Nicholas Wolterstorff: "Though in the course of his discussion Locke often speaks as if he were a realist concerning the existence of universals, his official position is clearly nominalism."[15] As evidence for Locke's nominalism, Wolterstorff adduces the following passages from the *Essay*: "All things, that exist, [are] particulars." And,

> Words are general . . . when used, for signs of general ideas; and so are applicable indifferently to many particular things; and ideas are general, when they are set up, as the representatives of many particular things: but universality belongs not to things themselves, which are all of them particular in their existence, even those words, and ideas, which in their signification, are general. When therefore we quit particulars, the generals that rest, are only creatures of our own making, their general nature being nothing but the capacity they are put into by the understanding, of signifying or representing many particulars.[16]

Just prior to the second passage quoted by Wolterstorff, Locke says this: "*General and Universal,* belong not to the real existence of Things; but *are the Inventions and Creatures of the Understanding,* made by it for its own use, *and concern only Signs,* whether Words, or *Ideas.*"[17] In these passages Locke seems to give about as clear an affirmation as possible of the sort of nominalism introduced by Ockham (or of the later medieval nominalists that followed in his wake). Indeed, these passages seem to admit of no other interpretation.[18]

Scholars like Samuel Zinaich Jr. prefer to describe Locke as an "anti-essentialist"—that is, as one who denies the existence of real, universal essences, as one who denies what Aristotle affirmed.[19] And Locke clearly rejects Aristotelian forms: "Those therefore who have been taught, that the several *Species* of Substances had their distinct internal *substantial Forms*; and that it was those *Forms*, which made the distinction of Substances into their true *Species* and *Genera*, were led yet farther out of the way by having their minds set upon fruitless Enquiries after *substantial Forms*, wholly unintelligible, and whereof we have scarce so much as any obscure, or confused Conception in general." Rather, "our *ranking*, and distinguishing natural *Substances into Species consists in the Nominal Essences* the Mind makes, and not in the real Essences to be found in the Things themselves."[20] In the next section of the same chapter, Locke proceeds to deconstruct the notion of species:

> In all the visible corporeal World, we see no Chasms, or Gaps. All quite down from us, the descent is by easy steps, and a continued series of Things, that in each remove differ very little from the other. There are Fishes that have Wings, and are not Strangers to the airy Region: and there are some Birds, that are Inhabitants of the Water. . . . There are Animals so near of kin both to Birds and Beasts, that they are in the middle between both: Amphibious Animals link the Terrestial and the Aquatique together; Seals live at Land and at Sea, and Porpoises have the warm Blood and Entrails of a Hog. . . . There are some Brutes, that seem to have as much Knowledge and Reason, as some that are called Men: and the Animal and Vegetable Kingdoms, are so nearly join'd, that if you will take the lowest of one, and highest of the other, there will scarce be perceived any great difference between them; and so on till we come to the lowest and most inorganical parts of Matter, we shall find everywhere, that the several *Species* are linked together, and differ but in almost insensible degrees.[21]

According to Locke, the *real essences* of things are unknowable, and the idea of substantial form is entirely unintelligible. He categorically rejects the strong realism of Plato and the moderate realism of Aristotle and Aquinas when it comes to what we can know and how we should reason about the world. But the passage quoted immediately above seems not only epistemic but ontological as well. Locke's rejection of substantial form entails not only the deconstruction of particular species but deconstruction of the concept of species itself—so much so, that there appears to be no *qualitative* difference between inorganic matter, vegetative life, and human beings. And Locke proceeds to unravel the particular "*Species* of *Man*": "Wherein then, would I gladly know, consists the precise and *unmovable Boundaries of* that *Species*? 'Tis plain, if we examine, there is *no* such thing *made by Nature*, and established by Her amongst Men. The real Essence of that, or any other sort of Substances, 'tis evident we know not; and therefore are . . . undetermined in our nominal Essences, which we make our selves."[22] The implications are not trivial. According to Jeremy Waldron, Locke's anti-essentialism "leaves him with no naturalistic basis whatsoever for distinguishing those creatures one is allowed to hunt, exploit, enslave, or eat from those that must not be treated in any of these ways." Indeed, "the point about Locke's anti-essentialism is that it leaves the field wide open for anyone to draw the boundaries of humanity wherever he likes."[23]

Given that Locke sometimes speaks "as if" he were a "realist" or a "moderate realist" in certain passages but refrains anywhere from expressly affirming metaphysical realism, whereas in the passages above he expressly affirms metaphysical nominalism and anti-essentialism, I believe I am on firm ground in treating Locke as a metaphysical nominalist (and, correlatively, as an anti-essentialist). But for those who nevertheless remain hesitant to call Locke a nominalist, I will use *metaphysical nominalism* to mean only what Locke says in the passages referenced above: universals do not belong to the real existence of things, and so universal essences do not really exist or, as Aristotle would have it, really inhere in things; universals are signs created or invented by us to represent many particulars; only particulars have "real existence." My argument is that there is a deadly fissure in Locke's argument, given his own account of universals and particulars. But I think my conclusion also follows from Locke's anti--essentialism taken by itself (whether framed mainly as epistemic or in ontological terms as well).

Nominalism and Natural Law

I have sided with Nicholas Wolterstorff in affirming that Locke is a metaphysical nominalist. There are those who demur from this interpretation. After all, say some, there are passages in the Lockean corpus that suggest that Locke is a moral realist. Now, whether or not Locke is correctly described as a metaphysical realist, there is something right about this position. For, as I argued in chapter 3, moral and metaphysical realism seem to go together such that moral realism assumes, as a necessary condition, metaphysical realism. That is, you can't really be a moral realist unless you are also a metaphysical realist. And this leads to a simple conditional: if moral realism, then metaphysical realism. Because metaphysical realism and nominalism are contradictories (and exhaustive of the options at that; for either general ideas are real or they are not), it follows, by application of the disjunctive syllogism, that affirming one requires denying the other. So the argument would work much like this: (1) if moral realism, then metaphysical realism; (2) Locke is a moral realist (by stipulation and arguendo here); (3) given (1) and (2), and by application of modus ponens, Locke must also be a metaphysical realist.[24] Therefore, (4), given (2) and given that realism and nominalism are contradictories that are exhaustive and mutually exclusive, by application of the disjunctive syllogism, Locke must *not* be a nominalist. So if one affirms that Locke is a moral realist, then one has good reason for denying (at least by implication) that he is a nominalist.

Conversely, if Locke is a nominalist and he (sincerely) affirms a doctrine of natural law, then one has good reason to believe that the account of natural law in question is a voluntaristic one.[25] More generally, if Locke holds that there is a such a thing as obligation and he is also committed to metaphysical nominalism, then his account of obligation must be voluntarist. And this is more or less the conclusion that Francis Oakley reaches. Locke is an Ockhamist through and through, as Oakley sees it.[26] For this conclusion Oakley adduces a sophisticated argument as well as considerable textual evidence. I will come to that later. For the moment, I'm interested only in the reason one might hold the proposition just described: if one holds some account of obligation (obligation in general but also of moral obligation in particular), o, and one posits metaphysical nominalism, n, then one must subscribe to a voluntaristic account, v, of obligation in general and of moral obligation in particular. This can therefore be framed as a conditional symbolized as follows:

(1) If both obligation and nominalism ($o \cdot n$), then metaethical voluntarism (formally: $(o \cdot n) \supset v$). Granted this conditional, then the logical rules of modus ponens and modus tollens apply. Thus,

(2) If not voluntarism ($\sim v$), then not both obligation and nominalism ($\sim(o \cdot n)$).

(3) According to DeMorgan's rule, not both obligation and nominalism ($\sim(o \cdot n)$) is equivalent to either not obligation or not metaphysical nominalism (either not o or not n; $\sim o$ or $\sim n$). Now,

(4) Locke clearly has a theory of obligation (a natural law theory of moral obligation and a consent-based account of political obligation); therefore he affirms obligation. Given double negation, obligation is equivalent to *not* not obligation (i.e., o is equivalent to $\sim\sim o$). And

(5) Given the disjunctive syllogism, the foregoing necessarily entails *not* nominalism ($\sim n$); that is, the rejection of metaphysical nominalism.

Thus, if Locke rejects voluntarism and affirms a theory of moral obligation, then he cannot, as a matter of logical entailment, be a nominalist. But I've suggested that the evidence cuts in favor of Locke being a metaphysical nominalist and that Locke posits a theory of moral obligation (i.e., he is not a moral anarchist, which explains, perhaps, the dramatic difference in his construction of the state of nature from that of Thomas Hobbes).[27]

Do we have good reason to posit the conditional framed above such that we can apply the rules of inference to it? Well, consider. Nominalists like Ockham or Locke reject forms or ideas as having any objective reality.[28] There are no general or abstract realities. Rather, only particulars exist. Apparent similarities are given the same name, which is to say that the generalities exist only in the mind and do not correspond to some larger reality. Nominalism is therefore a theory offered as an alternative to realism—the notion that there are such things as universals or forms or ideas, such things as abstract properties (or intangible, incorporeal properties) that are nevertheless quite real (like triangularity, humanity, or goodness). According to Plato, forms or ideas do not exist in the material world or in the human mind. Rather, forms transcend the particulars that instantiate them to some faltering degree. For Aristotle, however, forms do not transcend particulars.[29] Forms are still quite real. But the immaterial form always inheres in a particular object. There is for Aristotle no Platonic heaven of perfect forms detached from particulars. While Plato and Aristotle disagree about the *locus* of forms, they nevertheless very much agree about their *status*—namely, they exist. And any sound presentation of reality must give an account of them.[30]

Now suppose, with Ockham and Locke, that one both rejects the existence of universal forms, on the one hand, and yet maintains that there is such a thing as moral obligation (or *lex naturale* or *ius naturale*), on the other. The ground for right or obligation cannot be that the action required by natural law (or that is morally mandatory) is required just because (or in part because) the act in question is good. The ground for an obligation such that we are required *not* to act in a certain way (say murder or theft are proscribed) cannot be because such actions are intrinsically evil in the sense that they are opposed to goodness.[31] And that's because, for the nominalist (or the anti-essentialist), there is no such property or real universal as goodness. Likewise, it is incompatible for the nominalist to predicate a metaphysically real property of obligatoriness. If we are obligated to act in some way, x, or to refrain from acting in some way, y, then it can only be because there are commands of a certain sort that are called obligatory or that are called prescriptions of natural law. And those sorts of commands will be backed up by a will that we *call* authoritative—perhaps because it is sufficiently strong—omnipotent, as Ockham might say, or irresistible, to borrow Hobbes's turn of phrase. For Ockham certainly maintains that there is a natural law, known by reason, and that contains primary precepts such that they are binding on all persons, at all times, and in all places.[32] Given his nominalism, the only source to which he has recourse for the normative force of such a law is the omnipotent will of God. For Hobbes it may be the case that a mortal Leviathan does the trick.[33] But either way, force is the ground of obligation just because there is no such real idea or property such as obligatoriness. Nor, for nominalists, is there any higher (or highest) order form, such as Plato's good, to ground obligation. Given the foregoing, the options available to nominalists are only two—either they must reject the idea of obligation altogether and opt for moral anarchy or they must subscribe to a voluntaristic (i.e, a will-based) account of moral obligation. More precisely, if realism (the proposition that universal essences really exist) is false, then one must subscribe either to moral anarchism (the denial that moral norms and obligations exist) or to a voluntaristic ground of obligation. There are no other options. Letting r stand for realism, a stand for moral anarchism, v stand for voluntarism, the foregoing train of reasoning can be rendered formally as follows: $\sim r \supset (a$ or $v)$ (if not moral realism, then either moral anarchism or voluntarism). Given their anti-essentialism, nominalists reject realism (i.e., $\sim r$). They therefore affirm the antecedent of the conditional. Pursuant to modus ponens, they must affirm the consequent, which, in this case, is the disjunct just stipulated: either moral anarchism or voluntarism (a or v). But given that they affirm the idea of moral obligation, o, and given that o is equivalent to the rejection of moral anarchism, $\sim a$, nominalists who do not reject the idea of moral obligation must, by virtue of the disjunctive syllogism, embrace voluntarism, v. Given the foregoing and given that nominalism, n, entails the rejection of moral realism, or $\sim r$, there is good reason to subscribe to the conclusion with which this train of reasoning began: if both obligation and nominalism, then voluntarism (formally: $(o \cdot n) \supset v$).

To reiterate a point previously made—Locke is a metaphysical nominalist. He also, by nearly all accounts, has a theory of moral obligation (even if some dispute just what that theory is).[34] Locke refers to this account of moral obligation as the law of nature. Given that he is a nominalist and that his law of nature is an account of moral obligation, it follows, by logical implication, that Locke's law of nature must be voluntaristic. That is, the ground for the binding force (the *potestas*) of his law of nature, to remain consistent with his ontology, cannot be goodness as such. He cannot maintain, that is, that the precepts of natural law are binding because, at least as a matter of necessity, they all participate in or instantiate the good or goodness. He must, as a corollary, maintain that all requirements of the law of nature are binding just because they are required by an authoritative will. The will of an all-powerful superior is the only ground of the binding force of natural law allowed by his metaphysics.

Locke and the Ontological Foundations of the Law of Nature

When it comes to the ontological ground for the binding force of the law of nature, Locke says this: "the *foundation of obligation* [in both the natural law and the divine positive law] is the same, that is, *the will of the supreme divine power* [*numen*]."[35] Prior to this claim, in the course of answering Question 8 ("Is the Law of Nature binding on men?"),

Locke maintains, "*we are bound by God*, who is best and greatest, *because he wills*; in effect, *the declaration of his will determines the principle of* [our] *obligation* and our obedience, because we are only bound to what a legislator has in some manner made known and published as his will." "Beyond this," says Locke, "some things are binding of themselves, and by their own force; others by something else, and by virtue of something else." And "*the will of god is binding of itself and by its own force*, and only in this manner, whether it is knowable by the light of nature . . . or whether [it is] revealed by men 'inspired of god' or some other means, and is thus a positive divine law."[36] Subsequent to these comments, Locke seeks to show "that the law of nature is binding on all men, before any other law, both of itself, and by its own force."[37] Locke maintains that it is binding on all human beings just "because this law meets all the requirements [necessary] for the obligation of any law; for God, the author of this law, willed it to be the rule of our conduct and life, and he published it sufficiently that anyone could know it." Consequently, "since nothing more is required for bringing obedience about than the authority and just power of the ruler and [the fact] of his will having been made clear, no one can doubt that the law of nature is binding upon men."[38] And what is the ground of God's authority and just power over us? Well, it seems to be his superiority. Superiority as to what? The answer seems to be his superiority in power: "Since god is superior to all things, [and] he holds as much right and authority over us as we cannot hold over ourselves, since we owe to him and him alone our body, soul, life, whatever we are, whatever we possess, and also whatever we can be, it is right that we live [obedient] to the prescription of his will. God has created us out of nothing and, if it is his pleasure, he will return us to nothing again. We are, therefore, subject to him by supreme right and absolute necessity."[39] And, to drive the already driven nail, he adds, "This law is the will of this all-powerful legislator which becomes known to us by the light and principles of nature."[40] It is in the next paragraph that Locke writes the words with which this section began.[41]

So Locke is a nominalist with a theory of moral obligation, a theory he puts under the heading of the law of nature. I have argued that he must, as a matter of entailment, be a voluntarist. This is because there is no other possible ground of obligation available to a metaphysical nominalist. This is the route Ockham seems to have followed. And it is the way Locke seems to go as well.[42] Given the preceding chapters, it is not unproblematic if Locke subscribes to a voluntaristic account of moral obligation. Moral (or metaethical) voluntarism is self-referentially incoherent. Voluntarism is not a viable metaphysics of morals. Be that as it may, the passages above seem clearly to indicate that Locke is a voluntarist.[43] What greater affirmation is there for which a voluntarist could hope? Yet there are those who argue that Locke is not a voluntarist or that these passages notwithstanding, Locke's position is equivocal. It bears considering some of the passages these folks have in mind.[44]

The reader may perhaps recall, from having studied Aristotle and Aquinas (whose account of natural law summarized here will be elaborated in greater detail in chapter 6), that a dominant form of moral realism not only advances an objective notion of the good but also posits that the good (with respect to finite things) is teleological in nature.[45] That is, x can be stipulated to be good just in the case that x is good for some thing y. And x will be good for some thing y just in the case that x is perfective of y, that is, just in the instance that y is the goal at which x's nature is aimed. On this view, the proper function of y is to achieve or attain x (or the realization of x, where x may perhaps be some condition or state of affairs—say the state of *eudaimonia*). It is worth noting that no less a moral realist than Thomas Aquinas thought of natural law in just this way. When he speaks of the natural inclinations of human persons (first as substances, then as animate substances, and finally as rational, animate substances) he is speaking of the inclination (*inclinatio*) of the human essence. That is, human nature is, to borrow a turn of phrase from Anthony Lisska, a dispositional essence—an essence aimed at the achievement of some goal. And that goal at which human nature is aimed (or those goals at which it is aimed, given that human nature is complex) is the good for human persons as such.[46] The first precept of natural law, says Aquinas, is that good is to be done (or pursued or preserved) and evil, its contrary, avoided.[47] So natural law requires the pursuit of the good or goods perfective of the human being as such. But those goods are, essentially, teleological in nature. Thus, Aquinas's account of human nature is a teleological account in which the first precept of natural law, fully unpacked, mandates that human persons fulfill their proper function (or functions) and refrain from acting contrary to it.[48]

How is Saint Thomas relevant here? Well, the theory of natural law elaborated in Locke's *Questions Concerning the Law of Nature* presents itself as a teleological—that is, a proper function—account of natural law.[49] And there is at least one passage in the Second Treatise that also points strongly in this direction. Thus, in his *Questions*, Locke writes that we can infer (at least partly) "the principle of our duty and its certain rule from the constitution of man himself and the equipment of the human faculties, since man is not made by accident, nor has he been given these faculties, which both can and ought to be exercised, to do nothing." Moreover, "It seems that the function of man is what he is naturally equipped to do; that is, since he discovers in himself sense and reason, and perceives himself inclined and ready to perform the works of god, as he ought, and to contemplate his power and wisdom in these works, and then to offer and render him the laud, honor, and glory most worthy of so great and so beneficent a creator." Having ascertained the proper function (i.e., the rightful use of his capacities) in relation to the worship of the deity, Locke turns to society: "Then, [he perceives that he is] impelled to form and preserve a union of his life with other men, not only by the needs and necessities of life, but [he perceives also that] he is driven by a certain natural propensity to enter society and is fitted to preserve it by the gift of speech and the commerce of language." And finally, reflecting upon natural tendencies or propensities, the rational person finds that "he is obliged to preserve himself, since he is impelled to this part of his duty, and more than impelled, by an inner instinct [*instinctu*], and no man has been found who is careless of himself, or capable of disowning himself."[50]

Now, I am not suggesting that Locke follows Saint Thomas in every respect. He clearly does not. Aquinas, for instance, quite clearly maintains that the most fundamental precepts of the natural law are both right for all and known to all.[51] For Locke, while some commands and prohibitions of the law of nature are absolute, binding on all persons, at all times and places, he is rather less certain that there are moral truths known to all.[52] However, he is quick to point out

that the merely empirical fact of disagreement over moral requirements does not entail that the natural law does not exist.[53] Whether
or not the evidence bears out the Thomistic or the Lockean claim, the
argument against the law of nature (or natural law) from the fact that
people sometimes disagree in their moral convictions has always been
a glaring non sequitur.[54] Consequently, Locke's skepticism concerning moral principles known to all cannot be translated into (or read as)
skepticism concerning moral principles right for all—cannot, at least,
without conflating epistemology and ontology. The disagreements
between Thomas and Locke notwithstanding, Locke does infer the
duties of human nature in a way quite similar to Aquinas—he reasons
from the notion of proper function and the natural capacities of the
human person. In furtherance of the point just made, Locke says,
"by [the phrase] 'bond of law' one must understand the bond of the
law of nature by which everyone is constrained to discharge a debt
of nature, that is to perform that duty which it is incumbent on each
individual as something which must be performed by reason of one's
own nature."[55]

In addition to arguing from the proper function of human nature
to moral obligation (treating human nature as, at a minimum, the
proximate cause of moral obligation), Locke maintains that the binding power of the law of nature is perpetual and universal. Indeed,
he says its decrees are eternal. And this affirmation of the eternality
of the natural law suggests that its requirements are in some sense
necessary. That is to say, when Locke speaks of the requirements
of the law of nature as perpetual and eternal as well as universal,
he describes the law of nature in what seem to be strongly realist
terms. When Locke says "that the obligation of the Law of nature is
perpetual and universal," he means "that there is no time in which a
man would be permitted to violate the precepts of this law; here there
exists no interregnum, no holidays or Mardi Gras, nor any periods
of liberty or license under this rule." Rather, "The bonds of this law
are eternal and coeval with the human race; they are born with it and
they die with it."[56] Among those precepts, which can never be violated, Locke mentions prohibitions against murder and theft—there
is no time and place at which these are morally permissible. The law
of nature always prohibits such acts. There are other things the law

of nature always requires. Locke lists here "reverence and fear of the divinity, a sense of duty toward one's parents, the love of one's neighbor, and other feelings of this kind. To these we are bound forever."[57] To be sure, there are yet other duties of the law of nature that only apply to relevant circumstances or conditions. But worth noting here is Locke's subscription to the realist claim that the duties of the law of nature flow from human nature and that, given the fixity of human nature, certain of those duties always obtain.

When Locke refers to the obligation of the law of nature as "universal," he means that "the law of nature holds its force undiminished and unshaken throughout all the ages and over the entire globe."[58] He doesn't mean, however, that all persons fall under *all* the same obligations (though all fall under some). Rather, he means that, in addition to the absolute requirements of the natural law, binding on all persons, at all times and places, there are certain requirements that apply to any person who finds himself in particular circumstances, even though not everyone will find himself in those circumstances. Thus, the duties of being a father are binding upon all those who find themselves in the circumstance of being a father. Clearly not all persons find themselves in those circumstances. But given this qualification, Locke believes the claim made in the quote with which this paragraph began to be sound. Thus, the law of nature is "a fixed and eternal rule of conduct, dictated by reason itself, and for this reason something fixed and inherent in human nature. And it would be necessary for human nature to change before this law could either change or be abrogated."[59] Moreover, "this natural law [*jus*] will never be abrogated, since men cannot alter this law [*legem*]. They are subject to it and it is not for subjects to refashion laws at their own pleasure. Nor surely would god will this, since out of his infinite and eternal wisdom he created man such that these duties *necessarily* follow from his very nature." Consequently, "the law of nature stands and falls together with human nature as it now exists." To be sure, "God could have created men such that they had no eyes and no need of them; but provided they make use of the eyes they have and are willing to open them and, provided the sun shines, they must of necessity come to know the alternation of day and night, perceive the differences among colors, and see with [these] eyes the difference between the straight and curved." The law of nature "depends not on a will which is fluid and changeable, but *on the eternal order of things.*"[60]

To the foregoing evidence from the *Questions,* I would adduce the following passage from the Second Treatise: "Truth and keeping faith belong to men as men and not as members of society."[61] For the affirmation that there is such a thing as "men as men"—such a thing as human nature—to which certain goods are proper surely fits better within the realist school of thought than within nominalism. Within their respective philosophical systems, Plato and Aristotle affirmed with ease that there was such a thing as human nature. But the metaphysical nominalist's affirmation, that there are only particulars and no kinds (save those generalizations that occur without or minds), denies, as a matter or entailment, the very notion of human nature. It is true that nominalists such as Ockham and Hobbes and Locke sometimes speak *as if* there is such a thing as human nature. But the "as if" qualifier is here all important. Their philosophy prevents them from simply affirming that there is such a thing. The sorts of abstractions or generalities necessarily bound up with talk of "nature" or "essence" is, for the nominalist, only apparent. Moreover, in the *Essay Concerning Human Understanding,* Locke is an explicit anti-- essentialist who denies that a universal human essence, a real human nature, exists.

This brings us to a profound difficulty in Lockean moral philosophy. Locke seems rather clearly to affirm voluntarism. But he seems clearly to affirm moral realism as well. And voluntarism and moral realism are contradictories such that voluntarism implies the negation of moral realism and moral realism the negation of voluntarism. So by affirming voluntarism, Locke implicitly rejects moral realism. And by embracing moral realism, he implicitly rejects voluntarism. Locke's ethical theory seems to founder on the shoals of self-- contradiction. Is there anything that can be done about this? Francis Oakley provides us with the most sophisticated attempt to date of a coherent and comprehensive account of Locke's moral philosophy.[62] Oakley's brilliance notwithstanding, I argue that that the attempt to render Locke coherent or cogent ultimately fails, thereby leaving the jeopardy to his political theory intact.

The Attempt to Reconcile the Moral-Realist and Voluntarist Strands in Locke's Moral Philosophy

Over a series of published works, Francis Oakley argues that the *apparent* tensions in Locke's thought—between the passages that seem voluntarist and those that seem realist—are not really tensions at all and that we will understand this if we only think carefully through medieval nominalism.[63] Oakley argues that Locke followed the path pioneered by William of Ockham and medieval nominalism. Because I lay out Ockham's position in detail in chapter 6, I move more quickly here, focusing only on whether Oakley's account of Ockham provides, as he thinks it does, the key for resolving the apparent tensions in Locke.

Medieval nominalism did not reject the idea of natural law. Rather, medieval nominalism placed natural law upon a metaphysical foundation distinct from that of the *via antiqua* (the ancient way), the name given to the realist school of thought (including the moderate realism of the so-called schoolmen). In contrast to the *via antiqua*, adherents to the nominalist school of thought, which came to be called the *via moderna* (the modern way), rejected the notion of substantial forms or of universal essences or ideas in either the Platonic or the Aristotelian sense. Only particulars really exist. When it came to ethics, the adherents to the Ockhamist school of thought replaced the Good (or Goodness) as the ground of moral obligation (Goodness having been considered convertible with the divine nature, or more aptly, with divine Being, by adherents to the *via antiqua*) with divine will. Returning to an old Socratic dilemma (which from the time of Augustine of Hippo had been considered to pose a false dichotomy by classical theorists within the Christian tradition), Ockham and his progeny maintained that it was *not* the case that God commanded or willed something because what He commanded was in fact good. *Rather*, God commanding something made it good. His prohibiting some act made that act evil. From this perspective there were no actions such that they were intrinsically good or such that there intrinsically evil, no actions right of their own accord or wrong per se.[64] Good and evil were functions of the divine will, which was authoritative just because of divine omnipotence. Consistent with this view, Ockham quite readily affirmed that God could have commanded that we hate Him, thereby making hatred of the deity morally obligatory for His human creations.[65] Fortuitously, God actually commanded that His creatures love and worship Him and commanded other things conducive to human felicity. Even so, the obligatoriness of divine commands and their correspondence to human happiness was an unrelated, even if fortunate, coincidence. God could have commanded otherwise had He so chosen. Fortunately, He did not so choose.

This view of ethics is frequently described as a divine command theory. As such, it has usually been taken to be opposed to natural law theories of ethics. Indeed, many think such a view of ethics requires the promulgation of that which is morally obligatory through supernatural revelation. Ockham, however, did not take such a view. To be sure, he believed that whatever the deity promulgated through sacred revelation was in fact morally obligatory for his creatures. But Ockham maintained that this was not the only way in which the deity revealed his will. Ockham held that there are basic moral requirements both right for all, at all times and places, and known to all through human reason (or at least known to all who exercised their faculty of reason). And Ockham described the basic requirements of natural law as the requirements of a right reason that "in no case fails." Thus, for Ockham, there were certain moral requirements that could be understood as necessary or eternal. And these commands were the commands of reason.[66]

To put all of this more simply, when Ockham speaks of the natural law and its requirements, there seems to be very little distance between his theory and that advanced by Aquinas. But when Ockham speaks of the good and of goodness there is revealed, between his theory and Aquinas's, an unbridgeable divide. Both Aquinas and Ockham believe that the requirements of natural law are the edicts of natural law, which in no case fails. But Ockham believes that divine *will* is the *sole* cause of (is necessary and sufficient for) something being good or just. Just here we are inclined to ask how this is possible. If Ockham affirms both a voluntaristic, divine command account of the ontology of moral obligation *and* a right reason, natural law account of the moral order that in fact obtains, one that includes eternal and immutable laws, doesn't this make his position schizophrenic?

Doesn't this mean that there are two Ockhams rather than one or that somewhere along the way he changed his mind? According to Oakley, it does not. Oakley asks us to consider Ockham's theory of natural law (and Locke's) in light of the medieval distinction between the *potentia dei absoluta* and the *potentia dei ordinata*—that is, the distinction between the absolute and the ordained powers of God.[67] Let's consider, by way of illustration, the *potentia dei absoluta* in relation to the creation of the cosmos. The absolute power of the deity has to do with the options available to him before he creates a particular world. There are, at least arguably, infinitely many possible worlds God could create. And all of those possible worlds fall within the purview of his absolute power. That is, He could have created any of them. In contrast, the *potentia dei ordinata* refers to the world (or cosmos) He in fact chooses to create. That is, the ordained power of God refers to the order of things that He in fact wills to obtain.

Now, from the standpoint of Ockham, the only constraints upon the divine will when actualizing a possible world are divine existence (since he holds that God necessarily exists) and the law of noncontradiction.[68] That is, God cannot (of necessity) actualize or create a world in which He fails to exist or in which the law of noncontradiction fails to hold. But beyond these stipulations, the divinity is neither metaphysically nor morally constrained with respect to the world He chooses to create. So when Ockham maintains that God could have commanded that we hate Him, thereby making it morally obligatory for us so to do, he is referring to the *potentia dei absoluta*. He is speaking about a possible world God could have created, had he so chosen. By way of contrast, when Ockham speaks of the commands of natural law (which are just the same as those delineated by Aquinas) and when he says those commands are right for all persons at all times and places and are known by means of right reason, which in no case fails—thereby suggesting that these commands are in some sense necessary or even eternal—he is speaking in terms of the *potentia dei ordinata*, in terms of an initially possible world that God has in fact actualized. God could have created differently and could have chosen to relate to that creation differently. But, in setting the world up in a particular way, God has both established a certain order of things (which accounts also for natural regularities, from the

Ockhamist point of view) and has chosen to interact with that created order in a certain way. Within the confines of the possible world that God in fact actualized, there are some acts that are right for all (and, conversely, some that are wrong for all) at all times and places. Within the confines of the created order, such commands are known through "natural reason," which in no case fails. That is, though the world could have been created otherwise, given that it has been created in the way that it has, some things are always right for those human beings who find themselves within this created order. And they can know those things, always (in this given order), through the exercise of right reason.

Oakley contends that Locke is a thoroughgoing Ockhamist.[69] Thus, when Locke speaks of the divine will as the foundation of the law of nature, we should understand him as referring to the *potentia dei absoluta*. That is, the bedrock of Locke's law of nature, consistent with his metaphysical nominalism, is the omnipotence of the deity that, when ordaining a particular world, finds itself in no way constrained. The deity can make the world however He chooses. But when Locke speaks of the law of nature in teleological terms—when he speaks, that is, of the requirements of the natural law as being promulgated through the proper function of human nature—*and* when he speaks of the law of nature as eternal and standing for as long as human nature as it now is remains, then (says Oakley) we should understand Locke as referring to the *potentia dei ordinata*—to that, and nothing more.[70] Thus, the ontological foundation for the binding power of the law of nature, in Locke, is nothing other than the omnipotent will of God, who could have created us in any way that he pleased, but has chosen to create us as we are. *Human nature* is but a *proximate cause* of human, moral obligation. In particular, proper function is the *way in which* God has made the declaration of his will manifest. God could have chosen to create the world differently than He did. He could have chosen to promulgate the requirements of his will differently than he has. But the world as we have it, and human nature as we have it, is in fact how he has made his will known.

The foregoing suggests that we consider as a logically possible state of affairs the following scenario (from a modal logical standpoint, we would say that we are considering a possible world with a world-book that contains in it the following).[71] First, the only things absolutely necessary are God's existence and the basic laws of logic (identity, noncontradiction, and the excluded middle). Second, there are no universals or forms or ideas in the sense to which any species of realism refers. Third, there is no such thing as goodness as such. Rather, some action is good or right *if and only if* God requires that it be done. And some action is evil or wrong *if and only if* God proscribes the performance of that act. Fourth, in choosing to actualize a possible world, God has in fact willed that what is good is teleological in nature such that what is good for the human person is that which accords with the proper function of human beings as such. Fifth, some things accord with the proper function of human beings as such at all times and in all places and therefore are right for everyone, everywhere, always. Sixth, human persons ascertain their proper function through the exercise of natural reason, which in no case fails—that is, the requirements of natural law are the requirements of right reason [*recta ratio*]. Such a way of thinking about the requirements of the natural law and the good is *both* voluntaristic *and* teleological. What we have is, on the one hand, an Ockhamist metaphysic, providing an Ockhamist foundation (or ultimate ground) for moral obligation, and, on the other, a Thomistic system with respect to the proximate cause of human obligation (you might almost say that an Ockhamist metaphysics is tied to a Thomistic physics or causal theory with respect to human nature). And in such a system, it does seem that the requirements of natural law can both be contingent upon the world actualized and necessary for those who find themselves within a particular world. In light of the foregoing, has Oakley saved Locke?

The Self-Contradiction of Lockean Metaphysics with His Metaethics

On one level, Oakley's account of Locke's theory of natural law does seem to save Locke from contradiction by providing what initially seems to be a coherent account of the apparently contradictory elements in his moral philosophy—of the voluntaristic element, on the one hand, and the teleological element, on the other. But on another level, rendering Locke's theory consistent by making the teleological element dependent on the voluntarist element leaves Locke vulnerable to a damning indictment. For if Locke is in fact a voluntarist when it comes to the ontological foundations of the law of nature, then his theory cannot be salvaged precisely because voluntaristic accounts of obligation in general and of moral obligation in particular is self-referentially incoherent. If Locke is a voluntarist when it comes to the deep ontology of his moral philosophy, then his moral theory is fatally flawed. To the degree that his political theory rests on his moral theory, his political theory is in jeopardy as well.

Oakley's powerful and sophisticated argument notwithstanding, I am not convinced that Locke is a thoroughgoing voluntarist. By virtue of his nominalism, he ought to be. And he certainly says things that sound unequivocally voluntaristic. But included in the Lockean corpus are explicit denials of ethical voluntarism as well as arguments that entail the rejection of voluntarism. Consider this fragment, in which Locke strongly denounces voluntarism:

> Whatsoever carries any excellency with it, and includes not imperfection, it must needs make a part of the idea we have of God. *So that with being, and the continuation of it, or perpetual duration, power and wisdom and goodness must be ingredients of that perfect or super-excellent being which we call God*, and that in the utmost or infinite degree. But yet *that unlimited power cannot be an excellency without [i.e., unless] it be regulated by wisdom and goodness.* For since God is eternal and perfect in his own being, he cannot make use of that power to change his own being into a better or another state; and therefore all the exercise of that power must be in and upon his creatures, which cannot but be employed for their good and benefit, as much as the order and perfection of the whole can allow each individual in its particular rank and station; and therefore looking on God as a being infinite in goodness as well as power, we cannot imagine he hath made anything with a design that it should be miserable, but that he hath afforded it all the means of being happy that its nature and estate is capable of, and though justice be also a perfection which we must necessarily ascribe to the supreme being, yet we cannot suppose the exercise of it should extend further than his goodness has need of it for the preservation of

his creatures in the order and beauty of the state that he placed each of them in. For since our actions cannot reach unto him, or bring him any profit or damage, the punishments he inflicts on any of his creatures, i.e., the misery or destruction he brings upon them, can be nothing else but to preserve the greater or more considerable part, and so being only for preservation, *his justice is nothing but a branch of his goodness,* which is fain by severity to restrain the irregular and destructive parts from doing harm; for to imagine God under a necessity of punishing for any other reason but this, is to make his justice a great imperfection, and to suppose a power over him that necessitates him to operate contrary to the rules of his wisdom and goodness, which cannot be supposed to make anything so idly as that it should be purposely destroyed or be put in a worse state than destruction (misery being as much a worse state than annihilation, as pain is than insensibility, or the torments of a rack less eligible than quiet sound sleeping). *The justice then of God can be supposed to extend itself no further than infinite goodness shall find it necessary for the preservation of his works.*[72]

There are hardly words that are of a less Ockhamist tenor. The resonances are, in fact, quite anti-Ockhamist. Here Locke says that God's omnipotence cannot be considered a divine excellency *unless* that power is regulated by wisdom and goodness. That is, for divine power to constitute a divine excellence or perfection, a necessary condition is that this power be regulated or governed by divine wisdom and divine goodness. And the passage would collapse into sheer nonsense if the source of the divine goodness that must regulate the divine will in order for the divine power to be considered a perfection were itself merely an exercise of that will or created by it. Moreover, Locke's concluding words in this fragment are that divine justice (or divine right) "extend[s] no further than infinite goodness shall find it necessary for the preservation of his works." In other words, the justice of God in relation to his creation is limited by his infinite goodness. Correlatively, God's power over his creation is *not* unlimited, the infiniteness of that power notwithstanding. This passage is a rather straightforward rejection of ethical voluntarism.

There are other passages where a rejection of voluntarism is clearly implied. For instance, Locke at many times refers to the divinity as just and good;[73] he also refers to the commands of God, delivered in nature's law as well as in special (i.e., supernatural) revelation, as both just and good. But, as Leibniz maintained, predicating justice and goodness of God and His actions is unintelligible if something is good or just simply because God wills that it is.[74] This would make all such predications, including those in the Lockean corpus, tautological. But the problem goes even deeper. There would be literally nothing, on the voluntarist count, to which those terms (justice and goodness) would refer. There would be a signifier-referent problem of the first order. So the problem is not just linguistic or semantic, though it is that; it is also metaphysical. To refer to God Himself as just or good or to his commands as right and good is to presuppose a standard of goodness not reducible to sheer will.

Moreover, Locke grounds the normative force of human law in natural law. For if human law is not grounded in natural law, so he argues, then human law is nothing else but an arbitrary exercise of will or a mere exercise of power.[75] Just as such, Locke says, it would not be binding. Moreover, there would be no possibility of distinguishing authority from tyranny. But, as Leibniz points out, this same problem remains fully in force on the voluntaristic account of moral obligation or of natural law.[76] For if Ockham's account of natural law is correct, then the ground of natural law is nothing but an arbitrary exercise of sheer will—albeit of a powerful will at that. Such a will might compel me. But in what circumstance would I think that just because I could be compelled I was also obligated? All the arbitrariness Locke hopes to avoid comes rushing back in, at but one remove, if he subscribes to a voluntaristic account of natural law. And if the commands of human law become mere (i.e., nonbinding) commands when they are not grounded in natural law, how is it that the commands of God are not mere commands or arbitrary and therefore nonbinding commands if they do not effectuate, through their commanding, some objective right or good?

So there we have it: Locke is a metaphysical nominalist, *n*, who also posits the existence of moral obligation, *o*. His theory of natural law must, by entailment, be a voluntaristic theory of natural law, *v*.

And he says things that suggest he holds such a theory (even though he also says things that clearly reject it). Consequently, we can say the following:

(1) If both nominalism and obligation, then metaethical voluntarism, or $(n{\cdot}o)\supset v$.

(2) Some ambiguous passages notwithstanding, Locke seems clearly to affirm metaphysical *nominalism*. Thus, *n*.

(3) Locke has a theory of moral *obligation*, which he refers to as the law of nature. Thus, *o*.

(4) The rules of inference allow us, on the basis of (2) and (3), to say *both* nominalism *and* obligation, or $(n{\cdot}o)$.

(5) Given the conditional stipulated in (1) (and defended above) and given (4), by application of modus ponens, voluntarism, or *v*, follows. However,

(6) Both by entailment and explicitly (as in the passage above), Locke also rejects voluntarism. Locke wants a nonarbitrary foundation for human law. But that means the ontological ground of his moral law must also be nonarbitrary. In view of these considerations, the conclusion that Locke rejects voluntarism of the Ockhamist variety also seems clear. Thus, *not voluntarism*, or ~*v*. But,

(7) Given (1) and (6), the rejection of both nominalism and obligation, ~$(n{\cdot}o)$, follows by virtue of modus tollens.

(8) Not both nominalism and obligation, or ~$(n{\cdot}o)$, per DeMorgan's rule, is logically equivalent to *either* not nominalism *or* not obligation, or ~*n* or ~*o*.

(9) Given double negation, obligation, *o*, is equivalent to not, not obligation, or ~~*o*. Thus, given (3), which says Locke holds *o*, he also holds ~~*o*.

(10) Given the disjunctive syllogism, (9), and (8), Locke must reject metaphysical nominalism; that is, he must hold not nominalism, or ~*n*.

(11) Given (2) and (10), Locke holds both nominalism and not nominalism, or $n{\cdot}$~*n*, which violates the law of noncontradiction.

(12) Given (1)–(5) and (6), Locke holds both voluntarism
and not voluntarism, or $v \cdot \sim v$, which also violates the law of
noncontradiction. The relation of his metaphysics to his moral
ontology therefore commits a double self-contradiction and is
incoherent on both counts.

Conclusion

In sum, Locke is a nominalist who holds a theory of moral obligation. This means that he is, by implication (and whether he likes
it or not), committed to voluntarism (a self-referentially incoherent
proposition). However, he expressly rejects ethical voluntarism. And,
given that he holds a theory of moral obligation, he rejects, by entailment, nominalism. So he expressly affirms, but by implication
rejects, metaphysical nominalism. And he expressly rejects but by
implication affirms ethical voluntarism. There is therefore a double
self-contradiction running through the relation of his ethical theory
to his metaphysics. Given the self-referential incoherency of voluntaristic accounts of obligation, there are only two ways out for Locke.
He can reject metaphysical nominalism in favor of metaphysical realism. Or he can reject the notion of moral obligation. But between
these options, he must choose.[77] Or, more aptly, given that we are
some years removed from his tenure among the living, between these
options we must choose. For, as we saw at the conclusion of the last
chapter, there is no third way.

Moreover, because his political theory is at its foundation an application of the norm of promissory obligation, Locke requires a coherent foundation for moral obligation. And we have seen that even
sophisticated voluntarism provides no such foundation.

CHAPTER 6

Reason and Will in Natural Law:
The Necessity of Real Goodness and Prescriptive Will for Moral Obligation

Introduction

IN *Bondage of the Will*, Martin Luther writes, "God is He for Whose will no cause or ground may be laid down as its rule and standard; for nothing is on a level with or above it, but is itself the rule of all things. . . . What God wills is not right because He ought, or was bound, so to will; on the contrary, what takes place must be right, *because He so wills it*."[1] So stating, Luther took sides in a dispute over the nature of moral law that the Middle Ages bequeathed to the age of Reformation and the modern period. Indeed, Luther expressly identified himself with the school of William of Ockham and the *via moderna* (the modern way) over and against the *via antiqua* (the ancient way) associated with Thomas Aquinas.[2] In the passage just cited, Luther asserts *metaethical voluntarism*: an act (such as repaying benefits) is right or good or obligatory such that we ought to perform it *if and only if* (because and only because) God wills that it be so by prescribing it; correlatively, an act is wrong or bad or an act from which we are obligated to refrain (for instance, theft or murder) *if and only if* (because and only because) God has forbidden it. On the opposite side of the divide from Ockham and the *via moderna* stands Thomas Aquinas, who contended that "to say that justice depends *simply* on the will [of God] is to say that the divine will does not proceed according to the order of wisdom, and that is blasphemous."[3] Rather, for Aquinas, intrinsic goodness and divine wisdom lay at the foundation of natural law. Indeed, on Aquinas's realist ontology of moral obligation, an act is right or obligatory such that we ought to perform it *because* (or at least in significant part because) it is good; correlatively, an act is wrong or morally proscribed (illicit) *because* (or at least in significant part because) it is evil (i.e., contrary to good). Given the incoherence even of sophisticated voluntarism, I argue that Luther and Ockham are wrong and Aquinas right.

I will go beyond this historic dispute between voluntarists and realists to argue that prescription and goodness are each insufficient for moral obligation. Prescription, by itself, is an instance of sheer will. Prior chapters showed that metaethical voluntarism is self-referentially incoherent. The upshot is that sheer will and prescription alone are unable to ground or generate moral obligation. To avoid collapse into self-referential incoherence, moral obligation requires a real goodness transcendent of human will. Yet the intrinsic goodness of an act is not enough by itself to make the act morally obligatory. For among intrinsically good acts, some are merely permissible, some obligatory, and some supererogatory (that is, some acts are better than what obligation requires of us). But if not all good or intrinsically good acts are obligatory, then obligation is not conceptually included in and does not analytically follow from *good* or *intrinsically good*. It follows that goodness (or intrinsic goodness), though necessary, is not sufficient for moral obligation. Moral obligation requires *both* intrinsic goodness and prescription by someone who possesses the authority to prescribe. We can call this the *compound property* or *dual foundation* account of moral obligation.

Of course, just because someone commands us to perform some intrinsically good action, it does not follow that we are bound. For prescription to bind us, the person who prescribes must possess *authority* to prescribe. Thus, moral obligation requires an authoritative prescriber. As G. E. M. Anscombe argues, moral law requires a moral *lawgiver*.[4] Contra Anscombe, H. L. A. Hart claims that the "characteristic tenets" of natural law "have not been logically dependent" upon "belief in a Divine Governor or Lawgiver of the universe."[5] In what follows, I maintain that Hart is wrong and Anscombe right. The lawgiver is ineliminable from any coherent conception or intelligible account of moral obligation and therefore of natural law. The real alternative we face is affirming the lawgiver or abandoning moral obligation altogether. Consequently, an account of political foundations that depends on promissory obligation, such as consent theory, requires a coherent conception of moral obligation more generally.

Two Kinds of Natural Law

Setting aside "the civil or canon lawyers" who "often meant by natural law something rather different than did the philosophers or theologians" and focusing on "the theologians of the later Middle Ages," Francis Oakley says "two influential poles" dominated natural law theorizing: the rationalists and the voluntarists or the realists and the nominalists. Oakley adds, "The most prominent of the medieval realists was, of course, Thomas Aquinas, and the most coherent of the later medieval nominalists was William of Ockham."[6] In the early seventeenth century, Francisco Suárez provided perhaps the best summary (and contrast) of realism and voluntarism, as they had developed to that point. Suárez describes the realist (or intellectualist) position as follows:

> The natural law is not a preceptive law, properly so-called, since it is not the indication of the will of some superior; but . . . on the contrary, it is a law indicating what should be done, and what should be avoided, what of its own nature is intrinsically good and necessary, and what is intrinsically evil. . . .
>
> The natural law is not derived from God as Lawgiver, since it does not depend upon His will, and . . . in consequence, God does not by virtue of that law, act as a superior who lays down commands or prohibitions. Indeed, on the contrary, Gregory [of Rimini] . . . says that even if God did not exist, or if He did not make use of reason, or if He did not judge of things correctly, nevertheless, if the same dictates of right reason dwelt within man, constantly assuring, for example, that lying is evil, those dictates would still have the same legal character which they actually possess, because they would constitute a law pointing out the evil that exists intrinsically in the object.[7]

The realist position—as the antipode of voluntarism—need not consider God unnecessary for moral obligation, as Suárez claims Gregory of Rimini did and as the early modern Hugo Grotius intimates.[8] One might hold that "God is the efficient cause and the teacher . . . of the natural law; but it does not follow from this, that He is its legislator, for the natural law does not reveal God issuing commands, but indicates what is in itself good or evil, just as the sight of a certain object reveals it as being white or black, and just as the effect produced by God, reveals Him as its Author, but not as Lawgiver."⁹ On the intellectualist thesis, then, any act *a* (e.g., keeping one's word) is obligatory for any person *p* if and only if *a* is intrinsically good. The intrinsic goodness of *a* is necessary and sufficient for the obligatoriness of *a*. Likewise, any person *p* is obligated to refrain from performing any act *b* (e.g., murder or theft) if and only if *b* is intrinsically evil. The intrinsic evil of *b* is necessary and sufficient for an obligation to refrain from *b*-ing.

By way of contrast, Suárez describes the voluntarist account of natural law, which he traces to Ockham, Jean Gerson, and Pierre d'Ailly as follows:

That the natural law consists entirely in a divine command or prohibition proceeding from the will of God as the Author and Ruler of nature; that, consequently, this law as it exists in God is none other than the eternal law in its capacity of commanding or prohibiting with respect to a given matter; and that, on the other hand, this same natural law, as it dwells within ourselves, is the judgment of reason, in that it reveals to us God's will as to what must be done or avoided in relation to those things which are conformable to natural reason.

This is the view one ascribes to William of Occam (on the *Sentences*, Bk. II. Qu. 19, ad 3 and 4), inasmuch as he says that no act is wicked save in so far as it is forbidden by God, and that there is no act incapable of becoming a good act if commanded by God; and conversely . . . whence he assumes that the whole natural law consists of divine precepts laid down by God, and susceptible of abrogation or alteration by Him. . . . Gerson also inclines to this position . . . [Pierre] d'Ailly . . . too, defends this view at length . . .

These authorities also add that *the whole basis of good and evil in matters pertaining to the law of nature is in God's will, and not in a judgment of reason, even on the part of God himself, nor in the very things which are prescribed or forbidden by that law.* The foundation for this opinion would seem to be that actions are not good or evil, save as they are ordered or prohibited by God; *since God himself does not will to command or forbid a given action to any created being, on the ground that such an action is good or evil, but rather on the ground that it is just or unjust because He has willed that it shall be done.*[10]

On the voluntarist account of natural law, as Suárez presents it (and credibly attributes it to Ockham), any person p has an obligation to perform any act a if and only if God has commanded that a be done. God commanding people to perform a is necessary and sufficient for them to have an obligation to perform it. Likewise, any person p has an obligation to refrain from performing any act b if and only if God has forbidden anyone to p to b. Divine prohibition is both necessary and sufficient for individuals to have an obligation not to b.

Voluntarist Natural Law
WILLIAM OF OCKHAM'S SOPHISTICATED VOLUNTARISM

William of Ockham is a metaphysical nominalist who denies the reality of universal forms or essences—that is, he's an anti-essentialist.[11] According to Marilyn McCord Adams, "Ockham regarded the view that universals are real things other than names as 'the worst error of philosophy' . . . because he found it contradictory." Indeed, "Ockham identifies universals with universal names and denies that there are any universal things other than names."[12] According to Philotheus Boehner, Ockham claimed that "everything that exists is individual and singular."[13] William J. Courtenay writes, "No one disputes the fact that Ockham gave primacy to the singular and rejected the idea that there existed a 'common nature,' which inhered in the things that 'look alike' and which produced their resemblance."[14] For his part, Ockham says terms such as "genus," "species," "universal," and "predicable" are "names" that "signify only mental contents, which are natural signs or conventional signs."[15] He also claims, "the humanity of Plato is one thing and the humanity of Socrates another" and "what no power can cause to belong to several things no power can make predicable of several things; now no power can make such a nature, if it is really the same thing as the individual difference, belong to several things, because in no manner can [something really identified with one individual] belong to another individual; therefore, no power can make it predicable of several things, and consequently *no power can make it universal.*"[16] Ultimately, "a universal . . . is *only* a kind of mental picturing."[17] Now in the last chapter, I argued that a metaphysical nominalist who espouses the existence (or even just the conceptual possibility of) obligations must, by logical implication, affirm a voluntarist ontology of obligation (or metaethical voluntarism): if both metaphysical nominalism and obligation, then metaethical voluntarism (or $(n \cdot o) \supset v$). Given Ockham's metaphysical nominalism (and concomitant rejection of universal essences or forms), if he affirms that we do (or even just can) have obligations, then he should be a metaethical voluntarist. I submit that the evidence shows not only that he affirms voluntarism with respect to the ultimate ground of moral obligation but that he is a *sophisticated* voluntarist.

In *Questiones in librum secundum Sententiarum* (Ockham's *Commentary on the Sentences of Lombard*), Ockham claims that acts that are now vicious—such as robbery, adultery, or even hatred of God—could be made virtuous "if they were to agree with the divine precept just as now *de facto* their opposites agree with the divine precept."[18] Ockham provides two grounds for this claim: (1) "evil is nothing other than the doing of something opposite to that which one is obliged to do," and (2) God is "obliged to the causing of no act."[19] As well, Ockham holds that "God can do (or make or create) everything which does not involve a contradiction."[20] Ockham (and later medieval nominalists) hold that only God's existence and the law of noncontradiction are absolutely necessary.[21] And God's power to command (or forbid) are limited by these alone. Correlatively, on Ockham's view, nothing—in particular, no act—is intrinsically (or simply and absolutely) good or evil. God makes certain acts good or obligatory by commanding them; He causes other acts to be wrong or morally impermissible (such that there is an obligation to refrain from performing them) by forbidding them.[22]

Like Thomas Aquinas and his teacher Albertus Magnus (Albert the Great), Ockham distinguishes the absolute and ordained powers of God (the *potentia dei absoluta et ordinata*).[23] According to Aquinas, "What is attributed to [his] power considered in itself, God is said to be able to do by his absolute power. . . . As for what is attributed to his power as carrying out the command of his *just* will, he is said to be able to do by his ordained power. . . . Accordingly, it should be said that by his absolute power God can do things other than those he foresaw that he would do and preordained to do."[24] God's absolute power (*potentia dei absoluta*) refers to all the possible worlds that God could actualize or create. God's ordained power (*potentia dei ordinata*) refers to the world—the order of things—that He in fact created. For Albert and Aquinas, on the one hand, and Ockham and later medieval nominalists, on the other, God's absolute power refers to His freedom to create. God was not bound to create the world at all or to create it as He did. God could have created the world quite differently than He in fact created it.[25]

The difference between Ockham's view and Albert and Aquinas's involves Ockham's *radicalization* of the *potentia dei absoluta*. For Albert and Aquinas (and later realists like Hooker), there are doubtless an infinite number of possible worlds (possible orders of things) that God could actualize or create. But on their view, there are *imaginable* and even *logically* possible worlds that an essentially Good and Wise Being (one for whom Goodness and Being are convertible) could not create—perhaps even infinitely many. Thus, for Albert and Aquinas there are substantial metaphysical constraints on what God can will in establishing a particular order—though these limits derive from His Being or nature. According to the seventeenth-century Anglican divine Richard Hooker, "The being of God is a kind of law to his working."[26] Suppose, for instance, that lying is intrinsically evil (we need not take this to mean that deception of every sort is always wrong). And suppose that God is essentially Good (indeed Goodness itself) such that lying is metaphysically impossible for God. In that case, God cannot create or actualize a world in which God tells a lie or in which God calls lying good or even in which God commands someone to lie—*even if* such a world is imaginable or logically possible. But for Ockham and later medieval nominalists such as Gabriel Biel, the only limits on the set of actualizable worlds that God can choose to ordain are God's own existence and the law of noncontradiction. Thus, Ockham writes, "God can make certain things by ordinate power and others by absolute power. This distinction . . . must be understood thus; 'to be capable of something' is sometimes considered according to the laws ordained and instituted by God. God is said to do those things by ordinate power. Otherwise, 'to be capable of something' is taken as 'to be able to produce everything which does not entail a contradiction to be done,' whether or not God ordained that He would do it since He can ordain many things which He does not wish to do."[27] And on Ockham's view, God could either command or proscribe lying, murder, theft, and adultery without contradiction.

From the foregoing, it follows that on Ockham's view God could have created (or actualized) a world in which bearing false witness, theft, murder, and adultery are right, by commanding these acts, and in which honesty, not taking the property of others, protecting innocent life, and fidelity are wrong, by forbidding them. But Ockham holds that God has in fact established an order of things according to which bearing false witness, murder, theft, and adultery are wrong, by in fact forbidding these actions (though he could have commanded them) and their opposites (honesty, preserving innocent life, refraining from taking what belongs to others, and fidelity) right, by prescribing these actions (though he could have forbidden them). Moreover, Ockham holds that murder, theft, adultery, and bearing false witness are simply and absolutely wrong—wrong for everyone, everywhere, always—and their opposites simply right—right for everyone, everywhere, always. As Oakley has argued, Ockham takes the most fundamental requirements of natural law "to be absolute, immutable, and admitting of no dispensation."[28] Thus, Ockham affirms a morality with not only the same content but also the same degree of obligation in its most fundamental requirements as that affirmed by Albert, Aquinas, and other realists.[29]

Further still, in the *Dialogus* Ockham describes natural law as "a natural commandment," the first principles of which are either self-evident (*per se nota*) or "follow or are taken from such self-evident principles of morals." And "about such natural laws no one can err or even doubt." Certainly someone might be ignorant of or fail to know the most fundamental principles of morality "because it is possible not to think and never to have thought of them." Even so, "such natural laws occur [to us] immediately when we are obliged to do or omit something in accordance with them, unless we will proceed to act, or to omit such act without any deliberation and rule of reason." Yet, because the very first principles of natural law occur to us the moment we think about them, ignorance of these principles can only be the product of negligence on our part. Consequently, someone ignorant of them is morally culpable. According to Ockham, if an individual tempted to kill an innocent person "will deliberate, even briefly, about whether he should kill him, it will occur [to him] that he should not kill him. . . . Therefore, if without any deliberation he kills him, such ignorance does not excuse him."[30]

In addition to the first principles of natural law, Ockham also describes secondary principles that "are drawn plainly and without great consideration from the first principles." Finally, a third group of principles are inferred from more fundamental principles only by well-studied experts. And even these experts can get tertiary principles wrong. But disagreement among well-studied experts notwithstanding, there is a right answer as to what these principles are and what acts they require. All these principles of natural law—fundamental, primary principles, their immediate entailments, and those principles apprehended only by a few—are "dictates of natural reason" and can be described as rationally necessary: "That is called natural law which is in conformity with natural reason *that in no case fails.*"[31] Put another way, the requirements of natural law are apprehended by right reason that in no case fails.[32] God could have established an order of things—actualized a world—in which basic moral requirements are the opposite of what they now are and in which those requirements are conveyed only via direct, supernatural revelation. He has in fact created a world with moral requirements that include refraining from murder, theft, adultery, and bearing false witness and require love of God, in which these requirements are absolute, and in which they are apprehended by the faculty of reason.

Following Oakley, I submit that the voluntarist element of Ockham's thought belongs to his deep ontology of moral obligation and refers to his understanding of God's absolute power (*potentia dei absoluta*). His claims about natural law and right reason that in no case fails refers to the order God has in fact established—the world He has chosen to actualize—and so to the ordained power of God (*potentia dei ordinata*).[33] That is, Ockham affirms the reality of natural law. But the deep ontology of natural law is *not* divine wisdom or goodness but, rather, omnipotent power and divine *will*. As Ockham puts it, "by the very fact that the divine will wills [or commands] it . . . right reason dictates what is to be willed [by man]."[34] We might call this way of combining the voluntarist and natural law elements of Ockham's thought *sophisticated voluntarism*. On sophisticated voluntarism, natural reason (and right reason) that in no case fails and which apprehends absolute and immutable moral principles provides a *proximate* foundation for right and wrong and moral obligation. But the *ultimate* foundation remains the divine will constrained only by the necessity of divine existence and the law of noncontradiction. On this view moral obligation consists in reason and will (or prescription). But reason is subordinated to will.

And, as we saw with Oakley's voluntarist interpretation of Locke, sophisticated voluntarism can be cashed out in terms of a natural law wed to classical teleology, as one finds it in Aquinas. On such an account, divine omnipotence—constrained only by the necessities of divine existence and noncontradiction—could have established an order according to which the good or well-being or thriving of any particular thing consists in the performance of a proper function distinctive to it (perhaps that which it uniquely does or does better than anything else) and therefore where the good of a thing is its aim or goal—its telos. In such a divinely established order, human beings also have a proper function—or perhaps human nature consists in an ordered tier of proper functions (corresponding to rational and animal nature and that of existing things). And human good or well-being consists in the performance of that function (or those functions), which is the human telos. As well, in this divinely established order, God prescribes those actions that fulfill the human telos (or teloi— hierarchically ordered with rational nature at the summit) and forbids those actions that subvert it. Here we have natural law, apprehended by reason, the dictates of which correspond to the aim(s) or goal(s) of human nature. Moreover, God prescribes these requirements of right reason. At the same time, insofar as the account is voluntarist, natural law, right reason, and the normativity of human teleology are all subordinated to a divine will that created the world this way but also could have created the world such that reason does not apprehend the requirements of right and wrong and such that the moral law proscribes those actions that comport with the aim or telos of human nature (or some aspect of it) and prescribes those that subvert it. That is, on this view, a morally unconstrained, omnipotent will remains the sole ultimate cause of right and wrong and moral obligation.

Now metaethical voluntarism is self-referentially incoherent because it makes an instance (or certain instances) of sheer will normative or binding for all exercises of will on the basis of will alone. Sophisticated voluntarism, however, distinguishes between the ultimate and proximate causes of moral obligation, holding that reason and human nature (or the aims of human nature as such) provide proximate foundations for *oughtness* while divine will or prescription provides the ultimate foundation. Does sophisticated voluntarism escape self-referential incoherence by virtue of this distinction? It does not. Rather, sophisticated voluntarism simply pushes the problem of self-referential incoherence back one step, from the proximate to the ultimate cause. While the *proximate* cause of right and wrong or moral obligation does not result in self-referential incoherence on sophisticated voluntarism, because the proximate cause is not sheer will, the *ultimate* cause of right and wrong nevertheless remains sheer will and is therefore self-referentially incoherent. Put another way, the deep ontology of sophisticated voluntarism, even on the version that affirms a teleological account of human nature as the proximate cause of moral norms obligation, is self-referentially incoherent. And the incoherence of the deep ontology of sophisticated voluntarism necessarily infects the rest of the theory, rendering it logically invalid.

PUFENDORF'S ATTEMPT TO SALVAGE SOPHISTICATED VOLUNTARISM FROM HOBBESIAN COLLAPSE

The early modern moral and legal theorist Samuel von Pufendorf provides another version of sophisticated voluntarism. Pufendorf affirmed the mechanistic philosophy of modernity (together with its notion of material substance); concomitantly, he rejected classical teleology (the notion that things or substances have inbuilt ends or purposes the attainment of which constitutes their good).[35] On the one hand, Pufendorf grounds moral obligation in the decrees of a superior.[36] On the other hand, he explicitly rejects Hobbes's contention that sheer strength—even omnipotent strength—suffices to impose obligations on others. Thus, though Pufendorf is often described as a voluntarist (and rightly so), he is nevertheless *not* a Hobbesian voluntarist or a proponent of voluntarist natural law on what we might call the standard Ockhamist model. And we might wonder whether his particular brand of voluntarism can rescue the position from the self-referential incoherence that stalks the other variants or strains.

Let's begin with Pufendorf's distinction between natural (or purely physical) and moral entities. With respect to natural entities, he writes, "we see that all things which collectively make up this universe, consisting as they do of principles assigned and fitted to each of them by the Great and Good Creator Who constituted their respective essences, have their own particular characteristics. These issue from the arrangement and aptitude of the substance and express themselves in certain actions according to the measure of strength imparted to them by their Creator." Such things are "usually" called "natural," he claims, "since the term 'nature' has customarily designated not only the entirety of created things as such, but also the modes and activities flowing from their innate strength, which produces the infinitely varied motions whereby we see everything in this universe to be stirred."[37]

In contrast to those things that either lack sensations or, possessing only "minimally reflective sense, are driven by natural instinct alone," human beings have a "special light of the mind" by means of which they "can more accurately comprehend and compare matters, infer the unknown from the known, and judge of the proper arrangements among things." Due to this ability, human beings are not determined or "compelled to act always in the same manner." Rather, they can "exert, suspend, or moderate [their] actions as seems fit."[38] More concisely, people possess rational judgment and free will and so are able to direct their will by means of reason.

Moral entities Pufendorf defines as "certain modes superadded by intelligent beings to physical things and motions for the special purpose of directing and regulating man's free, voluntary actions, and for giving human life a certain order and grace." Where classical,

Aristotelian philosophy distinguished between a substance and its accidents, Pufendorf proposes a distinction between substance and mode instead: "This distinction between mode and substance makes it abundantly clear that moral entities are not self-subsistence but depend on substances and their motions, which they only affect in a certain manner." Moral modes "are superadded to physical things and their modes by an intelligent power." Moral modes are not properties of physical things. Rather, moral entities are imposed on them. And while Pufendorf contends that human beings are able to make (or impose) them (indeed, he says human beings create most of them), "Their primary author . . . is the Great and Good God" who desired human life to be different from the "brutes."[39] God desired human life to include culture and mores and for human behavior "to be tempered by certain principles"—which requires moral entities.

Thus, physical—or natural—entities are produced by "creation" and moral entities by "imposition" on already created things: "For moral entities do not arise from the intrinsic substantial principles of things but are superadded to things already existent and physically complete, and to their natural effects, by the will of intelligent beings who alone determine their existence." Moreover, moral entities are "assigned certain effects [for instance, sanctions] by these same causes [i.e., intelligent beings], at whose pleasure they can be destroyed again without any physical alteration in the thing to which they were superadded." Moral entities do not produce "physical motion or change in things by means of their own internal efficacy." Rather, they show human beings "how they ought to regulate their free actions" and render them "fit to receive some benefit or harm." God institutes moral entities by circumscribing the free will of human beings within certain limits, the violation of which He threatens with sanction and thereby "turns the recalcitrant in whatever direction He wishes." He possesses the right to circumscribe human free will and to impose sanctions for transgression of the limits He imposes "by right of creation."[40] That is, God has the right to impose moral limits (moral entities understood as limits on free will, where the limits are backed by sanction for transgressing them) because He has created us. So, on Pufendorf's account, moral entities are not natural or physical entities—all of which are complete in themselves. Nor do moral entities supervene on natural things. Nor are moral entities causal in relation to natural or physical substances. Moral entities are not final causes.

How do God and human beings create moral entities? *By imposing law on those under their authority:* "In general, law seems best defined as a decree whereby a superior obligates someone subject to himself to conform his actions to the superior's prescription."[41] While law must be made known in order to bind, "oral or written promulgation" is not necessary. Rather, promulgation via the "natural light" suffices. In this Pufendorf disagrees with Hobbes's claim that the laws of nature are "conclusions of reason" but not laws proper—except insofar as they are "orally promulgated by God in the Sacred Scripture."[42] Pufendorf also rejects Hugo Grotius's definition of law. For Grotius, says Pufendorf, law obligates us to what is just and right in and of itself. But in that case, "something just and right is given before any law and norm, so that the law of nature does not create what is right but only points to something right already existing."[43] Pufendorf denies that something right exists prior to law. Rather, *moral modes or entities are created by law.*

Though Pufendorf defines law as the decree of a superior and holds that God is author of the natural law,[44] he rejects the notion that moral obligation arises from strength alone or the Hobbesian contention that God's right or authority to rule is grounded in nothing other than His irresistible might. To be sure, "an obligation is properly introduced into a man's mind by a superior" where a superior is "someone who not only has the strength to threaten some evil against those who resist him, but also legitimate reasons allowing him to demand that our freedom be restricted at his discretion." But—especially in light of the "legitimate reasons" qualification—*"the right to lay an obligation on another, or in other words to command and prescribe laws for him, does not arise from strength alone,* nor even from a superiority [*huperochē*] or preeminence of nature." When another insists that I obey them *only* on the basis of their greater power over me, there is no reason why I should not endeavor "in every way to shake off that power and assert my freedom if I deem it in my own interest."[45] According to Pufendorf, "compulsion and obligation are different." And while natural strength can compel us, such strength exercised in relation to us does not obligate us. Thus, contra Hobbes, *"God's right to rule, or His sovereignty* (insofar as it denotes the power to impress an obligation on men's minds) *should in no way be derived from his bare omnipotence alone."* Thus also, Pufendorf rejects Hobbes's invocation of God's treatment of Job to demonstrate that God's right to rule over his creatures is "based on power alone."[46]

As for preeminence, "natural preeminence does not always entail an ability to govern someone else less well endowed by nature, nor are diverse grades of perfection among natural substances automatically linked with subordination and the dependence of one on the other."[47] Moreover, human beings have both judgment and free will. They are capable of regulating their own behavior according to their own discretion. Accordingly, there is no reason to think such a creature violates the dictates of conscience in acting according to his own discretion rather than a superior's.

Given the insufficiency of strength and preeminence for the right of one person to impose an obligation on another—"strength alone is not sufficient for an obligation to arise for me from another's will"—in order for someone to obligate me, that person "should also have procured some notable goods for me, or else I myself must have consented voluntarily to his direction." To the extent that any person p imposes an obligation on any other person q, it must be the case not only that p is stronger than q but also that p has benefited q in some notable or substantial way. But if p's "good intentions and . . . better ability to provide" for q "have also been confirmed," then "there is no clear reason why" q "should want to oppose his sovereignty." That is, Pufendorf holds that q has good reason for accepting the sovereignty of p over q given this state of affairs.[48] And we "owe" God "our very existence." Moreover, God gave us our free will. Consequently, does not God possess "the right to restrict some small portion thereof?"[49]

Though strength (or superior strength) is insufficient for moral obligation, it is, nevertheless, necessary. For any person p to impose an obligation on any person q, p must be capable of directing q and credibly threatening q with sanction for failure to comply with p's directives to q. Thus, while Pufendorf *rejects* "the overly crude assertion of certain writers that right is what pleases the stronger," he *affirms* that "laws can hardly attain their external end unless they are equipped with strength capable of prodding even the unwilling." The approbations and torments of conscience for either fulfilling or failure to fulfill our obligations come from the "strength of Almighty God"—before Whose tribunal all "who have neglected their duty" will be judged.[50]

Law—which is the decree of a superior—creates moral entities. According to Pufendorf, "The formal principle of the goodness and badness of actions consists . . . in their bearing or determinative relation to a directive norm which we call a law." Thus, "an intentional action which proceeds from and is undertaken in accordance with what a norm prescribes, so that it agrees exactly with the norm, is said to be good." Likewise, an evil or bad action is one "undertaken against what the norm prescribes, or is discrepant with it."[51] Thus, the law laid down by a superior creates (moral) good by prescribing and creates (moral) evil by forbidding; it creates moral obligation by imposing behavioral requirements upon us. With Pufendorf we have a form of normative constructivism according to which moral entities really are generated and so have a kind of existence, albeit one utterly detached from physical reality or natural things. And both God and human beings make moral entities—God's creation being the law of nature and human creations being the state and human law. Moreover, Pufendorf's account is clearly voluntaristic (God is free to actualize any possible world He chooses) without the arbitrariness of Ockham or Hobbes's reduction of obligation to sheer omnipotence or irresistible power.

As a voluntarist Pufendorf categorically *rejects* "an eternal rule for the morality of human actions beyond the imposition of God." Such a rule would establish an eternal principle outside of God that God "had to follow in the assignment of forms to things." [52] Such a principle would have limited God's freedom in the creation of human beings. According to J. B. Schneewind, Pufendorf holds that divine freedom precludes the existence of "any eternal and independent moral properties in things." Rather, "Morality first enters the universe from acts of God's will, not from anything else."[53] God was free to create or not to create human beings. And God was free to give human beings a nature other than the one they in fact have.

At the same time, Pufendorf holds that once God endowed human beings with a rational and social nature, "it was impossible for the natural law not to agree with his constitution, and that not by an absolute, but by a hypothetical necessity. For if man had been bound to the opposite duties, no social animal but some kind of wild and bestial creature would have been produced."[54] As Schneewind puts it, "God does not contradict his own will."[55] Thus, Pufendorf holds that God's will imposes moral obligations by creating human beings in a certain way, by endowing them with a particular nature. God could not make murder, theft, or adultery right for us without altering our basic constitution.

Schneewind's description of Pufendorf's project merits quoting at length:

> The ontological significance of the doctrine of moral entities is fairly definite. It is a major effort to think through a new understanding of the relation of values and obligations to the physical world. It presents a new response to the developing scientific view of the world as neutral with respect to value. Accepting the concept of a purely natural good dependent on the physical relation of things to humans, Pufendorf refuses to see it as the sole kind of value, and insists that moral norms and conventional values of all kinds are conceptually independent of it. He denies the old equation of goodness with existence, and the Grotian assertion of special moral qualities built into the nature of things. He equally repudiates the reductionism of Hobbes and [Richard] Cumberland, the definition of all evaluative terms by means of terms descriptive of the physical world. Moral entities involve ideas and beliefs that do not in any way represent the way things are in the world. Their whole point is to guide action. Moral entities are inventions, some of them divine, most of them human. Their ontological status gives no reason to doubt their ability to serve their purpose.[56]

The unavoidable upshot of Pufendorf's view is that morality and moral goodness are utterly meaningless when applied to God: "It is of course clear on Pufendorf's view that God, having no superior, can never be under a law and therefore can never be obligated. . . . The whole conceptual apparatus of our morality, therefore, since it derives from law, has no pertinence when we think of God."[57]

We might ask whether Pufendorf has provided a more tenable version of sophisticated voluntarism than those proffered by Ockham, Hobbes, and Locke (as interpreted by Oakley). I submit that he does not. First, as with Ockham and Oakley's Locke, Pufendorf merely defers the problem of voluntarism's self-referential incoherence. He pushes it back a level. The deep ontology of his theory still collapses into incoherence. For at the foundation, Pufendorf holds that *morally* unlimited divine will invents and imposes moral obligation simply by exercising itself in prescription or prohibition. Moreover, the incoherence of the deep ontology of Pufendorf's voluntarism entails, necessarily, that the ethical theory built on this foundation is incoherent as well.

Second, there is also a contradiction in Pufendorf's position. Recall that Pufendorf grounds God's authority not in sheer strength or bare omnipotence but also in the fact God has provided us with benefits— existence foremost among them. But how do we get from benefaction to an obligation to obey? According to Schneewind, Pufendorf's position is this: "The appropriate response to someone who is good to us is gratitude. And the only way to show gratitude to a being who needs nothing is to try to comply with his wishes." Given God's great benefits to us, we ought to do our best to discern what God wishes us to do and then to conform our actions to those wishes. But this poses a problem: "The appropriateness of repaying benefits with gratitude must itself be a moral entity imposed by God, which raises the question of its justifiability."[58]

Let's make Schneewind's argument a bit more systematic. For Pufendorf, our most fundamental moral obligations derive from the law of nature; they are produced by the law of nature being imposed on us. Why obey the law of nature? Because someone with authority— namely God—has imposed it on us. But what is the basis of God's authority? Either the basis of God's authority is sheer will—indeed, bare strength or irresistible power alone—or there must be something in addition to God's omnipotent will or bare strength that makes it obligatory. If Pufendorf grounds moral obligation in bare strength or omnipotent will alone, then he espouses a voluntarist ontology of obligation, which is self-referentially incoherent. But Pufendorf expressly distinguishes force or compulsion from obligation. So there must be something in addition to irresistible power or omnipotence that makes obeying God's will obligatory for us. Pufendorf says this additional something is God's benefaction to us and the corresponding duty of gratitude that we owe to Him—gratitude that can only be tendered by obedience. But now we must ask where our obligation to requite God's benefits comes from. Only two answers are possible: (1) it is itself imposed by divine decree resting on nothing more than bare strength or sheer will (in which case the position is self-referentially incoherent), or (2) it is *not* grounded in bare strength or sheer omnipotent will alone but also in divine benefaction and a correlative duty to gratitude that can only be tendered by obedience.

Either the duty to gratitude in (2) is a real moral obligation not grounded in strength alone—in which case it is an intrinsic duty or an eternal moral reality of precisely the sort Pufendorf expressly rejects—or it is imposed by omnipotent will alone, thereby conflating bare strength or compulsion with obligation. And once again the same dilemma presents itself. We are ultimately presented with three mutually exclusive and exhaustive alternatives: either (*a*) there is an infinite regress concerning the duty to show gratitude for divine benefaction by obeying God's law—in which case the obligation is never grounded, never *justified*; or (*b*) the duty to show gratitude for divine benefaction is a moral entity created by imposition of divine will alone—in which case Pufendorf's ontology of obligation is self-referentially incoherent; or (*c*) the duty in question is a real moral obligation (for Pufendorf, a moral entity) antecedent to any divine decree. On the one hand, (*c*) is necessary for any noncircular (non-viciously question-begging) justification of God's authority to impose the natural law and our obligation to obey it. But (*c*) is also—necessarily—a non-voluntaristic grounding of moral obligation. And (*a*) and (*b*) are incoherent. Thus, the only coherent grounding of God's authority over us and our correlative obligation to obey available to Pufendorf is one that rejects voluntarism. Yet, as Schneewind shows, Pufendorf expressly affirms voluntarism in order to protect God's freedom in creation. And that means Pufendorf is stuck with rejecting voluntarism in order to affirm it—a self-contradiction. To wit, Pufendorf provides no path out of the incoherence that stalks the voluntarist ontologies of obligation in the natural law accounts proffered by Ockham, Hobbes, and Locke (as interpreted by Oakley). Moral obligation requires the very sort of property or eternal principle Pufendorf sought to deny but that proves necessary for the coherence of his own theory. Moreover, it seems clear that any account of normative constraints that rejects moral and metaphysical realism faces this problem.

Realist-Intellectualist Natural Law

AQUINAS AND THE MORAL REALIST ACCOUNT OF NATURAL LAW

According to Knud Haakonssen, most scholars trace the "realist-intellectualist" tradition ultimately to Thomas Aquinas.[59] To be sure, following Otto von Gierke, a few scholars have tried to convert Aquinas into a kind of voluntarist. According to Gierke, Aquinas "derived the content of the Law of Nature from the Reason that is immanent in the Being of God and is directly determined by that *Natura Rerum* which is comprised in God Himself" *but* "traced the binding force of this Law to God's Will."[60] Stephen J. Grabill follows Gierke, claiming that "what ultimately makes something obligatory" on Aquinas's view "is God's command."[61] Indeed, according to Grabill, "on the question of the ultimate origin of moral obligation, namely the divine will, Aquinas, Scotus, and Occam . . . maintain general agreement. . . . Like Scotus and Occam, Aquinas held that divine will initially generates the moral obligation to do and pursue that which is good and avoid that which is evil."[62] For what we might call the Gierke Interpretation of Aquinas (advanced by Gierke and Grabill), the realist explanation of the *content* of moral obligation is accurate. But the *binding power* of moral precepts and the natural law is entirely voluntarist in character. The vast majority of Aquinas's interpreters (including Oakley and Haakonssen), however, reject the Gierke Interpretation and consider Aquinas the headwaters of the realist-intellectualist natural law tradition.

Before we consider the interpretations of others, however, we should first recall the passages in Aquinas's *Summa Theologiae* (namely, those in I-II, Q. 94, art. 2) upon which those interpretations are based.[63]

Aquinas writes, "The precepts of natural law are to the practical reason what the first principles of demonstration are to the speculative [or theoretical] reason, because both are self-evident principles." Now, the first principles of both theoretical and practical reason do not admit of demonstration. They are first principles because we reason from rather than to them. With respect to speculative or theoretical reason, the first principle is noncontradiction (something cannot both be and not be in the same way or relation and at the same time). With respect to practical reason, the first indemonstrable principle is that good is to be done and evil, its contrary, avoided: "As 'being' is the first thing that falls under the apprehension simply, so 'good' is the first thing that falls under the apprehension of the practical reason, which is directed to action, since every agent acts for an end under the aspect of good. Consequently, the first principle in the practical reason is one founded on the notion of good, viz., that *good is that which all things seek after.* Hence this is the first precept of natural law, that *good is to be done and ensued, and evil is to be avoided.*"[64] Aquinas adds, "All the other precepts of natural law are based on this."[65]

But what does it mean to define *good* as that which all things seek? According to Aquinas, the good of any particular thing *t* is an end to which *t* is by its nature inclined or disposed. He writes, "Since . . . good has the nature of an end, and evil the nature of a contrary, hence it is that all those things to which man has a natural inclination are naturally apprehended by reason as being good and, *consequently,* as objects of pursuit, and their contraries as evil and objects of avoidance."[66] Note Aquinas's construction. He employs the language of *entailment.* He says reason apprehends those things to which human beings are naturally inclined as "good . . . and, *consequently,* as objects of pursuit." To this Aquinas adduces the further claim that "the order of the precepts of the natural law is according to the order of natural inclinations." That is, the precepts of natural law derive from those goods to which human beings are naturally inclined. Likewise, the contraries of good are apprehended by reason "as evil *and* as objects of avoidance."[67] Aquinas implies that such objects are objects of avoidance *because* they are evil.[68] Consequently, entailment in this passage seems clearly to run from goods and evils to the precepts of natural law (i.e., the precept, and so the obligation, derives from the goods and evils).[69]

Aquinas distinguishes three sorts of inclinations by which human nature is defined. He holds these to be hierarchically ordered. First, human beings are substances. And every substance seeks its own preservation. Thus, human beings are naturally inclined to the preservation of human life. Consequently, "whatever is a means of preserving human life and of warding off its obstacles belongs to the natural law." Second, human beings are animals. Thus, "those things are said to belong to the natural law 'which nature taught to all animals,' such as sexual intercourse, education of offspring, and so forth." Finally, human beings possess reason. Humans are rational animals: "thus man has a natural inclination to know the truth about God and to live in society; and in this respect, whatever pertains to this inclination belongs to the natural law, for instance, to shun ignorance, to avoid offending those among whom one has to live, and other such things regarding the above inclination."[70]

Given the connotations of *inclination* in contemporary English, we should consider what Aquinas does *not* mean when he uses the Latin *inclinatio*. Natural inclinations, in Aquinas's sense, are *not* equivalent to desires or preferences in the usual psychological or social scientific use of those terms. As Anthony J. Lisska says, natural inclinations are not, in and of themselves, "conscious" drives or "intentional" acts.[71] Nor are natural inclinations biological instincts in the Darwinian (or neo-Darwinian) sense of that term. Natural inclinations are not spontaneous or automatic responses or drives to act in certain ways (say, in order to survive or preserve the species). Rather, natural inclinations are what Lisska calls dispositional essences:

> What then is an essence for Aquinas? It is a "supreme set of dispositional properties." Using terminology gained from Aristotle, Aquinas argues that a temporal essence is made up of matter and form. A form is what specifically differentiates one kind of thing from another kind of thing. This is Aquinas's concept of a "substantial form." The properties which make up a substantial form, which in turn specify the content of an essence are dispositional in character. They are not static. . . . The model of a tulip bulb

developing during the Spring is closer to Aquinas's concept of an essence than the definition of a triangle.[72]

Aquinas's theory of essence (to which his theory of good is tied) is developmental, where development is understood as development toward a particular end-state. And this makes the theory teleological (where teleology refers to "the metaphysics of finality" rather than to consequentialist theories like Utilitarianism).[73] As Aquinas says, "Nature acts for an end." For Aquinas, as for Aristotle before him, "the end or 'telos' is the point at which the dispositional properties in the primary substance reach their development or perfection. . . . In Aquinian terminology, the potency or disposition has reached a state of actualization."[74]

Given that natural inclinations are dispositional essences and given that (on Aquinas's view) human persons have three kinds of natural inclinations, human essence is "essentially a set of dispositional properties divided into three sets." And human good consists in the actualization of that toward which these properties are disposed. In view of Aquinas's claim that good has the nature of an end (telos) and the Aristotelian understanding of natural inclination, Lisska says, "the completion of a developmental process—the natural termination point—is a good."[75] On this view, the good of human beings consists in reaching the natural termination point of those dispositional traits in which human essence consists—or by which human nature is constituted. Following Aristotle, Aquinas also defines human good in terms of proper function. The good of anything consists in performing its proper function well. The human good is achieved when human beings function well. And, says Lisska, human beings function well when they reach (or perhaps aim to reach) the "developmental potential of [their] essential properties."[76]

On Lisska's interpretation, Aquinas holds that the elements of natural law arise in accordance with the dispositional properties of which human nature is composed.[77] Thus, "When the essence of a human person is determined, then this becomes the normative ground for what human beings are to be and to become. It is the foundation for *eudaimonia*, which is the functioning well of the essential properties common to the individual in a specific natural kind."[78] Immoral actions are immoral because they obstruct a natural developmental process. An act is wrong *because* it "prevents the completion—the self-actualization, as it were—of the dispositional properties which determine the content of human nature."[79] This account of moral norms provides Aquinas with a clear answer to the "famous" Euthyphro dilemma: "To paraphrase the text of the *Euthyphro* modestly, an act is right, not because the gods command it, but the gods command it because it is a right action. . . . What makes an act right or wrong is that it is either in accord or not in accord with the fundamental developmental properties central to the concept of human nature."[80] Thus, "An act is right, Aquinas argues, because it is in accord with the requirements of human nature, not because it is reducible to a divine command." God's will is not irrelevant here. For God could have made the world other than he did. "But once human nature had been established, certain moral rules follow from the divine archetype of human nature."[81] Or so argues Lisska. And there is much in Lisska's argument to commend it. According to Mark C. Murphy, for instance, "On Aquinas's account, the binding power of moral norms—their obligatoriness—is to be understood by reference not to divine commands but to the human good, promotion, protection, and respect for which is dictated by those norms." For Aquinas, "That one is obligated to adhere to a certain precept means that the following of that precept is required for one to attain the good of the agent, 'the end of virtue.' "[82]

Lisska's reference to "the divine archetype of human nature" brings to mind Oakley's account of how Aquinas frames the relation of eternal to natural law in the *Summa Theologiae*:

Assuming the primacy of reason over will, not only in man but also in God, [Aquinas] regarded what in later parlance would be called the physical laws of nature, and also the moral and juridical natural law, in comparatively "Greek" fashion as, both of them, the external manifestation of an indwelling and immanent reason. Thus, law in general being for him "something pertaining to reason," he viewed the divine "reason," which directs "the government of things" and exists "in God as ruler of the universe," as itself possessing "the nature of 'law' in which all beings, in some manner, participate . . . [deriving] . . . from it certain inclinations to those actions and aims which are proper to them." That "eternal law," then, orders to their appropriate ends all created beings, irrational "as well as rational," and it is to be understood as "nothing other than the idea of divine wisdom insofar as it directs all acts and movements" and governs "the whole community of the universe."[83]

Noting that Aquinas reserves the term *natural law* for the participation of rational creatures in the eternal law, Oakley describes Aquinas's account of natural law in thoroughly intellectualist terms:

> Aquinas's position, then, amounts basically to this: that there is an eternal law, an immanent order guiding all created things to their appointed ends emanating from divine ideas, forms, archetypes, or patterns in accordance with which God created those things. Insofar as it concerns man as such—created in his very essence as a rational, moral being, participant by his god-like reason in the divine idea of the good, co-member with God (to use Leibniz's language) in "a community of justice," caught up alike in a common web of morality—thus far, the *eternal law* is called the *natural law*.[84]

Having thus summarized Aquinas's position, Oakley suggests that "Aquinas's doctrine of moral or juridical natural law . . . emerges as something that at least approximates [Alfred North] Whitehead's doctrine *of laws of nature as immanent and springing from the very nature of things*."[85] Oakley subsequently contrasts this intellectualist-realist account of natural law with the voluntarist account inaugurated by Ockham and advanced, in their own ways, by Hobbes and Locke, a view in which order is, as it were, imposed from the outside.[86]

Perhaps no one captures the intellectualist interpretation of Aquinas better than John Finnis in *Natural Law and Natural Rights*. Finnis writes, "Aquinas's reason for saying that law is an act of intellect . . . has nothing to do with the will of a superior needing to be made known, but only with the fact that it is intelligence that grasps ends, and arranges means to ends, and grasps the necessity of those arranged means, and this is the source of obligation."[87] As we will see, this sort of realist account of moral obligation won't work. Nor would I attribute it to Aquinas (who is also clearly no voluntarist).

The early modern theorist Hugo Grotius differs from Aquinas in many crucial respects. Yet he was also a prominent proponent of realist or intellectualist natural law (even if, as some might contend, a thinned-out version of it). Indeed, Grotius frames his entire project against Carneades, the skeptical second-century head of the Academy, at least as Cicero depicts Carneades's position in his *De re publica*. In the "Preliminary Discourse" to *The Rights of War and Peace*, Grotius writes,

> Laws [according to Carneades] were instituted by Men for the sake of Interest; and hence it is that they are different, not only in different countries, according to the Diversity of their Manners, but often in the same Country, according to the Times. As to that which is called NATURAL RIGHT, it is a mere Chimera. Nature prompts all Men, and in general all Animals, to seek their own particular Advantage: So that either there is no Justice at all, or if there is any, it is extreme Folly, because it engages us to procure the Good of others, to our own Prejudice.[88]

Grotius holds that Carneades's doctrine "must by no means be admitted." The proposition "that every Creature is led by Nature to seek its own private Advantage . . . must not be granted."[89] Rather than personal advantage, "Sociability . . . or this Care of maintaining Society in a Manner conformable to the Light of human Understanding, is the Fountain of Right, properly so called; to which belong the Abstaining from that which is another's and the Restitution of what we have of another's, or the Profit we have made by it, the Obligation of fulfilling Promises, the Reparation of a Damage done through our own Default and the Merit of Punishment among men."[90] It is just a bit after this passage that Grotius makes his (in)famous claim: "And indeed, all we have now said would take place, though we should

REASON AND WILL IN NATURAL LAW 213

even grant, what without the greatest Wickedness cannot be granted, that there is no God or that he takes no Care of human affairs." He immediately notes that the contrary is true, namely, that God exists, and that He "ought to be obeyed by us in all Things without exception" on account of His "infinite Goodness and Almighty Power."[91]

In Book I of *The Rights of War and Peace*, Grotius clearly takes the intellectualist side in the intellectualist-voluntarist controversy. He notes that there is a "Sense of the Word *Right*, according to which it signifies the same Thing as *Law*, when taken in its largest Extent, as being *a Rule of Moral Actions, obliging us to that which is good and commendable*."[92] Moreover, "Natural Right *is the Rule and Dictate of Right Reason, shewing the Moral Deformity or Moral Necessity there is in any Act, according to its Suitableness or Unsuitableness to reasonable Nature*, and consequently that such an Act is either forbid or commanded by GOD, the Author of Nature."[93] Further, "The Actions upon which such a Dictate is given, are *in themselves* either *Obligatory* or *Unlawful*, and must *consequently*, be understood to be either commanded or forbid by God himself."[94] Indeed, in its most fundamental precepts, "the Law of Nature is so unalterable, that God himself cannot change it. For tho' the Power of God be infinite, yet we may say, that there are some Things to which this infinite Power does not extend, because they cannot be expressed by Propositions that contain any Sense, but manifestly imply a Contradiction. For Instance then, as God himself cannot effect that twice two should not be four; so neither can he, that what is intrinsically Evil should not be Evil. And this is *Aristotle's* Meaning, when he says . . . *Some Things are no sooner mentioned than we discover Depravity in them*."[95]

For Grotius, obligation to act a certain way is determined by the intrinsic goodness of the act. Correlatively, moral obligation to refrain from performing some act is determined by the intrinsic evil or baseness of the act. The relation of divine will to moral obligation is simply that God commands that which is good because it is good and forbids that which is evil because it is evil. But moral obligation is a function of intrinsic good and evil. Grotius seems to maintain, then, that we would have objective (and intrinsic) good and evil and, therefore, moral obligation even if (per impossible) God did not exist.

FINNIS AND THE NATURE OF MORAL OBLIGATION
IN NEW NATURAL LAW THEORY

The so-called new natural law theory of Germain Grisez, Joseph Boyle, and John Finnis provides us with a contemporary version of the intellectualist account.[96] Proponents of new natural law describe the ends of human action as certain irreducible and incommensurable intrinsic goods that provide ultimate, noninstrumental reasons for action. These goods are thus described as intrinsically reasonable. Thus, the rule and measure for human action, on new natural law theory, is intrinsic reasonableness. And intrinsic reasonableness is the ground of our obligation to act in certain ways and to refrain from acting in others. Because it bears on my argument in this volume, I will focus exclusively on Finnis's account of obligation in his discussion of promissory obligation in *Natural Law and Natural Rights*.

According to Finnis, "The word 'obligation' etymologically relates particularly to the 'binding force' (*ligare*, to bind) of promissory or quasi-promissory commitments." Philosophers and moralists, argues Finnis, use the term *obligation* to cover a number of different "notions": "that there are things, within our power either to do or not to do, which (whatever we desire) we *have* to do (but not because we are forced to), or *must* do, which it is our *duty to* do, which it is *wrong not to* do, or *shameful not to*, which one *morally* (or *legally*) *ought to* do." Moreover, Finnis thinks philosophers are justified in using the term *obligation* to cover these various notions: "[These notions] all seem to relate to what can be experienced as a demand of conscience, a claim upon one's commitment, decision, action. Or again (since those experiences are characteristically related to the process of responsible rational assessment and practical judgment), *all those expressions and notions may be related to some form or forms of rational necessity*." Finnis goes on to equate "rational necessity" with the "*requirements* of practical reasonableness."[97]

We can best see how Finnis derives obligation from rational necessity (or the requirements of practical reasonableness) by considering his account of promising. Finnis begins his analysis with a discussion of that in which a promise consists: "A promise is constituted if and only if (i) A communicated to B his intention to undertake, by that very act of communication (in conjunction with B's acceptance of it), an obligation to perform a certain action (or to see that certain actions are performed), and (ii) B accepts this undertaking in the interests of himself, or of A or of some third party, C."⁹⁸ This tells us what it means to make a promise. But in what does the obligation of keeping our promises consist? That is, why is one morally (or legally) *obligated* to keep one's promises?

According to Finnis, everyone "has reason to value the common good—the well-being alike of oneself and of one's associates and potential associates in the community, and the ensemble of conditions and ways of effecting that well-being." And "the practice or institution of promising-and-therefore-performing-or-accepting-the justice-of-reproaches-etc. is greatly to the common good." Thus, the practice of promising "provides an effective means of maintaining cooperation, once initiated, over the span of time necessary for the fulfillment of any human project." Consequently, "if one is to be a person who favours and contributes to the common good, one *must* go along with the practice of promising. Similarly, and secondarily, if one is not to be a 'free-rider' who unfairly takes the benefits of beneficial social institutions but repudiates the burdens, then one *must* go along with the practice when one has promised, as much as when one has been promised."⁹⁹

In this explanation of promising, necessity is connoted by the word *must*—"And these necessities . . . are not affected by the fact that breach of the promise will go undetected either by the promisee or by others."¹⁰⁰ Just a few pages later, Finnis writes,

> [The] common good (including the good of the promisee or other ascertained beneficiary) can be realized with reasonable impartiality *only* if one performs on one's promise; *and this necessity is the obligation of his promise* (both the general, moralists' obligation, and the obligation owed to the promisee or beneficiary). "I *cannot* be one who acts for the common good *unless* I go along with the practice of performing on this promise." Secondarily, "I *cannot* be one who is rationally impartial *unless* I take the burdens of the practice as well as the benefits, and perform on this promise . . .". The conclusion, in each case, is: "*Therefore*, I *must* perform."¹⁰¹

So it is that Finnis grounds promissory obligation in rational necessity. And Finnis takes promissory obligation to be paradigmatic of obligation generally speaking. Thus, I submit, Finnis grounds obligation per se in rational necessity or in the requirements of practical reasonableness.

The Insufficiency of Intellectualist Natural Law

To see how the intellectualist account of natural law ultimately fails, we need to have in hand an understanding of moral obligation or even of obligation more generally. We can get at this matter by considering a distinction Grotius makes in Book I of *The Rights of War and Peace*. Therein Grotius distinguishes law as "a rule of moral actions" that imposes obligations upon us to do that "which is good and commendable" from *counsel*. Counsels, "however honest and reasonable they be, lay us under no Obligation" and so "come not under this notion of *Law*."[102] Laws impose obligation, whereas counsels do not. What's the difference? Counsels give advice concerning what it would be good for one to do without placing one under a moral requirement to follow that advice. Put another way, counsels leave individuals with discretion as to what to do. Obligations remove discretion. They impose non-optional requirements upon individuals. In his seminal *Finite and Infinite Goods*, Robert Merrihew Adams writes, "The obligatory, we may say, is what we *have* to do. Part of what we mean in saying this is that doing something that would otherwise be good *instead* of something obligatory would normally be grounds for serious moral criticism."[103] Likewise, speaking of "the *nature* of moral obligation," Nicholas Wolterstorff writes, "at the center of any account of the nature of moral obligation has to be an account of the *requiredness* that is an ingredient of obligation. An act that I am obligated to perform is not merely an act that would be good for me to perform. It is one that I am *required* to perform."[104] With this understanding in hand, let's turn to criticisms of intellectualist natural law.

In *God & Moral Law*, Mark Murphy advances a distinctively theistic critique of Thomistic natural law *on the intellectualist* interpretation of it.[105] In contrast to Grotius's *impious* hypothesis, the intellectualist interpreters of Saint Thomas understand him to affirm

God's necessity for natural law. But in their account, God is necessary as *creator*, not as *lawgiver*. God causes things with particular natures to exist. But he does not *directly* create moral obligation or relations of moral necessitation. Rather, moral necessity or obligation arise directly from certain relations—in particular, relations of actions necessary to or necessarily subversive of what is good for human beings. According to Murphy, "The status of the norms of the natural law *as law* require us to appeal to God, but the status of those norms as *binding precepts* requires, on Aquinas's view, no such appeal."[106] Yet, on Christian theism in particular, God is the explanans of all that is—of everything that exists or, as Murphy puts it, of everything that is "explanation eligible." In that case, God ought to figure preeminently not only in the explanation of natural law's *existence* but also in the explanation of its *binding power*. Murphy's contention is that, on theism, God cannot be reduced to the efficient cause of moral obligation. God (meaning God's being, goodness, and will) must enter its ontological ground. His complaint is that Aquinas's account of natural law fails to do this.[107] As it happens, I think both Gierke and Grabill, on the one hand, and Lisska and Murphy, on the other, get Aquinas wrong on this point. But let's postpone that for the moment. Whether or not he gets Aquinas right, Murphy gives us good reason to think that intellectualism or mere moral realism provides an inadequate account of moral obligation *given theism*. I will argue that intellectualism also fails on its own terms.

In our prior discussion of Hobbes, following Hampton, I argued that hypothetical imperatives (and moral norms construed as conditionals), just as such, lack any oughtness.[108] Hypothetical imperatives take the following form: If you want some good g and you must φ (where φ stands for performing some action or other; for doing something) in order to obtain g, then you ought to φ. But where does the *ought* come from? It seems inserted into the conditional by sheer stipulation. Removing the purely stipulated ought, the conditional should be framed like this: In order to obtain g, you must φ (therefore if g, then j). That is, all the causal relation of g to φ entails is that j-ing is necessary for the attainment of g; φ-ing is a necessary condition for g. The conditional merely describes a causal relation. But no more follows. Just because φ-ing is causally related to g or a necessary condition from bringing g about, it doesn't follow that anyone ought to φ—*even if* or *however much* they happen to want g. For any person p who desires some good g for which φ-ing is necessary to obtain g, it only follows that p ought to φ if g is such that p ought to seek g. The oughtness in all such cases logically precedes the conditional. Put another way, the prescription of g is logically antecedent to any conditional concerning actions that ought to be taken to procure g. We might put it this way: hypothetical imperatives can tell you that you ought to take some step necessary to attaining a good *only if* the good is already such that you ought to attain it (whether or not you want to attain it). Thus, the only hypothetical imperatives that convey any oughtness at all must ultimately rest on a categorical imperative as to what ought to be done. A morality of hypothetical imperatives all the way down can't be made to go. For again, hypothetical imperatives as such merely describe causal relations—and we can only be bound to act according to them if the end is first such that it ought to be brought about.

Given the foregoing, arguments that endeavor to derive oughtness or obligation from hypothetical imperatives or conditionals commit a non sequitur. Suppose, for instance, that someone seeks peace and also that keeping one's covenants made is necessary to keeping peace. According to a moral system constituted wholly by hypothetical imperatives, the conditional would be this: If you seek peace, then you should keep your covenants. But *should* is being packed into the conditional by sheer stipulation. In reality, this conditional necessarily supposes a logically prior categorical prescription: namely, seek peace. We ought to keep covenants, if keeping covenants is necessary to keeping peace, not *merely* because keeping covenants is necessary to seeking peace but also, necessarily, because we ought to seek peace. That we ought to seek peace, categorically, is necessary for the logical validity of the conditional "If you seek peace, then you ought to keep your covenants, given that keeping covenants is necessary to keeping peace." In an account in which moral obligation is constituted by hypothetical imperatives all the way down, the conditional pretends to include analytically what is really a necessary and distinct premise, or it merely stipulates that oughtness supervenes on necessary causal connections with no account of how or why this is so.

While the preceding argument obviously applies to Hobbes's ethical system, it also applies to ethical systems of a realist bent that are constituted by hypothetical imperatives all the way down. We can imagine someone who holds that there are real or objective goods—indeed, that there are some actions or states of affairs that are intrinsically good and others that are intrinsically evil—*and* who holds that natural laws are hypothetical imperatives (or conditionals) in relation to those goods. For instance, we might follow Aquinas in holding that human life is an intrinsic good. We might then note that certain actions (such as not murdering or not letting a neighbor in dire straits starve to death) are necessary for preserving human life. Here again we have a conditional or a hypothetical imperative: If you seek to preserve human life (which is intrinsically good), then you must refrain from murder (or, insofar as you seek to preserve human life, you ought not murder). The foregoing argument entails that this conditional (or hypothetical imperative) by itself—*even with the stipulation that human life is intrinsically good*—does not tell us that we ought to refrain from murder. As a conditional (or qua conditional), it simply describes the causal connection. Even if refraining from murder is necessary to preserving human life (as it clearly is), it can only be the case that we ought not murder if it is first the case that we ought to preserve human life. Full stop. The categorical imperative with respect to the intrinsic good necessarily precedes any logically plausible hypothetical imperative. And the oughtness is given by the categorical imperative. Oughtness or obligation in the categorical imperative is necessary for any oughtness in the conditional. To reiterate, conditionals and hypothetical imperatives just as such are incapable of grounding obligation. And this follows for moral realism just as it does for subjectivism, emotivism, or any other sort of antirealism with respect to the good.[109]

What I've argued still holds even if we speak of the good (or at least of finite good) in the teleological language of purpose and proper function. Suppose we speak of the pursuit of truth (or apprehension of truth) as the proper function of human beings as rational animals. That is, we have a rational faculty—one that sets us apart from other animals—the purpose of which is theoretical and practical knowledge. Human life, given that we are rational animals, is aimed at knowing truth. And, indeed, human persons just as such cannot flourish or thrive—cannot achieve well-being (the fulfillment of their proper function with excellence)—without reason serving the function of seeking and apprehending truth. What follows from this is that reasoning and living according to reason is necessary for human well-being. Humans cannot achieve well-being unless they live according to reason. But all that follows so far is a causal connection with respect to human well-being or objective flourishing. It does not follow that we ought to live according to reason—that we ought to fulfill the human purpose—*unless* we are first bound to achieve well-being, and to do so as the sort of beings that we are (i.e., as rational animals). Put another way, a teleological account of real good (or of the objective good for human beings), though *necessary* for natural law, is nevertheless *not sufficient*. Natural law as law, natural law in order to be obligatory, requires more than stipulation as to what is necessary for human well-being or for human beings to fulfill their proper function with excellence. We need more than conditionals for truly moral precepts.

Now, the intellectualist interpretation of Thomistic natural law, the moral realism of Hugo Grotius, and the new natural law account of moral obligation advanced by Finnis all frame moral obligations as conditionals, as hypothetical imperatives. This is what it means to describe moral obligation as a *relation* of necessitation (where x is necessary for y, or if x, then y). Finnis explicitly grounds moral obligation in a necessary causal relations. I must keep my promises, for instance, because I cannot act for the common good unless I keep my promises. If we let A_{cg} stand for *acting for the common good* and P stand for *performing one's promises*, then Finnis's position is $A_{cg} \supset P$: if we act for the common good, then we must keep our promises; keeping our promises constitutes a necessary condition of acting for the common good. More generally for Finnis, if any act a is obligatory for any person p, then a-ing must be necessary for the attainment of some real good. But, in fact, obligation does *not* supervene on relations of necessitation. Rather, statements of such relations are merely descriptive. I can only be obligated to perform my promises, because keeping my promises is for the common good, if I am already obligated to act for the common good and not against it—simply and absolutely, categorically, unconditionally. But in that case, the relation of necessitation between keeping promises and being for the common good does not generate the obligation (or, at least, does not do so by itself). Rather, the obligation most fundamentally derives from a logically prior categorical obligation to act for the common good. Full stop. Given that I have this obligation to act for the common good and that I cannot act for the common good unless I keep my promises, it follows that I am bound to keep my promises. Grounding moral obligation in relations of necessitation is a non sequitur—it seeks to generate a conclusion without the major premise.

Finally, recall our earlier formulation of the intellectualist thesis in the discussion of Suárez: any person *p* has an obligation to perform an act, *a*, if and only if *a* is intrinsically good; correlatively, *p* has an obligation to refrain from *b* if and only if *b* is intrinsically evil. On this way of thinking, obligation follows analytically or conceptually from goodness. Obligation is contained within goodness. According to Adams, this way of thinking about obligation is fundamentally flawed.[110] As he notes, there are various kinds of goods. For instance, there is the good of a beautiful portrait such as Rembrandt's *Return of the Prodigal Son* or of a profound musical composition such as Beethoven's *Ninth Symphony* or Mozart's *Requiem*. And then there is good in action. Insofar as a good scene or portrait or piece of music really is good and a good action really is good, and insofar as only the latter can be obligatory, it follows, necessarily, that obligation is not analytically packed into the idea of good. Suppose the intellectualists insists that we confine our argument to the good in action—indeed, to intrinsically good acts. Even so, we can still distinguish various kind of good acts. There are intrinsically good acts that are licit (permissible) but not obligatory. For instance, Saint Paul says that—given the circumstances—it is better to remain single than to marry.[111] Clearly he believes remaining single out of devotion to God is intrinsically good. But he also considers marriage to be intrinsically good.[112] And he leaves it to the discretion of individual Christians to choose either state. Neither is obligatory. Or suppose that someone has the ability—indeed, at least initially, the talent—to be an exceptionally gifted classical vocalist *or* an exceptionally talented football coach but not both (given that use of one's voice as a coach precludes using it as a classical vocalist). And suppose both courses of life are intrinsically good. Each of these is permissible for such a person. Neither is obligatory or required. And, in fact, I believe we can conceive many intrinsically good acts that are in no way obligatory for anyone.

Clearly, however, some actions are obligatory. For instance, we ought to tell the truth (or bear truthful witness) and keep our legitimate promises; we ought not lie or murder or steal. So we can distinguish intrinsically good acts that are permissible but not obligatory from intrinsically good acts that are required and obligatory for us (e.g., telling the truth, not lying). Moreover, some actions are supererogatory. They are better than we have to do. They go beyond what our obligations require of us. In this class of acts we might include laying down one's life for a friend or, like the Good Samaritian, taking care of a wounded stranger who has been robbed, beaten, and left for dead on the road at personal expense. And whatever else the obligations of a soldier include (for instance, holding the line in the heat of battle), surely Socrates standing over a wounded and fallen Alcibiades at Potidaea, to defend him against attackers, at hazard to Socrates's own life, goes beyond what morality and common good require of him. Now according to Adams, the *mere conceptual possibility* of supererogatory actions (even if there are in fact no such acts) entails necessarily that obligation does not follow analytically from good (or intrinsic good or goodness). Rather, the obligatory marks off a subset of good (or intrinsically) acts.[113]

To adapt my critique of conventional contractarianism and metaethical voluntarism to intellectualism, we can conceive of a set of all intrinsically good actions (actions that are good but merely licit, actions that are obligatory, actions that are supererogatory).[114] We could represent this set of all logically possible, intrinsically good acts as follows: $(GA_1, GA_2, GA_3 \ldots GA_n)$. Some of these actions are good (indeed, intrinsically good) but not obligatory—that is, some are merely licit and some are supererogatory. Others are both good (indeed, intrinsically good) and obligatory. And we cannot tell which are intrinsically good and obligatory and which are intrinsically good but not obligatory (which are merely licit or supererogatory) on the basis of intrinsic goodness alone. For all the members of the set of intrinsically good actions—both those that are obligatory and those that are not—are intrinsically good. Intrinsic goodness is the property that defines the set. And we cannot distinguish among the members of a set on the basis of the predication of the property or the properties by which the set is defined. It follows that if some intrinsically good acts are obligatory such that we are required to perform them whereas other are not, then there must be some property transcendent of *or at least not simply reducible to* goodness or intrinsic goodness that singles out some intrinsically good acts as obligatory. And given that hypothetical imperatives cannot generate obligation or normativity (but, in fact, simply presuppose it), relations of moral necessitation cannot do the trick.

Intellectualist natural law fails to ground or account for obligation. In particular, it fails to explain why some intrinsically good acts are required whereas others are not. And it fails in this because it lacks prescription.

Moral Obligation as a Compound Property

If we consider our treatment of voluntarist natural law, the argument shows that will alone (even omnipotent or irresistible will) is *insufficient* for moral obligation. Prescription plus raw power won't do the trick. Prescriptive will lacks something. And the thing it seems to lack is the goodness (ultimately the intrinsic goodness) of what is prescribed. That is, intrinsic goodness seems clearly *necessary* to distinguish instances or exercises of prescriptive will that bind or obligate from those that do not. Intrinsic goodness is requisite to making prescription more than just an exercise of will, more than bare strength or mere power, more than just compulsion or force. The self-referential incoherence of voluntarist ontologies of obligation demonstrates the *necessity* of intrinsic goodness for moral obligation and, indeed, for normativity at all. At the same time, the argument of the section above shows that intrinsic goodness is *insufficient* for binding moral norms. Intrinsic goodness, contra the intellectualist interpretation of Aquinas, Grotius, and (I submit) Finnis, requires prescription—requires a prescribing will. We might call this the dual-foundation view of moral obligation or, more aptly, the compound property view. Intrinsic goodness and prescription, reason and will, are *both* constitutive elements of obligation just as such. In which case it would be logically wrong to claim that real goodness provides only the content of morality and prescriptive will alone provides its binding power (as Suárez seems to claim).[115] For such a view still instantiates a voluntarist ontology of obligation. The binding power of moral precepts cannot come from prescriptive will alone, given the incoherence of metaethical voluntarism. Rather, prescriptive will and intrinsic goodness are both at the foundation, both essential ingredients of moral obligation.

But though intrinsic goodness and prescriptive will are both necessary for moral obligation, they are not together sufficient for it. We still need something more. Consider a hypothetical case in which Antigone tells her younger sister Ismene to do something intrinsically good. Maybe this intrinsically good thing is for Ismene to help Antigone bury their dead brother, Polyneices, whose unburied body, pursuant to Creon's decree, lies above ground outside the city, carrion for birds and dogs. Suppose for the sake of argument that even though Polyneices has done something truly awful (like betraying and seeking to destroy his home city of Thebes), nevertheless burying him is right and good. Suppose also that Antigone is not requesting aid but, in fact, commanding Ismene to help her in this task and that Antigone has therefore prescribed something intrinsically good to Ismene. Does Ismene now have a moral obligation to perform the task? Not unless Antigone possesses the authority to issue this prescription to Ismene. Perhaps things are somewhat murky, since Antigone is Ismene's older sister, her only remaining immediate relative, and daughter of a former king of Thebes. Strip all that away. Make Ismene the older sister and Antigone the younger. Make them subjects rather than royalty in Thebes. Does Antigone create a moral obligation for Ismene by so prescribing? She does not. Not *merely* by prescribing to Ismene what is intrinsically good. Moral obligation requires prescription. But the prescription must come from someone possessed of the *authority* to prescribe.[116] Per our argument so far, sheer omnipotence, irresistible power, bare strength, however great, is not enough. Authority to prescribe does not arise from the power to compel. Nor does being really powerful and also benefiting someone suffice. But suppose the prescriber were not only omnipotent but, more importantly, infinitely wise and infinitely good—indeed Goodness itself, indeed Being itself, indeed, *fullness* of Being. It is immensely difficult to see how Being as such could fail to possess, could fail to *be* authority as such and so authoritative in relation to us. Absent such Being, however, it is equally difficult to see how moral law or even moral norms could exist at all, since neither sheer power nor intrinsic goodness are sufficient to bind.

In her seminal essay "Modern Moral Philosophy," Anscombe argues that "morally ought" (including *right* and *wrong* insofar as these are added to and not simply synonyms for *just* and *unjust*) "has no reasonable sense outside a law conception of ethics."[117] Correlatively, she contends that the notion of moral obligation (that, for instance, we have an obligation to be just and an obligation to refrain from injustice) or being morally bound (e.g., we are bound to be just or bound to refrain from injustice) requires a "*law* conception of ethics." Moreover, "it is not possible to have such a conception unless you believe in God as a law-giver; like Jews, Stoics and Christians."[118] Thus she rejects as "absurd" Immanuel Kant's notion of "legislating for oneself." For "the concept of legislation requires superior power in the legislator."[119] Now, it would be one thing if Kantian autonomy means that we recapitulate the transcendent moral law in our own willing, as John E. Hare reads Kant.[120] Though even then I think Anscombe's objection has real teeth. But if Kantian autonomy (literally, legislating for ourselves) means that we create the moral law (or obligation) for ourselves or that we are the sole source of the moral law's imposition *and that* no moral law antecedent to and normative for human willing (to which human will ought to conform itself) exists, then the view is entirely incoherent (and for reasons Hobbes saw concerning the incoherence of self-imposed obligation).[121] For any law we make for ourselves, we are likewise free to unmake whenever we see fit, in which case we were never really bound. Unless there is a moral law antecedent to and normative for human willing, then there is no possibility of considering a prior act of will binding or normative for later ones. Without a moral law antecedent to and normative for human willing, a later act of will *undoing* prior self-legislation possesses just as much normative force. Consequently, any law we create for ourself we can uncreate at will. More simply, either

Kant's putative self-legislation is an instance of conforming our will to an already extant moral law, in which case we aren't legislating (i.e., binding) in Aquinas's sense but are in fact already bound, *or* self-legislation is an exercise of will trying to bind other instances of will on the basis of will alone, in which case self-legislation is voluntaristic and self-referentially incoherent.

In contrast to Murphy, I think Aquinas holds that divine prescription or command is *necessary* to the binding power of natural law. Aquinas holds that it is of the essence of law to bind, that law qua law is *not only* an ordinance of reason for the common good but also that it is *made* by the person with the care of the community (ST, I-II, Q. 90, art. 3, resp.), and that God is that person for the whole of the created order in general and humanity in particular (ST, I-II, Q. 91, art. 1, resp.).[122] If natural law is law proper, as Aquinas holds, then it follows that natural law has been laid down by God. *And* if it is the essence of law *to bind*, then for P to legislate for Q just is for P to bind Q. And in that case, P enters immediately into the explanation of Q's obligation. Thus, if God lays down the natural law, then it seems that God enters immediately into the explanation of the moral obligations imposed by that law and of its power to bind. To frame the argument more formally:

(1) Aquinas holds that the essence of law (*lex*) is to bind (*ligare*).

(2) Aquinas also holds that law is "a dictate of practical reason emanating from the ruler who governs a perfect [i.e., complete] community" (ST I-II, Q. 91, art. 1).

(3) Aquinas also holds that "the end of divine government is God Himself, and His law is not distinct from Himself" (ST, I-II, Q. 91 art. 1, ad. 3).

(4) Premises (1) and (2) together entail that the binding power of the natural law emanates from God.

(5) Taken together, (3) and (4) entail that the binding power of God's law—and so of the natural law—is not distinct from God (ST, I-II, Q. 91, art. 1, ad. 3).[123] And (5) seems clearly to entail that

(6) God is the immediate cause of the binding power of law per se and therefore of the natural law qua law.

Consider in this context the second objection and reply in article 5 of Question 94 in I-II of the *Summa Theologiae*. Aquinas there considers the question of whether the natural law can be changed. The second objection reads: "Further, the slaying of the innocent, adultery, and theft are against the natural law. But we find these things changed by God: as when God commanded Abraham to slay his innocent son; and when He ordered the Jews to borrow and purloin the vessels of the Egyptians; and when He commanded Osee to take himself 'a wife of fornications.' Therefore the natural law can be changed."[124] Now, this argument is an objection *against* the position that Aquinas defends—namely, that when it comes to its first principles, the natural law is unchangeable in the sense that something that once accorded with natural law cannot cease to belong to it. Nevertheless, Aquinas's reply to the objection is telling:

> All men alike, both guilty and innocent, die the death of nature; which death of nature is inflicted by the power of God on account of original sin, according to I Kings ii. 6: 'The Lord killeth and maketh alive.' Consequently, by the command of God, death can be inflicted on any man, guilty or innocent, without any injustice whatever. —In like manner adultery is intercourse with another's wife, who is allotted to him by the law emanating from God. Consequently intercourse with any woman, by the command of God, is neither adultery nor fornication. —The same applies to theft, which is the taking of another's property. For whatever is taken by the command of God, to Whom all things belong, is not taken against the will of its owner, whereas it is in this that theft consists. *Nor is it only human things that whatever is commanded by God is right, but also in natural things*— whatever is done by God is, in some way, natural, as stated in the First Part.[125]

Now, this passage certainly sounds voluntaristic and perhaps bears some responsibility for those few scholars who take the angelic doctor to espouse a voluntaristic ontology of moral obligation. Nevertheless, this passage must be taken together with the intellectualist-realist passages in article 2 of Question 94, where Aquinas says that "the first principle in the practical reason is one founded on the notion of good" and that "all other precepts of the nature law are based upon" the first precept, "that good is to be done and pursued, and evil is to be avoided." The reply to the second objection in article 5 of Question 94 must also be interpreted in light of the passage from *De veritate* with which this chapter began. Rather than making the reply to an objection in article 5 of Question 94 the interpretative basis of the argument Aquinas advances in article 2 of the same question and the passage from *De veritate*, and rather than ignoring the central importance of divine command for moral obligation in the response, I propose reading Aquinas as a proponent of the compound theory of moral obligation. As I see it, for Aquinas moral obligation consists in intrinsic goodness and in authoritative prescription. At any rate, if Aquinas's response to the second objection of article 5 makes him a voluntarist, then it renders his own account of natural law not only incoherent but also, by his own contention in *De veritate*, "blasphemous." Rather than reading Aquinas against himself, I submit he advances a realist ontology of moral obligation—but one for which authority and prescription are also necessary, constitutive ingredients.

Conclusion

Insofar as voluntarist ontologies of moral obligation are incoherent, they cannot ground a moral obligation to keep our promises, and therefore cannot ground political contractarianism or political legitimation by consent. Insofar as mere moral realism or intrinsic goodness are insufficient, even though necessary, for moral obligation, then moral realism or intrinsic goodness are likewise insufficient to ground promissory obligation, and therefore insufficient to ground the necessity of consent. Grounding political authority and obligations on consent requires a prior obligation to keep our valid promises and agreements. Neither voluntarism nor intellectualism provide such a ground. Any viable political contractarianism or theory of consent requires *both* that fidelity and keeping our valid agreements is intrinsically good (or in service of some intrinsic good) *and* that it is required of us by someone with the authority to prescribe. Absent both real goodness and a moral lawgiver, consent theory and political contractarianism are unintelligible nonsense.

PART III

COVENENTAL REALISM:
THE ESSENTIAL DEPENDENCE OF COVENANT
AND CONSENT ON CLASSICAL NATURAL LAW

CHAPTER 7

Whose Covenant? Which Social Contract Theory?:
Covenant *versus* Natural Law or Covenant *and* Natural Law

Introduction

WHEN IT COMES TO THE study of the history of political thought,
nothing is more common than the dichotomization of two distinct
models of political organization: the covenant (or social contract)
model and the Aristotelian (or organic) model. Classical natural law
is usually placed with the organic model of political organization.
The basic idea is that the Aristotelian and the covenant (or social
contract) models of political organization are mutually exclusive such
that one can affirm one or the other but not both. Quite a bit of
scholarship on the American founding and framing exemplifies this
argumentative framework. Thus, a number of scholars argue that the
political philosophy of the US founders and framers, the Declaration
of Independence, various state declarations of rights, and the
Constitution crafted by the Philadelphia Convention of 1787 belong
on the social contract theory (or covenant model of political organization) side of the leger and therefore reject Aristotle and classical (or
Thomistic) natural law. By virtue of embracing government founded
on consent, these all reject organicism in political organization. I
maintain that this way of thinking depends on a misunderstanding of
Aristotle and, given Aristotle rightly understood, a false dichotomy.

To be sure, the framers (and others of the founding generation)
speak both of social compact and consent and of natural law (or of the
law of nature). The question is not whether they affirmed contractarianism (or covenantalism) *or* natural law. Rather, properly nuanced,
the question has to do with the relation of covenant (or social contract)
and natural law. According to proponents of the covenant model, the
idea of the law of nature is subsumed under the organizing idea of

231

covenant (or social contract). On the other hand, there are natural law theorists who insist that grounding political authority upon consent is just one way a polity could be organized—that is, consent *may* be part of a constellation of conditions together necessary and sufficient for legitimate political order. But—for such theorists—consent is *not* a necessary condition of political authority or political obligations or legitimate government. There may be regimes in which rightful authority is acquired in other ways. For covenantal and contractarian thinkers, by contrast, consent comprises a necessary condition for political authority as such.

In what follows I will argue that this way of thinking—one that sets Aristotelian political theory and classical natural law in conflict with covenant and consent theory by positing mutual exclusion and contradiction—is false. Those who frame social contract against Aristotle rely on an unsound conception of Aristotle's political theory. Aristotle posited that the polis is a natural whole. But he did not hold that it is an organic whole. For, on Aristotle's political theory, while all organic wholes are natural wholes, not all natural wholes are organic. The polis, for Aristotle, is a natural *associational* whole rather than a natural *organic* whole. Thus there have been theorists of covenant and consent and social compact who also embrace metaphysical and moral realism as part of their organizing frame. They embrace both classical natural law (or something very much akin to it) *and* covenant or social contract. Such a position is logically possible. Indeed, this dual commitment (of a certain sort of contractarian or covenantal theorist) makes sense given that natural law of the morally and metaphysically realist variety comprises a necessary condition of any intelligible theory of covenant or social contract. Affirming covenant or social contract theory without classical natural law results in logical collapse.

Covenant versus Natural Law: The Conflict Thesis

A number of the most prominent scholars who work in the area of Revolutionary-era American political thought accept a frame for thinking about the founding that opposes covenant or social contract theory, on the one hand, to Aristotelian organicism and Thomistic natural law, on the other. These are taken to be mutually exclusive alternatives. And so, just because the American framers embraced social contract theory and government by consent, they are therefore taken to reject classical natural law.[1] The argument is rendered as a form of the disjunctive syllogism (though it could also be cashed out as an instance of modus ponens). Michael P. Zuckert presents this idea in its starkest form. Social contract theory "was always controversial; well before the American founding, Aristotle firmly asserted what the social contract theory appeared to deny—that political life is natural and that human beings are naturally political beings. Even more to the point, he spoke explicitly of a contractually based polity as a grossly deficient political association. Aristotle, then, is an important authority against social contract thinking and thus apparently against the American founding."[2] So according to Zuckert, Aristotelian political theory excludes the social compact theory of the American founders, and the social compact theory of the American framers excludes Aristotle's political theory.[3]

While Zuckert's primary concern is not to provide an argument for the opposition of the American founding thought to Aristotle, we can ascertain how the argument for this claim likely goes from his treatment of William Blackstone's reflections on the social compact. After all, Zuckert maintains that Revolutionary American thought on law (including natural law) and social compact was deeply impacted by Blackstone. As Zuckert depicts him, Blackstone affirmed modernist rather than classical political philosophy.[4]

Let's begin by considering Blackstone's account of the social compact as rendered by Zuckert. Zuckert notes Blackstone's rejection of a historical or original compact. He cites Blackstone's claim that "this notion of an actually existing unconnected state of nature, is too wild to be seriously admitted."[5] Rather, says Zuckert, "the social compact account of the origins [of society] 'in nature and reason must always be understood and implied,' because it expresses the fundamental truth underlying the function, nature, and proper operation of society and government." He continues:

The core is Blackstone's understanding of "the natural liberty of mankind." Even though human beings never lived detached from one another as the state of nature story says, still the basic

moral fact about mankind is "natural liberty," that is, "a power of acting as one thinks fit, without any restraint or control,
unless by the law of nature" ([*Comm.*] I, 121). Human beings
are naturally free, naturally not subordinate to the rule of others. . . . This equality reflects the human status as "a free agent,"
a being possessed of the 'faculty of free will' ([*Comm.*] I, 121).
This "natural freedom" describes human beings whether they
live in families, tribes, or large cities. The idea of the state of
nature expresses the massively important notion that de facto
power is not authority, that merely established subordination is
not thereby justified subordination. The idea of natural liberty
implies (or is equivalent to) the idea of the state of nature, which
implies the idea of the social compact, that is, the idea society,
government, authority, and law exist as made (not natural) entities, to be best understood as contracted or consented to by those
subject to them.[6]

A bit later Zuckert adds, "Authority or legitimacy derives ultimately
from consent."[7] This claim is ambiguous. To claim that authority or
the right to govern derives from consent leaves open whether consent
is only a necessary condition for the authority of some persons over
others or whether it is a sufficient condition or whether it is both necessary and sufficient. It is also ambiguous as to whether consent is the
ground of the political authority of some human persons over others
or whether it is merely the *occasion* on which some individuals acquire
authority over others. To say that authority or legitimacy derive from
consent—and to leave it at that—is not yet to say much. Be that as
it may, the putative mutual exclusion of Aristotle and social contract
theory is now, perhaps, a bit clearer. For social contract theorists,
according to Zuckert, political association is *made* or *constructed* (via
consent) rather than *natural*. By way of contrast, for Aristotle political
association is natural to humans as such. The mutual exclusion would
seem to consist in the dichotomization of that which is natural, on
the one hand, and that which is constructed or artificial, on the other.
    Modern political philosophy's notion of the social contract, accord-
ing to Zuckert, goes hand in hand with a radically revised account of
natural law:

Blackstone's doctrine of natural law differs in all the most significant ways from the (by his time) traditional laws of nature as
expounded by [Christopher St. Germain's] Doctor [in the *Doctor
and Student*] and Thomas Aquinas. The most important difference lies in the core or first principle of the law of nature. For
Blackstone . . . that first principle is self-love; for earlier thinkers
it was *synderesis*, the faculty of soul that contained the first precepts of actions: seek the good and flee the evil. Blackstone's law
of nature is accordingly the means to achieve what our self-love
impels us to (our pursuit of happiness), where the medievals
formulated the law of nature as the dictates embodying an orientation to the various forms of good suited to the character of
human beings. Blackstone's law of nature, then, is unmistakably
of the modern variety, reminiscent of Hobbes' certainly, but
borrowing a good deal as well from Pufendorf's effort to tame
Hobbes by combining him where possible with more traditional
natural law writers, especially Grotius, and borrowing from also
from Locke's somewhat different attempt to tame Hobbes.[8]

Blackstone—whose influence over the framers, according to Zuckert,
was immense—posited laws of nature that yield hypothetical (rather
than categorical) imperatives. The laws of nature are instrumental
and descriptive of a certain causal relation. They provide necessary
conditions for pursuing (and obtaining) individual happiness. This
depiction of the laws of nature—as causal laws that describe certain
causal relations in the production of individual, human happiness, on
the one hand, and as hypothetical imperatives addressed to agents
free to choose or reject those imperatives, on the other—is thoroughly modernist.

Zuckert claims that Blackstone was "obviously under the spell of
a modern scientific view of nature."[9] Contrasting Blackstone's conception of eternal laws with Aquinas's (and St. Germain's), he writes,
"The paradigmatic instances of [eternal] laws [for Blackstone] are
'the laws of motion, of gravitation, of optics, or mechanics.' " Thus,
"Where St. Germain and Aquinas emphasize that the good is the
end to which the eternal law ordains all things, Blackstone emphasizes instead the necessity that characterizes his laws: 'When he put that

matter into motion, he established certain laws of motion, to which all movable bodies must conform' ([*Comm.*] I, 38). These are 'unerring rules,' which determine action in a 'fixed and invariable' way ([*Comm.*] I, 38–39)." Blackstone, says Zuckert, "seems most impressed with the ability of the Newtons of the human race . . . who have . . . laid out the real principles of action in the world."[10]

Underlying social compact theory, then, is a modernist rather than a classical account of natural law. Lying at the foundation of modern natural law is mechanistic philosophy. While Zuckert doesn't make the implication explicit, his argument rather obviously entails that social compact theory rejects classical metaphysics. For mechanistic philosophy was premised on just such a rejection.[11] In other words, the mutual exclusion between Aristotle and social compact theory, on Zuckert's view (or upon a necessary entailment of it), goes all the way down—to the most fundamental level. Let's call this thesis— that social contract theory and Aristotelian political theory depend upon opposed metaphysics—Zuckert Contractarianism (or the ZC view, for short). This is not the only way to think about covenant, consent, and metaphysics.

When it comes to opposition of consent to classical political philosophy, Zuckert Contractarianism is not the only game in town. The most comprehensive and sophisticated work on the idea of covenant in political theory (and political theology) is almost certainly the magisterial work of Daniel Judah Elazar. Elazar considers three distinct— and mutually exclusive—models of political organization, two of which are the organic model of ancient Greek political theory (and so of Aristotle) and the covenantal model, originally conceived in Jewish thought and practice and given modern articulation by Reformed thinkers such as Heinrich Bullinger and Johannes Althusius.

According to Elazar, "Organic evolution involves the development of political life from families, tribes, and villages into large polities in such a way that institutions, constitutional relationships, and power alignments emerge in response to the interaction between past precedent and changing circumstances *with the minimum of deliberate constitutional choice.*" Moreover, "Classical Greek political thought emphasized the organic evolution of the polity and rejected any other means of polity building as deficient or improper."[12] To this Elazar adds the claim that "the organic model is closely related to the concept of natural law in political order. Natural law informs the world, and, when undisturbed, leads in every polity to the emergence of natural power relationships, necessarily and naturally unequal, which fit the character of its people."[13] By way of contrast, "Covenantal foundings emphasize the deliberate coming together of humans as equals to establish bodies politic in such a way that all reaffirm their fundamental equality and retain their basic rights." Indeed,

> Even the Hobbesian covenant—and Hobbes specifically uses the term—which establishes a polity in which power is vested in a single sovereign, in principle maintains this fundamental equality. Polities whose origins are covenantal reflect the exercise of constitutional choice and broad-based participation in constitutional design. Polities founded by covenant are essentially federal in character, in the original meaning of the term, whether they are federal in structure or not. That is to say, each polity is a matrix . . . compounded of equal confederates who freely bind themselves to one another so as to retain their respective integrities even as they are bound in a common whole.[14]

But what is the covenant through which individuals or groups choose to associate or combine themselves? Says Elazar, "A covenant is a morally informed agreement or pact based upon voluntary consent, established by mutual oaths or promises, involving or witnessed by some transcendent higher authority, between peoples or parties having independent status, equal in connection with the purposes of the pact, that provides for joint action or obligation to achieve defined ends . . . under conditions of mutual respect, which protect the individual integrities of all the parties to it." Covenant always involves "consenting . . . and promising."[15]

For Elazar, the organic model endemic in Greek political philosophy emphasizes natural, almost unconscious growth and development. Political association is not, on that model, brought into being by choice or consent. Over and against the organic model, the covenant model "expresses the idea that people can freely create communities and polities, peoples and publics, and civil society itself through such morally grounded and sustained compacts (whether religious or civil in impetus), establishing thereby enduring partnerships."[16] So, for Elazar, it's either classical Greek organicism or Jewish (and Reformed) covenantalism.[17] Aristotle and classical natural law belong in the former camp. Social contract theory and the American founders and framers belong in the latter. Just because the American founders and framers thought of the polis as created through covenants or compacts, they (by implication) rejected the classical Greek model.

To be sure, covenantal theorists (from the early Reformation through Hobbes and later) still used the language of natural law. But natural law was reconceived in light of the primacy accorded to the covenant idea: "The covenant idea, with its derivatives and cognates, offers a particular orientation to the great questions of politics in theory and practice. Perhaps the clearest indication of this special orientation is to be found in Thomas Hobbes's translation of the principles of natural law in what he called articles of peace, that is, the articles of the original covenant."[18] This idea of a conception of natural law radically revised in light of the priority of covenant appears in the earlier work of Charles S. McCoy and J. Wayne Baker. In what many consider their path-breaking *Fountainhead of Federalism*, McCoy and Baker note that for "federalists" (i.e., covenantal thinkers), "the created order is based on the covenant of God, so that the divine commandments permeate the nature of things. Federalism [i.e., covenantalism], therefore has its *lex naturae* in a manner similar to what can be found in the Scholastic tradition. *But this moral order in creation derives from the faithful will of God in covenant, not from some rational or natural rigidity at the core of reality.*"[19] Reflecting on the work of the Reformed syndic of Emden, Johannes Althusius, McCoy and Baker argue that although Althusius assumes "that the covenant of God in creation infuses the entire world with moral order," nevertheless "this order cannot be identified with a Stoic/scholastic law of nature, which societal law must seek to replicate."[20] The covenantal notion of natural law rejects "the scholastic reliance on rational insight into natural law."[21] Instead, on the covenantal (and social compact) account, "The law of nature rests on the *will* of God."[22]

Resting the law of nature on the will of God would seem to make the covenantal account of natural law an instance of ethical voluntarism and therefore self-referentially incoherent. Moreover, as I've noted in prior chapters, ethical voluntarism has often been linked to metaphysical nominalism. To be sure, there are those (perhaps Duns Scotus, for instance) who may have been metaphysical realists and ethical voluntarists.[23] That is, there have been some who are realists about essences, forms, and properties but who think ethical obligation (or most all ethical obligation) derives exclusively (or almost entirely) from divine prescription (Scotus seems to exempt the love of God from an otherwise voluntaristic account of ethics). On the other hand, if one affirms both nominalism and ethical obligation, the only possible account of obligation seems clearly to be the voluntaristic account (though that account is self-referentially incoherent). So voluntarism does not necessarily entail nominalism even if nominalism and obligation together entail voluntarism. Even so, some scholars note the tendency of these two things to go together (in Ockham and Hobbes, for instance).[24] Some scholars attribute the emergence of the covenantal model for human relations (including political relations) to late medieval nominalism. According to the great medievalist and early modern scholar Heiko Oberman, whom Elazar cites on this point, late medieval nominalism included "an emerging new image of God. . . . God is a covenant God, His *pactum* or *foedus* is his self-commitment to become the contractual partner in creation and salvation. . . . In the nominalist view man has become the appointed representative and partner of God, responsible for his own life, society, and world, on the basis of and within the limits of the treaty or *pactum* stipulated by God."[25]

Yet Elazar (following McCoy and Baker) rejects any essential connection of the covenant idea to nominalist (or antirealist) ontology: "The problem with the effort to seek a nominalist link in the covenantal chain is that while nominalist ideas of covenant were present in and some ways even pervasive early in the sixteenth century, its basis in the Pelagian doctrine of justification would not at all have appealed to Bullinger [author of the first major treatise on the covenant idea]. Moreover, Bullinger himself was educated in the *via antiqua*, while nominalism was considered the *via moderna*."[26] Elazar's argument concerning nominalism and the Pelagian doctrine of justification is problematic. Martin Luther adhered to the *via moderna* and was both a nominalist (or, in his words, a terminist) and a metaethical voluntarist, on the one hand, and anti-Pelagian, on the other.[27] Yet a kernel remains to be separated from the chaff. Bullinger, the modern fountainhead of the covenant idea, was educated in the *via antiqua*. And he makes claims about God's goodness (and the wisdom and goodness of God's commands) that are only intelligible on metaphysical and moral realism.[28]

Elazar's argument comes to this:

(1) Covenant as a model of political organization or as a ground of political order must be distinguished from the organic model of classical Greek philosophy (including Aristotle).

(2) The covenant idea is *not* committed to a nominalist ontology and perhaps not to a voluntaristic account of moral obligation either.

(3) Classical natural law belongs to the organic model of political organization and not to the covenantal model, which reconfigures natural law to account for the priority of covenant.

(4) In view of premises (1) through (3), there is the possibility of a covenant model of political organization wedded to metaphysical and moral realism that nevertheless rejects the organic model of political order Elazar attributes to Aristotle and Aquinas.

What then is the difference between the covenant and organic models? For Elazar, that difference may not consist in ontology as it does for Zuckert. Rather, the difference consists in distinguishing political orders or regimes that are made through consent from those that are simply imposed from the top down (as in the case of conquest) or that develop organically. Covenant belongs under the more general heading of deliberate political construction. The organic model rejects construction.

On Elazar's view, the American founders and framers embraced consent and construction in political organization and so rejected political organicism. Consequently they (as well as anyone who embraces consent and construction) rejected classical Greek political philosophy. For the purposes of analytic precision, let's call the thesis that frames covenant (or consent and political construction) and organicism (and classical Greek thought) as mutually exclusive but that also allows for the possibility that covenantalism embraces or at least is not hostile to ontological realism (or, conversely, that covenantalism is not essentially wed to voluntarism or nominalism or modern mechanistic philosophy, etc.) Elazar Covenantalism (or EC for short).

While I think EC is more nuanced and, indeed, provides a better account of covenantal political order than ZC, I maintain that both EC and ZC pose a false dichotomy. To see why, we must turn to that allegedly organicist theorist, Aristotle.

Aristotelian Political Theory: The Polis Is Natural but Not Organic

My argument in this section is that Aristotle does not advance the so-called organic model of political organization. But first we should consider why some might think Aristotle embraces the organicist model and rejects the covenant model. So far as I can tell, the primary reason Aristotle is considered an organicist is because he holds that human beings are by nature political animals and, concomitantly, that the polis exists by nature. The idea seems to be that something is either natural or artificial. If the polis is constructed or conventional, then it is not given by nature. Conversely, if the polis is given by nature, then it is not constructed.

Aristotle says that "the state [polis] belongs to the class of objects which exist by nature, and that man is by nature a political animal."[29] Moreover, the polis exists by nature as the terminus of a *natural* process of development: "The final association, formed of several villages, is the [polis]. For all practical purposes the process is now complete; self-sufficiency has been reached, and while the [polis] came about as a means of securing life itself, it continues in being to secure the *good* life. Therefore every [polis] exists by nature, as the earlier associations too were natural. This association is the end of those others, and nature is itself an end; for whatever is the end-product of the coming into existence of any object, that is what we call its nature, of a man, for instance, or a horse, or a household."[30] Finally, he claims that human beings are naturally impelled toward political association: "Among all men . . . there is a natural impulse towards this kind of association."[31]

In addition to his claim that the polis exists by nature, Aristotle also appears to reject covenant or agreement as the ground of political order: "Any polis which is truly so called, and is not merely one in name, must devote itself to the end of encouraging goodness. Otherwise, a political association sinks into a mere alliance, which only differs in space from other forms of alliance where the members live at a distance from one another. Otherwise, too, law becomes a mere covenant—or (in the phrase of the Sophist Lycophron) 'a guarantor of men's rights against one another'—instead of being, as it should, a rule of life such as will make the members of a polis good and just."[32] For Aristotle, a genuine polis aims to make citizens "good and just." An agreement to refrain from injuring each other is not enough.

Further, whereas social contract theory focuses on the preservation of individuals and securing individual rights—as the purpose of political association—Aristotle prioritizes the polis and the common good over individual advantage. Thus, "the [polis] has a natural priority over the household and over any individual among us. For the whole must be prior to the part. Separate hand or foot from the whole body, and they will no longer be hand or foot except in name, as one might speak of a 'hand' or 'foot' sculptured in stone. That will be the condition of the spoilt hand, which no longer has the capacity and function which define it. So, though we may say they have the same names, we cannot say that they are, in that condition the sane things. It is clear then that the [polis] is both natural and prior to the individual."[33] The common good for Aristotle is a corporate good (the good of our association together and not merely the good of each taken one at a time—though it is that too); the priority it enjoys is clearly normative. But on social contract theory, at least of the Hobbesian variety, the individual would appear to enjoy a normative priority such that political association is ordered to individual advantage (namely, preservation) rather than the other way around.

Finally, and most obviously, covenant and social contract theory posit human equality. Social contract theory is said to begin with the state of nature wherein individuals are claimed to have natural liberty and natural equality. Aristotle, by way of contrast, grounds authority in natural subordination. Aristotle famously says that "some things are so divided right from birth, some to rule, some to be ruled."[34] The idea seems clearly to be that ruled-ruler relations are founded in nature. Some are fitted by nature to rule, others fitted by nature to be ruled. And fitness to rule is determined by one's share in reason—those who possess a share in reason sufficient for ruling (sufficient for directing others) should rule. They have a title, claim, or right to it. Those who have only a share sufficient for being ruled (sufficient only for apprehending and following directions from others) should be ruled. They have a concomitant obligation. In keeping with natural subordination, Aristotle says that only "some are free" "by nature." For all that, there is some ambiguity in Aristotle's position. For instance, does he mean that the natural superiority of x over y is a necessary condition of x's right to rule y? Is it a sufficient condition? Is it both?

All the foregoing seems to redound to the conclusion that Aristotle embraces the organic model of political organization. But I maintain that Aristotle can plausibly understood as an organicist only if "natural" is equated with "organic." Aristotle clearly affirms that the polis is a natural whole. He also considers all organic wholes to be natural wholes (and paradigmatically so). But the argument that Aristotle is an organicist with respect to political association confuses genus with species. For while all organic wholes are natural wholes, not all natural wholes are organic wholes. So, from the claim that political association exists by nature or that it comes to be through a natural process, it *does not follow* that the polis is organic. As I suggested earlier, we can distinguish between *organic* natural wholes and *associational* natural wholes. But if the Aristotelian polis is natural but not organic, it follows that Aristotle is not *inherently* opposed to polities that are made or constructed through deliberation and choice. And it follows that Aristotelian political theory may be amenable to political societies constructed through consent.

Let's begin with my contention that Aristotle holds that the polis, though natural, is not an organic whole. I maintain that, for Aristotle, organic wholes can only be those entities that are a substantial unity of form and matter—a tree, a squirrel, an individual human being. But a polis is not a substance in the Aristotelian sense. Consequently, a polis cannot be an organic whole. Second, though at one level Aristotle describes the process by which the polis comes to be, his focus is on final causation. Consequently, when describing the development of human associational life from households to polis in book 1, chapter 2, of his *Politics*, Aristotle says little about the mechanism of efficient causation. The polis (or political association) is *natural* to human beings in the teleological sense that human beings cannot achieve well-being outside of a polis. Life in political association is necessary to and at least in part constitutive of human flourishing. The polis exists by nature in the sense that human nature (or essence) is naturally disposed to political life; and human beings are naturally disposed to political life in the sense that human essence cannot achieve its proper function or specific good without political association.[35] But this claim is entirely compatible with the claim that the polis is constructed or made *rather than* organic. Moreover, this claim—about the naturalness of political association and that human beings are political by nature—is compatible with the claim that polis is *made* by or through human consent. Indeed, taking these correlative claims by themselves (the polis exists by nature, and man is a political animal or political by nature), they are entirely consistent with the claim that consent is a necessary condition of legitimate authority. Let's call the claim that the polis exists by nature and that human beings are political animals (or by nature political) P_n. Let's call the claim that the polis is constructed or made *rather than* organic P_c. There is no formal contradiction between P_n and P_c. Indeed, I see no contradiction of any kind. Let's call the further claim of the covenantal model and social contract theory—that consent is a necessary condition of the political authority of some over others—C_n. There is no contradiction between P_n and C_n. There is certainly no formal contradiction. One can claim with logical consistency that human beings can only fulfill their proper function with excellence within political society and that consent is a necessary condition for some to exercise political authority over others. One has not fallen into incoherence by claiming both these things.[36]

I am not claiming that Aristotle would have been friendly to contractarianism. I am claiming that although he was committed to the notion that a polis is a natural whole, he did not reject the idea that political association is—or at least can be—made or constructed and that it can be constructed with deliberation and choice. Indeed, Aristotle's understanding of lawgivers stands in sharp contrast to the organic model of political organization. As Fred D. Miller notes, "Aristotle speaks of the lawgiver, i.e., politician, as a craftsman who shapes material (population and land) into a finished polis (see *Pol.* VII 4 1325ᵇ40–1326ᵃ5). He mentions Lycurgus and Solon as craftsmen of the constitutions of Sparta respectively (II 12 1273ᵇ32–3)."[37] A good lawgiver shapes a polis by giving it a good constitution—which is to say, by giving it a good form. The law*making* activity of the lawgiver stands in no tension with Aristotle's claim that the polis exists by nature and is natural to human beings, for that claim refers to final rather than efficient causation. The work of making, in general, and of the lawgiver (as conceived by Aristotle), in particular, belongs to the realm of efficient causation. Thus, immediately after saying that human beings have a "natural impulse towards" political association, he proposes that "the first man to *construct* a state deserves credit for conferring very great benefits."[38] Aristotle claims in one breath that political association is both natural and constructed without any sense of contradiction between these claims.

What about Aristotle's claim concerning the priority of the common good? According to Zuckert, and other contemporary proponents of social contract theory, contractarian thought focuses on protecting the rights of individuals (something he takes to be a distinctively modern concern).[39] But for Aristotle the common good (or the good of the whole) has a priority to the advantage of each individual. And the common good is corporate rather than the good of each, taken one at a time. Here I can only note that one committed to the proposition that political authority or legitimate government derives from the consent of the governed stands in no tension with the claim that the end or goal of political association is the common good (where the common good is not merely the good of each but also a corporate good). Indeed, I see no tension between the claim that the government exists to protect certain rights (even absolute rights) of individuals and that that the final cause of political association is the good of the whole. For if the common good is a metaphysically substantive notion, then it is at least a priori possible that the violation of certain fundamental rights of individuals always subverts the common good (or can never really be for it). Aristotle thought that all just regimes are ordered to the common good and that the good of the whole has a priority to the benefit or advantage of each part. He also held that justice is rendering to each person his or her due. And from the Aristotelian vantage there is no tension between those two claims. On Aristotle's view (1) we ought always render others that which is due them (goods should always be distributed to individuals based on what they merit),[40] and (2) the purpose of political association is the good of the whole—which trumps the benefit of each part.[41] At any rate, there is no more problem with positing the common good as the end of political association and affirming that individuals have certain rights that must never be violated than with Aristotle's claim that we ought always render individuals their due and that the common good has a priority to the benefit of each part.

But what about Aristotle's rejection of the conception of the polis as a "mere alliance" and of the conception of law as a "mere covenant" or a mere "guarantor of men's rights against one another"?[42] What of his claim that the polis "is not an association of people dwelling in the same place, established to prevent its members from committing injustice against each other, and to promote transactions"?[43] Are these statements not quite obviously rejections of the social compact or covenantal account of political association? I can't see how. Aristotle holds that none of these are enough for a polis. They are *insufficient*. But at least some of the things listed are *necessary*. Having said that a polis "is not an association of people dwelling in the same place, established to prevent its members from committing injustice against each other, and to promote transactions," he goes on to claim that "all these features must be present if there is to be a [polis]."[44] In other words, it seems rather apparent that Aristotle is distinguishing necessary and sufficient conditions. The necessary conditions for a polis *also* include the aim of political association toward the proper end— "living *well*" or "a perfect and self-sufficient life."[45] A state or polis is more than the elements listed in the contractarian account. Insofar as it restricts itself to those elements, a contractarian account (say that of Hobbes) is deficient. But political association is not less than those things. Indeed, at least some of those elements are necessarily included in a full-blown account of political order. But if the problem

with the contractarian account of the polis is that it specifies necessary conditions that are not yet sufficient for political association just
as such, it's very hard to see how there's anything like contradiction
here. One could even insist on the necessity of agreement and covenant for political authority, while holding that for the agreement to
produce a genuine *political* order, it must produce a regime concerned
with the virtue of its citizens.

This leaves us with one item—Aristotle's doctrine of natural inequality and natural subordination. I maintain that Aristotle's doctrine of natural subordination yields only a conditional that is most
likely something like this: if x has natural (political) authority over y,
then x is naturally superior to y. In this case, natural superiority is a
necessary rather than sufficient condition of the (political) authority
of x over y. But the Aristotelian doctrine may also be rendered as
follows: x has a natural right to rule over y (politically) *if and only if x*
is naturally superior to y. In this case, natural superiority is necessary
and sufficient for the right of one person to exercise political rule
over another. Though I think it unlikely, some may hold that the
Aristotelian doctrine is this (and only this): if x is naturally superior
to y, then x possesses natural authority (or a natural right) to exercise
political rule over y. In that case natural superiority is sufficient for
the authority of one person over another but neither necessary nor
both necessary and sufficient.

Notice how the first two arguments are compatible with consent
or social contract theory. For the social contract theorist might
well subscribe to either of those conditionals and simply deny the
consequent—no person x is naturally superior to any person y because
all persons are naturally equal. Given modus tollens, this would entail
a denial of the antecedent: no person x has natural, political authority
over any person y (or there is no instance such that any person x has
natural, political authority over any person y). It may be the case that
Aristotle affirmed the antecedent and the consequent in the first two
conditionals. But rejection of the consequent and therefore of the antecedent seems consistent with his political theory (Aristotle would
then be factually but not theoretically wrong).

But what if his claim is that the natural superiority of x to y is
sufficient for x to exercise political authority over y? This would be a

strange claim. One would think that there must be other conditions for x to rule y (like x and y reside in the same territory, and y is not already subject to z, etc.). In that case, we're back to the claim that natural superiority is necessary but not sufficient for political rule. For the sake of argument let's ignore these other conditions. Even if Aristotle stipulates a sufficient condition (that is, makes the natural superiority of x to y the antecedent of the conditional) and even if Aristotle affirms the antecedent, on what he considers the merits, one could nevertheless hold (consistent with Aristotle's larger theory) that he is wrong about that. In other words, one could refuse to affirm the antecedent in the conditional. Now, negation of the antecedent does *not* entail negation of the consequent; that would be to commit the fallacy of denying the antecedent. Even so, if we refrain from affirming the antecedent, then the consequent does not follow from it. If there is no other premise (or no other sound proposition) that entails the consequent, then it does not follow at all (though this returns us to the claim that natural superiority is necessary and sufficient for the political authority of some over others). And I judge that one might—consistent with the rest of Aristotle's political theory—refrain from affirming the antecedent and maintain that there is no other true proposition that entails the consequent.

Or, one might simply reject what Aristotle says about natural subordination and hold that it bears no essential relation to the rest of his political theory. One might hold that Aristotle was wrong to suggest there are or might be natural slaves but that what he says about the priority of the common good or the naturalness of political association is spot on. In this case, though there is a real conflict between Aristotle's conception of natural subordination and covenantal or social compact thought, there is no contradiction between the rest of Aristotle's political theory and covenant or political contractarianism.

In support of the foregoing, consider this passage: "Among those who are equal and alike, it is neither just nor expedient that one man should be sovereign over all the rest, whether he rule with laws or without (he himself then being law instead), or whether he is a good man ruling over good men, or not-good over not-good; nor even if he is superior in virtue—except in some circumstances."[46] What Aristotle says here about one man would seem to apply to a few (i.e., to aristocracy) as well. This passage seems clearly to entail that human equality rules out or negates natural authority. Now, Aristotle does not take such equality to entail the contractarian or covenantal claim that consent is a necessary condition of the political authority of some over others. Rather, natural equality suggests that individuals should rule and be ruled in turn.[47] But natural human equality does not obviously entail taking turns ruling and being ruled rather than direct democracy or rather than covenant or social compact. Minimally, we can, I think, extract this proposition: Insofar as human beings are naturally equal, then the authority of some over others is *not given by nature*. Early modern contractarians, though rejecting Aristotle and Scholasticism at many points, embrace something very much like this proposition.

I conclude that Zuckert and Elazar make arguments that turn on an unsound dichotomization of *natural* and *made*. This is a necessary premise in their framing of the founding. But the premise seems clearly false.

Classical Christianity and Political Contractarianism: Concord

Social contract theorists usually affirm the proposition that humans are naturally equal. Some scholars insist that the ideas of natural equality and natural liberty are distinctly modern ideas that help mark off the modern turn.[48] The ancients and medievals, we are often told, subscribed to the notion of natural inequality. While there seems to be no doctrine of natural equality in classical Greek or Roman political philosophy, the doctrine makes its appearance in ancient and medieval Christian writers—and, indeed, in ancient Christian writers who subscribed to some variant or other of classical metaphysics (or who, at any rate, in no way affirmed any of the propositions central to variants of modern philosophy).[49]

In his *Divine Institutes*, Lactantius (tutor to Constantine the Great's son) writes,

The second constituent part of justice is *equality*. I mean this not in the sense of "equity," the virtue of giving judgment, praiseworthy as this is in a just man, but in the sense of treating others as one's equals—what Cicero calls "equability." For God who

gives being and life to men wished us all to be equal, that is,
alike. He laid down the same terms of life for us all, making
us capable of wisdom and promising us immortality, excluding
nobody from the benefits of heaven. And so, as he gives us all a
place in the daylight, waters the earth for us all, provides nour-
ishment and precious relaxing sleep, *no less does he endow us all
with moral equality. With him there is no slave or master.* Since we
all have the same father, *so we are all alike his freeborn children.*
No one is poor in his eyes, except for want of justice; no one is
rich except in moral qualities. No one is prominent, except in
being incorruptible; no one is famous, except for works of mercy
performed on a grand scale; no one has the title "Excellency"
without accomplishing all the stages of moral growth.[50]

Excoriating those who pursue wealth and gain for the sake of acquir-
ing more, Ambrose of Milan thunders,

How far can you take this mad acquisitiveness, you rich? Will
you make yourselves the only inhabitants of the earth? Why
grasp at nature's possessions, and keep nature's companions at
bay? The earth was created for all in common, rich and poor
alike. Why arrogate to yourselves a sole and exclusive right?
Nature knows no rich men, she makes us all poor at birth. We
are born without clothing, given life without gold and silver. We
are brought forth naked to the light, in need of food, clothing,
and drink. And naked as it produced us the earth receives us
back, and can accommodate no broad landholdings in the grave.
The narrower covering of turf is room enough for poor and rich
alike; clay, which had no hold on the rich man's affections while
he lived, holds the whole of him at last. *Nature makes no distinctions*, either when we are born or when we die. *It creates us all
equals*, as equals it enfolds us all in the grave's embrace. Who can
tell the classes of dead men apart?[51]

Gregory I synthesizes the foregoing claims of natural equality with
the Augustinian claim that mastery and servitude are products of the
fall rather than given by nature:

It is clear that *nature produced all men equal*; but, through variation in the order of their merits, guilt puts some below others. But the very diversity which has accrued from vice is ordered by divine judgment, so that, since all men cannot stand on an equal footing, one should be ruled by another. *Hence all who are over others ought to consider in themselves not the authority of their rank, but the equality of their condition*, and rejoice not to be over men, but to do them good. For indeed our ancient fathers are said to have been not kings of men, but shepherds of flocks. And when the Lord said to Noah and his children: "Increase and multiply, and replenish the earth" (Gen. 9:1), he at once added, "And let the fear of you and the dread of you be upon all the beasts of the earth." Thus it appears that, whereas it is ordered that the fear and the dread should be upon the beasts of the earth, it is forbidden that it should be upon men. *For man is by nature preferred to the brute beasts, but not to other men*: and therefore it is said to him that he should be feared by the beasts, but not by men; since to wish to be feared by one's equal is to be proud against nature.[52]

The foregoing Patristic and early medieval statements on natural equality cannot be equated with social contract theory or the claim that government derives its just powers from the consent of the governed. Nevertheless, they necessarily entail that political authority cannot be grounded in *natural* subordination. And they reject this claim of natural inequality without moving in the direction of modern metaphysics or modern moral and political philosophy.

Granting that early Christian thought, usually steeped in classical metaphysics, frequently posited natural equality, one might rightly wonder if it also posited that the polis or political life is natural to man. The first humans, say Gregory and Augustine, were "shepherds of flocks" and not "kings of men." This sounds like political association and government are a product of the fall rather than of the created, natural order. Be that as it may, there is nothing in what they say that is also opposed to the claim that political association is natural. Thomas Aquinas was persuaded both that human beings are social and political by nature, such that they cannot flourish outside of political society, and that human beings are by nature equal.

Indeed, as Aquinas saw it, human equality imposes practical limits on human authority:

> Nevertheless, man is bound to obey his fellowman in things that have to be done externally by means of the body; yet, *since by nature all men are equal*, he is not bound to obey another man in matters touching the nature of the body, for instance, in those relating to sustenance of his body and the begetting of children. Wherefore slaves are not bound to obey their masters, nor children their parents, in the matter of contracting marriage or of remaining in the state of virginity or the like. But in matters concerning the disposal of actions and human affairs, a subject is bound to obey his superior within the sphere of his authority.[53]

I am not suggesting that, when it comes to political order, Saint Thomas's thought is proto-modern. I mean only to underscore his affirmation of three claims: (1) life in political association is natural to human beings as such—that is, human beings cannot attain well-being outside of or without political association; (2) human persons are by nature equal; and (3) human equality imposes jurisdictional limits on the exercise of authority. Just because human beings are naturally equal, there are some ways in which no person can rightly command another (as to whether to marry or to have children). And this means human equality is of some import for political order—not just for prelapsarian humanity.

As with natural equality, the notions of natural liberty and of the state of nature arise before Thomas Hobbes and the so-called social contract tradition and arise in metaphysical contexts quite other than those resulting from the modern turn. I should first like to take up the late medieval and early modern Thomists (and primarily those in the Salamancan school). In what follows I draw substantially (but not exclusively) on Quentin Skinner's argument in the second volume of *The Foundations of Modern Political Thought*. Having looked at some salient passages, I will then turn to thinkers thoroughly grounded in classical thought and yet committed to covenant and consent: Johannes Althusius and the Anglican divine Richard Hooker.

According to Skinner, Luis de Molina "refers at several points to the condition of man '*in statu naturae*', and he imagines the '*status naturae*' as that situation in which all men may be said to have found themselves after the Fall and before the inauguration of political societies." According to Skinner, "The basic assertion which the Thomists make about this original or natural condition is that it must be pictured as a state of freedom, equality and independence." He cites Domingo de Soto's claim that "all men are born free by nature." Likewise, he records Suárez's contention that "in the nature of things all men are born free." Suárez adds that "no one man can ever be said in the nature of things to possess any power greater than the power of anyone else." In addition to the foregoing, Skinner notes Molina's claim that "the *status naturae* includes no right of dominion" and Suárez's affirmation (here quoting Suárez) that "since all men are in the nature of things born free, it follows that no one person has political jurisdiction over any other, just as no one person can be said to have dominion over anyone else."[54] When Sidney and Locke later affirmed natural liberty, they did so in order to reject Sir Robert Filmer's denial of it. Sir Filmer's denial of natural liberty was, in turn, an explicit rejection of Bellarmine's and Suárez's affirmation of it (a point about which Sidney was forthright).[55]

To return to the Salamancans, as I noted in the first chapter, they affirmed that life in the *status naturae* would be chaotic, discordant, conflictual, bereft of those goods requisite to human flourishing, one in which individuals would always be vulnerable to the predations of others and possess no means of redress. Life in such a state would be miserable due to human selfishness and the fall. According to Molina, "It is . . . easy . . . to ignore many aspects of morality and to be uncertain of many others" because "of our loss of innocence." According to Suárez, "Ordinary men find it difficult to understand what is necessary for the common good, and hardly ever make any attempt to pursue it themselves." Human life in this condition, he adds, would lack "the offices and arts necessary for human life" and be "without any means of gaining a knowledge of all the things we would need to understand." Moreover, "families would become divided amongst themselves." Consequently, "peace could scarcely be preserved amongst men," "no injuries could be properly averted or avenged," and "each private individual will be concerned only with his own private advantage, which will often be opposed to the common good." Thus, "for lack of any power to govern such a community" the *status naturae* would be one of "total confusion."[56]

Given natural freedom and equality, Skinner's "later Thomists" had to posit some mechanism by which legitimate political society is brought into existence. They had to answer, he writes, "the question of how it is possible for the change from a situation of natural liberty to the constraints of political society to be legitimately made." The answer: "The concept of consent is thus invoked by all these writers in order to explain how it is possible for a free individual to become the subject of a legitimate commonwealth."[57] Yet the evidence he adduces for this claim in the preceding paragraph all seems refer to corporate or communal consent to choose rulers or authorize government rather than individual consent.[58] Be that as it may, the later Thomists that come before Hobbes outline the idea of the state of nature together with the constitutive ideas of natural equality and natural liberty before these ideas make their appearance in his work. Moreover, as Daniel Schwartz argues, Suárez can certainly be read to posit "two different acts of consent: the individual's consent to constitute a political community ('constitutive consent') and the community's consent required by a would-be ruler to hold office."[59]

Skinner also emphasizes two qualifications that later Thomists made concerning the state of nature and natural liberty. First, "These writers circumscribe their commitment to the idea of man's natural condition as one of complete freedom and independence. They insist . . . that in describing this condition as one in which there would be no positive laws, they are by no means implying that it would be a state of pure lawlessness. They maintain on the contrary that the state of nature would be governed at all times by a genuine law." Thus Molina "stresses [that] the law of nature is equally available and known to all men in every condition in which they find themselves." Suárez "declares that this law is known to all mankind as 'a single law at all times and in every state of human nature.' . . . 'It derives not from any particular state in which human nature is found, but rather from the essence of that nature itself.' " Second, the *status naturae* would never be "a solitary or a purely individual state." Later Thomists "specifically attack the stoic belief—which Cicero had defended and a large number of humanists had more recently espoused—that men began as solitary wanderers before the formation of civil society." According to Skinner, "All the Thomists" rejected "the suggestion that man in his original condition must have lived a life of individual solitude" because that view "embodies a mistaken view of human nature." Rather, they considered it "inherent in human nature to live a social and communal life."[60]

So the later Thomists all affirm the Aristotelian-Thomistic position that human beings are social by nature (and, indeed, that they cannot live well outside of society), while describing a pre-political (though not pre-social) state they call the state of nature and while affirming natural equality and the natural freedom of individuals. And they all insist that political society is brought into existence by human willing. That is, they hold that political association is made, rather than organic. The dichotomy with which we began—whether framed by Zuckert or Elazar—does not appear in these theorists. The same can be said for Hooker and Althusius.

When it comes to moral philosophy, Richard Hooker rather clearly affirms the Thomist position or something very close to it. He affirms the natural law and grounds it in classical metaphysics.[61] Hooker is a natural law theorist who is both a metaphysical and moral realist. But Hooker also posits human equality, has the concept (without using the language) of the state of nature, and, I submit, insists on individual consent (or the consent of the heads of families) for the original establishment of the political authority of some individuals over others (though I think his argument on this front has implications that reach beyond the original establishment of civil society). Speaking of natural law, Hookers says,

> The laws which have been hitherto mentioned, do bind men absolutely, even as they are men, *although they have never any settled fellowship, never any solemn agreement amongst themselves what to do or not to do.* But forasmuch as we are not by ourselves sufficient to furnish ourselves with competent store of things needful for such a life as our nature doth desire, a life fit for the dignity of man: therefore *to supply those defects and imperfections, which are*

*in us living, single, and solely by ourselves, we are naturally induced
to seek communion and fellowship with others. This was the cause of
men's uniting themselves at the first politic societies,* which societies
could not be without government, nor government without a
distinct kind of law from that which hath been already declared.
Two foundations there are which bear up public societies, the
one, *a natural inclination, whereby all men desire sociable life and
fellowship,* the other *an order expressly or secretly [i.e., tacitly] agreed
upon, touching the manner of their union in living together.* The
latter is that which we call the law of a commonweal, the very
soul of a politic body, the parts whereof are by law animated,
held together, and set on work in such actions as the common
good requireth.[62]

So here we have the Aristotelian ideas that the common good is the
end or goal of political association, that human beings are naturally
inclined to political society, and that human beings cannot live well
(but only deficiently) without political society (i.e., political society
is necessary for human well-being), together with the concept of the
state of nature and the idea of societies established by agreement—
either tacit or express.

The following passage implies the concept of the state of nature
even more clearly:

We all complain of the iniquity of our times: not unjustly; for
the days are evil. But *compare them with those times, wherein there
were no civil societies, with those times wherein there was as yet no
manner of public regiment established* . . . and we have surely good
cause to think God hath blessed us exceedingly, and hath made
us behold most happy days. *To take away all such mutual grievances, injuries, and wrongs, there was no way, but only by growing
unto composition and agreement amongst themselves, by ordaining
some kind of government public, and by yielding themselves subject thereunto, that unto whom they granted authority to rule and
govern, by them the peace, tranquility, and happy estate of the rest
might be procured.* Men always knew that when force and injury
was offered, they might be defenders of themselves; they knew

that howsoever men may seek their own commodity, yet if this were done with injury unto others, it was not to be suffered, but by all men and by all good means to be withstood; finally *they knew that no man might in reason take upon him to determine his own right, and according to his own determination proceed in maintenance thereof, inasmuch as every man is towards himself and them whom he greatly affecteth partial; and therefore that strifes and troubles be endless, except they gave their common consent all to be ordered by some whom they should agree upon: without which consent, there were not reason, that one man should take upon him to be Lord or Judge over another;* because although there be according to the opinions of some very great and judicious men a kind of natural right in the noble, wise, and virtuous, to govern them which are of servile disposition; nevertheless for manifestation of this their right, and men's more peaceable contentment on both sides, *the assent of them who are to be governed, seemeth necessary.*[63]

Here, in Hooker—prior to Locke, prior to Hobbes—are the main lineaments of Lockean social contract theory. He speaks of the natural moral law that binds human persons as human persons even if there is "never any settled fellowship" or "solemn agreement" among them. He says we seek "communion" or society with others in order "to supply those defects and imperfections, which are in us living, single, and solely by ourselves." *And*, in concurrence with Aristotle, he says the "natural inclination" to seek "fellowship with others" "was the cause of men's uniting themselves at the first politic societies." In other words, political societies were created by human beings seeking social life in order to remedy the defects of individuals living "single, and solely by ourselves." In order to exit the condition of living "solely by ourselves" and to escape the deficiencies of that condition, individuals "expressly or secretly" agree to establish an "order" "touching the manner of their union in living together." In the second passage Hooker speaks of "those times" in which "there were no civil societies" or "public regiment" (i.e., no government). The "grievances, injuries, and wrongs" of life in that condition, however, could not be "taken away" without the establishment of government. Individuals seeking to establish government do so by means of "composition and agreement amongst themselves." To establish government, they tender their consent—"without which consent, there were not reason, that one man should take upon himself to be Lord or Judge of another." This passage speaks rather clearly of individual consent. And Hooker seems clearly to stipulate that this consent is a necessary condition of the political authority of some human persons over others ("the assent of them who are to be governed, seemeth necessary").[64]

The foregoing passages seem to make quite clear why Locke invoked Hooker in *The Second Treatise*. And yet, precisely because of the Aristotelian and Thomistic elements of Hooker's thought, some insist that Locke's invocation of Hooker was insincere. Hooker, they say, lacked any conception of the state of nature.[65] Thomas Pangle, for instance, says Locke was fully aware of the strangeness of his "particular version of the state of nature" and that many would find it objectionable. " 'Tis often asked as a mighty Objection," Locke writes, "*Where are*, or ever were, there any *men in such* a *State of Nature?*" Now Pangle:

> By quoting the "Judicious Hooker," the greatest political theorist of the established church and the direct Anglican heir to Thomas Aquinas's synthesis of Aristotle and the Bible, Locke claims to demonstrate that his doctrine of the state of nature derives from the most authoritative and patriotic interpreter of both Christianity and classical political philosophy. In other words, immediately after drawing attention to the alien character of his teaching, Locke loudly asserts its familiar and traditional origin.
>
> This invocation of Hooker has always proven enormously successful in establishing Locke's credentials with most readers as a pious and relatively conservative English gentleman. Yet attentive or questioning readers, once they recover from the barrage of authority and poke their heads up out of the trenches, must ask just where it is in Hooker's text that one discovers an endorsement of anything like the state of nature Locke has been describing. For surely there is nothing of the kind in the passage Locke here adduces, nor in the lengthy passage he quoted a few sections previously (II 5). And when one refers to the whole of the *Laws of Ecclesiastical Polity* one finds that Hooker never so much as mentions, let alone embraces, the concept of the state of

nature. On the contrary: in the very passages Locke quotes, one sees—once one reads them for what they actually say (and restores them to their original contexts)—that Hooker, following his teachers Thomas and Aristotle, is insisting that man's natural condition is that of a being dwelling in, or "naturally induced to seek," "Politick Societies." Hooker teaches that human existence (since the Fall of Adam) outside of political society, or prior to it, is existence in an unnatural state.[66]

Here we are quite clearly dealing with the dichotomy—one that I've suggested is false—that appeared in Zuckert and Elazar (their profound differences notwithstanding). Hooker insists that political association is natural to human beings. Man is "naturally induced to seek" political society. And Pangle takes this to entail that human life "outside political society" is unnatural. So the state of nature of social contract theorists such as Locke is unnatural to Hookerian individuals.

What are we to make of Pangle's argument? As Nicholas Wolterstorff asks, "Was it really deceptive of Locke to cite this passage from Hooker in support of his position?" I concur entirely with Wolterstorff's reply to Pangle:

I judge that Locke was indeed justified in believing that he found his idea of the state of nature in the Hooker passage. The laws of nature bind men, says Hooker, even though they never had any solemn agreement among themselves as to what to do and what not to do. Living without any solemn agreement among themselves—and thus perforce living without any executive to enforce that solemn agreement—is exactly what Locke means by living in a state of nature. Nowhere in all his writings, says Pangle, does Hooker use the term *state of nature*. I take his word for that. The idea can be present without the term being used.

But suppose Locke disagreed with Hooker's statement at the end of the passage that "we are naturally induced to seek communion and fellowship with others." Would it then be deceptive on his part to quote Hooker as he does? Locke's claim that some people live in the state of nature with respect to each

other carries no implications, one way or the other, as to what it
is that induces human beings to seek communion and fellowship
with each other. To say it again: On Locke's concept of the state
of nature, for two or more people to live in a state of nature with
respect to each other is just for there to be no executive authority
over them to enforce laws or compacts.[67]

If we read Hooker beyond the short passage cited by Locke, I think
the wrongness of Pangle's claim—that the idea of the state of nature
is nowhere present in Hooker—is more apparent. I also think it's
worth underscoring Wolterstoff's point that the concept of the state
of nature (or the Lockean version) "carries no implications, one way
or the other," as to why human beings seek to leave it. Locke lists reasons for which people leave it (certain "inconveniencies").[68] Locke's
"inconveniencies" sound remarkably similar to Hooker's "defects
and imperfections" (especially as recounted in the second passage).
So perhaps Locke gives us a proximate cause as to why people seek
to leave the state of nature. But there is no contradiction of any of
Locke's claims about the state of nature, the inconveniencies of that
state, and the fact that people leave it by consent or agreement that
yields a formal contradiction (or any other sort of contradiction) with
the claim that individuals are naturally induced to seek communion
with others in political societies.[69] That they leave the state of nature
(or give up natural liberty) only by consent is entirely compatible
with the claim that they are disposed or moved to do so by a natural
impulsion.

This brings me, finally, to Johannes Althusius. At the commencement of his *Politica methodice digesta* (*Politica* henceforth), Althusius
describes the political art in Aristotelian terms: "Politics is the art of
associating (*consociandi*) men for the purpose of establishing, cultivating, and conserving social life among them. Whence it is called
'symbiotics.' " To this he adds a covenantal wrinkle: "The subject
matter of politics is therefore association (*consociatio*), in which the
symbiotes pledge themselves each to the other, by explicit or tacit
agreement, to mutual communication of whatever is useful and necessary for the harmonious exercise of social life." Having claimed that
politics appertains to the cultivation of social life, Althusius proceeds

to give an Aristotelian justification of political association: "The end of political 'symbiotic' man is holy, just, comfortable, and happy symbiosis [living together], a life lacking nothing either necessary or useful." Concomitantly, human well-being requires political association: "Truly, in living this life no man is self-sufficient (αὐτάρκης), or adequately endowed by nature. For when he is born, destitute of all help, naked and defenseless, as if having lost all his goods in a shipwreck, he is cast forth into the hardships of this life, not able by his own efforts to reach a maternal breast, nor to endure the harshness of his condition, nor to move himself from the place where he was cast forth." Though in fact impossible, Althusius considers arguendo the case in which someone is born and manages to survive "well nourished in body" *without* human society. Even in that case, such a one "cannot show forth the light of reason." Human rationality requires human association. Moreover, the radical dependency of newborn and the young continues into adulthood: "Nor in his adulthood is he able to obtain in and by himself those outward goods he needs for a comfortable and holy life, or to provide by his own energies all the requirements of life." Consequently, "as long as he remains isolated and does not mingle in the society of men, he cannot live at all comfortably and well while lacking so many necessary and useful things. As an aid and remedy for this state of affairs is offered him in symbiotic life, he is led, and almost impelled, to embrace it if he wants to live comfortably and well, even if he merely wants to live."[70] Althusius also notes the responsibility of those who govern: "It pertains to the office of a governor not only to preserve something unharmed, but also to lead it to its end."[71] And this entails that government, rightly conceived, tends to "both the soul and the body" of those over whom rule is exercised.[72] Finally, Althusius affirms Aristotle's twin claims that human beings are by nature political and that political association exists by nature: "Aristotle teaches that man by his nature is brought to this social life and mutual sharing." Indeed, "man is a more political animal than the bee or any other gregarious creature, and therefore by nature far more of a social animal than bees, ants, cranes, and such kind as feed and defend themselves in flocks." "No man is able to live well and happily to himself," he writes; "necessity therefore induces association. . . . For this reason it is evident that the commonwealth, or civil society, exists by nature, and that man is by nature a civil animal who strives eagerly for association."[73]

For Althusius political association is natural to man as such. And he adopts the teleological position that human beings cannot live well outside of or without political association. At the same time he claims that human association is constructed or made. Indeed, it is the product of human agreement or consent. He conjoins both these claims by appropriating the Aristotelian causal schema: "The efficient cause of political association is consent and agreement among the communicating citizens," while "the final cause of politics is the enjoyment of a comfortable, useful, and happy life, and of the common welfare."[74] Althusius thus identifies the principle of consent with efficient causality while adopting the Aristotelian position concerning the final cause of political association. So doing, he conceives a frame in which covenant and Aristotelian political theory lie down together in peace. Concord, not conflict (to borrow Plantinga's turn of phrase).

Althusius's claim about the efficient cause of political association might (at least prima facially) be taken as a claim about the consent of *individuals* to political association. But Althusius's position is more complex. Individuals consent (or covenant) to form or join private associations—families and collegia. Families and collegia consent (or covenant) to form the first level of political association—the city. He writes, "The community is an association formed by fixed laws and composed of many families and collegia living in the same place. It is elsewhere called a city (*civitas*) in the broadest sense, or a body of many and diverse associations. . . . It [the city] is called a representational person and represents men collectively, not individually." Again, "The members of a community are private and diverse associations. These persons, by their coming together, now become not spouses, kinsmen, and colleagues, but citizens of the same community."[75] Political association is formed by the consent of prior (private) associations, which were themselves created by the consent or agreement of their members.

As a covenantal or federal theorist, Althusius is firmly committed to the doctrine of popular sovereignty—which is distinct from his insistence on the consent either of individuals or of prior associations to the establishment of political order. Popular sovereignty is the idea that the community (as a corporate entity) possesses authority over those who exercise rule. As Althusius puts it, "The superior is the prefect of the community appointed by the consent of the citizens. He directs the business of the community, and governs on behalf of its welfare and advantage, exercising authority (*jus*) over the individuals but not over the citizens collectively."[76] A few sentences later he writes, "Such a superior is either one or more persons who have received the power of governing by the consent of the community. . . . And so these general administrators of the community are appointed by the city out of its general and free power, and can even be removed from office by the city."[77]

The city constitutes only the first level of political (or public) association. The province is the second level of political association. But the most comprehensive level ("the universal and major public association") is called the realm or commonwealth: "In this association many cities and provinces obligate themselves to hold, organize, use, and defend, through their common energies and expenditures, the right of the realm (*jus regni*) in the mutual communication of things and services." Universal association is a "mixed society, constituted partly from private, natural, necessary, and voluntary societies" and "partly from public societies." Universal association "is a polity in the fullest sense, an imperium, realm, commonwealth, and people united in one body by the agreement of many symbiotic associations and particular bodies and brought together under one right. *For families, cities, and provinces existed by nature prior to realms, and gave birth to them.*"[78] Notice that Althusius says families, cities, and provinces "existed by nature." What is not clear in this statement, but clear from the rest of the work, is that each of these was also made or created. Moreover, consent constituted a necessary condition for the creation of these. The consent of individuals (at least with respect to marriage) formed a necessary condition of families. The consent of families and collegia was a necessary condition for the formation of cities. And so on. There is not the slightest sense of any tension between the two claims that each of these exists by nature and that each was created by voluntary agreement. The reason for this has to do with the fact that the primary sense of "natural" in the claim that political association exists by nature refers to final rather than efficient causation.

Likewise, there is no tension between the claims that the purpose of political association is the common good (or the public welfare) and the claim that public authority is established only by consent.

Let's return briefly to sovereignty and universal public association. At the beginning of his discussion Althusius claims that "ownership of a realm belongs to the people."[79] In the case of a monarchy, *administration* of the realm may belong to a king. But the king does not (and cannot) own the realm. A few pages later Althusius speaks of the "right of the realm," also called "the right of sovereignty." He contrasts the right of the realm "with the right that is attributed to a city or province." And he says that "the universal power of ruling (*potestas imperandi universalis*) is called that which recognizes no ally, nor any superior or equal to itself. . . . this supreme right of universal jurisdiction is the form and substantial essence of sovereignty (*majestas*)."[80]

The *realm* possesses sovereign power. But we must be careful to ascertain just what this means. First, the "right of sovereignty, does not belong to individual members, but to all members joined together and to the entire associated body of the realm." Put another way, "the people rules each citizen."[81] Second, those individuals who administer the government of the realm (those who exercise rule) "are not themselves in control of the supreme power."[82] This ties to the previous claim—namely, that ownership of the realm belongs to the people (which is to say, *not* to officials). In other words, Althusius espouses a doctrine of the authority of the community over government. There is no power of the state (of the realm or commonwealth) that transcends the community or that is sovereign with respect to it. Government (and the state) are but delegates and servants of the people—of the society—that owns the realm. Third, there is no political power (even of the people) that is absolute. The reason for this is that absolute power (meaning, almost certainly, *potestas absoluta*—given that there is an intelligible, non-Ockhamist sense of *potentia absoluta* employed by Albert and Thomas) is unjust.

In his rejection of absolute power, Althusius contends that "by absolute power justice is destroyed." Further, "Absolute power is wicked and prohibited. We cannot do what can only be done injuriously. Thus even almighty God is said not to be able to do what is evil and contrary to his nature." This he follows with the claim that "the precepts of natural law (*jus naturale*) are to 'live honorably, injure no one, and render to each his due.' *Law is also an obligation by which both prince and subject are bound.*"[83] Using Aristotelian terminology for natural law (and citing a passage from Saint Paul's Epistle to the Romans that Hooker also invokes), Althusius says,

> Common law (*lex communis*) has been naturally implanted by God in all men. "Whatever can be known about God has been manifested to men, because God has made it manifest to them." As to knowledge (*notitia*) and inclination (*inclinatio*), God discloses and prescribes the reason and means for worshipping him and loving one's neighbor, and urges us to them. "For there was reason derived from the nature of the universe," Cicero says, "urging men to do right and recalling them from wrong-doing and this reason did not first become law at the time it was written down, but at its origin." It is commonly called the moral law (*lex moralis*).

Following the traditional conception of natural law, Althusius also affirms that conscience is "the knowledge [of the moral law] imprinted within us by God." By means of conscience "man knows and understands law (*jus*) and the means to be employed or avoided for maintaining obedience to law." Indeed, "By this innate inclination, or secret impulse of nature, man is urged to perform what he understands to be just, and to avoid what he knows to be wicked."[84]

So Althusius holds that (1) human beings are political (and social) by nature and, concomitantly, political association exists by nature. By this he means to affirm the Aristotelian claim that human beings cannot live well—cannot flourish or attain well-being—outside of or without political association. Political association is a necessary and constitutive condition of human well-being. He also holds (2) a rather traditional (Aristotelian-Thomistic) conception of natural law (rather than an Ockhamist or voluntaristic conception of it) and of the priority of natural law to the commands of rulers such that commands contrary to natural and divine law lose their power to bind.[85] Finally, he maintains that (3) political association, though natural, is made or created by private associations covenanting together to

create it. Consent, he says, is the efficient cause of political association. He links this claim to popular sovereignty: "the people is
prior in time and more worthy by nature than its magistrate, and has
constituted him. And so no realm or commonwealth has ever been
founded or instituted except by contract entered into one with the
other, by covenants agreed upon between subjects and their future
prince, and by an established obligation that both should religiously
observe." Popular sovereignty places restrictions on the power of rulers (or magistrates). Thus, "When this obligation is dishonored, the
power of the prince loses its strength and is ended."[86] The respective
positions of Zuckert and Elazar discussed at the beginning of this
chapter require showing that (1), (2), and (3) are mutually exclusive
such that no person could (intelligibly) affirm all three. That requires
showing some contradiction of holding (3) together with (1) or with
(2), or with (1) and (2) together. No one has yet done any such thing.
And the argument that covenant or compact address *how* political
association comes to be (efficient causality) rather than *what* it is (its
quidditas or formal cause) or *why* it exists (its telos or final cause)
demonstrates that no contradiction in fact exists.

Conclusion

With the above distinctions in hand, it becomes clear that there is
no formal contradiction between Aristotelian political theory (the
objective reality and priority of the common good, human beings as
political by nature, the polis as existing by nature) or classical natural
law (wedded to moral and metaphysical realism), on the one hand,
and covenant or consent (natural equality, political order as made
rather than given by nature or organic, consent or agreement as a
necessary condition of the political authority of some over other), on
the other. The relation between these is not one of conflict. It's possible that human equality necessitates consent for political authority
and obligations and that political order is necessary for human beings
qua human to attain well-being. If so, then the relation would seem
to be one of concord rather than conflict.

CHAPTER 8

The Essential Dependence of Government by Consent on Natural Law

Introduction

AS WE SAW IN THE preceding chapter, prominent scholars argue that covenant (or social contract theory) and classical natural law (or natural right—to wit, classical moral and metaphysical realism) are mutually opposed and exclusive models of political organization.[1] Such theorists essentially argue for this disjunct: either classical natural law (more generally, either moral and metaphysical realism) or the covenantal model of political organization, social contract theory, and the necessity of consent for political authority and obligations. Over and against this regnant dichotomy, I have argued that these are not actually mutually opposed. There is no formal or metaphysical or any other sort of contradiction between classical natural law and a model of political organization that posits the necessity of consent for some persons to exercise political authority over others or one that posits the authority of society over government. In this chapter I wish to extend the argument one step further. Herein, drawing together lines of argument from ground we've previously covered (and therefore traversing again but also rearranging some of that topography), I argue that any intelligible theory of consent (or covenant or social contract) *must* be grounded upon moral and metaphysical realism. Put another way (and a bit more formally), classical natural law (moral and metaphysical realism) is a necessary condition of any logically coherent or valid theory of consent or covenant or social contract. To press the point a bit further, any theory of consent or social contract not grounded in moral or metaphysical realism collapses into self-referential incoherence. For the purposes of this chapter, I will set aside the question of whether or not social contract theory or standard forms of consent theory have other potentially fatal defects (e.g., the practical difficulty of securing meaningful consent from a sufficient number of people to authorize a regime). I restrict myself only to a necessary condition of a viable (i.e., of a coherent or valid) theory of consent. I will not enter the realm of sufficient conditions or conditions both necessary and sufficient for such a theory.

The argument for the proposition stated above can be summarized as follows: (1) Social contract theory makes consent a necessary condition of political obligations and of the political authority of some over others (or of the state or sovereign representative over citizens or subjects). (2) Hypothetical consent (as in the case of Hobbes, for instance) won't suffice to ground political authority or obligations for two reasons: *first*, there is no moral norm obliging one to observe hypothetical agreements; *second*, hypothetical imperatives just as such fail to generate actual obligations. Consequently, (3) real consent is necessary if political authority and obligation are to be grounded upon consent. (4) Real consent can be seen as generating bonds of obligation between subjects and the political authority *only insofar* as tendering consent constitutes an instance of promising (in which the individual makes an agreement or promise to obey duly established authority—perhaps under certain conditions). (5) Promises only bind insofar as making legitimate promises brings us under a moral requirement that we ought to (or, more strongly, *must*) keep our legitimate promises. (6) Promissory obligation cannot be grounded on will alone—whether we refer to convention (a moral norm constructed by the community), a law laid down by sovereign power, or sheer omnipotence (or irresistible power)—for the reason that obligation as such cannot be established by will alone. The sheer fact of commanding will (whomever is doing the commanding) fails to generate any obligation in anyone to comply with the command. (7) Premise (6) rules out a voluntaristic account of natural law in which promissory obligation is established by nothing other than omnipotent will. (8) The incoherence of grounding obligation in will alone entails the necessity of an objective good to distinguish instances of will that bind from those that do not. Correlatively, promissory obligation can only be grounded in moral realism. (9) But moral realism is an instance of metaphysical realism and entails metaphysical realism. This argument can be run from another direction. As I've argued above, rejecting voluntarism and affirming obligation entails rejecting nominalism and therefore affirming metaphysical realism.[2]

Consent Must Be Actual and Not Merely Hypothetical: Premises (1) to (5)

Consent is necessary for political authority and obligation. Whatever else political contractarians hold, the proposition that consent forms a necessary condition for political authority and obligation is what sets their position apart from other justifications of the authority of the state (divine right, natural subordination, the title of the wise and the good). But many contractarians (moral and political) insist that hypothetical consent will do the trick. I maintain it does not. That it does not entails, necessarily, that *if* consent is necessary for political authority and obligation, then the consent must be real rather than hypothetical. Moreover, when we consent together to do something, we enter into an agreement with each other—we engage in the practice of making promises to each other. But in that case, the coherence of consent depends on the moral obligation to keep our word. Let's unpack this argument by beginning with hypothetical consent (which I elaborate more fully in chapter 9; so here I'll move through the argument more quickly).

Hobbes clearly takes real consent as sufficient to ground political obligation—if you actually consent to sovereign power, Hobbes holds that you are bound.[3] But I find more interesting what strikes me as his argument from hypothetical consent—an argument that is somewhat tacit in *Leviathan*, albeit clearly there. Hobbes explicitly holds that the state of nature never existed the world over.[4] He is not trying to establish a historical state of nature.[5] Correlatively, he is not arguing that states emerged from actual covenants or contracts.[6] As noted earlier, Hobbes generally rejects the inductive and empirical science of the Royal Society in favor of a geometric, deductive approach. The principal purpose of his *Leviathan* is not history but, rather, to show the sorts of steps necessary to forestall the state of nature. He tries to show citizens and sovereigns what they must do to keep from falling into it.[7] How then are we to understand how consent functions in his theory? The answer, I think, goes something like this. Hobbes holds sovereign power is justified because *if* you found yourself in the state of nature, you certainly *would* consent to its establishment (this follows from the desire for self-preservation together with the fact that preservation cannot be secured in the state of nature but only with the establishment of sovereign power; indeed, Hobbes holds, on deductive grounds, that the best-case scenario in the state of nature is worse than the worst-case scenario under sovereign power). Consent in Hobbes's theory (the covenant of everyone with everyone of chapter 17, paragraph 13; and in contrast to Locke's theory) is *as if* consent.

Though they change the locus from the legitimation of political authority and obligation to justice, consent in Kant and Rawls is also hypothetical rather than actual.[8] For Rawls, principles of justice are authoritative for us because they are what we *would have* agreed to in the original position, even though he concedes that actual persons cannot get behind the veil of ignorance.[9] Actual consent to the principles of justice for which he argues is not the ground of their normativity. The fact that we would have consented to them is what binds us—at least insofar as consent enters the picture (the picture for Rawls is a bit more nuanced, to be sure: what binds us to his two principles of justice is the fact that *moral personalities*, shorn of all contingencies, would have agreed to them, together with the claim that the decision of moral personalities or their consent to such principles is authoritative for us).

Now, it's easy to understand why certain social contract theorists emphasize hypothetical consent. When it comes to the agreement to establish political authority and to incur political obligations, on the one hand, or to adopt principles of justice, on the other, obtaining the requisite level of consent (namely, unanimity *or* the consent of the vast majority of any given society) appears to be a practical impossibility. Such consent has not existed, nor does it, nor, in all likelihood, will it.[10] Consent theory (or social contract theory) does us little good if the required consent is unobtainable. Consequently, a number of theorists evade the practical impossibility of obtaining a sufficient level of actual consent by shifting to hypothetical consent.[11]

But, of course, hypothetical consent is considerably problematic. Consent theory is an attempt to account for political obligations (or for binding principles of justice, in Rawls's theory, for instance).

Obligations are, of course, requirements. To be obligated to φ (again where φ just stands for some action or other and φ-ing for performing some action or other), I must be required to φ. That is, φ-ing must be nonoptional for me. To be required to perform an action is no longer to have discretion as to whether I may perform it. From a somewhat different angle, we might say that moral obligations just as such are (or impose) categorical rather than hypothetical imperatives. Now, when it comes to actions that I am required to perform, to acts that are nonoptional for me, I think it's evident (per se nota, in fact) that there is no moral obligation to perform actions that I would have agreed to had I found myself in a particular state of affairs (say, for instance, if I found myself in the state of nature) *but do not now and, in fact, have never* actually found myself in. I am not bound to do that which I would have agreed to do but did not in fact agree to do. Perhaps given the right set of circumstances, John would have married Jane. But in fact he married Penelope instead. It doesn't follow that, just because he would have married her but in fact did not, John has spousal obligations in relation to Jane. To frame this even more precisely (and more technically): there is no *categorical* imperative such that I must do that which I would have agreed to do even if I have not in fact agreed to do it. Call this the covering norm (or the genus). It follows that there is no categorical imperative such that I incur political obligations (or obligations of justice—arguendo since there's no intelligible account of justice as the product of agreement) I would have agreed to incur in a state of nature (or original position) but did not in fact consent to incur since I've never found myself in the state of nature. Not only is there no such categorical imperative. There's no such imperative or moral norm at all.

Insofar as consent theory or social contract theory has a point, the point is to account for *particular* political obligations—the political obligations of particular individuals to a particular society, to a particular political community, to a particular government.[12] Consent theory seeks to do this by appropriating the norms and obligations attendant to the practice of promising. As noted before, consent or agreements are instances of making promises. As instances of promises, they bring one under the natural law norm (or moral obligation) that one ought—that one is bound—to keep one's legitimate promises (though I am obviously not bound to keep a "promise" that I had no business making in the first place). And there is a categorical imperative such that I am bound to keep my legitimate promises. John Locke refers to this as an instance of an obligation that belongs to men as men, to humans qua human, and not merely as members of society.[13] If I am bound to keep my promises and if agreeing to incur political obligations (by joining a society) is an instance of promising, then, necessarily, I am bound to fulfill those obligations I have incurred by joining that society. This is the basic form of social contract theory and of consent theory more generally. But this method of grounding political obligations only works if the consent in question is actual rather than merely hypothetical.[14] Hypothetical consent in Hobbes and others gets whatever veneer of plausibility it has by borrowing capital from the moral obligation attendant to actual consent as an instance of promising.

From the foregoing, I think we can posit this conditional: if consent is a necessary condition of political authority and obligation, then the consent in question must be actual rather than hypothetical. The conditional follows from the absence of any moral norm binding us to us to agreements we would have made in hypothetical scenarios or possible worlds that might have obtained but that have not in fact been actualized. The consent must be an actual instance of promising where the promise is secured by a moral norm—indeed, by a categorical imperative—that we are bound to keep our legitimate promises.

Promissory Obligation Requires Moral and
Metaphysical Realism: Premises (6) to (9)

Consent theory is intelligible only if consenting to political authority or obligations is making a promise and only if we are morally obligated to keep our valid or legitimate promises. But now we must ask a yet deeper question. What binds us to keep our legitimate promises? That is, in what does the metaphysical or ontological ground of binding promises consist? As we've seen in previous chapters, convention cannot do the trick. Nor can hypothetical imperatives. Nor also can a voluntaristic account of natural law (or of moral obligation) that grounds promissory obligation in nothing more than prescriptive will. We are compelled to conclude that promissory obligation is only intelligible on moral realism (or a moral realist account of natural law). But moral realism necessarily entails metaphysical realism.

For the sake of argument, consider the proposition that promissory obligation (as obligatory) is grounded in nothing other than the conventions of a community. The community has adopted a certain promissory practice that defines legitimate promises and then posits an obligation to keep promises made in accord with the governing convention. Suppose we adopt this account of promissory obligation. As applied to consent theory (and insofar as consent is an instance of promise making), political and legal obligation would not be grounded in a moral obligation transcendent of and normative for human will. Rather, it would be grounded in the convention of the community.[15] The community has adopted a norm that we must keep our valid promises (and it has defined, at least roughly, what constitutes a valid or invalid promise). To consent is to make a promise. So we incur political obligation by giving consent just because in so doing we have made a promise, in accordance with a norm adopted by the community.

Suppose, then, that a community has adopted a convention concerning the practice of promising. They've adopted or constructed a norm—one that is a norm only insofar as the community has chosen to make it so—that one ought to keep one's valid promises. Call it C_p. And suppose there is no other source for the obligatory force of binding promises—the community's convention and the act of making a promise under that norm are it. There's nothing more to promissory obligation. We must then ask this question: Why are we obligated to obey the conventions adopted or constructed by the community? What is it about the community's act of adopting or constructing that could make any such norm, including C_p, binding? Clearly obligation is not analytically packed into the concept of convention. It is not analytically or conceptually true that just because C_p is a convention adopted or constructed by some community that C_p is binding for the members of the community. And this holds for any convention adopted by any community. Indeed, it seems evident—to anyone who will but reflect on actual conventions—that while some conventions or customs are just and even authoritative, others are not. Conventions or customs surrounding slavery or segregation were not just or binding. Customs or conventions concerning the keeping of legitimate promises are. The former Hindu custom of sati (the immolation of a widow on her husband's funeral pyre) is not binding. Conventions barring the targeting of noncombatants in war are. So some conventions or customs are good and just and can bind us. Others are none of these.

Now imagine a set of all the various conventions that exist within a given society as well as across societies. What defines the set is the fact that these conventions or customs are simply conventions. That's the property defining the set. As I argued earlier, a general principle of sets is the impossibility of intelligibly distinguishing among the members of a set on the basis of the predication of the property or properties by which the set is defined. Applied to conventions, that means that it's impossible to distinguish among conventions (or customs) intelligibly on the basis of convention. Thus, if some conventions are binding and others are not, the basis for distinguishing binding from nonbinding conventions *cannot be conventions, cannot be some particular convention, insofar as it's a convention, or qua convention,* but, rather *must be some property of obligation transcendent of and normative for conventions.* This makes conventionalism (as an account either of moral and political obligation or of justice or of promissory obligation) self-referentially incoherent.[16] Consequently, the reason that consent binds cannot be because it is an instance of promissory obligation, where the reason promises bind is just because the community has adopted or constructed a governing norm (or norms) concerning the making and observance of valid promises.

The conclusion above can be reached via a slightly different route. For the sake of argument, suppose that we view all norms as social constructs. Is there a problem with this? There is. So viewing norms leaves one caught on the horns of dilemma. For where does the norm that we *ought* to obey socially constructed norms come from? Either that norm is *not* a social construct, in which case not all norms are social constructs, and the claim that they are, together with the claim that we *ought* to obey socially constructed norms, is self-referentially incoherent. *Or* that norm *is* socially constructed, making the claim that we ought to obey socially constructed norms viciously circular. So the claim that all norms are socially constructed, together with the claim that we ought to obey such norms (or even just some such norms), is either self-referentially incoherent or viciously circular. Either way the proposition is logically invalid.

Above I noted the distinction between categorical and hypothetical imperatives. The early modern Thomas Hobbes and the contemporary moral philosopher J. L. Mackie both understand all moral obligations as hypothetical imperatives (with respect to Hobbes, at least insofar as we view moral imperatives from the standpoint of reason alone).[17] For Hobbes and Mackie (and Hume as well), reason is instrumental. There are no substantial, rational ends that we are bound to pursue because they are intrinsically, or simply and absolutely, good or desirable—such that we ought to desire them whether or not we do. Desire itself sets the end. Reason simply directs us in attaining it. The idea with hypothetical imperatives is that if any person p wants some good g (where g is a good for p just because p desires g) and if φ-ing is the only way for p to obtain g (φ-ing is necessary for p to obtain g), then p ought to φ. The oughtness is entirely bound up with the conditional. Put another way, p ought to φ only because φ-ing is necessary for p to obtain g. But if p does not want g—perhaps p never wanted g or perhaps p no longer wants g or perhaps some preference for another good is now greater than it was for g—then φ-ing is not obligatory for p. That is, φ-ing is not, in that case, obligatory for g (unless, of course, φ-ing is necessary for some other good or goods p seeks to obtain).

How would this account of hypothetical imperatives and instrumental rationality apply to consent or social contract theory? On instrumental rationality the binding power of promising (and so of consenting or entering into an agreement) consists in the connection of promising to some end set by desire. In the case of Hobbes, one could argue that consent (to the degree that actual consent—or something much weaker, like assent—is on the table) is obligatory because it ultimately serves the end of preservation (and does this by allowing individuals to affirm together terms of peace). But ends are not set for us. When it comes to modern, instrumental rationality, there are no objective goods such that we ought to desire them whether or not we do. For Hobbes, Hume, Bentham, Mill, Mackie, and others, the goods that reason instructs us how to obtain are good or desirable only because they are desired.[18] Reason does not give the *what* of pursuit. It only provides the *how*. So the oughtness of φ-ing in order to obtain *g* is not given in φ-ing itself but only because we in fact desire *g*. If we did not, we would not be bound to φ.

Another version of instrumental rationality is also relevant to our discussion here. For we could construe the ends that human persons aim to achieve as chosen by an act of human will rather than as given by desire.[19] Some good *g* is good for some person *p* just because *p* *chooses* to obtain *g* or chooses to seek *g* or chooses *g* as her end (whatever her desires).[20] In this case (as above), reason only commands *p* to φ because φ-ing is necessary for obtaining *g*. The oughtness of φ-ing is not given by φ-ing itself (because φ-ing is intrinsically good, for instance) but rather because *g* cannot be obtained without φ-ing. Oughtness as such is still hypothetical or conditional. It is given by the relation of the means (φ-ing) to obtaining *g*, where *g* is good for *p* just because *p* has chosen *g*.

This brings us to a question not seriously considered by Hobbes, Hume, Bentham, Mill, or Mackie, but which, drawing on Jean Hampton, I raised earlier in this work: Do hypothetical imperatives actually impose obligations? Or rather: Does the hypothetical imperative account of moral obligation simply give up the game, eliminating obligation itself by providing a nonobligatory account of moral obligation? With Hampton, I maintain that hypothetical imperatives cannot ground moral obligation. Rather, on the hypothetical imperative account, moral obligation itself simply dissolves. Why?

Consider again the nature of moral obligation. What is it to be under a moral obligation in the proper sense? Suppose Odysseus has a son named Telemachus. In that case, Odysseus has a moral obligation to care for Telemachus. Setting aside the content of this obligation, we need to know what sort of thing this obligation is. In older parlance, if Odysseus is obligated to care and provide for Telemachus, then Odysseus is *bound* to provide for Telemachus. In the language of contemporary moral and legal theory, we would say that Odysseus is *required* to care for Telemachus. For any person *p* to have a moral obligation to φ (letting φ stand for any possible action to which one might have a moral obligation), then *p* must be *required* to φ. But to be required to perform some act is to be in a state of affairs such that not performing the act (not φ-ing) is nonoptional for *p*. So if Odysseus is obligated to care and provide for Telemachus, then he has a requirement to care for Telemachus such that not caring for Telemachus is normatively nonoptional for him—it's not a matter of discretion.

As we saw earlier, for theorists of hypothetical imperatives and instrumental rationality, oughtness is given with respect to the means necessary for bringing about ends selected either by desire or by human will. The oughtness is given in (or just is) the means-end relation in this causal structure. But we are compelled to ask whether this is an account of oughtness at all. Again, with Hampton, I submit that it is not. So-called hypothetical imperatives are, as Hampton notes, descriptions of causal relations. She focuses on Hobbes's account, in which desire sets the end and reason ascertains necessary conditions (or conditions together necessary and sufficient) for attaining the end. But the position is formally the same if will rather than desire chooses the end. In both cases, the proponent of instrumental rationality and of moral obligations as hypothetical imperatives seeks to construct norms "entirely out of non-normative ingredients."[21] The goal is to avoid moral objects that Mackie calls "queer" or strange or quixotic or, relatedly, metaphysical objects that Hobbes considers nonsense (like he considers a round quadrangle to be nonsense—the strangeness of a philosopher who claimed to have squared the circle considering a round quadrangle nonsense notwithstanding).[22] This is the goal of so-called naturalist theories of ethics (at least as that term is usually used in contemporary, analytic philosophy). According to Hampton, Hobbes and company seek to avoid positing "strange moral objects, prescriptive properties or a divinely revealed truth." Rather, Hobbes (among others) seeks to explain moral "laws as true in the same way that any conditional cause-and-effect proposition in a physical science is true."[23] And it's just this task—the endeavor to build norms out of nonnormative ingredients, or moral precepts or obligations out of antecedent building blocks that are not themselves moral—that I contend is utterly unintelligible.

The first thing to note about this account, then, is that the oughtness is in the hypothetical imperative. And the ingredients going into the imperative are supposed to be nonnormative or premoral. There is no oughtness in seeking peace. Rather, for Hobbes, I desire my preservation, and seeking peace with others insofar as they will seek it with me is necessary to attaining it. I cannot avoid a life that is solitary, nasty, poor, brutish, and short and in which the probability of sudden and violent death is high *unless* I seek peace with others insofar as they will also seek it with me. Given Hobbes's subjectivity concerning good and evil, oughtness must have the property of supervening on something. There are two possibilities—irresistible power (on which I'll say more below) or means-end causal relations. But the thing to note about such causal relations is that they do not include oughtness (or obligation) analytically or conceptually. Nor do they entail it. From the fact that I cannot seek peace with others without laying down the right of nature (granting this claim arguendo), it does not follow that I ought (or am obligated) to lay down the right of nature. All that follows is that I cannot seek peace with others unless I lay down the right of nature; that if I retain the right of nature, then I am not seeking peace with them; and that if I do lay down the right of nature, then I am taking a step essential to seeking peace with them. In other words, what follows from such conditionals is yielded by the disjunctive syllogism, modus ponens, modus tollens, the law of the excluded middle, noncontradiction, and the other rules of inference. And none of these rules of inference yield or (*magically*) produce oughtness or obligation from ingredients that have nothing moral or normative in them. Indeed, the only way laying down the right of nature could even be obligatory is if laying that right down is necessary to seeking peace *and* if seeking peace is *already* obligatory *apart from the causal connection.* It should be clear, then, that any attempt to get norms (of any kind) from nonnormative ingredients is a glaring non sequitur. Not one of the canons of valid argument can produce oughtness from hypothetical imperatives composed entirely from nonnormative ingredients. What we first require is a categorical imperative such that any person p is bound (required or obligated) to φ if φ-ing is necessary to obtain any desired object g (or some most strongly desired object g). But then, at the base of a morality the content of which is given by hypothetical imperatives, we would have a normative, categorical imperative. And so we would not have a morality built from nonnormative ingredients at all. Moreover, we wouldn't have a hypothetical imperative account of moral obligation either. Thus, the only intelligible account of moral obligation as hypothetical imperatives really isn't a hypothetical imperative account after all.[24]

We might put it this way. Either the causal relations that are said to ground hypothetical imperatives entail nothing concerning obligation or oughtness or normativity, *or* they do, but only because such hypothetical imperatives are grounded in a prior categorical imperative that gives hypothetical imperatives (or certain of them) what binding power they have. In either case, oughtness is not produced by the causal means-end relation itself. And in either case, hypothetical imperatives fail to ground or generate normativity of any sort. In particular, hypothetical imperatives of themselves cannot ground any moral obligation, for the reason that I am not bound to will the means to some end if I am not also bound to will the end. The fact that I do will some end or other, of itself, has no relevance to what I am obligated to do. The foregoing ought to be enough, by itself, to reject any attempt to ground either promissory obligation or social contract theory or consent theory in hypothetical imperatives. Indeed, I think the argument here completely suffices for that conclusion. But we can advance another argument sufficient for it as well.

David Hume well understood the implications of instrumentalist rationality (and of subjectivity concerning the good) for moral obligation. Consider again that passage in which he so vividly lays out the implication of a purely instrumentalist account of reason: " 'Tis not contrary to reason to prefer the destruction of the whole world to the scratching of my finger. 'Tis not contrary to reason for me to chuse my total ruin, to prevent the least uneasiness of an *Indian* or person wholly unknown to me. 'Tis as little contrary to reason to prefer even my own acknowledg'd lesser good to my greater, and have a more ardent affection for the former than the latter."[25] Hume's position comes to this: instrumental reason entails the indifference of reason to the ends pursued. But in that case, it follows that instrumental rationality is also indifferent as to whether I pursue self-preservation or choose, instead, to seek self-destruction. Instrumental rationality is, necessarily, indifferent as to whether I seek peace or pursue the destruction of society and humankind. In short, the most that instrumental reason can prescribe (and I maintain that it can't even prescribe this, in view of the argument above) is that I should perform actions conducive to self-preservation *if I desire self-preservation*. The most that instrumental reason can tell me is that I should take actions conducive to seeking peace with others, if I desire to seek peace with others. (In both propositions we could replace "desire" with "choose.") But instrumental reason—and a causal relation between my preservation and seeking peace with others—cannot tell me that I ought to seek the preservation of my nature or that I am bound to seek peace with others. Moreover, if what I desire (or choose) is the destruction of myself or society or of humanity, then instrumental rationality (to the extent it is even able to prescribe) tells me I ought to take the steps requisite to the fulfillment of those desires or chosen ends, *whatever they happen to be*. In other words, Humean consistency points out that oughtness, on instrumental rationality and the hypothetical imperative account of moral obligation, is completely open-ended. Any person p could be bound to φ, where φ-ing could be anything at all. But the fact that any person is bound only to do what they want to do (provided their actions are well calculated to yield the satisfaction of desire) or whatever they choose to do (so long as their actions are well calculated to produce the chosen end) should be considered the reductio ad absurdum refutation of the theory that entails this conclusion. Oughtness includes the idea that there are some standards or norms that I ought to follow—and that are normative for human willing—whatever I now choose or want to will. But it's hard to see how I ought to do anything at all if the actions required of me could be anything at all—if murder could be proscribed or prescribed, all depending on desire or choice. Such an open-ended theory of obligation empties obligation of any normativity at all.

It seems clear to me that trying to ground promissory obligation or consent theory or the social contract in hypothetical imperatives comes at the price of promissory obligation itself—comes at the price of any normativity associated with making promises. For if we ground morality or normativity in hypothetical imperatives all the way down, then we end up with imperatives that are not actually imperative.

In view of the foregoing, a viable theory of consent therefore requires holding that moral obligation is antecedent to those obligations, political or otherwise, established by convention. Consequently, moral obligation cannot be merely the product of social construction. A valid theory of consent also requires an account of moral obligation that is not framed entirely in terms of hypothetical imperatives as well as one that does not seek to build normativity or moral obligation from nonnormative or premoral ingredients. Ultimately, we require a theory in which promissory obligation (as to valid promises) is a categorical imperative of the natural or moral law.

As we saw in chapter 6, there are two standard accounts of natural law.[26] They are sometimes denominated as the voluntarist account and the intellectualist account. Because this dichotomization conflates ontological and epistemological matters, I prefer to distinguish them as the voluntarist account and the realist account. On the voluntarist account, the exclusive foundation of moral obligation is omnipotent divine will. On the realist account, moral obligation is founded on divine goodness and wisdom. I have argued that moral obligation is a complex or compound property comprised of intrinsic goodness together with prescription.[27] I have also argued that the voluntarist account of natural law or of moral obligation is self-referentially incoherent. I will summarize the argument below. The point of including the argument here is that if promissory obligation (and so consent) cannot be grounded in social construction or convention and cannot be grounded in hypothetical imperatives built from nonmoral or premoral elements, and so must be grounded in an objective moral law, then it must *also* be grounded in a coherent account of moral law. And the voluntaristic conception of moral law is not such an account.

On metaethical voluntarism, moral obligation is entirely the product of a prescribing or commanding will. There are secular versions of the theory. But these are formally identical to their theological progenitor—an account of natural law whose strongest proponent in the medieval period was William of Ockham. There are what seem (on first approximation) to be two strands in William of Ockham. On the one hand, there is the so-called divine command strand of his thought. On the other hand, there are those passages where he speaks of natural law and of natural reason that in no case fails. As for the divine command passages, Ockham seems rather clearly to hold that any person p is under a moral obligation o to perform or refrain from φ-ing *if and only if* God has commanded or forbidden p to φ. God's commands are necessary and sufficient conditions for moral obligation.

Moreover, divine command, for Ockham, is not grounded in infinite goodness or wisdom. Ockham distinguishes the *potentia dei ordinata*—the world or order (including the moral order) that God chooses to create or actualize—from the *potentia dei absoluta*, which has to do with possible worlds God could have actualized logically antecedent to the world He did in fact actualize (since none of God's decisions occur in time).[28] The *potentia dei absoluta et ordinata* distinction predates Ockham. It was deployed by Albertus Magnus and Thomas Aquinas. But for Thomas and Albert the *potentia dei absoluta* was metaphysically, and so substantially, constrained in ways it was not for Ockham. For Ockham the *potentia dei absoluta* was constrained only by God's existence (God cannot actualize a world in which God does not exist) and the law of noncontradiction (God cannot actualize a world in which the law of noncontradiction does not exist or is violated). But with those two caveats, Ockham held that God could cause a world with any other state of affairs to obtain.[29] For instance, God could ordain a world in which murder, theft, and adultery are all right or just and their opposites wrong or unjust. In fact, God has created a world in which murder, theft, and adultery are wrong (and not just wrong, but wrong for all people at all times and in all places). But it could have been otherwise.[30]

All that on the one hand. And yet, on the other hand, Ockham subscribed to a natural law, apprehended by right reason that in no case fails, and that, as to the content of moral obligations, was identical to Saint Thomas's. Thus, Ockham holds that that murder is wrong—indeed, that it is always and everywhere wrong—that the wrongness of murder is apprehended by right reason, and that the only way to fail to see the wrongness of murder is to fail to exercise reason with respect to the taking of innocent human life. Substantively, the moral world he describes is much the same as Aquinas's. Moral obligations are grounded in necessary truths apprehended by right reason. Further still, following the moral law would seem, for Ockham, to redound to human well-being or happiness. Of course, there are important differences. Ockham rejected Aquinas's (and Aristotle's) account of formal cause.

Given all the data (and as noted earlier), scholars have debated as to which Ockham is the real one—the divine command theory Ockham or the natural law Ockham—or whether Ockham is a house divided against himself. Oakley, as we saw, argues that there is one Ockham rather than two.[31] And his way of reconciling these two strands seem to me the best and maybe the only way to account for all the material. According to Oakley, when Ockham posits the contingency of morality—that murder could have been lawful or morally mandatory for us had God commanded us (and so also with hatred of God)—he refers to the *potentia dei absoluta*. With respect to the absolute power of God, morality—in particular, the content of our moral obligations—is radically contingent. There was no necessity that God ordain a world in which murder was wrong. By way of contrast, when Ockham speaks of the natural law—about natural or right reason that in no case fails and about moral precepts that are necessary and always hold—he refers to the *potentia dei ordinata*. In the world as we have it, the most fundamental moral precepts are right for all and known to all who exercise their reason. The most fundamental precepts of the natural law are inviolable. And they are necessary. Yet this necessity is conditional. The most fundamental moral precepts are necessary, given the world God has ordained. Such precepts, if you will, have a kind of de facto necessity. But they are not absolutely necessary. God could have ordained or actualized a different world in which very different moral obligations obtained. In his absolute power, God chose to ordain a world in which a natural law account describes ethics and moral obligation as we have them.

To return to a point above, Ockham himself rejected both Platonic and Aristotelian theories of ideas (or universals) and forms.[32] And Platonic or Aristotelian metaphysics usually grounds classical ethical theories such as Saint Thomas's. But one could imagine a doubly sophisticated Ockhamist who described the world as we have it in Thomistic terms (Aristotelian forms, the classical account of final causation and of motion/change, and so forth) but who also advanced an Ockhamist account of the *potentia dei absoluta* (something Saint Thomas rejected as blasphemous). This would seem to give us a

teleological account of natural law and human good grounded, ultimately, on an exercise of omnipotent and unrestrained divine will to
actualize such a possible world.

On the Ockhamist account, there is no objective or transcendent
goodness in which to ground moral obligation. There is no necessary
Good or Goodness. Only divine existence and the law of noncontradiction are necessary. And this leaves will (in this case omnipotent
will—but clearly not a good will, *since good and evil are the constructions of divine will*) as the only basis for moral obligation. But, of
course, grounding morality in nothing but will is self-referentially
incoherent.

Suppose someone holds that the strongest will binds or (with
Ockham and Hobbes) that acts of omnipotent or irresistible will
are binding for those not possessed of omnipotence or irresistibility.
Then the ground of obligation is not will so much as strength, omnipotence, or irresistibility. But of course strength, the ability to will
all things, and possession of irresistible powers are not of themselves
moral properties. Once again we have an attempt to brew normativity out of nonnormative ingredients. From the fact that someone
stronger than me has willed that I perform some act, all that follows
is that a person stronger than me has willed that I perform the act
(and that they can compel me if they so choose). That an irresistible
power (say, for instance, a mortal God such as Hobbes's Leviathan
state) has commanded me to do something only entails that a power
irresistible in relation to me has commanded and can compel me to
do something. Likewise, omnipotence (understood simply as the
power to will all things) by itself is insufficient for moral obligation.
Omnipotent will as will is not obligatory. Irresistible will qua will
and omnipotent power qua power are not obligatory.

In order for me to be bound by some act of will, there must be
some objective standard that tells me which instances of will bind
and which do not *because* the prescribing will prescribes what is good
or right. The only intelligible account of moral obligation or natural
law is one that grounds moral obligation in an objective good or right
that is transcendent of and normative for acts of will (with the exception of God, who is identical with Goodness and so whom goodness
does not transcend; but nor is goodness a divine creation; it is, rather,

the essence of divinity as such).[33] *The foregoing entails, necessarily, that the only intelligible account of natural law or of moral obligation is one grounded in moral realism. But if the only intelligible account of moral obligation is the moral realist account, then, necessarily, the only intelligible account of promissory obligation is one grounded in moral realism. And if consent is an instance or application of promissory obligation, then the only intelligible account of consent (or of the social contract) is one ultimately grounded in moral realism.*

To be sure, *mere* moral realism is not enough. I argued in chapter 6 that we can distinguish among intrinsically good acts. Some intrinsically good acts are obligatory (or required, or nonoptional), while others are merely licit or supererogatory. We cannot coherently or nonarbitrarily distinguish intrinsically good acts that are obligatory (required and nonoptional for us) from those that are not (because they are merely permissible or better than we have to do) on the basis of intrinsic goodness alone. What makes intrinsically good acts obligatory—required or nonoptional for us—is that they have been prescribed. Prescription requires a prescriber. But in order for one person to prescribe for another, the prescribing person must possess the authority to prescribe. Thus, prescriptive will and authority to prescribe—together with real goodness—are constitutive elements or ingredients of obligation. Obligation is a compound property. Even so, the compound theory of moral obligation is still an instance of moral realism.

Now moral realism is an instance (or part and parcel) of metaphysical realism (as I argued at the end of chapter 3). If we must, we can consider metaphysical realism (as to forms, essences, properties, and so forth) the genus and moral realism a species. Perhaps we can imagine a kind of metaphysical realism that does not include moral realism.[34] Perhaps Scotus affirmed something like this position (save with respect to our obligation to love and obey God).[35] So metaphysical realism does not (or at least, prima facially might not) entail moral realism. At any rate, my argument as here advanced remains agnostic on that claim and unaffected by whether or not an intelligible account of metaphysical realism entails moral realism. That notwithstanding, since moral realism is a species of the larger genus of metaphysical realism, it necessarily follows that if moral realism is true, then metaphysical realism is as well. Put another way, *given the genus-species relation, metaphysical realism is the necessary entailment of moral realism. So if moral obligation presupposes metaphysical realism—for its very intelligibility—so also does promissory obligation (insofar as promissory obligation is an instance of moral obligation) and so also does consent or social contract theory, as an application of promissory obligation to political obligation.*

Given the hypothetical syllogism and modus tollens, denying moral realism necessarily entails the rejection of promissory obligation and therefore the rejection of any intelligible social contract theory or consent-based ground for political obligation and legitimate political authority.[36] These would simply dissolve. This poses an interesting disjunct: *either* moral and metaphysical realism *or* we must deny the very possibility of consent as a legitimate ground of political authority and obligation. The irony is that some theorists have maintained just the opposite: *either* social contract and consent theory *or* moral and metaphysical realism. But we can now see that this position is not logically tenable.

There is, of course, more than one species of moral realism. I have argued in previous work that Kantian deontoligical realism is logically untenable and that the only intelligible account of moral realism is teleological (where *teleological* refers to the metaphysics of finality and not to consequentialism or Utilitarianism): just because it is impossible to distinguish among exercises of will on the basis of will alone, it is impossible to distinguish a good will from a bad one on the basis of nothing but will. The argument above entails that one can only distinguish a good will from a bad one (or a right will from a wrong one) with reference to some good (or right) external to will as such and normative for it. Correlatively, contra Kant, the will can only be judged good or bad, right or wrong, insofar as it *aims* or fails to aim at that external good (or right).[37] Thus, my argument entails the incoherence of a purely deontological realism. Traced all the way out, I maintain this leaves us with only the non-consequentialist, teleological realism of Aristotle and Aquinas.[38] I will not recapitulate the argument here. But if my conclusion in prior work is right, promissory obligation and consent theory can only be intelligibly grounded in classical, teleological natural law.

Conclusion

The foregoing means not only that covenant, political contractarianism, and the necessity of consent for political authority and obligation are *compatible* with classical natural law, as argued in chapter 7, but also that covenant, political contractarianism, and the principle of consent *essentially depend* on classical natural law for their coherence. There is no coherent account of covenant (and not just in political theory) or of the necessity of the consent of the governed for rightful political authority without metaphysical and moral realism—including a teleological conception of the good. And this solves the de jure problem for *political* contractarianism with which this volume began. *Political* contractarianism is coherent only if established on the sort of metaphysical foundation rejected by Ockham, Hobbes, and Locke and on the sort of ethical ontology rejected by Ockham and Hobbes (with respect to which Locke is perhaps equivocal). This leaves us with one remaining thread—the de facto problem. Namely, is *real* consent possible in practice?

CHAPTER 9

The Paucity of Consent:
Can Consent Theory's De Facto Problem Be Overcome?

Introduction

IN WHAT FOLLOWS I INTEND to argue that social contract and consent theory have a de facto problem concerning the paucity of meaningful individual consent. The only sort of intelligible consent theory treats consent as a *necessary*, rather than as either a sufficient or a necessary and sufficient, condition of political authority and obligation. Moreover, the consent required is actual rather than hypothetical or merely rationally implied. But no nation-state possesses the actual consent of a substantial number of individuals within the territory it purports to govern. A. John Simmons argues that the necessity of real consent, together with its paucity, entails the absence of political authority and obligations—a position he calls philosophical anarchism.[1] The question I take up herein is whether consent theory ultimately terminates in philosophical anarchism, as Simmons maintains, or whether it can be constructed in a way to justify political authority and obligation. I maintain that, when it comes to a society of any substantial size, *either* human equality should be taken to ground popular sovereignty *or* individual consent should be given up for corporate consent along the lines spelled out by Johannes Althusius.

Consent Theory's De Facto Problem: The Paucity of Individual Consent

CONSENT'S NECESSITY AND PAUCITY

As I noted in chapter 1, though consent theory comprised the regnant Western account of the ground of political authority and obligation from the latter seventeenth through the first part of the twentieth century, it was subjected to heavy fire from legal and political

289

philosophers in the latter twentieth century. Leslie Green and A. John Simmons were among those who advanced the most compelling arguments against it.[2] Their arguments focus on the paucity of the requisite individual consent to ground political authority and obligation. According to Simmons, (1) Locke is right (given human equality) that consent is *necessary* for political authority and obligations; (2) Hume is right that there is a paucity of actual consent (since most people at most times and places have not tendered consent to government or those who administer it, to exercise authority over them, or thereby taken on obligations to obey it); consequently, (3) most people in most regimes are not under political authority and do not have political obligations. Simmons calls this claim that most people lack political obligations and are not under political authority "philosophical anarchism."[3] We thus find ourselves confronted with the question as to whether consent theory or some form of political contractarianism can avoid this implication.

If most people have not tendered express consent (and if we cannot practicably expect them to in very large, modern nation-states, even in the case of constitutional democracies), then the options seem to be hypothetical or tacit consent. If neither hypothetical nor tacit consent are viable, then Simmons's conclusion seems to follow—*insofar* as we affirm that individual consent is *necessary* for political authority and obligation, that is. Before turning to the problems with hypothetical and tacit consent, however, I want to say something more about consent as a necessary condition of political authority and obligation and also about the Humean denial that most people have given meaningful consent to the regimes by which they are governed.

As Simmons argues, for Locke, consent is neither *sufficient* nor both *necessary and sufficient* for political authority and obligations. Rather, consent is *necessary* for these. Given the argument of chapter 1, the positions that consent is sufficient or both necessary and sufficient for political authority and obligations are both self-referentially incoherent. They both reduce consent to exercises of mere will and thereby seek to make some instances of human will normative or obligatory for others on the basis of will alone—which cannot coherently be done. Thus, only the version of consent theory according to which consent is necessary—but *not* sufficient and *not* both necessary and sufficient for political authority and obligations—is logically coherent. Thus, Locke rightly frames consent as *insufficient* for a legitimate regime. As Simmons argues, because Locke rejects the sufficiency of consent for political obligation, he "escapes . . . the charge that his account of consent would obligate all residents . . . to obey even unjust or tyrannical regimes."[4]

If we turn to Locke's *Two Treatises*, we see several passages on the limits of the power or authority of political society, of government generally, and of legislative power—limits that if transgressed dissolve the authority of a regime over those it claims the right to govern. Consider, for instance, the limits on legislative power that Locke affirms on the basis of a moral law—the law of nature—that imposes both negative obligations (not to harm) and positive obligation (to help) on individuals in relation to others in the state of nature and on the basis of the rejection of self-ownership. Though he describes the state of nature as one of "perfect Freedom," yet this freedom "to order their Actions, to dispose of their Possessions, and Persons as they see fit" for the preservation of themselves and others, only obtains "within the bounds [i.e., the boundary] of the Law of Nature."[5] For "The *State of Nature* has a Law of Nature to govern it, which obliges everyone." This law of nature imposes obligations on individuals not "to harm another in his Life, Health, Liberty, or Possessions." And we ought not do this because others are God's property, and that because they are God's workmanship. Likewise, even in the state of nature, the law of nature requires not only preserving oneself (and not committing suicide) but also preserving "the rest of Mankind" at least insofar as one's "own preservation comes not in competition" with it.[6] These requirements of the moral law—predicated on divine ownership of ourselves and others—forbid us from enslaving ourselves to others by placing ourselves under their absolute power: "For a Man, not having the Power of his own Life, *cannot*, by Compact, or his own Consent, *enslave himself* to any one, nor put himself under the Absolute, Arbitrary Power of another, to take away his Life when he pleases. No body can give more Power than he has himself; and he that cannot take away his own Life, cannot give another power over it."[7] On Locke's view, divine ownership and the moral law entail that we have only limited power (or authority) over ourselves. But on Locke's view, political society receives what authority or power it has over subjects by transfer from them via consent.[8] Since the individuals who consent to make political society have only limited authority over themselves to give, political society can only receive limited authority from them. In which case political society can only ever have and rightly exercise limited authority over them. And when a political society in turn delegates the exercise of its authority to government, it can only delegate limited authority to it. Thus, with respect to the Legislative, "the *Supream* Power in every commonwealth":

> It is *not*, nor can possibly be absolutely *Arbitrary* over the Lives and Fortunes of the People. For it being but the joynt power of every Member of the Society given up to that Person, or Assembly, which is Legislator, it can be no more than those persons had in a State of Nature before they enter'd into Society, and gave up to the Community. For no Body can transfer to another more power than he has in himself; and no Body has an absolute Arbitrary Power over himself, or over any other, to destroy his own Life, or take away the Life or Property of another. A man, as has been proved, cannot subject himself to the Arbitrary Power of another; and having in the State of Nature no Arbitrary Power over the Life, Liberty, or Possession of another, but only so much as the Law of Nature gave him for the preservation of himself, and the rest of Mankind; this is all he doth or can give himself, and the rest of Mankind; this is all he doth, or can give up to the Common-wealth, and by it to the *Legislative Power*, so that the Legislative can have no more than this. Their Power in the utmost Bounds of it, is *limited to the publick good* of the Society.

Consequently, the legislative (and government more generally) "can never have a right to destroy, enslave, or designedly to impoverish the Subjects."[9] Indeed, "the Law of Nature stands as an Eternal Rule to all Men, *Legislators* as well as others. The *Rules* that they make for other Mens Actions, must, as well as their own and other Mens Actions, be conformable to the Law of Nature, *i.e.*, to the Will of

God, of which that is a Declaration, and the *fundamental Law of Nature* being *the preservation of Mankind*, no Humane Sanction can be good, or valid against it."[10]

If government transgresses these limits, then it exercises "Power beyond Right,"[11] in which case the bond between government and society dissolves and society acquires a right to depose and replace the existing government. But note that for Locke political society also lacks the authority or right to empower such a government. And these limits not only on the power of government but also on what political society can do—limits imposed from by the law of nature, the requirements of the common good, and natural rights—necessarily entail that consent is not *sufficient* for political authority and obligation. Citizens cannot be obligated to obey a regime that exercises force beyond right, *even if they consented to establish it*—otherwise Locke's right of revolution (to depose and replace tyrannical governments) would be sheer nonsense. But in that case, consent, for Locke, supplies only a necessary condition—a position necessary to any logically coherent version of the theory.

It was precisely the insistence on consent as necessary for political authority and obligation that Hume attacked. In his discussion of an original contract, Hume seems clearly to think that consent *suffices* for these. "If we trace government to its first origin in the woods and des[e]rts," we discover that "the people . . . are the source of all power and jurisdiction, and voluntarily, for the sake of peace and order, abandoned their native liberty, and received laws from their equal and companion." Indeed, if this is what the phrase "original contract" means, then "it cannot be denied, that all government is, at first, founded on a contract, and that the most ancient rude [i.e., rudimentary] combinations of mankind were formed chiefly by that principle." To be sure, historical inquiry could never unearth these original contracts: "It was not written on parchment, nor yet on leaves or barks of trees," for "it preceded the use of writing and all the other civilized arts of life." But examination of human nature reveals "equality, or something approaching equality . . . in all the individuals of that species." And since "a man's natural force consists only in the vigour of his limbs, and the firmness of his courage; which could never subject multitudes to the command of one," it follows that "nothing but their own consent, and their sense of the advantages resulting from peace and order, could have had" that effect.[12]

Notwithstanding the origin of political authority and the establishment of government in consent, "Were you to preach, in most parts of the world, that political connexions are founded altogether on voluntary consent or a mutual promise, the magistrate would soon imprison you, as seditious, for loosening the ties of obedience; if your friends did not before shut you up as delirious, for advancing such absurdities. *It is strange, that an act of the mind, which every individual is supposed to have formed,* and after he came to the use of reason too, otherwise it could have no authority . . . *should be so much unknown to all of them, that, over the face of the whole earth, there scarcely remains any traces or memory of it.*"[13] On Hume's argument, insisting on the necessity of consent entails holding that the vast majority of regimes or political orders that have existed over the course of human history have been illegitimate. Insistence on the necessity of consent subverts almost all political authority. And this for the reason that the vast majority of people in the vast majority of regimes have never consented to the establishment of political authority over them and have never promised to obey. Thus, instead of providing a basis for political authority and obligation, insistence on the necessity of consent seems to place political legitimacy (at least for the most part) out of reach.

THE FAILURE OF HYPOTHETICAL CONSENT

Given what appears to be the paucity of express individual consent of the governed to those who govern (or to political society or to the form of government more generally), some theorists have tried to render the claim that consent is necessary for political authority and obligation more plausible by arguing that actual consent is not necessary. Hypothetical consent—sometimes described as rationally implied consent (i.e., a rational person would consent to the establishment of political authority in light of certain considerations)— they claim, will do the trick. Insofar as political contractarianism is concerned, there is a version of hypothetical consent that emerges from Hobbes and another that emerges from scholarly commentary on Locke.[14]

I begin with Hobbes.[15] By saying Hobbes's political theory rests political authority and obligation on hypothetical consent, I don't mean to say he rejects real consent. Hobbes will take real consent if he can get it. Real consent certainly suffices (for Hobbes) to place one under another's authority—whether that consent is given at the founding of a commonwealth or tendered to an existing commonwealth in which one resides or given under duress because the sword of the conqueror is at one's neck and one has been offered the choice to submit or die.[16] But I maintain that such real consent is *not necessary on Hobbes's view*.

As previously noted, in the world of science, Hobbes positioned himself in the geometric, deductive camp *over and against* those (such as Robert Boyle) who insisted on an observational and experimental science.[17] In the debate with Boyle over whether vacuums can exist in nature, Boyle claimed to have proved their existence experimentally (and subsequent science seems to have proven him right, especially as regards the conclusion—for atomic and subatomic particles oscillate in void space). Hobbes, however, rejected Boyle's corpuscularist position on purely a priori, deductive grounds. As Hobbes saw it, materialism necessarily entails that vacuums do not exist—in which case Boyle could not have proven that they did; in which case something must have been flawed with his experiment (air seeped in, or Boyle didn't really get it all out).[18] For Hobbes, *science* in the proper sense of the word refers to "*a priori* demonstration only of those things whose generation depends on the will of men." Geometry counts as pure science because "the generation of the figures depends on our will." Physics, by way of contrast, depends in part on a posteriori demonstration from our experience of the effects caused by "natural things" that "are not in our power" (but, rather, depend on "the divine will"). Consequently, Hobbes considers physics "mixed mathematics" rather than science in the proper sense—"for those sciences are usually called mathematical that are learned not from use and experience, but from teachers and rules." Science proper, for Hobbes, in no way depends on human experience but derives entirely from human construction. The foregoing might seem a tangent save that Hobbes considered ethics and politics to be demonstrative sciences. In contrast to physics, but like geometry, "politics and ethics . . . can be demonstrated *a priori*; because we ourselves make the principles."[19]

As such, ethics and politics proceed geometrically—deductively—
from axioms to necessary conclusions (thus Hobbes's claim to have
proven every claim in *Leviathan* save one: the superiority of monarchy to other regimes).[20] Thus, when Hobbes speaks of the state of
nature or covenants by which the state of nature is left—though the
state of nature may instantiate to some degree in human history and
though it's possible for people to establish political order by means
of covenant—the historicity or existential reality of the pure state of
nature in chapter 13 of Leviathan and of the covenant of everyone
with everyone in chapter 17 is entirely beside the point.

Let's begin with Hobbes's state of nature. The basic features of the
state of nature are generally well understood, and I have treated them
in prior work.[21] Prior to chapter 13 of *Leviathan*, Hobbes describes
human beings as being moved by one desire after another.[22] To be
unmoved by desire after desire (for good after good or satisfaction
upon satisfaction) is to be dead. Human desire is therefore in principle unlimited. Indeed, when it comes to preservation, Hobbes says
we can never rest content with what we have. We can never be sure
that we have enough to secure our preservation. Thus, human beings
always desire more.[23] But Hobbes also describes human competition
over goods desired by two or more people that they cannot both or
all have.[24] The notion he's getting at here is that the basic goods that
animate human action lack what economists call jointness of supply.[25]
They are zero sum. And they are finite in number. Thus, Hobbes
describes a world in which human desire outstrips the goods that are
present in it.[26] The goods of the world are therefore scarce. We might
say they are scarce relative to human desire rather than relative to
human need.[27] But in the natural condition, Hobbes says desire is the
only measure of human need.[28]

Competition over goods that individuals judge requisite to their
preservation—because of the relative scarcity of those goods—
produces conflict. In the course of pursuing a good deemed requisite
to survival that two or more individuals cannot all enjoy, they become
enemies.[29] The fact that individuals become enemies in pursuit of a
good they cannot all share might be of no consequence if a particular individual (or individuals) possessed substantially greater ability
to apprehend the good than everyone else pursuing it—and if that

individual were able to succeed against others repeatedly.[30] But, says, Hobbes, individuals in the natural condition and in the absence of a commonwealth or sovereign power are sufficiently equal in ability such that no one competing over goods desired for the sake of preservation backs down.[31] More precisely, Hobbes describes individuals in the natural condition as equal in strength and prudence. The equality of strength is actually an equality of *weakness*.[32] Everyone is equally vulnerable to death at the hands of others: no one is so strong that they cannot be killed by anyone else, acting either alone or in a group and by means of sheer strength or cunning. No one is so weak that they cannot kill anyone else.[33] Likewise, Hobbes says individuals possess equal prudence. For prudence is just experience, which equal time bestows equally on all who will but equally attend to it.[34] And the point here must be that life in the state of nature prevents anyone from attending to their experience with such care that they might learn from it. So the equality in view seems to be an equal *lack* of prudence—otherwise Hobbes's caveats concerning time and attention entail that prudence is in fact *not equal*. Hobbes takes these equalities of strength and experience together to constitute an equality of ability *to attain goods desired for the sake of preservation*. Equality of ability produces equal hope *in successfully obtaining those goods*.[35] Thus, in a competition for such goods, no one backs down. Were ability substantially unequal or the goods not thought requisite to preservation, individuals might back down from such conflicts. Just because of human equality, they don't.

Hobbes says individuals in the state of nature invade for three reasons: competition (for the sake of obtaining objects desired for preservation); diffidence (for the sake of security); and glory (for the sake of reputation).[36] The previous paragraph focuses primarily on the first reason. As to the second, Hobbes has in view the suspicion individuals have of others that those others will invade them.[37] To secure their lives, individuals apprehensive of being invaded by others strike preemptively. With respect to glory, the good in view is reputation. The point seems to be that a certain kind of reputation in the natural condition redounds to preservation, perhaps by getting others to back down. Hobbes, after all, regards as mad those who court death on the field of the battle for the sake of immortal fame.[38] But if the state of nature is a state in which individuals invade each other for these reasons, then the state of nature is a state of war—of every person against every person.[39]

Hobbes says that *state of nature* and *state of war* are two turns of phrase that refer to the same phenomenon such that anything true of one is also true of the others.[40] He speaks the language of predication. The state of nature *is* a state of war (and vice versa). And in the state of war, nothing is right or wrong. Neither just nor unjust have any place in that state of affairs. Consequently, says Hobbes, there is no property (no mine and thine distinct; no dominion). And this means that no killing can be called murder. No taking can be called theft. Rather, in contrast to the civil state, in the natural condition force and fraud are virtues.[41] And individuals possess what Hobbes calls the right of nature: the right to everything and to do anything in order to survive.[42] The state of nature is, consequently, one in which life is "solitary, poor, nasty, brutish, and short."[43] There is no agriculture, navigation, building/architecture, learning (for example, history), arts, and so forth. Hobbes suggests individuals in the state of nature have no time to learn the principles behind moving heavy objects (perhaps he has in mind the inclined plane, leverage, pulleys). As Hobbes sees it, the best-case scenario in the state of nature is still worse than the worst-case scenario under civil society. Consequently, anyone who found themselves in a state of nature would seek to leave it if they could. More aptly, insofar as individuals have any concern for their own preservation (and this, says Hobbes, is each person's chief concern), they will seek to escape or avoid the state of nature.

A chief criticism leveled by Hobbes's seventeenth-century opponents is that the state of nature never existed. But as A. P. Martinich notes, these critics misunderstood Hobbes's argument.[44] In chapter 13 of *Leviathan* Hobbes says he believes the state of nature in its purest form (as a state of conflict of every individual against every other individual) "was never generally so over all the world."[45] To be sure, he thinks there are three states of affairs that instantiate the state of nature to some real degree. He believes (wrongly, as it happens) that Native Americans lived under the government of small families. On Hobbes's telling, each family constitutes something like a petty kingdom, and the state of nature/war obtains across families. He likewise maintains that civil war instantiates the state of nature/war within a society.[46] And the nations of the world exist in a state of nature with respect to each other. Individuals within each nation are in a civil state, while a state-of-nature relation obtains across kingdoms or commonwealths.[47] In these instances we do not have the war of every man against every man. We do not have the pure state of nature. But these situations, according to Hobbes, are nevertheless state-of-nature relations. These variants of the state of nature illuminate the point at hand. Hobbes's concern is *not* to help individuals escape an original state of nature. Individuals in a pure state of nature would lack understanding (because they would lack language). As individuals in that condition would lack the time for agriculture, navigation, architecture, or to learn the principles for moving heavy objects just because they would be constantly occupied with their own survival, such individuals would lack both the time and inclination to study Hobbes's own work or any similar work or to otherwise develop such an argument on their own. Rather, Hobbes's concern is to help individuals within society understand what the state of nature would be like, were they to find themselves in one. He means to show people that if they found themselves in such a condition, they *would* escape it if they could. His point is entirely in the subjunctive mode, and his reasoning entirely hypothetical.

Against this backdrop, Hobbes's laws of nature are not first and foremost steps for escaping (or getting out of) the state of nature so much as means for avoiding or forestalling it. Hobbes's laws of nature are necessary conditions to prevent descent into the natural condition. Thus, the first law of nature directs individuals to seek peace with those others who will seek it with them as a *means* of securing their preservation (preservation is not the first law of nature but the good to which all of Hobbes's laws of nature redound).[48] The second law of nature—laying down the right of nature—comprises what Hobbes takes to be the necessary (indeed, analytically necessary) means of seeking peace.[49] Insofar as one possesses the right of nature, he remains in state of war with respect to everyone else. And, of course, Hobbes holds that mere renunciation is an insufficient means for laying the right of nature down—covenants without the sword, after all, are mere words and lack any power to secure one's life.[50]

Thus, Hobbes says the right of nature must be laid down by means of transferring it to another—to a sovereign power.[51] The covenant is the means by which this transfer is made.

There are many interesting things we might say about the covenant—for instance, that the sovereign is not party to it;[52] consequently, that the sovereign does not lay the right of nature down;[53] consequently, that the sovereign remains in a state of war relation vis-à-vis his subjects;[54] that the covenant establishes a sovereign that possesses absolute power or authority and is above and in no way subject to civil law;[55] that individuals can never lay down the right to defend themselves from force by force;[56] that concessions Hobbes must make concerning the liberty of subjects and the dissolution of sovereign power, when the sovereign can no longer protect them, ultimately means that subjects never really lay down private judgment concerning what redounds to their preservation; that subjects retaining private judgment about what redounds to their preservation, including whether to obey the sovereign based on their assessment of whether or not obedience threatens their preservation or whether or not the sovereign is able to protect them, means they retain the right of nature; that subjects therefore never really transfer the right of nature away from themselves;[57] and thus that the subjects never really empower an absolute sovereign. Jean Hampton says many interesting things on these points. And I addressed some of them in chapters 1 and 4. So I'll refrain from elaborating them further here.[58] For my purposes, it suffices to think of what Hobbes's covenant of every person with every other person (the sovereign representative excepted) must be in light of the hypothetical nature of the pure state of nature.

A covenant among individuals to escape a hypothetical state of nature must itself be hypothetical. The consent tendered in such a covenant would therefore be hypothetical rather than actual. Hobbes's point is that individuals who found themselves in the state of nature *would* consent to leave it by establishing an absolute sovereign if they were able to do so. Put another way, your consent to political authority in a commonwealth is rationally implied by the fact that you *would* give it if you truly understood the alternative: a condition in which life is "solitary, poor, nasty, brutish and short." Moreover, since anyone in the state of nature would consent to leave it for the civil state, such persons *would* also consent to the means by which the state of nature is left (i.e., to the laws of nature). The point at hand is that the deductive nature of Hobbes's philosophy compels him to affirm a hypothetical state of nature (one indifferent as to whether it really occurred historically) and therefore to posit hypothetical consent as the means by which it is left.[59] Indeed, if Hobbes were to insist on the *necessity* of actual consent to authorize sovereign power or incur obligations to obey, then his covenant would fall into the realm of experience and therefore, by his own definition, cease to be part of demonstrative science—contrary to his claim that ethics and politics are demonstrative sciences. Hobbes certainly thinks actual consent suffices to bind one to sovereign power. But the entire cast of his theory militates against him thinking actual consent is strictly necessary. As Gregory S. Kavka contends, "Hobbes is essentially a *hypothetical* contract theorist. For him, the social contract is not an actual historical event, but a theoretical construct designed to facilitate our understanding of the grounds of political obedience."[60]

But, again, Hobbes will take real consent if he can get it. Actual consent *suffices* to take on political obligations and authorize sovereign power. Before leaving Hobbes, we should consider the role of actual consent in his thought. In this vein, he speaks of commonwealths being established in one of two ways: by institution or by acquisition. People establish a commonwealth by institution "when [they] agree amongst themselves to submit to some man, or assembly of men, *voluntarily*, on confidence to be protected by [the sovereign] against all others."[61] A commonwealth is established by acquisition when "the sovereign power is acquired *by force*; and it is acquired by force when men . . . for fear of death or bonds do authorize all the actions of that man or assembly that hath their lives and liberty in his [or their] power."[62] The vast majority of citizens or subjects in the vast majority of commonwealths, however, have never participated in the creation of a commonwealth (commonwealth by institution) or expressly agreed to submit to a conquering power in order to avoid "death or bonds" (commonwealth by acquisition). Most people are born into a commonwealth. Does Hobbes say anything that addresses them?

Perhaps. If so, the consent he has in view is not express consent. In chapter 21 of *Leviathan*, Hobbes considers "what rights we pass

away when we make a commonwealth, or . . . what liberty we deny
ourselves by owning all the actions without exception of the one man
or assembly we make our sovereign." How do we authorize the sovereign and take upon ourselves an obligation to obey?

> For in the act of our *submission* consisteth both our *obligation*
> and our liberty, which must be inferred by arguments taken
> thence, there being no obligation on any man which ariseth not
> from some act of his own; for all men equally are by nature free.
> And because such arguments must either be drawn from the
> express words *I authorize all his actions*, or from the intention
> of him that submitteth himself to his power (which intention
> is to be understood by the end for which he so submitteth), the
> obligation and the liberty of the subject is to be derived, either
> from those words (or others equivalent) or else from the end of
> the institution of sovereignty, namely, the peace of the subjects
> within themselves, and defense against a common enemy.[63]

If Hobbes intends this passage to include those born into a commonwealth, then to submit must mean to obey the sovereign's commands.

Let's suppose Hobbes means to say that obedience to the sovereign
tenders consent to obey and thereby authorizes the sovereign's power
over us. Such a view is deeply problematic. For Hobbes, covenant or
consent is supposed to ground—to be the cause of—an obligation to
obey the sovereign. If obedience to the sovereign grounds the obligation to obey the sovereign, then one and the same thing becomes
its own cause and effect at the same time, which, as Locke argues,
is nonsense.[64] Taking obedience to the sovereign as the cause of our
obligation to obey the sovereign is like taking an agreement to keep
our agreements to be the cause of an obligation to keep our agreements. Both positions are viciously circular. Moreover, obedience to
the laws is at most an exceedingly equivocal instance of tacit consent.
You might obey the laws for any number of reasons that have nothing to do with tendering consent. For instance, perhaps you strongly
prefer to avoid the punishment for felony theft—and so you obey
the law simply for that reason. Finally, since obeying the sovereign
is not actually consenting to obey the sovereign, when you submit

to sovereign power (without express words of authorization) it's *as if* you've covenanted to obey. Which strikes me as hypothetical consent.

Given his account of science and his inclusion of ethics and politics under the heading of demonstrative science, Hobbes's project is not historical or chronological or predicated on temporal experience at all. It's constructive. He means to describe human nature as we have it here and now. And he means to build from human nature as we have it here and now to a justification of political authority and of the obligations of subjects here and now. Given that life without sovereign power *would be* solitary, poor, nasty, brutish, and short, characterized by constant fear of sudden and violent death at the hands of others, individuals here and now, who really understood this, *would* consent to authorize sovereign power in order to avoid that state of affairs. For Hobbes, that suffices to justify sovereign power and, ceteris paribus, to bind us to obey.

There are, of course, many difficulties with the Hobbesian theory. He arguably weds his contractarianism to materialism, which runs up against several objections that seem impossible for it to overcome.[65] Materialism turns out *not* to be the conclusion of an argument (scientific or metaphysical) but, rather, is usually held fideistically.[66] Moreover, the object of Hobbesian consent is an absolute sovereign power. Many (myself included) find such political absolutism objectionable and even morally reprehensible. As well, at the foundation of Hobbes's thought is nominalism concerning universals, subjectivism and relativism concerning good and evil, a rejection of a greatest (or highest) good with the character of a final end, and an express rejection of the rule of law (contained in Hobbes's denial that the sovereign can in any way be bound or limited by positive law). Finally, Hobbes rests his political theory on a moral foundation (on an account of oughtness) that is comprised of hypothetical imperatives all the way down *or* on moral contractarianism (or normative constructivism) *or* on a theistic-voluntaristic ontology of obligation where the laws of nature really are laws *because and only because* they are the commands of an irresistibly powerful God or of the mortal god (to wit, the state). Here I only briefly note that moral contractarianism, normative constructivism, and grounding obligation or oughtness in omnipotence or irresistible power alone are all instances of metaethical voluntarism,

which I have already shown to be self-referentially incoherent. I also
built on Jean Hampton's argument that moral theory constituted
by hypothetical imperatives all the way down ultimately lacks any
normativity or oughtness at all.[67] Consequently, a theory of consent
or political contractarianism grounded on a Hobbesian moral foundation (whichever of the foregoing turns out to be the proper account
of that foundation) is ultimately incoherent.

But perhaps we can salvage hypothetical consent from problems part and parcel of Hobbes's larger philosophy and his theory
of sovereignty by detaching hypothetical consent from absolute or
unlimited sovereign power and relativism concerning good and evil.
Some have interpreted Locke along these lines. Some scholars (for
instance, Hanna Pitkin) have argued that central to Locke's argument is the character or quality of the government.[68] What matters
most in his theory of consent is the *object* of consent—is the sort of
government or political society to which one can rightly or rationally
give consent. From Locke's vantage, the only sort of society or government to which individuals can rightly or rationally consent is one
that is limited. Individuals cannot consent to political power that is
absolute or arbitrary over the lives of citizens or subjects. There is a
sense in Locke in which one *ought not* try to do this. But I think the
main point for Locke is that one *cannot* do this even if one tries. As
we saw earlier, Locke repeatedly claims that one *cannot* give more
power than one has and, importantly, that one lacks absolute and
arbitrary power or authority over one's own life. Consequently, one
cannot transfer such power to political society. Political society, in
turn, cannot delegate such authority to government. In keeping with
this inability to enslave oneself, one cannot give to political society
or to the legislative it ordains authority to act beyond or contrary to
the common good or contrary to natural rights or natural law. To
put all this another way, Lockean individuals can only consent to a
political society or government animated by certain ends and operating within certain limits. And Pitkin (among others) takes this to
be what matters most in Locke's thought—but does so in a way that
actual (or historical) consent falls out and is replaced, it would seem,
with hypothetical consent.[69] That rational individuals would consent
to a government of this kind (but not to one that exercised absolutely

or arbitrary power over the lives of citizens and not to one that acted beyond or contrary to the common good) is sufficient to justify it. But in that case what justifies government is that it's the sort of thing to which rational individuals *would* consent if they were in a position to consent. Again we are dealing with hypothetical rather than actual consent. The consent in question is depicted in the subjunctive mode.

Now, I think Locke is interested in actual rather than hypothetical consent. But let's grant the hypothetical-consent interpretation for the sake of argument. Will it work? I think there are several objections against hypothetical consent. To be sure, the character or quality of political society and the government it ordains matters a great deal to Locke. But Simmons is surely right that when it comes to the sort of society or government to which rational individuals *would* (or *could*) consent, we are dealing with a necessary condition of authoritative political order rather than a sufficient one (or rather than one that is both necessary and sufficient).[70] To say that individuals can only consent to a political order of a certain kind (broadly construed— perhaps—to include constitutional monarchy, republican form, mixed regimes, etc.) is to say that if consent is or *were to be* tendered to something else, then the regime would not be authorized after all. And in that case, the requirement that the regime possess a certain character or quality is a necessary condition of political authority and obligation. But to specify a necessary condition is not to specify a sufficient one or one that is both necessary and sufficient. It's to say only that the regime *must be* of a certain kind to be authoritative. It is emphatically *not* to say that if the regime is indeed of a certain kind, then it's authoritative. In short, the quality-of-regime version of the hypothetical consent position seems to be something of a non sequitur.

Moreover, if what matters is the sort of regime to which individuals could rationally or rightly consent, then we are compelled to ask how individuals might be bound to one good regime rather than another.[71] Presumably we think the character of the regime *where they reside or of which they are a citizen* is what matters when it comes to political authority. But in that case the character of the regime (to which rational individuals would consent) does not matter by itself. An additional criterion to that of the regime's character (or rationally implied consent on account of its character) is being introduced to explain why individuals have political obligations to one good regime rather than another. Relatedly, as Simmons notes, with a hypothetical consent position that focuses on the character of the regime, consent seems to fall out of the picture entirely. The position seems another way of saying that it's only the character of the regime that truly matters.

Finally, we might keep in mind the claim that hypothetical contracts aren't worth the paper they're not written on.[72] As I noted in chapter 1, there is no moral norm to the effect that one is bound to keep promises or agreements that one would have made under certain conditions (or perhaps even should have made) but in fact did not make. There is a moral norm concerning promissory obligation: namely, that I ought to keep legitimate promises or agreements. To be sure, a promise to my neighbor to kill someone who has offended him is not binding because everyone has an obligation to refrain from such action—I cannot enter a binding promise to do something morally illicit. But when it comes to things I may promise or to which I may agree, then there is—as Locke notes in several places—an obligation (a natural moral obligation) to keep my promises and agreements. Indeed, consent theory is an application of the norm of promissory obligation to political authority and obligation. But in the case of hypothetical (or rationally implied) consent, there is no actual promise or agreement. And promissory obligation applies *only* to agreements and promises I did in fact make *just because* there is no obligation to abide by agreements or promises I would have but did not in fact make. This returns us to the non sequitur problem with the quality/character-of-regime version of hypothetical consent. What is missing in that argument is a major premise—where the major premise is a moral precept or requirement (indeed, a categorical imperative) such that promises or agreements I would have made *even though I did not* are nevertheless binding upon me. But such a moral precept—though necessary to drive any version of the hypothetical consent argument—is utterly absurd. It seems to be the sort of precept one would only posit to save the argument. But it also seems to be the only candidate for the major premise in the hypothetical consent argument.

THE INADEQUACY OF TACIT OR IMPLIED CONSENT

The failure of hypothetical consent to ground political authority and obligations entails that any coherent political contractarianism or theory of consent requires actual consent—only with actual consent is the moral norm that we ought to keep our promises or abide by our agreements, a norm on which Locke expressly relies, brought into the theory. But of course hypothetical consent is an attempt to save consent theory from the apparent paucity of individual consent. When it comes to individual consent, very few individuals have expressly consented to political authority over them or to take on obligations to obey.[73] Naturalized citizens have expressly consented.[74] Arguably we can add members of the military (especially insofar as we are dealing with an all-volunteer force rather than draftees compelled to serve and who therefore do not tender free consent in a military oath of service) and those who work in the government or who are elected or appointed to office—all of whom must swear an oath of office to uphold the laws.[75] But all these people together comprise only a minority (according to Simmons a very small minority) of any modern state—including regimes such as modern liberal democracies, like the United States, that claim to be founded on consent.[76] The Pledge of Allegiance recited by schoolchildren in the United States hardly seems a good candidate for meaningful express consent.[77] But in that case, if we rely on express consent as requisite for political authority and obligations, only a minority (and perhaps only a small proportion) of those who reside within a state's borders can be said to have obligations to obey and the state can only be said to have authority over a small number of individuals within its territory (a point underscored by Simmons, Green, and Wolterstorff). Yet the point of consent theory is the authorization of political authority that extended to more than a small percentage of those who reside within a state's territory. Because express consent seems clearly to entail that very few—even in liberal democracies—have political obligations and that modern states have authority over only a minority of those that reside within their territories (and perhaps only over a very small minority), indeed, because Locke, among early modern theorists, was aware of this problem, consent theorists (or political contractarians) have usually retreated to the weaker standard of tacit or implied consent.

Because, as Simmons argues, the obligations incurred by consent are so substantial and significant, even with tacit consent, both the giving of consent and the object of consent must be clear. Consequently, the sorts of actions by which tacit consent to political authority and obligations are given are of real importance. Some have suggested that political participation—in particular, voting—counts as giving consent to political authority and obligations. Locke suggests residence (though here we need to add residence with the real possibility of emigration from a state's territory) as well as using the roads or inns or, more broadly, enjoying the benefits a state provides.[78] Let's consider each of these possible instances of tacit consent—voting, residence, enjoying the benefits of a state (such as using roads or inns), as well as acquiescence (or going along)—in turn. For each is subject to considerable difficulties.

Let's begin with participation and, in particular, voting. According to some, to participate or vote is to agree to abide by the outcome. Several difficulties with voting as a sign of tacit consent immediately present themselves. Here I follow Simmons's argument. First, not everyone votes. Indeed, as Simmons notes, "many citizens in existing democracies fail to vote in particular elections, many vote in none at all, and very few citizens vote in *all* democratic elections."[79] If voting is choosing to take on political obligations, then what about those who refrain from voting? By refusing to participate or vote, it would seem that they are, at best, withholding consent to political authority and obligation and, at worst, doing nothing at all. Or maybe refraining from voting merely conveys frustration with the options with which one is presented. At best, then, the choice not to vote is deeply equivocal. But in that case, not voting is *not* a clear or unambiguous way of indicating whether one means to give or, more aptly, withhold consent. As Simmons says, "nonvoters cannot be understood to have consented at all."[80] Setting aside those regimes that do not grant subjects rights of participation (and so where participation is virtually nonexistent), the fact that many citizens in liberal democracies— where rights of participation are most extensive—do not vote leaves us with a substantial number of citizens who lack any political obligations and over whom the state has no authority at all—*insofar as we take voting as a sign of tacit consent.*

Perhaps in light of the fact that many citizens of liberal democracies refrain from voting, some scholars have taken the *right to vote* for tacit consent. But the mere possession of a right—including the right to participate—cannot be construed as tendering something and, in particular, as tendering consent.[81] Possessing the right to φ and φ-ing are, quite obviously, modally distinct. Just because Joe has the right to marry Jane does not mean that he has in fact married her. Moreover, if the right of participation amounted to consent, then rulers or governments of regimes in which subjects or citizens did not yet have the right to vote could compel their consent to the regime just by *giving* them the right to vote. But this proposition is absurd. The regime doing something for individuals is quite obviously *not* individuals doing something with respect to the regime. Indeed, possessing the right to vote does not involve the citizen in *doing* something at all. Yet Locke believes giving consent is something individuals *do*. If we have consented by virtue of possessing rights of participation, then we have not exercised a choice. Indeed, if the regime extracts consent from us by giving us the right to vote, then we have consented both without any action on our part and without any choice. As Simmons repeatedly notes, however, if what we seek is a theory of consent in which citizens deliberately choose to move from a state of natural freedom to one of political society by taking on political obligations and establishing political authority, then the choice must be voluntary and one made in light of real alternatives.[82]

According to Simmons, the most damning argument against voting as tendering tacit consent has to do with the fact that in voting (or refraining from voting) I don't do anything as an individual.[83] Rather, voting determines what the majority does. Voting is participation in a corporate act. But how am I bound by the majority? If I have not antecedently consented to political society and, consequently, to be determined or concluded by the majority when it comes to the decisions and actions of the community, then the answer would seem to be "Not by consent." Voting is how we determine majority rule with respect to things like laws or elected officials. And we can be bound by the majority in a way consonant with individual consent only if we have antecedently consented, as individuals, to be so determined. Thus, though Simmons doesn't put it just this way, taking voting for individual consent either represents a serious misunderstanding of the nature of voting or (viciously) begs the question, since to have the right to vote and to vote one must already be a citizen subject to the laws of the regime that empower citizens to participate in this way.

What about residence? The first point to make is that residence must be expanded to *residence together with the right of emigration*. This idea—that one consents to political authority and takes on an obligation to obey if one chooses to remain in a place (a state, commonwealth, or polis) when one could have left—originates in antiquity (in the speech that Socrates imagines the Laws make to him in the *Crito*).[84] Is residence together with the right to emigrate (when one has come of age) a way of giving consent to political authority and obligations?[85] There are reasons to be skeptical. First, consider the fact that everyone resides in a territory. If the problem of explicit consent is its paucity, the problem of tacit consent tendered via residence is that everyone gives it. Now, if consent is either sufficient or necessary and sufficient for political authority and obligation (though such a position is in fact self-referentially incoherent), then everyone in every regime, even the most oppressive, would be fully obligated and every regime—however oppressive—would be fully authoritative and legitimate. Consent theory is intended to distinguish legitimate or authoritative regimes from those that are not. But if residence counts for consent and if residence is sufficient or necessary and sufficient for political authority and obligation, then no such distinction is possible. The way out of this difficulty—at least initially—seems to be by holding that consent is never sufficient or both necessary and sufficient for political authority and obligation but only *necessary* for these. The character of the regime matters too. So consent can only authorize some regimes and not others. In that case residence as the mechanism of tacit consent does not result in the absurd consequence that all regimes are authoritative and that citizens have obligations to obey in every regime, however oppressive. Still, taking residence as a sign of consent would result in the authorization of every good regime. And in that case it seems like only the character of the regime counts, and consent doesn't really matter at all.

Moreover, as Simmons notes, residence doesn't present us with an instance of a clear, voluntary choice between two alternatives.[86]

Because everyone resides where they live, they have *already* "consent-ed" unless they leave. In other words, without having done anything at all, they are consenters. Doing something vis-à-vis residence would mean emigration. Thus, so far as I can tell, the idea here ends up being something like this: you've consented, unless you withdraw your consent. That seems reductio ad absurdum false. Consider again the case of marriage. One consents to take on the obligations of mar-riage. Those obligations are not in place prior to the giving of consent. What sense could there possibly be in saying that one has already given consent to marriage and its obligations unless one decides to walk away? Or consider purchasing a home. What sense could there possibly be in saying you have, a priori, given consent to buy a house unless you do something to withdraw it? Locke wants to hold that individuals consent to take on political obligations, including to obey the law, and have no such obligations unless they have consented. Taking residence for tacit consent is equivalent to saying something quite different: that one is born into such obligations unless one em-igrates to another place. Put another way, residence (conjoined with the right of emigration) entails that one has political obligations on account of where one is born ceteris paribus. These obligations are not indefeasible. They are defeasible if one exercises the right to emigrate elsewhere. But ceteris paribus, on residence they are automatic rather than consciously undertaken. And, again, this is the very account of political authority and obligation that Locke meant to reject.

Moreover, even if I have the *right* to emigrate to another place, it does not follow that I have the *ability* to emigrate. Indeed, I think Simmons and Hume are right to hold that most people at most times and places would have found emigration impossible.[87] Among other things, language and expense pose obstacles to emigration. Moreover, there may be little by way of good alternatives. Thus, contra Locke, emigration might be quite difficult. And even where concerns such as language and financial ability present no difficulty, there may be rea-sons one feels compelled or simply chooses to remain. For instance, one might remain out of a sense of familial obligation. Perhaps a family member requires care, and one chooses to remain not as a way of consenting to political authority and obligation but in order to care for the family member. Thus, even with a right of emigration, we may not be able to choose emigration. And one might choose to remain (and not to exercise the right of emigration) for reasons that have nothing to do with political authority and obligation. And this means the condition of voluntary choice and the condition of performing an act that clearly gives consent to political authority and obligations are not met by residence.

That leaves us with enjoying the benefits of the state—including such things as use of roads and inns (and of course we might add other items to Locke's list). Here Simmons contends (and I concur) that Locke has conflated a benefaction justification of political authority and obligation with consent.[88] Like consent theory, a benefaction account seeks to explain particular ties (of particular individuals to particular political societies), something a number of other accounts of political authority and obligation fail to do. Even so, benefaction has its problems. Suppose someone sets up a trust fund for Jane. She has never met this person. The person in question remains anonymous. Now suppose this trust pays for her expenses at all the best schools at every stage of her education; and suppose that after she completes her education, Jane lands a well-paying and highly satisfying job. After she's spent some time in this career, her benefactor reveals himself. It turns out the benefactor was a dear friend of her parents. Jane is of course very grateful for the extraordinary gift provided by her benefactor. But suppose the benefactor says that since Jane has enjoyed his good gift, she is bound to obey him. To make the example more plausible, let's posit that the expectation is not one of absolute obedience to every command but only to those commands that in no way violate the moral law or the rights of others. Does Jane have any such obligation? It's hard to see how. With benefaction there is, of course, an obligation to be grateful. Ingratitude would be a moral failing and an injustice to the benefactor. We could even argue there is an obligation to in some way or other return the favor. Perhaps after the benefactor passes on, his grandchild is in dire need. Perhaps Jane has an obligation to help the benefactor's grandchild if she can. But there is nothing in the benefaction itself that entails an obligation to obey the commands of the benefactor even ceteris paribus. Nor is it plausible to argue that obedience is somehow necessary to showing gratitude or reciprocating.

Now, I can imagine someone claiming that obedience is the only way to show gratitude for or reciprocate the kind of benefits provided by political society or the state. Indeed, something like this proposition would be a necessary premise for the benefaction account of political authority and obligation. But precisely here we are compelled to ask why such a premise would hold. Locke has provided no argument that it does. Indeed, I'm aware of no theorist who has gone beyond assertion to arguing that *obedience* is necessary for fulfilling obligations of gratitude or reciprocity for the benefits provided by political order.

But the main point is this: even if benefaction turned out to be a workable theory of political authority and obligation, we should not confuse benefaction with consent and believe that we have thereby found a mechanism of tacit consent. Indeed, with benefaction, the ground of political authority again precedes voluntary choice. For the state or the regime benefits you long before you can choose whether or not to receive such benefits.

Drawing on John Dunn's interpretation of Locke, there is one further account of consent that we might consider under the heading of tacit consent: acquiescence.[89] We might call this *weak consent*. The idea here is that in *going along* with the existing political order, I acquiesce (or consent) to its authority. Acquiescence or going along is sufficiently weak that it can hardly count as taking on political obligations.[90] There are, after all, lots of reasons one might go along. For instance, if the robber has a gun pointed at you and says, "Give me your wallet," you might well go along. But no one could seriously maintain that you had voluntarily taken on an obligation to obey.[91] Rather, you decided to go along in order to preserve your life. Likewise, one might *go along* with the state because the price of not going along is too steep. And so one acquiesces. Those who advance the acquiescence theory of consent, as Simmons suggests (or at least insinuates), "pry apart" political authority and obligation rather than taking them as correlatives.[92] Thus, going along or acquiescence is taken to ground the authority of the state rather than political obligations.

Will acquiescence—or weak consent—work to establish political authority even if something stronger is still needed to ground political obligations? I can't see how. First, whether or not political authority and obligation can be pried apart at all depends on what political authority is. G. E. M. Anscombe (who is followed in this by Jean Hampton and Nicholas Wolterstorff, among others) defines *authority* as a right to be obeyed.[93] Insofar as one has authority, one has a right to be obeyed within a domain of action. Consequently, the authority of the state is a right of the state to be obeyed (we need not say that this is a comprehensive or unlimited right; we can define the authority of the state as a right to be obeyed within a limited domain). Now if Anscombe, Hampton, and Wolterstorff are right (and I think they are), then whether or not the political authority and obligation can be pried apart depends on what a *right* is. For Hobbes, rights are sheer liberties that do not, just as such, correlate to obligations.[94] Thus, the sovereign has a right to punish me by means of imprisonment or death. But, according to Hobbes, I have no concomitant obligation to obey the sovereign in this.[95] Indeed, I have a right to resist the sovereign if the sovereign poses such a threat. For, according to Hobbes, I can never covenant away the right to defend myself from force by force.[96] Likewise, though I have a right to resist a sovereign seeking to take my life, the sovereign has no concomitant obligation to refrain from taking it.[97] Hobbes defines rights in such a way that rights qua rights do not entail obligations. They are sheer liberties.[98] Contra Hobbes, W. N. Hohfeld, Anscombe, and Wolterstorff (especially in *Justice: Rights and Wrongs*) establish that rights and obligations are necessary correlates.[99] As I see it, they rightly argue that rights and obligations always correlate. But even if they (and I following them) are not right that rights and duties always correlate, political authority—as a right to be obeyed—seems only intelligible as a *claim* right that imposes obligations upon those over whom the right is exercised. If either all rights are claim rights *or* authority in general (and so political authority in particular) is a claim right, then, necessarily, political authority and obligation cannot be pried apart.

Moreover, I cannot see why *going along* should suffice to convey consent to political authority if it cannot suffice to take on political obligations. In going along with the gunman, not only am I *not* taking on an obligation to obey, but I am also *not* implying that he possesses authority over me. I am simply going along in order to preserve my life. To be sure, if I take someone to have authority over me, I may well go along with their command. But it's not the going along that explains or grounds the authority; it's the authority that explains or grounds the going along. The problem with taking acquiescence as consent is that what we have here is a *per consequens* explanation of the phenomenon we are seeking to explain. In colloquial terms, we've put the cart before the horse.

CAN PHILOSOPHICAL ANARCHISM BE AVOIDED?

In light of the foregoing, there is strong reason to suspect that we lack clear tacit consent that represents a voluntary choice between alternatives, where one alternative represents giving and the other withholding consent. But in that case tacit consent fails to ground political authority and obligations. Thus, as things presently stand, neither hypothetical nor tacit consent appears capable of justifying political authority and obligation. If consent is a necessary condition of political authority and obligation, then the consent in question must be express. But, as we noted before, following Simmons, to the degree that (*a*) express individual consent is necessary for political authority and obligations, and (*b*) individuals have not given such consent, then (*c*) individuals will not have political obligations, and political authority will not be justified with respect to them. That is, if we take seriously the necessity of consent (together with the implausibility of hypothetical and tacit consent) *and* the paucity of consent, we seem driven to affirm philosophical anarchism (or the absence of political authority and obligation) for at least the vast majority of citizens.

At this point we might ask why Locke insists on real consent. Clearly he wants an account of political authority and obligation that ties particular people to particular communities. But why consent? Simmons argues rather persuasively that Locke insists on the necessity of consent on account of the natural liberty of human persons.[100] Human beings come under political authority and take on political obligations only if they give consent just because they are *not* born into political subjection to anyone else. Political ties are not given by nature. This idea is, of course, older than Locke or, for that matter, Hobbes. Salmancan Thomists—especially Suárez—affirmed expressly that individuals are not under political jurisdiction by nature:

"In the nature of things all men are born free; so that, consequently, no person has political jurisdiction over another person . . . nor is there any reason why such power should, [simply] in the nature of things, be attributed to certain persons over other persons, rather than *vice versa*."[101] Indeed, Locke criticizes Filmer for rejecting natural liberty, which occurs at the point where Filmer criticizes Bellarmine and Suárez for affirming it (though Locke refrains from mentioning this).[102] But wherever Locke came by the idea, natural liberty—in the sense of not being born into political subjection—is the basis of Locke's claim that consent is necessary for political authority and obligation. It bears mentioning that it's not clear in Locke whether natural liberty is necessary, sufficient, or both necessary and sufficient for the necessity of consent. I suspect he takes natural liberty either to be sufficient or to be both necessary and sufficient for the proposition that consent is necessary for political authority and obligation. The only point I wish to make here, however, is that Locke posits an essential connection. He seems to consider the necessity of consent to be an entailment of natural liberty. Thus, for Locke, to deny the necessity of consent for political authority and obligations is to deny natural liberty (here there would seem to be a straightforward application of modus tollens).

If Locke is right—if the necessity of consent is the entailment of natural liberty—and if actual (as opposed to hypothetical) consent is necessary and tacit consent does not present a viable way to give actual consent, then we are faced with the alternative *either* of affirming the necessity of express consent and, given its paucity, of affirming philosophical anarchism (the claim that individuals or that most individuals in modern states lack political obligations and that modern states lack authority over at least most of those they claim the right to govern) *or* of giving up natural liberty. Consequently, we might well wonder about the ground on which natural liberty is affirmed. Simmons says we have a fundamental moral intuition that we are not naturally under the political authority of (or bound to obey) some person or group. But if Simmons is right, this intuition does not seem to have been widely shared over most of the course of human history. As Francis Oakley notes, when it comes to the most appropriate form of political order, the common sense of mankind has overwhelmingly affirmed *sacral monarchy*.[103] From the deep recesses of the Neolithic period into the nineteenth century, sacral monarchy has been the form of political order adopted by the vast majority of human communities. The era of the Greek *poleis* and the Roman *res publica* constitutes so considerable an anomaly in antiquity (and human history more broadly) that scholars denominate it the "republican parenthesis." Renaissance republics and liberal democracies in the twentieth and twenty-first century do not make non-monarchical regimes less anomalous to any meaningful degree. And for anyone who has spent time studying sacral monarchy (and its attendant cosmic religiosity) in its various permutations, nothing seems more alien to that form of political order than the idea of natural liberty. If those human beings who have resided in sacral monarchies possessed natural liberty (and I am amenable to the claim that they did), they neither knew it nor affirmed it. The long experience of humanity strongly suggests that natural liberty is not, or at least has not been, a widely shared *intuition*. That does not make it false. But given that Locke and Simmons rest so much on natural liberty, it would be good if natural liberty had a better foundation than a moral intuition that has not been widely shared over the course of human history.

What Does Equality Entail?
EQUALITY AND NATURAL LIBERTY

I maintain that the ground of natural liberty (in Locke as well as more generally) is not a putatively (but perhaps not actually) widespread intuition—natural liberty is not ontologically or morally basic—but, rather, human equality. Natural liberty is an inference from natural equality. The reason that some persons are not under the authority of others without giving their consent to be governed is because human beings are equal when it comes to the authority and jurisdiction they have by nature, whether or not this equality is perceived or affirmed.[104] No person has been invested by nature with a clear title to rule others; no one has been invested by nature with obligations to obey particular persons. Insofar as some persons exercise authority over those who are their equals, this can only be on the basis of consent. Or so the argument goes. But insofar as such consent is absent, then equal individuals are not under political authority or obligation.

They retain possession of natural freedom. But does equality really have this implication?

DISENTANGLING SOCIAL CONTRACT, CONSENT,
AND POPULAR SOVEREIGNTY

As Wolterstorff notes, the notion of a social contract (perhaps of an original contract), the necessity of individual consent for political authority and obligation, and popular sovereignty are commonly conflated or taken to be bound together.[105] But, he quite rightly notes, these are not only analytically distinct but also, at least arguably, separable. Thus, the principle of consent itself—the necessity of consent for political authority and obligation—says nothing about whether any society was founded by an original contract. Likewise, there might be a regime that instantiates popular sovereignty—the supremacy of society to its government—as determined by the majority, but that was not founded by an original contract and that neither seeks nor possesses the consent of each individual to its authority.

It seems obvious that equality does not entail the necessity of an original contract, at least insofar as consent can be secured or equality otherwise paid its due without it. But does equality entail consent rather than popular sovereignty? Indeed, according to Aristotle, insofar as people are equal, then they should take turns ruling and being ruled.[106] And we might ask why natural equality doesn't entail ruling and being ruled in turn *or* a regime in which the people as a corporate whole—as determined by the majority—are supreme with respect to the government *rather than individual consent*. Unless natural equality *just is natural liberty*, it's hard to see why natural equality entails natural liberty rather than the alternatives just mentioned.

But if in fact Suárez and the Salamancan Thomists, as well as Locke and Sidney, are right in holding that individuals are not born under political jurisdiction (that is, are not born politically bound), then we must ask if there is any way in which consent theory can be salvaged from its paucity. I submit that the only way consent theory can be so salvaged is along lines described by the seventeenth-century syndic of Emden, Johannes Althusius.[107] Althusius's account of political order grounded on consent builds from the ground up. As he describes it, individuals covenant to enter into pre-political primary associations. The primary, voluntary associations he has in mind are families (where he has in view marriage and not the parent-child relation) and collegia (such as professional and trade guilds).[108] The first level of *political* association, the city, is created by a covenant or agreement. But the agreement is not among individual persons but, rather, among primary associations.[109] Individuals consent to associations that in turn consent to cities. Likewise, provinces are created by a covenant among cities and towns. The most comprehensive political association—which Althusius calls universal political association—is the realm or commonwealth.[110] Though he rejects Jean Bodin's claim that sovereign power is indivisible as well as Bodin's claim that sovereignty is exercised by the state (or the prince) over the realm, holding instead that sovereignty is possessed by the society over its so-called rulers, Althusius locates sovereignty with universal association rather than cities or provinces.[111] The commonwealth or realm, like collegia, cities, and provinces, is brought into existence by agreement. The members that agree together to create a realm are cities and provinces and not individuals, families, or collegia.[112]

The point here is that individual consent is first given to private, pre-political associations. From the moment he turns to political association, Althusius has corporate or communal consent in view. As things stand, I think the only sort of consent theory that has any possibility of securing a sufficient level of real consent and that incorporates actual individual consent to some degree is one that moves along path laid out by Althusius: a theory that builds consent and political association from the ground up—put another way, an account that is both corporate and federal.[113] The only other alternatives seem to be giving up natural liberty or embracing philosophical anarchism or affirming an account of popular sovereignty without individual consent at any level. Of course, a theory of popular sovereignty sans individual consent also seems a rejection of natural liberty. If individuals are in fact equal by nature in the sense that entails or just is natural liberty, then jettisoning consent as a necessary condition for political order is not an option. In that case, we require a corporate account of consent and a federal political order, *or* we must embrace philosophical anarchism.

I'm not arguing that following Althusius alleviates all the difficulties attendant to consent theory, though if there's a route through, I suspect it must be this way. Moreover, even granting natural liberty— which a number of theorists seem to take as axiomatic, even though its basicality is not at all clear—we have only been considering the plausibility of a necessary condition of political authority and obligation. In chapter 1, I established that consent is neither sufficient nor both necessary and sufficient. It can at best be necessary. Thus, a plausible account of consent does not get us all the way to political authority and obligation. Whether or not both consent and the character of the regime together suffice, the character of the regime also seems necessary for political authority and obligations. My point here is that a plausible or practicable account of government by consent must build from the ground up, instantiating a pattern that can only be called *federal*, broadly speaking.[114]

Put another way, self-government only occurs when citizens exercise the powers of government—not when they merely choose those who govern them by means of election. And citizens can only exercise the powers of government—by and large—in concrete local communities of which they are members.[115] This does not obviate the need for regional and national government or for checks on the excesses of local governance by more comprehensive political associations. But genuine self-government—and real consent to it—require building political order from the ground up and therefore require rejecting statist conceptions of political order such as those we find in Bodin and Hobbes.

Conclusion: Either Popular Sovereignty or Corporate Consent

The de facto problem for political contractarianism and consent theory ultimately proves more difficult to resolve than the de jure problem. Solving the de jure problem requires rejecting the metaethics (or ethical ontologies) and metaphysics of modernity and grounding political contractarianism and the principle of consent in moral and metaphysical realism. Solving the de facto problem is not impossible— though it will require adopting an approach to constitutional design fundamentally at odds with the modern theory of sovereignty explicated by Jean Bodin, Thomas Hobbes, and those who have followed in their steps. Resolution of the practical difficulty remains a logical possibility. In large nation-states, however, this resolution requires reversing long-established, deeply entrenched trends that are often accepted with little thought—it would require rejecting, for instance, the sovereignty of the state over society, rejecting the consolidation of power in strong national governments, and rejecting the idea of mass national democracy. It would also require adopting a position according to which pre-political and political incorporations less comprehensive than the state (or the realm or commonwealth) are *real* wholes with ontological status and agency and not just fictions (contra Alexander Hamilton, as it happens).[116]

Distinguishing popular sovereignty from consent theory, Wolterstorff notes that "the doctrine of popular sovereignty, that is, the right of the people to sovereignty with respect to the actions of their state" is "usually ignored" today; but "if it is taken note of and understood, it is usually rejected, either because its implicit ontology is unacceptable to those of a nominalist persuasion or because it is confused with . . . the doctrine of the consent of the governed."[117] What Wolterstorff says about the "ontology implicit in the doctrine of popular sovereignty" applies equally to political order built from the ground up where primary, pre-political associations consent to create the first level of political order (the town or city) and where cities or towns consent together to create provinces, and so on. The idea of associational wholes capable of giving or withholding consent to political order or to more comprehensive levels of political order only makes sense on supposition of a realist ontology. That's because in order to speak at all coherently of wholes and of the parts in relation to the whole and to speak intelligibly of the agency of corporate wholes, we require the ideas of predication and participation. Participation (like that of a member or part in a given whole) and predication (e.g., Socrates is a citizen of Athens), just like distinguishing some acts of will (or some interests or desires) from others, require real universals, require universal essences. Consequently, the only solutions to the paucity of consent, given human equality, seem to be popular sovereignty (the authority of the community over its government) or corporate consent from the ground up or both. And both depend on a realist ontology of wholes, and therefore entail rejecting nominalism.

Conclusion

IN THIS VOLUME I HAVE argued that conventional contractarianism is self-referentially incoherent and that government by consent depends on classical natural law or, at the very least, on moral and metaphysical realism for its coherence.[1] The relation between political contractarianism and realist natural law is not only one of concord rather than conflict but also one of necessary dependence of the former on the latter. The relation between moral contractarianism and political contractarianism, however, is one of conflict rather than concord. Over and against the regnant view, I have sought to demonstrate systematically and analytically that moral and political contractarianism are logically, intractably, at odds.

According to a position I'll call *fiat contractarianism*, the consent of those governed to those who exercise political rule (or to political society) is either sufficient or necessary and sufficient for political authority and obligation. On this view consent—given in the authorization of the political order—is either all that is needed for political authority and obligation *or* it's both needed and all that is needed. We might also call this position *pure contractarianism* because it is political contractarianism without anything else added to ground political authority and obligation (thus my use of *fiat* for this position). Why is *fiat* or *pure contractarianism* incoherent? To recapitulate the earlier argument, consent is an instance of human will and, therefore, an instance of will. To ground political authority and obligation in nothing other than consent (or in consent and consent alone) is therefore to ground such authority and obligation in nothing other than will (or in will and will alone). In short, pure political contractarianism (or fiat contractarianism) depends upon or is an instance of a radically

323

voluntaristic ontology of obligation. But any voluntaristic ontology of obligation is self-referentially incoherent. A voluntaristic account of obligation asks us to distinguish some instances of will from others (to take some instances of will as normative for others) on the basis of will alone. Yet it is impossible intelligibly to distinguish instances of will on the basis of nothing but will. All such attempts are self-referentially incoherent. And thus, fiat or pure contractarianism is also self-referentially incoherent.

The self-referential incoherence of political contractarianism *by itself* and with no other foundation entails that we need some basis of right or good outside of the consent by which political authority might be established to ground consent. We need a logically and metaphysically plausible basis on which to say some instances of will (for instance, those grounded in consent or emerging from a regime established by consent) are binding upon others (for instance, as to what sort of actions are licit or forbidden to citizens). Let's call that standard of right or good in human action *justice*. There are those, of course, who affirm a *conventional* account of justice. For conventionalists, justice—or the content of justice—is the product of human agreement as to what is right and good. Perhaps human agreement as to what is right and good—perhaps an agreement prior to the establishment of political society or government; perhaps a tacit agreement embedded in custom—can provide a basis for distinguishing some acts of human will as normative for subsequent acts. Perhaps human agreement can construct a standard of right normative for and capable of grounding political contractarianism. We can call this position *moral contractarianism* or *normative constructivism* or *deep conventionalism*. But as I argued earlier in this volume, normative construction and *moral* contractarianism—or any conventionalist account of justice or right—suffer from the same problem as fiat political contractarianism. All conventional or constructivist accounts of right (or norms more generally) are instances of voluntarism and so are self-referentially incoherent. And to ground political authority and obligation in an incoherent moral theory is to leave them ungrounded—and to fall back into the self-referential incoherence to which fiat political contractarianism fell prey. The upshot is that we need a moral norm or ground of obligation that transcends human will, including instances of human will such as consent or agreement, in order to ground any intelligible account of political authority and obligation, including any intelligible consent-based theory of such authority and obligation.

The only way to salvage consent theory from the ruins of voluntarism (when it comes to the ontology of obligation) is to ground political authority and obligation in moral precepts or requirements that transcend *human* will and are normative for it. I maintain that the only intelligible version of contractarianism grounds consent in natural law. Consent theory applies the natural law obligation to keep our licit promises and agreements to political foundations.[2] But, as Francis Oakley maintains, the medieval era bequeathed to us two variants of natural law. On one account—which we might call the Thomistic account—moral obligation is ultimately grounded in divine wisdom and goodness. In the other—the Ockhamist account—moral obligation is grounded in divine will and omnipotence.[3] According to preceding argument, Ockhamist (or voluntarist) natural law is self-referentially incoherent, even in the most sophisticated varieties such as those advanced by Ockham or Pufendorf. An intelligible account of moral obligation (or of obligation more generally) requires that obligation be grounded in a realist ontology of the good. But real goodness, though necessary for moral obligation, is not sufficient. For good acts—indeed, intrinsically good acts—include not only those that are morally obligatory but those that are merely licit (or permissible) and those that are supererogatory (better than we have to do) as well. Real or intrinsic goodness alone is not sufficient to distinguish intrinsically good acts that are required of (or nonoptional for) us from those that are not. Because it is incoherent to think of obligation as conceptually or analytically contained in good, prescriptive will is also necessary. Moral obligation is a compound property comprised of intrinsic goodness and prescriptive will exercised by someone possessed of the authority or right to prescribe.[4] Minimally, the sort of natural law required to ground consent theory is an instance of moral realism.

Grounding political contractarianism, consent theory, or government by consent in moral realism (or in morally and metaphysically realist natural law) rather than in moral contractarianism, normative

positivism, normative constructivism, or voluntarist natural law solves
the de jure problem with which we began. Political contractarianism is
in principle possible.[5] But is it possible in practice? In the last chapter
I argued that the paucity of individual consent, to authorize political
power and to take on political obligations, poses a substantial *practical*
obstacle to consent theory. The only practicable solutions consonant
with the natural equality of human beings, I suggested, were either
popular sovereignty (the authority of the community over its government) or a regime built from the ground up and in which, by the time
we reach the first level of political association, individual consent has
already fallen out of view and corporate consent (of families, congregations, guilds, and various other pre-political associations) has
already replaced that of individuals, or both of these together. Both
popular sovereignty and corporate consent to political order require
affirming that associational wholes have ontological status—that
they really exist.[6] And affirming natural, associational wholes, able
to exercise agency (like giving and withholding consent), implies a
realist ontology of the nature of things fundamentally at odds with
metaphysical nominalism's denial that real, universal essences exist.
The alternatives, I submit, are abandoning government by consent
for an alternative justification or embracing the philosophical anarchist's denial of political authority and obligation. The problem with
alternative justifications, however, is that these seem predicated on
denying the natural equality of human beings. Taking either popular
sovereignty (or communal authority) or corporate consent seriously,
however, will require giving local communities considerable, though
not unlimited, discretion to govern themselves—will require rejecting the modern theory of sovereignty, its centralizing tendency, and
the idea of mass national democracy. Popular sovereignty and meaningful corporate consent require a policy of local self-government for
many matters of policy, at least ceteris paribus, as a matter of principle
and not just prudence.

   In sum, government by consent requires a moral basis—moral
norms not created by but normative for human willing and behavior.
We are, however, incapable of creating these norms. They depend on
a real goodness that cannot be created by bare strength, sheer power,
or even omnipotent will. The coherence not only of government by

consent but also of moral obligation and normativity in general depend on goodness being at the foundation of reality. The alternative to moral realism is not conventionalism or moral constructivism but the loss of obligation and normativity altogether. In Book VI of Plato's *Republic*, Socrates say this: "We say that there are many beautiful things, many good, and many other such things, thereby distinguishing them in words. . . . We also say that there is a beautiful itself and a good itself. And so, in the case of all the things that we then posited as many, we reverse ourselves and posit a single form belonging to each, since we suppose there is a single one, and call it what each is."[7] Ockham, Hobbes, Pufendorf, Locke, Gauthier, and Rawls all reject this route (whether in the form of Plato's strong realism or the moderate realism of Aquinas). So doing, they yank the rug completely out from under not only government by consent and covenant but also out from under moral obligation and moral norms in general. The price of metaphysical nominalism is *oughtness*. Correlatively, the price of oughtness is moral and metaphysical realism. That is the beginning of the matter . . . and also the end of this book.

FINIS

Notes

Introduction

I borrow the title's framing from Alvin Plantinga's wonderful work on religion, science, and naturalism *Where the Conflict Really Lies* in which he argues that there is no real conflict between science and religion but, rather, one of both science and religion, on the one hand, with metaphysical naturalism, on the other.

1. I lay out the Thomistic account of natural law in chapter 6 of this volume. See also chapter 5 of DeHart, *Uncovering the Constitution's Moral Design.*

2. See a transcript of the Declaration of Independence at the National Archives: https://www.archives.gov/founding-docs/declaration-transcript.

3. The presence of political contractarianism in documents such as the Virginia Declaration of Rights of 1776, the Massachusetts Constitution of 1780, and the Essex Result is undeniable. On the pervasiveness of the idea of the state of nature in Revolutionary-era American thought, see Somos, *American States of Nature.* On social compact theory in founding thought, see Muñoz, *Religious Liberty*, 42–52; and Lutz, *Origins*, chaps. 3, 6, 7, and 9. Though I substantially disagree with Thomas West about the moral underpinnings and deep ontology of the American constitutional order, I concur, at least in broad outline, with his contention concerning the import of social compact and consent to American founding thought. See West, *Political Theory*, esp. chaps. 5 and 6. On the ontological and normative underpinnings of American constitutionalism, see DeHart, *Uncovering the Constitution's Moral Design.*

4. On these various theories and their problems, see chapter 1 of Hampton, *Political Philosophy.*

5. Hobbes, for instance, found national equality in strength and prudence, or ability, and therefore of hope in attaining desired goods. Hobbes, *Leviathan* 8.1–3, pp. 74–75. John Locke locates human equality in a naturally equal "power," as he puts it, or authority, and "jurisdiction," equal possession of the same "faculties," sameness of species (and of rank within species), and the absence of any natural subordination or subjection. Locke, *Two Treatises*, Second Treatise 2.4, p. 269.

6. See, for example, Deneen, *Why Liberalism Failed*, 5–6, 30–35, 99–101; McWilliams, "Democracy and the Citizen," 86–88; Hanby, "Birth of the Liberal Order"; Pangle, *Spirit of Modern Republicanism*, esp. 35, 114, 115, 119, 132–33; Zuckert, "Do Natural Rights Derive"; Zuckert, "Social Compact"; Gauthier, *Morals by Agreement*,

9, 15, 17, 55, 310; and Gauthier, "Why Contractarianism?," 15–16, 18–19, 30. See also Feser, *Locke*, 108–17; and Hill, *After the Natural Law*, 29–30, 133–44, 213–16. According to Hill, "With Hobbes, Rousseau, and other social contract thinkers, Locke helped invert the classical understanding of the relationship between the individual and the State. The entire classical political tradition from Aristotle on held that 'the state is by nature prior to the individual.' By this Aristotle had meant that the State was formally prior to the individual, as form is prior to matter. It is the State, conceived as society and all its institutions, that gives us our humanity. But this priority also means that the state is a natural end of the individual, a natural outgrowth of our human essence. Society and its political institutions are an organic expression of the human telos. For Locke and the social contract theorists, on the other hand, the State was artificial, the product of a contract grounded in self-interest. . . . Locke declared that the chief end of government is the protection of 'property,' a term he used to refer not simply to one's estates and possessions but to the totality of one's individual rights." Hill, *After the Natural Law*, 137–38.

7. Pangle describes "eighteenth-century political thought in America and Europe" as "dominated (though not monopolized) by the diverse and competing offshoots of a profoundly *anti*classical conception of human nature and politics." Pangle, *Spirit of Modern Republicanism*, 35 (emphasis in original). He also holds that "the conceptions of Thomas Hobbes, Benedict Spinoza, and John Locke shattered" the "foundations" of "premodern constitutionalism" exhibited "in the early foundations of government in the American colonies" (112, 114). His point of contrast is seventeenth-century colonial constitutionalism, as displayed in documents like the Mayflower Compact, and "moral language" with the eighteenth-century thought of the American founders, influenced by the distinctly modernist contractarianism of Locke. Manent says that Hobbes discerned the "decisive element" in the different state of nature and social contract theories of the "founders of modern natural right"—namely, considering "society or the city . . . as if it had been dissolved or reduced to its elements—in order then to recompose it in a more rational manner. . . . We suppose that it is possible to reduce the human world to a kind of 'degree zero,' to nothing or almost nothing, to dismember it entirely in order then to reconstruct or recompose it entirely." Manent, *Natural Law*, 51–52. See also Manent's *Intellectual History of Liberalism*, especially chapters 2-4.

8. See, for example, Elazar, *Covenant & Commonwealth*, 45. See also Simmons, *Moral Principles*, 59.

9. McCoy and Baker, *Fountainhead of Federalism*, 52, 56, 78, 92; and Elazar, *Covenant & Commonwealth*, 23, 24, 38, 84.

10. According to David Novak, a "biblically based theology" of covenant and rights "enables one to formulate a biblically based natural law theory, one that does not fall into the Platonism that makes some natural law theories, whether in more Aristotelian or more Stoic form, so problematic theologically." Novak, *Covenantal Rights*, 15. Further, while "*good* seems to many to be a more basic moral term than *right*, either in the classical sense ('it is *right* to do that') or in the modern sense ('he or she *has a right* to do that')," *good* (or the good) "is still insufficient to structure

morality in general, and certainly the morality of the Jewish covenantal tradition. . . . Justice as the order of rights is the more basic ethical-political term than good or *the* Good" (16). Finally, "Nature itself in general and human nature specifically are the obedient results of God's command. All law must be originally justified by divine law: what is to be obeyed in and of itself. . . . How fundamentally different all this is from seeing natural law as some sort of translation of a higher nature down to the actual affairs of human beings. In that view, there is no primary voice, but only a vision of a polity that might conform to a higher paradigm in the heavens. It is duty without an originating right/claim" (24–25).

11. I lay out a shorter version of the argument in DeHart, "Whose Social Contract?," 3–21.

12. See Simmons, *Moral Principles*, chaps. 3 and 4; Simmons, *Edge of Anarchy*, chaps. 7 and 8; and Leslie Green, *Authority of the State*, chaps. 5 and 6.

13. A conclusion for which Simmons argues in *Edge of Anarchy*, chaps. 7 and 8.

14. Deneen, "Liberalism's Logic." According to Deneen, by the time of the American founding "the idea of 'natural law' . . . had been considerably re-defined" by social contract theorists. "The meaning of 'natural law,'" he writes, "had been fundamentally changed from its medieval understanding in order to support the individualist premises of social contract theory. For Locke, as well as Hobbes, the 'Law of Nature' is primarily a law of self-preservation. We are not by nature political animals who flourish through the cultivation of virtue in political communities; rather, we are by nature rational calculators of individual advantage." According to Wilson Carey McWilliams, on the modern social contract theory of the American framers, "Our consent creates obligation," and consequently "nothing can evaluate our consent: Whatever we consent to will be 'right.'" McWilliams, "Democracy and the Citizen," 86–87.

15. According to Deneen, the Constitution is "the 'applied technology' of liberal theory": "The Constitution is the embodiment of a set of modern principles that sought to overturn ancient teachings and shape a distinctly different modern human." Deneen, *Why Liberalism Failed*, 101. See also Rosen, *American Compact*, chap. 2, esp. 15–16, 29. Against this interpretation, see DeHart, "Why *Why Liberalism Failed* Fails."

16. Oakeshott, *Hobbes on Civil Association*, 7–8. The third tradition is of more recent vintage—its "master-conception is the Rational Will," and Hegel's *Philosophy of Right* is the work that best represents it.

17. Hobbes, *De Homine* 10.5, pp. 42–43.

18. Hobbes, *De Cive* 10.5, p. 292; and Hobbes, *Leviathan* 31.5, p. 235.

Chapter 1

An earlier version of this chapter appeared in *Perspectives in Political Science*, though it has been considerably revised for this project. See DeHart, "Covenantal Realism."

1. According to Richard Franklin Bensel, "All modern states claim that they rule by popular consent." Bensel, *Founding of Modern States*, 2; see also p. 4.

2. See Somos, *American States of Nature*, Hulliung, *Social Contract in America*, chap. 1; Muñoz, *Religious Liberty*, 42–52; and West, *Political Theory*, esp. chaps. 5 and 6.

3. James Madison to Nicholas P. Trist, February 15, 1830, in Kurland and Lerner, *Founders' Constitution*, 1:239–40.

4. Texts in political theory and political science often take for granted the idea that the authority and legitimacy of the state are founded in some way or other on popular consent. For instance, in his popular introductory text *Power & Choice*, W. Philips Shively defines authority as "power based on a general agreement" (150). He then specifies the terms of the agreement. But it is clear that the *agreement* is what grounds the power. He says on the next page, "Remember that authority exists because it 'generally agreed on'; that is, most people believe [agree] it exists" (151).

5. See Hooker, *Laws of Ecclesiastical Polity* 1.8.7, 1.10.4; Bellarmine, *De Laicis*, chap. 6, p. 22; Bellarmine, *De Clericis*, chap. 7, cited in Rager, "Bellarmine's Defense," 513, where Bellarmine says, "In a commonwealth all men are born naturally free and equal"; Suárez, *Treatise on Laws* 3.2.1-4, pp. 429–33, and 3.3.6, 439; Sidney, *Discourses Concerning Government* 1.2, p. 8; and Locke, *Two Treatises*, Second Treatise 2.4, p. 269, 4.22, pp. 283-84, and 8.95, pp. 330–31. Sir Robert Filmer framed his rejection of natural liberty and natural equality (and popular sovereignty) as a rejection of Bellarmine. Filmer, *Patriarcha*, chap. 1, esp. pp. 2-6; see also *Patriarcha*, chap. 2, pp. 15-16.

6. On the place of equality in John Locke's political theory, see Waldron, *God, Locke, and Equality*. See also Waldron, *One Another's Equals*. On the absence of the equal worth or dignity of human beings in antiquity prior to the advent of Christianity, see Roman historian Kyle Harper's "Christianity and the Roots of Human Dignity in Late Antiquity." According to Harper, Roman Stoics "say nothing to the effect that all humans possess [*dignitas*]. In the mind of Seneca, *dignitas* was still very much a sliding scale of worthiness," p. 129.

7. With respect to the rules of inference and logical terminology, I rely throughout this volume on Hurley, *A Concise Introduction to Logic*. According to modus tollens, (1) if A, then B (formalized as A⊃B), (2) not B (formalized as ~B), therefore (3) not A (~A). According to DeMorgan's rule, not both A and B, represented as ~(A•B), is equivalent to not A or not B, represented as ~A or ~B. Letting *e* stand for natural equality, *a* stand for political authority, and *c* stand for the necessity of consent for political authority and obligation, the conditional in the main text would be (*e•a*)⊃*c*. To reject *c* (i.e., ~*c*) would entail ~(*e•a*), which is equivalent to ~*e* or ~*a*—that is, either human equality or political authority would have to be denied. Given the disjunctive syllogism—(1) either A or B (A v B), (2) not A, therefore (3) B—and double negation—A is equivalent to *not* not A (~~A)—human equality (~~*e*) would entail ~*a*, the rejection of political authority.

8. Hobbes can certainly be read this way, especially insofar as he treats assent as the basis of obligation in later work such as *Leviathan* or his exchanges with Bramhall, as Gauthier argues in "Hobbes: The Laws of Nature." See chapter 4 of this volume.

9. Regarding the idea that natural law does not exist: in fact, the so-called fact-value or is-ought dichotomy—famously announced by David Hume in his *Treatise*

of Human Nature, 3.1.1 (pp. 468-70 of the Selby-Bigge edition), and widely adopted by scholars in various disciplines subsequent to Hume's work—ultimately eliminates moral values or the moral law from the class of existing things; that is, the dichotomy entails that there are no moral facts not reducible to personal tastes, expressions of emotion, individual preferences, will, or social conventions. Some philosophers go further, claiming that putatively moral and scientific "facts" are on the same ontological and epistemic footing, both warranting skepticism. According to Nietzsche, "It is still a *metaphysical faith* upon which our faith in science rests." Nietzsche, *The Gay Science*, 283 (italics in original). And he quotes this precise passage in his *Genealogy of Morals* (third essay, sec. 24, in Nietzsche, *Basic Writings*, 584–89), in that part of the text wherein he questions not just moral values but the value of truth per se. I find this position to be more consistent than the fact-value or is-ought dichotomy, but also self-defeating, insofar as it is impossible to critique truth without presupposing the truth of the critique being made. In contrast to both positions, thoroughgoing realists affirm the ontological reality and the epistemic intelligibility of both (nonreductive) moral and scientific realities or truths (and if this is what is meant by facts, then of moral facts) and, indeed, of truth as such. The realist position has the virtues of consistency and of not being self-referentially incoherent. See also Budziszewski, *The Resurrection of Nature*, 43–44.

Regarding the idea that natural law is irrelevant to the authority of the state: in legal theory, the Utilitarians John Austin and Jeremy Bentham predicated legal positivism on the is-ought dichotomy. See for example Austin, *The Province of Jurisprudence*, lecture 5, p. 184. In the twentieth century, Kelsen wed affirmation of the is-ought dichotomy to normative positivism (and so moral antirealism) in *Pure Theory of Law* (esp. pp. 66–68; but see also 48–50) and *General Theory of Law*. See also Kelsen's "Natural Law Doctrine and Legal Positivism," in *General Theory of Law*, 396–97. Hart rejects predicating law and legal analysis on noncognitive ethical theories. But he espouses the separation of law and morals and considers moral truth claims irrelevant to what counts as law. See Hart, "Positivism," esp. 626. In political science, proponents of the behavioral approach made the is-ought dichotomy central to scholarly analysis of politics. See Truman, "Political Behavior Research," 39; and Dahl, "The Behavioral Approach," 768, 770–71. Rational choice theorist William H. Riker says the rational choice model takes moral values, like personal tastes, as given but has nothing to say about their origin—which is to say, it regards what is true and false in matters of morals as irrelevant to political and constitutional analysis. Riker, "The Future of a Science of Politics," 29–30.

10. This logical incoherence amounts, I would argue, to an enormous fissure in the ontological ground of the theory, which in turn suggests that the flaw is fatal.

11. One sort of objection to my argument might be to concede that conventional social contract theory is or may be logically flawed and then to ask why the logical failure of the theory (or of its ontological foundation) matters. The answer is simply that social contract theory constitutes an attempt to justify the authority of the state. As a result, it endeavors to put in place a benchmark against which the legitimacy of the state can be evaluated. But a logically incoherent benchmark is incapable of

performing any evaluative function. An evaluative standard must be intelligible in order to evaluate. And a self-referentially incoherent benchmark is certainly not an intelligible one.

12. ~~Which is not to say those same theorists removed the necessity of divine del~~egation altogether. On the problems attendant to other modes of justifying political authority, see chapter 1 of Hampton, *Political Philosophy*.

13. Early moderns clearly affirmed the conditional that if human persons are equal, then voluntary consent is necessary for some persons to possess political authority over others. And they provided arguments (of varying quality) for natural equality. That said, so far as I can tell, no one has argued on behalf of this conditional.

14. Simmons, *Edge of Anarchy*, chap. 1, esp. 197–202.

15. Höpfl and Thompson, "History of Contract," 919–44. See also Oakley, "Legitimation by Consent"; Oakley, *Watershed of Modern Politics*; Skinner, *Foundations*, vol. 2; and McCoy and Baker, *Fountainhead of Federalism*.

16. For instance, Elazar, *Covenant & Polity*. See also Novak, *The Jewish Social Contract*; and Novak, *In Defense of Religious Liberty*, 167–77, where he raises some important challenges not only to Hobbes but to New England Puritans as well.

17. Other roots are undeniable too (such as conciliarism and Counter-Reformation thought). Moreover, a full history of social contract theory would, of course, have to take note of passages in the Platonic corpus, the conciliarists, and Counter-Reformation theologians and philosophers. See Oakley, "Legitimation by Consent"; and Skinner, *Foundations* 2:174–84.

18. Bullinger, *De testamento*, translated as "A Brief Exposition of the One and Eternal Testament or Covenant of God" by McCoy and Baker in *Fountainhead of Federalism*, 99–138. The part of *Fountainhead of Federalism* preceding the translation of Bullinger's work is the first major exposition of the covenantal tradition in recent times. For a history of covenantal/federal theology and political thought from Jewish thought to early modern Western political thought, see Elazar, *Covenant & Polity*; and Elazar, *Covenant & Commonwealth*.

19. McCoy and Baker, *Fountainhead of Federalism*, 20.

20. McCoy and Baker, 104.

21. McCoy and Baker, 113.

22. McCoy and Baker, 20.

23. McCoy and Baker, 20, 116.

24. For instance, Heiko Oberman describes "an emerging new image of God" according to which "God is a covenant God, his *pactum* or *foedus* is his self-commitment to become the contractual partner in creation and salvation. . . . In the nominalist view man has become the appointed representative and partner of God, responsibility for his own life, society and world, on the basis of and within the limits of the treaty or *pactum* stipulated by God." Oberman, "The Shape of Late Medieval Thought," 15.

25. The *via antiqua* and the *via moderna* refer to two schools of thought that differ with respect to the status of universals. Broadly speaking, the former corresponds to the moderate realism of scholastic thought, which affirmed the existence

of universals (or of universal essences), and the latter to the nominalism of William of Ockham (or at least to a school of thought that followed in his wake), which denied they existed at all. As to the relation of Bullinger's thought to the *via antiqua*, see McCoy and Baker, *Fountainhead of Federalism*, 15; and Elazar, *Covenant & Commonwealth*, 84.

26. Bullinger, *De testamento*, 105.

27. Bullinger, 109.

28. Bullinger, 110 and 109–11 more generally; see also 104–5.

29. Jacob cited in Höpfl and Thompson, "History of Contract," 938. Höpfl and Thompson take the citation from Förster, *Thomas Hobbes*, 96.

30. John Cotton, Richard Mather, and Ralph Partridge, "A Platform of Church Discipline" (1649), in Frohnen, *The American Republic*, 48–63.

31. Cotton, Mather, and Partridge, "Platform" 4.2–4, p. 50.

32. It scarcely needs said that the congregational model of church government described in the "Platform" differs substantially from all preceding models in Christian history and is a de novo innovation of British Separatists.

33. Cotton, Mather, and Partridge, "Platform" 10.2, p. 54.

34. Cotton, Mather, and Partridge 10.5–6, pp. 54–55.

35. Höpfl and Thompson, "History of Contract," 938. Oakley, cites this passage approvingly and writes:

> In relation to the Church . . . Protestant and Catholic alike, continued, by and large to think in terms of an all-inclusive Church, a compulsory body in the medieval mold embracing society as a whole. . . . Only when some Elizabethan Puritans had finally abandoned their earlier scruples and had come to think in terms of reform "without tarrying for any" did the sectarianism of the Radical Reformation begin to make truly significant inroads upon one of the established strongholds of Protestantism, bringing with it the idea of the Church as a voluntary society of true believers who have entered it "on the basis of conscious conversion," a restricted fellowship or sect that eschews talk of institutional sanctity, stressing instead the holiness of its individual members and demanding of them the type of freely-undertaken life commitment to which the many may periodically aspire but which only a few can long sustain. (Oakley, "Legitimation by Consent," 332)

Noting that modern "democracy is a product of the fusion of the Greek and the Christian heritage and therefore can survive only in this foundational connection," Joseph Ratzinger (Benedict XVI), in a passage to which Gunnar Gundersen pointed me, contends:

> Democracy as understood today need not and did not automatically spring from this root but, in fact, was first shaped under the special circumstances of the American congregationalist type, that is, apart from the classical

European traditions of the church-state relationship that developed histor-
ically here [in Europe]. Hence it is only in a very qualified sense that the
Enlightenment led to democracy, as Hannah Arendt has shown in her book
On Revolution (London, 1962). The European Reformation with its ideas
about the state church had been even less capable of blazing the trail. . . .
All this, on the other hand, should not obscure our view of the existence
of fundamental democratic elements in prerevolutionary Christian society.
(Ratzinger, *Church, Ecumenism, and Politics,* 203)

Ratzinger cites Bien and Maier, "Demokratie"; and Maier, *Katholizismus and
Demokratie.*
    36. Jacob cited in Höpfl and Thompson, "History of Contract," 938 (emphasis
added); who in turn are citing citing Förster, *Thomas Hobbes,* 97.
    37. In addition to Höpfl and Thompson on the English Separatist and Puritan
appropriation of church covenants for the foundations of civil government in their
North American colonial settlements, see also Lutz, *Origins,* 25–27, and chapter
3 more generally. Lutz writes, "The appropriation of biblical covenant idea by the
dissenting Calvinist sects and the centrality of religion to their lives are reflected in
town records showing that almost the first thing many colonies did was to covenant
a church among themselves. One of the first church covenants, that of Charlestown-
Boston Church on July 30, 1630 is typical." He then compares the Charlestown-
Boston Church Covenant with the Mayflower Compact.
    38. Thomas Hooker as recorded by Henry Wolcott, cited in Hall, *Roger Sherman,*
17.
    39. Or so argue McCoy and Baker: "The first systematic, fully developed artic-
ulation of federal political thought came from Johannes Althusius in his *Politica*
published in 1603." *Fountainhead of Federalism,* 27. They also note his frequent references to the Huguenot Philipe du Plessis-Mornay (likely the pseudonymous Junius
Brutus), though it's worth noting with Höpfl and Thompson ("History of Contract,"
931–32) and Oakley ("Legitimation by Consent," 324–26) that *individual* consent
does not factor into *Vindiciae contra tyrannos.*
    40. Höpfl and Thompson, "History of Contract," 935.
    41. See Althusius, *Politica*; and Elazar, *Covenant & Commonwealth,* 315–31.
According to Höpfl and Thompson, Althusius "apparently . . . made the first attempt to bring contractual language explicitly derived from Huguenot and [French
Catholic] *Ligue* sources and the scholastics' conception of civil society together
into a self-consciously political theory. In *Politica methodice digesta* . . . Althusius
insisted on interpreting *all* significant relationships within the *societas perfecta* as
contractual. The relationships were not simply consensual—that was a scholastic commonplace—but were founded on covenants (*pacta, foedera,* or *conventus*)."
Moreover, "Althusius plainly could no longer characterize a legitimate association
or account for legitimate authority without recourse to ideas of will, artifice, and
consent." At the same time, Höpfl and Thompson hold that Althusius did not move
as far in the direction of a thoroughly contractarian account of political order as

the Separatists / congregationalists, since he "did not contemplate a covenant between *individuals* equipped with natural rights." Rather, "The bearers of rights in his conception are still unmistakably associations, groups, and corporations of various sorts, not individuals." Höpfl and Thompson, "History of Contract," 935–36. Oakley suggests that all medieval and early modern theorists prior Elizabethan Puritans, the Levellers, and Hobbes and Locke, understood consent as the consent "of free communities, possessed at a minimum of the original right to choose their rulers, perhaps also to choose the form of government under which they were to live, maybe even to participate on some sort of continuing basis in the governmental process" but *not* as "the assent of a concatenation of free and equal individuals imposing on themselves an obligation which of their ultimate autonomy they could avoid." Oakley, "Legitimation by Consent," 324. Individual consent, he argues, plays no substantial role in the thought of De Soto, Molina, or Suárez, on the one hand, or Mornay, Althusius, Rutherford, and Hooker, on the other. My enormous regard for Oakley's scholarship notwithstanding, I think individual consent plays a substantial role in Althusius (as well as Hooker and, I'd argue, Suárez)—which is not to deny the importance of corporate consent in their accounts.

42. Althusius, *Politica* 1.2, p. 17.

43. Althusius 1.29, p. 24.

44. At least insofar as such associations are *political associations*, in the proper signification of both terms.

45. Althusius, *Politica* 19.11, p. 122. I'm not suggesting here that Althusius's conception of natural law is precisely the same as that of Aquinas or the Scholastics. Rather, Althusius's natural law theory falls in the classical stream because of the realist and anti-voluntarist position espoused in passages such as this. On Althusius's theory of natural law, see Witte, *Reformation of Right*, 156–69. See also Grabill, *Rediscovering the Natural Law*, chap. 5.

46. Elazar, *Covenant & Commonwealth*, 45.

47. Simmons, *Moral Principles*, 59. To Simmons's list we might add Algernon Sidney's *Discourses Concerning Government* (published posthumously by John Toland in 1698). In *Locke and the Theory of Sovereignty*, Julian H. Franklin suggests that George Lawson references Althusius's *Politica* and that that Lawson influenced Locke: "The starting point for the political part of Lawson's treatise [*Politica sacra et civilis*] is a quasi Aristotelian idea for the origin of human groups for which he is avowedly indebted to Althusius" (69); and "Lawson's . . . idea of dissolution was taken up by Locke" (ix–x). Setting the relation of Lawson to Locke aside, the alleged reference to Althusius is at least dubious. Conal Condren writes, "Lawson's generic reference to 'Authors of Politics' who follow Aristotle is misread [by Franklin] as a reference to the singular *Politica methodice digesta* of Althusius." "Resistance and Sovereignty," 674n5.

48. On this see chapter 1, "The Problem of Political Authority," in Hampton, *Political Philosophy*.

49. Gierke, *The Development of Political Theory*, p. 91, cited in Höpfl and Thompson, "The History of Contract," 923.

NOTES FOR CHAPTER I

50. Höpfl and Thompson, "History of Contract," 926.

51. Tierney, *The Growth of Constitutional Thought*, 78.

52. Woolhouse, *Locke*, 9.

53. Oakley, "Legitimation by Consent," 326, follows d'Entréves's interpretation of Hooker in *The Notion of the State*, 197n2: Hooker considered equality "a source of duties, not of rights" and considered "consent" to be "the expression of the corporate life of the whole society, not of single, individual wills." Höpfl and Thompson seemingly acknowledge the importance of *individual* consent in Hooker's theory but maintain that Hooker was "the finest English writer" in the genre that located "the foundation of political authority in *consent*, not covenant." "History of Contract," 934 (italics in original).

54. Skinner, *Foundations* 2:159.

55. Skinner, 2:159.

56. Skinner, 2:160.

57. Skinner, 2:162.

58. Skinner, 2:174. This claim notwithstanding, Skinner contends that it would be "a considerable overstatement to think of these writers [i.e., 'the counter reformation theorists'] as the chief originators of a modern 'democratic' view of politics. To interpret their writings in this way is to overlook the fact that, while they were prepared to adopt various features of a radical and secularized theory of *Imperium*, they were no less concerned to counteract what they took to be the excessively populist concept of sovereignty which the followers of Bartolus as well as Ockham had begun to articulate" (178–79). Nevertheless, reflecting on the French Protestant resistance writer Philippe de Mornay, Skinner writes:

> When [Mornay] turns to the question of tyranny in the *Defence*, he explicitly refers us to Aquinas, Bartolus, Baldus and the codifiers of the Roman law. And when he considers the central question of the right to resist, he reveals a close dependence on the radical background of conciliarist political thought. He quotes several decisions made at Constance and Basle, refers us on two occasions specifically to the "Sorbonnists," and employs the theories of Gerson, Almain and Mair in order to defend the idea of an exact analogy between the thesis of conciliarism in the Church and of popular sovereignty in the commonwealth. . . . [Thus,] although it has become usual in recent discussions of reformation political theory to speak of the "the Calvinist theory of revolution," it will now be evident that there are virtually *no elements in the theory which are specifically Calvinist at all*. The arguments used by the first Calvinist revolutionaries in the 1550s were largely Lutheran; the new arguments added in the 1570s were largely scholastic; and since the arguments taken by the Calvinists from the Lutherans had originally been taken by the Lutherans from the civil and canon law, *we may say with very little exaggeration that the main foundations of the Calvinist theory of revolution were in fact constructed entirely by their Catholic adversaries*. (321; emphasis added)

Mark David Hall replies that while

> as a matter of the genealogy of ideas this may be the case . . . these ideas
> were most extensively developed, defended, and applied with the Reformed
> tradition. Within a generation of Calvin, virtually every Reformed civil and
> ecclesiastical leader was convinced that the Bible taught that governments
> should be limited, that they should be based on the consent of the governed,
> that rulers should promote the common good and the Christian faith, and
> that unjust or ungodly rulers should be resisted or even overthrown. These
> ideas are not unique to Calvinists, but the Reformed tradition became a ma-
> jor means by which they became a part of American political culture. (Hall,
> *Roger Sherman*, 16)

59. Filmer, *Patriarcha*, chaps. 1 and 2; Sidney, *Discourses Concerning Government*
1.2, 1.6, and 2.1; and Althusius, *Politica*, chap. 9, esp. p. 70. On Sidney's invocation
of Bellarmine and Suárez, see Lutz, *Origins*, 118.

60. The term *nominalism* refers to the doctrine, commonly attributed to William
of Ockham and affirmed by Hobbes and Locke, that there are no universal essences
but only particulars. Particulars that appear similarly may be given the same name
(thus "nominal"), but they do not instantiate a shared, universal essence. *Voluntarism*
refers to the idea (again tracing to Ockham but also to Duns Scotus) that moral
obligation or rightness is determined by nothing other than will—in the case of
Ockham and Scotus, the will of God; in the case of later voluntarists such as Gauthier, the will of some human person or persons. Such will may be expressed in the
conventions of the community. See Angeles, *Dictionary of Philosophy*, 205, 334. It is
worth noting that in theorists like Ockham and Hobbes, nominalism and voluntarism are connected.

61. As to Hobbes, see Martinich, *Two Gods of Leviathan*, 133; and Hampton,
Hobbes and the Social Contract, 128–29. Concerning Locke's nominalism, see Wolterstorff, *John Locke*, 17–18. Voluntaristic ethics seems a clear implication of nominalistic metaphysics. Yet whether Locke was a voluntarist or a realist in his ethics is
a vexed question. Wolterstorff, for instance, argues that Locke should be understood
as a kind of moral realist (134–48). On the other hand, A. John Simmons thinks that
Locke's ethical theory has more than one strain, but that the predominant strain is
metaethical voluntarism. See Simmons, *Lockean Theory of Rights*, 33–34.

62. Hobbes, *Leviathan* 31.5, pp. 235–36. See also Martinich, *Two Gods of Leviathan*, 92–99.

63. David Gauthier proffers a social contract account of morality in *Morals by
Agreement*.

64. Of obligation qua obligation or just as such—and so of moral, political, and
legal obligation.

65. Jean Hampton understands Hobbes's contractarian justification of sovereign
power this way: "Hobbes believed that moral imperatives were commanded by God,

340   NOTES FOR CHAPTER I

but this justification of them is different from the contractarian justification that he
also uses to defend them. The contractarian method seeks to define the nature and
authority of moral imperatives by reference to the desires and reasoning abilities
of human beings, so that regardless of their religious commitments, all people will
see that they have reason to act morally." Hampton, "Two Faces of Contractarian
Thought," 33n6.

66. See Gauthier, *Logic of Leviathan*, esp. 93–98; and Gauthier, "The Social Contract as Ideology," 130–64.

67. Gauthier, "Thomas Hobbes: Moral Theorist," 547.

68. In the introduction to his recent anthology of essays on Hobbes, Gauthier
writes "Increasingly I have found Hobbes's ideas similar to my own." *Hobbes & Political Contractarianism*, xiii.

69. Gauthier in fact incorporates the argument from "The Social Contract as Ideology" in his treatment of *homo economicus* in *Morals by Agreement*, 316–317, which
I discuss in chapter 3.

70. Bernard Gert rejects Gauthier's description of Hobbesian individuals as utility
or self-interest maximizers: "Gauthier . . . claims that Hobbes holds the maximizing
conception of rationality, and what is maximized is the satisfaction of subjective
preference. . . . Gauthier himself, Rawls, Brandt, and most other contemporary philosophers and economists claim that they hold such a view. But, besides being an
absurd view, this is clearly not Hobbes's view of rationality." "Hobbes's Account of
Reason," 560. See also Gert, "Hobbes on Reason." As Gert sees it, Gauthier fails to
appreciate that for Hobbes "self-preservation remains the standard of rationality."
But given paragraphs 1 and 2 of chapter 11 of Hobbes's *Leviathan*, I wonder whether Gert hasn't perhaps created something of a false dichotomy. Preservation is, after
all, instrumentally necessary for preference maximization and Hobbes defines felicity as the satisfaction of one desire after another where the satisfaction of any desire
is instrumental to the satisfaction of subsequent desires. And Hobbes characterizes
human beings as animated principally by the acquisition of "more." Even so, most all
of the criticisms of Hobbesian political and moral theory in this volume stand even
if Gert's criticism of Gauthier's interpretation of Hobbes is right.

71. This seems to be part of the reason (perhaps a significant part) for the many
opportunities individuals have to get away with disobeying the edicts of the state,
thereby defaulting on the requirements of the social contract.

72. Hampton, *Hobbes and the Social Contract*; and Hampton, *Political Philosophy*,
cited above.

73. Hampton's terminology may require some elaboration. Hampton uses "*agency
social contract*" to refer to an argument assuming that political authority is granted by
the people to the ruler as a loan" and "*alienation social contract*" to refer to an argument
assuming that political authority is given as an irrevocable grant." *Political Philosophy*,
41. So in Hobbes's alienation social contract, "each person gave up the 'right to govern' herself or himself and bestowed that right on the sovereign. So [the sovereign]
can now rightfully command each of them because he now 'owns' these governing

rights" (50). In Locke's agency theory, the person or persons who govern(s) holds political office as a revocable trust but cannot be said to "own" governing rights.

74. See, for example, Hobbes, *Leviathan* 13.3, 75. Though neither Hobbes's argument nor Hampton's critique requires that he holds so strong a premise (which he nevertheless certainly affirms). Rather, Hobbes could hold that whether or not each individual is chiefly concerned with his own preservation, each individual is absolutely concerned with it. Perhaps each individual holds preservation to be a lower order preference but also one absolutely requisite to the satisfaction of any greater object of desire (where for Hobbes this only means *more desired* objects).

75. Hobbes, *Leviathan* 17.1, 106.

76. Hobbes, *Leviathan* 17.13, 109 and 18.3, 110-11.

77. Hobbes, *Leviathan* 18.4, 111-12.

78. Hobbes, *De Cive* 6.18, pp. 187–88; Hobbes, *Leviathan* 19.12, pp. 123–24, and 29.9, p. 213; and Hampton, *Hobbes and the Social Contract*, chap. 4, pp. 98–105.

79. Hobbes, *Leviathan* 21.12–17, pp. 142–43, and 21.21, p. 144. See also, 20.10, p. 131, where Hobbes says slaves have no obligation to obey those who hold them in bondage.

80. Hampton, *Political Philosophy*, 51.

81. Hampton, 51.

82. Hampton, 51.

83. Hampton, 52.

84. I suppose one might object to Hampton's argument here by suggesting a certain reconstruction of the Hobbesian argument. Why can't we just remove the qualifications (or riders) on the obligation of the subject or citizen to obey the sovereign power? Why not stipulate that the establishment of sovereign power entails the obligation of citizens or subject to obey, even if the sovereign is no longer capable of protecting the lives of his (or her or their) subjects? For that matter, why not remove the right of the individual to resist the sovereign whenever the citizen perceives the sovereign as threatening her life? The problem with this suggestion, however, is that these qualifications which dissolve the obligation to obey the sovereign *follow* from Hobbes's theory. The only reason anyone would consent to enter a civil state governed by a sovereign power is for the protection of his life. To surrender the right to protect one's own life against the sovereign would be establish a sovereign power contrary to the purpose for which sovereign power is authorized or established in the first place. As well, if one is compelled to obey the sovereign even when the sovereign jeopardizes one's own life or even when the sovereign is no longer capable of protecting one's own life, then one is in a state of affairs relative to the sovereign that one was in, relative to everyone else, in the state of nature. One would have in effect traded one state of nature for another—and given the focused strength of sovereign power, one's latter condition would arguably be worse than the former. So the coherence of the Hobbesian argument requires his qualifications on sovereign power. But these qualification of sovereign power is the very thing that prevents Hobbes's social contract, his wishes notwithstanding, from being an alienation contract.

342

NOTES FOR CHAPTER 1

85. Hampton, *Political Philosophy*, 53.

86. Hampton, 63.

87. Hampton, 63.

88. I consider Hampton's argument against alienation social contract theory dispositive. But her argument against agency social contract theory perhaps commits the fallacy of composition. After all, the people as a corporate whole, a real whole not reducible to the sum of its parts (i.e., to an aggregation of the individuals of which it is comprised) might—through chosen agents or delegates—exercise authority over each. This of course depends on an ontology of wholes and parts quite at odds with metaphysical nominalism and, in fact, requires something much like metaphysical realism.

89. See Green's *Authority of the State*. Nicholas Wolterstorff is among the critics I have in mind.

90. I am not distinguishing contractarianism and consent theory in this volume in the way that Green does, save in this treatment of Green.

91. Wolterstorff, "Accounting for the Political Authority of the State," 267, and 267–69 more generally.

92. Wolterstorff, " 'For the Authorities Are God's Servants.' " The precise passage I'm citing here comes from the original paper delivered at the "Theology, Morality, and Public Life" conference at the University of Chicago Divinity School in 2003 and does not appear in either of the published versions of this essay, though there are analogues in both. This way of putting the point best fits with the argument I'm framing herein and is used with Wolterstorff's gracious permission.

93. Wolterstorff, "Accounting for the Political Authority of the State," 267. In " 'For the Authorities Are God's Servants,' " Wolterstorff writes, "the ability of the state to establish and secure the social good in question does not require that its valid dictates be seen as placing its subjects under *obligation* to obey those dictates. It's sufficient that its subjects see conformity to those dictates either as in their own rational self-interest or as a morally good, but not obligatory, thing to do. This argument seems to me decisively correct. Attempts to ground the authority of the state in the requirements of social order have failed" (58).

94. Green, *Authority of the State*, 188.

95. Williams, "Ideas and Actuality."

96. And here we ought to keep in Ronald Dworkin's contention, in critique of Rawls, that "a hypothetical contract is not simply a pale form of an actual contract; it is no contract at all." Dworkin, "Original Position," 501.

97. Nathanson, *Should We Consent*, 23. See also "The Argument from Tacit Consent," chapter 4 of Simmons, *Moral Principles*.

98. In chapter 3 of *Moral Principles*, Simmons writes:

How is the consent theorist to avoid the charge that if unanimous consent is required for legitimacy, no government will be legitimate? The answer, for Hobbes, Locke, and Rousseau, is found in the notion of "tacit consent through residence." For if mere residence can be taken to be a sign of consent, then unanimous consent is *guaranteed*. This, however, seems to show more than the consent theorist wanted, for it seems to show not just that some governments are after all legitimate, but rather that *all* governments are legitimate. The problem, of course, is that in order to find some "sign of consent" which all citizens in *some* states could be taken to have given, Hobbes, Locke, and Rousseau were forced to accept one which all citizens in *all* states could be taken to have given. (73–74)

99. Green writes, "Not many of us have, in fact, consented. It follows then that the state has legitimate authority only over some of its citizens." *Authority of the State*, 188. Likewise, in "Accounting for the Political Authority of the State" Wolterstorff writes, "I . . . have never made any such promise, nor have most of my fellow citizens" (263). In "Right of the People to a Democratic State" he notes, "Few present-day thinkers, myself included, find the doctrine of consent plausible" (227).

100. Wolterstorff, " 'For the Authorities Are God's Servants,' " 59.

101. In which case, it seems political authority is unnecessary. If so, authorization of political authority is likewise unnecessary. In which case authorization of political authority by means of consent in unnecessary. In other words, this argument raises a significant objection to the necessity of consent central to early modern social contract theory.

102. See for instance Rawls, *Theory of Justice*; Rawls, *Political Liberalism*; Habermas, *Between Facts and Norms*; Habermas, *Justification and Application*; Habermas, *Moral Consciousness*; and Fishkin, *Dialogue of Justice*. For a devastating critique of the Rawlsian project, see Seung, *Intuition and Construction*, esp. chaps. 1–3. For a similarly devastating critique of Habermas's and Fishkin's attempts to create justice out of dialogue, see Williams, "Dialogical Theories of Justice."

103. This point is perhaps too obvious to merit further elaboration. But see Gauthier, "Thomas Hobbes: Moral Theorist"; and Gauthier, *Morals by Agreement*.

104. See also chapter 4 of DeHart, *Uncovering the Constitution's Moral Design*.

105. It is true that some properties are absolutely predicated of a given thing such that the thing in question either has the property or lacks it, whereas other properties may be predicated to some degree. Given this, suppose we are speaking of a property that a thing may possess to a greater or lesser degree. For instance, suppose we are speaking of the property of being full after Thanksgiving dinner. I may be simply full or I may be very full or I may be fuller than I've ever been. Even given this distinction, the point I am making here still holds. For in the case where a property may instantiate to a greater or lesser degree and so may be predicated to a greater or lesser degree, even so you cannot distinguish among objects wherein the property instantiates *on the basis of* the predication of that property to those objects. But, given this, my argument remains unscathed by the distinction between properties that are predicated absolutely and those that may be predicated to some degree.

106. It should be mentioned just here that obligation is a property quite distinct from sheer will.

107. According to C. S. Lewis,

> The idea that, without appealing to any court higher than the instincts them-
> selves, we can yet find grounds for preferring one instinct above its fellows
> dies very hard. We grasp at useless words: we call it the "basic," or "fun-
> damental," or "primal," or "deepest" instinct. It is of no avail. Either these
> words conceal a value judgment passed *upon* the instincts and therefore not
> derivable *from it*, or else they merely record its felt intensity, the frequency of
> its operation, and its wide distribution. If the former, the whole attempt to
> base value upon instinct has been abandoned: if the latter, these observations
> about the quantitative aspects of a psychological event lead to no practical
> conclusion. It is the old dilemma. Either the premisses already concealed an
> imperative or the conclusion remains merely in the indicative. (*Abolition of
> Man*, 36–37)

See also Plato, *Republic* 4.435e–449e, pp. 122–27: "Then if anything in [the soul/
self] draws it back when it is thirsty, wouldn't it be something different from what
thirsts and, like a beast, drives it to drink? For surely, we say, the same thing, in the
same respect of itself, in relation to the same thing, and at the same time, cannot
do opposite things" (quote at 4.439b, p. 127).

108. Locke, *Questions Concerning the Law of Nature*, Q. 7, pp. 199–201.

109. Locke, Q. 8, pp. 213–15.

110. The alternative is a thoroughly will-based or voluntarist ontology of legal
obligation, which, consequently, is self-referentially incoherent.

111. As I see it, this is compatible with the claim that moral obligation generally
(i.e., usually) under-determines legal obligation in the sense of leaving room for human legislators to enact positive laws in a way that takes differences of circumstance
into account.

112. DeHart, "Dangerous Life," 389. See also DeHart, *Uncovering the Constitution's Moral Design*, 138–39 and 168–78. The foregoing argument notwithstanding,
one frequently hears asserted the claim that, at the very least, there must some
"morally indifferent" laws. But the assertion is in fact false so long as the above
argument holds. So someone who asserts the possibility of *altogether* morally indifferent laws must show that some premise of the argument is unsound or that the
inference from the premises to the conclusion is in some way invalid. I suspect what
the objector really has in view is the fact that with respect to some law *l*, there may
be more than one morally acceptable way to frame *l*—and indeed, that these different ways may be equally acceptable. Moreover, if there is more than one equally
acceptable way to frame *l*, then how *l* is framed, so long as it is framed in one of
the acceptable ways, arguably is a matter of moral indifference. But even if there is
more than one equally acceptable way to frame every conceivable law, it leaves my
argument unaffected. For consonant with that argument, I would maintain that in
each such case we have an instance of morally bounded indeterminacy (as opposed

to the radical indeterminacy assumed by the objector). The objector, so I maintain, relies on an equivocation of indeterminacy with radical indeterminacy. But the former does not entail the latter.

113. Hobbes, *Leviathan* 14.27, p. 86. This passage is central to Martinich's interpretation of Hobbes's in *Two Gods of Leviathan*, 84.

114. Martinich, *Two Gods of Leviathan*, 82–83.

115. Martinich, 83.

116. Hobbes, *On the Citizen* 15.5, p. 173. In his own translation of the passage, Hobbes writes, "God in his *natural kingdom* hath a right to rule, and to punish those who break his laws, from his sole *irresistible power*." Thus, "God *Almighty* derives his right of sovereignty from the *power* itself." Hobbes, *De Cive* 15.5, p. 292. In *Leviathan*, Hobbes writes, "The right of nature whereby God reigneth over men, and punisheth those who break his laws, is to be derived, not from his creating them (as if he required gratitude, as of obedience for his benefits), but from his *irresistible power*" (31.5, p. 235). Reflecting on these passages in Hobbes, Leibniz writes, "Plato in his dialogues introduces and refutes a certain Thrasymachus, who, wishing to explain what justice is, gives a definition which would strongly recommend the position we are combating, if it were acceptable: for that is just (he says) which is agreeable or pleasant to the most powerful." Leibniz contends that Hobbes is Thrasymachus's progeny: "A celebrated English philosopher named Hobbes, who is noted for his paradoxes, has wished to uphold almost the same thing as Thrasymachus: for he wants God to have the right to do everything, because he is all powerful." Leibniz finds this view deeply problematic: "This is a failure to distinguish between right and fact. For what one can do is one thing, what one should do another." Moreover, on this view, "there would never be a sentence of a sovereign court, nor of a supreme judge, which would be unjust, nor would an evil but powerful man ever be blameworthy. And what is more, the same action could be just or unjust, depending on the judges who decide, which is ridiculous. It is one thing to be just and another to pass for it, and to take the place of justice." Leibniz, "Meditation on the Common Concept of Justice," in *Political Writings*, 46–47.

117. Locke, *Questions Concerning the Law of Nature*, 213.

118. While Locke seems to suggest above that the binding power of the natural law derives from the will of God, he also maintains that the will of God is necessarily regulated by goodness. See, for example, the fragment "Of God's Justice" in Locke, *Political Essays*, 277–78, which is quoted at length in chapter 5 of this volume.

119. As Rousseau says, "Force is a physical power; I do not see how its effects could produce morality." *Social Contract* 1.3, p. 52. We might add here, *contra* Hobbes, that "irresistibleness" is not a *moral* property either.

120. Arkes, *First Things*, 33.

121. On this see Adams, *Finite and Infinite Goods*, esp. chaps. 1 and 11, where Adams says that "it is only the commands of a definitively good God . . . that are a good candidate for the role of defining moral obligation" (250); Adams, "Modified Divine Command Theory"; and Adams, "Divine Command Metaethics."

122. It would be a non sequitur to infer from the foregoing that God is incapable of grounding morality. The argument only entails that sheer will—even if omnipotent, irresistible, or just the strongest—is incapable of grounding morality.

123. I elaborate ~~conventionalism~~ and the ~~philosophical difficulties attendant to the~~ concept in chapter 4 of DeHart, *Uncovering the Constitution's Moral Design.*

124. Arkes, *First Things*, 34–35. Wolterstorff notes that the argument requires "authority" in the place of "power" in the middle sentence of the quote (personal correspondence), which, I take it, is what Arkes means by "power" in this context.

125. To render the point formally, letting C stand for consent and E stand for human equality, (1) If E, then C; (2) not C; therefore (3) not E (modus tollens).

126. Of interest here is Waldron, *One Another's Equals.*

127. Budziszewski, "Comments on Wolterforff's " 'For the Authorities are God's Servants,' " 4. Cited with slight revision by and permission of the author. I should note that Budziszewski's position is that there is an initial presumption of consent— because God created humans free—that is nevertheless *not* indefeasible but, rather, can be overridden. Following Augustine and Aquinas, he holds that if a people becomes considerably corrupt (e.g., Augustine's example of a people selling their votes), then, morally (whatever happens in practice), they forfeit the right or privilege of choosing their magistrates. See Budziszewski, *Commentary on Aquinas's "Treatise on Law,"* 44–47. For Aquinas, see *Summa Theologiae* I-II, Q. 97, art. 1. There is, however, a difficulty with this position—especially if one affirms human equality or, with Bellarmine and Suárez, that God transmits political authority to the community and (given human equality) not to some particular individuals over others: What human has rightful authority to revoke the right of a people to choose its magistrates? As well, the proposition that the corrupt character of a people results in forfeiture of authority to rule depends on a more general premise that entails that corrupt, nonpopular rulers (kings, aristocratic or oligarchic assemblies, other magistrates) forfeit authority on account of their corruption. There seems no reason to restrict the corrupt character principle from broader application unless one denies natural equality. We might say that a corrupt people, like a corrupt king, don't deserve to exercise rule. That doesn't mean that any other human being has the right to take it from them and place it elsewhere.

128. In this volume generally I define metaphysical nominalism as Hobbes and Locke define it. According to Hobbes, there is "nothing in the world universal but names; for the things named are everyone of them individual and singular." Hobbes, *Leviathan* 6.6, p. 17. See also Hobbes, *Elements of Law* 1.5.6, pp. 36–37; and Hobbes, the first section of *Elements of Philosophy, Concerning Body (De Corpore)*, 2.9, pp. 19–20. Locke writes in his *Essay Concerning Human Understanding,* "All things, that exist, [are] particulars" (3.3.1, p. 409). Universals "are Inventions and Creatures of the Understanding, made by it for its own use. . . . When . . . we quit particulars, the generals that rest, are only creatures of our own making" (3.3.11, p. 414).

129. I elaborate a somewhat different argument for this contention in chapters 5 and 6 of DeHart, *Uncovering the Constitution's Moral Design.*

130. Drawing on my article "Fractured Foundations" and on chapter 5 in this volume, the preceding argument can be formalized as follows: Let *n* stand for

nominalism (understood as the denial of universal essences and/or the proposition that only particulars exist), *o* for obligation, *v* for voluntarism, and *r* for realism. I claim that the only account of obligation a nominalist can give is a voluntarist account. That gives us (1) *n•o* (if nominalism and obligation, then voluntarism concerning obligation). Voluntarism, per the argument above, is self-referentially incoherent. Thus, (2) ~*v* (not voluntarism). By application of modus tollens, ~*v* (not voluntarism) entails (3) ~(*n•o*) (not both nominalism and obligation). The rules of logical equivalency tell us that ~(*n•o*) is equivalent to (4) ~*n* or ~*o* (either not nominalism or not obligation). Now suppose we affirm, by way of argument or perhaps as properly basic, that some person or persons has some obligation or other, *or*, less ambitiously, that there is some possible world such that persons in it have some obligation(s) or other—that is, that obligations are conceptually possible. In that case, we would affirm *o* (obligations exist in some possible state of affairs). But o is logically equivalent to (5) ~~*o* (*not* not obligation). Given the disjunctive syllogism, ~~*o* entails (6) ~*n* (not nominalism). I have also suggested that realism and nominalism (concerning universal essences) are mutually excusive. Thus, (7) *r* or *n* (realism or nominalism). Given (6) and the disjunctive syllogism, we have (8) *r* (realism). The argument holds as long as we are warranted in affirming, either as properly basic or for good reasons, that some person (or persons), either actual or purely possible, falls under some obligation or other. The cost for maintaining nominalism, namely, the rejection of all obligations, is a price I believe most of us would be unwilling to pay.

131. The disjunctive syllogism holds the following: (1) Either A or B, (2) not A, (3) therefore b.

132. I don't think it necessary to establish by argument that we have obligations. It strikes me as likely the case that certain of our obligations are properly basic. We know that we have certain obligations, and such knowledge is not held or acquired on the basis of anything else we know or believe.

133. Hobbes, *Leviathan* 4.6, p. 17; and Locke, *Essay Concerning Human Understanding*, 3.3.1, p. 409, and 3.3.11, p. 414, quoted briefly in n. 100 above and in chapters 4 and 5 more extensively.

134. A type of Hobbesian reply might be that materialism rules out universals or substantial forms (or other concepts on which metaphysical realism depends). This reply turns on the presence of a valid and sound deductive argument for materialism or, at least, of a cogent inductive argument for it. In passages of *Leviathan* such as chapters 34 (esp. secs. 1–5, 18, 23, and 24) and 46 (esp. secs. 14–19), Hobbes affirms materialism (or the notion that material or bodily substance is the only sort that exists) on what he takes to be the implausibility of incorporeal substance. He even asserts that incorporeal substance constitutes something of a self-contradiction (this last claim occurs at 4.21). But Hobbes only ever asserts the incomprehensibility of incorporeal substance. He never establishes it. Indeed, there is good reason to think that he could not, and that materialism consequently operates more as an assumption than as a conclusion in philosophic and scientific argumentation. Moreover, the case for materialism has not fared well since the time of Hobbes. As it happens, there is a dearth of valid and sound deductive arguments or of cogent inductive arguments

for it. See the essays in Koons and Bealer, *Waning of Materialism*. In his contribution to that volume, Laurence BonJour claims that "as far as I can see, materialism is a view that has no very compelling argument in its favor and that is confronted with ~~very powerful objections to which nothing even approaching an adequate response~~ has been offered." BonJour, "Against Materialism," 3. As the highly regarded and philosophically adept physicist Stephen Barr surmises, *all* of the arguments for materialism "seem to boil down in the end to 'materialism is true, because materialism must be true.' The fact seems to be that the philosophy of materialism is completely fideistic in character." Barr, *Modern Physics*, 16. See also DeHart, *Uncovering the Constitution's Moral Design*, 247–48.

135. As to this, see Zimmerman's introduction to Van Inwagen and Zimmerman, *Persons: Human and Divine*: "But the positivists' dogma that theology (and metaphysics and ethics and . . .) is meaningless was not part of analytic philosophy at its origins; and it was soon rejected, as positivism passed from the scene. Initially, 'the philosophy of analysis' meant a fully metaphysically-loaded commitment to *realism* in opposition to the idealisms of Bradley, Bosanquet, and others. Its founders—Russell and Moore—never went along with the extreme positivist dogmas of the early 1930s, which led Carnap, Ayer, and others to consign theology to the same dustbin as metaphysics" (9).

136. See, for example, Koons, *Realism Regained*; Adams, *Finite and Infinite Goods*; Seung, *Intuition and Reconstruction*; Sayre-McCord, *Moral Realism*; Wolterstorff, "The World Ready Made" in Wolterstorff, *Practices of Belief*, 12–40.

137. With respect to his rejection of Hobbes's metaphysical nominalism, see "Preface to an Edition of Nizolius" in Leibniz, *Philosophical Papers*. Leibniz says, "Nominalists are those who believe that all things except individual substances are mere names; they therefore deny the reality of abstract terms and universals forthright" (128). Nominalism, he writes, originated with Roscelin of Brittany, was "eclipsed" and then "revived" by William of Occam; "Gregory of Rimini, Gabriel Biel, and many of the Augustinian order agreed with [Occam], and Martin Luther's earlier writings also show clearly a love of nominalism" (128). According to Leibniz, "Occam himself was not more nominalistic than is Thomas Hobbes now, though I confess that Hobbes seems to me to be a super-nominalist," who, "not content like the nominalists, to reduce universals to names . . . says the truth of things itself consists in names and what is more, that it depends on the human will, because truth allegedly depends on the definitions of terms, and definitions depend on the human will. This is the opinion of a man recognized as among the most profound of our century, and, as I said, nothing can be more nominalistic than it. Yet it cannot stand. In arithmetic, and in other disciplines as well, truths remain the same even if the notations are changed, and it does not matter whether a decimal or a duodecimal number system is used" (128). Contra Hobbes (and Nizolius), "If universals were nothing but collections of individuals, it would follow that we could attain no knowledge through demonstration . . . but only through collecting individuals and induction. But on this basis knowledge would straightway be made impossible, and the skeptics would be victorious" (129). Leibniz's rejection of Locke's nominalism appears in his

New Essays on the Human Understanding, book 3, chap. 6, pp. 317–28; book 3, chap. 10, pp. 343–46; and book 4, chap. 6, pp. 400-402. See Jolley, *Leibniz,* 121–23. Locke's nominalism entails a complete deconstruction of the notion of species in the *Essay Concerning Human Understanding.* Leibniz rejects this total deconstruction. Given modus tollens, it follows he rejects Locke's ground for it—namely, Lockean nominalism. To be sure, Robert Merrihew Adams says, "Like other early modern philosophers, Leibniz was no Platonist about universals. The only universals he recognized were concepts and 'possibilities in resemblances' ([*New Essays*] 323f.). And since he thought that relations between substances exist only in the mind, he would have to say that a lion's resemblance to other animals is contained, strictly speaking, in the concept that a mind forms of lions by comparing them with other animals, rather than in the lion itself." Adams, *Leibniz,* 71; but see also 178–80 (where Adams says Leibniz affirms "a theistic modification of Platonism" in which "necessary truths, and more generally the being of the objects of logic and mathematics" are "ideas in the mind of God....They exist necessarily, since God's having and understanding them follows from the divine essence," p. 180). On this point I think Jolley's analysis better captures other passages in *New Essays,* esp. 3.6, 325–26f and 3.10, 345f. Consider Leibniz's argument that "justice follows certain rules of equality and of proportion [which are] no less founded in the immutable nature of things, and in the divine ideas, than are the principles of arithmetic and of geometry. So that no one will maintain that justice and goodness originate in the divine will, without at the same time maintaining that truth originates in it as well: an unheard-of paradox by which Descartes showed how great can be the errors of men." Leibniz, "Opinion on the Principles of Pufendorf" (1706), in *Political Writings,* 71.

138. On this score, see Williams, *Rousseau's Platonic Enlightenment,* chaps. 1 and 2.

139. An anonymous reader for the *Perspectives in Political Science* version of this essay noted that some might object to the argument for grounding any viable theory of consent on moral and metaphysical realism because, "historically speaking, the reign of realism correlates with the reign of social and political *inequality.*" I've always found this objection to be a red herring. The historical record is more ambiguous than the objection lets on. But, even worse, the objection has self-referential incoherence difficulties. For if the objection is a *moral* or *normative* objection, then the validity of the objection requires a *real* moral standard by which inequality can deemed morally objectionable. Even worse, the entailment relation from equality to consent requires an equality of human nature such that the human nature in question imposes (indeed, is capable of imposing) obligations upon others to treat it in a certain way. Not just any equality will do. Hobbesian equality of strength, prudence, and hope, for instance, entails nothing concerning the necessity of consent for legitimate government. The sort of equality needed—the equality of a real *human nature* that is normative for human behavior—is most at home within moral and ontological realism. As C. S. Lewis writes, "Subjectivism about values is eternally incompatible with democracy. We and our rulers are of one kind only so long as we are subject to one law. But if there is no Law of Nature, the *ethos* of any society is the creation of its rulers, educators, and conditioners; and every creator stands above

and outside his own creation." Lewis, "The Poison of Subjectivism," 81. I address this objection in DeHart, *Uncovering the Constitution's Moral Design*, 252–58.

Chapter 2

1. Hampton, "The Two Faces of Contractarian Thought," 32. See Gauthier, *Morals by Agreement* and his summary of that argument in "Why Contractarianism?"

2. See Gagarin and Woodruff, *Early Greek Political Thought*.

3. I don't intend to argue that Hobbes's moral philosophy is purely or thoroughly conventionalist. I maintain only that there is a conventional strain. The argument might construed as an analysis of Hobbes's account of justice insofar as his account is conventional. Other interpretations of Hobbes's moral philosophy are considered in chapter 4 of this volume.

4. In addition to Gauthier and Rawls, we must add Mackie, *Ethics*; Kelsen, *Pure Theory of Law*, esp. 62 ("Moral norms, precisely like legal norms, are created by custom and by acts of will" and "morals, like the law, because actually posited, are positive"); and Hart, *Concept of Law*. For my argument that Hart is best understood as a conventionalist, given his account of rules of recognition, see chapter 6 of DeHart, *Uncovering the Constitution's Moral Design*.

5. Aquinas, *Questiones Disputatae de Veritate*, Q. 23, art. 6.

6. See Wolterstorff, *Justice*, 143–44, where he speaks of human lives as noninstrumental goods and identifies the good as that which is worthy of approbation (the inverse of Hobbes, who considers objects of approbation or praise to be good insofar as they receive approbation or praise); Adams, *Finite and Infinite Goods* (see, e.g., 281); Rist, *Plato's Moral Realism*; and Seung, *Intuition and Construction*.

7. Dworkin, *Justice for Hedgehogs*.

8. In this section I to some extent build on my argument in DeHart, "The Dangerous Life." That essay can also be read to supplement arguments advanced here.

9. See Copleston's *A History of Philosophy*, vol 1, *Greece and Rome* (cited herafter as *Greece and Rome*), 87.

10. All quotations for Protagoras are from Steinberger, *Readings in Classical Political Thought*, 20–21.

11. Copleston, *Greece and Rome*, 87–88.

12. As Graham Walker writes, "Plato presents Protagoras's doctrine as pertaining in the first instance to perception of physical nature, making the natural realities around us wholly dependent on human perception and construal, thus making ontology strictly contingent on human epistemology." Walker, *Moral Foundations*, 35.

13. My critique of Protagorean antirealism or Protagorean conventionalism does not depend on whether the individualist or collectivist reading of his *homo mensura* is correct.

14. Steinberger, *Readings in Classical Political Thought*, 20–21.

15. Antiphon in Steinberger, 26.

16. *The Essential Thucydides* 5.89, pp. 164–65. For the entire dialogue, see 5.85–5.116.

17. Thucydides 5.90, p. 165.

18. Thucydides 5.105, p. 168.

19. Plato, *Republic* 1.338c, p. 15. As Reeve translates it: "I say justice is nothing other than what is advantageous for the stronger."

20. Plato 1.338e–39a, p. 15.

21. Plato, *Laws* (trans. Saunders) 4.714, pp. 172–73. See also C. D. C.'s recent translation of Plato's *Laws*.

22. Plato, *Laws* (trans. Saunders) 4.714–15, p. 173.

23. Plato 4.715, p. 173.

24. Plato, *Gorgias*, lines 483b–484b, pp. 73–74.

25. Plato, *Republic* 2.358e–359b.

26. See Gauthier's treatment of Glaucon's argument in chap. 10 of *Morals by Agreement*, esp. 307–10. See also MacIntyre, *A Short History of Ethics*, 17–18, 34–36.

27. See Plantinga's treatment of what he calls "creative anti-realism" in "How to Be an Anti-Realist," esp. 47–54.

28. See Rist, *Real Ethics*, pp. 10-11, on "contemporary perspectivism". According to Rist, "Contemporary perspectivism" goes "beyond the view that we can only describe 'events' partially, and that our viewing is irremediably determined by our subjective stance, its history and the tradition to which it belongs" to the "philosophical theory that 'truth' itself, in history as in morality, is unobtainable and therefore an illusion; indeed that the past itself is to be collapsed into the present or constructed out of our desires and wishes for the future." Rist rightly notes, "Such bold inferences . . . are far from self-evident and face dialectical threats—as can be recognized if we deconstruct the project itself."

29. See also DeHart, *Uncovering the Constitution's Moral Design*, 120n8, 247.

30. Indeed, the self-referential incoherence would be as embarrassingly obvious as that of the cornerstone of logical positivism: namely, the criterion of empirical verifiability.

31. My point here is analogous to Hadley Arkes's argument that moral relativism is self-refuting. Arkes, *First Things*, 132.

32. For the rules of inference see Hurley, *A Concise Introduction to Logic*. According to simplification $p \cdot q$ entails p. According to a rule called commutativity, $p \cdot q$ is equivalent to $q \cdot p$. And, given simplification, $q \cdot p$ entails q. Thus, a proposition that affirms both A and not A ($a \cdot {\sim} a$), given commutativity, is equivalent to both not A and A (${\sim}a \cdot a$), from which ${\sim}a$ follows. The upshot of simplification and commutativity together is that either term of a conjunct follows from the conjunct.

33. Cicero, *The Laws* [*De legibus*], in *"The Republic" and "The Laws"* 1.42–43, pp. 111–12. This argument occurs in a dialogue between himself (Marcus), his brother (Quintus), and his friend (Atticus) in *De legibus*. Cicero is responding to the account of justice that Thrasymachus espouses in Plato's *Republic*.

34. Cicero, *Laws* 1.43–44.

35. My argument that justice conceived entirely in terms of interest turns out to be an empty concept has clear parallels with the argument of J. Budziszewski that rule utilitarianism is an empty concept, given that it ultimately collapses into act utilitarianism. Budziszewski, *Written on the Heart*, chap. 11, esp. 148–58.

36. I underscore here that (2) refers to one's perceived interest. For moral realists certainly hold that justice is in one's *true* interest. To borrow a turn of phrase from Alexis de Tocqueville, justice accords with one's interest rightly understood. But, of course, it might conflict with one's perceived or immediate or selfish interest.

37. Socrates, of course, makes this point against Thrasymachus's contention that justice is nothing other than the interest of the stronger party. Plato, *Republic* 1.339c–340a, p. 16.

38. Self-interest can refer either to *perceived* interests (one's interests are just whatever one considers them to be) or to *true* interests (we have real interests that we may sometimes wrongly perceive). If self-interest means perceived interests, and justice is a function of interest, then everything is right and nothing is wrong. The terms *right* and *wrong* lose all meaning because they cannot distinguish some acts as right from others that are wrong. But if interest refers to genuine or true interest, such that our perceptions may get our interests right or wrong, then we have introduced an ideal and normative account of interest that is no longer conventional. And what could true or genuine interests, as distinguished from perceived interests, be other than interests the pursuit of which is *good for* human beings? In which case distinguishing true from perceived interests requires an account of human good not reducible to interest alone.

39. Even David Gauthier, who seeks to justify moral constraints on the straightforward maximization of self-interest as maximizing one's interest in the long run, commences *Morals by Agreement* with this: "Were duty no more than interest, morals would be superfluous. Why appeal to right or wrong, to good or evil, to obligation or duty, if instead we may appeal to desire or aversion, to benefit or cost, to interest or to advantage? An appeal to morals takes its point from the failure of these latter considerations as sufficient guides to what we ought to do. . . . It is only as we believe that some appeals do, alas, override interest or advantage that morality becomes our concern." Gauthier, *Morals by Agreement*, 1. I think Cicero's point is precisely this: that if we reduce justice or duty to sheer interest, then morality is indeed superfluous. But Gauthier fails to see how this observation subverts the rest of his project, as I seek to show in chapter 3.

40. Gauthier, "Thomas Hobbes: Moral Theorist," 547. Bernard Gert rejects Gauthier's contention that Hobbes affirms both value subjectivism and the "maximizing conception of rationality." See Gert, "Hobbes's Account of Reason," 559–60. See also Gert, "Hobbes and Psychological Egoism"; Gert, "Hobbes, Mechanism, and Egoism"; and Gert, "Hobbes on Reason." Gert notwithstanding, from the vantage of nature—or of human beings taken by themselves—I think Hobbes is clearly a subjectivist about good and evil; from the vantage of human beings in civil society where law prescribes, then public good and evil are relative to civil law. Moreover, the conventionalist (or moral contractarian) interpretation of Hobbes does not require interpreting him to say that humans are rational maximizers.

41. Gauthier, "Thomas Hobbes: Moral Theorist," 547–48.

42. For my analysis here, I'm adapting a comment that Hampton makes concerning the relation of God to the laws of nature in *Hobbes and the Social Contract*

(96) and about Hobbes's divine command and contractarian justifications of moral imperatives in "Two Faces of Contractarian Thought" (p. 33n6). One way to read Hobbes's comment about the laws of nature becoming laws proper when they are commanded by God (*Leviathan* 15.1, p. 100), on the one hand, or when commanded by the commonwealth (*Leviathan* 26.8, p. 174), on the other, is as providing two independent foundations for them. And we might ask whether his account of the laws of nature is coherent on either foundation. I maintain it is not, but here I propose to focus just on the conventionalist or moral contractarian strain.

43. Hobbes, *De Homine* 11.4, p. 47. See also *Elements of Law* 1.7.3, p. 44. Note that Hobbes uses the language of predication. He is not referring to psychology or epistemology (though these are relevant) rather than ontology. As I will argue in chapter 4, his subjective or relativist account of good and evil is an application of his metaphysical nominalism—and it's impossible for metaphysical nominalists to posit any sort of real or intrinsic or simple and absolute good.

44. Hobbes, *De Homine* 8.8, p. 68.

45. Hobbes 8.8, pp. 68–69.

46. Hobbes 8.9, p. 69 (emphasis added).

47. Hobbes, *De Cive* 6.16, pp. 185–86.

48. Richard, *Twelve Greeks and Romans*, 33–34. See also Rahe, *The Spartan Regime*, 26.

49. Richard, *Twelve Greeks and Romans*, 32. See also Rahe, *The Spartan Regime*, 9, 23–24, 49.

50. Hobbes, *Leviathan* 13.13, p. 78.

51. Hobbes, *Leviathan* 14.1, p. 79, and 14.4, p. 80.

52. Hamilton, "The Farmer Refuted," 258. Hamilton is responding to the Loyalist Seabury's critique of his earlier vindication of the measures of the Continental Congress.

53. Hobbes, *Leviathan* 15.1, p. 89.

54. Hobbes 15.2, p. 89.

55. Hobbes 15.3, p. 89.

56. Hobbes 17.2, p. 106.

57. Hobbes 15.3, p. 89 (emphasis added).

58. Hobbes 15.2, p. 89.

59. Hobbes 30.20, 229.

60. Hobbes 15.4, p. 90.

61. Hobbes, 15.5, pp. 91–92.

62. Gauthier, "Thomas Hobbes: Moral Theorist," 555–56.

63. Hobbes, *Leviathan* 5.3, p. 23.

64. Gauthier, "Thomas Hobbes: Moral Theorist," 557. Though here "conventional reason"—in Gauthier's account—seems to abstract from or broaden Hobbes's solution. The reason Hobbes proposes is an instance of conventional rather than natural rationality, to be sure. But the conventional reason is that of an arbitrator or judge individuals set up to resolve the conflict—ultimately, the sovereign power of chapter 17.

65. Gauthier, "Thomas Hobbes: Moral Theorist," 557 (emphasis added).

66. Of course, justice on the Hobbesian view is inapplicable to a situation in which each individual pursues their own self-interest in an unconstrained way—such a condition is the state of nature/war; and in that state neither just nor unjust has any place. So on the Hobbesian view, justice is only relevant to constrained pursuit—and must have to do with the constraints. As to this, Gauthier certainly captures Hobbes's view, though I think this means he runs headlong into the problem I've just laid out.

67. Hobbes, *De Homine* 10.4, p. 41.

68. Hobbes 10.5, pp. 42–43.

69. See also Alasdair MacIntyre's argument that Hobbes's position is "ruined by an internal self-contradiction": Hobbes "wishes [the original contract] to be the foundation of all shared and common standards and rules; but he also wishes it to be a contract, and for it to be a contract, there must already exist shared and common standards of the kind he specifies cannot exist prior to the contract." MacIntyre, *Short History of Ethics*, 136–37.

70. Cuneo, *Speech & Morality*, 2.

71. Hume, *A Treatise of Human Nature* (ed. Mossner), 545–47. While later in life Hume seems to distance himself from his youthful *Treatise* (he calls it a "juvenile work"), the essay on *justice* in his later *Enquiries* lays out the same position as the parallel section in the *Treatise*. Indeed, he claims that his "philosophical Principles are the same in both" works; only his manner of presentation changes between the two. In the later work he writes, "Thus, the rules of equity or justice depend on the particular state and condition in which men are placed, and owe their origin and existence to that utility, which results to the public from their strict and regular observance. Reverse, in any considerable circumstance, the condition of men: Produce extreme abundance or extreme necessity: Implant in the human breast perfect moderation and humanity or perfect rapaciousness and malice: By rendering justice totally *useless*, you thereby totally destroy its essence, and suspend its obligation upon mankind." A few paragraphs later, he comments that the "*poetical* fiction of the *golden age* is, in some respects, of a piece with the *philosophical* fiction of the *state of nature*; only that the former is represented as the most charming and most peaceable condition, which can possibly be imagined; whereas the latter is painted out as a state of mutual war and violence, attended with the most extreme necessity. On the first origin of mankind, we are told, their ignorance and savage nature were so prevalent, that they could give no mutual trust, but must each depend upon himself and his own force or cunning for protection and security. No law was heard of: no rule of justice known: no distinction of property regarded: Power was the only measure of right; and a perpetual war of all against all was the result of men's selfishness and barbarity." He rejects the historical existence of the state of nature: "Whether such a condition of human nature ever could exist, or if it did, could continue so long as to merit the appellation of a *state*, may justly be doubted. Men are necessarily born in a family-society, at least; and are trained up by their parent to some rule of conduct

and behavior. But this may be admitted, that, if such a state of mutual war and violence was ever real, the suspension of all laws of justice, from their absolute inutility, is a necessary and infallible consequence." Hume, *Enquiries Concerning the Human Understanding* 1.3, p. 188–90.

72. Hume 1.3, p. 188.

73. In his *Questions Concerning the Law of Nature*, Q. 10, pp. 221–33, Locke distinguishes natural law obligations that bind everyone simply or absolutely and those that apply to certain conditions. That is, I am bound to keep my promises, only insofar as I have made promises. One is bound to perform the function of a father only if one is a father. We might call these obligations conditional—they obtain for one on the condition that one has made a promise or become a father. These obligations don't obtain for those who have made no promises or for those who are not fathers. But though they do not in fact apply to all people—but only if the relevant condition(s) obtain—they are nevertheless objective or real. They are not on account of their conditionality artificial, constructed, or conventional.

74. Hume, *A Treatise of Human Nature* 3.2.2, p. 545 (Mossner ed.).

Chapter 3

1. Seung, *Intuition and Construction*, xiii; and *Plato Rediscovered*, 242 (and chap. 7 more generally).

2. Gauthier, "Why Contractarianism?," 15–16.

3. Gauthier, 18–19.

4. Gauthier, *Morals by Agreement*, 4. With moral contractarianism, Gauthier writes, "we have a mode of justification that does not require the introduction of moral considerations." Gauthier, "Why Contractarianism?," 19.

5. Gauthier, *Morals by Agreement*, 8. In "Why Contractarianism?" he writes:

Since in representing our preferences we become aware of conflict among them, the step from representation to choice becomes complicated. We must, somehow, bring our conflicting desires and preferences into some sort of coherence. And there is only one plausible candidate for a principle of coherence—a maximizing principle. We order our preferences, in relation to decision and action, so that we may choose in a way that maximizes our expectation of preference fulfillment. And in so doing, we show ourselves to be rational agents, engaged in deliberation and deliberative justification. There is simply nothing else for practical rationality to be. (Gauthier, "Why Contractarianism?," 19–20)

6. See also T. K. Seung's treatment of Gauthier's account of instrumental rationality in chapter 5 of *Intuition and Construction*.

7. Gauthier, *Morals by Agreement*, 9.

8. Gauthier, 6.

9. Gauthier, 1.

10. Gauthier, 59. A few pages earlier Gauthier claims, "The defence of subjectivism is the primary task facing anyone who identifies value with the measure of considered preference." He adds that he "finds the case for subjectivism compelling" (55).

11. Gauthier, 9.

12. Gauthier, 310.

13. Gauthier, 17.

14. "The key idea is that in many situations, if each person chooses what, given the choices of others, would maximize her expected utility, then the outcome will be mutually disadvantageous in comparison with some alternative—everyone else could do better. . . . Given the ubiquity of such situations, each person can see the benefit, to herself, of participating with her fellows in practices requiring each to refrain from the direct endeavor to maximize her own utility, when such mutual restrain is advantageous." Gauthier, 22–23.

15. "It is rational to dispose oneself to accept certain constraints on direct maximization in choosing and acting, if and only if so disposing oneself maximizes one's expected utility." Gauthier, "Why Contractarianism?" pp. 25–26.

16. Gauthier, *Morals by Agreement*, 14.

17. Gauthier, 15. The proviso, he says, is a *condition* on rational agreement—necessary for any agreement among preference maximizers—and so is not a "product" of agreement.

18. Gauthier, 15.

19. Gauthier, 16.

20. Gauthier, 16. Here he describes "the Archimedean point" not only as one of "assured impartiality" but also as "the position sought by John Rawls behind the 'veil of ignorance.' "

21. Gauthier, "Why Contractarianism?," 26.

22. Gauthier, 27.

23. Gauthier, 27.

24. Gauthier, 27.

25. Gauthier, 28.

26. Gauthier, *Morals by Agreement*, 316.

27. Gauthier, 316–17.

28. Gauthier, 316.

29. Gauthier, 316.

30. Plato, *Republic* 2.360e–361b5, p. 39.

31. Gauthier, *Morals by Agreement*, 317.

32. Gauthier, "Why Contractarianism?," 30.

33. On teleology in Aristotle and Aquinas, see Lisska, *Aquinas's Theory of Natural Law*, chaps. 4 and 5; and Feser, *Aristotle's Revenge*, esp. chap. 1.

34. There is another strain of argument entangled with his contention about what *we* can no longer accept. We might call this the *alternative-explanation* line of argument. On this line of argument, we need no longer explain the cosmos as purposively ordered because teleological explanation of the world has been replaced by an alternative explanation—namely, that of modern science. Teleological explanation is

no longer necessary. Of course, the possibility of explaining the world both in tele-ological and nonteleological terms does not constitute a refutation of the former or an argument for the latter. Rather, says Gauthier, the explanations of modern science simply ignore teleological explanation. But in that case, the weight of the argument must remain with what his anonymous *we* can accept. See Gauthier, "Why Con-tractarianism?," 21. See also Strauss's comments about the advent of nonteleological natural science in *Natural Right and History*, esp. 166. For the argument that this change is philosophical rather than scientific and an untenable philosophy of sci-ence at that, see the arguments of Peter van Inwagen, Stephen Barr, Thomas Nagel, Edward Feser, and Robert C. Koons referenced below.

35. Gauthier, "Why Contractarianism?," 20.

36. Gauthier writes that religion faces "a comparable foundational crisis" to that of morality: "Religion demands the worship of a divine being who purposively or-ders the universe. But it has confronted an alternative mode of explanation." To be sure, "evolutionary biology and, more generally, modern science do not refute reli-gion. Rather they ignore it, replacing its explanations by ontologically simpler ones." Gauthier thinks that "religion, understood as affirming justifiable worship of a divine being, may be unable to survive its foundational crisis." But this claim is asserted rather than argued. "Why Contractarianism?," 21.

37. Gauthier, 17.

38. Gauthier, *Morals by Agreement*, 1.

39. Barr, *Modern Physics*; Polkinghorne, *Faith of a Physicist*; Polkinghorne, *Belief in God in an Age of Science*; Barrow and Tipler, *The Anthropic Cosmological Principle*; Davies, *God and the New Physics*; and Davies, *The Mind of God*.

40. Gilson, *From Aristotle to Darwin*; Frederick Copleston, debate with Bertrand Russell on the existence of God, BBC Radio, 1948; Van Inwagen, "The Compati-bility of Darwin and Design" (see essays by Richard Swinburne and Paul Davies in the same volume); Nagel, *Mind and Cosmos*; Flew, *There Is A God*; Koons, *Realism Regained*; and Feser, *Aristotle's Revenge*.

41. Smith, *What Is a Person?*

42. Adams, *Finite and Infinite Goods*; Taylor, *Sources of the Self*, esp. 74; MacIntyre, *After Virtue*; Rist, *Real Ethics*; Cuneo, *Normative Web*; Cuneo, *Speech and Morality*; Finnis, *Natural Law & Natural Rights*; Anscombe, "Justice of the Present War"; and Stump, "Aquinas's Theory of Goodness."

43. Lewis, *Abolition of Man*; and Lewis, "Poison of Subjectivism."

44. Arkes, *Philosopher in the City*; Arkes, *First Things*; Budziszewski, *Line Through the Heart*; and Holloway, *The Way of Life*.

45. Smith, *To Flourish or Destruct*. See also the devastating critique of attempts to construct a science of morality, from the Englightenment to the present, in Hunter and Nedelisky, *Science and the Good*.

46. Hampton, *The Authority of Reason*; George, *In Defense of Natural Law*; and Seung, *Intuition and Construction*, chap. 5.

47. Plantinga, *Warrant: The Current Debate*, esp. 138–42; Plantinga, *Warrant and Proper Function*; Plantinga, *Warranted Christian Belief*, esp. 116 (I believe Plant-inga misconstrues Aristotle, but he puts his finger on a problem fundamental to

construing reason simply as means-end rationality); Wolterstorff, *Practices of Belief*; Wolterstorff, *Justice*, 229–32, 301–2; and Cuneo, *The Normative Web*.

48. MacIntyre writes,

> Moral judgments are linguistic survivals from the practices of classical theism which have lost the context provided by these practices. In that context moral judgments were at once hypothetical and categorical in form. They were hypothetical insofar as they expressed a judgment as to what conduct would be teleologically appropriate for a human being: "You ought to do so-and-so, if and since your *telos* is such-and-such" or perhaps "You ought to do so-and-so, if you do not want your essential desires to be frustrated." They were categorical insofar as they reported the contents of the universal law commanded by God: "You ought to do so-and so: that is what God's law enjoins." But take away from them that in virtue of which they were hypothetical and that in virtue of which they were categorical and what are they? Moral judgments lose any clear status and the sentences which express them in a parallel way lose any undebatable meaning. Such sentences become available as forms of expression for an emotivist self which lacking the guidance of the context in which they were originally at home has lost its linguistic as well as its practical way in the world. (MacIntyre, *After Virtue*, 60)

49. On this point I would then register a disagreement with MacIntyre. I hold normativity or oughtness to require both teleology (understood in the Aristotelian, non-consequentialist sense) and divine prescription. That is, there is no normativity, rightness, or oughtness to be had from hypothetical imperatives alone.

50. Cited in Gauthier, *Morals by Agreement*, 17. Gauthier cites a manuscript of Locke's quoted in Dunn, *The Political Thought of John Locke*, 218–19.

51. Gauthier, *Morals by Agreement*, 17. See also Nussbaum, *Frontiers of Justice*. She writes, "The core moral idea in the [social contract tradition] is that of mutual advantage and reciprocity among people who need to make such a contract" (16).

52. Gauthier, *Morals by Agreement*, 268. According to Nussbaum, "classical [social contract] theorists . . . omitted from the bargaining situation women . . . children, and the elderly"; and "no social contract doctrine . . . includes people with severe and atypical physical and mental impairment in the group of those by whom basic political principles are chosen." Nussbaum, *Frontiers of Justice*, 14–15. She notes that in the revised original position of Rawls's *Political Liberalism*, "the parties are designing principles for citizens who, like themselves, are human beings possessed of no serious mental or physical impairments" (17).

53. Baier, "Pilgrim's Progress," 320.

54. Baier, 322.

55. Locke, *Two Treatises*, First Treatise 6.57, pp. 181–82, referencing Garcilaso de la Vega's *Le Commentaire Royale, ou L'Histoire des Yncas, Roys du Peru* published in 1633.

56. Garcilaso, cited in Locke, First Treatise 6.57, p. 182. According to Baier, in "Pilgrim's Progress" (323), Locke is citing Filmer's quotation of Garcilaso. (323). But Laslett notes that Locke had Garcilaso's *Commentarios Reales* in his Oxford study in 1681 and referenced it "frequently" (6.57n, p. 182).

57. Baier, "Pilgrim's Progress," 323.

58. Gauthier, "Moral Artifice," 404.

59. On the Inca, see Handwerk, "Inca Child Sacrifice Victims"; and Corthals et. al., "Detecting the Immune System Response." There has been considerable debate over claims of extensive child sacrifice in Carthage. See Xella, Quinn, Melchiorri, and Dommelen, "Phoenician Bones of Contention."

60. Baier raises this matter at the end of her critique of Gauthier's *Morals by Agreement*. On the widespread practice of *expositio* of infants in the Greco-Roman world, see Bakke's magisterial study, *When Children Became People*, especially chaps. 2 and 4. *Expositio* was not criminalized in the Roman empire until 374 AD / CE. Prior to that date, "*expositio* [of newborns] was well-known and societally accepted in both the eastern and western regions of the empire. There is no consensus among scholars about what happened to these children; some were rescued and looked after, and most of these ended up as slaves, but the sources also indicate that a relatively large number of such children died. A number of reasons led parents to take this step. Mostly, poverty was the cause of *expositio*, but we know of instances where even wealthy Romans exposed their children. Other common reasons were illegitimacy or a handicap, though it was probably more common to kill children born with deformities, or those judged not strong enough to grow up. It is also reasonable to assume that more girls than boys were exposed" (51). Bakke notes that a few Stoic philosophers opposed the widespread practice as contrary to nature and that from the second century AD / CE forward the authorities in a number of Italian cities opposed *expositio* because it cut too deeply into the supply of workers. Their concern was entirely pragmatic. Besides ancient Rome, we might note the extensive infanticide the Spartans practiced in the name of a eugenics project aimed at ensuring a population of strong warriors.

61. Locke, *Two Treatises*, First Treatise 6.56n, pp. 180–81. According to Peter Laslett, Locke is criticizing Filmer and Bodin, on whom Filmer draws:

In *Patriarcha* (77–78) Filmer shows, with an example from Roman history, that fathers could punish their children with death, and in the *Directions* (231) he says: "God also hath given the Father a right . . . to alien his power over his children . . . whence we find the sale and gift of children . . . much in use in the beginning of the world . . . the power of castrating . . . much in use." These statements come unaltered from Bodin's *République*, where it is said that it is "needful to restore unto parents . . . their power of life and death over their children." (*Two Treatises*, First Treatise 6.56n, pp. 180–81)

62. Gauthier, *Morals by Agreement*, 17–18, 268. Gauthier speaks of "Locke's criticism of the scope of contractarian morality" (18) as evidenced in this fragment from

Locke: "An Hobbist . . . will not easily admit a great many plain duties of morality" (17).

63. Again, I do not mean to say that moral contractarianism is the whole of Hobbes's normative theory (see chapter 4).

64. Hobbes, *Leviathan* 20.5, pp. 129–30. See also Hobbes, *De Cive* 9.2–7, pp. 212–15.

65. Baier, "Pilgrim's Progress," 319–20.

66. Gauthier, *Morals by Agreement*, 269.

67. To the modus tollens of Gauthier's argument, we might reply with modus tollens instead.

68. Locke, *Questions Concerning the Law of Nature*, Q. 7, 199–201.

69. And here we might note that Gauthier is certainly guilty of smuggling moral properties into his putatively nonmoral foundation. Consider the agreement reached at the Archimedean point in his theory. It is not really interest or preference maximization—or at least, it's not these alone—that makes the hypothetical agreement binding. Rather, it is *impartiality*—the fact that all interests are treated equally and the interests of all parties to the agreement adjudicated fairly (on his account of fairness). But if impartiality has no objective, normative hold on us, then, when it comes to moral justification, there is no reason whatsoever for moving from the given norms of a society or from an actual agreement to a hypothetical one. Thus, Gauthier's premoral foundation is not really premoral at all.

70. On this, see the references to Seung, *Intuition and Construction*, below.

71. See Dyer, *Natural Law*, 170–72; also DeHart, "Political Philosophy after the Collapse," 40–51.

72. Rawls, *Theory of Justice*, 137.

73. Rawls, 152–53. See also Hampton, *Political Philosophy*, 139.

74. Rawls, *Theory of Justice*, 60.

75. Rawls, 15.

76. Rawls, 27.

77. Rawls, 3.

78. Rawls maintains that "certain principles of justice are justified *because* they would be agreed to in an initial situation of equality" (21; emphasis added).

79. According to Rawls, "A conception of justice cannot be deduced from self-evident premises or conditions on principles" (21).

80. Rawls, 17.

81. Rawls, 8 (emphasis added).

82. Rawls, 18–19 (emphasis added).

83. Rawls, 21 (emphasis added).

84. Rawls, 19.

85. Rawls, 20.

86. Rawls, 20.

87. For the purposes of my critique of Rawls, this need not be a radical lack of fit. My criticism supposes only some lack of congruence between the two.

88. The original position "excludes knowledge of those contingencies which sets men at odds and allows them to be guided by their prejudices." Rawls, *Theory of*

Justice, 19. And why seek to prevent humans from being guided by their prejudices in choosing principles of justice? Presumably because this would be wrong—wrong because unfair to others, because it would treat others in a way they don't deserve to be treated.

89. T. K. Seung gave a talk laying out this argument in late 2002 or early 2003 (I remember the performance like it was yesterday but I've forgotten the specific year he gave it). He framed the argument succinctly in personal correspondence with me.

90. Seung, *Intuition and Construction*, 63.

91. Seung, *Intuition and Construction*, 64. Seung also notes Michael J. Sandel's contention that, insofar as Rawls holds that the justification of the original position derives from widely accepted assumptions embedded in our culture, then his position is question begging. See Sandel, *Liberalism and the Limits of Justice*, 45.

92. Seung, *Intuition and Construction*, 65.

93. Seung, 65.

94. Even on the dual perspective thesis, however, we are still affirming some culturally embedded ideals (perhaps connected to transcendent ones) on the basis of other culturally embedded ideals (also perhaps connected to transcendent ones). And there is no way to decide which to favor on the basis of cultural ideals alone. We still need access to a score that is not simply culturally embedded and can therefore tell us which culturally embedded ideals express real, binding norms.

95. Rawls, "Kantian Constructivism," 522.

96. MacIntyre, *After Virtue*; Taylor, *Sources of the Self*; Sandel, "The Procedural Republic"; and Rist, *What Is a Person?*

97. Sandel, "The Procedural Republic." See also Sandel, *Liberalism and the Limits of Justice*.

98. And that even if Rawls thinks it's the right view; though, to be sure, he was always uneasy with Kantian metaphysics.

99. See Rawls, "Kantian Constructivism." See also Pakaluk, "Rawls and the Rejection of Truth." On this point, I disagree with Seung's contention that "in his Dewey Lecture . . . Rawls expresses not only Kantian conventionalism, but also Kantian transcendentalism." Seung, *Intuition*, 65. According to Seung, Rawls "repeats the familiar assertion that there are no moral facts apart from the principles adopted in the original position (*KC* 519, 568)," but also contends that "this problematic assertion appears to presuppose Kantian transcendentalism. Until the Kantian ideals are brought down from the noumenal to the phenomenal world, there can be no moral rules or facts. This assertion makes no sense whatsoever, if it is taken in the context of Kantian conventionalism." Seung, 65. Though I agree with Seung's last claim (in terms of what coherence requires), I take Rawls, in the passages Seung cites, to be rejecting any sort of transcendent principles and to be giving expression to conventionalism.

100. Rawls, "Kantian Constructivism," 519 (emphasis added). Rawls adds, "A well-ordered society . . . is effectively regulated by a public conception of justice . . . in which every one accepts and knows that others likewise accept, the same first

principles of right and justice" where these "public principles of justice are themselves founded on reasonable beliefs as established by society's generally accepted methods of inquiry" (521). Moreover, "the members of a well-ordered society are, and view themselves and one another in their political and social relations . . . as, free and equal moral persons . . . as free persons, they think of themselves not as inevitably tied to the pursuit of the particular final ends they have at any given time, but rather as capable of revising and changing these ends on reasonable and rational grounds" (522). Thus, so far as the public conception of justice is concerned, the final ends of individuals are not given by nature but *chosen* by them.

101. Rawls, "Kantian Constructivism," 564.

102. Rawls, 568 (emphasis added). On the same page he also writes, "The notion of radical choice, commonly associated with Nietzsche and the existentialists, finds no place in justice as fairness. The parties in the original position are moved by their preference for primary goods, which preference in turn is rooted in their highest order interests in developing and exercising their moral powers." Moreover, "in the model-conception of a well-ordered society, citizens affirm their public conception of justice because it matches their considered convictions and coheres with the kind of persons they, on due reflection, want to be" (568). Yet, "Our society is not well-ordered: the public conception of justice and its understanding of freedom and equality are in dispute. Therefore, for us—you and me—a basis of public justification is still to be achieved" (569).

103. Rawls, "Kantian Constructivism," 571 (emphasis added).

104. See Rawls, 568–69, and the note above—though Rawls does not show how Kantian constructivism in fact avoids radical choice. But my argument contra Rawls does not depend on whether he affirms radical choice but only on his contention that choice is not governed by antecedent moral principles (whether or not that contention ultimately devolves into radical choice, as some have suspected it does).

105. Rawls, "Kantian Constructivism," 569.

106. Rawls, "Justice as Fairness: Political not Metaphysical."

107. Rawls, 230 (emphasis added).

108. Rawls, 230–31.

109. On the idea of a *forced option*, see William James's "The Will to Believe," a response to William Clifford's "The Ethics of Belief," an epistemic catastrophe of an essay. As Hadley Arkes has long reminded us, Lincoln clearly saw that when Stephen Douglas claimed that his doctrine of "popular sovereignty" was neutral on the question of slavery, the policy in fact favored the pro-slavery position—that the enslaved is not fully human or entitled to equal, inalienable rights. Neutrality on the rightness or wrongness of slavery was not neutral at all. See Arkes, *First Things*, 24. See also Sandel, *Liberalism and the Limits of Justice*, 199–201.

110. On the impossibility or "Myth of Moral Neutrality," see chapter 3 of J. Budziszewski's *The Revenge of Conscience*, previously published in the journal *First Things*, June 1998.

111. Rawls, *Political Liberalism*, 135.

112. Rawls, 137.

113. Hampton, "Should Political Philosophy be Done."

114. Rawls, *Political Liberalism*, 134.

115. Rawls, "Overlapping Consensus," esp. 10–12.

116. According to Sandel, "In *Political Liberalism* Rawls pulls back from this purely pragmatic account" of justice advanced in "Kantian Constructivism," an account for which Richard Rorty welcomed him to the "thoroughly historicist and antiuniversalist" camp. Sandel writes, "Although justice as fairness begins 'by looking to the public culture itself as the shared fund of implicitly recognized basic ideas and principles,' it does not affirm these principles simply on the grounds that they are widely shared." Sandel bases this conclusion on Rawls's distinction between an overlapping consensus and a mere modus vivendi in *Political Liberalism*—since, in an overlapping consensus, adherents of different comprehensive views endorse shared principles of justice "for reasons drawn from within their own conceptions." Sandel, "Political Liberalism" republished as an appendix to the second edition of *Liberalism and the Limits of Justice*, 194–95. As I read Rawls, however, *Political Liberalism* does not depart from the deep conventionalism resulting from his method of avoidance laid out in "Justice as Fairness."

117. Rawls, *Political Liberalism*, 217, 248, 253; and also the preface to the paperback edition, xliv, xlvi, l–li, liv.

118. My treatment of Rawls's political liberalism, beginning with "Justice as Fairness," through this argument concerning its self-referential incoherence adapts (with substantial revision) my argument in "Political Philosophy After the Collapse," 40–51. That essay contains my full argument concerning the epistemic incoherence of public reason liberalism, as Wolterstorff denominates the position.

119. I am grateful to David Williams for pointing me to Dworkin's criticism of Walzer.

120. Walzer, *Spheres of Justice*, 312–313.

121. Walzer, 313.

122. Walzer, 314.

123. Dworkin, "What Justice Isn't," in *A Matter of Principle*, 217. Originally published as "To Each His Own" in the *New York Review of Books*, April 14, 1983.

124. Dworkin, *A Matter of Principle*, 217.

125. Dworkin, 219.

126. Dworkin, *Justice for Hedgehogs*, 9. See also Dworkin, "Objectivity and Truth: You'd Better Believe It," which is criticized by Sharon Street in "Objectivity and Truth: You'd Better Rethink It." A pre-published version of Street's argument is criticized from the vantage of moral realism in Cuneo, *Speech & Morality*, 228–47.

127. Dworkin, *Justice for Hedgehogs*, 9. The early modern voluntarist Samuel von Pufendorf (whose position I take up in chapter 6) is the only theorist I know of who speaks of moral *entities* and who therefore approximates Dworkin's characterization of moral realists. But Pufendorf was certainly no realist. And even in his case, the notion of a moral particle would be a caricature. Dworkin's account of moral realism in no way captures the positions of Plato, Aristotle, or Aquinas.

128. Dworkin, *Justice for Hedgehogs*, 9.

129. Dworkin, 10.

130. Dworkin, 11. Dworkin here, again, misbegets the realist's position.

131. On early modern mechanistic philosophy see Feser, *Locke*, chap. 2; and Forde, ~~*Locke, Science, and Politics*, chaps. 1 and 2.~~

132. Suppose we let PA stand for Protagorean antirealism and MIT stand for mind-independent truth. Protagorean antirealism denies the existence of any MITs. So we get this conditional: If PA, then not MIT (PA⊃~MIT). Dworkin affirms mind-independent moral principles, which are MITs. So he affirms MIT, which is equivalent to ~~MIT (*not* not MIT). Given modus tollens, according to which denial of the consequent of a conditional entails denial of the antecedent, ~PA (that is, not Protagorean antirealism) necessarily follows.

133. Of course, a realist need not hold that objective truths are mind-independent. The realist holds that there are eternal and immutable truths. That's compatible with holding that all such truths are necessarily contained in the mind of God. My point is only that Dworkin's attempt to exclude metaphysics fails on its own terms.

Chapter 4

1. Gauthier, "Hobbes: The Laws of Nature."

2. It bears mention here that the ensuing argument and my conclusion do not depend on reading each interpretation as sharply disjunctive with or exclusive of every other interpretation.

3. According to Strauss, "mechanistic psychology . . . is by no means the necessary assumption of Hobbes's political philosophy. Hobbes's characteristic theories—the denial that 'altruism' is natural, the theses of man's rapacious nature, of the war of every one against every one as the natural condition of mankind, of the essential impotence of reason—can also be maintained on the indeterminist assumptions." Strauss, *Political Philosophy of Hobbes*, 3. I take Strauss to mean determinism is not essential to his political theory. Whether he is right or wrong, by starting my presentation of his philosophical commitments here with metaphysical nominalism rather than with materialism or determinism, I mean to bracket that dispute. Strauss also writes, "The period between Hooker and Locke had witnessed the emergence of modern natural science, of nonteleological natural science, and therewith the destruction of the basis of traditional natural right. The man who was the first to draw the consequences for natural right from this momentous change was Thomas Hobbes." Strauss, *Natural Right and History*, 166. At the same time, Hobbes's "notion of philosophy or science has its roots in the conviction that a teleological cosmology is impossible *and in the feeling that a mechanistic cosmology fails to satisfy the requirement of intelligibility*" (176; emphasis added). Hobbes's solution, says Strauss, was to make the "most compelling end posited by human desire . . . the highest . . . organizing principle" (177).

4. Hobbes, *Leviathan* 4.6, p. 17. See also Hobbes, *Elements of Law* 1.5.6, pp. 36–37; and Hobbes, *Elements of Philosophy, Concerning Body (De Corpore)* 2.9, pp. 19–20, where he writes, "Of names, some are *common* to many things, as a *man, a tree*; others *proper* to one thing, as *he that writ the Iliad, Homer, this man, that man*. And a common name, being the name of many things severally taken, but not collectively

all together (as man is not the name of all mankind, but of every one, as Peter, John, and the rest severally) is therefore called an *universal name*; and therefore this word *universal* is never the name of any thing existent in nature." Universal names are just "names common to many things."

5. Together with his nominalism concerning essences, Hobbes also rejects final causation in any classical sense. See below.

6. I maintain that Hobbes lies downstream from late medieval nominalism and ultimately from William of Ockham. According to Marilyn McCord Adams in her landmark study *William of Ockham*, Ockham rejected both Platonic "extreme realism" and the "moderate realism" of Aristotle and Aquinas: "Ockham regarded the view that universals are real things other than names as 'the worst error of philosophy' " (1:13). He "identifies universals with universal names and denies that there are any universal things other than universal names" (1:71).

7. DeHart, "Fractured Foundations," 120–26, and chapter 5 in this volume.

8. See Suárez, *De legibus, ad Deo legislatore* (*Treatise on Laws and God the Lawgiver*); and the treatment of the relevant passage in Haakonssen, *Natural Law and Moral Philosophy*, 17.

9. Stated formally: Letting n stand for nominalism, o stand for obligation, and v stand for voluntarism, $n \cdot o \supset v$.

10. But see Hare, *God and Morality*, chap. 2.

11. David Gauthier notes that Bernard Gert, in his introduction to Hobbes's *Man and Citizen* (pp. 13-18; Gauthier's citations are to the original Anchor Books edition, pp. 13-16), mistakenly "denies that [Hobbes] is a subjectivist, while granting he is a relativist." Gauthier, *Morals by Agreement*, 51. Indeed, in his introduction to *Man and Citizen*, Gert interprets Hobbes as a kind of moral realist standing in the "great philosophical tradition stemming from Plato" (18) Over and against Gert's strained interpretation of Hobbes, Gauthier argues that Hobbes provides "perhaps the classic philosophic formulation of a conception of value both subjective and relative" (51). Likewise, "Hobbes links subjectivism with relativism—the view that value is dependent on appetite or preference with the view that value is relative to each individual" (51). Referencing the passage from chap. 6 of *Leviathan* discussed below, Jean Hampton writes, "In this passage Hobbes is clearly defining 'good' as 'what we desire,' and 'bad' as 'what we are averse to.' Note that whereas Aristotle said that we desire what is good and hate what is evil, Hobbes says the opposite: What is good is simply what we desire, and what we hate is simply what is bad." And "this is a baldly subjectivist ethical understanding of 'good' " that "Hobbes seems not only to admit but also to welcome." Thus, in chap. 11 of *De Homine*, "in opposition to Aristotle," Hobbes says that "one cannot speak of something as being *simply good* . . . good is said to be relative to person, place, and time" (11.4, 47)—something Aristotle denies in both *Rhetoric* (1.13.1373b, 102-103) and *Nicomachean Ethics* (2.6.1107a9–26, p. 1748). See Hampton, *Social Contract Tradition*, 29 and, more broadly, 27–34. I find Hampton's case for Hobbes's subjectivist account of good and evil and her critique of scholars advancing views to the contrary dispositive. For the purposes of my argument, however, I take subjectivism concerning good and evil to be how Hobbes

defines these terms in the passages from *Leviathan* and *De Homine* quoted above. For my purposes, subjectivism means that good is a name for objects of desire, evil for objects of aversion, and that nothing is simply or absolutely good (or evil)—these are relative to desire and aversion and not given in the nature of things. If others define subjectivism differently and seek to argue that Hobbes is therefore not a subjectivist, that is neither here nor there for my argument. See also the discussion of good and evil in Hobbes's thought in Martinich, *Hobbes*, 57–63.

12. Hobbes, *Leviathan* 6.7, pp. 28–29.

13. Hobbes 15.40, p. 100. And here we must recall the claim Hobbes makes in *De Homine*, that "one cannot speak of something as being *simply* good; since whatever is good is good for someone or other. . . . Therefore good is said to be relative to person, place, and time. What pleaseth one man now, will please another later" (11.4, p. 47). Hobbes also says those "who consider men by themselves and as though they existed outside of civil society, can have no moral science because they lack any certain standard against which virtue and vice can be judged and defined." *De Homine* 8.8–9, pp. 68–69. In *Elements of Law* Hobbes writes:

> Every man, for his own part, calleth that which pleaseth, and is delightful to himself, GOOD; and that EVIL which displeaseth him: insomuch that while every man differeth from other in constitution, they differ also one from another concerning the common distinction of good and evil. Nor is there any such thing as ἀγαθόν απλός, that is to say, simply good. For even the goodness which we attribute to God Almighty, is his goodness to us. And as we call good and evil the things that please and displease [us]; so call we goodness and badness, the qualities or powers whereby they do it. (1.7.3, p. 44)

See also Hobbes, *De Cive* 3.31, p. 150. The contention of Hobbes in chap. 15 of *Leviathan*, chaps. 11 and 13 of *De Homine*, chap. 3 of *De Cive*, and chap. 7 of *Elements of Law* is clearly ontological rather than psychological—an application of his metaphysical nominalism to the meaning of *good* and *evil*. In *Leviathan* 6.7, Hobbes denies the *existence* of anything simply or absolutely good ("there *being* nothing simply or absolutely so [i.e., good]").

14. Hobbes, *Leviathan* 15.40, p. 100.

15. Hobbes 11.1, p. 57. See also Hobbes, *Elements of Law* 1.7.6–7, pp. 44–45; and Hobbes, *De Homine* 11.15, pp. 53–54 ("Of goods, the greatest is always progressing towards even further ends with the least hindrance"). What strikes me as an implausible interpretation of this passage (and the parallel passages in *Elements* and *De Homine*) claims that Hobbes only rejects a greatest good or final end, as is spoken of by the old moral philosophers, in this life but not in the next one. But Hobbes never says any such thing. He concludes that the felicity of this life does not consist in the repose of a mind satisfied but, rather, in the satisfaction of desire after desire (11.1, p. 57). To be sure, in chapter 6, having defined felicity as "*continual success* in

obtaining those things which a man from time to time desireth," Hobbes there adds, "I mean the felicity of this life. For there is no such thing as perpetual tranquility of mind, while we live here; because life itself is but motion, and can never be without desire, nor without fear, no more than without sense. What kind of felicity God hath ordained to them that devoutly honour Him, a man shall no sooner know than enjoy, being joys that now are as incomprehensible as the word of school-men *beatifical vision* is unintelligible" (6.58, pp. 34-35). But the *incomprehensibility* of the felicity of the life to come is no basis for taking Hobbes to hold that there is a summum bonum or finis ultimis, a highest good or final end (in any sort of Aristotelian, Ciceronian, or Augustinian sense), in the next life. Such a claim is an argumentum ex silentio at best and an unjustifiable and problematic interpolation at worst. Moreover, in chapter 11, the sentence following his definition of felicity, as "a continual progress of the desire, from one object to another, the attaining of the former being still but the way to the latter" (11.1, p. 57), commences with "For" and provides the grounding reason for the conclusion (i.e., his definition of felicity). In that grounding premise, Hobbes simply says that the greatest good or final end spoken of by the old moral philosophers does not exist. Full stop. He does not qualify the nonexistence of a highest good or final end (as Aristotle or Cicero speak of it, for example) with "in this life." It does some violence to his hatred of Aristotle to suggest that he merely excoriates Aristotle (and Cicero) for locating the final end in this life, as if Hobbes were something of a classical Augustinian. Hobbes considers the union of Aristotelian philosophy with Christianity to be the "Kingdom of Darkness." In part 4 of *Leviathan*, he writes, "I believe that scarce anything can be more absurdly said in natural philosophy than that which is now called *Aristotle's Metaphysics*; nor more repugnant to government than much of what he hath said in his *Politics*; nor more ignorantly than a great part of his *Ethics*." Hobbes, *Leviathan* 46.11, p. 457.

16. See also *Elements* 1.7.7, p. 45; and *De Homine* 11.15, pp. 53–54: "For of goods, the greatest is always progressing towards even further ends with the least hindrance."

17. Hobbes, *Leviathan* 6.57. See also Hampton, *Hobbes and the Social Contract*, 34–42, where Hampton shows how Hobbes's language of *apparent* and *seeming* good can be reconciled with his subjectivism concerning good and evil and his instrumentalist rationality. See also Hampton, "Hobbes and Ethical Naturalism."

18. See Hobbes, *Leviathan* 8.18, p. 41; Hobbes, *De Homine* 12.9, p. 60; Hobbes, "Dialogue," 88; and the treatment of these passages in Hampton, *Hobbes and the Social Contract*, pp. 36–42; and Hampton, "Hobbes and Ethical Naturalism," pp. 340–43.

19. Hobbes, *Elements of Philosophy, Concerning Body* (*De Corpore*), 2.7, pp. 131–32.

20. Copleston, *History of Philosophy*, vol. 5, *Modern Philosophy: The British Philosophers* (hereafter cited as *The British Philosophers*), 22. With respect to formal cause, Hobbes says:

> *Entity, essence, essential, essentiality* . . . are . . . no names of things, but signs by which we make known that we conceive the consequence of one name or attribute to another (as when we say *a man is a living body*, we mean not that

the *man* is one thing, *the living body* another, and the *is* or *being* a third, but that the *man* and the *living body* is the same thing, because the consequence *if he be a man, he is a living body* is a true consequence, signified by that word *is). Therefore, to be a body, to walk, to be speaking, to live, to see,* and the like infinitives (also *corporeity, walking, speaking, life, sight,* and the like that signify the same) are the names of *nothing,* as I have elsewhere more amply expressed. (*Leviathan* 46.17, p. 460)

Hobbes subsequently speaks of the "errors which are brought into the Church from the *entities* and *essences* of Aristotle." He then suggests that Aristotle may have known his account of essences (i.e., formal causes) was false but espoused it, "fearing the fate of Socrates" (46.17, p. 460).

21. Hobbes, *Leviathan* 5.2, pp. 22–3. See Holloway's account of instrumental rationality in Hobbes in *The Way of Life*, 32–36.

22. Hobbes, *Leviathan* 3.4, p. 13.

23. Hobbes 8.16, p. 41.

24. Hobbes 10.1, p. 57.

25. Hobbes 10.16, p. 51.

26. Hampton, "Forgiveness, Resentment and Hatred," 46.

27. Hobbes, *De Cive* 1.10, p. 117.

28. According to Gert (*Hobbes: Prince of Peace*, 53), whereas Hume views "reason as only instrumental, i.e., [as] having no goals of its own," Hobbes holds that "it is irrational not to avoid death, pain, or disability." For Hobbes, reason has the goal of self-preservation. Thus, Gert claims, Hobbes does not affirm purely instrumental rationality *because* reason has a "greatest evil," a "*summum malum*"—namely, avoidable death. And "the primary goal of reason is a negative one, avoiding an avoidable death" (72). Reason also has "the goal of avoiding pain and disability" (50). Gert concludes, "The negative goals of reason put limits on the contents of the desires to be satisfied when obtaining felicity. Hobbes . . . would not consider a person to be continually prospering if he has continual success in satisfying his desires to cut off his fingers one at a time in a food processor" (51).

Nevertheless, it's difficult to see how Gert's argument entails that Hobbes does not adopt a thoroughgoing instrumental rationality. For Hobbes's view of reason to be noninstrumental, it seems (on his argument) that death (or avoidable death) would have to be intrinsically—that is, simply and absolutely—evil and self-preservation instrinsically—that is, simply and absolutely—good. But Hobbes repeatedly says that nothing is simply or absolutely good or evil and that these are relative to desire and aversion in the state of nature and to the commands and prohibitions of law in civil society. Put another way, holding that reason has an overriding goal of self-preservation or avoiding death is insufficient to show that Hobbes does not affirm instrumental rationality. Moreover, Hobbes espouses the relativity of evil, in the relevant passages, just as he does the relativity of good. Perhaps avoidance of death (or self-preservation) is instrumental to the fulfillment of every other desire. Finally, Gert's argument seems entirely contrary to Hobbes's contention that there can be "no moral science" of men considered by themselves (i.e., in themselves) "because" there would be no "standard against which virtue and vice can be judged and defined" (*De Homine*, 13.8, pp. 68-69).

29. Hume, *Treatise of Human Nature* 2.3.3 (p. 416 in Selby-Bigge ed. and p. 463 in Mossner ed.).

30. Given debates among Hobbes scholars concerning instrumental rationality in Hobbes, the argument that follows only depends on taking Hobbes to affirm two things: (*a*) reason is instrumental to avoiding sudden and violent death at the hands of others and, correlatively, instrumental to self-preservation, and (*b*) since, according to Hobbes, nothing is simply or absolutely good or evil, then, necessarily, death (or sudden and violent death at the hands of others) is not simply or absolutely evil, and preservation not simply and absolutely good.

31. Hobbes, *Leviathan* 13.11, p. 77.

32. In the Latin edition of 1668, Hobbes seems to suggest that there indeed has been a war of all against all: "But someone may say: there has never been a war of all against all. What! Did not Cain out of envy kill his brother Abel, a crime so great he would not have dared it if there had at that time been a common power which could have punished him?" Even so, Hobbes means his argument to apply to readers who are quite obviously not living in a natural condition. Consequently, his argument (to work) must at best be indifferent to whether or not the state of nature historically obtained. I concur with Martinich. Hobbes critics, who took him to be arguing for a historical state of nature when in fact there never was such a state, misunderstood his argument. See Martinich, "Law and Self-Preservation in *Leviathan*," pp. 45-48.

33. Warrender, *Political Philosophy of Hobbes*, 99. Warrender goes on to say that, given such a view of the laws of nature, "political obligation would turn out like natural law to be no more than another prudential maxim" (99–100). Leo Strauss is clearly among the "commentators" Warrender has in mind; see Strauss, *The Political Philosophy of Hobbes*, 123–25. According to Strauss, "The belief that man is exposed by a Nature which is not ordered and ordering, but the principle of disorder, to all hazards; in other words, the denial of creation and providence, is the presupposition for Hobbes's conception of the state of nature" (123). See also Strauss, *Natural Right and History*, 181–83; Cooke, *Hobbes and Christianity*, chap. 3, esp. pp. 52–61; and Forster, "Divine Law and Human Law," 203–9.

34. Hobbes, *Leviathan* 15.41, p. 100. To be sure, Hobbes continues, "But yet if we consider the same theorems, as delivered in the word of God, that by right commandeth all things; then they are properly called laws." *Interpretation I* tends to downplay this additional comment and underscores the absence of this qualification in the ensuing quotation. See also *Leviathan* 26.8, p. 174.

35. Hobbes, *De Cive* 3.33, p. 152.

36. Strauss is clearly among those who view the laws of nature as hypothetical imperatives: "The fundamental change from an orientation by natural duties to an orientation by natural rights finds its clearest and most telling expression in the teaching of Hobbes, who squarely made an unconditional natural right the basis of all natural duties, the duties being therefore only conditional." Thus, Hobbes "is

the classic and the founder of the specifically modern natural law doctrine." Strauss, "Hobbes' Political Philosophy," 418. In *Political Philosophy of Hobbes*, Strauss speaks of the "conditional character" Leibniz "attributes to the propositions of natural law" (viii), and notes this view "was held by Hobbes before Leibniz" (viii, n. 1). "Hobbes . . . starts, not as the great tradition did, from natural 'law', i.e., from an objective order, but from natural 'right', i.e. from an absolutely justified subjective claim which, far from being dependent on any previous law, order, or obligation, is itself the origin of all law, order, or obligation" (viii).

37. Hampton, *Authority of Reason*, 125.

38. Mackie, cited in Hampton, *Authority of Reason*, 127.

39. Or, at least, sufficient ceteris paribus.

40. See for example, *Leviathan* 5.5, p. 24 and 5.12, p. 25.

41. Hampton, "Hobbes and Ethical Naturalism," esp. pp. 333, 336, and 350.

42. Here we must again bear in mind Hobbes's claim in *De Homine* 13.8, pp. 68–69, that moral science is impossible taking men as men (i.e., humans just as such).

43. Hampton, "Hobbes and Ethical Naturalism," 345.

44. Hobbes, *Leviathan* 26.8, p. 174 (emphasis added).

45. Hobbes, 26.10, p. 175.

46. Recall our earlier conditional: $n{\cdot}o{\supset}v$ (if nominalism and obligation, then voluntarism). If we reject voluntarism because it's self-defeating ($\sim v$), then, given *modus tollens*, we have $\sim(n{\cdot}o)$. $\sim(n{\cdot}o)$ is logically equivalent to $\sim n$ or $\sim o$ (either not nominalism or not obligation). Given the disjunctive syllogism and double negation, n, which is equivalent to $\sim\sim n$, entails $\sim o$ and o, which is equivalent to $\sim\sim o$, entails $\sim n$. See DeHart, "Fractured Foundations," 120–26.

47. Perez Zagorin, for instance, treats Hobbes as a kind of positivist. See Zagorin, *Hobbes and the Law of Nature*, 54. On Bentham and Austin, see Hart, "Positivism"; Austin, *Province of Jurisprudence*. Mark Murphy demonstrates how pervasive the positivist interpretation of Hobbes is in "Was Hobbes a Legal Positivist?," esp. 846–49.

48. See Murphy, "The Natural Law Tradition"; Murphy, *Natural Law in Jurisprudence*, 1, 21n5, 61–62 (though on p. 62 Murphy concedes that "peace is a common good for Hobbesian agents" only in "a very weak sense" and considers it "a point in favor of natural law credentials of a conception of the common good" if "it fulfills the 'commonness' desideratum more fully than a Hobbesian conception does"); and Murphy, "Was Hobbes a Legal Positivist?"

49. See for instance, DeHart, "The Dangerous Life," 389; DeHart, *Uncovering the Constitution's Moral Design*, 168–71; and DeHart, "Fractured Foundations," 113–16. See also chapters 1 and 5 of this volume.

50. Koons, *Realism Regained*, 275–76; and DeHart, *Uncovering the Constitution's Moral Design*, 171–78. See also my unpublished essay, "The Poverty of Positivism: The Self-Referential Incoherency of Legal Positivism."

51. Letting O stand for obligation: $O_{legal} \supset O_{moral}$.

52. Formally, (1) $O_{legal} \supset O_{moral}$ (2) $\sim O_{moral}$ therefore (3) $\sim O_{legal}$ (modus tollens).

53. Gauthier, "Hobbes: The Laws of Nature," 260.

54. Hobbes, *Leviathan* 21.10, p. 141.

55. Hobbes, 21.10, p. 141 (emphasis added). His actual position in this passage is perhaps a bit more complex. The fuller quotation reads as follows: "The obligation and liberty of the subject is to be derived, either from those words (or others equivalent) or else from the end of the institution of sovereignty, namely, the peace of the subjects within themselves, and their defence against a common enemy."

56. Gauthier, "Hobbes: The Laws of Nature," 260.

57. In *Of Liberty and Necessity* Hobbes says this: "And whereas he [the Bishop] saith, the law of nature is a law without our assent, it is absurd; for the law of nature is the assent itself that all men give to the means of their own preservation." Cited in Gauthier, "Hobbes: The Laws of Nature," 269. Likewise, in part 3 of *Leviathan*, Hobbes asks, "Who it was that gave to these written tables [of the Decalogue] the obligatory force of laws? There is no doubt but they were made laws by God himself, but because a law obliges not, nor is law to any but to them that acknowledge it to be the act of the sovereign, how could the people of Israel . . . be obliged to obedience to all those laws which Moses propounded to them?" Hobbes, *Leviathan* 42.37, cited in Gauthier, "Hobbes: The Laws of Nature," 270. Says Gauthier (quoting Hobbes), "The answer, of course, is that the people of Israel 'had obliged themselves . . . to obey Moses'; 'Moses, and Aaron, and the succeeding high priests were the civil sovereigns' " (270).

58. Gauthier, "Hobbes: The Laws of Nature," 266.

59. Hobbes, *De Cive* 14.2, p. 272–73.

60. Gauthier, "Hobbes: Laws of Nature," 270.

61. Hobbes, *On the Citizen* 6.14, p. 84 (p. 183 in the Hackett edition of *De Cive*).

62. Hobbes, *Leviathan* 27.6, p. 174. The fuller quotation runs as follows: "The sovereign of a commonwealth, be it an assembly or one man, is not subject to the civil laws. For having power to make and repeal laws, he may, when he pleaseth, free himself from that subjection by repealing those laws that trouble him and making of new; and consequently, he was free before. For he is free that can be free when he will; nor is it possible for any person to be bound to himself, because he that can bind can release; and therefore, he that is bound to himself only is not bound."

63. Hobbes, *Leviathan* 13.13, p. 78.

64. Connolly, *Political Theory & Modernity*, 32.

65. Connolly, 35–6.

66. Hobbes, *Leviathan* 15.1, p. 89.

67. Hobbes, 14.27, p. 86.

68. "If a covenant be made wherein neither of the parties perform presently but trust one another, in the condition of mere nature (which is a condition of war of every man against every man) upon any reasonable suspicion it is void. . . . For he that performeth first has no assurance the other will perform after, because the bonds of words are too weak to bridle men's ambition, avarice, anger, and other passions, without the fear of some coercive power, which in the condition of mere

nature, where all men are equal and judges of the justness of their own fears, cannot possibly be supposed." Hobbes, *Leviathan* 14.18, p. 84. "But because covenants of mutal trust where there is a fear of not performance on either part . . . are invalid, though the original of justice be the making of covenants, yet injustice actually there can be none till the cause of such fear be taken away, which while men are in the natural condition of war, cannot be done" (15.3, p. 89). "And covenants without the sword are but words, and of no strength to secure a man at all" (17.2, p. 106). See also Hobbes, *De Cive* 2.11, p. 127.

69. Martinich, *Two Gods of Leviathan*, 82–83.

70. Hobbes, *Leviathan* 18.4, p. 111.

71. Hobbes, 14.5–9, pp. 80–82, and 7.13, p. 109; Hobbes, *De Cive* 2.3–9, pp. 123–26.

72. Hobbes, *Leviathan* 28.2, p. 204.

73. I believe that I owe this point about Hobbesian sovereigns and subjects being in a state of war with each other to personal correspondence with A. P. Martinich some years back.

74. See Martinich, "Law and Self-Preservation in *Leviathan*," 46–47.

75. In addition to chapter 1, see Williams, "Ideas and Actuality."

76. Lloyd, *Morality in the Philosophy of Thomas Hobbes*, 263–64. See also Lloyd, "Hobbes's Self-Effacing Natural Law Theory."

77. Hobbes, *Leviathan* 43.3, p. 398.

78. Hobbes 43.23, p. 410. Together with this passage, we should keep in view Hobbes's consignment of the Kingdom of Christ to "the last day" and until after "the general resurrection" when there is "a new heaven and a new earth" (41.3, p. 328). Hobbes seeks to prevent the Kingdom of Christ from impinging on the domain of the civil sovereign and to prevent the law of Christ from competing or conflicting with the civil sovereign's command. Indeed, Hobbes says,

> our Savior Christ hath not given us new laws, but counsel to observe those laws we are subject to (that is to say, the laws of nature and laws of our several sovereigns), nor did he make any new law to the Jews in his sermon on the Mount, but only expounded the laws of Moses, to which they were subject before. The laws of God, therefore are none but the laws of nature, whereof the principal is that we should not violate our faith, that is, a commandment to obey our sovereigns, which we constituted over us by mutual pact with one another." (Hobbes 43.5, p. 399)

79. Hampton, *Hobbes and the Social Contract*, 96. See also chapter 5 of Bobbio, *Hobbes and the Natural Law Tradition*. On Bobbio's interpretation of Hobbes, "natural law founds the legitimacy of, and makes obligatory the positive legal order as a whole, not the individual norms which comprise it. Civil power is instated on the basis of the law of nature. But once civil power is instituted, the individual norms of the system derive their validity from the authority of the sovereign, and no longer from particular laws of nature" (166–67); "once the state has been instituted, only

one law of nature survives. This is the law that imposes on human beings the obligation to obey civil laws" (165).

80. Hobbes, *Leviathan* 14.3, p. 79.

81. Hobbes 14.5–7, pp. 80–81.

82. Hobbes 19.12, pp. 123–24, 20.18, p. 135, 26.6, p. 174, 28.2, p. 204, 29.3–5, pp. 211–12, 29.9, p. 213, 30.20, p. 229; and, preeminently, Hobbes, *De Cive* 6.14, pp. 183–84, and 6.17–18, pp. 186–88. See also Hampton, *Hobbes and the Social Contract*, chap. 4; and DeHart, "Leviathan Leashed," 11–17.

83. See Hampton, *Hobbes and the Social Contract*, chap. 7; see also Hampton, "Two Faces of Contractarian Thought," esp. 33–37.

84. Hobbes, *Leviathan* 21.12–15, p. 142.

85. Hobbes 21.21, p. 144.

86. Hampton, *Hobbes and the Social Contract*, 197–207. For a critique of Hampton, see Gauthier, "Hobbes's Social Contract," reprinted in Gauthier, *Hobbes and Political Contractarianism*.

87. Taylor, "The Ethical Doctrine of Hobbes"; Warrender, *The Political Philosophy of Hobbes*; and Martinich, *Two Gods of Leviathan*. See also Martinich, Vaughan, and Williams, "Hobbes's Religion."

88. Hobbes, *Leviathan* 15.1, p. 89.

89. Hobbes 30.1, p. 219.

90. Hobbes 19.11, p. 123. To be sure, Hobbes follows this passage with an argument about the absolute and unlimited power of the sovereign: "That king whose power is limited is not superior to him or them that have the power to limit it; and he that is not superior is not supreme, that is to say not sovereign" (19.12, p. 123).

91. Hobbes, 21.7, p. 139. See also 29.9, p. 213: "It is true that sovereigns are all subject to the laws of nature, because such laws be divine, and cannot by any man or commonwealth be abrogated. But to those laws which the sovereign himself, that is, which the commonwealth maketh, he is not subject."

92. Hobbes 31.5, pp. 235–36. See the corresponding passage in Hobbes, *De Cive* 15.5–7, pp. 292–94.

93. Hobbes writes, "God in his *natural kingdom* hath a right to rule, and to punish those who break his laws from his sole *irresistible power*," and adds, "They therefore whose power cannot be resisted, and by consequence God *Almighty* derives his right of sovereignty from the *power* itself." Hobbes, *De Cive* 15.5, p. 292. In a marginal note in *Leviathan* (31.5, p. 235), Hobbes writes, "The right of God's sovereignty is derived from his Omnipotence." See also Martinich, "Natural Sovereignty," chap. 10 in *Hobbes's Political Philosophy*, esp. 196–97.

94. As Warrender notes in *The Political Philosophy of Hobbes*, Hobbes holds that "natural law is the will of God, and ought to be obeyed for that reason" (279), and that "the laws of nature oblige because they are commanded by God, and not that God commands them because they are right or just" (281). See also Oakley, *Natural Law*, esp. 93–94.

95. In addition to this volume, see DeHart, "Reason and Will in Natural Law," esp. pp. 23–26 and chapter 6 in this volume.

96. Warrender, *The Political Philosophy of Hobbes*, 282.

97. Warrender, 279.

98. Here I have in mind Hobbes's claim in *Leviathan* (15.41, p. 100) that the laws of nature are not laws proper but "dictates of reason" or "conclusions or theorems concerning what conduceth to the conservation and defence of themselves," except insofar as they are "delivered in the word of God, that by right commandeth all things" and "then are they properly called laws"; and in *De Cive* (3.33, p. 152) that "those which we call the laws of nature . . . are not in propriety of speech laws, as they proceed from nature. Yet, as they are delivered by God in holy Scriptures . . . they are most properly called by the name of laws. For the sacred Scripture is the speech of God commanding over all things by greatest right." Of relevance here is the distinction Hobbes makes between law and right (14.3, p. 79) and between counsel and command (25.2–4, pp. 165–66), and his contention that "law in general is not counsel, but command" (26.2, p. 173), where command is a "declaration . . . of the will of him that commandeth (by voice, writing, or some other sufficient argument of the same)" (26.12, p. 177) and where one commanding has the right to command (15.41, p. 100).

99. See Hart, *The Concept of Law*, 187–88: "Natural law has, however, not always been associated with belief in a Divine Governor or Lawgiver of the universe, and even where it has been, its characteristic tenets have not been logically dependent on that belief."

100. Warrender, *The Political Philosophy of Hobbes*, 81–82. He quotes the following passage in *De Cive* (8.9, p. 209): "For no man is understood to be obliged, unless he know to whom he is to perform the obligation." He also notes Hobbes's position in *Leviathan* that children and madmen are "exempted from obligation to natural law" just because they "have not the proper use of reason." Hobbes writes,

> From this, that the law is a command, and command consisteth in declaration or manifestation of the will of him that commandeth (by voice, writing, or some other sufficient argument), we may understand that the command of the commonwealth is a law only to those that have the means to take notice of it. Over natural fools, children, or madmen there is no law, no more than over brute beasts; nor are they capable of the title of just or unjust, because they had never power to make any covenant or to understand the consequences thereof, and consequently, never took upon them to authorize the actions of any sovereign, as they must do that make to themselves a commonwealth. And as those from whom nature or accident hath taken away the notice of all laws in general, so also every man from whom any accident (not proceeding from his own default) hath taken away the means to take notice of any particular law is excused, if he observe it not; and to speak properly, that law is no law to him. (Hobbes, *Leviathan* 26.12, p. 177)

Chapter 5

An earlier version of this essay appeared as "Fractured Foundations: The Contradiction between Locke's Ontology and His Moral Philosophy," *Locke Studies* 12 (2012): 111–48, and is used here with their permission.

1. As with William of Ockham, some scholars describe Locke as a conceptualist rather than a nominalist. For my purposes in this chapter, I will define nominalism in terms of what Locke affirms. My argument follows not from the label we give to Locke's (or Ockham's) position but, rather, from his own account of particulars and universals.

2. Other theorists who hold that Locke is inconsistent include Peter Laslett, in his introduction to Locke, *Two Treatises*; Wolterstorff, *John Locke*, 138; Harris, *Mind of Locke*, 264–77, 308; and Zinaich, "Locke's Moral Revolution." Over and against the view that Locke is logically inconsistent, see Colman, *Locke's Moral Philosophy*; and Colman, "Locke's Empiricist Theory." My way of framing the inconsistency in Locke's argument is, of course, distinct from the foregoing accounts.

3. For instance, Rawls, "Justice as Fairness"; and Rawls, "Overlapping Consensus." See also chapter 3 in this volume.

4. Rawls, *Political Liberalism*, xlviii–xlix, 224–25, 442–44. See also pp. 134-135 where Rawls says that "no comprehensive doctrine is appropriate as a political conception [of justice] for a constitutional regime."

5. Hampton, "Should Political Philosophy."

6. Seung, *Intuition and Construction*, chaps. 1–3.

7. In relation to this, see arguments concerning the incoherence of legal positivism in Koons, *Realism Regained*, 177–78; DeHart, "Dangerous Life," esp. 389; DeHart, *Uncovering the Constitution's Moral Design*, chaps. 4 and 5; and DeHart, "Covenantal Realism."

8. Locke, *Questions Concerning the Law of Nature*, Q. 8, pp. 213–15 (emphasis added).

9. Saint Augustine writes:

Justice being taken away, then, what are the kingdoms but great robberies? For what are robberies themselves, but little kingdoms? The band itself is made up of men; it is ruled by the authority of a prince, it is knit together by the pact of the confederacy; the booty is divided by the law agreed on. If, by admittance of abandoned men, this evil increases to such a degree that it holds places, fixes abodes, takes possession of cities, and subdues peoples, it assumes the more plainly the name of a kingdom, because the reality is now manifestly conferred on it, not by the removal of covetousness, but by the addition of impunity. Indeed, that was an apt and true reply which was given to Alexander the Great by a pirate who had been seized. For when that king had asked the man what he meant by keeping hostile possession of the sea, he answered with bold pride, "What thou meanest by seizing the whole earth; but because I do it with a petty ship, I am called a robber, whilst though who dost it with a great fleet art styled emperor." (*City of God* [*De civitate dei*] 4.4, pp. 112–13)

What Saint Augustine means here is that justice is a necessary condition for distinguishing the commands of legitimate authority from what Elizabeth Anscombe calls "sophisticated banditry." See Anscombe, "Authority of the State," 135.

10. Locke, *Questions Concerning the Law of Nature*, Q. 11, p. 247.

11. See Hardin, "Tragedy of the Commons."

12. Locke, *Questions Concerning the Law of Nature*, Q. 1, pp. 115–17.

13. According to Zinaich in "Locke's Moral Revolution," Locke's later *Essay Concerning Human Understanding* is logically inconsistent with his earlier *Questions Concerning the Law of Nature* in that the earlier work represents the sort of Christian--Aristotelianism rejected by the *Essay* (Zinaich's essay as a whole argues this point; the specific claim occurs on pp. 79–80). Now Zinaich's point is that the Locke of the *Essay* arrives at a different point than the Locke of the *Questions* just because in each work Locke begins from a different starting point. His point is not primarily chronological (though it does also seem to be that). Even so, the fact that the *Essay* is written rather later than the *Questions* has led some to conclude that Locke changed his mind. Concomitantly, one might argue that while the later Locke is inconsistent with the earlier Locke, nevertheless the Locke of each period is consistent with himself (i.e., internally or logically consistent). Now if Locke in fact changed his mind about the law of nature, then my critique of Locke seems to depend upon an unsound premise. Over and against the foregoing, I believe the early Locke and the later Locke (which is to say, the Locke of the *Essay*) both affirm the "law of nature." Locke, after all, was working on the *Essay* and the *Two Treatises* at the same time and, of course, published them both in the same year. Moreover, Locke in later writings such as *A Paraphrase and Notes on the Epistles of St. Paul* in *The Works of John Locke in Nine Volumes*, vol. 7 (on this, see Colman, "Locke's Empiricist Theory," 106), and *The Reasonableness of Christianity* (and his *Vindication* and *Second Vindication*) in *The Works of John Locke*, vol. 6 (on which see Harris, *Mind of Locke*, 308–9), continues to affirm the law of nature. Finally, the contradiction I am going to elaborate holds so long as Locke has a notion of obligation (in general and of moral obligation in particular), whether or not it is a natural law notion. In other words, for Locke to evade my argument, he must reject the notion of obligation altogether. But Locke employs the notion of obligation in later as well as in earlier work. Moreover, given that the *Essay* purports to advance what Wolterstorff in *John Locke* aptly calls an epistemic ethic, I maintain that Locke cannot be construed to have done this. For in the essay, Locke maintains that we have an obligation to regulate our believing in a particular way.

14. Copleston, *The British Philosophers*, 71.

15. Wolterstorff, *John Locke*, 17.

16. Cited in Wolterstorff, 17. See Locke, *Essay Concerning Human Understanding* 3.3.1, p. 409, and 3.3.11, p. 414.

17. Locke, *Essay Concerning Human Understanding* 3.3.11, p. 414.

18. To be sure, in the *Essay Concerning Human Understanding* Locke distinguishes between *real* and *nominal* essences. And one might initially take this to be the

NOTES FOR CHAPTER 5

language of moderate realism or of the *via antiqua* as regards universals or forms. I think this would be a mistake. For realists ancient and medieval, *real* refers to universal essences or formal properties that instantiate in particulars. For such realists, particulars are emphatically *not* all that exist. Nor, for the realist, are universals the invention and creation of *human* intellect. Rather, the human intellect apprehends or discovers such universals as constituting the world we inhabit. In contrast, late medieval nominalism affirmed that particulars are all that exist and that general ideas are the invention of the human understanding. Given this, I think it quite obvious that Locke must mean something fundamentally different from moderate realism (or from realism of any sort) when he distinguishes *real* and *nominal* essences. I suspect a nominal essence for Locke is nothing other than a particular as it appears to the senses whereas a real essence is nothing but the inner constitution of that which appears to the senses even while remaining distinct from the appearance. Even so, that inner constitution is not a form or something general. It's more like the distinction between how Socrates appears to the senses and the underlying reality of blood, bone, nerves, cells, etc. On this, see chapter 3, "Species and the Shape of Equality," in Waldron, *God, Locke, and Equality.*

19. In his argument against Colman, Zinaich argues for the same conclusion (i.e., that Locke is a nominalist). Rather than calling Locke a nominalist, Zinaich calls Locke an anti-essentialist. For this argument he invokes (among others) the passages cited above. Locke's anti-essentialism is evident in his denial of universals; and his denial of universals is contained not only in the claim that only particulars exist but also in the concomitant claim that general ideas are *made* by the understanding. Zinaich, "Locke's Moral Revolution," 84–86. Zinaich advances a second line of argument for Locke's anti-essentialism: he notes that Locke subscribed to Boyle's corpuscularism and that corpuscularism implies that only particulars exist (109–110). But then corpuscularism evidently entails anti-essentialism or nominalism.

20. Locke, *Essay Concerning Human Understanding* 3.6.10 and 3.6.11, respectively, p. 445.

21. Locke 3.6.12, pp. 446–47.

22. Locke 3.6.27, pp. 454-55. See also Waldron, *God, Locke, and Equality*, 60–63.

23. Waldron, *God, Locke, and Equality*, 63. Given Locke's handling of *species* and *man* in the *Essay Concerning Human Understanding*, Waldon concludes that "in order to make Locke's account of equality in the *Two Treatises* consistent with his discussion in Book III of the *Essay*, we have to forget about real essences, and abandon the emphasis on species altogether." Instead, "we should focus . . . on what Locke is prepared to concede—namely, real resemblances between particulars" (66). Waldron seems not to realize that there is no anti-essentialist or nominalist way to cash out coherently the idea of resemblances (much less real resemblances). See also Forde, *Locke, Science, and Politics*, 83–86: "Whatever else [Locke's] account of species accomplishes, it destroys any possibility of drawing from a species concept 'man' any universally valid moral law, in the fashion of the old philosophic schools. There is no 'form' of man, no essence of humanity, no perfection of man implicit in his nature" (86).

24. Modus ponens holds (1) if A, then B; (2) A; therefore, (3) B.

25. According to Zinaich, Locke cannot be regarded as a natural law theorist insofar as he rejects universals (or essentialism), final causes and concomitantly intrinsic goodness *and* insofar as Locke embraces a subjectivist account of good and evil and corpuscularism. See, for instance, "Locke's Moral Revolution," 86, where Zinaich writes, "Locke is not a natural-law philosopher, because he advocates in the *Essay* a subjectivist and relativistic account of good and evil." Put another way, Zinaich views essentialism and an objectivist account of the good as a necessary condition not only of natural law but also of a theory of natural law. The Locke of the *Essay* rejects these necessary conditions of natural law theory and so cannot be a natural law theorist. But whether a voluntarist or a nominalist theory of natural law is *a good theory* of natural law (I will suggest that it is *not*) is quite different from whether a voluntarist or nominalist theory of natural law is *a theory* of natural law. Ockham, after all, is a nominalist who rejects essences or universals and who advances a theory (though a very flawed one) of natural law.

26. Oakley and Urdang, "Locke, Natural Law, and God"; Oakley, "Locke, Natural Law and God—Again"; and Oakley, *Natural Law*.

27. Here I mean that Hobbes's pure state of nature, or condition of mere nature, is morally unconstrained; in the state of nature "nothing can be unjust." Hobbes, *Leviathan* 13.13, p. 78.

28. See Adams, *William of Ockham*, 1:13, 1:71; Ockham, *Philosophical Writings*, 39, 41, 58; and the beginning of chapter 6 in this volume.

29. On the locus of forms or universals in Plato and Aristotle, see Hill, *After the Natural Law*, 37–41. On Plato's "Doctrine of the Forms," see Copleston, *Greece and Rome*, chap. 20, esp. pp. 164–77. On "The Metaphysics of Aristotle," see Copleston, *Greece and Rome*, 301–305.

30. For a discussion of the metaphysics of Plato and Aristotle, see Copleston, *Greece and Rome*, pt. 3, chap. 20 and pt. 4, chap. 29.

31. Put another way, on nominalism, there is no object or state of affairs to which the word "good" refers—at least, not in any meaningful sense. Rather, there is the term *good* that we use to denominate certain things, acts, or states of affairs that appear similar to us. But the similarity is our own doing or, more aptly, our own perceiving. There is nothing truly in common with respect to things, acts, or state of affairs that we refer to as good.

32. Thus, Ockham expressly maintains this: "That is called natural law which is in conformity with natural reason that in no case fails." "A Dialogue" (hereafter simply "Dialogue" or *Dialogus*), part 3, tract 2, book 3, chapter 6 (hereafter I will just cite book and chapter for references to part 3, tract 2 of the *Dialogus*), p. 286. Included here is the idea that natural law contains absolute prohibitions that bind all persons, at all times, and in all places: "About such natural laws no one can err or even doubt" (1.15, p. 273). It is not possible for one who exercises her reason, with respect to them, never to have thought of them.

33. Hobbes, *Leviathan* 26.8, p. 174.

34. As to possible accounts of moral obligation in Locke, see Colman, "Locke's Empiricist Theory," 109–10, 112–15.

35. Locke, *Questions Concerning the Law of Nature*, Q. 8, p. 213 (emphasis added).
36. Locke, Q. 8, p. 211 (emphasis added).
37. Locke, Q. 8, p.211.
38. Locke, Q. 8, p. 211.
39. Locke, Q. 8, p. 211–13.
40. Locke, Q. 8, p. 213. Earlier in *Questions Concerning the Law of Nature*, Locke writes, "Thus, for anyone to know that he is bound by law, he must first know that there is a legislator, a superior; that is, some power to which he is rightfully subject." And "We must also know that there is some will of that superior power as regards the things we must do; that is, that that legislator whoever he may prove to be, wills us to do this, or to refrain from that, and demands of us that the conduct of our life be in agreement with his will" (Q. 5, p. 159). This sounds very much like a voluntaristic account of law as such. Given that the law of nature is a kind of a law, a necessary condition for it to be a *law* of nature is that it meets the necessary conditions of laws as such. Thus if the definition of law or the obligation of law is voluntaristic, it follows that the law of nature must be voluntaristic as well. The quotes above could then be understood as Locke unpacking what it means for the law of nature to be a law.
41. Wolterstorff highlights a fissure that emerges at just this point in Locke's theory. Wolterstorff notes the passage in the Second Treatise (2.6, p. 271) where Locke says that "men being all the workmanship of one omnipotent, and infinitely wise maker; all the servants of one sovereign master, sent into the world by his order, and about his business; they are his property whose workmanship they are, made to last during his, not one another's pleasure." Reflecting on this passage, Wolterstorff says:

> The right to which Locke is here appealing appears to be the right to dispose of one's property as one wishes and we are God's property. But how, in Locke's system, are we to understand the status of such a right? Earlier in the *Essays* Locke had remarked that "right is grounded in the fact that we have the free use of a thing, whereas law is what enjoins or forbids the doing of a thing." On this understanding, for one to have a right do so-and-so is for the relevant laws of obligation to *permit* one to do so-and-so. But obviously, God's right to command obedience of us cannot be understood as consisting in God's being permitted to do so by the laws of obligation, if the laws of obligation are just God's laws. Locke offers no alternative analysis, however; and I fail to see what alternative analysis he could offer. There is, here, a deep fissure in Locke's theory. (Wolterstorff, *John Locke*, 138)

42. In addition to Oakley (cited above), see Schneewind, *Invention of Autonomy*, 149–52, 157–59; and Hill, *After the Natural Law*, 136: "For Locke, the natural law was purely external and largely prohibitive in character. It was imposed from the outside, grounded in the commands of God, and buttressed by God's natural sanctions, pain and pleasure" (see also p. 143).
43. In addition to the passages already discussed, in an entry in his Commonplace Book, Locke maintains that "the punishments and rewards which God has annexed

to moral rectitude or pravity as proper motives to the will . . . would be needless if moral rectitude were in itself good and moral pravity evil." "Voluntas," 1694, MS Locke c. 28, fol. 114, in Locke, *Political Essays*, 321. Based on this passage, Colman claims that "in Locke's opinion there is nothing *intrinsically* attractive in virtuous or right conduct and nothing *intrinsically* repellant in vice." Colman, "Locke's Empiricist Theory," 113.

44. See Soles, "Intellectualism and Natural Law." Soles argues that the concept of the law of nature advanced in Locke's Second Treatise can be construed as intellectualist rather than as voluntarist. Soles, however, wrongly equates voluntarism with a theistic account and intellectualism with a secular account of natural law. Copleston argues that if we take Locke to mean "that the criterion of moral good and evil, of right and wrong actions, is the arbitrary law of God, there would be a flagrant contradiction between what he says in the second book of the *Essay* and what he says in the fourth," where he suggests our duties have a foundation not only divine power but in divine goodness and wisdom as well. Copleston, *The British Philosophers*, 125–26.

45. Here I employ the word *teleology* not in the sense of "consequentialism" or "utilitarianism" but in the sense of what Anthony Lisska calls "the metaphysics of finality" (see the note below). Lisska, *Aquinas's Theory*, 107. See chapter 6 in this volume for a discussion of Lisska on the metaphysics of Thomistic natural law.

46. See Lisska, esp. 96–109.

47. See Aquinas, *Summa Theologiae* I-II, Q. 94, art. 2.

48. The Latin *inclinatio* carries no connotation of instinct or subjective desire; psychological motives are not what is in view. According to Lisska, on "the metaphysics of finality . . . an end is to be attained, not because of a subjective desire or wish on the part of the agent, but because the end itself determines the well-functioning of the human person. The disposition has, as a part of its very nature, a tendency toward a specific end. This end, when realized, contributes to the well-being of the individual." Lisska, *Aquinas's Theory*, 107. See also Budziszewski, *Aquinas's "Treatise on Law,"* 246–55; and the treatment of Aquinas's theory of natural law in Wolterstorff, *Justice*, 38–42.

49. Locke's reflections on natural law published in *Questions Concerning the Law of Nature* were first translated and published under the title *Essays on the Law of Nature*, edited by W. von Leyden. The two editions, however, are separate translations and the introductions present rival interpretations of Locke's account of natural law.

50. Locke, *Questions Concerning the Law of Nature*, Q. 5, p. 167–69.

51. He says, "It is therefore evident that, as regards the general principles whether of speculative or of practical reason, truth or rectitude is the same for all and is equally known by all." Aquinas, *Summa Theologiae* I-II, Q. 94, art. 4. For a defense of Saint Thomas on this count, see Budziszewski, *What We Can't Not Know*; and Budziszewski, *Aquinas's "Treatise on Law,"* 263–77.

52. Locke, *Questions Concerning the Law of Nature*, Q. 7, 181–201, Q. 10, 219–29.

53. Locke, Q. 1, 109–113: from the fact that "in one place one thing is considered to be a law of nature, in another something else," "it hardly follows that there exists

no law of nature." See also Q. 7, esp. p. 199 (where he argues that the law of nature cannot be inferred from the consensus of mankind, in part because such a consensus does not exist), and Q. 8, esp. pp. 211–15 (where he argues that that the law of nature is necessary for the binding power of civil law).

54. Moreover, as Hadley Arkes argues, the position that moral disagreement means there is no moral truth is self-refuting. *First Things*, 132.

55. Locke, *Questions Concerning the Law of Nature*, Q 8, 205.

56. Locke, Q. 10, 219.

57. Locke, Q. 10, 221.

58. Locke, Q. 10, 227.

59. Locke, Q. 10, 227.

60. Locke, Q. 10, 229. The fuller passage reads, "[T]his law depends not on a will which is fluid and changeable, but *on the eternal order of things*. In my opinion, some states of things seem to be immutable, and some duties, which cannot be otherwise, seem to have arisen out of necessity; not that nature (or, to speak more correctly) god could not have created man other than he is, but, since he has been created as he is, provided with reason and his other faculties, there follow from the constitution of man at birth some definite duties he must perform, which cannot be other than they are. For it seems to me to follow as necessarily from the nature of man, if he be a man, that he is bound to love and reverence god, and to perform other duties which are in conformity with a rational nature—that is to observe the law of nature—as it follows from the nature of a triangle, if it be a triangle, that is three angles are equal to two right angles" (229; emphasis added). This appears to be a very strong affirmation of moral realism, indeed.

61. Locke, *Two Treatises*, Second Treatise 2.14, p. 277.

62. Though see also Colman, "Locke's Empiricist Theory"; and Colman, *Locke's Moral Philosophy*.

63. Oakley and Urdang, "Locke, Natural Law, and God"; Oakley, "Locke, Natural Law and God—Again"; and Oakley, *Natural Law*.

64. Ockam himself clearly states that no vices are such that they are necessarily vicious nor any virtues such that they are necessarily virtuous. Vices and virtues are only contingently so. See *Ockham: Philosophical Writings*, 144–147.

65. On the foregoing see Oakley, *Natural Law*, 75–76.

66. In addition to the references above, see also Oakley, *Natural Law*, 76–77.

67. Oakley, *Natural Law*, 77–80. See also Oakley, *Omnipotence, Covenant, & Order*, 48–50, 81–82. Oakley notes that this distinction in fact predates Ockham and is employed by Aquinas—though Aquinas and Ockham understand the *potentia dei absoluta* quite differently. See also Courtenay, *Capacity and Volition*, 87–91.

68. See Philotheus Boehner's introduction to *Ockham: Philosophical Writings*, xix.

69. Oakley, *Natural Law*, 86.

70. Oakley, 84–85.

71. I do not wish to be understood as suggesting that such a state of affairs is actually or metaphysically possible. In fact, the argument that follows will suggest that there are logical difficulties with these propositions taken together. I am suggesting

that it is only an a priori possibility that presents itself in light of the sort of voluntaristic theory of natural law that Oakley attributes (and not without reason) to Locke.

72. From "Of God's Justice" in *Locke: Political Essays*, 277–278 (emphasis added).

73. In Book 4 of the *Essay*, Locke says, "The idea of a supreme being, infinite in power, goodness, and wisdom, whose workmanship we are, and on whom we depend; and the idea of ourselves, as understanding, rational beings, being such as are clear in us, would, I suppose, if duly considered, and pursued, afford such a foundations of our duty and rules of action, as might place morality amongst the sciences capable of demonstration," book 4, chap. 3, sec. 18 (4.3.18), p. 549. This is, of course, one of the most famous passages in Locke. What is relevant for our purposes is that Locke thought it insufficient to refer to infinite and supreme power as a foundation for moral obligation. Rather, he felt compelled to mention God's goodness and wisdom as well.

74. See Leibniz's "Meditation on the Common Concept of Justice," esp. pp. 46–47, and his "Opinion on the Principles of Pufendorf," esp. p. 71, both in *Leibniz: Political Writings*. Richard Price leverages an argument along these lines directly against Locke: "Mr. Locke . . . places [our moral ideas] among our ideas of relations, and represents rectitude as signifying the conformity of actions to some rules or laws; which rules or laws, he says, are either the will of God, the decrees of the magistrate, or the fashion of the country: From whence it follows, that it is absurdity to apply rectitude to the rules and laws themselves; to suppose the divine will to be directed by it; or to consider it as itself a rule of law." Price endeavors to lighten the blow by suggesting, "it is undoubted, that this great man would have detested these consequences." See Price, *Review of the Principal Questions* 1.3, p. 609.

75. See *Questions Concerning the Law of Nature*, Q. 1, pp. 115–17, and Q. 8, p. 213. And consider the passages of Filmer that frame human law entirely in terms of the will of the father or the sovereign that Locke rejects in *Two Treatises*, First Treatise 2.8, pp. 146–47.

76. Leibniz argues that the idea that whatever God wills is good and just simply because He wills it "would destroy the justice of God. For why praise him because he acts according to justice, if the notion of justice, in his case, adds nothing to that of action? And to say *stat pro ratione voluntas*, my will takes the place of reason, is properly the motto of a tyrant. Moreover this opinion would not sufficiently distinguish God from the devil," "Meditation on the Common Concept of Justice," 46. Later in the essay he writes, "A celebrated English philosopher named Hobbes . . . has wished to uphold almost the same thing as Thrasymachus: for he wants God to have the right to everything because he is all-powerful," 47.

77. According to Locke's friend James Tyrell, "some thinking men at Oxford," the so-called Oxonians, with whom Tyrell discussed Locke's *Essay*, seem to have concluded that Locke rejected the notion of moral obligation. They allegedly accused Locke of holding that "there is no moral good or evil, vertue, or vice but in respect of those persons, that practice it or thinke it so." They concluded that Locke was a "Hobbist." See Harris, *Mind of Locke*, 275.

Chapter 6

A few paragraphs in this chapter have, with revision, been drawn from DeHart, "Reason and Will in Natural Law" in *Natural Law and Evangelical Political Thought*, edited by Jesse Covington, Bryan McGraw, and Micah Watson, 125–52; and De-Hart, "Nature's Lawgiver: On Natural Law as *Law*," which appeared in the *Catholic Social Science Review*. They are used here with permission.

1. Luther, *Bondage of the Will*, 209. According to Irving Babbitt, Jonathan Edwards echoes this voluntarism in his infamous Sermon "Sinners in the Hands of an Angry God": "By the mere pleasure of God, I mean his sovereign pleasure, his arbitrary will, restrained by no obligation." *Democracy and Leadership*, 113.

2. Luther referred to William of Ockham as "my master Ockham." His right-hand man in leading the German Reformation was Philip Melanchthon, who in his *Life of Luther* wrote that Luther "read Occam much and long and preferred his acumen to that of a Thomas and Scotus." Cited in Reilly, *America on Trial*, 131. For his part, Luther said, "The terminists, among whom I was, is the name of a school of the universities. They oppose Thomists, Scotists, and Albertinists, and are called Occamists, from Occam their founder. They are the very latest sect and most powerful in Paris, too. The dispute was over whether 'humanitas' and words like it meant a common humanity, which was in all human beings, as Thomas and others believe. Well, say Occamists or terminists, there is no such thing as a common humanity, there is only the term 'homo' or humanity meaning all human beings individually. . . . Occam is a wise and sensible man, who endeavored earnestly to amplify and explain the subject." Birch, *De Sacramento Altaris of Ockham*, xxiii. See also Oberman's treatment of Luther's affirmation of terminism/nominalism in Oberman, *Luther*, 119–23, 169–70. To be sure, Luther's position is more complex. See the note in chapter 7 on Luther's apparent affirmation of Augustinian Platonism against Aristotelian Scholasticism in his early "Disputation against Scholastic Theology" (1517) and "Heidelberg Disputations" (1518).

3. Aquinas, *De Veritate*, Question 23, art. 6 (emphasis added).

4. Anscombe, "Modern Moral Philosophy," 30.

5. Hart, *Concept of Law*, 187–88.

6. Oakley, "Medieval Theories of Natural Law," 65.

7. Suárez, *Treatise on Laws*, book 2, chap. 6, sec. 3 (2.6.3), pp. 208–9.

8. According to Knud Haakonssen, Suárez "distorts [Gregory's view] in a significant way. Gregory did not say . . . that without God the dictates of right reason would still have the same 'legal character' (*rationem legis*) nor that they would constitute a *lex ostensiva*. He said only that, even without God, there would be sin, or moral evil (*peccatum*). By imputing to Gregory the former view, Suárez is suggesting that the earlier thinker had the idea that there could be obligation without God, a point Suárez obviously took to be absurd," *Natural Law and Moral Philosophy*, 20–1.

9. Suárez, *Treatise on Laws* 2.6.2, p. 208.

10. Suárez 2.6.4, pp. 209–10 (emphasis added).

11. In his most recent work, *What Is & What Is in Itself*, Robert Merrihew Adams affirms "that universals exist." But he says there are three answers to the question

as to "in what the existence of a universal consists." The first answer is Platonism: "It is the view that universals exist necessarily and eternally, independently of being instantiated or realized by any particular thing, and independently of being thought or understood by any thinker." Thus, "the Platonist must hold that life, as a universal, would have existed even if nothing had ever lived and there had never been any thought of life." According to the second view—Aristotelianism—"universals exist only in being instantiated or realized in particular things. . . . What exists in particular things when they have a property seems not be universal but particular—not the life that is common to all plants and animals, for example, but the particular life of the particular plant or animal, which could not also be the life of another plant or animal." The third account of universals, which Adams favors, "is that universals, as such, exist only as intentional objects of the thought or understanding of actually existing thinkers." This view is "Widely known . . . as Nominalism or Conceptualism," 69. Adams here seems to take nominalism (or conceptualism) as an account of universals rather than as a rejection of them. By way of reply to Adams, I would note the following. First, he seems to have neglected Thomistic *moderate* realism, which holds that universals exist necessarily and eternally, instantiate in particular things, and must also be objects of the divine mind. Second, setting Ockham to the side, moderns like Hobbes and Locke frame nominalism as a rejection of real universals and not as an account of them. Third, Adams interpretation of Ockham is problematic. According to Étienne Gilson, Ockham ultimately preferred an account "of the nature of concepts in the mind" that "identifies the concept with subjective intellection, or 'intention,' which is, in the mind, a real singular quality, naturally pointing out a plurality of possible objects." And Ockham rejected "the reality of universality." *History of Christian Philosophy in the Middle Ages*, 492. See also Copleston, *Ockham to Suarez*, 53–59. According to Copleston, for Ockham, "universals are terms (*termini concepti*) which signify individual things and which stand for them in propositions. Only individual things exist; and by the very fact that a thing exists it is individual. There are not and cannot be existent universals." Copleston, *A History of Philosophy*, vol 3, *Ockham to Suárez* (hereafter cited as *Ockham to Suárez*).

12. Adams, *William of Ockham*, 1:13, 1:71.

13. Boehner, introduction to Ockham, *Philosophical Writings*, xviii.

14. Courtenay, "Nominalism," 36.

15. Ockham, *Philosophical Writings*, 58.

16. Ockham, 39 (emphasis added).

17. Ockham, 41 (emphasis added).

18. *Guillelmi de Ockham: Quaestiones in librum secundum Sentatiarum* (*Reportatio*), II, Q. 15, cited in Oakley, *Natural Law*, 75. I follow Oakley's translation of the Latin here and in the next quotation.

19. Ockham, *Quaestiones* II, Q. 3–4, p. 59, cited in Oakley, *Natural Law*, 75–76.

20. Boehner, introduction, xix. Boehner cites *Quodlibeta* VI, Q. 6., which is reproduced in Latin and translated into English in *Ockham: Philosophical Writings*, p. 25-27: "Anything is to be attributed to the divine power, when it does not contain a manifest contradiction" (p. 25). See also the quotation from *Quodlibeta* VI, Q. 1,

in Clark, "Ockham on Right Reason": "God is able to produce everything that does not entail a contradiction to be done," 31. On Ockham and the later medieval nominalist Gabriel Biel, see also Oberman, *Harvest of Medieval Theology*, 37.

21. Oakley, *Natural Law*, 75; Clark, "Voluntarism and Rationalism," 77.

22. In recent decades John Kilcullen has argued that Ockham's account of natural law is *not* an instance of metaethical voluntarism. According to Kilcullen, Ockham holds that absolute requirements of natural law (to refrain from murder, adultery, bearing false witness) may be overridden by God's commands. On his theory, basic or primary requirements of natural law constitute a rational, non-positive morality—one not wholly dependent on omnipotent will that are indefeasible *except in one instance*—whenever God commands to the contrary. See Kilcullen "Natural Law and Will in Ockham"; and Kilcullen "Medieval Theories of Natural Law" (redacted and published as Kilcullen, "Natural Law"). I find Kilcullen's argument unpersuasive. See DeHart, "Leviathan Leashed," esp. 5–6 and 28–29, nn15–17. As we've seen, Ockham was a metaphysical nominalist who affirmed that "everything that exists is individual and singular" (Boehner, introduction, xviii), and who considered the view that universals are something other than names "the worst error of philosophy." Adams, *William Ockham*, 1:13. He also clearly has a theory of moral obligation. So Ockham affirms *n•o*. But, again, *n•o* entails metaethical voluntarism, *v*. Thus, (*n•o*)⊃*v*. Kilcullen holds Ockham is not a voluntarist—or ~*v*. But, as we've already seen, that ultimately entails ~*n* or ~*o* (not nominalism or not obligation). So if Kilcullen is right, Ockham is deeply inconsistent. In contrast to Locke, I don't think Ockham is deeply inconsistent (though I hold his theory is ultimately logically invalid). Moreover, Kilcullen's claim—that the natural law provides a body of fundamental, rational precepts that hold ceteris paribus and are defeasible if (but also only if) God commands to the contrary—strikes me as incompatible with Ockham's contention that natural law in its primary principles is "immutabile…et invariabile ac indispensabile" (see *Dialogus* III, II, III, ch. 6, line 65 cited in Oakley, "Medieval Theories of Natura Law, 71n29). I find the evidence for Ockham's voluntarism presented by Boehner (introduction to *Ockham: Philosophical Works*), Oakley ("Medieval Theories of Natural Law" and *Natural Law*), and Clark ("Voluntarism and Rationalism" and "Ockham on Right Reason"), cited in this chapter, overwhelming and dispositive. See also Osborne, "Ockham as a Divine-Command Theorist"; Haldane, "Voluntarism and Realism"; Lisska, "Right Reason"; and Gillespie, *Theological Origins of Modernity*, 23.

23. See Oakley, *Omnipotence, Covenant, & Order*, 48–49; Courtenay, *Capacity and Volition*, 87–91; and Oakley, *Omnipotence and Promise*.

24. Aquinas, *Summa Theologiae* Ia, Q. 25, art. 5 (emphasis added). Cited in Oakley, *Omnipotence, Covenant, & Order*, 49.

25. Prior to Albertus Magnus, Alexander of Hales wrote that "the absolute power pertains to those things concerning which there is no divine preordination; the ordained power . . . to those things which have been preordained or disposed by God." Oakley, *Omnipotence, Covenant, & Order*, 50. According to Courtenay, God's absolute power refers "to the total possibilities *initially* open to God, some of which

were realized by creating the established order; the unrealized possibilities are now only hypothetically possible. Viewed another way, the *potentia absoluta* is God's power considered absolutely, that is, without taking into account the order established by God. *Potentia ordinata*, on the other hand, is the total ordained will of God, the complete plan of God for his creation." Courtenay, "Nominalism," 39.

26. Hooker, *Laws of Ecclesiastical Polity* 1.2.2, p. 54.

27. *Quodlibeta* VI, Q. 1, cited in Clark, "Ockham on Right Reason," 31.

28. Oakley, *Natural Law*, 80

29. "That is called natural law which is in conformity with natural reason that in no case fails." Ockham, "Dialogue" 3.6, p. 286. The natural law contains absolute prohibitions binding on everyone, everywhere, always. Here Ockham mentions absolute prohibitions such as "Do not commit adultery," "Do not lie," and "Do not bear false witness." Moreover, the absolute requirements of natural law are self-evident (or are necessarily drawn from them from such principles). Thus, "about such natural laws no one can err or even doubt." It is not possible for those who exercises their reason, with respect to them, never to have thought of them. See Ockham 1.15, p. 273. See also my treatment of Ockham's theory of natural law in DeHart, *Uncovering the Constitution's Moral Design*, 162–65, esp. notes 8 and 13.

30. Ockham, "Dialogue" 1.10, p. 261, and 1.15, pp. 273–74.

31. Ockham 1.15, p. 274, and 3.6, p. 286.

32. Passages like these lead Brian Tierney to claim that "nominalism and voluntarism . . . seem to have little relevance for Ockham's ideas on natural law and natural rights." For "Whenever Ockham discussed natural law or natural rights he persistently appealed to right reason as the ground of his argument." In fact, "All medieval and early modern thinkers . . . realized that both reason and will were necessary for the conduct of human affairs." But "if we have to divide them into rationalists and voluntarists according to their emphases, Ockham clearly belongs in the rationalist camp," Tierney, *Idea of Natural Rights*, 199. My great respect for Tierney notwithstanding, I think Oakley, Clark, and Lisska (in the various works cited above) demonstrate that Ockham subordinates *recta ratio* to omnipotent will.

33. Oakley, "Medieval Theories of Natural Law," 71–72; and Oakley, *Natural Law*, 77–80.

34. *Scriptum in librum primum Sententiarum (Ordinatio)*, dist. 41, qu unica, p. 610, cited (and translated) in Oakley, *Natural Law*, 78.

35. See Knud Haakonssen, *Natural Law and Moral Philosophy*, 38: for Pufendorf, "The moral and the physical world are two self-contained spheres, which is to say that there is no moral quality or purpose inherent in the physical world. Values are not among the natural qualities. The *entia moralia* are simply 'modes' that are introduced into the natural world supervening upon the particular substances of human nature. In order for things or events in nature to acquire value, they have to be related to a norm, and this can be done only by beings who can understand norms as prescriptions for actions and who can act upon this understanding, that is, beings of intellect and free will, who may or may not follow the prescription and will thereby do either right or wrong. Value is thus imposed upon that which in itself is morally

neutral, when a rule is prescribed to guide a will." Schneewind notes that "Pufendorf breaks with a long-standing tradition in which goodness and being are equated" to which Grotius "would have been at least sympathetic" and that Cumberland simply affirmed. *Invention of Autonomy*, 123. See also Forde, *Locke, Science, and Politics*, 101: Pufendorf "has constructed a theory in which divine legislation is the only possible origin of morality. As the new science teaches, nature is morally vacuous; moral law is not part of the natural order. Morality can arise only by the imposition of moral modes upon nature, by intelligent agents. So far as nature is concerned, no actions are good or evil in themselves."

36. As he writes in *On the Duty of Man and Citizen*, "Actions in accordance with law are called good; contrary to law bad," 30.

37. Pufendorf, *On the Law of Nature* 1.1.2, p. 99.

38. Pufendorf 1.1.2, p. 100.

39. Pufendorf 1.1.3, p. 100.

40. Pufendorf 1.1.4, p. 100–101.

41. Pufendorf 1.6.4, p. 120.

42. Pufendorf quotes *De Cive* 3.33 in his rejection of Hobbes's position.

43. Pufendorf, *On the Law of Nature* 1.6.4, p. 121.

44. Pufendorf 1.6.7, p. 122.

45. Pufendorf 1.6.9, p. 123 (emphasis added).

46. Pufendorf 1.6.10, p. 124 (emphasis added).

47. Pufendorf 1.6.11, p. 125.

48. There are substantial problems with Pufendorf's argument here. First, his language conflates q having no reason to oppose the sovereignty of p over q with q having good reason to accept the authority of p over q. These are not equivalent. But let's take him only to mean the second formulation. Pufendorf clearly conflates q having good reason to accept or consent to the authority of p over q with q having in fact consented to it. But maybe q has no reason to oppose the authority of p or has good reason to accept the authority of p and nevertheless does not consent to it. Moreover, are the benefits p provides q necessary or sufficient for the authority of p over q. Minimally, benefaction does not always give the benefactor authority over the beneficiary or create an obligation of the beneficiary to obey the benefactor. But in that case, p benefiting q seems only to provide a necessary and not a sufficient condition for the authority p over q. Is Pufendorf saying p benefiting q and being sufficiently powerful to compel q are together necessary and sufficient? In that case, it would seem any person p could exercise authority over any person q where p provides q certain benefits (perhaps ones q could not have procured for himself) and p is sufficiently stronger than q. That seems problematic indeed.

49. Pufendorf, *On the Law of Nature* 1.6.12, p. 125.

50. Pufendorf 1.6.12, p. 126. By "certain writers," Pufendorf means Hobbes, and clearly has in view passages in *De Cive* such as 1.14, p. 119: "The conqueror may by right compel the conquered, or the strongest the weaker" and "irresistible power confers the right of dominion and ruling over those who cannot resist."

51. Pufendorf, *On the Law of Nature* 1.7.3, p. 129.

52. Pufendorf 1.2.6, cited in Schneewind, *Invention of Autonomy*, 122

53. Schneewind, *Invention of Autonomy*, 122.

54. Pufendorf, *On the Law of Nature and Nations* 2.3.4, cited in Schneewind, *In-vention of Autonomy*, 122.

55. Schneewind, *Invention of Autonomy*, 122.

56. Schneewind, 138–39.

57. Schneewind, 139.

58. Schneewind, 136.

59. Haakonssen, *Natural Law and Moral Philosophy*, 16.

60. Gierke, *Political Theories of the Middle Ages*, 172 cited in Grabill, *Rediscovering the Natural Law*.

61. Grabill, *Rediscovering the Natural Law*, 61.

62. Grabill, 58. According to Grabill, "Oakley correctly points out that Gierke, and, by implication, Crowe, d'Entrêves, and Rommen, offer no documentation for the caricature of the nominalist theory of natural law as grounded in a series of possibly arbitrary divine commands," 61. This statement profoundly *misrepresents* Oakley's position. Oakley says that even in the *Dialogus*, "in at least two places . . . Ockham says that certain moral precepts cannot be defended by reason. Indeed, he goes so far as to admit that God is not bound by natural law because He can dispense from its precepts. Such statements can only serve to indicate that the natural law, far from possessing any intrinsic rationality or any ontological foundation, is grounded solely in the decisions of a sovereign Divinity." Oakley, "Medieval Theories of Natural Law," 68–69. And if we turn from the *Dialogus* to Ockham's *Commentary on the Sentences of Peter Lombard*, "Here Gierke would seem to find support in a long series of text which enunciate the voluntarist position in terms which admit of no equivocation. In the second book of the *Sentences* we are told that hatred of God, adultery, robbery—all such vices—could be stripped of their evil and rendered meritorious 'if they were to agree with the divine precepts just as now, *de facto*, their opposites agree with the divine precept,'" 69. As we shall see, Grabill's framing of Aquinas as a voluntarist concerning moral obligation runs equally afoul of Oakley's scholarship.

63. For quotations from the *Summa Theologiae* that follow, I rely on Bigongiari, *Political Ideas of Aquinas*, unless otherwise indicated. The translation is usually that of the Fathers of the English Dominican Province, though a few select passages have been translated by the editor. At points I make use of the Blackfriars edition—Aquinas, *Summa Theologiae* (1a2æ. 90–97), edited by Thomas Gilby.

64. Lisska renders this passage as follows: "Good is what each thing tends towards." Lisska, *Aquinas's Theory*, 274.

65. Aquinas, *Summa Theologiae* I-II, Q. 94, art. 4, pp. 44–45.

66. Aquinas I-II, Q. 94, art. 4, pp. 45 (emphasis added). See the treatment of this passage in Budziszewski, *Aquinas's "Treatise on Law,"* 245–46.

67. Aquinas I-II, Q. 94, art. 4, pp. 45 (emphasis added).

68. The Blackfriars edition renders the passage as follows: "Now since good has the meaning of being an end, while being an evil has the contrary meaning, it follows

that reason of its nature apprehends the things towards which man has a natural tendency as good objectives, and therefore to be actively pursued, whereas it apprehends their contraries as bad, and therefore to be shunned." *Summa Theologiae* 28 (1a2ae. 90–97), *Law and Political Theory*, 81. The Latin does not have *per consequens* after *mala*. But it seems clearly implied.

69. This paragraph advances a common interpretation of Aquinas. I think his theory of obligation is more complex than the common interpretation suggests. Aquinas doesn't say or imply, for instance, that good is to be done (or that goods are objects of pursuit) *just* (or *only*) *because* it is (or they are) good. To say that good is to be done or pursued *because* it is good is to leave open the possibility of additional grounds for doing or pursuing the good. For instance, it is possible that we are obligated to act in a particular way *both* because what we are obligated to do is intrinsically good *and* because we are required (perhaps by the command of God as impressed upon the very structure of the practical intellect) so to act.

70. Aquinas, *Summa Theologiae* I-II, Q. 94, art. 4, pp. 45–46.

71. "In analysing the concept of *inclinatio* as disposition, a disposition is not, of itself, a conscious drive or the object of consciousness. It can become the object of consciousness when the mind, reflecting upon human experience, decides upon a certain construct as a possible explanation of the concept of human nature. But a disposition in and of itself is not necessarily a conscious drive." Lisska, *Aquinas's Theory*, 104. As Budziszewski comments, "The sorts of 'things' that seek or desire the good are things with substantial unity, with natures. They desire it, not necessarily in the psychological sense, which requires a mind, but in the ontological sense. For example, though an acorn is oriented toward becoming an oak, its orientation is certainly not reflected in the thought, 'Gosh, I wish I were an oak.' " Budziszewski, *Aquinas's "Treatise on Law,"* 245.

72. Lisska, *Aquinas's Theory*, 97.

73. "Aquinas is not considering teleology in a manner akin to that of Bentham or Mill. . . . Utilitarianism—and most other teleological theories—consider that moral theories are justifiable in terms of the ends developed. . . . William Frankena argues that teleological theories are determined by the attainment of non-moral ends or goods. Hence, the realm of value is determined by the process and attainment of certain ends, which ends themselves are morally neutral. Given this neutrality, most ends considered in teleological theories are determined by the subjective wants, interests, or desires of the human agents." In contrast, "the metaphysics of finality . . . argues that an end is to be attained, not because of a subjective desire or wish on the part of the agent, but because the end itself determines the well-functioning of the human person." Lisska, *Aquinas's Theory*, 107.

74. Lisska, 99.

75. Lisska, 102.

76. Lisska, 103.

77. Lisska, 101–2.

78. Lisska, 105.

79. Lisska, 104.

80. Lisska, 114.

81. Lisska, 115.

82. Murphy, *God & Moral Law*, 77–78. See also Murphy's Plantinga Fellow Lecture, "God and Moral Law." Murphy's interpretation of Aquinas echoes John Finnis's: "Aquinas's reason for saying that law is an act of intellect . . . has nothing to do with the will of a superior needing to be made known, but only with the fact that it is intelligence that grasps ends, and arranges means to ends, and grasps the necessity of those arranged means, and this is the source of obligation." Finnis, *Natural Law*, 1st ed., pp. 54–55. C. Stephen Evans agrees that intellect certainly "grasps ends, and sees what means are necessary for those ends" thereby giving a person "a reason for acting in some ways rather than others." *Yet* this "ought" is not moral obligation: "moral 'ought' has a different character." Evans, *God & Moral Obligation*, 70.

83. Oakley, *Natural Law*, 50.

84. Oakley, 72.

85. Oakley, 72 (*emphasis* added).

86. With respect to Hobbes, see Oakley, 87–94; and with respect to Locke, Oakley, 82–86.

87. Finnis, *Natural Law*, 54–5.

88. Grotius, *Rights of War and Peace*, "The Preliminary Discourse," para. 5, p. 79.

89. Grotius, "Preliminary Discourse," para. 6, p. 81.

90. Grotius, para. 8, pp. 85–86.

91. Grotius, para. 11, pp. 89–90.

92. Grotius, *Rights of War and Peace* 1.1.9, pp. 147–48.

93. Grotius 1.1.10, pp. 150–51.

94. Grotius 1.1.10, pp. 151–52 (emphasis added).

95. Grotius 1.1.10, pp. 155–56.

96. See, for instance, Grisez, Boyle, and Finnis, "Practical Principles, Moral Truth."

97. Finnis, *Natural Law* (2nd ed.), 297 (emphasis added).

98. Finnis, 298–99.

99. Finnis, 303.

100. Finnis, 303-304.

101. Finnis, 307 (emphasis added).

102. Grotius, *Rights of War and Peace* 1.1.11, p. 148.

103. Adams, *Finite and Infinite Goods*, 232.

104. Wolterstorff, *Justice*, 266–67.

105. My goal herein is not to capture Mark Murphy's position in its entirety, which is complex and which has developed over time. See Murphy, *Natural Law in Jurisprudence*; Murphy, *Essay on Divine Authority*; and Murphy, *God's Own Ethics*.

106. Murphy, *God & Moral Law*, 78.

107. Evans thinks Murphy's argument depends on "too strong" of a "requirement that God be the immediate ground of morality." Evans, *God & Moral Obligation*, 58.

108. To be fair, Hampton does not sharply distinguish instrumental rationality and hypothetical imperatives. Rather, I'm suggesting that her own argument tells against any conceivable account of a moral system constituted entirely by hypothetical imperatives.

109. One could argue that this is why Aquinas presents the first and most fundamental precept of the natural law—"that good is to be done and pursued, evil is to be avoided" (*Summa Theologiae* I-II, Q. 94, art 2)—as a categorical imperative. He then proceeds to describe certain goods to which human beings have natural inclinations. But human obligation with respect to these goods is not constituted merely by the fact that they are goods to which human beings have a natural inclination but also by the categorical prescription found in the first and fundamental premise of the natural law.

110. Adams, *Finite and Infinite Goods*, 232.

111. 1 Corinthians 7:25–28.

112. Or at least that seems to be the implication of Ephesians 5, where he analogizes Christian marriage to Christ and the Church.

113. "There are things it would be good to do that we don't have to do. I think there are even things it would be best to do (indeed, morally best to do) that we don't have to do; actions that are better than we have to do are *supererogatory*. It is controversial whether any action is supererogatory in this sense, but supererogation is at least conceptually possible. Someone who says something would be morally best but one isn't morally *required* to do it may be making a substantive ethical mistake, but surely need not be manifesting a deficiency of linguistic understanding or an aberration of linguistic usage. This is one way in which the concept of the obligatory marks off a potentially smaller territory than that of the good." Adams, *Finite and Infinite Goods*, 232. On supererogation see also Swinburne, *Responsibility and Atonement*, 18–24.

114. See DeHart, "Covenantal Realism"; DeHart, "Leviathan Leashed"; and De-Hart, "Reason and Will in Natural Law."

115. According to Suarez, "Although the obligation imposed by the natural law is derived from the divine will, in so far as it properly a preceptive obligation, nevertheless that will presupposes a judgment as to the evil of falsehood, for example, or similar judgments." Suárez, *Treatise on Laws* 2.6.13, pp. 220–21. See Haakonssen's comment on Suárez's solution in *Natural Law*, 22. According to Gierke, Suárez and Aquinas both "regarded the substance of Natural Law as a judgment touching what was right, a judgment necessarily flowing from the Divine Being and unalterably determined by that Nature of Things which is comprised in God; howbeit, the binding force of this Law, but only its binding force, was traced to God's Will. Thus, Aquinas, Caietanus, Soto, Suárez." Gierke quoted in Grabill, *Rediscovering the Natural Law*, 60. Even if Gierke has Suárez right, he has Aquinas wrong (though not in the way Grabill thinks).

116. A potential objection to my claim about the necessity of *authority* for *moral obligation* emerges from Robert Paul Wolff's influential *In Defense of Anarchism*, 4–18. Wolff claims that morality and authority are mutually exclusive. This mutual exclusion derives from his definition of morality as autonomy, where *autonomy* means that we alone judge what moral constraints bind us; we alone judge what our moral obligations are. The truly autonomous person is not subject to someone else's will. Authority, by contrast, consists in issuing commands. And I obey a command only when I do what I am commanded to do because the person commanding me tells me to do it, bracketing my own reasons for acting or not acting as commanded.

Thus, insofar as I act morally (i.e., autonomously), I don't act under another's authority; insofar as I act under another's authority, I don't act morally. Wolff's argument, however, depends on misunderstanding authority, on the one hand, and a very controversial and eminently contestable account of morality—one that seems to render the very idea of moral obligation complete nonsense—on the other. As to the implausibility of Wolff's conception of authority, see Wolterstorff, "Accounting for the Authority of the State," 250–53. As Wolterstorff argues, the practical reasoning account of authority (one advanced not only by Wolff but also, he says, by H. L. A. Hart, and Joseph Raz, p. 250) "gets things backwards in the way it characterizes binding directive authority; it's an example of what medieval philosophers called a *per consequens*... explanation" (252). You might say such accounts put the cart before the horse. With respect to autonomy, Leslie Green notes, "Wolff has moralized this dilemma, by postulating a primary duty to be autonomous. Not everyone, however, thinks of autonomy in this way, as a duty. More often, it is seen as a capacity or skill for significant self-determination." Green, *Authority of the State*, 25. Green seeks to recast Wolff's dilemma. So doing, however, he retains the practical reasoning account of authority that is *per consequens*.

117. Anscombe, "Modern Moral Philosophy," 32.

118. Anscombe, 30.

119. Anscombe, 27. See Evans's treatment of Anscombe's argument or of what he calls "the Anscombe intuition" in *God & Moral Obligation*, 9–22. Evans argues that Socrates has a notion of moral obligation according to which "our moral duties are linked to a God or gods to whom we are responsible" and "who ought to be *obeyed* because he has authority," 18–20 (and pp. 16–29 more broadly). Thus, the notion of moral obligation predates Christianity and occurs outside the Jewish and Christian orbit, on the one hand, and connects God to moral obligation, embodying the Anscombe intuition, on the other.

120. According to Hare, autonomy for Kant is the appropriation of the already extant moral law for oneself: "Autonomy on this reading is more nearly a kind of submission than a kind of creation." Hare, *God's Call*, 96. See 94–96 for Hare's critique of the creative antirealist interpretation of Kant advanced in Schneewind, *Invention of Autonomy*. Hare notes that while Kant "says we should recognize our duties as God's commands to us. . . . Kant denies that God is the author or creator of the moral demand, because he thinks this demand does not strictly have an *author* at all. But if it does not have an author, then *we* cannot be its author or its creator either. So *creative* anti-realism must be wrong" as an interpretation of Kant. Thus, "In his Lectures on Ethics from 1775 to 1780 Kant says that the laws of morality are necessary, like the fact that a triangle has three angles. Only contingent laws . . . can have an author. Necessary laws do not have an author, but they can have someone who promulgates or declares them" who can "in that sense" be considered their "lawgiver" (94). See also Hare, *God and Morality*, chap. 3.

121. Hobbes, *De Cive* 6.14, p. 183; and Hobbes, *Leviathan* 26.6, p. 174.

122. Aquinas, *Summa Theologiae* I-II, Q. 90, art. 3, resp., and Q. 91, art. 1, resp., in *The Political Ideas of St. Thomas*, 7–8, 11–12.

123. Aquinas I-II, Q. 91, art. 1, ad. 3, p. 12.
124. Aquinas I-II, Q. 94, art. 5, obj. 2, p. 51.
125. Aquinas I-II, Q. 94, art. 5, ad 2, p. 52 (emphasis added). One might take Aquinas's point here while demurring from his interpretation of the binding of Isaac. Given the prohibitions on child sacrifice in the Torah (Deuteronomy 12:29–32) and Prophets (Jeremiah 7:31 and Ezekiel 20:25–26), we might understand the story in story recounted in Genesis 22:1–9 as God showing Israel that He forbids child sacrifice. The most important part of the story, in that case, is God telling Abraham not to go through with it, to stop. This interpretation gains plausibility when we consider that Hebrew Scripture presents child sacrifice as a widespread practice among the nations surrounding Israel and that the Torah aims to establish a people distinct from the surrounding nations—including, specifically, with respect to this abhorrent practice. As the late Rabbi Jonathan Sacks writes, "The Binding of Isaac is a polemic against, and a rejection of, the principle of *patria potestas*, the idea universal to all pagan cultures that children are the property of their parents." So understood, "the Binding of Isaac is now consistent with the other foundational narratives of the Torah, namely the creation of the universe and the liberation of the Israelites from slavery in Egypt." Sacks, "Binding of Isaac." I concur with Sacks. But see also Kierkegaard, *Fear and Trembling*; Adams, *Finite and Infinite Goods*, chap. 12; Evans, *Kierkegaard's Ethic of Love*, chap. 3. On Aquinas's reply to the second objection in Q. 94, art. 5, see Budziszewski, *Aquinas's "Treatise on Law,"* 285–88. Against Adams's interpretation, Edwin Curley reads the passage from Ezekiel 20 in a way contradictory not only to Jeremiah 7 (which he realizes) but also in contradiction to Deuteronomy 12 (which he seems not to realize). Curley, "God of Abraham." Curley seems unfamiliar with Jewish interpretations of these passages such as the contextually sensitive one offered by Rabbi Sacks, who concludes (rightly in my estimation), that "The Torah is horrified by child sacrifice, which it sees as the worst of all sins." Sacks, "Binding of Isaac." As I read Ezekiel, when God says "I gave them . . . ordinances by which they could not live," context suggests (contra Curley) that Israel disobeyed the prohibition on child sacrifice in the Torah (Deuteronomy 12) and imitated the surrounding nations by practicing child sacrifice and was defiled by this disobedience.

Chapter 7

1. Barry Alan Shain is perhaps a rare exception to the rule. He seems to hold that Revolutionary-era Americans (with the exception of at least some national super-elites) affirmed natural law and an organicist conception of political order and rejected the idea of a contractarian or compact foundation for political society. See Shain, *Myth of American Individualism*, 56–57.
2. Zuckert, "Social Compact," 235–36. The passage from Aristotle that Zuckert has in mind is *Politics* 3.9.1280a34–1281a2, pp. 196–98 (all quotations of Aristotle's *Politics* in this volume are from the Sinclair and Saunders translation unless otherwise noted). I take Aristotle's point to be different from the one Zuckert attributes

to him. Zuckert takes Aristotle to reject a polis based on a pact or covenant. I take Aristotle only to say a pact or covenant is not enough.

3. Contra Zuckert on the relation of Aristotle to American founding thought, see Rubin, *America, Aristotle*. I concur with Arkes, *Philosopher and the City*, 15–16. See also DeHart, "Whose Social Contract?"; and DeHart, *Uncovering the Constitution's Moral Design*, esp. chapter 4.

4. For a different interpretation of Blackstone, see Conklin, *Pursuit of Happiness*. Conklin underscores elements of Blackstone's thought elided by Zuckert's interpretation. She contends that Blackstone articulated "a conception of happiness that harmonizes with Aristotle's . . . discussion in *The Nicomachean Ethics*" (Conklin, 26). At the same time, he rejected "the scholastic tradition . . . as unnecessarily complex and ultimately unknowable" by the average person, and blamed the "complexity of [deductive and syllogistic] scholastic method of jurisprudence" for "the inconsistencies in the common law" (19–20). Conklin also argues that both Hooker and Newton influenced Blackstone's account of the laws of nature (25). Conklin advances a nuanced interpretation of Blackstone. For all that, I think she perhaps misses the degree to which he caricatures Scholasticism. Aquinas, for instance, did not think that the first principles of law—in particular, of natural law—were reached through a long train of metaphysical deductions. For the first principles of natural law and their immediate implications are not deduced or inferred at all. They are apprehended as epistemically basic. As well, Blackstone's claim that Parliament's power is both absolute and uncontrollable rejects a central—and not a peripheral—tenet of Thomistic and (classical) scholastic natural law.

5. Zuckert, "Social Compact," 255.

6. Zuckert, 255–56.

7. Zuckert, 259.

8. Zuckert, 251–52.

9. Zuckert, 246.

10. Zuckert, 245–46. Zuckert's argument seems to depend on the proposition that Newtonian mechanics rules out Aristotelian physics and metaphysics. This rests, I think, on a misunderstanding of both Aristotle and Newton. Edward Feser, in "Motion in Aristotle," demonstrates that there is no necessary contradiction here. See also Feser, *Aristotle's Revenge*. And Samuel Gregg notes in *Reason, Faith* (56) that, in his "Scholium Generale," [General Scholium]" added as an appendix to the 1713 edition of *Principia Mathematica* and written to repudiate "divine clockmaker Deism," Newton speaks of the necessity of a God with final causes:

We know [God] only by his most wise and excellent contrivances of things, and final causes; we admire him for his perfections; but we reverence and adore him on account of his dominion. For we adore him as his servants; and a God without dominion, providence, and final causes, is nothing else but Fate and Nature. Blind metaphysical necessity, which is certainly the same always and every where could produce no variety of things. All that diversity of natural things which we find, suited to different times and places, could arise from nothing but the ideas and Will of a Being necessarily existing. (Newton, "General Scholium," 942).

See Gregg, *Reason, Faith*, 53–56.

11. On this point, see Feser, *Locke*, 9–27, 60–61; and Feser, *The Last Superstition*, chap. 5, esp. 178–9.

12. Elazar, *Covenant & Polity*, 36 (emphasis added).

13. Elazar, 36–37.

14. Elazar, 38.

15. Elazar, 23-24. See also Lutz, *Origins*, 12, 25–27; and Lutz, "From Covenant to Constitution."

16. Elazar, *Covenant & Polity*, 24.

17. On Jewish covenantalism, see also Novak, *Covenantal Rights*, and Novak, *Jewish Social Contract*. Like Elazar, Novak also sharply distinguishes Jewish covenantal and Greek philosophical thought when it comes to natural law. See *Covenantal Rights*, 15–16, 24–25. On Reformed Protestant covenantalism, see Elazar, *Covenant & Commonwealth*.

18. Elazar, *Covenant & Polity*, 23.

19. McCoy and Baker, *Fountainhead of Federalism*, 52 (emphasis added).

20. McCoy and Baker, 56.

21. McCoy and Baker, 78.

22. McCoy and Baker, 92 (emphasis added).

23. See treatment of Scotus in Hare, *God's Call*, esp. pp. 59–62; and Hare, *God and Morality*, chap. 2, esp. 97–105 and 111–113.

24. See Oakley, *Natural Law*, 69–70, 97–99.

25. Cited in Elazar, *Covenant & Commonwealth*, 83.

26. Elazar, 84.

27. To be sure, in the list of philosophical theses in his early "Heidelberg Disputations" (1518), Luther seems to excoriate Aristotle in order to elevate Plato: "Aristotle wrongly finds fault with and derides the ideas of Plato, which actually are better than his own" and "The mathematical order of material things is ingeniously maintained by Pythagoras, but more ingenious is the interaction of the ideas maintained by Plato." Luther, *Basic Theological Writings*, 33. One might take the Heidelberg Disputations and the 1517 "Disputation Against Scholastic Theology" to affirm Augustinian Platonism against medieval Aristotelian Scholasticism. If so, Luther nevertheless rejected the moral realism of Augustine in favor of metaethical voluntarism: "God is He for Whose will no cause or ground may be laid down as its rule and standard; for nothing is on a level with it or above it, but it is itself the rule of all things. If any rule or standard, or cause or ground, existed for it, it could no longer be the will of God. What God wills is not right because He ought, or was bound, so to will; on the contrary, what takes place must be right, because He so wills it." Luther, *Bondage of the Will*, 209. Moreover, Luther claimed to be a *terminist* and an *Occamist*:

"Terminists" was the name of one sect of the university to which I, too, belonged. They take a stand against the Thomists, Scotists, and Albertists, and were also called Occamists after Occam, their founder. . . . The dispute was over whether 'humanitas' [humanity] and words like it meant a common humanity, which was in all human beings, as Thomas and the others believe. Well, say the Occamists or terminists, there is no such thing as a common humanity, there is only the term "homo" [human] or humanity meaning all human beings individually, the same way a painted picture of a human being refers to all human beings. (Oberman, *Luther*, 169–70)

Luther's *Bondage of the Will* is also an anti-Pelagian treatise, though we must note that Luther's polemic does not provide the only path for avoiding Pelagianism. See remarks on the second Council of Arles in Hittinger, *First Grace*, xi.

28. See chapter 1.

29. Aristotle, *Politics* (trans. Sinclair), 1.2.1253a1, p. 59.

30. Aristotle 1.2.1252b27, p. 59.

31. Aristotle 1.2.1253a29, p. 61.

32. Aristotle 3.9.1280a34–1280b12. This quote from Ernest Barker's translation, 119, quoted in Sandel, *Democracy's Discontent*, 7.

33. Aristotle, *Politics* (trans. Sinclair) 1.2.1253a18, pp. 60–1.

34. Aristotle 1.5.1254a17, p. 67.

35. The polis stands in a similar relation to human nature that the virtues do. The virtues are natural to human beings in the sense that they are essential to human well-being. Humans cannot live well without them. They are perfective of human nature. But they virtues *are not given by nature*. They are therefore acquired rather than *natural* in the sense of being given by nature. So also the Aristotelian polis is not given by nature. It's made. But it's essential to human well-being. And so political association is natural in the sense of being perfective of human nature (which is what I mean by natural in a teleological sense). On this, see Miller, *Nature, Justice, and Rights*, 60.

36. Fred D. Miller adduces two important arguments against the organicist interpretation of Aristotle. First,

there are . . . important differences between organisms and communities. In the former, the part typically has a function or end which is distinct from and subordinate to the end of the whole. For example, the primary end of Socrates' eyebrows is to protect his eyes . . . and the end of his lungs is to breathe or provide the body with air . . . whereas the end of Socrates himself is rational activity. . . . But in the community the end of the whole is a common good in which the parts must directly share in order to qualify as parts: "For there must be some one thing that is common and the same for those who have [something] in common (*tois koinonois*), whether they partake [in it] equally or unequally, e.g. food, an amount of land, or something else of this sort." (*Pol.* VII 8 1328ª25-8). Hence, the realization of the end must *include*, rather than transcend or supersede, the fulfillment of the parts." (Miller, *Nature, Justice, and Rights*, 54)

And second,

Aristotle also rules out the organic interpretation of the polis, in the course of his criticisms of Socrates' ideal constitution as depicted in Plato's *Republic*. Aristotle ascribes to Socrates the hypothesis that it is best for the polis to be as far as possible one, which [Aristotle] objects will destroy the polis: ". . . for the polis is with respect to its nature a sort of multitude [*plethos*], and if it becomes more one it will become a household instead of a polis, and a human being instead of a household; for we would say that a household is more one than a polis and one human being is more one than a household . . ." (II 2 1261ª18-21). It is evident from this that a polis does not possess the innate unity which is characteristic of an Aristotelian substance. Its superiority lies instead in its completeness and self-sufficiency (1261ᵇ10-15). (Miller, 54–55)

Mary Keys notes "that the vision of political community Aquinas appropriates from Aristotle is not an organic one but rather an action-based, associational theory. As was the case in Aristotle's usage, the organic argument is a metaphorical one not to be read *ad litteram.*" Keys, *Aquinas, Aristotle*, 77–78.

37. Miller, *Nature, Justice, and Rights*, 59–60.

38. Aristotle, *Politics* (trans. Sinclair) 1.2.1253a29, p. 61.

39. "The point of political community, according to Blackstone, is 'to guard the rights of each individual member,' as it is with Locke (*Comm.* I, 48)." Zuckert, "Social Compact," 252.

40. Aristotle, *Nicomachean Ethics* 5.3.1131ª10–1131ᵇ20, pp. 1785–86.

41. Aristotle, *Politics* (trans. Sinclair), 1.2.1253a18–1253a39, pp. 60–61.

42. Aristotle, *Politics* (trans. Barker), 3.9, p. 119. Quoted in Sandel, *Democracy's Discontent*, 7.

43. Aristotle, *Politics* (trans. Sinclair) 3.9.1280b29, 197–98.

44. Aristotle 3.9.1280b29, 198.

45. Aristotle 3.9.1280b29, 198.

46. Aristotle 3.9.1287b36, p. 229.

47. Reflecting on Aristotle's account of rulership, C. S. Lewis writes, "The justice or injustice of any given instance of rule depends wholly on the nature of the parties, and not in the least on any social contract. Where citizens are really equal then they ought to live in a republic where all rule in turn ([*Politics*] I, 12; II, 2). If they are not really equal then the republican form becomes unjust (ibid. III, 13)." Lewis, *Preface to Paradise Lost*, 74.

48. According to Thomas Pangle in *The Spirit of Modern Republicanism*, for instance, in the premodern, classical world, "there was much talk of duty for most men,

and of royal or noble or priestly prerogative for a tiny few; little talk of natural rights, and hardly any reference to the rights of man or the rights belonging to human beings. Consent was at most a consent to the preordained rule of natural or divine superiors" (114). Thomas Hobbes, Benedict Spinoza, and John Locke "shattered" the "foundations" of this premodern world. Heirs to the revolution of Hobbes, Spinoza, and Locke—and over and against the premodern, classical view—the American founders and their "new [i.e., modern] republicanism" affirmed "Natural Equality and the Rights of Men, including the right of resistance or revolution; religious toleration and freedom of conscience; and 'No Taxation without Representation!' " (35), as well as popular sovereignty, according to which all authority to govern derives from the people (114). I maintain that natural equality, natural liberty, liberty of conscience, natural rights, separation of church and state, government by consent, popular sovereignty, and the right of a people to depose and replace tyrannical leaders (and change their form of government) all predate the putative revolution of Hobbes, Spinoza, and Locke. In addition to this chapter, see DeHart, "Whose Social Contract?"; and see DeHart, "Return of the Sacral King" on separation of church and state in Christian and modern thought. Pangle's position concerning religious liberty and liberty of conscience strikes me as dispositively disproven by Wilken, *Liberty in the Things of God*. See also essays by Wilken, Timothy Samuel Shah, and Kyle Harper, among others, in Shah and Hertzke, *Christianity and Freedom*, vol. 1.

49. With respect to antiquity, see Kyle Harper's argument that for Roman Stoics like Seneca, *dignitas* was measured "on a sliding scale of worthiness," "Christianity and the Roots of Human Dignity,"129.

50. Lactantius, *Divine Institutes*, book 5, in O'Donovan and O'Donovan, *From Irenaeus to Grotius*, 52 (emphasis added).

51. Ambrose of Milan, *The Story of Naboth*, in O'Donovan and O'Donovan, *From Iranaeus to Grotius*, 76 (emphasis added).

52. Gregory I, *Pastoral Rule*, in O'Donovan and O'Donovan, *From Irenaeus to Grotius*, 197 (emphasis added). In the next page Gregory compares rulers who refuse to acknowledge their equality with those over whom they exercise rule to the "apostate angel":

> But commonly a ruler, from the very fact of his being pre-eminent over others is puffed up with elation of thought; and, while all things serve his need, while his commands are quickly executed after his desire, while all his subjects extol with praises what he has done well, but have no authority to speak against what he has done amiss, and while they commonly praise even what they ought to have reproved, his mind seduced by what is offered in abundance from below, is lifted up above itself; and, while outwardly surrounded by unbounded favour, he loses his inward sense of truth; and, forgetful of himself, he scatters himself on the voices of other men, and believes himself to be such as he outwardly hears himself called rather than such as he ought inwardly to have judged himself to be. He looks down on those who are under

him, nor does he acknowledge them as in the order of nature his equals; and those whom he has surpassed in the accident of power he believes himself to have transcended also in the merits of his life; he esteems himself wiser than all whom he sees himself to excel in power. For indeed he establishes himself in his own mind on a certain lofty eminence, and, though bound together in the same condition of nature with others, he disdains to regard others from the same level; and so he becomes to be even like him of whom it is written: "He beholdeth all high things: he is a king over all the children of pride" (Job 41:34). Nay, aspiring to a singular eminence and despising the social life of the angels, he says: "I will place my seat in the north, and I will be like unto the Most High" (Isa 14:13). Wherefore through a marvelous judgment he finds a pit of downfall within himself, while outwardly he exalts himself on the summit of power. For he is indeed made like the apostate angel, when, being a man, he disdains to be like men (197–98).

It's worth noting that Gregory had a much greater grasp of the Hebraic understanding Leviathan—even in the book of Job—than Hobbes ever did. Saint Augustine's rejection of natural subordination occurs in book 19, chapter 15, of *City of God*:

But in the households of the just man who lives by faith, those who command really serve. Though they appear to command, their commands do not issue from a craving to dominate, but from a readiness to take care, not from a pride which asserts mastery, but from a compassionate acceptance of responsibility. This, of course, is what the arrangements of nature require; it is how God created mankind. "Let him have dominion over the fish of the sea, and over the birds of the air . . . and over every creeping thing that creeps upon the earth" (Gen. 1:26). The rational creature made in God's image was given dominion over irrational creatures, no more: not man over man, but man over beast. . . . That is why God made the first righteous men shepherds of flocks, not rulers of men: to point out the difference between the system of created beings and the requirements of sin. For the state of servitude is rightly understood as a measure imposed on sinners. . . . It was a term required by the fact of guilt, not by nature. . . . Sin, then, is the first cause of servitude, which binds one man in subjection to another, something arising only from God's judgment. (Cited in O'Donovan and O'Donovan, *From Irenaeus to Grotius*, 157–58)

53. *Summa Theologiae* II-II, Q. 104, art. 5, in Aquinas, *On Law, Morality, and Politics*, 243 (emphasis added).

54. Skinner, *Foundations* 2:155–56. The fuller passage from Suárez runs as follows: "In the nature of things all men are born free; so that, consequently, no person has political jurisdiction over another person, even as no person has dominion over another; nor is there any reason why such power should, [simply] in the nature of

things, be attributed to certain persons over certain other persons, rather than *vice versa.*" Suárez, *Treatise on Laws* 2.3.3, p. 430.

55. See Bellarmine, *De Laicis*, chap. 6, p. 22; Filmer, *Patriarcha and Other Writings*, chap. 1; and Sidney, *Discourses Concerning Government* 1.2, p. 8, 1.6, pp. 20–23, and 2.1, p. 77. As Lutz underscores, "Sidney quotes liberally from Aristotle, Plato, the Bible, and the Jesuits Bellarmine and Suárez. The last two, as has been demonstrated by Quentin Skinner in his *Foundations of Modern Political Thought*, were responsible for bringing contract theory to a high point of completion. In fact, most of what Locke has to say is found in their writings." Lutz, *Origins*, 118.

56. All cited in Skinner, *Foundations* 2:160.

57. Skinner, 2:161, 162.

58. According to Oakley,

> Consent appears . . . to have remained what it had been even for the most "advanced" of medieval consent theorists: not . . . the assent of a concatenation of free individuals imposing on themselves an obligation which of their ultimate autonomy they could well avoid, but the consent instead of free communities, possessed at a minimum of the original right to choose their rulers, perhaps also to choose the form of government under which they were to live. . . . In the sixteenth century it is true of the famous Huguenot tract, the *Vindiciae contra tyrannos*, and of its Catholic counterpart, the *De justa reipublicae christianae . . . authoritate* of William Rainolds (Rossaeus), of Spanish thinkers like Francisco de Vitoria, Domingo de Soto, and Luis de Molina. . . . In the seventeenth century it is true of the political thinking of the Jesuits Francisco Suárez and Juan de Mariana. (Oakley, "Legitimation by Consent," 324–25)

59. Schwartz, "Suárez on Consent," 62. Schwartz suggests Skinner conflates these two kinds of consent in his treatment of Suárez in *Foundations*, 2:162. On behalf of Schwartz, we might note that Suárez claims that (1) no person is born under the political jurisdiction of another, and (2) the only way out of the miserable and chaotic *status naturae* is by consenting to create a commonwealth would seem to entail the necessity of individual consent in some sense, which is how Schwartz reads book 3, chap. 2, sec. 4, pp. 432-33. Suárez says we can regard the "multitude of mankind" from two different standpoints: "The multitude of mankind should . . . be viewed with regard to the special volition, or common consent by which they are gathered together into one political body through one bond of fellowship and for the purpose of aiding one another in the attainment of a single political end" (432).

60. Skinner, *Foundations* 2:157-58.

61. Thus Hooker writes, "The being of God is a kind of law to his working: for that perfection which God is, giveth perfection to that he doth" (Hooker, *Laws of Ecclesiastical Polity* 1.2.2, p. 54). And,

The wise and learned among the Heathens themselves . . . all confess . . . in the working of [the] first cause, that *counsel* is used, *reason* followed, a *way* observed, that is to say constant *order* and *law* is kept, whereof itself must needs be author unto itself. Otherwise it should have some worthier and higher to direct it, and so could not itself be first. Being the first it can have no other cause than to itself be the author of the law it willingly worketh by. God therefore is a law both to himself, and to all other things besides. . . . God worketh nothing without cause. All those things which are done by him, have some end for which they are done" and the end for which they are done is a reason of his will to do them (1.2.3, 55-56).

62. Hooker 1.10.1, p. 87 (emphasis added).

63. Hooker 1.10.3-4, pp. 89–90 (emphasis added).

64. An important difference with Lockean consent theory must be addressed. According to Hooker, after a political society has been established, the consent of those who form it bind later generations in perpetuity, *unless consent to it is revoked by unanimous consent*: "Since men naturally have no full and perfect power to command whole politic multitudes of men; therefore utterly without our consent we could in such sort be at no man's commandment living. And to be commanded we do consent, when that society whereof we are part hath at any time before consented, without revoking the same after by the like universal agreement." For "we were then alive in our predecessors, and they in their successors do still live." Hooker, *Laws of Ecclesiastical Polity* 1.10.8, p. 93. Locke rejects the idea that we can be bound by our predecessors or bind our progeny to political society. *Two Treatises*, Second Treatise 8.116, pp. 345–46. Yet morally and metaphysically realist social contract theory (or consent theory) need not reject the necessity of the voluntary consent of individuals after the initial establishment of political society. Suárez argues that political authority "is given to the community of mankind by the Author of nature, but not without the intervention of will and consent on the part of the human beings who have assembled into this perfect community." Suárez, *Treatise on Laws* 3.3.6, p. 439. Replacing Hooker's claim that we consent through our predecessors with an insistence on the consent of individuals is entirely compatible with everything else Hooker affirms—that is, such a claim stands in no logical, metaphysical, or moral contradiction with anything else he affirms.

65. In addition to the passages from Pangle's *Spirit of Modern Republicanism*, treated below, see also Ward, *Politics of Liberty*, 226, 237–38. Arguing that although Locke invokes Hooker, his position nevertheless represents a significant and substantial break with Hooker's, Michael P. Zuckert speaks of a "chasm" between Locke and Hooker on natural law and "the natural executive power." Zuckert, *Natural Rights*, 18, 224–30. With Wolterstorff (see below), I think Pangle, Ward, and Zuckert have the logical relation between the positions of Hooker and Locke wrong.

66. Pangle, *Spirit of Modern Republicanism*, 132–33.

67. Wolterstorff, "God in Locke's Philosophy," 140–41.

68. *Two Treatises*, Second Treatise, 9.127, 352.

69. One real point of contrast between Locke and Hooker can be found in Hooker's claim that fathers are "natural superiors" within their families. Locke, by contrast, holds that *parents* are naturally superior to *children*. He underscores that authority in the family is of both parents over children.

70. Althusius, *Politica* 1.4, pp. 17–18. A bit later Althusius explicitly invokes the authority of Aristotle for the claim that humans are essentially social: "Aristotle teaches that man by his nature is brought to this social life and mutual sharing. For man is a more political animal than the bee or any gregarious creature, and therefore by nature far more of a social animal than bees, ants, cranes, and such kind as feed and defend themselves in flocks" (1.32, p. 24).

71. Althusius 1.13, p. 21.

72. Althusius 1.14, p. 21; see also 1.27, p. 23.

73. Althusius 1.32-33, pp. 24–25.

74. Althusius 1.29 and 1.30, p. 24. "The formal cause is indeed the association brought about by contributing and communicating one with the other, in which political men institute, cultivate, maintain, and conserve the fellowship of human life through decisions about those things useful and necessary to this social life"; "The material of politics is the aggregate of precepts for communicating those things, services, and right that we bring together, each fairly and properly according to his ability, for symbiosis and the common advantage of social life." Althusius 1.29 and 1.31, p. 24. So Althusius gives an analysis of political association in terms of Aristotle's causal theory.

75. Althusius 5.8-9, p. 40 and 1.10-11, p. 40.

76. Althusius 5.22-23, p. 40. This way of distinguishing the parts from the whole—such that the whole community, and those officials they elect, exercise authority over each individual but where these officials, do not have authority over the community itself—solves the problem Hampton framed concerning agency contract theory (discussed in chapter 1 of this volume), at least in principle. But I submit that the American experiment with popular rule at the state and local level suggests it works (or has worked) in practice too. American local communities in the seventeenth, eighteenth, and first half of the nineteenth century instantiated the authority of the community over both officials and community members and were exceptionally effective in exercising control over members. See Shain, *Myth of American Individualism*, 56–57, 88–89, 98–100.

77. Althusius, *Politica* 5.24-25, p. 41.

78. Althusius 9.1-3, p. 66 (emphasis added).

79. Althusius 9.4, p. 66.

80. Althusius 9.15, pp. 69–70.

81. Althusius 9.18, p. 70.

82. Althusius 9.19, p. 71.

83. Althusius 19.10-11, pp. 121–22 (emphasis added). See also his very Aristotelian/Thomistic discussion of the *lex moralis* and of the common law/proper law distinction, 21.19-41, pp. 139–48.

84. Althusius 21.20, 139–40.

85. To be sure, Althusius's conception of natural law in *Politica* is not fully traditional in every respect. While he holds that the first table of the Decalogue is inviolable and cannot be altered or abridged even by God (21.26, p. 141), he also holds that God (but only God) can dispense from or make exceptions to the second table (21.28, pp. 143-33). However, so far as I can tell, revising the Althusian position so that the second table of the Decalogue holds invariably and that God does not (or even, given human nature, cannot) dispense from it has no bearing upon my argument in this paragraph. If we make Althusius's position about the second table more consonant with Saint Thomas's (or Aristotle's position that adultery, theft, and murder are never right), my argument still holds.

86. Althusius, *Politica* 19.15-16, p. 122.

Chapter 8

1. Zuckert, "Social Compact," 235–36; Elazar, *Covenant & Polity*, 36–38, 23–24; and McCoy and Baker, *Fountainhead of Federalism*, 52, 56, 78, 92.

2. In what follows, I summarize and reorganize the arguments of previous chapters in order to demonstrate the essential dependence of government by consent and political contractarianism on classical natural law and to bring that central line of argument in this volume to its conclusion. Nevertheless, an important loose thread remains at the end of this chapter: namely, the practicability of government by consent, which I take up in the final chapter.

3. Which is surely what Hobbes has in mind when he speaks of commonwealths established by institution or acquisition in *Leviathan* 17.15, 109–10.

4. Hobbes, *Leviathan* 13.11, p. 77.

5. Martinich, "Law and Self-Preservation."

6. DeHart, "Leviathan."

7. This interpretation is necessitated not only by things Hobbes says but also by the fact that his work is one of political theory rather than of history or anthropology. Moreover, Hobbes takes his work to have normative rather than merely descriptive implications. And it is written for people in the state of civil society and not for people seeking to leave the state of nature. The best explanation of his account of the state of nature (given he says it is not a general historical phenomenon) and of how to leave it is that he is really describing how to avoid falling into it.

8. According to Kant,

> We need by no means assume that this contract (*contractus originarius* or *pactum sociale*), based on a coalition of the wills of all private individuals in a nation to form a common, public will for the purposes of rightful legislation, actually exists as a *fact*, for it cannot possibly be so. . . . It is in fact merely an idea of reason, which nonetheless has undoubted practical reality; for it can oblige every legislator to frame his laws in such a way that they would have been produced by the united will of a whole nation, and to regard each subject, in so far as he can claim citizenship, as if he had consented within

the general will. This is the test of the rightfulness of every public law. For if the law is such that a whole people could not *possibly* agree to it . . . it is unjust. ("On the Common Saying: 'This May Be True in Theory, but It Doesn't Apply in Practice,'" quoted in Hampton, *Political Philosophy*, 134).

See Williams, "Ideas and Actuality."

9. See the treatment of the original position in Rawls's *Theory of Justice* by Hampton in *Political Philosophy*, 133–44; and in Sandel, *Liberalism and the Limits of Justice*, 105–13.

10. On this, see Green, *Authority of the State*: the "scope [of "the traditional theory of consent"] is limited: not many of us have, in fact, consented. It follows then that the state has legitimate authority only over some of its citizens" (188). See also Wolterstorff, "Accounting for the Authority of the State," 268–69; and Simmons, *Edge of Anarchy*, chaps. 7 and 8.

11. Reflecting on "the Blackstonean modification of social contract theory" in "Social Compact, Common Law, and the American Amalgam," Zuckert writes, "The state of nature and social contract are not historical truths; the slow growth via custom of the common law signifies clearly enough to Blackstone that the social contract will never do as history. But they are moral political philosophical truths when understood correctly, i.e., as a rational reconstruction of the source of legitimate authority" (256).

12. See Simmons, *Moral Principles*, chap. 2.

13. "The Promises and Bargains for Truck, etc. between the two Men in the Desert Island, mentioned by *Garcilasso De la vega*, in his History of *Peru*, or between a *Swiss* and an *Indian*, in the Woods of America, are binding to them, though they are perfectly in a State of Nature, in reference to one another. *For Truth and keeping Faith belongs to Men, as Men, and not as Members of Society*." Locke, *Two Treatises*, Second Treatise 2.14, 277 (emphasis added).

14. The importance of actual promises (with an intimation to their relation to covenant/consent) is underscored in Locke's famous *Letter Concerning Toleration*: "Lastly, those are not at all to be tolerated who deny the being of God. Promises, covenants, and oaths, *which are the bonds of human society*, can have no hold upon an atheist. The taking away of God, though but even in thought dissolves all" (64). In his (until 1954 unpublished and almost completely unknown) *Questions Concerning the Law of Nature*, he writes, "There are two foundations on which human society seems to rest: namely, the fixed form of a commonwealth and constitution of a regime, and [second] the keeping of covenants. These removed, all community among men collapses, just as, were the law of nature removed, these [foundations] collapse themselves" (Q. 1, p. 115).

15. That is, moral obligation would be grounded in act of corporate or aggregate will. I maintain that these—corporate will and a mere aggregation of wills—are analytically distinct. But for the purposes of my argument concerning the logical impossibility of grounding promissory obligation in convention, it does not matter whether corporate will is viewed as a whole not reducible to the sum of its parts or

whether it is viewed as a mere aggregation of individual wills. My argument holds against either construal of conventionalism.

16. In addition to chapters 2 and 3 in this volume, see chapter 4 of DeHart, *Uncovering the Constitution's Moral Design*, in which I argue that procedural and preferential conventionalism are both self-referentially incoherent.

17. In addition to Hobbes and Hume, see Mackie, *Ethics*; and Hampton, "Hobbes and Ethical Naturalism."

18. On Mill, for example, see Budziszewski, *Written on the Heart*, 141: For Mill, "The good . . . is nothing but the desirable, and the desirable is nothing but what we actually desire." See Mill, *Utilitarianism*, p. 34.

19. Michael J. Sandel, for instance, understands what he calls the Kantian liberalism of John Rawls and Robert Nozick as a philosophy in which human ends are chosen by human will. See Sandel, *Liberalism and the Limits of Justice*, chap. 1; and Sandel, *Democracy's Discontent*, chap. 1.

20. It's worth noting that holding that human ends are chosen by will rather than given by desire does not rule out the influence of desire in the will's choosing. Nor does the Hobbesian, desire-based account rule out human will. Rather, these are distinct accounts of hypothetical imperatives in terms of what is treated as *most* fundamental. For Hobbes, for instance, human will is fully determined by desire— he defines will as the last appetite in deliberating. For Rawls, by contrast, will clearly has a more fundamental role than desire.

21. Hampton, "Hobbes and Ethical Naturalism," 338.

22. Hobbes, *Leviathan* 4.21, p. 21. Of course Hobbes was manifestly wrong about his having squared the circle and nevertheless right about the nonsense of a round quadrangle. On Hobbes's attempt to square the circle, see Douglas M. Jesseph, *Squaring the Circle: The War between Hobbes and Wallis*. His ethical subjectivism falls into the same camp as the squared circle (as does his thinking about infinity, incorporeality, etc.).

23. Hampton, "Hobbes and Ethical Naturalism," 338.

24. Also, on such a theory, it would seem to be the case that the satisfaction of all our desires would be obligatory, at which point the notion of obligation has become entirely superfluous. Suppose we then distinguish some desires from the rest as objects of pursuit by instrumental rationality. That distinction could not be made on the basis of desire without collapsing into self-referential incoherence or, quite obviously, on the basis of instrumental rationality (that is, on the basis of causal relations about courses of action that obtain objects of desire). The distinction could only be made on the basis of a standard transcendent of and normative for desire and therefore for instrumental rationality. And the imperatives about which desires to pursue would have to be categorical rather than hypothetical.

25. Hume, *Treatise of Human Nature*, 2.3.3, p. 463 (Mossner ed.). Two paragraphs earlier Hume (in)famously writes, "Reason is, and ought only be the slave of the passions, and can never pretend to any other office than to serve and obey them" (462).

26. On this see Oakley, *Natural Law*, chap. 3; and his earlier "Medieval Theories of Natural Law," 65–68. See also Lisska, "Right Reason"; and DeHart, "Reason and Will in Natural Law."

27. See also Evans, *God & Moral Obligation*, as well as Alasdair MacIntyre, *After Virtue*, 60. According to MacIntyre, on classical theism "moral judgments were at once hypothetical and categorical in form. They were hypothetical insofar as they expressed a judgment as to what conduct would be teleologically appropriate for human beings. . . . They were categorical insofar as they reported the contents of the universal law commanded by God." In other words, on classical theism, moral obligation as such is a compound reality.

28. On the *potentia dei absoluta et ordinata* distinction see Oakley, *Omnipotence, Covenant, & Order*; and Oakley, *Omnipotence and Promise*. See also Courtenay, *Capacity and Volition*.

29. In modal terms, for Ockham, God could actualize a world book with any moral content so long as it included God's own existence and noncontradiction.

30. As to the interpretation of Ockham and the divine powers, in addition to Oakley and Courtenay, see Lisska, "Right Reason"; DeHart, "Reason and Will in Natural Law"; and DeHart, "Leviathan Leashed."

31. See the relevant passages in Oakley's *Natural Law* concerning divine will and natural law Ockham's corpus.

32. See, for example, Adams, *William of Ockham*, 1:13, 1:71; and chapter 6 of this volume.

33. See Plato, *Republic*, 2.377c–383c, pp. 57–65, esp. 379a10-b, p. 59 ("Now, gods, of course, are really good, aren't they, and must be described as such?"), and 381c7–9, p. 62 ("It is impossible, then, for a god to want to alter himself. On the contrary, since each god is, it seems, as beautiful and as good as possible, he must always unqualifiedly retain his own form").

34. I would in fact reject such a position. But the unsoundess of such a position is neither here nor there for my argument in this volume.

35. On Scotus see Hare, *God and Morality*, chap. 2.

36. According to the hypothetical syllogism: (1) If A, then B, (2) if B, then C, therefore (3) if A, then C.

37. See Kant, *Grounding for the Metaphysics of Morals*, First Section, 7–8: "A good will is good not because of what it effects or accomplishes, nor because of its fitness to attain some proposed end; it is good only through willing, i.e., it is good in itself" (7). See also Walker, *Moral Foundations*, 29.

38. The preceding lines are taken, with slight modification, from DeHart, "U.S. Constitution of 1789 and Natural Law." See also the treatment and critique of Kant's deontological realism in DeHart, *Uncovering the Constitution's Moral Design*, 129–33, 146, 151, 259–60. See also my critiques of simple thin-teleological realism and complex-thin teleological realism in *Uncovering*, chap. 4.

Chapter 9

1. Simmons, *Edge of Anarchy*, chap. 7.

2. Green, *Authority of the State*; Simmons, *Moral Principles*, esp. chaps. 3 and 4; Simmons, " 'Denisons' and 'Aliens' "; Simmons, "Tacit Consent"; and Simmons, *Edge of Anarchy*.

3. Simmons, *Edge of Anarchy*, chap. 7, esp. 197–202.

4. Simmons, 203.

5. *Two Treatises*, Second Treatise 2.4, p. 270.

6. Second Treatise 2.6, p. 271.

7. Second Treatise 4.23, p. 284.

8. Second Treatise 11.135, p. 357.

9. Second Treatise 11.135, p. 357.

10. Second Treatise 11.135, p. 358.

11. Second Treatise 18.199, p. 398.

12. All quotations from Hume, "Original Contract," 468.

13. Hume, 470 (emphasis added).

14. When it comes to moral contractarianism, Immanuel Kant and John Rawls are both proponents of hypothetical consent.

15. The following draws on prior work I've published on Hobbes that substantiates the claims below. See DeHart, "Leviathan Leashed"; DeHart, "Leviathan"; and the passages that treat Hobbes in DeHart, *Uncovering the Constitution's Moral Design*.

16. See, for instance, Hobbes, *Leviathan* 17.1–2, pp. 109–10 and 20.1–2, p. 127. This submission, however, is not the same as enslavement or being held captive: "for by the word *servant* . . . is not meant a captive (which is kept in prison or bonds till the owner of him that took him, or bought him of one that did, shall consider what to do with him; for such men, commonly called slaves, have no obligation at all, but may break their bonds or the prison, and kill or carry away captive their master, justly), but one that, being taken, hath corporal liberty allowed him, and upon promise not to run away, nor to do violence to his master, is trusted by him" (20.10, pp. 131).

17. On which, see Martinich, *Hobbes*, 18–21; Martinich, "Law and Self-Preservation," 46–47; and Hobbes's account of "Science" in *De Homine* 10.4, p. 41.

18. Martinich, *Hobbes*, 18–21. See also Feser, *Locke*, 24–25.

19. *De Homine* 10.5, pp. 41–43.

20. Martinich, "Law and Self-Preservation in *Leviathan*," 46–47. But see the qualification of this point in Martinich, *Hobbes*, 156–57. That qualification does not affect adversely affect the argument I develop here.

21. DeHart, "Leviathan Leashed," 12–14; DeHart, "Leviathan," 888–90; and DeHart, *Uncovering the Constitution's Moral Design*, 184–86, 219–21.

22. Hobbes, *Leviathan* 11.1, p. 57.

23. Hobbes, 11.2, p. 58.

24. Hobbes, 13.3, p. 75.

25. See Mancur Olson's account of jointness of supply in relation to public or collective goods in *Logic of Collective Action*, 14n21.

26. Thus competition causes individuals in the state of nature to invade each other for the sake of gain. Hobbes, *Leviathan* 13.6–7, p. 76.

27. Gauthier, "Social Contract as Ideology," 145–48.

28. "*Good* and *evil* are names that signify our appetites and aversions. . . . And therefore so long as a man is in the condition of mere nature (which is a condition

of war) . . . private appetite is the measure of good and evil." Hobbes, *Leviathan* 15.40, p. 100. Hobbes also says it "is true" that "every private man is judge of good and evil actions . . . in the condition of mere nature, where there are no civil laws" (29.6, p. 212).

29. Hobbes 13.3, p. 75.
30. Hobbes 31.5, pp. 235–36.
31. Hobbes 13.3, p. 75.
32. This is especially apparent in Hobbes, *De Cive* 1.3, p. 114.
33. Hobbes, *Leviathan* 13.1, p. 74.
34. Hobbes 13.2, pp. 74–75.
35. Hobbes 13.3, p. 75.
36. Hobbes 13.6–7, p. 76.
37. Hobbes 13.4, p. 75.
38. Hobbes's regards those who seek death rather than their own preservation as sick or mad, as we saw in chapter 4 of this volume. See Hampton, "Hobbes and Ethical Naturalism," pp. 42-43.
39. Hobbes, *Leviathan* 13.8, p. 76.
40. Hobbes 13.9, p. 76.
41. Hobbes 13.13, p. 78.
42. Hobbes 14.4, p. 80.
43. Hobbes 13.9, p. 76.
44. Martinich, "Law and Self-Preservation," 45–48.
45. Hobbes, *Leviathan* 13.11, p. 77.
46. Hobbes 13.11, p. 77.
47. Hobbes 13.12, p. 78.
48. Hobbes 14.4, p. 80.
49. Hobbes 14.5, p. 80.
50. Hobbes 14.6, p. 81, 14.15, p. 83, 17.2, p. 106, and 18.4, p. 112.
51. Hobbes 14.7, p. 81, and 17.13, p. 109.
52. Hobbes 18.4, p. 111.
53. Hobbes 28.2, p. 204, and 18.4, p. 111.
54. I believe I owe this point to personal correspondence with A. P. Martinich.
55. Hobbes, *Leviathan* 20.18, p. 135, 21.7, pp. 138–39, 26.6, p. 174, 29.3, p. 211, and 29.9, p. 213.
56. Hobbes, 14.8, p. 82, 14.29, p. 87, and 21.11–17, pp. 141–3.
57. Hobbes, 21.21, p. 144.
58. Hampton, *Hobbes and the Social Contract*, chap. 7, esp. pp. 200–203. See also DeHart, "Covenantal Realism."
59. Again, Hobbes is certainly interested in real consent. But hypothetical consent best fits with his account of science, his treatment of politics as a science, and his claim that the state of nature in the purest science was not historical.
60. Kavka, *Hobbesian Moral and Political Theory*, 22.
61. Hobbes, *Leviathan* 17.15, p. 110.
62. Hobbes 20.1, p. 127.

63. Hobbes 21.10, p. 141. But see Hampton, *Hobbes and the Social Contract*, 173–74.

64. Locke, *Questions Concerning the Law of Nature*, Q. 7, pp. 199–201.

65. I think materialism entails metaphysical nominalism. But, in fact, one can be a metaphysical nominalist while denying that everything that exists is matter in motion (e.g., Ockham, late medieval nominalists, Locke). So nominalism does not require materialism. And when it comes to Hobbes's metaphysics, my argument only depends on his affirmation of metaphysical nominalism and his denial that anything simply or absolutely good or evil exists.

66. See Koons, *Waning of Materialism*; and Barr, *Modern Physics*.

67. Hampton, "Hobbes and Ethical Naturalism," esp. 57–60.

68. See Simmons, *Edge of Anarchy*, chap. 7, 204–6; and Pitkin, "Obligation and Consent—I," esp. 995–7. See also Pitkin, "Obligation and Consent—II." In the second installment, Pitkin speaks of a "new formulation" or "new interpretation of consent theory" derived from Locke's *Second Treatise* and Joseph Tussman's *Obligation and the Body Politic* according to which "legitimate authority is precisely that which *ought* to be obeyed, to which one ought to consent, which deserves obedience and consent, to which rational men considering all relevant facts and issues would consent, to which consent can be justified," 39.

69. See Simmons, *Edge of Anarchy*, 204–6.

70. Simmons, 208–10.

71. I am appropriating a point Simmons raises in his critique of natural duty theories of political obligations or a duty to obey the law. Political obligations are ties of particular citizens to particular regimes and are, therefore, an instance of special obligations. But natural duties refer only to general obligations we owe to everyone. Consequently, general obligations cannot explain why any person p has an obligation to obey the laws of any given country c or why c would have authority over p. See Simmons, chaps. 6 and 7, in Wellman and Simmons, *Is There a Duty*, esp. p. 110.

72. Hampton, *Political Philosophy*, 66. Hampton adopts a paraphrase, "usually attributed to Robert Nozick," of a remark made by Samuel Goldwyn, 69n46. Dworkin makes the same point: "A hypothetical contract is not simply a pale form of an actual contract; it is no contract at all," Dworkin, "Original Position," 501.

73. As Hume argues in the passage from "Original Contract" cited in the first section of this chapter. See also Simmons, *Edge of Anarchy*, chaps. 7 and 8: "Even in liberal democracies" "express consenters . . . who directly and explicitly authorize their societies or governments to make biding law or in other ways control them" are "rare" (219); Green, *Authority of the State*: "Not many of us have, in fact, consented. It follows that the state has legitimate authority only over some of its citizens" (188); Wolterstorff, "Accounting for the Authority of the State," 267–69; and Wolterstorff, "Right of the People to a Democratic State," esp. 227: "Few present-day thinkers, myself included, find the doctrine of consent plausible"; Wolterstorff seeks, instead, "to formulate the doctrine of popular sovereignty and free it of its association with the doctrine of the consent of the governed."

74. See the Naturalization Oath of Allegiance to the United States of America, Code of Federal Regulations, sec. 337.1: *"I hereby declare, on oath, that I absolutely and entirely renounce and abjure all allegiance and fidelity to any foreign prince, potentate, state, or sovereignty, of whom or which I have heretofore been a subject or citizen; that I will support and defend the Constitution and laws of the United States of America against all enemies, foreign and domestic; that I will bear true faith and allegiance to the same; that I will bear arms on behalf of the United States when required by the law; that I will perform noncombatant service in the Armed Forces of the United States when required by the law; that I will perform work of national importance under civilian direction when required by the law; and that I take this obligation freely, without any mental reservation or purpose of evasion; so help me God."*

75. Simmons certainly exempts military oaths taken by Americans in the past under legally enforced conscription: such "military oaths were both taken under threat of punishment for refusal (as were most 'loyalty oaths' in Locke's day) and regarded by those who did take it as a mere formality." *Edge of Anarchy*, 219.

76. A friend who wishes to remain anonymous undertook adding up the number of actual, express consenters in the United States a number of years ago. His informal count suggested to him that the percent might be as high as 40 percent in the United States. Suppose for the sake of argument we set 40 percent as the upward bound. Even so, 40 percent is only a substantial minority of the population. And modern states take themselves to have authority not merely over a substantial minority of their population but, rather, over everyone within their boundaries. Clearly 40 percent gets us nowhere near the 100 percent modern states claim the right to govern. Simmons, on the contrary, holds there is no evidence of meaningful consent for even a substantial minority of modern democratic (or putatively consent-based) states. Simmons, *Edge of Anarchy*, chap. 8, sec. 1–3, pp. 218-48 and also 8.4, p. 250.

77. See Simmons, *Edge of Anarchy*: "The pledge of allegiance to the flag . . . taken by American schoolchildren (and some others), can hardly bind persons who have yet to reach the 'age of consent'; and it is . . . so mechanical a performance for most that it could not be taken seriously as the extremely important act of making oneself a citizen." (219).

78. Locke famously observes, "every Man, that hath any Possession, or Enjoyment, of any part of the Dominions of any Government, doth thereby give his *tacit consent*, and is as far forth obliged to Obedience to the Laws of that Government, during such Enjoyment, as anyone under it; whether this his Possession be of land, to him and his Heirs for ever, or a Lodging only for a Week; or whether it be barely travelling freely on the Highway; and in Effect, it reaches as far as the being of anyone within the Territories of that Government," Second Treatise 8.119, p. 348. On voting, see the treatment and rejection of the position in Simmons, *Edge of Anarchy*, 218–25.

79. Simmons, 221.

80. Simmons, 221. Moreover, "one would have to assume that since what is typically voted *for* is a candidate for a political office of limited term, consent is given only to the authority of that candidate for that term" (221).

81. As Simmons observes, taking "having a right" to vote for consent "appears to conflate having the opportunity to consent with actually consenting"—*at best*. Simmons, *Edge of Anarchy*, 221.

82. Simmons, 226–28.

83. Simmons, 222.

84. *Crito*, in Plato, *Trials of Socrates*, lines 51d–52d, pp. 74–75.

85. In contrast to ancient Athens and a number of other cities (poleis) in ancient Greece, emigration from one community to another in colonial New England, at least in the seventeenth century, required getting permission from the community one was leaving. See Shain, *Myth of American Individualism*, 88–89; and Handlin and Handlin, *Liberty and Power*, 218.

86. Simmons, *Edge of Anarchy*, 227.

87. Simmons, 233. Hume asks rhetorically, "Can we seriously say that a poor peasant or artisan has a free choice to leave his country, when he knows no foreign language or manners, and lives from day to day, by the small wages he acquires?" He answers, "We may as well assert that a man, by remaining in a vessel, freely consents to the dominion of the master; though he was carried on board while asleep and must leap into the ocean and perish, the moment he leaves her." "Of the Original Contract," cited in Simmons, *Edge of Anarchy*, 233. Says Simmons, "Even when citizens understand the significance of the choice between residence and emigration . . . the latter option is not really one that is open to many citizens. Those who are poor or unskilled, for instance, could not emigrate without suffering disastrous consequences. And if a person is required to choose between two courses of action, of which only one is a real possibility, that person cannot really be understood to choose freely at all." Moreover, "It is not only the poor and unskilled for whom emigration is an extremely unattractive option. For most of us the most important things in our lives, like home, family, friends, style of life—are firmly tied to our countries of residence . . . it is a very hard thing to ask anyone, and especially to ask one just arrived at the age of consent, to seriously consider leaving all this behind for the uncertainties and alienation of emigration" (233–34).

88. Simmons, *Edge of Anarchy*, 202; and *Moral Principles and Political Obligations*, 83–95.

89. See Dunn, "Consent in the Political Theory of John Locke," in *Political Obligation*, 34–35, 47; and the treatment of Dunn's argument in Simmons, *Edge of Anarchy*, 210–17.

90. As Simmons notes, in *Essays on the Law of Nature* (Simmons cites the 1954 von Leyden edition of Locke's reflections on natural law; I've been quoting from the 1990 translation published as *Questions Concerning the Law of Nature*), Locke distinguishes "positive consent" from "natural consent" where the latter "occurs when people simply conform their actions to the customs of social life or 'give assent' to prevailing opinions." Simmons, *Edge of Anarchy*, 213. And according to Locke, natural consent is "by no means a sufficient reason for creating an obligation." Locke, *Essays on the Law of Nature*, 177, cited in Simmons, *Edge of Anarchy*, 213.

91. On "the gunman situation writ large," see Hart, *Concept of Law*, 6–7.

NOTES FOR CHAPTER 9

92. Simmons, *Edge of Anarchy*, 207 (in addition to the central paragraph, see also notes 23 and 26); and Simmons's subsequent treatment of Dunn's account of *acquiescence* (210–17).

93. "Authority on the part of those who give orders and make regulations is: a right to be obeyed. More amply, we may say: authority is a regular right to be obeyed in a domain of decision." Anscombe, "Authority of the State," 132. According to Hampton, "Whatever [authority] is, it is not the same as (sheer) power. Authority is about the *entitlement* to rule; mere power isn't enough to supply entitlement. . . . Rulers are said to have not only the power to make and enforce rules but also the entitlement to do so. And when they do so, they are said to have (political) authority." Hampton, *Political Philosophy*, 4. In the next paragraph, she notes, "Connected to this entitlement is the obligation the subjects have to obey the (authoritative) ruler's commands." Finally, Wolterstorff: "To have the authority to do certain things . . . is to have the permission-right to do certain things and the claim-right to be free to do those things. Intrinsic to most offices, perhaps indeed to all, is such authority . . . among the rights intrinsic to an office will often be the authority to issue commands of a certain kind." Wolterstorff, *Justice*, 270–71.

94. "Right consisteth in the liberty to do or to forbear." Hobbes, *Leviathan* 14.3, p. 79. See my treatment of Hobbes's understanding of rights as sheer liberties in DeHart, *Uncovering the Constitution's Moral Design*, 219–21.

95. Hobbes, *Leviathan* 21.12–17, pp. 142–3.

96. Hobbes 14.8, p. 82, and 14.29, p. 87.

97. Thus, "a man that is commanded as a soldier to fight against the enemy . . . may nevertheless in many cases refuse without injustice" yet "his sovereign have right enough to punish his refusal with death." Hobbes 21.16, p. 142. Consider as well that the exercise of the right of nature in the state of nature entails no obligation for others in that state to respect its exercise, since no action in that state of affairs is just or unjust, right or wrong. Hobbes 13.13, p. 78.

98. Though on his view the sovereign may have a right to command, even to demand my compliance, *and* I may have an obligation to obey (so long as what the sovereign commands does not place my preservation in jeopardy). These may instantiate together. But the ground of the obligation is my consent. Since he defines right, as such, as the liberty to do or forbear and given that in many possible instances the right of the sovereign to command and the obligation of subjects to obey may not instantiate together, it follows that on his view rights qua rights are not correlative to obligations.

99. See Anscombe, "Source of the Authority of the State," 138–46; and Wolterstorff, *Justice*, 241–63, where he defends a version of the position advanced in Hohfeld, *Fundamental Legal Conceptions*. Wolterstorff defends what he calls the "weak Hohfeld thesis," according to which "to every claim right there is a correlative duty," 249. In *Uncovering the Constitution's Moral Design* (209-17) I lay out and defend Anscombe's account of authority as a claim-right against an alternative account advanced by H. L. A. Hart ("Are There Any Natural Rights?") and Richard

Tuck (*Natural Rights Theories*, esp. 5–7, on the distinction between passive and active rights).

100. Simmons, *Edge of Anarchy*, 200, 204, 216, 228.

101. Suárez, *Treatise on Laws* 3.2.3, p. 430. On the Salamancan Thomists and natural liberty, see Skinner, *Foundations* 2:155–57.

102. Filmer, *Patriarcha*, in *Patriarcha and Other Writings*, chap. 1.

103. Oakley, *Kingship*; and Oakley, *Empty Bottles of Gentilism*, ix–xiii, 1–10.

104. Insofar as it has any normative implications, human equality is an ontological and not merely doxastic matter.

105. Wolterstorff, "Right of the People to a Democratic State," esp. 242–44.

106. See Aristotle, *Politics* (trans. Sinclair), 1.12.1259a37–1259b17, 2.2.1261a22, 3.5.1277b7, 3.6.1279a8.

107. On which, see Althusius, *Politica*; and Elazar, *Covenant & Commonwealth*, esp. chap. 16.

108. Althusius, *Politica*, chaps. 2–4, pp. 27–38.

109. Althusius 5.1, p. 39.

110. Althusius 9.1, p. 66, and 9.5, p. 67.

111. Althusius 9.18–21, p. 70–72.

112. Althusius 9.5, p. 67.

113. On the way political order was built from the ground up in the American context, see DeHart and Oakerson, "Are Local Governments Mere Creatures of the States?" See also Lutz, *Origins*, 25–28, 31–32, 42–49. In *Fountainhead of Federalism*, McCoy and Baker write, "Primary social entities such as families, congregations, occupational guilds, and commercial organizations exist by virtue of the tacit and explicit compacts defining relations among members and committing participants to the group. More comprehensive social structures are based on compacts among less inclusive groups. In political organization, a town is made up of a compact among families, a province of a compact among towns, a commonwealth of a compact among provinces, and international relations of compacts among commonwealths" (13) After a slightly more elaborate account of development from the ground up later in the volume, they write, "In each case [i.e., at each level of association], a covenant creates the more comprehensive level of political order. But the more inclusive entity does not negate the significance, participation, and consent of the covenanted groups that comprise it. Each level retains its integrity as an operative community with appropriate governmental functions" (58). There is, I think, a need here for building blocks that each have agency (and so jurisdiction) of their own.

114. DeHart and Oakerson, "Are Local Governments Mere Creatures," argues this is not just a matter of historical chronology. What matters is the whether the regime is designed from the ground up. The Northwest Ordinance of 1785 did something like this for the Northwest Territory (55). Political theorists and constitutional architects interested in building from the ground up would surely benefit from engaging Ostrom, *Political Theory*; Ostrom, *Meaning of American Federalism*; and Oakerson, "Reciprocity." To be sure, the argument of this chapter is somewhat at

odds with Ostrom's "individualistic assumption about political experience" (*Political Theory*, 30–35), though Ostrom also holds that "conceiving of individuals as being the basic units exercising responsibility in political relationships does not presume ~~that individuals as such exist apart from ordered social relationships with others in~~ a society" (34).

115. See my argument in DeHart, "What Is a Republic?"

116. In the debate over equal representation of the states in the Senate conducted from June 28 to July 2, 1787, at the Constitutional Convention, Hamilton rhetorically asked, "But as States are a collection of individual men which ought we to respect most, the rights of the people composing them, or of the artificial beings resulting from the composition[?] Nothing could be more preposterous or absurd than to sacrifice the former to the latter," Ketcham, *Constitutional Convention Debates*, 79–80. If Hamilton means to suggests political incorporations are not only constructed but fictions or in some sense lack genuine ontological status, then I think he is clearly mistaken. On corporate wholes and agency, consider March and Olsen, "The New Institutionalism," esp. 739–40.

117. "Right of the People to a Democratic State," 227. Wolterstorff finds the doctrine of consent implausible and also accepts the "ontology implicit in the doctrine *popular* sovereignty," which was "alive and well at the time of the American Revolution" and reaffirmed in Lincoln's Gettysburg Address (emphasis ibid).

Conclusion

1. See DeHart, "Covenantal Realism."

2. That is surely the implication of this passage from Locke's *Questions Concerning the Law of Nature*: "Without the law of nature the other foundation of human society collapses as well—that is, the keeping of contracts and agreements, for there would be no reason to expect a man to abide by an agreement, because he made a promise, when a more advantageous arrangement offered itself elsewhere, unless the obligation to fulfill promises came from nature and not from the will of men" (115–17).

3. Oakley, "Medieval Theories of Natural Law."

4. See DeHart, "Nature's Lawgiver"; and DeHart, "Reason and Will in Natural Law." See also Evans, *God & Moral Obligation*.

5. By resolving the de jure problem for consent theory, I refer only to consent as a necessary condition of political authority and obligation. That does not mean other conditions sufficient for political authority and obligation have been specified.

6. As David Novak writes,

Truly, without the presupposition of more original social or communal bonds, the idea of the social contract becomes incoherent since there are no real persons to come to it. Only full persons and not abstractions can contract with one another in any substantial way. Persons are social beings by nature, not by mutual agreement. There cannot be contracting persons, as distinct from humanoid phantoms, who are not *already* socialized. . . . Thus no contract between persons can create a primal community because a primal community, one's original society, hovers *around* persons before there are any real agreements *between* persons within it. . . . However, this pre-contractual, natural priority does not preclude a subsequent social contract. (Novak, *Jewish Social Contract*, 11–12)

I agree completely with this argument. However, Novak's rejection of the priority of the good (in *Covenantal Rights*, as noted earlier) suggests to me that he also rejects the implicit ontology necessary for the intelligibility of corporate wholes.

7. Plato, *Republic*, 6.507b1–10, p. 202.

Bibliography

Adams, Marilyn McCord. *William of Ockham*. 2 vols. Notre Dame: University of Notre Dame Press, 1989.

Adams, Robert Merrihew. "Divine Command Metaethics Modified Again." In *The Virtue of Faith*, 128–43.

———. *Finite and Infinite Goods: A Framework for Ethics*. Oxford: Oxford University Press, 2002.

———. *Leibniz: Determinist, Theist, Idealist*. Oxford: Oxford University Press, 1998.

———. "A Modified Divine Command Theory of Ethical Wrongness." In *The Virtue of Faith*, 97–122.

———. *The Virtue of Faith and Other Essays in Philosophical Theology*. Oxford: Oxford University Press, 1987.

———. *What Is & What Is in Itself: A Systematic Ontology*. Oxford: Oxford University Press, 2021.

Althusius, Johannes. *Politica: An Abridged Translation of Politics Methodically Set Forth and Illustrated with Sacred and Profane Examples*. Edited and translated by Frederick S. Carney. Indianapolis: Liberty Fund, 1995.

Angeles, Peter A. *The HarperCollins Dictionary of Philosophy*. 2nd ed. New York: HarperCollins, 1992.

Anscombe, G. E. M. *Ethics, Religion, and Politics*. Vol. III of *Collected Philosophical Papers*. Oxford, UK: Basil Blackwell, 1981.

———. "The Justice of the Present War Examined." In *Ethics, Religion, and Politics*, 72–81.

———. "Modern Moral Philosophy." In *Ethics, Religion, and Politics*, 26–42.

———. "On the Source of the Authority of the State." In *Ethics, Religion, and Politics*, 130–55.

Anstey, Peter R., ed. *The Philosophy of John Locke: New Perspectives*. London: Routledge, 2003.

Aquinas, Thomas. *On Law, Morality, and Politics*. Edited by William P. Baumgarth and Richard J. Regan, SJ. Translated by Richard J. Regan. Indianapolis: Hackett Publishing Company, Inc., 1988.

————. *The Political Ideas of St. Thomas Aquinas*. Edited by Dino Bigongiari. New York: The Free Press, 1997.

————. *Questiones Disputatae de Veritate, Questions 21–29.* Translated by Robert W. Schmidt, SJ. Chicago: Henry Regnery Company, 1954.

————. *Summa Theologiae*. Vol. 28, *Law and Political Theory* (Ia2ae. 90–97). Edited by Thomas Gilby. London: Blackfriars in conjunction with Eyre & Spottiswoode in London and McGraw Hill in New York, 1966.

Aristotle. *Nichomachean Ethics*. Translated by Martin Ostwald. Englewood Cliffs, NJ: Prentice Hall, 1962.

————. *Nicomachean Ethics*. In *The Complete Works of Aristotle: The Revised Oxford Translation*, edited by Jonathan Barnes, vol. 2, 1729–827. Princeton, NJ: Princeton University Press, 1984.

————. *Politics*. Edited and translated by Ernest Barker. Oxford: Oxford University Press, 1946.

————. *Politics*. Translated by T. A. Sinclair. Revised by Trevor J. Saunders. London: Penguin Books, 1981.

————. *On Rhetoric: A Theory of Civic Discourse*. Translated by George A. Kennedy. Oxford: Oxford University Press, 1991.

Arkes, Hadley. *First Things: An Inquiry into the First Principles of Morals and Justice*. Princeton, NJ: Princeton University Press, 1986.

————. *The Philosopher in the City: The Moral Dimension of Urban Politics*. Princeton, NJ: Princeton University Press, 1981.

Augustine. *The City of God*. New York: Modern Library, 1993.

Austin, John. *The Province of Jurisprudence Determined* and *The Uses of the Study of Jurisprudence*. Introduction by H. L. A. Hart. Indianapolis: Hackett Publishing Company, Inc., 1998.

Babbitt, Irvin. *Democracy and Leadership*. 1924. Indianapolis: Liberty Fund, 1979.

Baier, Annette C. "Pilgrim's Progress." *Canadian Journal of Philosophy* 18, no. 2 (June 1988): 315–30.

Bakke, O. M. *When Children Became People: The Birth of Childhood in Early Christianity*. Minneapolis: Fortress Press, 2005.

Barr, Stephen M. *Modern Physics and Ancient Faith*. Notre Dame, IN: University of Notre Dame Press, 2003.

Barrow, John D., and Frank J. Tipler. *The Anthropic Cosmological Principle*. Rev. ed. Oxford: Oxford University Press, 1988.

Bellarmine, Robert. *De Laicis (On Laymen or Secular People)*. In *On Temporal and Spiritual Authority*, edited and translated by Stefania Tutino, 1–120. Indianapolis: Liberty Fund, 2012.

Bensel, Richard Franklin. *The Founding of Modern States*. Cambridge: Cambridge University Press, 2022.

Bentham, Jeremy. *Of Laws in General*. In *The Collected Works of Jeremy Bentham: Principles of Legislation*, edited by H. L. A. Hart. London: Athlone Press, 1970.

Bergmann, Michael, Michael J. Murray, and Michael C. Rea, eds. *Divine Evil?: The Moral Character of the God of Abraham*. Oxford: Oxford University Press, 2011.

Bien, Günther, and Hans Maier. "Demokratie." In *Historisches Wörterbuch der Philosophie*, edited by Joachim Ritter, Karlfried Grunder, and Gottfried Gabriel, 2:50–55. Basel, Germany: Scheidegger and Spiess, 1972.

Birch, Bruce, ed. *The De Sacramento Altaris of Ockham*. Burlington, IA: Lutheran Literary Board, 1930.

Bobbio, Norberto. *Thomas Hobbes and the Natural Law Tradition*. Translated by Daniela Gobetti. Chicago: University of Chicago Press, 1993.

Bodin, Jean. *On Sovereignty*. Translated by Julian H. Franklin. Cambridge: Cambridge University Press, 1992.

BonJour, Laurence. "Against Materialism." In *The Waning of Materialism*, edited by Robert C. Koons and George Bealer, 3–23. Oxford: Oxford University Press, 2010.

Budziszewski, J. *Commentary on Thomas Aquinas's "Treatise on Law."* Cambridge: Cambridge University Press, 2014.

———. "Comments on Nicholas Wolterforff's " 'For the Authorities Are God's Servants': Is a Theistic Account of Political Authority Still Viable, or Have Humanist Accounts Won the Day.' " Delivered at the Theology, Morality, and Public Life Conference at the University of Chicago Divinity School, Chicago, March 2003.

———. "Two Theories, Not One." In *Theology and Public Philosophy: Four Conversations*, edited by Kenneth L. Grasso and Cecilia Rodriguez Castillo, 69-74. Lanham, MD: Lexington Books, 2012.

———. *The Line Through the Heart: Natural Law as Fact, Theory, and Sign of Contradiction*. Wilmington, DE: ISI Books, 2009.

———. *The Resurrection of Nature: Political Theory and the Human Character*. Ithaca, NY: Cornell University Press, 1986.

———. *The Revenge of Conscience*. Dallas, TX: Spence Publishing Company, 1999.

———. "Two Theories, Not One." In *Theology and Public Philosophy: Four Conversations*, edited by Kenneth L. Grasso and Cecilia Rodriguez Castillo. Lanham, MD: Lexington Books, 2012.

———. *What We Can't Not Know: A Guide*. Rev. ed. San Francisco: Ignatius Press, 2011.

———. *Written on the Heart: The Case for Natural Law*. Downers Grove, IL: InterVarsity Press, 1997.

Bullinger, Heinrich. *De testamento seu foedere Dei unico et aeterno*. 1534. Translated as "A Brief Exposition of the One and Eternal Testament or Covenant of God" in McCoy and Baker, *Fountainhead of Federalism*, 99–138.

Cicero. *"The Republic" and "The Laws."* Translated by Niall Rudd. Oxford: Oxford University Press, 1998.

Clark, David W. "Voluntarism and Rationalism in the Ethics of Ockham." *Franciscan Studies* 31 (1971): 72–87.

———. "William of Ockham on Right Reason." *Speculum* 48, no. 1 (January 1973): 13–36.

Clifford, William. "The Ethics of Belief." In Peterson, Hasker, Reichenbach, and Basinger, *Philosophy of Religion*, 104–9.

Colman, John. *John Locke's Moral Philosophy*. Edinburgh, Scotland: Edinburgh University Press, 1983.

———. "Locke's Empiricist Theory of the Law of Nature." In Anstey, *The Philosophy of John Locke*, 106–26.

Condren, Conal. "Resistance and Sovereignty in Lawson's *Politica*." *Historical Journal* 24, no. 3 (September 1981): 673–81.

Connolly, William E. *Political Theory and Modernity*. Oxford, UK: Basil Blackwell, 1988.

Conklin, Carli N. *The Pursuit of Happiness in the Founding Era: An Intellectual History*. Columbia: University of Missouri Press, 2019.

Cooke, Paul D. *Hobbes and Christianity: Reassessing the Bible in "Leviathan."* Lanham, MD: Rowman & Littlefield Publishers, Inc., 1996.

Copleston, Frederick. *A History of Philosophy*. Vol. 1, *Greece and Rome: From the Pre-Socratics to Plotinus*. New York: Doubleday, 1993.

———. *A History of Philosophy*. Vol. 3, *Ockham to Suárez*. London: Burns Oates & Washbourne Ltd., 1953.

———. *A History of Philosophy*. Vol. 5, *Modern Philosophy: The British Philosophers from Hobbes to Hume*. New York: Doubleday, 1993.

Corthals, Angelique, Antonius Koller, Dwight W. Martin, Robert Rieger, Emily I. Chen, Mario Bernaski, Gabriella Recagno, and Liliana M. Dávos. "Detecting the Immune System Response of a 500-Year-Old Inca Mummy." *PLoS One* 7, no. 7 (July 25, 2012): 1–9.

Courtenay, William J. *Capacity and Volition: A History of the Distinction of Absolute and Ordained Powers*. Bergamo, Italy: Pierluigi Lubrina Editore, 1990.

———. "Nominalism and Late Medieval Religion." In Trinkaus and Oberman, *The Pursuit of Holiness*, 26–59.

Covington, Jesse, Bryan McGraw, and Micah Watson, eds. *Natural Law and Evangelical Political Thought*. Lanham, MD: Lexington Books, 2002.

Cuneo, Terence. *The Normative Web: An Argument for Moral Realism*. Oxford: Oxford University Press, 2007.

———. *Speech and Morality: On the Metaethical Implications of Speaking*. Oxford: Oxford University Press, 2014.

Curley, Edwin. "The God of Abraham, Isaac, and Jacob." In *Divine Evil?: The Moral Character of the God of Abraham*, edited by Michael Bergmann, Michael J. Murray, and Michael C. Rea, 58–78. Oxford: Oxford University Press, 2011.

Dahl, Robert A. "The Behavioral Approach in Political Science: Epitaph for a Monument to a Successful Protest." *American Political Science Review* 55, no. 4 (December 1961): 763–72.

Davies, Paul. *God and the New Physics*. New York: Simon and Schuster, 1983.

———. *The Mind of God*. New York: Simon and Schuster, 1993.

d'Entréves, Passerin. *The Notion of the State*. Oxford: Oxford University Press, 1967.

DeHart, Paul R. "Covenantal Realism: The Self-Referential Incoherency of Conventional Social Contract Theory and the Necessity of Consent." *Perspectives in Political Science* 41, no. 3 (2012): 165–77.

———. "The Dangerous Life: Natural Justice and the Rightful Subversion of the State." *Polity* 38, no. 3 (July 2006): 369–94.

———. "Fractured Foundations: The Contradiction between Locke's Ontology and His Moral Philosophy." *Locke Studies* 12 (2012): 111–48.

———. "Leviathan." In *The New Catholic Encyclopedia Supplement, 2012–2013: Ethics and Philosophy*, edited by Robert L. Fastiggi, 888–90. Detroit: Gale, Cengage, 2013.

———. "Leviathan Leashed: The Incoherence of Absolute Sovereign Power." *Critical Review* 25, no. 1 (September 2013): 1–37.

———. "Nature's Lawgiver: On Natural Law as Law." *Catholic Social Science Review* 22 (2017): 53–71.

———. "Political Philosophy after the Collapse of Classical, Epistemic Foundationalism." In DeHart and Holloway, *Reason, Revelation, and the Civic Order*, 33–63.

———. "Reason and Will in Natural Law." In Covington, McGraw, and Watson, *Natural Law*, 125–52.

———. "The Return of the Sacral King: The Christian Subversion of the Roman Empire and the Modern State." *Catholic Social Science Review* 25 (2020): 51–65.

———. *Uncovering the Constitution's Moral Design*. Columbia: University of Missouri Press, 2007.

———. "The U.S. Constitution of 1789 and Natural Law: Concord or Conflict." Delivered to the Constitutional Thought and History Seminar at Pembroke College, Oxford University, February 26, 2015.

———. "What Is a Republic?" *National Affairs*, no. 56 (Summer 2023): 152–64.

———. "Whose Social Contract?: Hobbes versus Hooker and the Realist Contract Tradition." *Catholic Social Science Review* 26 (2021): 3–21.

———. "Why *Why Liberalism Failed* Fails as an Account of the American Order." *Catholic Social Science Review* 24 (2019): 19–31.

DeHart, Paul R., and Carson Holloway, eds. *Reason, Revelation, and the Civic Order: Political Philosophy and the Claims of Faith.* Dekalb: Northern Illinois University Press, 2014.

DeHart, Paul R., and Ronald J. Oakerson. "Are Local Governments Mere Creatures of the States?" *National Affairs*, no. 51 (Spring 2022): 51–64.

Deneen, Patrick. "Liberalism's Logic and America's Challenge: A Reply to Schlueter and Muñoz." *Public Discourse*, March 6, 2014.

———. *Why Liberalism Failed.* New Haven, CT: Yale University Press, 2017.

Dunn, John. *Political Obligation in Its Historical Context: Essays in Political Theory.* Cambridge: Cambridge University Press, 1980.

———. *The Political Thought of John Locke: An Historical Account of the Argument of the "Two Treatises of Government."* Cambridge: Cambridge University Press, 1969.

Dworkin, Ronald. *Justice for Hedgehogs.* Cambridge, MA: The Belknap Press of Harvard University Press, 2011.

———. *A Matter of Principle.* Cambridge, MA: Harvard University Press, 1985.

———. "Objectivity and Truth: You'd Better Believe It." *Philosophy & Public Affairs* 25, no. 2 (Spring 1996): 87–139.

———. "The Original Position." *University of Chicago Law Review* 40, no. 3 (Spring 1973): 500–533.

Dyer, Justin Buckley. *Natural Law and the Antislavery Constitutional Tradition.* Cambridge: Cambridge University Press, 2012.

Elazar, Daniel Judah. *Covenant & Commonwealth: From Christian Separation through the Protestant Reformation.* Vol. 2 of *The Covenant Tradition in Politics.* New Brunswick, NJ: Transaction Publishers, 1996.

———. *Covenant & Polity in Biblical Israel: Biblical Foundations & Jewish Expressions.* Vol. I of *The Covenant Tradition in Politics.* New Brunswick, NJ: Transaction Publishers, 1995.

Evans, C. Stephen. *God & Moral Obligation.* Oxford: Oxford University Press, 2013.

———. *Kierkegaard's Ethic of Love: Divine Commands & Moral Obligations.* Oxford: Oxford University Press, 2004.

Fastiggi, Robert L., ed. *The New Catholic Encyclopedia Supplement, 2012–2013: Ethics and Philosophy.* 4 vols. Detroit: Gale, Cengage, 2013.

Feser, Edward. *Aristotle's Revenge: The Metaphysical Foundations of Physical and Biological Science.* Neunkirchen-Seelscheid, Germany: Editiones Scholasticae, 2019.

———. *The Last Superstition.* South Bend, IN: St. Augustine's Press, 2008.

———. *Locke*. Oxford, UK: Oneworld, 2007.

———. "Motion in Aristotle, Newton, and Einstein." In *Neo-Scholastic Essays*, 3–27. South Bend, IN: St. Augustine's Press, 2015.

Filmer, Robert. *Patriarcha and Other Writings*. Edited by Johann P. Sommerville. Cambridge: Cambridge University Press, 1991.

Finnis, John. *Natural Law and Natural Rights*. Oxford: Oxford University Press, 1980.

———. *Natural Law & Natural Rights*. 2d ed. Oxford: Oxford University Press, 2011.

Firestone, Chris L. and Nathan A. Jacobs, eds. *The Persistence of the Sacred in Modern Thought*. Notre Dame: University of Notre Dame Press, 2012.

Fisher, Carlton. "Because God Says So." In *Christian Theism and the Problems of Philosophy*, edited by Michael D. Beaty, 355–77. Notre Dame, IN: University of Notre Dame Press, 1990.

Fishkin, James S. *The Dialogue of Justice: Toward a Self-Reflective Society*. New Haven, CT: Yale University Press, 1992.

Flew, Anthony. *There Is a God: How the World's Most Notorious Atheist Changed His Mind*. New York: HarperOne, 2007.

Forde, Steven. *Locke, Science, and Politics*. Cambridge: Cambridge University Press, 2013.

Forster, Greg. "Divine Law and Human Law in Hobbes's *Leviathan*." *History of Political Thought* 24, no. 2 (Summer 2003): 189–217.

Förster, Winfried. *Thomas Hobbes und Der Puritanismus: Grundlagen und Grudfragen Seiner Staatslehre*. Berlin: Duncker & Humblot, 1969.

Franklin, Julian H. *John Locke and the Theory of Sovereignty: Mixed Monarchy and the Right of Resistance in the Political Thought of the English Revolution*. Cambridge: Cambridge University Press, 1978.

Frohnen, Bruce, ed. *The American Republic: Primary Sources*. Indianapolis: Liberty Fund, 2002.

Gagarin, Michael, and Paul Woodruff, eds. *Early Greek Political Thought from Homer to the Sophists*. Cambridge: Cambridge University Press, 1995.

Gauthier, David. "Hobbes: The Laws of Nature." *Pacific Philosophical Quarterly* 82 (2001): 258–84.

———. *Hobbes and Political Contractarianism: Selected Writings*. Edited by Susan Dimock, Claire Finkelstein, and Christopher W. Morris. Oxford: Oxford University Press, 2022.

———. "Hobbes's Social Contract." *Noûs* 22, no. 1 (March 1988): 71–82.

———. *The Logic of Leviathan: The Moral and Political Theory of Thomas Hobbes*. Oxford: Oxford University Press, 1969.

———. "Moral Artifice." *Canadian Journal of Philosophy* 18, no. 2 (June 1988): 385–418.

———. *Morals by Agreement*. Oxford: Oxford University Press, 1987.

―――. "The Social Contract as Ideology." *Philosophy & Public Affairs* 6, no. 2 (1977): 130–64.

―――. "Thomas Hobbes: Moral Theorist." *Journal of Philosophy* 76, no. 10 (October 1979): 547–59.

―――. "Why Contractarianism?" In Vallentyne, *Contractarianism and Rational Choice*, 15-30.

George, Robert P. *In Defense of Natural Law.* Oxford: Oxford University Press, 1999.

Gert, Bernard. *Hobbes: Prince of Peace.* Malden, MA: Polity Press, 2010.

―――. "Hobbes, Mechanism, and Egoism." *Philosophical Quarterly* 15, no. 61 (October 1965): 341–49.

―――. "Hobbes and Psychological Egoism." *Journal of the History of Ideas* 28, no. 4 (October–December 1967): 503–20.

―――. "Hobbes on Reason." *Pacific Philosophical Quarterly* 82, nos. 3–4 (2001): 243–57.

―――. "Hobbes's Account of Reason." *Journal of Philosophy* 76, no. 10 (October 1979): 559–61.

Gierke, Otto von. *The Development of Political Theory.* Translated by Bernard Freyd. New York: W. W. Norton & Company Inc., 1939.

―――. *Natural Law and the Theory of Society, 1500 to 1800.* Translated by Ernest Barker. Cambridge: Cambridge University Press, 1950.

―――. *Political Theories of the Middle Ages.* Translated by Frederic W. Maitland. Cambridge: Cambridge University Press, 1951.

Gillespie, Michael Allen. *The Theological Origins of Modernity.* Princeton, NJ: Princeton University Press, 2008.

Gilson, Étienne. *From Aristotle to Darwin and Back Again: A Journey in Final Causality, Species, and Evolution.* Notre Dame, IN: University of Notre Dame Press, 1984.

―――. *History of Christian Philosophy in the Middle Ages.* Washington, DC: Catholic University of America Press, 2019.

Grabill, Stephen J. *Rediscovering the Natural Law in Reformed Theological Ethics.* Grand Rapids, MI: William B. Eerdmans Publishing Company, 2006.

Grasso, Kenneth L., and Cecilia Rodriguez Castillo, eds. *Theology and Public Philosophy: Four Conversations.* Lanham, MD: Lexington Books, 2012.

Green, Leslie. *The Authority of the State.* Oxford: Oxford University Press, 1988.

Gregg, Samuel. *Reason, Faith, and the Struggle for Western Civilization.* Washington, DC: Regnery Gateway, 2019.

Grisez, Germain, Joseph Boyle, and John Finnis. "Practical Principles, Moral Truth, and Ultimate Ends." *American Journal of Jurisprudence* 31, no. 1 (1987): 99–151.

Grotius, Hugo. *The Rights of War and Peace.* 1738. Edited by Richard Tuck. Translated by John Morrice. Indianapolis: Liberty Fund, 2005.

Haakonssen, Knud. *Natural Law and Moral Philosophy: From Grotius to the Scottish Enlightenment.* Cambridge: Cambridge University Press, 1996.
Habermas, Jürgen. *Between Facts and Norms.* Translated by William Rehg. Cambridge, MA: MIT University Press, 1996.
———. *Justification and Application.* Translated by Ciaran P. Cronin. Cambridge, MA: MIT University Press, 1993.
———. *Moral Consciousness and Communicative Action.* Translated by Christian Lenhardt and Shierry Weber Nicholsen. Cambridge, MA: MIT University Press, 1990.
Haldane, John. "Voluntarism and Realism in Medieval Ethics." *Journal of Medical Ethics* 15, no. 1 (1989): 39–44.
Hall, Mark David. *Roger Sherman and the Creation of the American Republic.* Oxford: Oxford University Press, 2013.
Hamilton, Alexander. "The Farmer Refuted" (1775). In *Classics of American Political and Constitutional Thought,* edited by Scott J. Hammond, Kevin R. Hardwick, and Howard L. Lubert, 257-63. Vol. 1 of *Classics of American Political and Constitutional Thought.* Indianapolis: Hackett Publishing Company, Inc., 2007.
Hampton, Jean. *The Authority of Reason.* Cambridge: Cambridge University Press, 1998.
———. "Forgiveness, Resentment, and Hatred." In *Forgiveness and Mercy,* edited by Murphy and Hampton, 35–87. Cambridge: Cambridge University Press, 1988.
———. "Hobbes and Ethical Naturalism." *Philosophical Perspectives* 6 (1992): 333–53.
———. *Hobbes and the Social Contract Tradition.* Cambridge: Cambridge University Press, 1986.
———. *Political Philosophy.* Boulder, CO: Westview Press, 1997.
———. "Should Political Philosophy be Done Without Metaphysics?" *Ethics* 99, no. 4 (July 1989): 791–814.
———. "The Two Faces of Contractarian Thought." In Vallentyne, *Contractarianism and Rational Choice,* 149-62..
Hanby, Michael. "The Birth of the Liberal Order and the Death of God: A Reply to Robert Reilly." *New Polity* 2, no. 1 (February 2021): 54–85.
Handlin, Oscar, and Lilian Handlin. *Liberty and Power, 1600–1700.* Vol. 1 of *Liberty in America: 1600 to the Present.* New York: Harper & Row, 1986.
Handwerk, Brian. "Inca Child Sacrifice Victims Were Drugged." *National Geographic,* July 29, 2013.
Hardin, Garrett. "The Tragedy of the Commons." *Science* 162, no. 3859 (December 13, 1968): 1243–48.
Hare, John E. *God and Morality: A Philosophical History.* Oxford, UK: Wiley-Blackwell, 2009.

——. *God's Call: Moral Realism, God's Commands, & Human Autonomy*. Grand Rapids, MI: William B. Eerdmans Company, 2001.

Harper, Kyle. "Christianity and the Roots of Human Dignity in Late Antiquity." In Shah and Hertzke, *Christianity and Freedom*, vol. 1, 123–48.

Harris, Ian. *The Mind of John Locke: A Study of Political Theory in its Intellectual Setting*. Cambridge: Cambridge University Press, 1994.

Hart, H. L. A. "Are There Any Natural Rights?" *The Philosophical Review* 64, no. 2 (April 1955): 175–91.

——. *The Concept of Law*. 2nd ed. Oxford: Oxford University Press, 1994.

——. *Essays on Bentham: Studies in Jurisprudence and Political Theory*. Oxford: Clarendon Press, 1982.

——. "Positivism and the Separation of Law and Morals." *Harvard Law Review* 71, no. 4 (February 1958): 593–629.

Hill, John Lawrence. *After the Natural Law: How the Classical Worldview Supports our Modern Moral and Political Values*. San Francisco: Ignatius Press, 2016.

Hittinger, Russell. *The First Grace: Rediscovering the Natural Law*. Wilmington, DE: ISI Books, 2003.

Hobbes, Thomas. *De Cive*. In Gert, *Man and Citizen*, 87–386.

——. *De Homine*. In Gert, *Man and Citizen*, 33–85.

——. "A Dialogue between a Philosopher and Student of the Common Laws of England." In *The English Works of Thomas Hobbes of Malmesbury*, edited by Sir William Molesworth, vol. 6. London: John Bohn, 1840.

——. *The Elements of Law, Natural and Politic: Part I, "Human Nature" and Part II, "De Corpore Politico."* Edited by J. C. A. Gaskin. Oxford: Oxford University Press, 1994.

——. *Elements of Philosophy: The First Section, Concerning Body*. In *The English Works of Thomas Hobbes of Malmesbury*, edited by Sir William Molesworth, vol. 1. London: John Bohn, 1839.

——. *Leviathan*. Edited by Edwin Curley. Indianapolis: Hackett Publishing Company, Inc., 1994.

——. *Man and Citizen: "De Homine" and "De Cive."* Edited by Bernard Gert. Indianapolis: Hackett Publishing Company, Inc., 1991.

——. *On the Citizen*. Edited and translated by Richard Tuck and Michael Silverthorne. Cambridge: Cambridge University Press, 1998.

Hohfeld, W. N.. *Fundamental Legal Conceptions as Applied to Judicial Reasoning*. New Haven, CT: Yale University Press, 1920.

Holloway, Carson. *The Way of Life: John Paul II and the Challenge of Liberal Modernity*. Waco, TX: Baylor University Press, 2008.

Hooker, Richard. *Of the Laws of Ecclesiastical Polity*. Edited by Arthur Stephen McGrade. Cambridge: Cambridge University Press, 1989.

Höpfl, Harro, and Martyn P. Thompson. "The History of Contract as a Motif in Political Thought." *American Historical Review* 84, no. 4 (October 1979): 919–44.

Hulliung, Mark. *The Social Contract in America: From Revolution to the Present Age*. Lawrence: University Press of Kansas, 2007.

Hume, David. *Enquiries Concerning the Human Understanding and Concerning the Principles of Morals*. 1777. Edited by L. A. Selby Bigge. 2d ed. Oxford: The Clarendon Press of Oxford University Press, 1902.

———. *Essays Moral, Political, and Literary*, edited by Eugene F. Miller. Indianapolis: Liberty Fund, 1987.

———. "Of the Original Contract." 1777. Part II, Essay XII in *Essays Moral, Political, and Literary*, edited by Eugene F. Miller.

———. *A Treatise of Human Nature*. Edited by L. A. Selby-Bigge. Oxford: The Clarendon Press of Oxford University Press, 1896.

———. *A Treatise of Human Nature*. Edited by Ernest C. Mossner. London: Penguin Books, 1969.

———. *A Treatise of Human Nature*. Edited by David Fate Norton and Mary J. Norton. Oxford: Oxford University Press, 2000.

Hunter, James Davidson, and Paul Nedelisky. *Science and the Good: The Tragic Quest for the Foundations of Morality*. New Haven, CT: Yale University Press, 2018.

Hurley, Patrick J. *A Concise Introduction to Logic*. 6th ed. Belmont, CA: Wadsworth Publishing Company, 1997.

Jacobs, Jonathan A., ed. *Reason, Religion, and Natural Law: From Plato to Spinoza*. Oxford: Oxford University Press.

James, William. "The Will to Believe." In Peterson, Hasker, Reichenbach, and Basinger, *Philosophy of Religion*, 71-79.

Jesseph, Douglas M. *Squaring the Circle: The War between Hobbes and Wallis*. Chicago: University of Chicago Press, 1999.

Jolley, Nicholas. *Leibniz*. 2nd ed. London: Routledge, 2020.

Kant, Immanuel. *Grounding for the Metaphysics of Morals; with, On a Supposed Right to Lie because of Philanthropic Concerns*. 3rd ed. Translated by James W. Ellington. Indianapolis: Hackett Publishing Company, Inc., 1993.

———. "On the Common Saying: 'This May Be True in Theory, but It Doesn't' Apply in Practice.'" In *Kant's Political Writings*, edited by Hans Reiss. Cambridge: Cambridge University press, 1970.

Kavka, Gregory S. *Hobbesian Moral and Political Theory*. Princeton, NJ: Princeton University Press, 1986.

Kelsen, Hans. *General Theory of Law and State*. Translated by Anders Wedberg. Cambridge, MA: Harvard University Press, 1945. Reprint, Clark, NJ: The Lawbook Exchange, Ltd., 2007.

———. *Pure Theory of Law*. Translated from the 2nd (Revised and Enlarged) German edition by Max Knight. Berkeley: University of California Press, 1967. Reprint, Clark, NJ: The Lawbook Exchange, Ltd., 2002.

Ketcham, Ralph, ed. *The Anti-Federalist Papers and the Constitutional Convention Debates*. New York: Signet Classics, 2003.

Keys, Mary M. *Aquinas, Aristotle, and the Promise of the Common Good*. Cambridge: Cambridge University Press, 2006.

Kierkegaard, Soren. *Fear and Trembling*. Translated by Alastair Hannay. London: Penguin Books, 1985.

Kilcullen, John. "Medieval Theories of Natural Law." Revised and published as "Natural Law." In *Encyclopedia of Medieval Philosophy: Philosophy between 500 and 1500*, edited by Henrik Lagerlund, 831–39. New York: Springer, 2011.

———. "Natural Law and William of Ockham." In *History of Philosophy Yearbook*, edited by Knud Haakonssen and Udo Thiel, vol. 1. Canberra: Australasian Society for the History of Philosophy, 1993.

Koons, Robert C. *Realism Regained: An Exact Theory of Causation, Teleology, and the Mind*. Oxford: Oxford University Press, 2000.

Koons, Robert C., and George Bealer, eds. *The Waning of Materialism*. Oxford: Oxford University Press, 2010.

Kurland, Philip B., and Ralph Lerner, eds. *The Founders' Constitution*. 5 vols. Chicago: University of Chicago Press, 1987.

Leibniz, Wilhelm Gottfried. *Leibniz: Political Writings*. Edited and translated by Patrick Riley. Cambridge: Cambridge University Press, 1972.

———. *New Essays on the Human Understanding*. Translated and edited by Peter Remnant and Jonathan Bennett. Cambridge: Cambridge University Press, 1996.

———. *Philosophical Papers and Letters, Synthese Historical Library*. Volume 2. Edited by Leroy E. Loemker. 1969. Reprint, Dordrecht: Kluwer Academic Publishers, 1989.

Lewis, C. S. *The Abolition of Man*. New York: HarperCollins, 2001.

———. *Christian Reflections*. Edited by Walter Hooper. Grand Rapids, MI: William B. Eerdmans Company, 1967.

———. "The Poison of Subjectivism." In *Christian Reflections*, 89–102.

———. *A Preface to Paradise Lost*. Oxford: Oxford University Press, 1942.

Lisska, Anthony J. *Aquinas's Theory of Natural Law: An Analytic Reconstruction*. Oxford: The Clarendon Press of Oxford University Press, 1996.

———. "Right Reason in Natural Law Moral Theory: Thomas Aquinas and William of Ockham." In *Reason, Religion, and Natural Law: From Plato to Spinoza*, edited by Jonathan A. Jacobs, 155-74. Oxford: Oxford University Press, 2012.

Lloyd, S. A. "Hobbes's Self-Effacing Natural Law Theory." *Pacific Philosophical Quarterly* 82, no. 3–4 (2001): 285–308.

———. *Morality in the Philosophy of Thomas Hobbes: Cases in the Law of Nature*. Cambridge: Cambridge University Press, 2009.

Locke, John. *An Essay Concerning Human Understanding*. Edited by Peter H. Nidditch. Oxford: Oxford University Press, 1975.

———. *Essays on the Law of Nature: The Latin Text with a Translation, Introduction, and Notes, Together with Transcripts of Locke's Shorthand in his Journal for 1676*. Edited by W. von Leyden. Oxford: Oxford University Press, 1954.

———. *Letter Concerning Toleration*. Buffalo: Prometheus Books, 1990.

———. *Political Essays*. Edited by Mark Goldie. Cambridge: Cambridge University Press, 1997.

———. *Questions Concerning the Law of Nature*. Edited and translated by Robert Horwitz, Jenny Strauss Clay, and Diskin Clay. Ithaca, NY: Cornell University Press, 1990.

———. *Two Treatises of Government*. Edited by Peter Laslett. Cambridge: Cambridge University Press, 1960.

———. *The Works of Locke in Nine Volumes*. 12th ed. London: Rivington, 1824.

Luther, Martin. *The Bondage of the Will*. Translated by J. I. Packer and O. R. Johnston. Grand Rapids: Fleming H. Revell, 1957.

———. *Martin Luther's Basic Theological Writings*. Edited by Timothy F. Lull. Minneapolis: Fortress Press, 1989.

Lutz, Donald S. "From Covenant to Constitution in American Political Thought." *Publius* 10, no. 4 (Autumn 1980): 101–33.

———. *The Origins of American Constitutionalism*. Baton Rouge: Louisiana State University Press, 1988.

MacIntyre, Alasdair. *After Virtue: A Study in Moral Theory*. 3d ed. Notre Dame, IN: University of Notre Dame Press, 2007.

———. *A Short History of Ethics: A History of Moral Philosophy from the Homeric Age to the Twentieth Century*. 2nd ed. New York: Macmillan, 1966.

Mackie, J. L. *Ethics: Inventing Right and Wrong*. London: Penguin Books, 1990.

Maier, Hans. *Katholizismus and Demokratie*. Freiburg, Germany: Herder, 1983.

Madison, James. "James Madison to Nicholas P. Trist, 15 February 1830." In Kurland and Lerner, *The Founders' Constitution*, vol. 1, *Major Themes*, chapter 7, Document 28, 239-41.

Manent, Pierre. *An Intellectual History of Liberalism*. Translated by Rebecca Balinski. Princeton, NJ: Princeton University Press, 1994.

———. *Natural Law and Human Rights: Toward a Recovery of Practical Reason*. Translated by Ralph C. Hancock. Notre Dame: University of Notre Dame Press, 2020.

Manson, Neil A., ed. *God and Design: The Teleological Argument and Modern Science*. London: Routledge, 2003.

March, James G., and Johan P. Olsen. "The New Institutionalism: Organizational Factors in Political Life." *American Political Science Review* 78, no. 3 (September 1984): 734–49.

Martinich, A. P. *Hobbes*. London: Routledge, 2005.

———. "Law and Self-Preservation in *Leviathan:* On Misunderstanding Hobbes's Philosophy, 1650–1700." In *The Persistence of the Sacred in Modern Thought,* edited by Chris Firestone and Nathan A. Jacobs, 38-65. Notre Dame, IN: Notre Dame University Press, 2012.

———. *Hobbes's Political Philosophy: Interpretation and Interpretations.* Oxford: Oxford University Press, 2021.

———. *The Two Gods of Leviathan: Thomas Hobbes on Religion and Politics.* Cambridge: Cambridge University Press, 1992.

Martinich, A. P., Sharon Vaughan, and David Lay Williams. "Hobbes's Religion and Political Philosophy: A Reply to Greg Forster." *History of Political Thought* 29, no. 1 (Spring 2008): 49–64.

McCord-Sayre, Geoffrey, ed. *Essays on Moral Realism.* Ithaca: Cornell University Press, 1989.

McCoy, Charles S., and J. Wayne Baker. *Fountainhead of Federalism.* Louisville: Westminster/John Knox Press, 1991.

McWilliams, Wilson Carey. "Democracy and the Citizen: Community, Dignity, and the Crisis of Contemporary Politics in America." In *How Democratic Is the Constitution?,* edited by Robert A. Godwin and William A. Schambra, 79-101. Washington, DC: American Enterprise Institute, 1980.

Mill, John Stuart. *Utilitarianism.* Edited by George Sher. Indianapolis: Hackett Publishing Company, Inc., 1979.

Miller, Fred. *Nature, Justice, and Rights in Aristotle's Politics.* Oxford: Oxford University Press, 1995.

Muñoz, Vincent Phillip. *Religious Liberty and the American Founding: Natural Rights and the Original Meanings of the First Amendment Religion Clauses.* Chicago: University of Chicago Press, 2022.

Murphy, Jeffrie G., and Jean Hampton. *Forgiveness and Mercy.* Cambridge: Cambridge University Press, 1988.

Murphy, Mark C. *An Essay on Divine Authority.* Ithaca: Cornell University Press, 2002.

———. "God and Moral Law." The 8th Annual Plantinga Fellow Lecture, delivered at the University of Notre Dame, October 2, 2009.

———. *God & Moral Law: On the Theistic Explanation of Morality.* Oxford: Oxford University Press, 2011.

———. *God's Own Ethics: Norms of Divine Agency & the Argument from Evil.* Oxford: Oxford University Press, 2017.

———. *Natural Law in Jurisprudence and Politics.* Cambridge: Cambridge University Press, 2006.

———. "The Natural Law Tradition in Ethics." In *The Stanford Encyclopedia of Philosophy,* edited by Edward N. Zalta. Stanford, CA: Metaphysics Research Lab, originally published September 2003 and substantially revised May 2019. http://plato.stanford.edu/archives/win2011/entries/natural-law-ethics/.

———. "Was Hobbes a Legal Positivist." *Ethics* 105, no. 4 (July 1995): 846–73.

Nagel, Thomas. *Mind & Cosmos: Why the Materialist, Neo-Darwinian Conception of Nature Is Almost Certainly False.* Oxford: Oxford University Press, 2012.

Nathanson, Stephen. *Should We Consent to Be Governed: A Short Introduction to Political Philosophy.* 2nd ed. Belmont, CA: Wadsworth, 2001.

Newton, Isaac. *The Mathematical Principles of Natural Philosophy.* Translated by Andrew Motte. London, 1713 and 1726.

———. "General Scholium," appendix to the 1713 edition of *Principia.* In *The Principia: Mathematical Principles of Natural Philosophy,* translated by I. Bernard Cohen and Anne Whitman, assisted by Julia Budenz, 939–46. Berkeley: University of California Press, 1999.

Nietzsche, Friedrich. *Basic Writings of Nietzsche.* Translated and edited by Walter Kaufmann. New York: Modern Library, 2000.

———. *The Gay Science.* Translated by Walter Kauffman. New York: Vintage Press, 1974.

Novak, David. *Covenantal Rights: A Study in Jewish Political Theory.* Princeton, NJ: Princeton University Press, 2000.

———. *In Defense of Religious Liberty.* Wilmington, DE: ISI Books, 2009.

———. *The Jewish Social Contract: An Essay in Political Theology.* Princeton, NJ: Princeton University Press, 2005.

Nussbaum, Martha. *Frontiers of Justice: Disability, Nationality, and Species Membership.* Cambridge, MA: The Belknap Press of Harvard University Press, 2006.

Oakley, Francis. *The Empty Bottles of Gentilism: Kingship and the Divine in Late Antiquity and the Early Middle Ages, to 1050.* New Haven, CT: Yale University Press, 2010.

———. *Kingship: The Politics of Enchantment.* Oxford, UK: Blackwell Publishing, 2006.

———. "Legitimation by Consent: The Question of Medieval Roots." *Viator* 14, no. 1 (1983): 303–35.

———. "Locke, Natural Law and God—Again." *History of Political Thought* 18, no. 4 (Winter 1997): 624–51.

———. "Medieval Theories of Natural Law: William of Ockham and the Significance of the Voluntarist Tradition." *Natural Law Forum* 6 (1961): 65–83.

———. *Natural Law, Laws of Nature, Natural Rights: Continuity and Discontinuity in the History of Ideas.* London: Continuum, 2005.

———. *Omnipotence, Covenant, & Order: An Excursion in the History of Ideas from Abelard to Leibniz.* Ithaca, NY: Cornell University Press, 1984.

———. *Omnipotence and Promise: The Legacy of the Scholastic Distinction of Powers.* The Etienne Gilson Series 23. Toronto: Pontifical Institute of Medieval Studies, 2002.

————. *The Watershed of Modern Politics: Law, Virtue, Kingship, and Consent, 1300–1650*. New Haven, CT: Yale University Press, 2015.

Oakley, Francis, and Elliot W. Urdang. "Locke, Natural Law, and God." *Natural Law Forum* 11 (1966): 92–109.

Oakerson, Ronald J. "Reciprocity: A Bottom-Up View of Political Development." In *Rethinking Institutional Analysis and Development: Issues, Alternatives, and Choices*, edited by Vincent Ostrom, David Feeny, and Hartmut Picht, 141–58. San Francisco: International Center for Economic Growth, 1988.

Oakeshott, Michael. *Hobbes on Civil Association*. Indianapolis: Liberty Fund, 2000.

Oberman, Heiko A. *The Harvest of Medieval Theology: Gabriel Biel and Late Medieval Nominalism*. Grand Rapids, MI: Baker Academic, 1963.

————. *Luther: Man between God and the Devil*. New York: Doubleday, 1982.

————. "The Shape of Late Medieval Thought: The Birthpangs of the Modern Era." In Trinkaus and Oberman, *Pursuit of Holiness*, 3–25.

Ockham, William. *Guillelmi de Ockham: Quaestiones in librum secundum Sentatiarum (Reportatio)*. Edited by Gedeon Gál and Rega Wood. New York: Franciscan Institute Publications, 1981.

————. *Ockham: Philosophical Writings*. Translated by Philotheus Boehner. Revised by Stephen F. Brown. Indianapolis: Hackett Publishing Company, 1990.

————. "A Dialogue, Part III, Tract II, On the Rights of the Roman Empire." In *William of Ockham: A Letter to the Friars Minor and Other Writings*, edited by Stephen McGrade and John Kilcullen, translated by John Kilcullen, 232–99. Cambridge: Cambridge University Press, 1995.

O'Donovan, Oliver, and Joan Lockwood O'Donovan, eds. *From Irenaeus to Grotius: A Sourcebook in Christian Political Thought*. Grand Rapids, MI: William B. Eerdmans Publishing Company, 1999.

Olson, Mancur. *The Logic of Collective Action: Public Goods and the Theory of Groups*. Cambridge, MA: Harvard University Press, 1965.

Osborne, Thomas M., Jr. "Ockham as a Divine-Command Theorist." *Religious Studies* 41, no. 1 (March 2005): 1–22.

Ostrom, Vincent. *The Meaning of American Federalism: Constituting a Self-Governing Society*. San Francisco: Institute for Contemporary Studies Press, 1991.

————. *The Political Theory of a Compound Republic: Designing the American Experiment*. 3rd ed. Lanham, MD: Lexington Books, 2008.

Pakaluk, Michael. "Rawls and the Rejection of Truth." *Law & Liberty* (April 1, 2021).

Pangle, Thomas L. *The Spirit of Modern Republicanism: The Moral Vision of the American Founders and the Philosophy of Locke*. Chicago: University of Chicago Press, 1988.

Peterson, Michale J., William Hasker, Bruce Reichenbach, and David Basinger, eds. *Philosophy of Religion: Selected Readings*. Oxford: Oxford University Press, 1996.

Pitkin, Hanna. "Obligation and Consent—I." *American Political Science Review* 59, no. 4 (December 1965): 990–99.

———. "Obligation and Consent—II." *American Political Science Review* 60, no. 1 (March 1966): 39–52.

Plantinga, Alvin. "How to Be an Anti-Realist." *Proceedings and Addresses of the American Philosophical Association* 56, no. 1 (September 1982): 47–70.

———. *Warrant: The Current Debate*. Oxford: Oxford University Press, 1993.

———. *Warrant and Proper Function*. Oxford: Oxford University Press, 1993.

———. *Warranted Christian Belief*. Oxford: Oxford University Press, 2000.

———. *Where the Conflict Really Lies: Science, Religion, and Naturalism*. Oxford: Oxford University Press, 2011.

Plato. *Gorgias*. Translated by James H. Nichols Jr. Ithaca, NY: Cornell University Press, 1998.

———. *The Laws*. Translated by Trevor J. Saunders. London: Penguin Books, 1970.

———. *Laws*. Translated by C. D. C. Reeve. Indianapolis: Hackett Publishing Company, Inc., 2022.

———. *Republic*. Translated and Introduced by C. D. C. Reeve. Indianapolis: Hackett Publishing Company, Inc., 2004.

———. *The Trials of Socrates: Six Classic Texts*. Translated by C. D. C. Reeve. Indianapolis: Hackett Publishing Company, Inc., 2002.

Polkinghorne, John. *Belief in God in an Age of Science*. Rev. ed. New Haven, CT: Yale University Press, 2003.

———. *The Faith of a Physicist*. Princeton, NJ: Princeton University Press, 1994.

Price, Richard. *A Review of the Principal Questions in Morals*. In Selby-Bigge, *British Moralists*, vol. 2, 103–84.

Pufendorf, Samuel. *On the Duty of Man and Citizen*. Edited by James Tully. Translated by Michael Silverthorne. Cambridge: Cambridge University Press, 1991.

———. *On the Law of Nature and Nations in Eight Books*. In *The Political Writings of Samuel Pufendorf*, edited by Craig L. Carr, translated by Michael J. Seidler, 95–268. Oxford: Oxford University Press, 1994.

———. *Political Writings of Samuel Pufendorf*. Edited by Craig L. Carr and Translated by Michael J. Seidler. Oxford: Oxford University Press, 1994.

Rager, John C. "The Blessed Cardinal Bellarmine's Defense of Popular Government in the Sixteenth Century." *Catholic Historical Review* 10, no. 4 (January 1925): 504–14.

Rahe, Paul A. *The Spartan Regime: Its Character, Origins, and Grand Strategy*. New Haven, CT: Yale University Press, 2016.

Ratzinger, Joseph. *Church, Ecumenism, & Politics: New Endeavors in Ecclesiology.* San Francisco: Ignatius Press, 2008.

Rawls, John. "The Idea of an Overlapping Consensus." *Oxford Journal of Legal Studies 7*, no. 1 (Spring 1987): 1–25.

———. "Justice as Fairness: Political not Metaphysical." *Philosophy and Public Affairs* 14, no. 3 (Summer 1985): 223–51.

———. "Kantian Constructivism in Moral Theory." *Journal of Philosophy* 77, no. 19 (September 1980): 515–72.

———. *Political Liberalism.* With a new introduction and the "Reply to Habermas." New York: Columbia University Press, 1996.

———. *A Theory of Justice.* Cambridge, MA: The Belknap Press of Harvard University Press, 1971.

Reilly, Robert R. *America on Trial: A Defense of the Founding.* San Francisco: Ignatius Press, 2020.

Richard, Carl J. *Twelve Greeks and Romans Who Changed the World.* Lanham, MD: Rowman & Littlefield Publishers, Inc., 2003.

Riker, William H. "The Future of a Science of Politics." *American Behavioral Scientist* 21, no. 1 (September and October 1977): 11–38.

Rist, John M. *Plato's Moral Realism: The Discovery of the Presupposition of Ethics.* Washington, DC: The Catholic University of America Press, 2012.

———. *Real Ethics: Reconsidering the Foundations of Morality.* Cambridge: Cambridge University Press, 2002.

———. *What Is a Person? Realities, Constructs, Illusions.* Cambridge: Cambridge University Press, 2020.

Rosen, Gary. *American Compact: James Madison and the Problem of Founding.* Lawrence: University Press of Kansas, 1999.

Rousseau, Jean-Jacques. *The Social Contract.* Translated by Maurice Cranston. London: Penguin Books, 1968.

Rubin, Leslie G. *America, Aristotle, and the Politics of a Middle Class.* Waco, TX: Baylor University Press, 2018.

Sacks, Jonathan. "The Binding of Isaac: A New Interpretation." *Covenant & Conversation.* https://rabbisacks.org/covenant-conversation/vayera/binding-of-isaac-new/.

Sandel, Michael J. *Democracy's Discontent: America in Search of a Public Philosophy.* Cambridge, MA: The Belknap Press of Harvard University Press, 1996.

———. *Liberalism and the Limits of Justice.* Second Edition. Cambridge: Cambridge University Press, 1998.

———. "The Procedural Republic and the Unencumbered Self." *Political Theory* 12, no. 1 (February 1984): 81–96.

Schneewind, J. B. *The Invention of Autonomy: A History of Modern Moral Philosophy.* Cambridge: Cambridge University Press, 1998.

Schwartz, Daniel. "Francisco Suárez on Consent and Political Obligation." *Vivarium* 46 (2008): 59–81.

Selby-Bigge, Lewis Amherst, ed. *British Moralists: Being Selections from Writers Principally in the Eighteenth Century*. Vol. 2. Oxford: Clarendon Press, 1897.

Seung, T. K. *Intuition and Construction: The Foundation of Normative Theory*. New Haven, CT: Yale University Press, 1993.

———. *Plato Rediscovered: Human Value and Social Order*. Lanham, MD: Rowman & Littlefield Publishers, Inc., 1996.

Shah, Timothy Samuel, and Allen D. Hertzke, eds. *Christianity and Freedom*. Vol. 1, *Historical Perspectives*. Cambridge: Cambridge University Press, 2016.

Shain, Barry Alan. *The Myth of American Individualism: The Protestant Origins of American Political Thought*. Princeton, NJ: Princeton University Press, 1994.

Shively, W. Philips. *Power & Choice: An Introduction to Political Science*. 10th ed. Boston: McGraw Hill, 2007.

Sidney, Algernon. *Discourses Concerning Government*. Edited by Thomas J. West. Indianapolis: Liberty Fund, 1996.

Simmons, A. John. " 'Denisons' and 'Aliens': Locke's Problem of Consent." *Social Theory and Practice* 24, no. 2 (Summer 1998): 161–82.

———. *The Lockean Theory of Rights*. Princeton, NJ: Princeton University Press, 1992.

———. *Moral Principles and Political Obligations*. Princeton, NJ: Princeton University Press, 1979.

———. *On the Edge of Anarchy: Locke, Consent, and the Limits of Society*. Princeton, NJ: Princeton University Press, 1993.

———. "Tacit Consent and Political Obligations." *Philosophy & Public Affairs* 5, no. 3 (Spring 1976): 274–91.

Skinner, Quentin. *The Foundations of Modern Political Thought*. Vol. 2, *The Age of Reformation*. Cambridge: Cambridge University Press, 1978.

Smith, Christian. *To Flourish or Destruct*. Chicago: University of Chicago Press, 2015.

———. *What Is a Person? Rethinking Humanity, Social Life, and the Moral Good from the Ground Up*. Chicago: University of Chicago Press, 2010.

Soles, David E. "Intellectualism and Natural Law in Locke's *Second Treatise*." *History of Political Thought* 8, no. 2 (Spring 1987): 63–81.

Somos, Mark. *American States of Nature: The Origins of Independence, 1761–1775*. Oxford: Oxford University Press, 2019.

Steinberger, Peter J., ed. *Readings in Classical Political Thought*. Indianapolis: Hackett Publishing Company, Inc., 2000.

Strauss, Leo. *Natural Right and History*. Chicago: University of Chicago Press, 1953.

———. "On the Spirit of Hobbes' Political Philosophy." *Revue Internationale de Philosophie* 4, no. 14 (October 1950): 405–31.

————. *The Political Philosophy of Hobbes: Its Basis and Its Genesis*, translated by Elsa M. Sinclair. Chicago: University of Chicago Press, 1952.

Street, Sharon. "Objectivity and Truth: You'd Better Rethink It." In *Oxford Studies in Metaethics*, edited by Russ Shafer-Landau. Oxford: Oxford University Press, 2016.

Stump, Eleonore. "Aquinas's Theory of Goodness." *The Monist* 105 (2022): 321–36.

Suárez, Francisco. *A Treatise on Laws and God the Lawgiver.* 1612. In *Selections from Three Works: A Treatise on Laws and God the Lawgiver; A Defence of the Catholic and Apostolic Faith; A Work on the Three Theological Virtues*. Edited by Thomas Pink. Translated by Gwlays L. Williams, Ammi Brown, and John Waldron. Indianapolis: Liberty Fund, 2015.

Swinburne, Richard. *Responsibility and Atonement*. Oxford: Oxford University Press, 1989.

Taylor, A. E. "The Ethical Doctrine of Hobbes." *Philosophy* 13, no. 52 (October 1938): 406–24.

Taylor, Charles. *Sources of the Self: The Making of Modern Identity*. Cambridge: Cambridge University Press, 2002.

Thucydides. *The Essential Thucydides: On Justice, Power, and Human Nature: Selections from "The History of the Peloponnesian War."* Edited and translated by Paul Woodruff. 2d ed. Indianapolis: Hackett Publishing Company, Inc., 2021.

Tierney, Brian. *The Idea of Natural Rights*. Grand Rapids, MI: William B. Eerdmans Publishing Company, 1997.

————. *Religion, Law, and the Growth of Constitutional Thought, 1150–1650*. Cambridge: Cambridge University Press, 1982.

Charles E. Trinkaus with Heiko A. Oberman. *The Pursuit of Holiness in Late Medieval and Renaissance Religion*. Studies in Medieval and Reformation Thought. Volume 10. Leiden, Netherlands: E. J. Brill, 1974.

Truman, David B. "The Implications of Political Behavior Research." *Social Science Research Council* 5, no. 4 (December 1951): 37–39.

Tuck, Richard. *Natural Rights Theories: Their Origin and Development*. Cambridge: Cambridge University Press, 1979.

Vallentyne, Peter, ed. *Contractarianism and Rational Choice: Essays on David Gauthier's "Morals by Agreement."* Cambridge: Cambridge University Press, 1991

Van Inwagen, Peter. "The Compatibility of Darwin and Design." In Manson, *God and Design*, 347–61.

Van Inwagen, Peter, and Dean Zimmerman, eds. *Persons: Human and Divine*. Oxford: Oxford University Press, 2007.

Waldron, Jeremy. *God, Locke, and Equality: Christian Foundations for Locke's Political Thought*. Cambridge: Cambridge University Press, 2002.

———. *One Another's Equals: The Basis of Human Equality*. Cambridge, MA: The Belknap Press of Harvard University Press, 2017.

Walker, Graham. *Moral Foundations of Constitutional Thought: Current Problems, Augustinian Prospects*. Princeton, NJ: Princeton University Press, 1990.

Walzer, Michael. *Spheres of Justice: A Defense of Pluralism and Equality*. New York: Basic Books, 1984.

Ward, Lee. *The Politics of Liberty in England and Revolutionary America*. Cambridge: Cambridge University Press, 2004.

Warrender, Howard. *The Political Philosophy of Hobbes: His Theory of Obligation*. Oxford: Oxford University Press, 1957.

Wellman, Christopher Heath, and A. John Simmons. *Is There a Duty to Obey the Law?* Cambridge: Cambridge University Press, 2005.

West, Thomas. *The Political Theory of the American Founding: Natural Rights, Public Policy, and the Moral Conditions of Freedom*. Cambridge: Cambridge University Press, 2017.

Wilken, Robert Louis. *Liberty in the Things of God: The Christian Origins of Religious Freedom*. New Haven, CT: Yale University Press, 2019.

Williams, David Lay. "Dialogical Theories of Justice." *Telos*, no. 114 (Winter 1999): 109–31.

———. "Ideas and Actuality in the Social Contract: Kant & Rousseau." *History of Political Thought* 28, no. 3 (Autumn 2007): 471–97.

———. *Rousseau's Platonic Enlightenment*. University Park, PA: Pennsylvania State University Press, 2007.

Witte, John, Jr. *The Reformation of Right: Law, Religion, and Human Rights in Early Modern Calvinism*. Cambridge: Cambridge University Press, 2007.

Wolff, Robert Paul. *In Defense of Anarchism*, with a new preface. Berkeley: University of California Press, 1998.

Wolterstorff, Nicholas. "Accounting for the Political Authority of the State." In *Understanding Liberal Democracy*, 245–74.

———. " 'For the Authorities Are God's Servants': Is a Theistic Account of Political Authority Still Viable Today Or Have Humanist Accounts Won the Day?" Delivered at the Theology, Morality, and Public Life Conference at the University of Chicago, Divinity School, March 2003.

———. " 'For the Authorities Are God's Servants': Is a Theistic Account of Political Authority Still Viable or Have Humanist Accounts Won the Day?" In *Theology and Public Philosophy: Four Conversations*, edited by Kenneth L. Grasso and Cecilia Rodriguez Castillo, 51-68. Lanham, MD: Lexington Books, 2012.

———. "God in Locke's Philosophy." In *The Persistence of the Sacred in Modern Thought*, edited by Chris L. Firestone and Nathan A. Jacobs. Notre Dame: University of Notre Dame Press, 2012.

————. *John Locke and the Ethics of Belief.* Cambridge: Cambridge University Press, 1996.

————. *Justice: Rights and Wrongs.* Princeton, NJ: Princeton University Press, 2008.

————. *Practices of Belief.* Vol. 2 of *Selected Essays,* edited by Terence Cuneo. Cambridge: Cambridge University Press, 2010.

————. "The Right of the People to a Democratic State: Reflections on a Passage in Althusius." In *Understanding Liberal Democracy,* 227-44.

————. *Understanding Liberal Democracy: Essays in Political Philosophy.* Edited by Terence Cuneo. Oxford: Oxford University Press, 2012.

Woolhouse, Roger. *Locke: A Biography.* Cambridge: Cambridge University Press, 2007.

Xella, Paolo, Josephine Quinn, Valentina Melchiorri, and Peter van Dommelen. "Phoenician Bones of Contention." *Antiquity* 87 (December 2013): 1199–1207.

Zagorin, Perez. *Hobbes and the Law of Nature.* Princeton, NJ: Princeton University Press, 2009.

Zinaich, Samuel, Jr. "Locke's Moral Revolution: From Natural Law to Moral Relativism." *The Locke Newsletter,* no. 31 (2000): 79–115.

Zuckert, Michael P. "Do Natural Rights Derive from Natural Law?: Aquinas, Hobbes, and Locke on Natural Rights." In *Launching Liberalism: On Lockean Political Philosophy,* 169–200.

————. *Launching Liberalism: On Lockean Political Philosophy.* Lawrence: University Press of Kansas, 2002.

————. *Natural Rights and the New Republicanism.* Princeton, NJ: Princeton University Press.

————. "Social Compact, Common Law, and the American Amalgam: The Contribution of William Blackstone." In *Launching Liberalism,* 235–73.

Index

absolute and ordained powers of God. See *potentia absoluta et ordinata*

Adams, Marilyn McCord: on Ockham's nominalism, 191; Ockham considered view that universals are real "the worst error of philosophy," 191, 365n6

Adams, Robert Merrihew, 91; obligatory acts as a subset of intrinsically good acts, 221–22; God's goodness and God's will, 38–39, 46; on Leibniz and universals, 349n137; the nature of obligation, 216; only commands of a good God can ground moral obligation, 345n121; and supererogatory acts, 222, 391n13; presents Ockham as providing an account of universals rather than as rejecting them, 383–84n11; critique of Adams's account of Ockham and universals, 384n11

Alcibiades, 222

Albert the Great (Albertus Magnus), 194, 383n, 396n27; on the absolute and ordained powers of God, 192–93, 264, 282, 385n25

Alexander of Hales: meaning of the absolute power of God, 385n25

American Founders and framers, the, 6, 11, 12, 231, 232–33, 238, 240, 330n7, 398n48; and popular sovereignty, 414n117

Althusius, Johannes, 236; affirms classical / traditional natural law, 265–66, 337n45; his account of natural law not traditional in every respect, 403n85; his Aristotelian account of the *lex moralis* and of the common law/proper law distinction,

402n83; consent as the efficient cause of political association, 19, 262, 266; on the covenantal foundation of political order, 18–20; employs Aristotle's causal schema, 262; final cause of politics, 262; on the formal and material causes of politics, 402n74; human beings are political by nature and political association exists by nature, 261–62, 265–66; individuals consent to form pre-political associations, which in turn consent to from the city, 18–19, 262; invocation of Vásquez, 21; invokes Aristotle's claim that humans are social and political by nature, 402n70; McCoy and Baker on his account of natural law and divine will, 238; on natural law as "naturally implanted by God," 264–65; necessity of human society to live well and simply to live, 261; political association formed by explicit or tact agreement, 260, 265–66; political order built from the ground up, 18–19, 318–19; and popular sovereignty, 262–64; 319; rejects absolute power (even of God), 264–65; his way of distinguishing the whole and the parts and Hampton's critique of agency contract theory, 402n76

Ambrose of Milan: on natural equality, 250

"Amor ti vieta" (an aria from the opera *Fedora*), 31

Anscombe, G. E. M., 91; on Kant's notion of self-legislation as absurd, 225; correlation of rights and obligations, 314; defines authority as a right to be obeyed,

INDEX 443

covenant model of political organization: contrasted with Aristotelian political theory, 231; said to conflict with classical natural law, 232–41; compatible with Aristotelian political theory, 241–49; compatible with classical Christianity and natural law, 249–66

Cudworth, Ralph, 46

Cuneo, Terence, 91; on Clarke's critique of Hobbes, 72–73

Curley, Edwin: rejects Robert Adams interpretation of the Binding of Isaac, 393n125

D

Dahl, Robert A.: predicates behavioralism on the is-ought dichotomy, 333n9

Davies, Paul, 90

De Tocqueville, Alexis: and self-interest rightly understood, 352n36

Declaration of Independence, 3, 11, 231, 329n2

d'Entréves, Passerin: claims Richard Hooker only affirmed corporate consent, 338n53

de facto criticism of social contract theory, the, 14, 27–31, 289–315

DeMorgan's rule (rule of inference), 12, 167, 185, 332n7 (defined)

Deneen, Patrick J., 5, 329n6; claims social contract theorists redefined natural law, 331n14; says Constitution sought to overturn "ancient teachings," 331n15

disjunctive syllogism (rule of inference), 42, 118, 122, 167, 168, 170, 185, 233, 278, 332n7 (defined), 347n130, 370n46

double negation (rule of inference), 168, 185, 332n7 (defined), 370n46

Dunn, John: on acquiescence, or going along, and consent, 313

Dworkin, Ronald, 46, 79; a hypothetical contract is no contract at all, 342n96, 409n72; affirms the objectivity and mind-independence of moral value, 81, 120, 121, 122; on "the metaphysical independence of value," 120; and the failure of his "metaphysical independence

of value" thesis, 121-23, 364n132; rejects moral and metaphysical realism, 81, 118–19, 120–21; rejects Walzer's relativism/conventionalism about justice, 119–20

E

Elazar, Daniel Judah: Althusius's influence early modern social contract theorists, 19; claims Aristotelian political theory and Thomistic natural law are instances of the organic model, 238; on the covenantal model of political order, 237–38; his definition of covenant, 237; on the Hobbesian covenant, 237, 238; on the organic model of political order, 236–37; provides a history of the covenant idea from ancient Israel to early modernity, 334n18; rejects any essential connection of covenant to nominalism, 239–40; social contract theory and the American founding belong to the covenantal model, 238

equality (natural), 12, 266, 332n7, 334n13, 413n104; American founders affirm, 12; in ancient and medieval Christian thought, 249–52; in Ambrose of Milan, 250; in Aquinas, 252; Aristotle rejects, 20, 242–43; Aristotle says equality entails people should take turns ruling, 249; Augustine says human beings are created equal, 399n52; Bellarmine affirms, 12, 332n5; Budziszewski on, 346n127; and classical Christian thought, 249–52; and the covenant model, 237; Filmer rejects Bellarmine's affirmation of, 332n5; Hobbes on, 297, 329n5; Richard Hooker affirms, 20, 255, 257; and Hume, 293–92; in Lactantius, 249–50; may not require individual consent, 318; in Gregory I (Gregory the Great), 251–52; in later Thomists (according to Skinner), 254–55; Locke on, 12, 329n5; and natural liberty, 234, 317–320; the necessity of consent for political authority and obligations, x, xii, 3, 4, 5, 14; only has normative implications if ontological and not merely

Grisez, Germain, 214

H

Haakonssen, Knud: Aquinas as a "realist-
intellectualist," 206; on Pufendorf and
the *entia moralia*, 386–87n35; says Suárez
distorts the Gregory of Rimini's position,
383n8
Habermas, Jürgen: dialogical theory of
justice, 31
Hall, Mark David: and Reformed tradition
as a major channel through which
government by consent was transmitted
to American political culture, 339n58
Hamilton, Alexander: on Hobbes as a moral
conventionalist, 63–64; held that states
are just collections of individuals and
artificial beings, 321, 414n116
Hampton, Jean, 14, 31, 91, 329n4, 334n12,
409n72; alienation and agency social
contracts defined, 340–41n73; critique
of Hobbes's alienation contract theory,
24–26, 154; critique of Locke's agency
social contract theory, 26–27; her
critique of agency social contracts
may commit the naturalistic fallacy,
342n88; distinguishes "moral" and
"state" contractarianism, 45; follows
Anscombe's definition of authority as
a right to be obeyed, 314, 412n93; on
Hobbes's "regress argument," 24–25; says
Hobbes's makes obedience to the civil
sovereign God's "premier command,"
152; Hobbes makes human value purely
instrumental, 134; Hobbes's subjectivism
concerning good and evil, 133, 365n11,
367n17; Hobbes's account of morality
opposed to Aristotle's, 365n11; inability
of hypothetical imperatives to ground
normativity, 91, 139–41, 157, 217,
276–77, 304; on instrumental rationality,
137; political philosophy should not
be done without metaphysics, 160; the
problem she poses for agency contract
theory solved by Althusius, 402n76; On
Rawls and ineliminable pluralism, 115;

two justifications of moral imperatives:
commands of God and contractarian
justification, 339–40n65; two foundations
for the law of nature: commanded by God
and commanded by the commonwealth,
352–53n42
Hanby, Michael, 329n6
Hare, John E.: his interpretation of Kant on
autonomy, 225, 392n120
Harper, Kyle: Seneca held *dignitas* is on a
sliding scale, 332n6, 398n129
Harris, Ian, holds Locke is inconsistent in
his treatment of natural law, 375n2
Hart, H. L. A., 158, 392n116, 412n99;
claims natural law not dependent on a
divine lawgiver, 188, 374n99; espouses the
separation of law and morals, 333n9
Hill, John Lawrence: claims Hobbes,
Rousseau, and Locke inverted the
classical understanding of the individual
and the state, 330n6; claims Locke's
natural law is "purely external" and
"imposed from the outside," 379n42
Hobbes, Thomas, 12, 15, 45, 46, 77, 123,
159, 176; cannot covenant away the
right to defend oneself, 314; Clarke's
objection to Hobbes's conventionalism,
72–73; commonwealth by institution and
acquisition, 301; and conventionalism
concerning justice, 60–69, 332n8;
covenants entered in the condition of
mere nature obligatory, 36–37, 149;
consigns the Kingdom of Christ until
after the general resurrection, 372n78;
covenants made in the condition of
mere nature void upon any reasonable
suspicion, 371n68; on divine omnipotence
and irresistible power, 37; ethics and
politics as demonstrative sciences,
ix, 7, 72, 295–96, 303; felicity as the
satisfaction of desire after desire, 132,
134, 366–67n15; God's sovereignty
derives from His irresistible power, ix–x,
7, 21–22, 37, 156, 200, 345n116, 373n93;
good and evil as relative and subjective,
61–63, 98, 112, 130–31, 352n40, 353n43,

(or teleological) account of natural law, 173; distinguishes real and nominal essences in the Essay, 376–377n18; his "real essences" probably refers to internal constitution of things, 377n18, 377n23; rejects Filmer's rejection of Bellarmine's and Suarez's affirmation of natural liberty, 253, 316; rejects the "Hobbist" view of morality, 92, 359–60n62; rejects idea that we can be bound by our predecessors or bind our progeny, 401n64; rejects strong realism of Plato and moderate realism of Aristotle and Aquinas, 165, 377n18; seems to deny moral rectitude good in itself and moral depravity in itself evil, 379–80n43; the self-contradiction of Locke's metaphysics and metaethics, 181–86; and the state of nature, 94, 258–60, 270, 291, 292, 330n6, 404n13; and tacit consent, 307–8, 309, 311, 312, 312, 342–43n98; 410n78; truth and keeping faith belong to men as men, 176, 272, 404n13; and voluntarism, 37–38, 166–70, 170–71, 176, 339n61, 379n40; his express rejection of metaethical voluntarism, 159, 182–83, 345n118; Wolterstorff on the fissure in Locke's moral theory, 379n41; Zinaich argues Locke's treatment of the law of nature is inconsistent across his works, 376n13

Lloyd, S. A.: Hobbes's law of nature underwrites unlimited sovereign power, 152

Luther, Martin, xi; as anti-Pelagian, 240, 396n27; as metaethical voluntarist, 187, 395n27; called Ockham "my master" and referred to himself as a terminist (i.e., nominalist), 383n2, 395–96n27; seems to affirm Augustinian Platonism against Aristotelian Scholasticism in "Disputation against Scholastic Theology" and the "Heidelberg Disputations," 383n2; 395n27

Lutz, Donald S., 329n3, 413n113; dissenting Calvinists appropriation of biblical covenant idea, 336n37; "Sidney

quotes liberally from Aristotle, Plato, the Bible, and the Jesuits Bellarmine and Suárez," 400n55

M

MacIntyre, Alasdair, 91, 109, 110; Hobbes's argument "ruined by an internal self-contradiction," 354n69; on the necessity of final causation or divine prescription for normativity, 91, 358n48; on classical theism moral judgments were both hypothetical and categorical in form, 406n27

Mackie, J. L., 10, 46, 114; morality as constituted by hypothetical imperatives, 137, 275, 276; seeks to construct moral norms entirely from non-normative ingredients, 277

Madison, James: letter to Nicholas Trist, 11

Manent, Pierre: modern state of nature and social contract theories seek to dismember and reconstruct the human world, 330n7

March, James G. and Johan P. Olsen: on the agency of institutions, 414n116

Martinich, A. P.: on covenants and the state of nature in Hobbes, 36, 149–50; on Hobbes's state of nature as hypothetical (and a matter of demonstrative science) rather than actual, 298–99, 369n32; self-preservation not the first law of nature, 153

Massachusetts Constitution of 1780, 329n3

materialism, 89, 303, 347n134, 364n3, 409n65; criticisms of, 348n134

Mayflower Compact, the, 18, 330n7, 336n37

McClay, Wilfred (Bill) M., xii

McCoy, Charles S. and J. Wayne Baker: Althusius provides first "fully developed articulation of federal political thought," 336n39; on Bullinger's account of covenant, 15–16; covenant has its own *lex naturae* that derives from the will of God, 238; in covenantal thought, primary social entities created by a compact among individuals, towns by a compact among primary social entities, provinces by a

454 INDEX

natural law (*continued*)
and government by consent, 3–7, chapter 7; and Finnis, 214–16; and Grotius, 212–14; Hart on, 158, 188; insufficiency of mere moral realism and intellectualist natural law, 216–23, 285; and Locke, 37, chapter 5; and natural inclinations, 173, 208–10; necessary for civil/human law, 34–35, 161–62, 292–93; and metaphysical nominalism, 166–70; and Ockham, 177–80, 191–97, 378n32, 386n29; and proper function in Locke, 173–4, 180; and Pufendorf, 197–206; realist natural law, 172–76, 187–88, 189–190, 206–16; voluntarist natural law, 10, 37, 170–72; 187, 190–91, 191–206, 281–84; requires a moral lawgiver, 158, 188, 224–26, 358n48, 358n49, 406n27; self-referential incoherence of voluntarist natural law, x, 37–39; 144, 147, 172, 197, 205, 239, 281–84, 325. *See also* Hobbes; Locke

natural liberty, 234, 242, 249, 319, 320; Bellarmine affirms, 253, 332n5; Filmer rejects Bellarmine and Suárez's affirmation of, 253, 316, 332n5; Locke affirms, 315–16; no necessary contradiction between natural liberty and humans being naturally inclined to political society, 260; problem with natural liberty as a fundamental moral intuition, 316–17; affirmed Molina, 253; affirmed by Sidney, 253; Skinner and the Salamancan School, 252–55; affirmed by Soto, 253; affirmed by Suárez, 253, 315

natural wholes: Aristotle on, 232, 243; imply a realist ontology, 326

Naturalization Oath of Allegiance to the United States, 410n74

Newton, Sir Isaac, 137, 236; Aristotelian metaphysics not incompatible with Newtonian mechanics, 394n10; on God and final causes in the "Scholium Generale," 394–95n10

Nietzsche, Friedrich: Gauthier rejects his prediction that morality will perish, 82; faith in science still a metaphysical faith,

333n9; questions not only moral values but the value of truth, 333n9; Rawls denies Kantian constructivism involves radical, Nietzschean choice, 111, 362n102

nominalism (metaphysical), 4, 5, 13, 21, 43, 326, 339n60, 346n128; contradictory with metaphysical realism, 167; and Hobbes, 129, 130, 143, 157, 346n128, 348n137, 353n43, 364–65n4; Leibniz critiques nominalism of Hobbes, Locke, and Nizolius, 349–49n137; and Locke, 159, 163–66, 180, 185–86, 346n128, 348–49n137; and Luther, 240, 383n2, 395–96n27; and materialism, 347n134, 409n65; and natural law, 166–70, 171–72; at odds with natural wholes and popular sovereignty, 326, 342n88; and Ockham, 130, 159, 168, 180, 191–92, 365n6, 384n11; price is oughtness, 327; and voluntarism, 41, 130, 143, 159, 164, 167–69, 176–78, 185–86, 192, 239, 269, 346–47n130n, 365n9

normative constructivism, x, 5, 6, chapter 3, 324, 326, 202; any coherent account of justice requires rejecting, 81; the incoherence of, 6, 97–99, 280–81, 303–4, 324–25

normative force, 29, 32, 34, 35, 51-52, 76, 139, 142, 149, 161, 184, 225. See also *potestas*

normative positivism, x, 43, 118, 119, 325–26; in Kelsen, 333n9; and Rawls, 108–9

Novak, David: juxtaposes a "biblically based" theology of covenant to Platonism, 330–31n10; 395n17; "There cannot be contracting persons . . . who are not *already* socialized," 414–15n6

Nozick, Robert, 45, 405n19, 409n72

Nussbaum, Martha: classical social contract theorists omitted women, children, and the elderly, 358n52; "core moral idea" in social contract tradition is mutual advantage and reciprocity, 358n51

O

R

Rattlesnake Point, Canada, 32

Ratzinger, Joseph (Benedict XVI): on modern democracy and American congregationalism, 335-36n35

Rawls, John, x, 6, 45, 46, 79, 327; "A conception of justice cannot be deduced from self-evident premises," 360n79; our considered convictions, 80, 103–4, 108; conventionalism, 80–81, 102–3, 104, 107–9, 361–62n100; on the "dominant tradition" in political philosophy, 115; and hypothetical consent, 270; the idea of an overlapping consensus, 115–16; the incoherence of Rawls's political liberalism, 81, 117–18; posits an ineliminable pluralism of incommensurable conceptions of the good, 114, 116; the instability of a mere modus vivendi, 115; on justice as political and not metaphysical, 114; Kantian constructivism, 79, 82, 99, 108, 109–13, 361n99, 369–70n100; Kantian transcendentalism, 81, 99, 108, 109; on the liberal principle of legitimacy, 114; Rawls's maximin principle, 101; on the moral duties of civility and reciprocity, 116; no comprehensive doctrine appropriate basis for justice for a constitutional regime, 375n3; the original position, 80, 100–3, 360–61n88; Seung's argument that the original position viciously begs the question, 107; political philosophy without metaphysics, 112–13, 114, 160; rejects radical, Nietzschean choice, 111, 362n102; reflective equilibrium, 80, 103–4; the incoherence of Rawls's reflective equilibrium, 104–7; rejects Utilitarianism, 101; the veil of ignorance, 31, 80, 100–1

Rawlsian Story, the, 13

realism (metaphysical), ix, x, 6, 240; and Aquinas 5, 81, 88–89, 172–73, 193, 208–11, 282–83, 286, 327, 380n45; and Aristotle, 88–89, 166, 168, 209, 232, 236, 245–46, 283–84, 286, 367n15,

394n10; compatible with covenant and government by consent, 240, 266, 267, and chapter 7 generally; moral realism presupposes, 41–43; Dworkin rejects metaphysical realism, 46, 81, 118–19, 12–21; criticism of Dworkin's rejection, 121–23, 364n132; Hobbes's rejection of, 129–30, 133; and human equality, 349–50n139; and Leibniz, 43, 184, 348–49n137; Locke's political theory logically dependent on, 160; Locke rejects, 163–66; moral realism presupposes and entails, 81–82, 166–67, 121–23, 268–69, 273, 285–86; nominalism and metaphysical realism contradictories 166–67, 346–47n130; objectivity of moral value presupposes, 81–82, 121–23; obligation as such requires metaphysical realism, 143, 157–58, 167–68 (together with 31–40 and 182–82), 169–70, 346–47n130; the ontology of wholes and popular sovereignty, 321, 326, 342n88, 414n117; and Plato, vi, 168, 327, 345n116, 349n137, 383–84n11; Rawlsian political philosophy neither confirms nor denies, 112–14; incoherence of Rawls's eschewal of metaphysical foundations, 117–18; required for the coherence of covenant and consent theory, x, 6, 39–43, 267, 268–69, 272–87, 323–27

realism (moral). *See* moral realism

reflective equilibrium, 80, 103-4

Rembrandt: *The Return of the Prodigal Son*, 221

Revolutionary-era Americans, 3, 11, 12, 232, 233, 329n3, 330n7, 331n14, 393n1

Richard, Carl J., 62-63

Riker, Willliam H.: says rational choice theory considers "true and false in . . . morals . . . irrelevant to political and constitutional analysis," 333n9

Rist, John, 46, 91; on contemporary perspectivism, 351n28

Rousseau, Jean-Jaques, 19, 20, 22, 45, 330n7, 342–43n98; force or physical power cannot produce morality, 345n119

Socrates, 50, 54, 83, 191, 222, 310, 321,
    327, 352n37, 368n20, 377n18, 392n119,
    396–997n36
Soto, Domingo de: "all men are born free by
    nature," 253; Oakley on, 337n41, 400n58;
    Gierke on, 391n115
Sparta: allowed adultery, 62; and infanticide,
    63, 93, 106, 359n60; Lycurgus and the
    Spartan constitution, 245
state of nature: in Hobbes, 13, 23, 25, 36–37,
    62, 63–64, 68, 70, 94, 129, 134, 135, 136,
    138, 145, 148–51, 151–53, 154–57, 242,
    269–70, 296–301, 341n84, 368–69n28,
    369n32; in Richard Hooker, 255–60;
    in Hume, 74, 75, 354n71; in Locke, 94,
    258–60, 270, 291, 292, 330n6, 404n13;
    Manent on, 330n7; in Revolutionary /
    Founding era thought, 329n3; in thought
    of Salamancan Thomists (Molina, Soto,
    Suarez), 21, 252, 253–54
Strauss, Leo: advent of nonteleological
    natural science, 357n34, 364n3; Hobbes's
    political philosophy does not presuppose
    mechanistic psychology / determinism,
    364n3; for Hobbes, nature "is not
    ordered and ordering, but the principle
    of disorder," 364n33; claims Hobbes
    views the laws of nature as conditional,
    369–370n36
Stump, Eleonore, 91
Suárez, Francisco, 6, 130, 224; all men born
    free by nature and therefore no one has
    political jurisdiction (by nature) over
    anyone else, 253, 315–16, 318, 399–
    400n54; Filmer rejects his affirmation
    of natural liberty, 21, 316; Gierke on
    Suárez's account of natural law, 391n115;
    Haakonssen says Suárez distorts Gregory
    of Rimini's position, 383n8; on life in
    the state of nature, 253–54; two accounts
    of natural law, 189–91; on natural law
    applicable to "every state of human
    nature," 254; on natural equality; 253;
    necessity of consent for political authority
    given natural equality, 12; Oakley denies
    individual consent in Suárez, 337n41,

400n58; obligation of natural law
    derives from divine will but that will
    presupposes judgments about good and
    evil, 391n115; political authority given to
    the community by God but not without
    the will and consent of human beings,
    401n64; on realist / intellectualist natural
    law, 189–90, 221; two acts of consent: to
    constitute a political community and to
    choose rulers, 254, 400n59, 401n64; on
    voluntarist natural law, 130, 189, 190–91

T
Taylor, Charles, 91, 109, 110
Thomists (later). *See* Salamancan school
Thompson, Martyn P. See Höpfl, Harro
    Martyn P. Thompson
Thrasymachus, 10, 46, 49–50, 51, 52, 56, 58,
    62, 77, 114, 345n116, 351n33, 352n37,
    382n76
Thucydides, 49, 51, 52, 56
Tierney, Brian, on relation of Althusius
    to American federalism, 20; rejects the
    voluntarist interpretation of Ockham and
    calls him a rationalist, 388n32
Trist, Nicholas, 11
Truman, David B.: weds behavioralism to
    is-ought dichotomy, 333n9
Tyrell, James: says Oxonians with whom he
    discussed Locke's *Essay* concluded that
    Locke was a Hobbist, 382n77

U
Uncovering the Constitution's Moral Design,
    329n1, 346n129, 350n139, 375n7, 394n3,
    405n16, 406n38, 407n15, 4122n94;
    on the normative underpinnings of
    American constitutionalism, 329n3

V
Van Inwagen, Peter, 90, 348n135, 357n34
Vázquez, Fernando, 21
via antiqua (the ancient way), 16, 177,
    239–40, 334–35n25, 377n18
via moderna (the modern way), 16, 177, 187,
    239–40, 334–35n25